# ISLINGTON

Please return this item on or before the last date stamped below or you may be liable to overdue charges. To renew an item call the number below, or access the online catalogue at www.islington.gov.uk/libraries. You will need your library membership number and PIN number.

6|12

2 9 JUN 2012

3 1 MAR 201'

10

# THE
# VICTORIAN ELLIOTS
## IN PEACE AND WAR

LORD AND LADY MINTO,
THEIR FAMILY AND HOUSEHOLD
BETWEEN 1816 AND 1901

## JOHN EVANS

AMBERLEY

*Once again, for Gillie*

First published 2012

Amberley Publishing
The Hill, Stroud
Gloucestershire, GL5 4EP

www.amberleybooks.com

British Library Cataloguing in Publication Data.
A catalogue record for this book is available from the British Library.

ISBN 978 1 4456 0507 4

Typesetting and origination by Amberley Publishing
Printed in Great Britain

# CONTENTS

# ILLUSTRATIONS

# Maps, Plans & Sketches

The following maps and illustrations can be found throughout the main text.

# ACKNOWLEDGEMENTS

Writing a book covering largely untrodden ground, except by one or two members of the family or scholars whose commentaries have generally only been published in dictionaries of biography, presents the writer with some difficulties. Working from the Highlands of Scotland and being dependent on receiving thousands of copied manuscript pages at considerable cost has few advantages, but for once the quality of handwriting made transcription easier, a task to which my wife and valuable amanuensis rose wonderfully despite having to live with my immobility.

The research, preparation and writing of this book has taken some five years on account of it being a composite biography with its style and content largely determined by the nature of the particular letters, diaries and journals left behind by each character. Since no writer could tackle a subject of this proportion without an army of invaluable, often white-gloved, librarians and archivists, and their contribution needs to be acknowledged from the outset, I have followed the convention of listing them here rather than the more modern position before the Bibliography at the end of the book.

The largest mine of material about the Elliot family is located in the National Library of Scotland and it is to Olive Geddes, Sally Harrower, Sheila Mackenzie and Yvonne Shand in Edinburgh that I would like to express my deepest thanks, especially for pointing out the significance of the journal written by the family's governess. They supplied me with copies of more than fifty individual manuscripts of varying lengths. The National Maritime Museum at Greenwich also proved to be a valuable source and in addition to Kate Jarvis and Martin Salmon in the Manuscripts Department, an ex-employee, Hannah Cunliffe, undertook very useful research into the voluminous correspondence between Admiral Sir George Elliot and his brother from 1836 to 1844.

Other copies of manuscripts and research material were supplied to me by British university libraries, including those at Aberdeen (Michelle Gait) and the Bodleian Library in Oxford (Patricia Buckingham and Elizabeth Elizabeth Crowley). Those Cambridge University colleges whose archivists and teaching staff researched information included Girton (Kate Perry), Gonville and Caius (Professor Richard Evans) and Peterhouse (Professor Brendan Simms, who was kind enough to read a draft text). In addition, the archivist and biographical Librarian (Malcolm Underwood and Fiona Colbert) of St John's College, and the archivist and manuscript cataloguer (Jonathan Smith and Adam C. Green) of Trinity College, along with Dr John Pollard of Trinity Hall, gave invaluable advice. Other university libraries included those at

Edinburgh (Arnott T. Wilson, Irene Ferguson, Ann Henderson), Glasgow (Joanne Docherty, Matt Leavey and April Hopkins), the Senate House Library at University of London (Ross Woollard), Reading (Professor Christopher Duggan), and the Hartley Library, in the University of Southampton (C. M. Woolgar, Mary Cockerill), whose record of the Foreign Office's dispatches during Lord Minto's duty in Berlin was a valuable source of information. The Professor of International History at the London School of Economics (Janet Hartley) was particularly helpful in throwing light on some of the characters involved in the negotiations with Johann Ancillon.

The assistance of a number of highly respected academic institutions outside the UK on a number of small matters was particularly valuable. These include the American Historical Association (Jessica Folmer); the McCord Museum of Canadian History; McGill University, which supplied several photographs; and the Ontario Archives & Collections Society (Betty Ann Anderson, who copied a paper by Fred Dreyer published in *Ontario History* about young Gilbert Elliot's service in the Toronto garrison). The Riksarkivet or the National Archives of Sweden (Lars Hallberg) searched the background of several diplomats the family encountered in Paris, and Yale University, Beinecke Library (Laurie Klein, Natalia Sciarini) kindly supplied a transcript of a letter written to Lord Minto in Florence.

Those local government librarians and archivists who provided much practical advice included those employed by Berwick Borough (Linda Bankier); the Borders Library, Selkirk (Helen Darling); the City of Westminster (Alison Kenney); Devon County Council (John Draisey and Brian Carpenter); the Hampshire Record Office (Gina Turner, Melissa Camp, Nicola Pink); Herefordshire (Rhys Griffith); and London Metropolitan Archives (Jeremy Smith). At the national level, the British Library, both through its European Collections staff (Chris Michaelides) and the Newspapers section (Jim Coyle), undertook a number of valuable searches, also supplying copies of the third earl Minto's correspondence, as did the National Archives at Kew (Vanessa Carr) concerning William Symonds, the Admiralty's famous surveyor.

Among the schools who were able to clarify the careers of their pupils featured in the story were Eton College and Rugby School and their respective archivists (Penny Hatfield and R. MacLean). Similar biographical and other searches were undertaken by the Borders Family History Society (Ronald Morrison and Elma Fleming), the Church of Scotland's depute clerk (Rev Dr Marjory A. MacLean), the President and Secretary of the Great Eastern Railway Society (John Watling and Bill King), the Grosvenor Estate Archivist (Louise Martin) and staff at Lambeth Palace and Lincoln's Inn, Archives Assistant (Krzysztof Adamiec) and Archivist and Assistant Librarians (Guy Holborn, Jo Hutchings and Mrs Frances Bellis respectively). I would particularly thank the Woburn Abbey Archivist (Mrs Ann Mitchell).

Governmental and semi-governmental organisations played their part. The Historians Team within the Foreign & Commonwealth Office (Dr Stephen Twigge, Grant Hibberd), supported by the Information & Technology Directorate (Pearl Taylor, Elaine King), helped establish the career moves of diplomats and others. The History of Parliament Trust (and section editor Dr Ruth Paley) has been an unparalleled source of information along with the Institute of Historical Research (Sandra Gilkes). Helping clarify the always obscure world of Scottish heraldry was Lord Lyon King of Arms (W. David H. Sellar) while a variety of questions about buildings were dealt imaginatively by the staff of the Royal Commission on the Ancient & Historical Monuments of Scotland (Sarah Dutch and Lydia Fisher) and the Royal Institute of British Architects (Catriona Cornelius).

Those galleries, organisations and individuals kindly permitting their illustrations, including maps, to appear in the book include the Bodleian Library in respect of an eighteenth-century plan and elevation drawing of Minto House, also a RCAHMS image, and the National Library of Scotland for photographs of some members of the Elliot family. Other photographs were supplied by Toronto's McCord Museum and Andrea Jahn of the Stadtmuseum in Berlin, while the rare portrait of Johann Ancillon was supplied by the Bildargentur für Kunst. More than a half a dozen portraits were supplied by the National Portrait Gallery in London (Robin Francis, Paul Cox) and several by the National Galleries of Scotland. Unexpectedly, the Victoria and Albert Museum (Frances Warrell and Catriona Cornelius) discovered a copy of George Elliot's *Thoughts on Bribery and Corruption at Elections*.

It gives me great pleasure in being able to thank several individuals for their help, including Norman Newton, now retired from his position as Reference Librarian for the Highland Council and its Library Support Unit, and Andrina Gammie whose responsibilities include obtaining volumes under the inter-library loan scheme across the country. With its strong maritime theme and the need to establish often critical detail, the book benefited enormously from Christopher Donnithorne's Naval Biographical database at the Royal Naval Museum library in Portsmouth, along with one or two specialist websites of great use to naval historians. Bjom Slettan, a retired Norwegian history teacher, helped confirm visits made to Mandal by George Elliot and William Vernon.

Every attempt has been made to obtain the permission of copyright owners in respect of the publication of manuscripts and illustrations but the use of short extracts from manuscripts has been deemed not to be an infringement of copyright law. Where for any reason I have failed to obtain or record my appreciation to any copyright owner, I can only offer my most sincere apologies.

Lastly, I should like to thank my publisher on this occasion for the excellent team that was put together to ensure a comfortable read for those who now hold the end product in their hands. Special thanks are due to Nicola Gale who masterminded the illustrations so essential in helping the reader appreciate the characteristics of different members of the family. Robert Drew's incisive yet light touch in editing my text, and the encouraging tone of Tom Furby's professional advice, were particularly valuable. However, a special long service award must go to Gill, my wife, for suggesting often subtle changes to drafts of the work, feeling under all manner of carpets and encouraging further examination of original handwriting in some manuscripts, proving beyond all doubt that an inaccurate transcription of one vowel can produce enormous errors.

# INTRODUCTION

This introduction provides the reader with a summary of the lives, loves and character of the book's principal *dramatis personae* – the second Earl and Countess of Minto, Gilbert and Mary Elliot, their five sons and five daughters, along with members of the household in the county of Roxburghshire, Scotland, between the end of the Napoleonic Wars and the turn of the century. Each man was made of different stuff, making his mark throughout the Victorian period whether as politician, diplomat, soldier, sailor or lawyer. Four of the daughters in the family made appropriate marriages and were able to develop their skills as hostesses, and in literature and appreciation of the arts as well as giving birth and nurturing numerous children. Their mother's encouragement in education and discovery made them independent spirits with plenty of gifts to support their husbands and share within their own society.

## Gilbert Elliot, Second Lord Minto

Born in France in 1782, Gilbert Elliot was the eldest son of Sir Gilbert Elliot, who had been made an earl in 1813 during his service as governor-general of India, and who died three years later. Lord Minto attended Eton for three years from 1796 and went on to Edinburgh University in 1891, and St John's College, Cambridge, in 1803. He married Mary Brydone of Lennel House near Berwick in 1806 when he was twenty-four years old, and the last of their children were to live beyond the turn of the century. Two periods as a Member of Parliament followed, one representing Ashburton (1806–07), the other for Roxburghshire (1812–14).

It was in 1832 that the second earl Minto became British ambassador to Berlin, where he underwent an apprenticeship in diplomatic negotiation. Often outmanoeuvred by Johann Ancillon, the Prussian foreign minister, Lord Minto turned frequently to Palmerston, his chief at the Foreign Office, for guidance or redirection. The height of his political career was probably reached during the six years from 1835 when he was a member of Lord Melbourne's cabinet and First Lord of the Admiralty. He was responsible for gaining parliamentary support for the coming age of steam and paddle, then screw-driven, warships. Family life at the Admiralty changed greatly in character from that of a diplomat in Prussia.

A period in the wilderness for Lord Minto followed until he became Lord Privy Seal in his son-in-law's administration (1846–52). Lord John Russell asked him to undertake a special mission to Switzerland and Italy, where there were delicate meetings with the Pope Pius IX, Metternich and Ferdinand II, King of the Two Sicilies. When Lord John was forced to resign as Prime Minister in 1852, Earl Minto continued to sit and vote in the House of Lords whenever possible. He stayed with Lady Minto for a time at Nervi near Genoa, the summer home of their eldest daughter Mary, but the countess died at Nervi in 1853. The earl was to die at his Eaton Square home in London six years later.

The family was to find that Lord Minto had been regarded by many if not as a failure then someone whose career had been undistinguished. Dozens of pleas from friends objected to the distressing falsehoods which appeared in the obituary notice published by *The Times* newspaper.[1] He was described, on the one hand, as 'a great statesman', and, on the other, as 'of small public account'. A truer account of his character and career would have made more use of such adjectives as distinguished, meticulous, responsible, hardworking, capable, and conscientious. He certainly had not been 'an aristocratic pro-consul', as the fourth Earl Minto was to be described,[2] nor someone with hubristic ambitions. In an age when forcefulness, and occasional high-handed arrogance, were to be seen, Lord Minto was probably guilty of demonstrating too little forcefulness in political matters. The poor and middle classes in Queen Victoria's Britain may have thought the aristocracy had won what was popularly described as the 'first prize in the lottery of life' but for the Elliots there were few such prizes. The word superiority was rarely used. Brilliance, whether in politics, diplomacy, the arts or a career, took second place to integrity, perseverance and quiet service to the country.

## Lady Minto

We meet Lord and Lady Minto with nine of their children for the first time in 1829 when they were preparing for an extended stay in Paris and Switzerland, one of its aims being to give the older children an introduction to society, art and geography. With all five of the Minto boys and four of the five Minto girls of an age when they could travel, and a nanny, governess and tutor appointed, an entourage of some twenty-four people crossed the Channel to Calais in July 1829. The tour was to follow a similar one made to Geneva in 1817 when Lady Minto had given birth to William, Lord Melgund, as the eldest son was called until his accession.[3] Although back in London by 1831, the family was soon off again the following year to Berlin.

During this period Lady Minto was able to blossom socially and show her great charm and creativity. In Paris, she enjoyed the Italian opera and attended numerous balls given by the wives of foreign diplomats. Life had become easier now that the older boys were at Eton during term times and the appointment of Catherine Rutherford as the children's governess had been a particular success. The latter quickly won their affection and taught them many of the habits so evident later in their lives. On their way to the Prussian capital the earl and countess had taken lunch in Brussels with King Leopold and Louise-Marie d'Orléans, but society in Potsdam was altogether less relaxed. M Bresson, the French minister, described Prussian society to Lady Minto as a place where 'les femmes tricotent, les hommes ferment'.[4] She had been brought up to expect to play a part in her husband's career and never had any intention of doing any knitting. Such success as Lord Minto achieved in the diplomatic world was much influenced by the good judgement she showed although, undoubtedly, there were times when she allowed her deprecatory view of politics to show.

While at the Admiralty Lady Minto was much preoccupied with the lives of her adolescent family and in 1841 she had the delicate task of guiding her twenty-six-year-old daughter, Frances, in her proposed marriage to Lord John Russell, a forty-nine-year-old widower. Quite apart from their difference in age, Lady Minto had been worried about who was going to care for his children by his first wife. The adjustment to the echelon of society her marriage demanded, called for great care and tact. The ten months that had to pass before Fanny and her mother accepted the future Prime Minister put an especial strain on both women. Misgivings about 'a nursery ready-made of children' steadily dissipated as the family took 'the simplicity and gentleness' of her son-in-law's character to heart.

Lady Minto's stamina was tested further when she was with her husband in Italy and aboard HMS *Hibernia*, which had taken them to Palermo. Such absences from the family had their downsides, where for instance neither parent could attend their second son's wedding. Lady Minto remained in the warmer Italian climate until her death in 1853 when she was brought home and buried at Minto House surrounded by the family. She had been loved by her husband for forty-seven years, and by all her children as well as those who served her in the Minto household. She was described early in life as beautiful but, as her great-niece wrote in 1880, 'her beauty [was] not her principal merit, as she is universally said to have a temper as fair'.[5]

## Catherine Rutherford

Catherine Rutherford's father, who had been in service with the Minto family, was killed while out riding sometime during the second decade of the century. The accident meant that his widow and two children, Catherine and her younger brother Gilbert, had to leave accommodation on the estate and move for some time to a village near Duns in Berwickshire. By 1825 the Rutherfords were living in Edinburgh, where Catherine managed to go to the theatre occasionally and hoped to improve her piano playing, but when the opportunity presented itself for her to return to Minto, which she always regarded as her home, she jumped at it. At first Lady Minto only wanted her to stand in for an absent French governess, a post she filled so successfully that her mistress made her a present of a small French watch. Then, late in 1828, Catherine was told that the family was going abroad for a year or two, and the countess invited her to go with them as governess to the younger children.

The five years' service Catherine was to give the Elliots would be remembered by all ten children during their lifetimes. None forgot the love or the contribution she made to their growing-up during walks and climbs of varying lengths after lessons in astronomy, poetry, drawing and painting. She sat with them through their childhood sicknesses and disappointments, and often combined her own role with that of nanny. After a short stay in Paris, the family reached Vevey in August 1829. They stayed beside Lake Geneva until the autumn of 1831, except for the winter when they returned to the French capital. Life in Switzerland was to be intensely happy. The sophistication of Paris was replaced by lengthy and almost daily expeditions on foot and aboard lake steamers and the family's yacht, with the two eldest boys returning to Eton when required. Long-planned climbs were led by Lord and Lady Minto to the slopes of Monte Rosa and Mont Blanc and included the older children, together with Mr Hildyard, William and Henry's tutor, and professional mountain guides whose job it was to cut footsteps for them in the ice or to hold out their poles for them to hold on to as they jumped over crevasses.

During the family's intensely prosaic life in Prussia, the children's temptation to tease visitors from many countries visiting their home in the Unter den Linden, had to be overcome by inviting the more colourful characters to join in their indoor games or even skating outside when this was possible. Often under-exercised, the youngest of Catherine's charges might grasp any excuse to come downstairs after having been put to bed. Looking out over the city at night, the children were usually the first to hear or see the fire brigade with its trumpets blowing, drums beating and bells ringing. Another of Catherine's duties was to instil some appreciation of the theatre in the older children wherever they were, in Berlin or later at Bad Freienwalde, but productions could be boring and neither governess nor charges took to the German language.

In 1833 Catherine heard that her mother had taken a house at Lanton in the Borders of Scotland and that there was every likelihood that she would have to leave the Elliot family's service to look after her. By chance Lady Minto's companion, Miss Drinkwater, was also leaving the Elliot family's service and the two girls (accompanied by Miss Drinkwater's brother) left Prussia earlier than the family. It was not long, however, before Catherine was writing to her erstwhile mistress, homesick for the place of her birth, to say nothing of all the family. Nevertheless, some six years or so later, when Ephraim Selby had taken over as estate factor from his rather unreliable father, Catherine and he were married. The couple had three sons, Robert, Gilbert and William. Both were to die in 1884.

## Lady Mary Elliot

The poet Sir Henry Taylor describes how at a party given by Lord John Russell he encountered 'a fine set of girls and women, those Minto Elliots; full of literature, poetry and nature'.[6] Lord and Lady Minto's eldest daughter Lady Mary, *La Penserosa* as their son-in-law described her, came out in 1829 at a ball arranged by Lady Lansdowne and met her future husband when the family was in Berlin. Ralph Abercromby, the son of the Speaker of the House of Commons, fell in love with her when he was secretary of legation in Berlin. They married in 1838 when Ralph was minister resident to the Grand Duke of Tuscany. Mary (Maillie), their only child, was born when he was plenipotentiary to the King of Sardinia. After retiring in 1849 he was made a KCB in 1851 and he accepted a special appointment as British ambassador to the Dutch court in The Hague. Life for Mary and Ralph on the outskirts of the capital proved particularly comfortable, their home being a property adjacent to the embassy where Mary's brother Henry was the secretary of legation. When Annie, Henry's wife, described the scene it was one of perfectly quiet mornings, when the ladies were able to see to their correspondence. Dining out was frequent and along with court balls there were opportunities to attend the opera. Ralph looked infinitely better and his cough was less frequent. They even built on two new rooms to their home and paid several visits to Ralph's father, the first Baron Dunfermline, before his death in 1858.

Mary and Fanny were great correspondents, the elder of the two sisters spending a lot of time with their mother during her last days at Nervi, both initially sharing the joys of motherhood and the political interests of their spouses. Ralph, who was a much-loved husband but always of a generally weak constitution, died when he was only sixty-five at the Abercromby home, Colinton House, Midlothian in July 1868 and Mary followed him six years later.

## Lady Frances Elliot

Fanny, as she was known, the second of the Elliot's girls, spent her fourteenth birthday in Paris, a month before the family moved to Switzerland for the summer of 1829. Other continental holidays followed but by 1832 Lady Francis was growing up fast in Prussia, where she waltzed with her father's colleagues and foreign diplomats. Three year later, with Lord Minto then at the Admiralty, Fanny joined the family for one of the great days in the London calendar, the opening of Parliament. A crucial event in Fanny's life took place at the start of November 1838 although she was not to realise its significance for some time. She was at Minto when the 'sad, sad news' of the death of Adelaide, Lady John Russell, was received. Well known to the family, she had died giving birth to her second daughter, Victoria, a sister to two-year-old Georgiana. Lord John Russell was to take some time to recover from his loss. Then Secretary of State for Home Affairs in Lord Melbourne's administration, he had to contemplate life with his two daughters and four children from his wife's previous marriage.

It was during the summer of 1840 that Fanny began to see more of Lord John Russell. In August, he and his stepson, Lord Ribblesdale, travelled north in the Minto carriage. All enjoyed his visit but it was Fanny who 'dreamed about him and waked all night'. She told her sister Mary that 'a proposal from Lord John Russell is at this moment lying before me. I see it lying, and I write to you that it is there, but yet I do not believe it.' Much to the relief of Lady Minto, Fanny turned him down and four days later a lovelorn Lord John sent her a very sad reply explaining he had deceived himself into 'a foolish notion' that she might have been 'prepared to throw herself away on a person of broken spirits'.[7] However, with the family back in London, where the couple unavoidably continued to meet, Fanny's hesitation was overcome and they became engaged in June 1841, the marriage taking place at Minto on 20 July. The couple had only just returned to 30 Wilton Crescent from their honeymoon at Bowhill House near Selkirk, when Lord John's children, one boy and five girls, arrived from Ramsgate.[8]

The following year the Russells' first child was born, John, Lord Amberley. Fanny could say 'now I am a mother'. Writing to sister Mary, Fanny had to admit that only those who had become 'in one moment, mother of six children, wife of the Leader of the House of Commons [or more correctly, leader of the Whigs], and mistress of a house in London' could imagine her situation.[9] While staying at Minto in 1844, Fanny's health deteriorated and she chose to move into Edinburgh where access to medical advice was better. In December there was 'utter consternation'. As Lord John wrote in his journal, 'sitting in the evening with my family at Douglas's Hotel, a waiter informed me that a person wished to speak to me'. He proved to be the bearer of a letter from the Queen in which Her Majesty desired him to attend her at Osborne House on the Isle of Wight, upon 'affairs of great public importance'. The final leg of Russell's three-day journey was completed on 11 December when he took an early train to Southampton and, after waiting there an hour, went on by the ordinary steamer to Cowes. He reached Osborne House before four o'clock and soon afterwards, and in the presence of Prince Albert, he had an audience with the Queen. Her Majesty said at once that she supposed he knew why he had been sent for. It was to form a government.[10] Fiercely proud of her husband, Fanny now desired that her husband 'should be the head of the most moral and religious government' the country ever had.[11]

In the spring of 1847, the couple accepted the Queen's offer of a house on the fringe of Richmond Park. Pembroke Lodge, which was to be their home for life, replaced Chorley Wood, a property near Rickmansworth which Lord John had bought the previous year. With a new routine in place, involving some nights of the week being spent in London, Fanny became used to times when 'each hour may bring an account of a new revolution somewhere, or worst of all, a rebellion in Ireland'.[12] As she developed her beliefs in home rule for Ireland, a broadening of the franchise, greater religious liberty and women's rights, Fanny took special interest in the French political scene after Louis Philippe's abdication and escape to England. With Prince Louis Napoleon Bonaparte (later Emperor Napoleon III) in power, she could not decide whether it was 'for good or evil' although certainly a disgrace. For here was 'a man to whom no party gives credit for either great or good qualities raised to the highest dignity in the new Republic'.[13] The couple's second child, George, was born in 1848, followed in July the following year by Francis Albert Rollo (always known as Rollo). During the summer of 1850 at Minto, Fanny spent some time driving 'daily with Mama – and such lovely drives!' fearing their time together was 'slipping away fearfully fast', but Lady Minto was to survive to 1853, the year in which the Russells' last child and only daughter, Mary Agatha, was born.

What Fanny called 'the Czar's misdeeds' led to the declaration of the Crimean War by the French and British governments in March 1854, but Lord John was initially preoccupied with an abortive attempt to bring in an electoral reform bill. It was only then that he turned his attention to the conduct of the war and during the summer he became increasingly disillusioned. By January 1855 he had deserted his colleagues and resigned. Whereupon the new Prime Minister, Palmerston, sent him to Vienna with his brother-in-law, Fanny's brother George, where her diplomat brother Henry had just arrived. She was to join her husband early in March but by the beginning of April it was clear that Lord John wanted to resign, a move Fanny deprecated as 'his reputation [could] not afford a fresh storm'.[14]

In July 1855 Lord John was forced out of office and resigned, and Fanny's 'dear and noble husband' was on the edge of a mental breakdown. He had put himself in something of a false position during the discussions in Vienna and when the *Daily News* said he had committed political suicide, Fanny urged her husband not to believe it. 'Depend upon it,' she wrote in her most forceful but loving manner, 'it is in your power, and it is therefore your duty to show that you can still be yourself.'[15] The following year Fanny and the children went to The Hague, where they were joined by Lord John and together they travelled to Switzerland and Italy.

By the time Fanny's father died, Lord John had regained his position in the Commons. The general election resulted in a win for Palmerston, who invited him to serve as his Foreign Secretary. Fanny, who always looked upon the part her husband had played in the liberation of Italy with great pride, was delighted when he sent his famous dispatch declaring that Her Majesty's government would look towards 'the gratifying prospect of a people building up the edifice of their liberties and consolidating the work of their independence'.[16] Lord John enjoyed his days at the Foreign Office although he was in two minds about the American Civil War. When Garibaldi came to England in 1864, a luncheon party at Pembroke Lodge went well. Her daughter, Agatha, gave their eminent guest a nosegay of flowers in Italian colours and Lord John presented him with a walking stick of British oak. In September there was news of Lord Amberley's engagement. Then, before the new parliament could meet after the general election of 1865, Palmerston died, and Fanny's husband was given the reins of power as Prime Minister for one last year. However, disunity within the party soon led to a conservative administration.

Two years later, Lord John died at Pembroke Lodge in May 1878 and was buried in the family vault at Chenies in Buckinghamshire. Fanny was to survive her husband by twenty years, her desire for knowledge never abating. On her eighty-second birthday, she thanked God that she was 'still able to love, to think, to rejoice, and to mourn' with those dear to her although she could also see 'failure on every side'. On 11 December, ninety-four old scholars from Petersham village school, which she had helped expand, visited Pembroke Lodge. Fanny was unable to see them in the drawing room but she got from her bedroom to her sitting room in the afternoon and all of them shook her hand in turn. However, six days after the start of 1898 Fanny was attacked by influenza which soon turned to bronchitis. Her doctor did what he could for her, and he sat beside his patient for ten days or so as the illness became worse. Fanny died on 17 January 1898 and was buried four days later beside her husband Lord John Russell at Chenies near Amersham in Buckinghamshire.

## Lady Elizabeth Elliot

The third daughter, 'Lizzy', as she was always known, married Frederick Romilly (1810–1887), the sixth son of Sir Samuel Romilly, at the end of November 1848, and the couple were to have a happy life together. They had three sons, Samuel Henry, Frederick William and Hugh Hastings,[17] and two daughters, Elizabeth Mary and Gertrude Emily. Frederick's brother, Sir John Romilly, who had been at Trinity, was made Attorney-General by Lord John Russell in 1850 before becoming Master of the Rolls the following year.

Lizzy's husband went into the Army when his father bought him a commission, first as an ensign in 1826 and then, also by purchase, as lieutenant, captain, and the brevet rank of major by 1846. When he retired at the end of the decade he was lieutenant colonel in the Scots Fusilier Guards. During this time it appears he played cricket for the Marylebone Cricket Club. In 1850, Frederick was elected the Liberal MP for Canterbury without opposition, but at the general election two years later he was defeated, whereupon it appears he fought a duel at Weybridge with one George Smythe, the eldest son of Lord Strangford. In 1864, the colonel was appointed a Commissioner of Customs, becoming deputy chairman of the Board of Customs in 1873. He was also a justice of the peace and deputy-lieutenant for Glamorganshire, in which county he possessed the Barry estate, near Cardiff.[18]

At the time of the 1871 census, the colonel and Gertrude were staying in Herefordshire with one of his brothers while Lizzy, Samuel, Hugh and Elizabeth, to say nothing of twelve servants, were at the family home in 55 Eccleston Square,

Westminster. Lizzy was charming, rather light-hearted in disposition, not a great traveller and with wide artistic interests. She enjoyed the Sunday breakfast parties at Lindsey Row in Chelsea during the 1870s for which James Whistler became known, and it was he who described her as 'one of the most charming people it was ever my happiness to meet, so kind, so natural, and with a courtesy so sweet'.[19] She had learned her political awareness from the family, her husband and his family.

Particularly friendly with Fanny as Lizzy was, the two ladies had often sat in the House of Commons to listen to Lord Russell, and when her brother George was standing for Parliament at Hawick she had given him every encouragement. Lizzy also demonstrated her support for Gilbert at the time of his 'scrape' in Canada and, soon after, Admiral Charles took up the post of commander-in-chief at Devonport in 1880, the colonel, Lizzy and Gertrude went to stay. She was to die in 1892, aged seventy-two.

## Lady Charlotte Elliot

It was the marriage in 1855 of Lady Charlotte to Melville Portal, the thirty-six-year-old son of John Portal, of Freefolk Priors and Laverstoke in Hampshire that was to cause considerable concern in the family. At first, all seemed to go well for thirty-one-year-old 'Lotty', or 'Bob'm' as she was also called, and her father gave Henry an 'excellent account' of Lotty, her husband and her home a year later. He had seen her 'fairly established' in December when he had been in London for the state visit of Victor Emmanuel II, the King of Sardinia. During the Crimean War she kept up a faithful correspondence with her soldier brother Lt-Col. Gilbert, and another brother, George, spent Christmas 1859 with the Portal family at Laverstoke House, halfway between Andover and Basingstoke, where he 'found Lotty and her belongings very flourishing'. She seemed 'very well and jolly' and although Melville was 'up to his ears in building plans for schools and cottages as well as alterations in the house', it had been a pleasant time. The couple were to have three sons and three daughters, Captain Melville Raymond, Gerald Herbert (later Sir Gerald) and Alaric were born in 1856, 1858 and 1862 respectively, along with Adela, Ethel and Katherine Charlotte, born in 1860, 1863 and 1867.

Melville Portal went to Harrow and Christ Church, Oxford, and was called to the bar in 1845. He spoke in the House of Commons for the first time in March 1851, having been elected the Tory Member for North Hampshire, two years or so before his marriage. He made no mark as a politician and he devoted the rest of his life to local affairs. In 1863, he became High Sheriff for Hampshire and he was chairman of quarter sessions between 1879 and 1903. Describing him as a prison reformer, his obituary noted his membership of the 'brilliant group of magistrates' who did so much for good government in Hampshire. It had also carried out Lord Carnarvon's proposals for Winchester gaol. The family's concern nevertheless stemmed from his actions as a husband and the contradiction of his public and private behaviour.

When Lotty and her daughters first encountered her husband's bullying behaviour is not known, but it seems to have developed when he was the senior magistrate, probably in the 1880s. It was in June 1890 that William, the third Earl Minto, came down from Minto in the hope of seeing more of Fanny at Pembroke Lodge and then went down by train to Laverstock to visit Lotty and her husband. The second day saw the two men sitting on the lawn after a walk together, and following church on the Sunday they went to see Melville's cornfield.[20]

In July 1893 Fanny heard that Lotty's Raymond, who had been her 'most dear and precious' son, had died of malarial fever.[21] When Fanny talked to her retired diplomat brother, Henry, they both

> felt almost frightened by it. She will be sanguine no longer but tremble at every telegram and never again be our bright and buoyant Lotty, feeling all the joyousness, the beauty, and the hopefulness of life far more than her good and devoted daughters to whom the dark side of life is the side they have for many years habitually seen, their young joy and spirits having been crushed out of them by their father.[22]

In February 1894, brother George, who had seen Lotty at Raymond's funeral, called on Fanny. Although Lotty had been 'wonderfully calm', he was 'imperturbably indignant' with Melville. Fanny could not bear to think what he was like at home, adding 'why did he ever win the love of such a one as Lotty'.[23] She died in 1899, a year after Fanny and five years after Melville Portal.

## Lady Harriet Elliot

Born four years after Lotty, Harriet was the last of Lady Minto's children and introduced to the reader in 1830 when the family was in Paris. Two years later when the family was again on the move, and at the French hilltop town of Cassel en route for Frankfurt and Berlin, Harriet was included in the inventory Catherine Rutherford gave of the coaches and those who were travelling in them. First was the fourgon (a covered wagon for carrying baggage), then the coach containing Lady Mary, Fanny and Lizzy, Miss Georgina Drinkwater (Lady Minto's companion) and Catherine herself, with a fifteen-year-old Henry riding in the dicky. Third in order was the chariot containing Charlotte, Gibby and Harriet, with a maid and a nurse on the dicky, two kittens in a basket in front. The fourth vehicle carried Lord and Lady Minto and the phaeton which brought up the rear contained the family's doctor, William and a coachman.[24]

Young Harriet seems to have had an especially soft spot for her youngest brother, enjoying a correspondence with Gilbert when he was serving in Canada, where the Army pay was poor, food often bad, and discipline prone to brutality. When the family began to build up a case against his marriage to a colonialist's daughter, Harriet put the case for her brother returning home so that he could be made aware of 'how superior English ladies are'. The two kept up their correspondence when her brother was fighting in the Cape, and during the Crimean War. He was the first to acknowledge the 'lots of letters' she had sent but he was anxious that she should not 'be in a fright about me when you read about our people being killed in the trenches'.[25]

Harriet was only to have a short life, having been a weakling through much of her childhood, but there were occasions before her death in 1855 when she showed glimpses of her light-hearted demeanour. She wrote a fascinating and well-crafted journal, living at Minto for most of her life. Her daily routine involved short walks and a more frequent use of a carriage. During her first London season, she joined Fanny in organising a three-day bazaar in the open at Chelsea to raise funds for a hospital.

Each had a stall and raised the tidy sum of £73. It had been hard work but 'most excellent fun'.[26] In 1844 she greatly enjoyed being at William and Nina's wedding in London and the subsequent stay at Ketteringham Hall in Norfolk.

## William Elliot (later third Earl Minto)

After completing his schooling at Eton, William went to Trinity College, Cambridge, where he seems to have had an undistinguished academic life. In 1835, two years after he had come down, he found himself almost by accident the Member of Parliament for a Kentish constituency. So far as his father was concerned, this experience confirmed that his eldest son was far from being either a natural diplomat or politician. Having decided not to stand at the next election, William went to stay with his brother Henry, who was then a paid attaché, nearly the lowest post at the British embassy in St Petersburg. There, the two young men's lifelong love of shooting quickly drove out concern about their future careers.

William would nevertheless sit for many years in Parliament, taking up the mantle of a simple politician again twice in the Commons between 1847 and 1859, and in the House of Lords on his father's death in 1859, six years after his mother died. A man with a strong social conscience, he was prepared to work hard for the Whig cause from the backbenches. He had no apparent ambition for high office and such diplomacy and negotiating skill as at least three of his brothers showed were used in his case to achieve social reform. William was to show himself as a warm, reliable and hard-working reformer without Henry's pomposity and egotism but with much of lawyer George's kind perspicacity and modesty. He regularly took exercise, a habit which Catherine Rutherford might have encouraged when the family were in Berlin and where he skated one day to Potsdam, a round trip of fifty miles. William never held office and much of his time was given over to the management of the estate, county business, country sports, and long periods of foreign travel. He chose what Buchan called the *fallentis semita vitae*, an unfulfilled path of life.

Although innately shy and withdrawn, William was fortunate to marry Emma, the only daughter of General Sir Thomas Hislop, in May 1844. During the following five years four sons were born to the couple, each of whose public life was substantial. In addition to Gilbert, who became the fourth Earl, governor-general of Canada and viceroy of India, Arthur Ralph Douglas became editor of the *Edinburgh Review* before entering Parliament as the Member for Roxburghshire and being appointed Financial Secretary to the Treasury by Arthur Balfour in 1903. Their third son, Hugh Frederick, represented Ayrshire North in the Commons between 1885 and 1895, while William Fitzwilliam reached the rank of lieutenant colonel in the Army and showed an artistic ability not unlike that of his mother. Having interested himself in matters relating to Border raids, he found there were many ballads which gave conflicting accounts of such events as the battles of Flodden in 1513 and of Philiphaugh in 1645, and he wrote three separate volumes on the subject.

During the decade before his father's death in 1859, William slowly got to grips with his responsibilities in running the Minto estate, something he did not find easy given the persistently delicate state in which its finances continued to be. It was a matter troublesome to each generation's steward. The family had neither rich patrons nor friends who could come to their aid. The web of connections so necessary for any politician seeking advancement was missing. In a period remarkable for its industrialisation, where invention led to the development of many new profitable products, it was strange that none of the Minto sons became inventors, architects or engineers.

When William finally settled down after his father's death and concentrated his attention on social reform in Scotland, he saw education as the key to wider prosperity and the elimination of poverty. Far from being a backwoodsman, he took the chair of the House of Lord's select committee on the 'Scotch Police System' in 1868, and became a member of the Privy Council's committee on education having worked for ten years with the National Education Association. He also introduced the School Establishments (Scotland) Bill and worked with pioneering feminists who were promoting women's employment, enlisting the support of penal reformers in a campaign to strengthen the role of procurator-fiscals in Scotland. By supporting the introduction of more thorough investigation into the causes of accidents, and examination of witnesses in what today would be termed 'health and safety' tribunals, William hoped to improve social justice. Evening schools and libraries for workers were also part of his concept. As Lord Moncreiff was to say, 'there were few public questions affecting Scotland on which he had not left the mark of his vigorous thought'. He was appointed to the Order of the Thistle in 1870.

Nina, as Countess Minto was known, was one of the few women in the family to undertake several family biographies when she started writing in the 1860s. Having produced a book of *Border Sketches* with a little support from Lord John Russell, she went on in 1868 to write *A Memoir of the Right Honourable Hugh Elliot*, which was published in Edinburgh. In 1874 notices about her literary work began to appear in the press after her three-volume *Life and Letters of Sir Gilbert Elliot, First Earl of Minto from 1751 to 1806* was published in London. Six years later in 1880, Longmans, Green & Co. handled the publication of *Lord Minto in India: Life and Letters of Gilbert Elliot, First Earl of Minto from 1807 to 1814*. Some criticism came from the *Standard* newspaper but Thomas Emerson Headlam, a retired MP who like William had been at Trinity College, wrote to record how much he had enjoyed reading both the life of Sir Gilbert as well as her work about her grandfather, Hugh Elliot. He thought Nina's books would live as long as there was anyone interested in history.[27] Louisa Beresford, the Marchioness of Waterford, was happy to acknowledge 'how well and cleverly' Nina had arranged her book.

At the start of winter in 1881 Lady Minto left Roxburghshire for Bournemouth. She had not enjoyed the best of health the previous year and she died there in April 1882. Gilbert, their eldest son, who had been aide-de-camp to Major-General Roberts in the Second Afghan War, was summoned south, and he subsequently brought her body back by train to Minto House for burial. William was to die aged seventy-six in 1891. His life as a widower had been occupied by visits to Fanny, Henry, George and other members of the family. When at Minto, where he spent much of the time, it was as if his life would end as it had started, shooting and riding out to hounds. Certainly there were many of his sporting partners at his funeral in Minto parish church.

## The Right Hon. Henry Elliot

The diplomat among Lord and Lady Minto's five sons turned out to be Henry Elliot, who was three years younger than his eldest brother William. When he returned in 1839 from Tasmania, where his father had sent him to be an aide to Sir John Franklin, it had been the 'merest chance', as he wrote later, that he came to enter the diplomatic service. His father had always evaded his son's questions about the career he might follow, answering that 'the army was a wretched profession and diplomacy a worse one'. After several junior postings as a précis writer in the Foreign Office and a paid attaché at St Petersburg from 1841 to 1847, he became secretary of legation in 1848, and occasionally chargé d'affaires, at the embassy in The Hague. In 1853, he at last achieved a major appointment as chargé d'affaires at Vienna, a post he held until the end of 1855. A two and a half year stint as envoy extraordinary and minister plenipotentiary at Copenhagen followed. It was at this point in his career that another 'merest chance' came his way. In 1859 when war between France and Sardinia on the one hand, and Austria on the other, was just starting, he was offered a special mission, initially described as one to go to Naples to congratulate Francis II on his accession, and to hold out the hope that Britain would re-establish its legation if he followed more liberal and humane policies.

With feelings in Whitehall strongly on the side of Austria, it was feared that the young Francis II, King of the Two Sicilies, might be induced to throw in his lot with the emerging liberals. Henry wrote in his autobiography, *Some Revolutions and Other Diplomatic Experiences*, that the Foreign Secretary's last words to him were 'an injunction to use every endeavour to dissuade the Neapolitan government from joining the Allies', but by the time he reached Naples the chance of this happening had disappeared and he was glad not to have to act on instructions he found repugnant. A man of 'singularly humane nature', as his daughter described Henry, found that Naples and Sicily were entirely governed by an irresponsible police, uncontrolled by any form of law and regardless of the 'most elementary considerations of justice', a system which he realised Francis II would not maintain. He was in Naples at the height of the war in Lombardy, where the battle of Magenta was being fought. Three weeks later the battle of Solferino took place in June 1859 and the peace of Villafranca put an end to what Henry called 'the preponderance of Austria in Italy'.[28]

In September 1860, Henry was on board HMS *Hannibal* in the Bay of Naples. Looking at him across the captain's desk was Guiseppe Garibaldi, who with his thousand 'red shirts' had seized Sicily in the name of King Victor Emmanuel. On Lord John's instructions, Henry had the task of interviewing him. London had decided on a policy of non-intervention and Henry managed to dissuade Garibaldi from attacking Venice. After a plebiscite in October, Sicily was annexed and integrated into the Kingdom of Italy, so leaving the British legation with no *raison d'etre*. Henry was obliged to return home.

Despite his first excursion to Italy achieving little, Henry went on to undertake a similar mission to Greece between 1862 and 1863, where he was again charged with encouraging the emergence of more liberal administrations. Discontent against King Otto had led to a coup against him and his exile in Bavaria. Henry was charged with agreeing terms with the provisional government whereby the second son of King Christian of Denmark could become the new Greek monarch. When the seventeen-year-old candidate was unanimously elected King George I by the National Assembly in March 1863, Henry was able to return home. He was, however, soon appointed by Lord John Russell as envoy extraordinary and minister plenipotentiary to the King of Italy, taking up residence first at Turin and then in 1865 at Florence, which had become Italy's capital. Promotion followed in 1867 when he became British ambassador to the Sublime Ottoman Porte (or government) at Constantinople in 1867 and he was almost immediately swept into troubles that had broken out on the island of Crete, where the Greek majority was under Turkish control. Diplomatic relations between Turkey and Greece broke down and the rebellion led to the loss of many lives together with the destruction of the Arkadi Monastery.

He was sworn a Privy Counsellor the following year and was knighted in 1869 and became Queen Victoria's representative at the opening of the Suez Canal during the winter of that year. In 1875, an insurrection occurred in the Balkans against Turkish rule and Henry took a hugely Turkophile line such that he found himself the central target of the campaign against what were called the 'Bulgarian atrocities'. Disraeli considered he had been ill-informed and frequently alluded to 'Sir Henry's lamentable want of energy and deficiency'. He felt that Elliot had acted 'stupidly', and if 'he had acted with promptitude, or even kept himself informed, these atrocities might have been checked'. Just as he deplored the failure of the Constantinople Conference in December 1876, where he acted as Lord Salisbury's assistant until the end of his life, so with Disraeli's remarks. At the end of 1877 he returned as ambassador in Vienna, a position his daughter described as 'exceptionally good', but seven years later he finally retired.[29]

Henry took a long time to grow to maturity and adjust to all the pitfalls and hazards of the diplomatic world. He was very much an egotist and also someone who found it difficult to make relationships outside his work. So far as his writing was concerned, Henry had a tendency to use three words where one would do, and often combined obscure phrases with colourful metaphors. When comparing the weather in Italy with that further north, he spoke of it being 'proportionately diluted by sundry degrees of latitude'.[30] In many of his concerns there was always a hint of disinterestedness. He was rarely seen going the extra mile and many of the mistakes and misjudgements Henry made, though never so serious as to ruin his career, could have and should have been anticipated. Without his marriage to Anne, Sir Edmund Antrobus's second daughter, Henry might have remained too aloof and introverted for his own good. Annie never became a great socialite due to extended periods of bad health after bearing Francis, their first child in 1851.[31] While the couple were at The Hague she insisted on 'quiet mornings' before attending the opera or a ball. Social life in Vienna, where Annie used a bath chair to get about, was relieved by breaks they took at their country house. The birth of their daughter Gertrude in 1855 occasioned a setback, especially as the medical profession in Vienna did 'absolutely nothing' to help.

On Henry's return to England the couple moved into Ardington House near Wantage, which had been lent to them and from whence he regularly rode to hounds between performing his duties as a local magistrate. Annie died at the turn of the century and Henry seven years later.

## Lieutenant Colonel Gilbert Elliot

Only fourteen short years separated a day in August 1829 when the three-year-old Gibby was being cared for at Vevey by Catherine Rutherford, the Minto family's governess, in the absence of his parents (who were both walking in the French Alps), and his arrival as a soldier in Corfu. He enjoyed a happy childhood even during Lord Minto's posting to Berlin, where he was to be seen riding 'Blot', his pony, past the Brandenburg

Gate or out with his brother William, as they had been on Easter morning in 1833. Gilbert was to be the only one of the boys to enter that 'wretched profession', as his father had called the Army. Acceptance of a commission in the Rifle Brigade had been forced on his father when it had become apparent that there were no openings for the young man in any of the Guards' regiments.

Although Gilbert found military life on an Ionian island 'the best place out of England, next to Canada', the subaltern was to endure three years of boring 'parades and inspections', a routine that was not to be broken until he came home on leave in 1846 and embarked the following year for Canada, where his regiment was quartered. To the family's chagrin he soon fell in love with a twenty-six-year-old girl and Lady Minto was irritated by the way he brushed her advice aside, to say nothing of his father's vexation. When marriage was contemplated, Charlie, his naval brother, was sent out to bring Gilbert home, such was the pressure that Victorian society could bring to bear. There were limits to which a young son could distress his parents and on a lieutenant's salary marriage would be out of the question.

By 1852, Gilbert was at war for the first time and in the middle of an intense and bloody guerrilla-style conflict against Kaffirs (or Bantu) in Cape Province, South Africa. He and his regiment had sailed aboard HMS *Magaera* to Algoa Bay some 400 miles east of the Cape of Good Hope at the end of March. The riflemen were then promptly marched by companies to Port Elizabeth and onward to Grahamstown, where the battalion was kept busy for the rest of the year with clashes in the Waterkloof valley, Fort Beaufort, Mundell's Krantz, Sabella and Balotta. Although the war was fragmented, and often involved small numbers of men, it was exhausting for the troops engaged such that by April 1853 Gilbert was looking out for news about which regiments had been selected to return to England, but he soon learned he was to be left behind in 'this detestable country'.[32]

The Crimean War started at the end of March 1854. It was to be a long and painful campaign so far as Gilbert was concerned. Already one hundred men of the 1st Battalion had readily volunteered to be transferred to the 2nd Battalion, which was then under orders to embark for Turkey. Many of these were veterans who had served through the Kaffir Wars. Now ready to join Lord Raglan's army, the first, commanded by Lt-Col. Beckwith, sailed from Portsmouth on the *Orinoco* on 14 July. The second, under Lt-Col. Lawrence, had left Southampton three months before aboard HMS *Vulcan* and HMS *Himalaya*. Both were to arrive at Malta and, after several mishaps, sail on through the Bosphorus to the Black Sea port of Varna. To the great gratification of the Riflemen, the 1st Battalion was placed in General Torren's brigade and attached to the 4th Division, which was commanded by Sir George Cathcart. The 2nd Battalion, which lost thirty men from cholera during July and August, was not so fortunate, being broken up into seven companies. Each sailed in separate vessels before making their rendezvous in Kalamita Bay off the west coast of the Crimean peninsula, where both battalions landed, bivouacking on the beach without tents in the rain.[33] Lord Raglan had predicted that it would take twelve days to capture Sevastopol.

Captain Elliot's daily exertions in this mountainous terrain, first during the battle along the Alma River, then bivouacking often without tents in rain, snow and mud during the unexpectedly long and frustrating siege of Sevastopol, took their toll and, rather too late, he found himself in quarters at Scutari within easy reach of doctors.

The family became increasingly anxious about Gibby's health although he returned to light duties which involved assisting those moving the wounded to the port at Balaclava for embarkation to Scutari. For his part, he was especially impressed by the fact that 'every man soon after he is put on board is put into a bath, if he is well-enough to stand it, and then into clean clothes'. He told Lotty, however, that 'I am not going to pretend that I like fighting, and I don't believe anyone really does like it till it is over'.[34]

HMS *Apollo* brought him home in 1857 but his service had left him with many symptoms of consumption. While he was at home on leave his health improved and he married Katherine, a daughter of the Bishop of Chichester, in August 1858. Soon after, Gilbert was posted to Malta, where, still on light duties, he invigilated Army examinations, and the couple were able to entertain several members of their families. Not being able to visit them personally, his brother George sent them the sum of £50 with which to increase their 'very small stock of spoons' as a present. In 1860, with Charlie in command of HMS *Cressy* and anticipating being able to give 'a lift from Malta sometime during the heat of the summer', and Henry hailed as 'the greatest man in Naples', the couple would have felt well cared for. However, two or three years later they were living in Ireland, a depot of the Rifle Brigade being in Co. Tipperary. Determined to fight his disease, Gilbert rode a little but by March 1865 Kate and her father and sisters, along with Nina and Lotty, were nursing him in Sussex.

Gilbert gave twenty-two years of his life to 'Queen and Country'. As a youthful soldier he constantly looked for fun whether it was shooting snipe in Albania or showing his horses the care they needed since they often provided the only exercise he could get. Kind, conscientious and possessing a keen sense of right and wrong, he never came up against military discipline. He did not condemn those of his fellows, particularly in Africa, who were racist and he had the ability to report the minutiae of action in war without exaggerating his own part or that of others. He was not, however, one who took the broader canvas into account and this may have contributed to his slow rate of promotion during the Crimean War. Even if the tuberculosis that showed itself in Russia had affected him more seriously, Gibby was surrounded much of the time by men suffering from cholera and all manner of gangrenous wounds and he knew, as an officer, that such matters were not spoken of outside the family. Some might say that his inability to accept that he was becoming an invalid showed poor judgement but he, like many others during the Victorian age, had received poor medical care from a variety of doctors and specialists. Brave, determined and generally cool-headed, the young soldier died of natural causes at the age of thirty-nine.

## The Hon. Charles Elliot

The Minto habit of having at least one son in each generation with a significant amount of salt in his blood was maintained by Charles, who went to sea at the young age of fourteen. He left the warmth of the family and the care of Catherine Rutherford in 1832 to join Sir Pulteney Malcolm, who was blockading the Scheldt estuary with the fleets of France and Spain also under his command.

When the story of Charlie's later life at sea starts, he is forty years old and captain of HMS *Cressy* in the Mediterranean. At Gibraltar, he caught sight of newspapers that referred to Palmerston's new cabinet and the news that his sister Fanny's husband, Lord Russell, had become Foreign Secretary. After a short stay at Malta, he sailed for Alexandria in Egypt, where he anchored in July 1859, but the Admiralty soon required his presence in the Bay of Naples, where his brother Henry had been sent by Lord John Russell to negotiate with King Francis II of the Two Sicilies. He spent 'a pleasant autumn' there, enjoying shooting with Henry until recalled in 1860 to Valetta, where he met up with Gilbert, who was recuperating after the Crimean War. There followed a strange mission to Morocco in support of the British minister's negotiations with the sultan, Mului Abbas, and his vizier.

He became a rear-admiral in 1861 but he was to be without a ship for three years. During this time he explored the Ionian Islands, where he was given passage to Messina in 1863 by an easy-going seafarer who turned out to be the step-nephew of Queen Victoria, and in December that year he married Louisa Blackett at Matfen Hall in Northumberland. The couple were to have four sons. In the spring of 1864, Charlie became commander-in-chief, south-east coast of America, and he and Louisa sailed on board his flagship, HMS *Bombay*, to Rio de Janeiro, a voyage that took forty-nine days. Quite apart from Anglo-Brazilian relations which Palmerston described as being 'marked by great neglect [and] the violation of treaty arrangements', Charles was soon confronted with the outbreak of civil war in Uruguay, where General Venancio Flores, a member of the Blanco party, was laying siege to Montevideo. Within a few months, a bloody war between Argentina, Brazil and Uruguay on the one hand, and Paraguay on the other, had started. It was to last until 1870.

A station commander's duties in the Navy included providing support for British diplomats and giving protection to British residents, but no sooner had Charlie arrived in Montevideo in the autumn of 1864, and established a presence at the mouth of the River Plate, than disaster struck. The captain of his flagship, HMS *Bombay*, had taken her to sea where, only just out of sight of the Elliots' quinta, the vessel caught fire and sank with substantial loss of life. Captain Campbell was exonerated after a five-day court-martial hearing on board HMS *Victory* at Portsmouth the following February, attended by the ship's officers and those of the crew who survived. Edward Thornton, the British minister at Buenos Aires, and his wife Mary became great friends of Charles and Louisa and their first child was born in the Argentinian capital. The admiral had to wait until June for his new flagship, the *Narcissus*. It arrived in Montevideo as Paraguay declared war against the Argentine Republic, which Charles described as a suicidal act on their part. He was to initiate a little gunboat diplomacy of his own up the River Paraná partly to show the flag, and partly to encourage the Brazilian admiral to get on with the war.

By September 1865, the rear-admiral had returned to Rio de Janiero and visited Petropolis with Louisa. Intending to visit the Falkland Islands, which weather eventually prevented, they took the opportunity to inspect several places on the way back to Montevideo in December with a view to establishing their usefulness to the Navy. These included Una Grande, with its fair anchorages, San Sebastian, Santos and Santa Catarina. Santos proved to be a low, unhealthy-looking town a few miles up a river which the *Narcissus* could go up if necessary but 'it would be a pinch'. Charles's motivation had been to find some action. He had enjoyed several months socialising in and around Rio but his official life threatened to become 'monotonous and unimportant'.[35]

After the handing over of HMS *Narcissus* in 1866 to her new commander-in-chief at Rio, the family sailed by the packet for Southampton. No sooner had they reached Edinburgh than their second child, Walter Charles Elliot, was born in December and the family moved into Bonjedward House, a property near Jedburgh which George had found for them in the village of the same name. Sadly, baby Walter died in February 1867 after barely two months of life. Charles was nevertheless at his wife's bedside in December that year for the birth of their third son, Bertram Charles Elliot, the only one of their children to reach adulthood and live into his sixties. In March 1870, a year that could easily be called an *annus horribilis*, Julian Arthur Elliot was born, but the family's happiness was to be destroyed when young Gilbert died, the happy, pony-riding youngster who had been born in Montevideo. His mother, whom it would seem had been greatly weakened by Julian's birth, then went to her grave on 17 July, at least ignorant of the baby's subsequent death on 18 October. Louisa's death came just sixteen days after the Admiralty announced Charlie's appointments as administrator of the fleet and commander-in-chief at the Nore.

In February 1873, it seems that the admiral had had enough of what proved to be a solely administrative appointment and the next year he married again, his new wife Harriette Liddell (always known as Har) being happy to accept young Bertram as her child. They were to have two daughters. At the beginning of 1880 Charles was brought back to active service and posted as commander-in-chief to Devonport, where he was to spend a pleasurable eighteen months entertaining a steady flow of royal visitors. Following Gladstone's election success, Charles was hugely delighted to hear that his name had been submitted to the Queen for a knighthood, and in 1882 Sir Charles Elliot found himself Admiral of the Fleet, a position he was to hold until his retirement from the Navy in December 1888. The family soon moved to their new home at Bitterne near Southampton in place of Admiralty House at Devonport. They were to take great pleasure in returning to 'Brydone' after several winter visits to Biarritz, which became their favourite French resort. It was 'a cheerful place without being over gay'.[36]

Charlie was always refreshed by change. He anticipated new responsibilities every eighteen months or so, and carried out his civil duties as a foil and stimulus to his naval ones. His knowledge of seamanship and man management at sea were valuable skills. When combined with a delicate diplomacy and tact that many Foreign Office appointees would have envied, Charlie's versatility was obvious. His writing was not only sympathetic, clear and expressive but, to whomsoever he wrote, his interest in his correspondents rarely faltered. He would discuss with them how incidents fitted into the political and diplomatic scene, and what their probable outcome might be. Charlie also possessed an encyclopaedic memory about naval vessels and all who sailed in them – rather like his uncle, Admiral Sir George Elliot – and having personally suffered the pain of court-martial proceedings, he sympathised with anyone caught up in such often lengthy actions.

The admiral died in 1895 after a life of great service, aged eighty six. When his name had been submitted to the Queen for the award of a KCB, he had written, 'I never felt the least desire to have the "Sir" … I had always felt that I would not care for getting it if it was bestowed when I was not serving … when it would appear to be given from seniority or rank rather than as a reward for service.' But on reflection, Charlie felt he could accept the knighthood as 'a valued honour bestowed by Her Majesty for past services'.[37]

## The Hon. George Francis Elliot

Intellectually, George was probably the brightest and most intelligent of the Elliot brothers. During his time at Rugby he benefited from being boarded in School House under the headmaster, Dr Thomas Arnold. During the four years he spent at Trinity College, Cambridge, Doddy (as he was known) passed the Mathematical Tripos, became a senior optime, and obtained a degree as a Master of Arts. Entering Lincoln's Inn in 1843, he was called to the bar three years later when he would have been twenty-four years old. No sooner had he been judged competent to plead in court, George found work at the bar difficult to obtain. Although it was to provide only a small income, he turned to practising as an equity draughtsman – first from chambers at 6 New Square, Lincoln's Inn, until 1853 and later at 3 Old Square, Lincoln's Inn. Such specialist barristers drafted complex written proceedings in actions brought in the Court of Chancery.

George joined the family party which went in 1847 to Italy, where his father had become Palmerston's special envoy. He visited Turin and the galleries and churches of Florence briefly before coming home via Switzerland. In 1847, a little before the general election in August, he put himself at his brother William's service during the latter's fight for a parliamentary seat at Greenock. The start of the Crimean War in 1854 saw George helping to brief William on the scope for legislation to improve Scotland's education system, and his attachment the following year to Lord John Russell's mission at the Vienna Conference. It was, however, the death of Lord Minto and William's subsequent inheritance which occupied the family solicitor at the end of the decade. It came as a shock to the whole family when George's examination of the Minto finances showed them to be in none too good a state. He had to advise the third earl to let the family's house in Chester Square and try to keep 'things as they were intended to be'.[38]

Between 1859 and the middle of 1866, the lawyer served as private secretary to Lord John Russell, then Foreign Secretary. This experience of the political scene tempted George to throw his hat into the parliamentary ring, but William thought this might be a mistake and, while George was to consider putting his name forward on several occasions, he never won a seat.

Fearing that his brother Henry 'had been having a tough time of it' in Constantinople, George went there in 1876 to give him support. He found him 'sadly persecuted by visitors' and 'hardly fit for his interview with the Sultan'.[39] Gossiping articles about his behaviour had been published in *The Times* at a time when he was involved with what came to be called the Conference of Ambassadors, attended by representatives from France, Germany, Austria-Hungary, Russia, Italy, Turkey and Britain, and whose purpose was to look for solutions to yet another crisis in the Ottoman Empire. George's interest was aroused not only by the diplomatic shuffling going on but by the way the government had sent out engineer officers to survey a line of defence for Constantinople extending from the Black Sea to the Sea of Marmora. It had been done 'very quietly' although it could not be kept secret.

Three years later, after the Russo-Turkish War of 1877–78 had liberated Bulgaria from Turkish rule, George was again having to defend his diplomat brother from 'remarkable stories' and untruths in the newspapers. This time the libellers included the *Hawick Advertiser* and the *Nottingham Daily Express* as well as *The Times*, their speculation alleging that more than twenty years before, Lord Russell had prematurely retired a diplomat, Sir James Hudson, in order to find a post for Henry. George had always been someone who held probity in high esteem – one of his earliest publications had been his *Thoughts on Bribery and Corruption at Elections* – and in 1886, after Hudson's death, he found time to publish what he called 'an historical rectification' – in effect a defence of Earl Russell's dealings with Sir James.

George was about to go north in 1880 to give William's son, Arthur, support at the election when the latter's agent for the Roxburghshire seat reported that the contest would be close. Gladstone professed confidence in his Midlothian campaign but the Tories, it was said, thought he had 'not a chance – and this was the general opinion'.[40] Once in Scotland he found the work was a 'great deal of trouble with the irregular hours' but when the national results were declared the Liberal Party had made a net gain of 110 seats. As George said, we 'had a narrow squeak ... and I never was more surprised than when the Sheriff read out the numbers – Elliot 859, Douglas 849'. Celebrations soon replaced post-mortems and at Minto the reception was 'enthusiastic and original. The kitchen bell and all the handbells that could be mustered sent forth a peel and Mrs Smart [the housekeeper] with a long broom worked away at the wires of all the other bells so that there was hardly one in the house but which tinkled out its welcome, and the Thurot gun [captured by Captain Elliot in 1760 from the French] fired with great effect'.[41] Such was the life of a family lawyer at election time.

Back in London at his house in Pont Street, George resumed his rather quiet existence. Between 1882 and 1898 George was a regular visitor to William Vernon's holiday home at Mandal in Norway. In the summer of 1886, for example, he found the fishing poor and the two men chose instead to visit Valle and Setesdal, a hundred miles from Kristiansand. The party travelled with its own carrioles and horses through fine scenery with a couple of his host's own men to look after them. True to the habit of the family, he read a batch of English newspapers regularly.

During the five years before William's death in the spring of 1891, George spent a good deal of time at Minto House not only at work on *The Border Elliots and the Family of Minto*, his 540-page history of family from the fifteenth to the end of the eighteenth century, but also in reorganising the terrace library. There were several incomplete sets of books with some missing volumes possibly residing at other Minto properties in London which George felt it would be well to send northward. He could only find the first four volumes of Lecky's *A History of England during the Eighteenth Century*, which had been published in 1880. At this time he was also pleased to see that 'in the opinion of competent authorities' William had made a good purchase of a property in Portman Square.[42]

When William's eldest son, Gilbert, became the fourth Earl Minto, it fell to George, who was himself then sixty-nine years old, to deal with his legal affairs. Gilbert had married the daughter of Queen Victoria's private secretary in 1883 and, after failing in his attempt to become the MP for Hexham, he returned to Minto, where he found his responsibilities and the tedium of fighting off the growing insolvency of the estate motives enough to seek the governor-generalship of Canada. This he achieved in 1898 through his wife's influence at court and the encouragement given him by his parliamentarian brother, Arthur. A variety of family concerns, including the deaths of Fanny and Lotty, were to occupy George until his death in 1901.

George was always the family's 'go-between', sorting out what his father sometimes called their 'foolish scrapes' along with family births, deaths and marriages, tensions and diseases. Much more than the family solicitor, he was the provider of advice and guidance across a number of disciplines. From a young age, his letters, which were rarely short, were well ordered and written so that the reader could follow the progression of his arguments. Not only were George's directions clear and usually perspicacious but members of the family came to recognise how much his good superintendence of various crises did in resolving problems. Although someone with a warm heart, and who appears to have enjoyed feminine company, he never married. He showed an enormous amount of brotherly care for those who needed his always practical advice. Typical of his concern and kindness was the care he gave to brother Gilbert and his new young wife, Katherine Ann Gilbert, the sixth daughter of the Bishop of Chichester, who were in Malta. On another occasion, when relaxing in Norway, the lawyer was soon on his way to Fanny's side after hearing of 'the unhappy state of things' between Frank, Viscount Amberley's eldest son, and his wife that eventually led to their divorce.[43]

George died when he was in his seventy-ninth year. He was to be the last of the Elliot brothers of this generation except for his diplomat brother Henry, who went to his grave six years later.

# 1

# THE FIRST AND SECOND EARLS OF MINTO

Gilbert Elliot Murray Kynynmound, the second Earl of Minto, was born at Lyon in France on 16 November 1782. His mother Anna Maria Amyand, aged twenty, and his father Sir Gilbert Elliot, who was thirty-one, were en route for Nice on the Cote d'Azur, which was then part of the Kingdom of Sardinia. They were to spend a winter on the Mediterranean coast 'after the lizard-like fashion of travellers from the north, basking all day on the rocks, exploring the coast, and doing nothing more laborious than was required to move from one spot of beauty to another'.[1] Family doctors, quite erroneously as it turned out, had suspected his father might be suffering from early tuberculosis.

With lands at Minto in Roxburghshire, Scotland, as well as Fife and Forfarshire, Sir Gilbert Elliot had become the fourth Baronet on the death of his father in 1777. A year before, he had been returned as MP for Morpeth, and the following year he was to become MP for Roxburghshire, a seat which he held until 1784. He was a barrister, shareholder in the East India Company, and a supervisor of prisons. In the Commons he became a member of the select committee on the Bengal justiciary.

In 1781 Sir Gilbert Elliot travelled to Russia to bring his wife's sister Harriet back to England, taking the opportunity to visit the more important courts of Central Europe, including Berlin, St Petersburg, Warsaw and Vienna.[2] Experiencing at first hand the enthusiasm there was in Europe for the American colonists, he reversed his own support for Lord North and concluded that they should be given their independence. When North was defeated in 1782, he followed Fox on to the Whig benches, and subsequently turned down the offer of an appointment to the Admiralty Board by the Earl of Shelburne, who had become first minister. Between 1784 and 1786 he was without a seat in the Commons but he won Berwick-upon-Tweed in September 1786, much to the delight of his friend Edmund Burke, who sent him 'a thousand congratulations'.[3] Although in acute financial straits on account of the debts his father had incurred when he had been Treasurer of the Chamber, he agreed 'to move and conduct the impeachment' of Sir Elijah Impey.[4] This proved to be an ill-judged decision when the evidence in the case against Impey collapsed.

During the Regency crisis his legal knowledge and verbal facility of expression were employed frequently by opposition leaders but he did not speak in the debates. In June 1789 he was for a second time the unsuccessful opposition candidate for the post of Speaker of the House. In the recess he decided to retire from parliamentary life but the offer of a seat at Helston in Cornwall brought him back to the Commons in December 1790. However, disenchantment was never far away and his differences of opinion with parliamentary colleagues of both parties during the next few years did not help.

In the autumn of 1792 the peace and calm of Roxburghshire was threatened by news of the massacre of the Swiss Guard and the removal of the King and Queen of France from the Tuileries to the Tour du Temple, the royal prison. The 'September massacres' followed, filling Europe with dismay. William Eden, first Baron Auckland, who married Eleanor, the youngest daughter of Sir Gilbert Elliot (third Baronet, 1722–1777) wrote to Sir Gilbert from The Hague in September 1792. He told how all his ideas of happiness had been shaken by 'the calamitous history of France', where it was not an exaggeration to say that above 20,000 cold-blooded murders had been committed within the last eight months.[5] In February 1793, France declared war against England.

Sir Gilbert, then forty-two years old, turned down the offer of the governorship of Madras in May 1793 just before Christ Church, Oxford, conferred the degree of Doctor of Laws on him, although he found the city 'a solitude, like in long vacation, but without a scout, a bed-maker, or any other living face' that he knew.[6] Early in August, Sir Gilbert was invited by the government to undertake a service which Lady Minto, the second Earl Minto's wife, later referred to as one particularly acceptable to him. This was principally on account of his acquaintance with French history, manners and language, and 'his natural moderation, candour and liberality of mind, joined to a temper of unfailing sweetness'. The plan was to send Sir Gilbert to Dunkirk, which was then under siege by British forces, so that he could receive its expected surrender; but before he could even leave London, the siege was lifted by the French – much to Pitt and the Duke of York's discomfort. A similar appointment was also doomed before it could begin. Sir Gilbert agreed to go in September to Toulon, where the expectation was that Britain's forces under General O'Hara would be able to resist any attacks by the French.[7] This time he did at least reach Toulon after a 56-hour journey from Dover to Ostend and a stay in Genoa. When the British evacuation came at the beginning of 1794, Sir Gilbert was still safely in Lord Hood's charge in the Bay of Hyères off the coast of Provence.

Instead of returning home, Sir Gilbert took a berth in the frigate HMS *Lowestoft* to reach Corsica, where he had the task of negotiating with the Corsican leader, Pascal Paoli, for the cession of Corsica to Britain. Lord Hood and the fleet were to follow a few days later. It was 3 January when he went ashore, some seventeen years to the day of his wedding to Anna Maria. It had been determined that he and the admiral, acting as 'Commissaries Plenipotentiary of the King of Great Britain' would send a confidential mission to Paoli charged with receiving his view on the possibilities of success in wresting Corsica from the French and the extent to which Corsicans might support such action. Sir Gilbert's first conference with Paoli convinced him that any calling together of the General Assembly was utterly impracticable. The Corsican leader himself would have to speak for the populace. During a week's residence on the island Sir Gilbert concluded that they were 'passionately attached to Paoli'. To show the state of life on the island, he told Lady Elliot that his 'drawing room windows were built about halfway up in brick, with loopholes to fire through' and that Corsica 'had one of the merits of Minto, that one [could] never walk many paces on a level'. The result of the mission was that Lord Hood soon concluded a convention with Paoli.[8]

By June that year, after being shipwrecked while transporting refugees from Toulon to Leghorn, and much to the relief of the administration, he agreed to become the first (and last) viceroy of Corsica, a post he eventually took up on 1 October. The delay to the receipt of his viceregal powers greatly annoyed Sir Gilbert, as did the excuse that the Crown lawyers had been unavoidably delayed in producing his commission. When Lady Elliot and the children arrived at Bastia, a new chapter in the family's life opened. As his great-niece was to write,

> a first introduction to foreign lands is an eventful moment in most lives; in those of the youthful Elliots it was probably a turning point ... transported at the most susceptible age from their quiet Scottish home to a scene where their daily existence depended on European complications and the fortune of war, their minds received an ineffaceable impression, determining the career of some and the tastes of all.

As Nina said, the boys learnt something about England's

> unswerving faith in her power and greatness, imbibing at the same time a passion for naval life which, in the case of George, the viceroy's second son, was gratified as soon as his age permitted his being entered as a midshipman on board the flag-ship. His eldest brother Gilbert [who was to become the second Earl Minto] meanwhile, better fitted by age and tastes to form wider sympathies, learnt not to love England less but Italy too.[9]

On his way home after the Duke of Portland had ordered the immediate abandonment of the island, the court of Naples gave Sir Gilbert a reception; the King and Queen showed him 'real kindness'. He met Lady Hamilton, whose unpolished manners were said to be those of a barmaid. With men her language and conversation were so exaggerated as to show the 'inveterate remains of her origin'. He sailed from Naples on 15 January and arrived at Porto Ferraio a week later. Scarcely was he with Nelson aboard HMS *Minerva* (Captain Cockburn's ship) when they were hotly pursued by two Spanish line-of-battle ships. Fortunately the Spaniards misinterpreted a manoeuvre by the English frigate. A day or so later he repaired on board HMS *Lively*, which had orders to proceed with him to England; but when it became clear that the battle of Cape St Vincent was about to commence, Sir Gilbert arranged to have the *Lively* wait until she could carry home the dispatches concerning the expected naval battle. Thus it was that he became an eyewitness to the battle and the proud possessor of a sword taken from the captain of the *San Josef* by Nelson himself and presented to him.[10]

HMS *Lively* was off St Ives on 1 March 1797 and Gilbert Elliot's party landed at Plymouth four days later. Writing to his wife on 5 October, Sir Gilbert told her that the King was to make him Baron Minto of Minto. He was to kiss hands on 11 or 12 October and he proposed to set off for Minto thereafter. During the ceremony, 'the King said over and over again that there was the greatest propriety in it, and that he did it with the greatest pleasure; that I had earned it, and should be of the greatest use in the House of Lords'.[11] He took the opportunity of adding the surnames Murray and Kynynmound to the family's name, which were subsequently confirmed by royal licence. While family and friends were generally delighted at the honour, the new Baron Minto's eldest son had hoped he would not accept a peerage or 'any of that nonsense'. Young Gilbert's objection was to be repeated.

Writing to his wife on 11 June 1798, Minto told her that he had slept several nights in Fulham with Mr and Mrs Legge, and that he was about to visit the Palmerstons then at Henley. Nelson had 'actually gone to the Mediterranean with only three sail of the line' he wrote, explaining that he had heard it from Admiral Gambier, who was a Lord of the Admiralty (and who fought at the battle of Copenhagen nine years later). He had 'met it out incautiously' since the navy was keeping the 'exact state of the affair back till they hear of Nelson having the whole of his squadron with him'. A fortnight later the state of the war was far from his mind. He wrote to Lady Minto with the news of the celebrated rebellion at Eton College, where their son Gilbert was a pupil, which had been terminated by a wholesale flogging of the school.[12]

In the House of Lords, Baron Minto spoke with the same diffidence he had shown previously in the Commons. Recognising this fact himself, he was relieved to be given another diplomatic mission in June 1799. Grenville, Pitt's Foreign Secretary between 1791 and 1801, sent him to Vienna as an envoy extraordinary in an attempt to improve Anglo-Austrian relations, which were at a low ebb. Ignored agreements and several acts of double-dealing by the Austrian government led to Lady Minto's journey to Vienna being deliberately postponed for a period. She eventually got as far as Dresden by March 1800, where she heard from her husband that her *estafette* (a message by express courier) had at least 'produced a grand rumour' in the Austrian capital. About his work he only told her how kind everybody had been in his 'vexations and disappointments' and that he expected to have taken a country house by the time she reached Vienna.[13] Writing to her sister Lady Malmesbury, Lady Minto told of life in the capital and how she had 'dined with Marshal Lacy, then 74 years old, at his small country estate in Dornbach, three miles from Vienna and not unlike a magnified Dunkeld'. She found that everywhere people confessed to being pleased or happy without fear of disgrace. They 'show civility to women without being accused of being in love with them'.[14]

The withdrawal of Russia from the war enabled Lord Minto to send a treaty to London in June 1800 which aimed to bring Austria and Britain into a new alliance. However, Grenville was not told until later that it contained articles omitted from previous drafts which he had seen. Minto was wrongly confident his action would be supported – 'the judgement formed in London of this question must depend almost entirely on the degree of that confidence which I may happen to possess'. In the same month, however, Austria attacked France at Marengo, losing the battle after a very successful French counter-attack. This defeat caused Austria to evacuate much of Italy. Another Austrian defeat, this time at Hohenlinden six months later, brought an end to their war with France and totally nullified the Anglo-Austrian alliance.

One of the first dispatches received by Lord Minto at the beginning of 1801 announced the resignation of Pitt on the grounds that the King was determined not to grant the political equality Irish Catholics had been promised. On 15 February, Lord Minto wrote to Lord Grenville asking for his recall from Vienna on the ground that the separate peace made by Austria was 'the natural conclusion of a mission destined solely to prevent such a consummation'.[15] Grenville accepted Minto's recall. Several times his actions had incurred the Foreign Secretary's displeasure, particularly as they affected Baron Thugut, the Austrian minister, and the Austrian court, while at the same time Lord Minto accepted that he had occasionally exaggerated events by the use of his 'elegantly composed but prolix dispatches'. He arrived back in London at the end of November.

Lady Minto, who left Vienna a short time before her husband, told of a call he had been able to make on Baron Thugut, then in retirement. The latter became Austria's 'director of foreign affairs' in 1793 but his policies left him with few friends. The British government nevertheless considered him a sure ally and worthy of vigorous support. It was, however, the French victory against Austria at the battle of Hohenlinden in December 1800 that made his position untenable and forced his retirement from public life in March 1801. Minto called on Thugut in the village of Pressburg, where he was then living. The place was 'most miserable' and a 'horrid residence for a man like Thugut'.[16] He had been warmly welcomed by the old baron 'dressed in an old green full-dressed coat with gold lace, and an arm-hat', the latter having apparently been squeezed into the form of a triangular pancake for many years. The baron took him to see the old castle in the village and was obviously enamoured by Minto's visit.

While the administration still nurtured hopes of sending Lord Minto to St Petersburg, he was now averse to foreign missions and when the Grenville ministry was formed in 1806, following the death of Pitt, he became President of the Board of Control for India in London, but without a seat in cabinet. In July, however, when the original candidate was found unacceptable to the directors of the East India Company, Minto found himself appointed governor-general of Bengal. It was to be an appointment where his 'zeal, activity and perseverance' found wider scope than in his previous offices and instead of his tenure in office being simply 'smooth and cautious' it proved both 'controversial and momentous'.[17]

His voyage to Calcutta aboard the frigate HMS *Modeste* – commanded by his second son, Captain George Elliot – involved a stay of two weeks in Madras for a new foremast to be fitted.[18] Writing to his wife in July 1807 from his final destination, he told her of the 'fussifications' associated with his arrival and accession. With crowds of servants and attendants bowing round him, he found the life wholly different from anything he had experienced before, and felt a 'little like Nell awaking in Lady Loverrule's bed'. The only difference was that it was not at all like his notions of paradise.[19] It took him time to adjust to riding or driving at five in the morning in order to have any air or exercise, and 'the only way of seeing ladies', he discovered, was after eight in the evening at table.[20] The weather, however, had 'been uncommonly favourable to beginners' such as himself and he soon got used to the 'tatty' (a hanging grass mat for doorways), an invention 'quite effectual' which made a 'temperate zone between the tropics'. In May, the first of the 'little rains' that preceded the monsoon proper arrived during a council meeting and 'it became so dark that we could not see our desks'.[21]

The following year, Minto's third son, John Edmund Elliot, who had been a writer in the East India Company's service from 1805 and the governor-general's private secretary once his father reached Calcutta, married Amelia Casamaijor. His seafaring son, Captain George, also married; his wife, Eliza Ness, was much admired in Calcutta society.[22] As Lord Minto told his wife, this greatly pleased him but, after describing the wedding, he told her of his 'domestic longings'. A governor's constant round, however diverse and colourful, was evidently becoming taxing and a strain on his health. Although he continued to assert how important the duty he owed the public was, and commanded the loyalty of those around him, Minto was still a very personal and lonely man who missed the presence and daily advice of a wife who had often accompanied him during previous appointments. Nevertheless, another celebration helped to restore Lord Minto's equilibrium temporarily.

Within a month or so of the new governor-general's arrival, plans had been submitted to Minto for the reduction of the French islands of Bourbon (Réunion) and Mauritius. Their capture went well so that by 1811 his attention could be turned to the Dutch island of Java, which had been included as another strategic target for reduction. Again Minto was successful and this time he took the extraordinary step of accompanying the expedition himself. He had chosen 'a clever, able, active and judicious man perfectly versed in the Malay language and manners to open communications with the Javanese chiefs, and to prepare the way for our operations' – one Stamford Raffles.[23] An eastern campaign on the island followed and was similarly successful, thus permitting Lord Minto to sail for Calcutta on 20 October. Writing home from Java he told his wife that Gilbert, his son, had written to warn him 'not to expect any great rewards'; also, that happy as he was to be heading towards one of his homes (Calcutta), it was the 'grand departure' (from India) that he was now anticipating.[24]

The prospect of some national act of approbation for her father's actions was the subject of a letter from Catherine Sarah Elliot, Minto's eldest daughter. Convinced that 'the great men of the age' were certainly not governed by 'great motives', she had to admit that 'it was not very easy to say … what will be thought or done by those who call themselves your friends'. Some directors of the East India Company wished that Mauritius had been seized for the company not the Crown.[25]

When Lady Minto wrote to her husband in April 1812 she told him something of the effect the war in Europe was having on the country. Riots, she said, 'have taken place in most of the great manufacturing towns, of a most formidable character … Royalty seems to court its downfall, and has already forfeited even artificial respect.' Then, following the assassination in May of Spencer Perceval, the Prime Minister, which had made 'everybody's hair stand on end', Lady Minto told her husband something about the state of society in London, where she was staying after five years at home in Minto. She found it more insipid than of old and the 'horrid phrase *well-mannered* meant 'silent, dull and *no-carey*'. Her severe remarks were, however, tempered by the pleasure she received from the society she found at Holland House (the home in Kensington of Henry Fox) and the elegant town house of the Marquess of Lansdowne in Berkeley Square. She wished she could 'board and lodge with them'.[26]

In the two years before he resigned his office, Lord Minto found himself with too much to do 'by several hours' work every day', and the death of his youngest son, born in 1788, who had begun his naval career as a midshipman aboard HMS *Modeste*, cast a painful shadow. Gilbert eventually received his recall to England in 1813 and was created Earl of Minto on 24 February 1814.[27] When the East India Company fleet arrived in Calcutta that year, it brought news of the general election and of his eldest son's return to the Commons as the Member for Roxburghshire.

Captain George Elliot was again to transport his father, this time back to England aboard the 35-gun HMS *Hussar*, and on 7 May 1814 Lord Minto wrote to his wife when they were off Southern Ireland. Good news was given to them by a passing frigate which signalled the words 'Peace with France, the old kingdom [of the Bourbons] restored'. An Irish vessel then told them that 'the Emperor of the West is sent to Elba – *relegates ad insulas*'. Eleven days later Lord Minto was in London writing to his wife, telling her how it was one of the happiest days of his life and that there was 'one happier still in store, when I shall have you once more in my arms'. He reckoned the longest he was likely to remain there was a fortnight.[28]

Ironically, Lady Minto had written to her husband at the same time, saying how she had begun to think that she 'did a very wrong thing to stay at home'. The couple had been separated for a long time and had she chosen to leave the arrangements for her husband's return in someone else's hands, she could have travelled to meet Gilbert in London. As it was, Lady Minto had 'shivered' in Scotland in sympathy with some Malay boys who had been among the first detachment of the homecoming party, changing 'their ship's clothing' for clothing made of flannel.[29] Meanwhile, Lord Minto was incurring another series of 'fussifications', this time in London, which included a court dinner given by the East India Company to which he did not feel equal either 'mentally or bodily'.[30]

Lord Minto's departure for Scotland had to be postponed when William Eden, first Baron Auckland, was found dead in bed by his daughters when they went to summon him to breakfast on 28 May. Minto quite naturally wanted to be able to comfort Eleanor, his sister, who had married William in 1776 and they attended the funeral at Beckenham together. The sad procession by road from London to Eden Farm, the family home, was followed by a funeral service lasting five hours. Four days later Lord Minto complained of a cold which was put down to his exposure at the funeral, where the burial had been in drizzling rain. He was ordered to stay indoors.

Determined to call on Lady Malmesbury at Park Place on his way north, although 'such a diversion added at least a day to the length of his journey', the family sent for another doctor, whose diagnosis was that Lord Minto was suffering from 'an attack of a most alarming disease, which under the treatment of those days, too frequently proved fatal'.[31] They managed to reach Stevenage but he died on the night of 21 June and all 'those hopes in the moment of their accomplishment, which had been the solace of seven years of separation' were dashed. When the last year's letters written to Lord Minto by his wife, so 'full of hope and joy', were found tied together with black string, their inscription included the two words 'Poor Fools'.[32] It fell to the lot of John Elliott, the third son, who had accompanied him from India,

to carry down the mournful and incredible tidings to the county alive with preparations for his reception. In the town of Hawick the people were in readiness to draw his carriage through the streets; on the hills the bonfires were laid, and under triumphal arches the message of death was borne to her who waited at home.[33]

He was buried in Westminster Abbey on 29 June 1814.

Gilbert succeeded his father as the second Earl of Minto at the age of thirty-two and took his seat in the House of Lords on 22 March 1816. He had been privately tutored for a period but when he reached the age of fourteen his father decided to send him to Eton, where Dr Heath was in his fourth year as headmaster. He remained there until Easter 1800. His father wrote to Lady Minto in May the following year saying how pleased he was that Gilbert was to go to Edinburgh University and that he would be together with Viscount Palmerston's son Harry. The Palmerstons were paying Professor Dugald Stewart £400 per annum for their boy's board and lodging and, according to Lady Minto, he was teaching both boys mathematics and nothing else.[34] The following year Gilbert was admitted to Edinburgh University, where he would have attended various classes after matriculating in the Faculty of Arts in 1801 although, in common with many students at that time, he probably would not have bothered with the formality of graduation.

In 1803 Gilbert went up to St John's College, Cambridge, where his name appears on the college's books continuously from 13 May to February 1804 when he seems to have then 'withdrawn'. In common with many of noble status, he is not listed in the residence register or in the exam class lists of the college. The young undergraduate had two tutors, Joshua Smith and James Wood (1760–1839), a mathematician who after attending St John's as a student himself had been elected Fellow of his college. His quiet manner and even temper endeared him to his students and during the twenty-five years he was a tutor he published numerous books, including his *Principles of Mathematics and Natural Philosophy*. When Gilbert arrived in Cambridge, Wood had just been made president, and the positions of master and vice-chancellor were to follow.

The young undergraduate became an admirer of the debating ability of Charles James Fox in the House of Commons in his late teens, much to the pleasure of his father, who regarded public affairs as his 'natural destination in the end'. His son's representation of the county of Roxburghshire in 1804 was 'a great object' but it was also thought to be 'distant and precarious', and so it proved. He had to be content with becoming the member for Ashburton in Devon in the 1806 general election where he beat Sir Hugh Inglis.[35] He was to sit for Roxburghshire from 1812 until 1814, taking his seat in the House of Lords on his father's death.

On August 28 1806, just before voting in the election got under way, and perhaps to the surprise of his mother, Gilbert married Mary Brydone (1786–1853), the eldest daughter of Patrick Brydone of Lennel House, Coldstream, near Berwick-upon-Tweed.[36] Writing to her husband, Lady Minto said,

> Mary is beautiful, but her beauty is not her principal merit, as she is universally said to have a temper as fair as her face. Her family dote on her and have brought her up with simple tastes, which will not jar with Gilbert's; so that we shall gain a daughter and not lose a son, which might have been the case had she been a London lady, apt to think Scotland a desert.[37]

The first of the couple's ten children to reach adulthood was not born until 1811.[38]

One immediate result of his marriage was the greater attention Gilbert gave to the Minto estate. It originally belonged to the powerful Turnbull family, one of whom became its factor in the eighteenth century. It was next sold to the Stewarts before passing into the ownership of the Elliot family. The parish of Minto in Roxburghshire contained the villages of Minto and Hassendean and was bounded by Lilliesleaf, Ancrum, Bedrule, Cavers and Wilton. The Teviot River ran generally along the southern and

Map of Minto House and estate in
Roxburghshire.

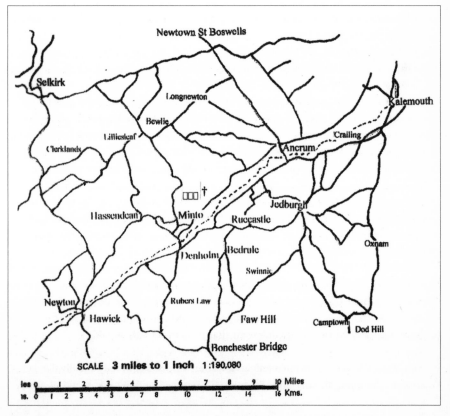

south-eastern boundary. The hills around were unlike the wild rugged mountains of the Highlands, having 'a soft and tender beauty of their own'.[39] Minto House, a four-storeyed building designed on an unusual V-plan, underwent numerous additions and alterations, including the creation in the 1720s of a large library by Sir Gilbert Elliot, the second Baronet, a facility rarely encountered at that time in Scotland. The sixteenth-century tower was encased by William Adam between 1738 and 1743 while he continued to work on Hopetoun House in Linlithgowshire. It was, however, the architect Archibald Elliot (1761–1823) – who may have been a relative and who by then had an office in Edinburgh – who reworked the property into an austere classical structure between 1809 and 1814. Born at Ancrum, he redesigned some of the largest and most imposing early romantic houses in Scotland. Lord Minto was to use the services of William Playfair (1790–1857) when he came to develop some of the estate properties.[40]

The couple seem to have spent time together not only planning design improvements and new plantings but learning what they could do for the best from other important landowners. Gilbert's journal for 16–17 July 1808 recorded their interests during a visit to the Duke of Atholl's estate at Blair. Subsequently the couple visited Dunkeld, Callander and Loch Katrine, returning to Edinburgh via Stirling, prompting Gilbert to write that

the duke plants principally larch, at about 9 feet distance in bad land and 18 in good, and fills up a little with hard wood. He is getting seed from Archangel in hopes of its being less subject to the insect; none of them has been found in the seedlings from A[rchangel] this year and the plants are earlier. They find sawdust better than sand or bushes in the nursery to prevent the frost from turning them out of the ground. A man only pits for and plants 150 four year old larch in a day.

The earl's notebook went on to explain that

emigration from this part of the country to Prince Edward Island has been pretty considerable of late and does not appear to have been the consequence of any change of system towards the tenants as the duke continues to let the small farms. But people have been going about the country holding out such golden prospects that the poor people cannot resist the temptation. Lord Selkirk does not appear to have been directly implicated in this system of kidnapping but his name has been made use of and it cannot be supposed that he should discourage what is so profitable to him. I fancy that the truth is that the people who go about are not his agents but persons who have made extensive purchases from him and afterwards retail them to the Highlanders whose pride and avarice make them easy dupes to a speculation which flatters both.

Returning to other problems facing Scottish landowners, the gardener who had been with them at Blair Castle gave them an excellent account of the duke's deer hunting. In winter the red deer came down to the low ground and did a great deal of mischief to the trees. Lady Minto wrote down all that he said on this subject:

[He] was a fine eager highlander and his affection seemed to be pretty equally divided between the trees, the deer and the duke. We returned by the same beautiful road to the Glen Cairn and the opposite side of the water from Fascally and the falls of the Tummel'.[41]

In 1812 the family became involved in a strange affair in which Gilbert, as his absent father's spokesman, played a part. The government was considering 'offering his father a viscountcy which the family thought inadequate for his services in India'.[42] Young Gilbert had an eye towards the value of the pension associated with an earldom, which was eventually conceded. Inadequate wealth with which to sustain the estate continued to be a problem, especially for one not given to corruption. His father's stipend as governor-general had only been £25,000 a year, the diarist Joseph Farrington being told wrongly that a fortune in excess of £200,000 had been acquired. Meanwhile, Gilbert went on to win the Roxburgh constituency but, as his political journal for the first half of 1813 makes clear, he took an increasingly poor view of the Prince Regent and his government.

Gilbert voted for Catholic relief on two occasions during the spring of 1813, and helped draw up the ill-fated bill. He privately feared that the Catholics would spoil their case by 'obstinacy and intemperance' and told his father that he had 'stood the long nights and bad air of the House of Commons' better than he expected, adding that he had very little reason to hope that either his head or his stomach 'would allow [him] to sit out a debate of four nights'. The following year he voted for Viscount Morpeth's motion that was critical of the Speaker, Romilly's attainder bill, and a motion against the blockade of Norway. He voted against new Corn Laws in May 1814.

Mary, young Gilbert's wife, was at Minto House when Earl Minto was expected back from India. She wrote to a friend telling her how 'the news spread through the house like wildfire, everybody was running here and there, not knowing how to show their joy. When I told them to go to the top of the house to cheer, in ten minutes there were about seventy people assembled; I gave them a quantity of guns, and we had volleys and cheering from that time to one o'clock.' Then, she added, 'Lady Minto behaved admirably; she was not overcome with all this joy but it was a long while before she durst trust herself to speak to me.'[43]

From the attendance records of the House of Lords it is clear that the new earl was otherwise engaged until 1818 when he returned to Westminster, attending twelve times in April and May. The following year saw him more fully committed to the House's business when he sat for some forty-nine days between February and December. In 1819 Lord Minto was in the House for the debates in December on the Seditious Libel Bill which proposed to punish libel by transportation.[44] But it was the Bill of Pains and Penalties, tabled the following year, that was to occupy him and the House of Lords for a great deal of time. During 1820 he attended on no less than sixty-seven days.

*The Times* reported that on 9 November 1820 Minto moved the suspension of a standing order so that he and other peers might have the opportunity of signing the protest against the bill 'to deprive her Majesty, Caroline Amelia Elizabeth, of the title, prerogatives, rights, privileges and exemptions of Queen Consort of this realm; and to dissolve the marriage between his Majesty and the said Caroline Amelia Elizabeth'. On 16 November, and as 'a proof of the real strength of the Queen's cause', the newspaper included Minto's name among the 'men of honour and justice, bound to vote for her'.[45] Divorce proceedings against Queen Caroline had been instigated by ministers to please the King, who was openly living with other women. The populace were in some doubt about the Queen's character but not that of the King when they discovered that Bartolomeo Pergami, an Italian witness of 'low station', had been brought to England to swear away his wife's good name before the Lords. The fiasco of what was called the 'Queen's Trial' provided material for Cruikshank, the principal caricaturist of the day. The vote when it came showed 125 members (including the Archbishop of Canterbury) for the second reading and 97 against, including Minto. Fortunately, Lord Liverpool withdrew his bill in a panic when all London was in uproar. More trouble would have ensued had it not been for the death of an unhappy, often foolish, queen in August 1821.

Lord Minto's attendance at Westminster then fell away and he only sat on a few occasions in the spring of 1821 and none at all the following year. After occasional attendances during the next two years and virtually none in 1823 and 1824, it was not until 1825 that he was assiduously in attendance on forty-two occasions, voting on the second and third readings of the Catholic Relief Bill, and against a motion by Lord Lansdowne for 'assimilating the state of the English with that of the Irish Catholics'.[46] Daniel O'Connell had established the Catholic Association and its crusading marked the first steps towards Catholic emancipation, which the Commons supported but the Lords did not. While he was to engage more fully in the affairs of the Lords after 1832 when he became a member of the Privy Council, and immediately before his first ambassadorial appointment, he was entirely absent in 1826 and only sat ten or so times in the period to May 1829.

# 2

# A Governess's First Year
## (1829-1830)

It was an early autumn day in Scotland when, on 13 September 1806, the wife of Thomas Rutherford, an employee on the Minto estate gave birth to a daughter. Her husband is variously described as the second Earl's footman, and on his daughter's death certificate as a private secretary. Four days later she was brought for baptism and christened Catherine. She was to have a brother named Gilbert but he was not born until 28 March 1815. Sometime between then and 1825, while her father was still in service at Minto House, he was killed while out riding, leaving his wife and the two children badly off and in search of alternative accommodation. They first moved to a village in Berwickshire and later to an address in Edinburgh.

Writing in October 1825 from West Fettes in Edinburgh to 'her dearest friend', Miss McGilchrist, the nineteen-year-old Catherine recalled the morning when she left Mungo's Walls at Duns in the Borders for a new life in Edinburgh. She would never forget 'the women flocking round to bid us farewell; they held out their hands and looked as if they would have spoken but their hearts were full; some were even sobbing aloud'. Gilbert, who was ten years old by then, had grown fond of his school and Catherine was preparing to attend classes in Edinburgh. She suggested her friend might watch out for her trudging along with books under her arm. Her mother intended to acquire a pianoforte for Catherine, who felt 'very dull without one'. She was anxious to go to a music class as soon as possible as she was fully aware how far she had fallen behind in that part of her education.[1]

Two months later she wrote a second letter to her friend, giving her more news of the new life that she, her mother and young brother were making for themselves. She had to admit having seen few Berwickshire people since the move north, except when she met up with one or two who attended Edinburgh's Hallow Fair, but the family now seemed to be reconciled to the change and settled as the result. Her mother had, however, had a severe fall. She was out one windy night and, having rolled herself up firmly in her cloak, was crossing a street when a violent wind threw her down, hurting her knee a good deal. Catherine had been to the theatre to hear Miss Catherine Stephens sing and on another occasion heard Miss Noel but, as she told Miss McGilchrist, she was not fond of the theatre and had refused several invitations.[2] Her mother had 'heard Mr Henderson every Sabbath since we came here' and had taken seats in his chapel. Robert Gordon 'preached there last Sabbath, making a most beautiful sermon'.[3]

On 13 September 1827, her twenty-first birthday, Catherine returned to Minto intending to stay there for a few weeks in order to help Lady Minto with the children's lessons following the departure of their French governess, and until she could appoint a replacement. She would never have undertaken the charge, even for a short period, had she not known them all so well. As for teaching them French, Catherine reminded Lady Minto that the older ones were already quite fluent. However, the arrangement proved a success and was extended by mutual consent, Catherine being happy to do all she could for someone who had been a mother to her in many ways when she was young. As a token of her satisfaction with the progress the children had made, Lady Minto presented Catherine with a small French watch. In the spring of the following year, Catherine and her mother appear to have travelled south, spending six weeks in Tunbridge Wells and some ten days at Portsmouth, where they may have been able to meet up with Gilbert, who was considering joining the Navy. By this time he was thirteen years old and as tall as his sister.

Catherine, who had been born and brought up on the estate, always felt it to be her true home. Writing to Miss McGilchrist in July 1828, she said that

> it would be impossible to tell how much I am attached to Minto. I think one always likes the place of one's nativity better than any other. Whenever I used to hear it spoken of my heart filled directly, and when I returned to it I ran like one wild all over my old haunts and pointed out almost every tree and bush which had been cut down in my absence.

She appears to have become a competent and imaginative teacher in a surprisingly short space of time, and came to her duties with little apparent knowledge of the educational theories popular in the 1830s or any preconceived ideas. She was quite unlike many governesses of her time who depended for their authority on the strictest of regimes, the belief that all children were inclined to wickedness and that punishment brought its own rewards. The deeper any religious temperament was, the more restrictive many governesses often became. Catherine's energy, confidence and cheerful disposition were probably in no small way due to the tenor of life in the Minto family and the fact that even those 'below stairs' seem to have been treated with a good deal of consideration. The countess had no difficulty in deciding that Catherine should fill the vacancy and was sure she had made a good choice.

One consequence was that by July 1828, eleven months after she had decided to stay at Minto, Catherine had only seen her mother and brother Gilbert once. She had probably concluded that her mother was well able to look after herself. Throughout this time Catherine lived at a house where another temporary occupant was Dr Aitkin, the parish minister. He was staying while a new manse was built for him. The village's medieval church was replaced by the new building in 1831. Their routines had never coincided and Catherine had to admit never having spoken to him.

Her expectation that summer was that she would probably return to Edinburgh to be with her mother, but Catherine heard that the family were planning to go abroad for a year or so in 1829 and Lady Minto offered her the post of governess if she would come with them. Her growing affection for the Minto children, and they for her, helped clinch her decision and she accepted. She would have been twenty-three years old when she first accompanied the earl and numerous members of the family to France. The earl was then forty-seven and his wife, the countess, four years younger.

The party left Minto about nine o'clock on 26 March 1829 and reached Newcastle late that evening in the dark.[4] The day had been very fine and warm and they had dined at Otterburn. Travelling in the coach, all were 'very merry' and enjoyed 'plenty of songs'. The following day on the way to Borough Bridge for the night they passed Durham, which looked 'quite beautiful', and later changed horses at Northallerton. It was not until they reached Doncaster for dinner on the 28th en route for Scarthing Moor that Catherine told her readers more about who was in the party, mention being made of Fanny (Lady Frances Anna Maria) and her going to the room they had shared the last time they were there. She also noted in her journal that her brother Gilbert had become fourteen years old that day. They all drank his health.

The next morning one of the wheels of the chariot broke as it was going up Gunnerby Hill. Lord Minto, Lady Mary (the Mintos' eldest daughter) and Lord Melgund (William Hugh Elliot) were obliged to stay at Grantham for a time until it was mended and they could all go on to Witham Common for dinner. That night they slept at Alconbury Hill and reached Stevenage about noon on the 30th. At this point Lord and Lady Minto went on to Richmond to look for a house where the party could stay. Meanwhile, Lord Melgund went out to see a coffin in which was a dead man who had been in it about 105 years. After tea the young played cards and 'had some very good fun'.

They arrived in Richmond at the Star and Garter on the last day of March at around 1 p.m. having gone off the London Road at Barnet for a journey of some 20 miles across country. They found that Lord and Lady Minto had taken a house on Ham Common which they visited the following day. Catherine reported that 'it has a very nice garden and hot house' but no sooner had they returned than it snowed quite hard and was very cold indeed. In what manner is not reported but 'Lord Minto made us all April fools', Catherine reported. His lordship attended the House of Lords from Ham on ten occasions in April and May before leaving for France. On 3 April the family moved in, the children arriving in the forenoon, and the adults after dinner.

Three weeks went by and Catherine reported going to London for a few days in April (between 22 and 24 April), where she stayed with Betsy Turnbull at Walcot Place.[5] On the first day the two friends were not put off by the constant rain and went to see 'the Bedlam', Bethlem Royal Hospital in St George's Fields, Southwark. This was followed by tea at Dr Armstrong's. The next day which turned out to be the King's birthday, both Betsy and Catherine were taken by Mr Turnbull to St Paul's, the Soho Bazaar and the Quadrant in Regent's Street. Returning home, they had dinner about six o'clock and afterwards went out to drink tea with a Mr Tomlins, where they also played vingt-et-un. Catherine told of being 'much amused by Alfred Tomlins who made me a great many fine speeches'. On their last day together, visits were paid to the 'British Gallery of pictures' (the National Gallery), where Tomlins liked 'all the sea pieces, of course' while Catherine particularly admired 'Mazeppa's punishment' by Jean Louis Géricault. Thereafter, they went on to the Burlington Arcade, the House of Lords and Commons, to Westminster Hall and Abbey, finally leaving her friends, and returning that night to Ham Common. Whether this had been her first visit to London was not recorded.

A fortnight later the family was still at Ham Common. On 9 May a walk to Richmond Bridge preceded their taking a boat to Kew, where they went to see the Botanic Gardens and later remarked how very old and ugly was Kew Palace. Lord Melgund and Mr Hildyard (the two elder boys' tutor) 'rowed us both there and back'. Several days later they set off after luncheon for Hampton Court, taking a boat at Teddington Lock which, once again, the two younger men rowed there and back. The palace obviously greatly impressed Catherine, who included a lengthy account in her journal of its history and very full descriptions of all the apartments, amounting to well over one hundred lines. She did, however, admit that 'it would be a very tiresome palace to live at; everything is so very formal and nothing looks natural, except the Wilderness'.

Ending a long entry in her journal for 14 May, Catherine concluded with the happy news that Lord and Lady Minto, and Lady Mary, their eldest daughter, were in London that day. Lady Mary was making 'her first appearance in the fashionable world at Lord Lansdowne's' in Berkeley Square, an event which occasioned Catherine to whisper a prayer for Lady Mary on so important an occasion. A few days afterwards a visit was made first to Bushy Park, the seat of the Duke of Clarence, and then to Henry VIII's tennis court at Hampton Court. As they returned along the avenue at Bushy Park, some soldiers played 'Hurrah for the Bonnets O'Blue', a Kelso song that would have been known to all the family.

It was Wednesday 13 July when the party finally set out for Kent, the English Channel and the Continent. They left Ham in a variety of coaches about twelve o'clock and, after changing horses in Camberwell and dining at Dartford, reached Rochester about eight in the evening. A very fine day became cold as they approached Gravesend. They eventually reached Dover on 16 July and went aboard the *Crusader* steam packet for Calais the next day. The rough crossing of three and a half hours made 'everyone of our party, consisting of 24 people' very sick apart from Lord and Lady Minto. Catherine could not help being amused in the middle of it all to see the deck covered with people stretched out at full length, and kind sailors running about among them with basins, glasses of warm water, stepping over some, holding another's head, covering them with coats and cloaks to keep off the spray – in short, doing everything in their power to make the family comfortable. When they reached Calais they progressed one by one along the plank from the steamboat to the pier, where they were conducted to the Customs House. They expected to be searched but no sooner had Lord Minto's passport come into view than they said, with the greatest civility, 'they would not detain us'.

They stayed the night at Dessein's, a 'charming old hotel, with its court, gardens and lordly kitchen', as Thackeray described it.[6] After breakfast the following morning, Catherine told of them going out to see the horses harnessed with ropes, and the postillions with their immense boots and hairy trousers and jackets. They made a great noise cracking their whips going through the town. The party dined at Boulogne but before dinner was ready 'we walked out to see the pier where the sea was very rough. We all felt very thankful that we had already crossed.' On Sunday 19 July they dined at Bernay en route for Abbeville. The landlady made many apologies about the melon not having been sent in with the soup which, as Catherine said, 'seemed to be the custom there'. A visit was paid to the cathedral which looked only half-finished and rather bare inside while the town 'looked rather deserted and the streets very dirty, there being no pavement for foot passengers'. The dress of the women, many of whom were remarkably pretty, was described as very neat.

They remained in Abbeville a day longer than was intended as a consequence of Lady Minto and Henry being rather unwell. Catherine describes a walk to the outer ramparts, where Lady Mary and Dr Williams, their physician, made a sketch of the cathedral. She bought a pair of tortoiseshell combs. Their departure the following morning was held back until half past ten as the Duc d'Orléans (later King Louis Philippe) had taken all the postillions, which provided an excuse for Catherine to go out and buy caps for the boys. They eventually dined at Airaines (west of Amiens) but afterwards Lady Mary 'took a very bad head-ache and was obliged to lie down' and a doctor was called for. Lord Minto and Robert went on to find where they were to stay that night. As it turned out, they found an inn at Grandvilliers which 'was so noisy that we could get no sleep till the morning'.

They dined at Beauvais during that day's travel and went to see the immensely high cathedral with its stained-glass windows. There had been a very steep hill on the journey and Lord Minto, the boys and Catherine had got out of the carriage to walk and look for plants. When they were near the top they saw the phaeton on its side in the middle of the road, with a great many people standing round it. The horses had apparently run away when the doctor and Robert were getting out to walk up the hill. Robert's arm and leg were bruised slightly but it was 'a great wonder that he was not killed or one of his limbs broken'.

Catherine described Thursday 23 July as 'a dreadfully hot day'. The party left Beauvais for Paris, changing horses at St Denis and seeing Versailles at a distance as well as Montmartre. Rooms were taken at the Hotel de Londres. Having bathed in tepid water and had dinner, they went to the Tuileries, where thousands of people were walking up and down. Catherine noted that the gardens were very formal but very pretty and gay while the palace was quite immense but looked dull. It was nevertheless the finest palace she had ever seen and she 'would have had no objections to living there – always provided that those we love were there too!' Carriages were continually passing and repassing in the Place Vendome, which housed their hotel and which she recorded as the only square in Paris where there was no garden in the middle. On Saturday towards the end of the month, a Monsieur and Madame Viaris called and in the evening they all went to the Palais Royal, 'an immense building in the form of a square built by Richelieu and given to the Bourbons'. They found shops and coffee-houses and a public garden in the middle which was 'lighted round and crowded with people'. A similar visit to the Jardin des Plantes to 'see the wild beasts' followed the next day, during which the animals 'almost all ate bread out of our hands'.

Two days later, Catherine went with Lady Minto first to the Champs-Élysées which 'were not at all pretty'. Baron Haussmann had yet to develop the area. There was 'nothing but straight rows of ugly croft trees'. At the Palais Royal it had been a different story and the boulevards were 'very pretty'. The following morning there were three deserters from their regiments dressed in grey with similar coloured capes drawn up under their windows. Ordered to take off their capes they listened as details of their crimes and disgrace were read out to the other soldiers. Later the family visited the tall bronze monument in the Place Vendôme, where they climbed 176 steps, each holding lanterns as it was quite dark inside, and on the evening of 28 July they all went to the Théâtre de Nouveautés, where one of the pieces was *Gilette de Narbonne*, a three-act operetta which Catherine 'understood well, considering'.

At the end of the month there was a rush to buy mementos of what had been a happy stay. Fanny, Lizzie and Catherine went to the '*vingt-cinq sous*' shop, and in the evening a party went to the Rue de la Paix. There, while Mme Viaris bought a copy of Bernardin de Saint Pierre's novel *Paul et Virginie*, Catherine acquired the complete works of Byron in one volume for 20 francs. They were held up for a day by their phaeton not being ready; the party finally left Paris for Fontainebleau on the last day of July, with Catherine mourning her departure. She had never been in any town she so liked, and where she would have liked to live. The sun shone over Paris and there was 'not a bit of smoke to be seen'. Travelling through the forest of Fontainebleau after they had dined, Catherine was reminded of Minto by the rocks all around. Going up a hill they got out to gather some plants, including blue veronica 'exactly as we had in the garden at the house', and plenty of bell heather, brambles, junipers and sloe bushes loaded with berries.

Staying overnight at the Hotel Britannique in Fontainebleau, they took tea on arrival, and Mr Hildyard, Dr Williams and the boys went to see the royal residence. Once they were under way again, the road became bad and the country filled with vineyards which Catherine thought 'very ugly things'. Crossing the Seine and the Yonne rivers during the afternoon, they arrived after a great deal of jolting at Sens. Lord Minto, the boys' tutor, Fanny and Catherine went to the cathedral the next morning but the party was soon off again, dining en route to Auxerre at Joigny-sur-l'Yonne. For the first time, those in the coach with Catherine spoke French to one another.

By 4 August they were in Dijon having passed through country about which Catherine could only say that 'nothing in Scotland could ever be half so ugly'. During the journey there had been eight inside the coach and two people on the dicky. Lady Mary had read aloud Lord Byron's poem *The Bride of Abydos* and Claudine, a maid, had told them a French story, and during their several days stay they had 'seen no bugs!' in their hotel. The party's first sight of the Jura came after they dined at Dole on the way to Poligny, and by 7 August the landscape became 'more lovely than anything' Catherine had ever seen. When they reached Moret (Morez) they sat for a moment in silence, looking at the lovely scenery round them, but there was a degree of puzzlement about the fact that, although they had climbed and climbed all day, the rivers still flowed in the direction they were travelling. The following day saw them leaving France, while the children, continuing the game they had started soon after leaving Dole, really did see Mont Blanc from their hotel at St Cergues. The Lake of Geneva and the Alps beyond were 'far too grand' for Catherine to describe, and as they were about to sit down for dinner Lady Minto sent to say that Mont Blanc was in sight. When she pointed it out, everyone called out 'Oh!' and 'stood gaping in astonishment for a thing so high far exceeded anything we had imagined'. Mr Hildyard then arrived with a map of the area which helped the children grasp where they were.

After breakfast, the family set off down towards Nyon. Catherine went in the phaeton with Mr Donald (probably a footman) as the boys were going to remain at

St Cergues until the following day. Lord and Lady Minto followed a few minutes later to go to Geneva overnight to look for a house for the party. On their first day in Nyon, Catherine and her girls were 'at lessons' when a carriage drove up and to her great surprise Colonel, Mrs and the Misses Drinkwater stepped down.[7] They were on their way to Geneva and had no idea that the Minto family was in the neighbourhood. A few minutes afterwards, the boys came from St Cergues and went on to bathe. After luncheon (a word used by the family for the first time) and while on a walk, Catherine met Lord and Lady Minto returning from Geneva, where they had been unsuccessful in their search for a house. A day or so later another sally also failed, with the result the party was obliged to move on to Lausanne, where they obtained temporary private lodgings overlooking the lake. On 13 August, Lady Mary, Fanny, Lady Minto and Catherine drove out to continue the search but the property that had been suggested proved too small and a long way from the lake. That evening it became clear that Lord Minto had settled the question of accommodation by taking a house for them near Vevey. Finding how every property was surrounded by almost continuous vineyards up and along the hillside above Vevey, Catherine bought herself a large coarse Leghorn bonnet since there was little shelter from the very hot sun.

The family's move into a property called the Château de la Tour had to be delayed for a few days as the rooms were not quite ready, but Lady Minto was 'delighted with it' – it was 'quite a romantic-looking ruined castle'. The old man from Geneva who owned it, a Monsieur Monnet, had agreed to let it for two months. Rather surprisingly her mistress told Catherine that it was once the residence of her father, Mr Brydone, when he was travelling in Switzerland and it corresponded exactly to the description of a Château he once described. It was an immense building, partly in ruins, with an old tower at one end. The entrance was through a very high wall covered with ivy into a courtyard – 'rather like Lennel', Patrick Brydone's last home in Berwickshire. It was large and convenient, with a terrace in front and a wall bounding the lake. Rather inevitably, it had a somewhat forlorn and melancholic appearance, but Catherine was convinced that they would very quickly grow fond of it.

Now that she could say that 'the mark of the wanderer' had been lifted from them, Catherine was able to concentrate more on the girls. One morning they had all run down to the lake before breakfast. Lady Minto had been there for some while and had sent Henry to tell her to bring Lady Mary and Fanny down to the pier. There were a great many people on it waiting for the lake steamer which could be seen at a distance. Catherine was astonished to see the lake foaming like a very rough sea and becoming a green colour as the clouds hanging halfway down the hills on the opposite side contributed to the coming storm.

With Lord and Lady Minto, Lady Mary, Mr Hildyard, Lord Melgund and Henry away visiting Chamonix in France for a few days, Catherine felt it necessary to keep Lady Minto abreast of all that was going on at the Château de la Tour, even to the extent of writing to tell her how well 'Gibby' or Gilbert, her youngest charge, was. However, the Chamonix party returned at the end of the month and told of the feat Lord Minto and the boys had performed. They had climbed over some glaciers in which the guides had to cut footsteps for them in the ice; by holding the poles of the guides they jumped over crevasses many feet wide. Their landing place on the other side was often a narrow ridge where they had scarcely room to stand. They threw stones down these crevasses and were astonished at the length of time they heard them bouncing from one side to the other before they reached the bottom. One small guide with them ran along the edge and sides of the rocks like a cat, making bridges for them. Lady Minto brought back a piece of heather for Catherine from the Tête Noire, along with three beautiful cut stones found on Mont Blanc, and Henry presented her with a 'beautiful little heart'. Three days later and rather belatedly, Lord Melgund gave her a brooch which he had bought for her at Chamonix.

At the beginning of September, snow topped the Dent de Morcles and the Vélan peeped through the clouds but the Dent du Midi remained elusive. Following dinner on the fifth of the month, Catherine went with the young in what the family called the 'bang up'[8] to Châtelard; but while going through Vevey, Robert nearly drove over a little boy about two years old. So near was he to being crushed that had the horse put down his foot another time he would have been killed. Robert pulled on the reins as hard as he could and a man passing by darted forward and snatched the child up in his arms. Later they had a walk close to the Château de Blonay and although Catherine and the girls were back home by seven o'clock, the boys came in later, being very pleased with their climb. It had enabled them to see towards the Oberland mountains and the Jungfrau. The following day turned out fine and the Prince of Bavaria (probably King Ludwig I), accompanied by twelve pages, came to the Hotel Trois Couronnes, a well-established inn on the Rue du Simplon. Catherine reported him as 'an old-looking man with a red face and white hair; very plainly dressed as were his pages'. They wore coarse-looking grey coats like the 'common homespun cloth of the poorer class in Scotland'.

The weather on Charlotte's fifth birthday (12 September) was as wet, cold and uncertain as it had been for some time. Lord Melgund told Catherine that he had given up any thought of a sunny autumn while they were in Switzerland. The next day, Catherine went up to her room after breakfast and found to her surprise a beautiful little bronze statue of Bonaparte on the chimney piece with a note addressed to her – 'A Birthday Present from Fanny, Henry, Charlie, Lizzie and Doddy – September 13th 1829'. They had bought it for her some days before and watched for the opportunity of putting it in her room. In her journal Catherine recalled with obvious feeling that it had been two years to the day since she had come to Minto fully intending to stay only a few weeks.

After failing to reach Vevey on Saturday 19 September as planned, Marie Louise, the second wife of Napoleon Bonaparte, arrived at the Château de la Tour the following day.[9] Crowds of people had assembled round the door in expectation of her arrival at eleven o'clock and they were not disappointed when a coach drawn by six horses, and followed by five carriages in attendance, pulled up. Catherine and the children watched from the top of the stairs to get a peep at her as she came up to the castle's old salon. She was dressed in a tartan cloak and seemed rather lame as she came upstairs. M. Monnet, the Minto's landlord, spoke to her as she was going into the salon. She turned round and the children got a very good look at her. She was very tall and very thin, by no means good-looking in the smallest degree, and with a rather melancholy expression in her countenance. Lord Minto supposed her to be about forty but with a much older appearance, and he explained that she had been married again since the emperor's death but that her husband was dead. Rumours were that she had lately refused Prince Leopold. There was another lady in the coach with her, a very little woman and two more ladies in the next. The rest were filled with gentlemen, one they called a 'chasseur' dressed in green regimentals with a star on his breast. Two couriers came at two o'clock that morning, apparently to order horses for her.

Catherine was standing in the passage with Gibby in her arms when Marie Louise came out from dinner. As she passed them she stopped the child and called him 'un joli petit enfant' and then looking at Catherine, 'il est bien joli'. Standing for a moment to admire him, one of her ladies-in-waiting, a Countess Valire, asked if he was Catherine's child and how old he was and a little later they spoke again downstairs and she gave Gibby a kiss. Another countess, a young lady, very nearly had a fall when getting into the carriage but M. Monnet kept a firm hold of her and, although the carriage went on very fast for about 20 yards, he continued to keep himself and her from being dragged below the wheel – although her back was rubbing against it all the time. It had clearly been an absorbing and colourful occasion for all concerned.

One day towards the end of September the family returned home to find Mr John Boileau, who had married Lady Catherine Sarah Elliot, the daughter of the first Earl Minto, some four years earlier.[10] He was on his way to Milan with a cousin of his, a Mr Manningham, who was in very bad health. On 24 September, and with the lease on the Château de la Tour coming to an end, Lord and Lady Minto went to Geneva by steamer to look for another property for them. Their present landlord, M. Monnet, took the opportunity to take Catherine and the children through the garden of the old château next to the pier, which was charming and beautifully kept although without a view on account of an avenue of horse chestnut trees. He was clearly much taken by the children and on another occasion showed them an enormous trout which had been caught locally and which weighed more than 27 lb. The house, however, was in a poor and smelly state, in Dr William's view 'like a dissecting room'.

Catherine was sketching on the first day of October when Lizzy and Doddy fell into the water near the marble works. Mr Boileau returned from Milan that day but he was very tired, having travelled two nights on roads which were all broken up, as they had been across Mt Cenis. The only way to Italy in his view was by Mt Simplon. The next day, Catherine had another attempt at sketching Chailly-sur-Clarens, and on the Saturday she and the children went out with Lady Minto in a boat and viewed a 'very fine thunderstorm'. Then there was news that the boys were not going to Eton (on their own). It had been settled that 'we are not going to Geneva at all but straight to Paris with the boys'.

Tuesday was market day in Vevey and Catherine had become used to seeing the wonderful displays of fruit and vegetables, including plums, peaches, pears and apples. Fine greengages were quickly and greedily gobbled up. On what was to be their last market day, she patronised another section where she bought a small pocket book for Henry and some gold beads to finish the bracelets she was making for Mrs Elliot. In the afternoon she went to a bookshop to choose a French book for Fanny and then to the steamer pier to meet a Mlle Bernard. Subsequently, it seemed as if each member of the party was buying presents. Those that were not started feverishly packing for their departure. Lord Minto bought Fanny and Lord Melgund watches each and Mr Hildyard purchased a new gold one for himself. Lady Minto and

Catherine trudged through the rain in their waterproof cloaks to a shop to buy some silk cord.

The Château's chef 'treated them with a splendid dinner' on account of their going away and since it was snowing so hard that no one could go out on the day before their departure the adults danced in Madame Monnet's room while George and Henry 'made dwarfs' that evening in Catherine's room. The next morning the party left for Orbe in the Vaud, dining at Lausanne en route and where they said goodbye to Mlle Bernard. Discovering that the pass at Orbe was 14 feet deep in snow, the party was forced to stay at Cossonay. While they waited to depart the following day, a report was received from a man who had crossed the Jura. He told of the roads being bad but not impassable. It nevertheless took nearly four hours to travel eight miles on their way to Orbe. The following morning Lord Minto pointed out both Mont Blanc and the top of the Jungfrau away in the distance. Catherine had been sad to bid the mountains goodbye but hoped that they would be able to return to Switzerland the next year.

After passing through the customs post at the border on 12 October, where their belongings were thoroughly searched, they dined and got back into their carriages. About half past three in the afternoon a dreadful row broke out between Renard, a servant, and the Maître de Poste about the horses. This grew in intensity and, as Catherine wrote, it was 'near 4 o'clock when we set off with five horses only in the coach and those belonging to the paysans which, being accustomed to draw one before the other, were yoked to the coach in that way. We had five postillions.' They had not gone many steps before a brace broke. That was mended but a few steps further and the pole which hung across to fasten the front horses also broke, causing two horses to run on without the coach. It was uphill but as the snow was very deep it prevented the coach from running back. After that had been mended the party set off again only for another brace to break. They thought they would never get through the village and when they tried once more, two pigs got in their way. The road being piled up with snow on each side, they were obliged to stop again to let them pass, given the danger of being overturned. By this time, people were crowding to their doors and windows and the women were all very much amused at their ineffectual efforts. The postmaster in a blue smock frock and white nightcap seemed quite in despair. At this last stoppage he lifted up his hands and eyes, calling out 'Oh! Dieu!' When they finally did get free, it was nearly dark by the time they reached Pontarlier, where they were to stay.

During the next stage of the journey they were able to see the salt works at Salines, where they were most impressed by the enormous fire which heated the boiler as well as the beauty of the white product it helped produce. The town was in a deep hollow with hills around and a fort which resembled Edinburgh Castle. Catherine made no mention of where the party stayed and it seems that by this time a decision had been taken to dispense with two of their carriages for want of horses. They had encountered another customs post during their journey that day and officers had taken their trunks down from the coaches after a little bustling and swearing so that they could be 'plombé – ed' (or sealed). En route for Dôle the following day they dined in a village where they had waited some considerable time for horses on the way south. There was a tame fox there which behaved just like a dog, licked their hands and frisked about the children – the 'prettiest of creatures'. Lord Minto had never seen anything like it. That night the party took rooms at a large inn.

It was an early start next morning. The countryside was alive with the vendange. They changed horses at Auxonne and arrived at Dijon just after midday, but there was some regret that at their next stop they did not have time to see the house or gardens of Buffon, the cosmologist and mathematician who lived in Montbard. After stops at St Florentin, where Lord Minto was charged more than he had ever paid at the best inns and the maids had not been given breakfast, and Sens, where they had been before and were reminded that the French paid no regard to Sunday, they set off for Melun on 19 October. The traffic on the roads was heavy and they met a great many diligences – the 'dilly' was how many British referred to the French stagecoach – which 'at a little distance, looked like immense castles' moving towards them. They were fearsome-looking things. One of their postillions had apparently fought with Bonaparte and been at the retreat from Moscow. Having enjoyed reading a handbill inviting them to stay at the Hotel de France which was written in bad English, they accepted the offer and took rooms there. After dinner, Catherine and the children had a game of 'wolf & lamb' in the immense salon and played 'a game at Casino' before going to bed.

Many of the houses in the villages between Melun and Paris looked 'new and white' and Catherine was struck by the appearance of the Parisians and how gay and happy they looked. Just how much interest the family's governess could have shown about the European political and social climate in 1829–30 is not clear, but by listening to her employer's frequent conversations and reading newspapers she would not have been left totally unaware of the growing unrest across Europe. In March 1829, as the war for Greek independence ended, Greece appeared to have gained some autonomy from the Ottoman Empire; but by July a trans-Balkan offensive had been launched by the Russian Field Marshall von Diebitsch which advanced to within 70 miles of Constantinople. Numerous monarchs were renewing despotic regimes as memories of Bonaparte and 1815 faded from their minds. The Emperors of Austria and Russia, and the King of Prussia formed their 'Holy Alliance' to suppress liberal opinion and demands for popular government in their own and their neighbours' dominions.

In France, the post-war generation had its own new train of priorities. Emigrant nobles returned in triumph, bringing with them old doctrines and forgotten watchwords. Fragments of many factions, which the Revolution had produced – liberals, republicans, jacobins, royalists and Napoleonites – strove to give their own direction to the future government. The restored Bourbon monarchy in France was reactionary and, although backed by foreign bayonets, it found itself too weak to re-establish the despotism of Louis XIV. An inept ruler, Charles X (1757–1836) inspired resentment among the middle class and in July 1829 he was to dismiss the Chambre des Députés, the lower house of parliament, when tighter control of the press and a more restricted franchise were introduced.

The family arrived in Paris on 20 October, staying for a few days at the Hotel de Londres, where they had lodged en route for Switzerland as the house in the Rue Monsieur which Lord Minto was to rent was not ready for them. Dr Williams chose to take lodgings in the Rue de l'Université and the boys' departure for England was fixed for the following Sunday.[11] It was the earliest day that bookings could be made and places for them had been reserved in the coupé of the diligence. Renard showed Catherine their passports, along with that of Mr Hildyard. Last-minute shopping on their behalf in the Rue Saint-Honoré produced some parchment required by Mr Hildyard. It was expected that when the party left for England on 25 October they would take dinner at Beauvais, then travel all night and reach Calais late on the following day, crossing on Tuesday 27 October.

The rest of the family had barely moved into their new house in the Rue Monsieur a week later when a Mary Square wrote to tell the family that both boys were well; Lord Melgund had got a long 'tailed' coat as prescribed by the authorities at Eton but Henry had not been obliged to have one. Both were required to wear white neckcloths but Mr Hildyard had been distressed about the way they had been so badly made. Back in Paris, the party found their new accommodation 'magnificent' and Catherine was particularly pleased to have been allocated the library of the house in Rue Monsieur as a schoolroom. The walls and doors in the drawing room were nothing but mirrored glass so that nobody could move without seeing themselves from head to foot. There was also a large garden.

Four days into November, on the birthday of Charles X, Catherine went in the carriage to the Champs-Élysées to 'see the amusements; there was an immense crowd all across the Pont de Louis Seize'. Returning from the Rue de la Paix a few days later, where Catherine had been shopping in Melinotte's for shoes for Fanny and herself, she learned that a soldier had been shot in the Champs de Mars for the murder of an officer. On her return home a letter from Mr Hildyard awaited her. He told of Lord Melgund getting through his examination very well, and although Henry had not done so well in his, both boys were in good spirits. They had rooms at a Mrs Valiancy's but they had been furnished with a bed only and Mr Hildyard had been obliged to buy other necessities for them.

On the Saturday following, the girls were introduced to Monsieur Faucher, who was to be the family's dancing master and the next day all but the earl went to the English Chapel in the Champs-Élysées and heard

a good sermon from the third chapter of St John's gospel. The minister seemed much shocked with the conduct of the English in Paris on the Lord's Day. In this worldly city, he said, their earnest prayer ought to be: 'Lord lead us not into temptation'.

On the Monday Catherine enjoyed a gallop in the Champ de Mars as far as the École Militaire, and soon afterwards received a letter from her mother posted from Chatham. Mrs Rutherford had travelled south with Gilbert, Catherine's brother, who was in good spirits and looking forward to joining HMS *Winchester*, a 52-gun vessel commanded by Captain Charles Austen.[12] She told Catherine that she hoped to come to Paris as soon as Gilbert had been fitted out. There was also a letter from Eton, where Lord Melgund and Henry were quite happy and had seen Mrs Rutherford for five minutes while she was passing through London.

Fanny's fourteenth birthday was on Sunday 15 November and she went with Catherine to the Chapel de Marbeuf, where Mr Montague preached a good sermon but, in Catherine's opinion, 'he was too violent against the Catholics whom he called blasphemers'. Monday turned out to be a busy day in the house. It was also Lord

Minto's forty-seventh birthday and the music mistress came in the morning. She was joined by a new drawing master and a young mistress to teach French, a Monsieur Constantin and Mademoiselle Baudier respectively. There was considerable excitement when Lady Minto took Catherine to the opera on the evening of 24 November to hear *La Muette de Portici*.[13] The opera house was soon complimented on its size and beauty. The 'dancing dresses and scenes were beyond anything … and finished by an irruption [*sic*] of Vesuvius which was quite magnificent'. Among those coming and going at the house on the Rue Monsieur that night, soon after Lady Minto and Catherine returned from the opera, were Sir Thomas and Lady Hislop, whose daughter would marry the Minto's son, William. A day or so later there was more news from Eton: Lord Melgund and Henry had become fags and 'toasted the bread of other boys', and they would be setting off for Paris on 9 December. Nearer their arrival Catherine took Charlie and George to have their hair cut, probably for the first time other than by their nanny.

The weather became bitterly cold but after they had all been to church on 6 December, and had called on Lady Hislop and Sir Thomas, who were staying at the Hotel de Brighton, Catherine was cheered by a letter from her mother, who was to arrive in Paris in the company of Lord Melgund and Henry. Every carriage which came into the courtyard of the house in the Rue Monsieur 'set them all listening' and it was not until about half past seven in the evening of 12 December, when Catherine had just gone up to her room, that Fanny and Lizzie came running to tell her to go down to the drawing room. As she prepared to join the girls, Betty, a nurse, burst into the room and asked her whether she had seen Henry 'for he had been in the nursery'. They could not believe her because they had expected to sit up late for both of the boys. Catherine let a bedroom candlestick drop out of her hand as she flew into the drawing room, where the first person she saw was her brother, Gilbert. She had not expected to see him for several years at least. At Dover he had joined their mother, who equally had no idea of his coming until he turned up there. The Elliot boys looked well: Henry was really quite fat and, furthermore, 'he did not look as odd in his [Eton] neck cloth as we had expected'.

The family went to Notre-Dame to attend mass on Christmas morning but Catherine found 'the whole thing quite unintelligible'; the music was beautiful but the church extremely cold. After the service the party went to the Louvre and, since Mr Hildyard was with them, Catherine 'had the pleasure of showing him his likeness'. A few days before when she had taken the children there on their own they had accidentally found someone who looked like the boys' tutor – 'the mouth in particular'. The following day there was an expedition to a very fine shop in the Rue du Coq, St-Honoré to see what Catherine described as their 'etiennes' or shoes and other expensive goods. All the boys were there except Catherine's brother Gilbert, who had gone with Monsieur LeFévre to the ambassador's residence to pick up his passport. He was to leave Paris a day or so later to join his ship.

On Sunday 27 December the intense cold was so 'terrible' that Lord Minto would not hear of the children going to church, but by the time the afternoon came he had relented, and Catherine and the boys went to the Champ de Mars, then round by the Champs-Élysées, crossed the Seine by the Pont Louis Seize and returned home by the boulevards. They dined at six, with her journal reminding the reader that there were some twenty-eight people in the house on that day, and a further eleven 'out a-doors'. Later that week Mlle Baudier returned after being away for three weeks while Lizzie and Catherine began Italian lessons with Signor Martelli. Lady Minto gave Catherine a beautiful pincushion for her Christmas box. The cold spell continued, so much so that members of the household could be seen wearing shawls, fur tippets and cloaks, and sitting close to the fireside. Outside, the boys had seen several people skating on the Seine. The eve of 1830 brought back memories for Catherine of the ball there had been at Minto the previous year.

At the start of the new decade, Catherine and the children repeated their visit to the Louvre to see an exhibition of royal porcelain, tapestries and mosaics, but it was overshadowed by the uncomfortablly low temperatures which gave her headaches. They also went back to the Gobelin museum with Mr Hildyard, the streets being 'frightfully slippery'. Lord Minto, who had brought the coach, found it was 'too much loaded' and had to get out and walk. Catherine bought Scott's poetical works as a present for her mother, along with some caricatures for 'the boys to hang up in their room at Eton'. Then, no sooner had the boys clambered into the coupé of the diligence on 19 January and left for Calais (a very rough crossing of four hours), than there was a complete thaw in Paris. Strong winds took the place of the cold and ice.

During Mrs Rutherford's stay over Christmas it seems Catherine had arranged for her to sit for a portrait, which arrived just after the boys had returned to Eton. Both women were pleased with the work done by Madame Bigarne, the artist; it was 'very like' her. Since she was leaving for England the next day, Catherine took her mother and the children out in the carriage on 23 January and in the evening to the Italian opera with Lady Minto and the two Counts Montesquieu to hear Malibran sing.[14] A little under a week later Lord Minto had a letter from Mr Hildyard which gave more details of the boys' crossing. It had been very disagreeable and their packet boat had struck the pier as they were entering the harbour at Dover. News also came that Catherine's mother had returned to England safely and was about to leave for Portsmouth from whence Gilbert and his ship, HMS *Winchester*, were to sail.

As the cold returned, confining the young to a small room next to the sitting room which was more easily kept warm, Catherine's routine became one of short expeditions and a little shopping. But even the purchase of a ribbon for Betty's cap brought its hazards – she was 'very near run over by a carriage'. Flakes of snow fell now and then all day and by the end of the first week in February the Seine had frozen over again. Catherine was much affected by the sufferings of the poor. A young beggar was found frozen to death at the foot of a tree and mothers had been found dead with their children; several had dropped down in the street. She told the tale of a 'dreadful circumstance' which happened near the Rue Monsieur:

A gentleman was sitting in his own room reading, when the door burst suddenly open, a man rushed in, and holding a loaded pistol to his throat demanded his purse. The gentleman, seeing no alternative, threw it on the table; the man opened it, took out ten francs, with which he made off. The gentleman's curiosity was awakened at so singular a theft that he determined to follow the man. He saw him run along the boulevard and go into a baker's shop and come out again with some bread and, running straight on, saw him enter a house. The gentleman asked the baker if he knew the man. He said he did not know his name but he knew he lived somewhere nearby. The baker explained that the man had owed him ten francs which he had just paid, and bought some bread. Determined to know the truth if possible, the gentleman rather imprudently followed him into the house and, running up stairs, opened a door into a cold miserable-looking room in which stood the man distributing the bread amongst his famished-looking children. The noise of the door opening made him turn round, but no sooner did he discover the gentleman he had just robbed had entered, than (either from shame or from fear of justice) he made a spring to the window, threw himself headlong from a balcony into the street where he was dashed to pieces.

The poor gentleman, Catherine said, blamed himself very much, but she hoped the fact that he had gone into the house with a good intention would 'console him'.

With bad weather continuing, it was not until St Valentine's Day that Catherine could go out in an open carriage. It was the first time in 1830 that this was possible. Driving in the Bois de Boulogne she passed the young Duc de Bordeaux coming from La Bagatelle, one of the city's manicured gardens, where he went every day.[15] It was about then that the fourteen-year-old Fanny, doubtless with Catherine's help, conjured up some verse which illustrated life in the household in the Rue Monsieur.

> Gibby's got a curly wig,
> But Pawkie and Bob will cut it
> Charlie likes to play a jig
> And sturdy Liz to foot it.
>
> Catherine's thin and falls away.
> O'er some Scotch love she's brooding.
> But Miss Baudier's brisk and gay,
> For she's got damn'd plum-pudding.
>
> Hun and Will are gone to school,
> But Baby's here to chatter,
> Doddy stays to play the fool,
> And Lot – to coax and flatter.
>
> Mammy went to Court one night
> and wandered through the kitchens,
> She didn't think the cooks polite
> But thought the King bewitching.
>
> Mary gives a solemn look,
> To Fanny who's a slattern,
> Cousin Ned don't like his book
> But likes to flirt with Cattern.
>
> Pappy wouldn't go, he said,
> Because he's not so loyal,
> And only has his breeches made
> To visit Palais-Royal.[16]

Among the illusions above was one that referred to Harriet Ann Gertrude, the last of the Elliot's ten children, who 'was here to chatter' and who had probably been born in 1827. 'Hun' was an alternative name for Henry. Cousin Ned, probably Edward Drinkwater, may have liked to flirt with Catherine but it was Fanny who described herself as a slattern, 'an untidy, dirty woman', and her elder sister Mary, always something of a butt, who had the solemn look of Rossetti's *La Penserosa*, as her husband would call her. The reference to Lord Minto, and the suggestion that he needed little prompting to leave the pomp of the court behind, was surprising given the diplomatic career he would shortly follow.

A week later, the children much enjoyed a great carnival in the Bois and on 23 February, to celebrate young Gibby's fourth birthday, Catherine took all her charges to an entertaining parade along the boulevards, where they laughed at three hunchbacks on horseback, and Robinson Crusoe and his Man Friday. Two days later, and with the temperature at 63 degrees Fahrenheit, it was possible for long walks to be taken at last in the warm sun. The unaccustomed exercise meant that they all felt very stiff when they reached home. In the Champ de Mars, young priests and different schools were also making the best of the fine weather. On the penultimate evening of the month, however, Catherine was disappointed at not being able to attend a ball given by Mlle Baudin on account of 'Gibby' being unwell. Madame Bigarne came to drink tea with them instead. All in all, the last two days of February were busy with visitors, and the sight of those who Catherine called 'the fashionables'. These included a Mr Haig, whom the children 'liked better than we had expected', Mr and Mrs Pelham seen riding in the Bois, Mr and Mrs Locke, and Miss Tollemache. Then, on the second day of March, Lord and Lady Minto went to the Chambre des Députés with their eldest daughter to hear Charles Dix make a speech at the opening. There were cries of '*Vive le roi*' both when he entered and as he left. Lady Minto told the children how the gentlemen wore velvet robes and threw their hats in the air. Fanny asked if the ladies did the same.

Lady Minto commissioned a portrait of Catherine from Madame Bigarne for which she started sitting at her house, 9 Rue Cassette, early in March. The artist asked her to be grandly dressed but Catherine begged that she might be painted in her ordinary dress as the picture was for her mother. Madame Bigarne consented with a little reluctance, Catherine suspecting that she thought that 'fine feathers made fine birds'. She also asked Catherine to sit for a few days after her portrait was finished as she wished to have a sketch of Catherine for herself – a 'fine compliment', as the journal recorded, '*n'est-ce pas?*' In the second half of the month, an important subscription ball for poor English people in Paris topped the social calendar. Lady Minto, who raised 2,000 francs, was one of the cause's patrons and when she found there was a spare ticket, Fanny went along too. Lady Mary opened the ball with the Duc de Chartres, the son of the Duc d'Orléans, Fanny dancing with a Colonel Craddock. The nineteenth of March was Lord Melgund's sixteenth birthday and the children had muffins for breakfast in his honour. This was followed the next evening by Catherine and a party of five attending the opera, where they again heard Maria Malibran – this time in a performance of Rossini's *La Gazza Ladra*.

On Sunday 28 March, Catherine referred in her journal to two more birthdays, one being 'baby' or Harriet, who was 'three years old', the other being that of her brother Gilbert, who was fifteen and 'sailing on the Atlantic'. With it being the last

Sunday in the month, Catherine went to the chapel at Marbeuf with Lady Mary after which they joined Lady Minto and Mr Edward Drinkwater to visit Lady Sinclair, a member of the Caithness family. Having lunched, they walked in warm sunshine to the Luxembourg Gardens with Fanny and Lizzy but the Parisian heat was soon preventing walks altogether. Catherine recalled that she and the family had been at Richmond just twelve months before, where they had had a heavy fall of snow.[17]

As April came in, Paris was enduring a temperature of 96 degrees before breakfast but it failed to deter Lady Minto, Lady Hislop, Catherine and Mr Hayter, a music teacher, from attending an important concert given by Malibran and Ferdinando Paer, the composer and pianist. In the audience was the Duchesse de Berri, whose expression Catherine liked, together with the Duke and Duchess of Hamilton and their daughter. Other guests included young Sir William Eden, probably the sixth Baronet, who was well known to the family. The boys reached Paris on 4 April for a month's holiday, Mr Hillyard bringing with him an atlas, a present for Catherine. It was not long before Good Friday was upon them and Catherine took Gibby to hear Mr Hayter play his guitar. Paris was en fête and some of the ladies' dresses were *magnifique* but the carriages and horses were far 'inferior to our English ones'. On Easter Sunday the family went to a children's theatre and came home 'much pleased with everything they had seen'.

The following day was the anniversary of Charles X's entry into Paris. There was to have been a review of troops in the Champs de Mars but it was postponed due to bad weather and a Minto party instead called on Lord Lansdowne at the Hotel de Londres. He was laid up with the gout.[18] When the review eventually took place, Catherine reported that everyone had a good view of the old king but 'it was a poor affair'. There was no firing, or manoeuvring, and the music was 'wretched'. The king did nothing but ride up and down the ranks on a white horse, and the young Duc de Bordeaux followed in a carriage with his mother, sister and several other ladies. The following Sunday saw the family at Père Lachaise, the boys in the phaeton and Catherine's group in the coach.

April and May were to be months anticipating the family's move to Switzerland for the summer. Paris had provided a pleasant winter sojourn during which opera, concerts and a wide social life had fed Lord and Lady Minto's mind and spirit, while the children had been introduced to architecture, art and ordinary life in a foreign country. It had been the first extended stay in the French capital that Lady Minto had enjoyed now that the Elliot family was complete. In generally warm weather, visits were made to Meudon with its fortified palace, Sèvres and the china manufactory, and Versailles where they toured the palace and its sumptuous state rooms. The boys left for Eton at the beginning of May soon after their mother and Lady Mary attended the first of several breakfasts given by Madame Apponyi, a leading hostess and the wife of the Austrian ambassador; but with news that His Majesty King George IV might be dying, Lord Minto decided his place was in London.

While the earl and countess were in England, Lady Mary and Catherine called on Lady Hislop and 'little Emma', William's future wife, and attended a concert given by the blind pupils of a school in the Rue St-Victor which Mr Hayter's son attended, having become blind after a bout of measles. It was 'very wonderful to hear them all playing together and keeping such good time ... two girls sung and one played the piano, the boys played on the clarinet, bassoon and violin'. Four days before Lord and Lady Minto returned from England, Catherine had been frustrated by the lack of a carriage to take the children to see the King and Queen of Naples in the Champs-Élysées but they were soon pleased to see the parents back, albeit 'covered with dust and very much sun burnt'. The children sat on the steps in front of the drawing room windows and heard all about London. The king had been close to death and was to die at the end of June. Lady Minto had been quite delighted with the visit she paid to Eton, a 'lovely place and the boys looking so happy' but she had been very struck by how dowdy English ladies appeared. Their petticoats were long and 'dragly', their headdresses ugly, and several ladies – wrote Catherine – wore velvet gowns which would have been thought 'outré', or perhaps more appropriately 'old-fashioned', in France.

Packing for the journey to Switzerland then began in earnest. Last-minute buying of books, and the packing of others, started the process. They were to avoid the events of July and August when the rumours about another revolution in France, which Catherine had mentioned in her journal, became a reality. She had written in March how the people thought Charles X was acting foolishly in his dealings with the houses of parliament and that 'everyone was angry with him'. Lady Minto, who had been at court the previous Sunday, referred to the disregard the King seemed to show about his position.

Riots were to break out in Paris on 25 July. They were followed by 'Three Glorious Days' during which the populace showed its dislike of the Ordinances of Saint-Cloud which had been announced by the King's first minister, Jules Armand de Polignac. The King and Polignac suspended the liberty of the press, dissolved the newly elected Chambre des Députés, reduced the number of députés in future chambers, and appointed new, reactionary Conseillers d'Etat. Clashes with the National Guard resulted in the death of some 1,800 Parisians and 300 soldiers. On 2 August, Charles X abdicated at Rambouillet and twenty minutes later his elder son, the Dauphin, also gave way to Henri, the ten-year-old Duc de Bordeaux, who was proclaimed Henri V, King of France and Navarre. It was, however, a fictive or imaginary reign that lasted only seven days. The National Assembly refused to confirm Henri as king and declared the French throne vacant. Seven days later the Duc d'Orléans became Louis Philippe, King of the French, and he appointed the Duc de Broglie as his prime minister.

# 3

# THE FAMILY RETURNS TO SWITZERLAND
# (1830-1831)

With warm weather replacing the only too memorable cold winter, Catherine Rutherford expected the family to leave Paris for Vevey in April, but there was still much to do and, in the event, the family did not depart until the end of May 1830.[1] The party arranged itself for the first part of the journey and a stay at Melun, with Lord and Lady Minto in the barouche, and Ellen (a maid) and Charlie on the dickey seat, leading the way. Behind was the coach with Lady Mary, Fanny, Lizzie, Doddy and Catherine, with William on the dickey. Betty and Irma with the three little ones followed in the chariot with Mr Friend on the outside seat. Doctor Williams and Robert travelled in the phaeton and came a little later, while Monsieur Guillaume, the cook, was in the 'bang up'. Three other listed members of the group were Tinker, who later turned out to be Lord Minto's horse, together with Pug and Jean, the children's pets.

Ten days later, the party reached Vevey, having stayed at the same places and hotels as they did the previous year. At Auxerre they encountered eight English priests in the hotel on their way to Rome, and in Dijon they took the same rooms for the third time. Irma's mother and father lived at Champagnole and she showed Catherine and the children a delightful park on the evening of their arrival. After passing St Cergues and the Dole, which they called their 'little hill', and spending a night at Nyon, they took the lake steamer, the *Leman*, to Vevey.[2] The family stayed on deck admiring those mountains not in the clouds until it began to rain, whereupon they went down to the cabin which was very large and 'prettily fitted up with books'. The vessel touched at Rolle, Morges and Ouchy to leave and take on passengers and as it approached Vevey a cannon was fired from the steamer, and another as the party landed. For Catherine, the captain answered the description of the Red Rover in Fenimore Cooper's book of that name and only wanted 'a little dignity to make him complete'.[3] By four o'clock on 4 June they were ensconced at the Hotel des Trois Couronnes, where they met up with a surprised M. Monnet, who had not expected them so soon.

The family soon moved back into the Château de la Tour and, after several days of tidying the borders in the garden and arranging themselves inside the mansion, everyone relaxed. The summer routine of long walks with Lady Minto and the children resumed along with the occasional trip by boat on Lake Geneva. Catherine wrote to her brother Gilbert, sending the letter to her mother for forwarding, although she thought HMS *Winchester* was at Nassau. She and Lady Mary resumed their sketching together but their walking could occasionally call for extreme measures – as on 24 June when her charge was forced to take off her stockings and shoes to wade across a stream near Chailly. They eventually made a sketch of Le Chatelard, probably with the camera lucida, an optical device used as a drawing aid by artists.[4] With the mountains and the lake in the foreground, it looked especially beautiful. Not unusually, the Dents du Midi remained enveloped in cloud except for its peak. When the pair reached home Catherine's feet were quite blistered and she felt a little stiff. The post had brought a letter from Mr Hildyard reporting that Lord Melgund had got his remove and had made a speech. For his part, Henry had got a medal for Greek and seemed quite happy at Eton. Both boys were to leave London at the end of June to join the family at Vevey. Then, in the evening after dinner, a party rowed out on the lake, where the sunset was beautiful and the snowy peaks of the Dents du Midi quite visible.

On the last Sunday in June, Fanny, Lizzy, Doddy and Catherine left the other children to attempt a climb up Mont Pèlerin since Lizzy and Doddy had not been with them when it was climbed the previous year. As they passed the church of St-Martin its clock struck three. It turned out to be a hot climb between the vineyard walls to Joigny and, seeing an old man at the door of a chalet, they asked him the best way to take. The grass in many places grew very thickly and it seemed a sin to tread on the vast array of scabious, gentians, rhododendrons, candytuft and 'loads of other garden flowers'. But the children were most delighted with the blaeberries and strawberries which made their mouths and fingers purple. Fearful that they might not reach the top before sunset, they pushed on steadily through woods of beech and chestnut, eventually reaching the peak after what had been a three-hour climb and saw around the whole lake, the snow-topped mountains and the softer Jura to the north. They sat down near a fountain and emptied their provision bag ravenously. In all, the expedition had taken five and a half hours and they returned at eight o'clock to a dinner which was waiting for them.

At dinner on the first day of July the family drank Henry's good health on his thirteenth birthday. There was also news of the other youngster of similar age, Catherine's Gilbert, who had apparently been very ill and had been taken to Providence on Rhode Island. For three weeks his life was despaired of and he was being sent home aboard Admiral Fleming's ship HMS *Barham* and was expected daily at Portsmouth. Catherine, who often felt alone in a world where a large and loving family enjoyed such good fortune, wrote in her journal that she would be 'miserable' until she received another letter. However, fuller and happier news from her mother and Gilbert arrived a week or so later. His ship had reached Barbados around the middle of March and went from there to Port Royal in Jamaica, where he was bled and sent to his hammock.[5] Next morning he was so ill that he was bled in both arms and more than 60 ounces of blood were taken from him. He was put into a cot and a sentry placed to allow no one to speak to him. Arriving in Port Royal he was swung overboard; all his messmates took their last look as they thought of him in hospital. After three weeks it was decided he was fit enough to be shipped home to Portsmouth in Admiral Fleming's ship, something Catherine already knew. Her reaction would not have pleased her brother. She hoped he would never be obliged to go to sea again 'for his own sake' as well as his mother's.

It was 6 July when Lord Minto, Lady Mary, Fanny and Catherine went on board the steamboat *Winkelreid* and had breakfast in their cabin, which turned out, as Catherine explained, to be smaller than that of her sister ship, the *Leman*; but it had a good view, as it was surrounded by glass, and had a parquet floor and marble tables. The captain was 'as different from the Red Rover as it was possible to imagine, being a dour stupid-looking man'. The vessel called at Ouchy, where seven Englishmen and four ladies 'disgusted and amused' the Minto party with their fine airs. They sailed to Sécheron which had 'quite a different sort of beauty from Vevey and the other end of the lake', arriving there about 4 p.m They were met by a boat sent for them by their host, Monsieur Dejean, at the Hotel d'Angleterre. After dinner, the party walked down to the lake which was 'studded as thick as possible with Châteaux and gentlemen's seats with gardens and trees quite like Kew or Richmond'. The next two days were spent visiting several family acquaintances, who included Mlle Bernard and Mrs Botte, together with some exploration of the botanical gardens, Madame de Staël's house and those of Voltaire and Byron. Mrs Botte's husband showed them 'most handsome things' which included 'a paper-weight with a crown on it set in pearls and a decorative cage in which there were two singing birds about the size of bumble bees. The return journey was accomplished by the steamer *Leman* taking the party off the small boat from Sécheron about halfway across the lake. Breakfast followed in their cabin. The captain seemed to be delighted to have the family back aboard his ship although the lake was pretty rough and the ship 'tossed and heaved a good deal'.

At the end of the month, when Lord Melgund and Henry were travelling to Switzerland, their father read in *Galignani's Messenger* that Charles X had stopped the liberty of the press in France and that the people were quite enraged about it.[6] The effect in Vevey was that there was neither a post nor newspapers for a few days. When letters did arrive, one from the boys – who were in Brussels – told of their plans to come south by steamer up the Rhine via Cologne, Coblenz, Strasbourg and Basle. Meanwhile, horrible accounts were coming through from the French capital. Charles X was said to have left Paris, the Dauphin had been killed, and the Rue de Rivoli had been covered with dead bodies; part of the Tuileries had also been set on fire. Additional news came through a surprising channel. Early on the morning of 3 August, when the boys had still not arrived by the diligence from Bern, the family decided to sail their boat, the *Bawsy*, on the lake.[7] It was too hot to do anything else. Later in the day they met the steam boat *Winkelreid* which towed them back. 'It felt', Catherine wrote, 'delightful to fly thro' the water as quick as the bateau de vapeur'. While this was going on, a member of the crew threw them a gazette which gave the news about 1,500 people being killed in Paris and an incredible number wounded. The Dauphin, she was happy to see, had not been killed but 'every vestige of anything belonging to the Bourbons ... pictures of Charles X along with his statue were thrown into the Seine'. They were to hear later that some of the fighting had taken place in the Rue de Babylone, which was very close to their house in the Rue de Monsieur and along which they went every day. All the troops had been forced to evacuate Paris which was now in the possession of the National Guard with General Lafayette, who had become leader of the revolution, at their head. Whenever he made an appearance, he was greeted with cries of '*Vive la nation, vive la liberté*'. It was similar to the situation in 1789.

Catherine's personal commentary was interesting if somewhat sentimental. She wrote that

> Paris is now quiet; the tri-coloured flag [instead of the white and fleur-de-lis] now floats over all the public buildings in that formal city and the people, having gained their object, seem now peaceably inclined. Letters from Paris say the people behaved exceedingly well throughout and as yet not one instance of barbarity has been discovered. To us who have left Paris not quite two months ago, all this appears like a dream. It was so quiet, and although it was well-known that the king was very much disliked, a revolution was never dreamt of. His own madness and stupidity have hastened his ruin and he will have few or none to lament his downfall. The Montesquieus, who were very intimate with the Duc d'Orleans, will benefit by the change of kings.

Four days into the month of August there was still no news of the boys. The family sat all day outside the Château walls in the shade, looking out for them. When the lake steamer came in sight, Lord Minto took 'Tinker' and rode to Vevey, where he found them. Catherine's first sight of Lord Melgund was him riding his father's horse as Mr Hildyard and Henry came on foot with Lord Minto. Both had on smooth frocks and looked remarkably well and much grown. They looked 'so fair beside us who are burned black' wrote Catherine. Later, all the family went out on the lake in their sailing boat except for Lady Minto and Catherine, who sat on the end of the pier. Unfortunately, the party afloat had great difficulty in coming back as the wind was blowing strongly against them. Men along the shore came running to their assistance and Catherine remarked on how readily they all lent their help, especially when several of them ran into the lake up to their waists to draw the boat on shore. After the young ladies had been rescued, the men towed the boat round into the harbour for good measure.

After breakfast the following day, Lord Melgund, Lady Mary and Catherine walked outside the walls of the Château and took a view of the Chancellerie with the camera lucida. Then after a bathe they went to Vevey with the boys, Mr Hildyard and Dr Gibson, finishing the day on the terrace, where they remained until midnight when the temperature was still above 80 degrees. The Eton party soon became acclimatised to the schedule of expeditions and on 6 August everyone with the exception of Lord and Lady Minto rose at five o'clock to climb the gentle slopes of the Pleiades, facing the Dent d'Oche. In the phaeton were Fanny, Henry and Charlie, Lady Mary, Dr Gibson and Mr Hildyard, while William and Catherine walked and reached quite a height by about 8 a.m. After cutting their names into a table they found there, they consumed some bread and milk, butter, eggs and cheese. Going on to the top they were afraid of a thunderstorm which they saw collecting in the valley with the result they only sat for a short while. Descending by the north side of the hilltop to Bains de l'Alliez, they bought some very cold mineral water although it tasted and smelt of rotten eggs. The boys were delighted at catching a large snake which they brought home. The rain which fell that night was the first they had seen for a month.

They enjoyed an expedition across the lake to St-Gingolph in the Haute-Savoie aboard the *Bawsy*, and dinner was ordered early the next day as the family was travelling to Bex in the Valais that evening, close to the town of Aigle. They left a little past 5 p.m. and reached their destination three and a half hours later. In the phaeton had been Lord Minto, Mr Hildyard, Charles, Robert and a Limousin guide, while Lady Minto, Lady Mary, Fanny, Henry, Lord Melgund and Catherine travelled in a caleche, a light carriage with two or four low wheels and a collapsible top. Lord Minto's vehicle was soon in the lead. When they were nearly at Chillon, a charabanc passed them. In it was Mr Coleridge, one of the masters at Eton. He turned back and spoke to the family, Henry being one of his pupils. The party then drove through Villeneuve and Aigle, across very low-lying and marshy land to Bex.

After breakfast they all walked about a mile up a beautiful valley full of chestnuts, oaks and larches towards yet another large salt mine. Readers will recall their visit to Salines the previous year. The area appeared more like a gentleman's park than anything natural. At first they were introduced to the saltwater filtering through faggots which were piled high, and then they were shown how putrefaction acted on pieces of wood over different lengths of time. Further up the hill they came to the salt mines proper, where, to some amusement, they had to put on greasy-looking frock coats with hoods which made them look like Eskimos. The guide lit lamps and they made their way to the mine entrance, leaving Lady Minto to wait for their return. After going straight along an immense way, they came to a huge echoing hall. When they returned to the surface and daylight after two hours in the mines, they were so dazzled they could not see anything and the atmosphere felt so hot. Lady Minto laughed when she saw the droll figures emerge, while Mr Hildyard signed 'the travellers' book'. It rained hard before they could reach Bex but, having dined, they set off for home, having 'good fun' on the journey. With five on a seat meant to hold only two in the caleche and with Fanny and Henry sitting on the others' knees, it surprised no one that the phaeton got home a full half hour before them.

A lengthy period of poor weather in the middle of the month restricted the number of expeditions the family could make. One exception was a lengthy tour on the way to Martigny and Chamonix between 20 and 22 August, which went ahead without Lord Minto, who felt unwell and wanted to save himself for the Monte Rosa. Catherine and the children thought the absence of father and perhaps mother meant that their mountain expeditions were now at an end. In the circumstances, Lady Minto came and Mr Hildyard was put in charge. The first day saw them across the Rhône and as soon as they arrived, the *chef des guides* was sent for so that the following day's journey could be planned. They left Martigny at six in the morning with three guides; Lady Mary's guide was Pillier, Fanny's was Jean Maurice, and Catherine had Hubert, along with a mule called Marquise. From the top of the pass they saw the Jungfrau and many snow-capped mountains, and at the bottom Martigny lay at their feet. Walking through a valley, Catherine saw a glacier for the first time with a few blue cracks in it. After some refreshment and when the mules had been rested, they rode up the Bois de Maria which was very steep, requiring the animals to rest every few minutes. The guides took hold of the hands of their charges in order to prevent the mules jerking them off their saddles. It was so steep that the poor beasts were almost standing on their hind legs, and after an hour and a half of such precipitous going, the air grew very cold as they approached the Mont Blanc chain. Coming down the col, the guides told them the names of all the dozens of mountains, needles and glaciers in view.

Never could 'the most polished gentlemen be more attentive', Catherine wrote. She never felt uneasy or frightened the whole day.

They stayed at the Hotel d'Angleterre at Chamonix and had a glorious view of Mont Blanc. In the restaurant, where they dined from the table d'hôte, besides themselves there were only three Germans. After dinner Mr Hildyard had a long conversation with one of the guides about the approach to climbing Lord Minto's Monte Rosa. He told them the way he had climbed Mont Blanc along with many of the stories which reflected life in the mountains – the hazards, escapes and catastrophes. Catherine found it amazing that only seventy years before, the area they had so enjoyed was largely uninhabited save for robbers and bandits. Two English visitors, William Windham and Richard Pococke, had, she wrote, been responsible in 1727 for opening it up to visitors. After riding nearly 30 miles on her mule that day Catherine felt 'uncommonly sleepy' and all the family were soon in bed.

Leaving Chamonix on the return journey the next day, with seven mules and three guides, the family party approached the Tête Noire, where the road became more beautiful, and they crossed the Eau Noire over a wooden bridge without parapets. Walking rather than riding soon became the order of the day but after a while Catherine got ahead of the group and almost immediately fell down by the side of the road. Charlie called for one of the guides' leather cups to get some water for her and in a moment everyone surrounded her, offering her various berries and even a peppermint lozenge. Some miles further on they came across an enormous pile of stones with an inscription in English and French which had been paid for by Lord Portsmouth and Lady Caroline North as a sort of monument 'in remembrance of a few happy hours they had passed there'. When they reached Trient, Caroline had some wine and water, and after a rest felt quite refreshed when 'the mules were brought to the door'. She then rode on to Martigny, where no sooner had they arrived than Lord and Lady Minto drove up in the phaeton from Vevey. Lord Minto, Lord Melgund and Mr Hildyard were to go to the top of the Monte Rosa while Lady Minto took the rest of the party to see what she called 'the kernel' of Switzerland.

It was past eight o'clock in the morning when they left Martigny. The Monte Rosa guides, some in a charabanc, and some riding mules, set off first. The 'bang up' followed with Lord Minto's party while Catherine's group had a coach with four horses. At Sion they ate lunch and, although disliking the flat uninteresting country, the Diablerets soon came into view, and the party arrived in the village of Turtmann around six o'clock. The next day 'we separated from the two lords', as Catherine put it, with Lord Minto's party taking the road to Zermatt and the other meeting their guides to conduct them to Leukerbad, which they reached at midday. En route for Frutigen the roads got steeper and steeper such that they could not be seen until one was on them. The stones got too slippery, the path too narrow and the precipices at one side too terrible-looking for them to ride any further. As they dismounted they were joined by two Englishmen and a Swede whom they had seen at Chamonix. The path was cut in the side of the rocks so that it hung over their heads. The guides screamed to let them hear the echo. When they got to a chalet they were relieved to find their mules waiting for them to mount. They were obliged to wrap themselves up as they were hot and the air at the top very bitter. When the top was reached they stayed a while looking at the snowy chain of the Matterhorn and Monte Rosa without a single cloud and 'touching the sky'. On the top there was a dismal lake and not a tree or leaf to be seen. On the descent they came to the gate which separated the canton of Bern from the Vallais, and where they found their mules again waiting them; they were soon in the valley of the River Kander which 'was too lovely to be described'. Arriving in the village of Kandersteg, they hired a charabanc and drove to Frutigen, where they arrived at their inn about five in the afternoon. The sun set on the Blümlisalp and the village looked quite new after a fire a few years ago wiped out the original buildings.

The following morning, Saturday 28 August, they hired two charabancs and left early for Interlaken and Lauterbrunnen. The smart people Catherine saw in the lakeside town led to her concluding that they spoiled it sadly. The walnut trees, however, fared better, being 'quite immense, spreading and beautiful' and the party walked about until dinner time when they met up with Lady Sophia Raffles, the widowed second wife of the founder of Singapore, and Ella, her young daughter.[8] Continuing their journey by charabanc, the party drove along the banks of the River Leutschen up the narrow valley to Lauterbrunnen, where they arrived around four in the afternoon. After breakfast in a private 'salle' the following morning they set out for Grindelwald, riding 'our great coach horses' with two German guides while ascending the Wengeralp. Although the going was steep, their horses 'trotted up hill' through a pine wood, reaching the top in rather more than three hours. The appearance of the Jungfrau 'in all her glory and tearfulness' prompted Lady Minto to recall many of the Alps she had visited and speak of how imposing the scene before them really was. Covered in snow 'it looked quite perpendicular and much more awful-looking than Mont Blanc'. As if to prove the point, the party caught the sound of what they thought was a clap of thunder until their guides pointed to the top nearby of the Jungfrau and said, 'Voilà une avalanche!' They watched as the snow poured down a gully in the rocks for the distance of 9,000 feet with a thundering noise the whole way. Before beginning their descent they dined on bread. They rode for a long while down the side of the hill, 'which looked exactly like a Scotch moor only covered with rhododendrons instead of heather', and were back at Grindelwald about six in the evening. There followed more singing by Swiss girls and it was a shame to go to bed but again everyone was very tired.

It was early on the penultimate day of August when they left, still with their four Lauterbrunnen horses and two guides. They had a fair view of the Wetterhorn, the Mönch and the Eiger. Their destination this time was Brienz and they sent their guides with the horses to the inn to order dinner while they walked up to the glacier of Rosenlau – immensely high and blue, and clear in a clear sky. Walking down to the inn they dined at the table d'hôte, where there was a noisy party of some eleven Germans but not, as Catherine wrote, 'so insufferable as the same number of English would have been'. After remounting, they had a most delightful ride into the valley of Meiringen, much broader than that at Lauterbrunnen. The banks of the River Aare were covered with large beech trees and the Reichenbach Falls were the largest and noisiest the party had seen. Lady Minto and Henry rode on to Meiringen to order a charabanc, which they found easily. There was some regret that they had not been able to stay a night there as 'it was such a lovely place'.

They left Brienz the next day by boat. It took their two men and three women rowers about two and a half hours to reach Interlaken, where Catherine showed more concern about the way the town was developing. It had 'become the resort of a set of fashionable English who think of nothing but balls and parties of pleasure, and I suppose, seldom think of the scenery'. She could not bear to see them; 'their fine silk gowns and gaudy ribbons seemed like a profanation of this lovely place'. They dined again with Lady Raffles and her daughter, along with two Englishmen, and afterwards Lady Minto showed them the house where she and Lord Minto had stayed on a previous visit. It began to rain when they got into a boat with an awning at Neuhaus and were rowed up the Lake Thun. They landed at Spiez expecting to find a charabanc but there was none to be had. In the event they lodged in an inn at Wimmis, which was particularly comfortable, and left the following morning in two charabancs. Following the Simmental, just before midday they reached Zweisimmen, where they ate, thereafter driving on to Saanen, where they hired two open charabancs. Driving into the canton of Vaud, they were delighted to hear all the people speaking French again and they reached Château-d'Oex a little before seven in the evening. As Catherine said, 'It had been a beautiful day and the evening promises well for the morrow.'

In the morning two charabancs were produced to take them the pleasant drive to the Col de Jaman, where they sat down a little while to look at the lake – 'our own dear lake' – and the Jura in the distance. A walk down to the Mont Avant was very steep but after having luncheon they turned towards Vernet, where they took a boat. They had endured what Catherine called 'seven hours of *penible* walking'. When the party neared the Château de la Tour they saw Lord Melgund in the 'barber's basin' somewhat to their horror and concluded that his party with Lord Minto had not succeeded in its attempt to climb Monte Rosa. But the question had to be asked, so all screamed 'had they been at the top?' to which they were delighted to hear the reply 'yes'. They had accomplished everything they set out to do. The little ones were in the arbour ready for bathing when Catherine slipped round the terrace wall and found Mr Hildyard sitting on one of the benches. He gave a great shout when he saw them, and Lord Minto, who had also heard the shout, came running. All three were exceptionally sunburnt and had apparently slept two nights on snow. Surprisingly, they had only arrived home from Martigny about an hour before Lady Minto's party.

The family was not to leave Switzerland for Paris until November and regular long walks were to feature during the remaining months of their stay. After a climb towards Mont Pèlerin with Dr Gibson, Mr Hildyard and the boys in the second week of September, Catherine enjoyed a sail the following day aboard the *Bawsy* to Vernet, where she and the boys landed and walked through orchards covered with crocuses until they reached the dark pine woods. They discovered an old ruin for which they had looked in vain the previous year and came down by a new path to the Pont de Brent. In the evening, there were fireworks on the pier.

A party rowed over to St-Gingolph on 17 September, a journey which took two hours. After an overnight stay on what was the French side of the lake, they set off early intending to reach the top of the Dent d'Oche. They had two guides and a horse without a side saddle for Lady Minto. The first part of their walk was along the banks of a roaring torrent which formed the boundary between Vallais and Savoy, but after one or two villages the scenery grew much barer and wilder. Lady Minto left the children and Catherine at this point 'as she was afraid of tiring herself'. It soon began to cloud over but when the children's mother had left them, every *dent* and *aiguille* became clear for a while. Eventually, the party was forced back by a violent shower of hail and, drenched to the skin and without a thing to change into, they returned to St-Gingolph after two hours. Catherine lit a fire in the room she shared with the young, where they stripped and sat in their nightgowns until the landlady sent Lady Mary some gowns for them, rather too wide for Fanny and Catherine. After dinner, and clothed with all the layers of gowns they could find, they rowed back across the lake, which fortunately was quite smooth. The final part of the journey was in the dark and they could hardly see to steer into the harbour at Vevey.

At the end of the month it was time for Lord Melgund, Henry and Mr Hildyard to return to Eton and a mail coach arrived from Sécheron to collect them. Catherine and the family were to miss them a great deal; it 'felt and looked so melancholy today at dinner without them, and everyone spoke so little that I was very glad when it was over'. Fortunately for them, the following day, when the boys would have been beyond the Jura and preparing to travel through the night, it was far from being cold. A couple of evenings later, Lord Minto read to the children from his journal about the ascent of Monte Rosa they had undertaken. He described how everyone suffered a good deal from cold on the first night, especially Mr Hildyard, while they waited on the Col du Cervin at 1,100 feet in the hope of the weather clearing. Next morning, in fine weather, they set off again and got to the top much more easily than anticipated. The Valley of St Nicholas they thought especially lovely. Cold was, however, a constant problem and Mr Hildyard's pulse rate had been very low.

A day or so later news from Paris told of the boys having arrived there safe and well. They had slept the first night at Orbe and the second at Salines while, once in Paris, they met Mrs Aitkin at the Tivoli and went with her to the theatre. Meanwhile in October the wine harvest was in full swing. There was no sermon in the church – people were so busy with their vintage. Vevey 'really stinks of wine cellars to a degree that is quite unacceptable', wrote Catherine. Irma, one of the family's nursery maids, left to stay for a while at Champagnole before rejoining them in Paris. On 19 October, Lord and Lady Minto, and Lady Mary, went to Geneva by the *Leman*, returning three days later by the same steamer. They brought back a present for Catherine of two beautiful drawings, no doubt realising the habit she had acquired of copying drawings by such local artists as Jean d'Aoste, Pierre Dronay and Michel de Liddes, the first two of whom came to visit her and the children one morning. At the end of the month the *Winkelried* passed the Château during the morning and fired a farewell salute to the family just as Gibby was having his curls cut off. There had been much consultation and hesitation about the decision but everyone agreed it was a great improvement. Fanny, Lizzy and Catherine 'bought stuff in Vevey for Guy Fawkes' and on 1 November it was the *Leman*'s turn to sail past on her last voyage that season. Catherine even saw the 'Red Rover' pacing the deck. It was 'very dismal to see everything disappearing'.

The journal entry for the day of the family's departure, 15 November, concluded wistfully: 'we left our dear old Château this morning about 9 o'clock'. Monsieur Monnet and everyone was at the door to say their goodbyes, and soon the travellers were past Lausanne despite the teeming rain which persisted all day. They stopped around two o'clock at Cossonnay, where the children dined, and eventually reached

Orbe, where they were to stay the night. Louise and the cook had gone on ahead in the 'bang up' to prepare beds and fires. Robert and the doctor travelled in the phaeton while the rest of the party travelled in their own carriages as usual. As they entered the town Catherine noticed that something about the new bridge, and the town arch, was different from when they were last there. They had to go round by a different way as a result. The journey had taken five and a half hours.

The following night they stayed at their familiar inn at Pontarlier, as they had the previous year, but soon after one of the springs of Catherine's carriage broke, thus delaying the party considerably. Nevertheless, the onward journey to Paris via Dijon, Montbard and Tonnerre was completed without further incident. It is noteworthy that the young Fanny seems to have started writing her diary at Melun while the family were travelling to Paris, a habit that was to last with a few breaks until 1898, the year of her death. A few days in a hotel followed; but soon after midday on 25 November, Lord and Lady Minto, Lady Mary, Fanny and Catherine arrived at their new home, 10 Rue de Courcelles on the recently developed right bank of the Seine. Writing about the new abode, Catherine noted that it was 'a most magnificent house, the furniture is all new and everything seems covered with satin and gold. The rooms feel quite hot, having hot pipes blowing into them on all sides.' The dining room was surrounded by pillars and lit from the top while its floor was made of different coloured marble. At each end of the room was a fountain with beautiful mirrors. The lustres (chandeliers) in the dining room, the music room and the drawing room were the finest Catherine had ever seen.

Three days into December, Lord Minto set off for London, where he wanted to attend the House of Lords on the 7th and 9th of the month, returning to Paris on the 13th. The Duke of Wellington's Tory government had lost a vote of no confidence and Charles Grey, the second Earl Grey, having become Prime Minister, appointed Lord John Russell as Paymaster-General. Lord Durham, the Lord Privy Seal, asked Russell to join a committee of four to draft an electoral reform bill. In Paris, where all Russians were being ordered to leave immediately as the result of an armed rebellion against the rule of the Russian Empire in Poland and Lithuania, the boys duly arrived from Eton in the care of Mr Hildyard. Catherine and Lady Mary had sat with the drawing room door open so as to see them come into the courtyard. In their luggage was another box of shortbread which Mrs Fraser had sent from Minto. After settling down quickly, the boys were soon busy shopping, leaving Catherine to start German lessons with Mme Viaris. She was also to have drawing classes with a Mr Roberts.

Lady Minto took a box at the Opéra de l'Académie Française de Musique and with Lady Mary, Fanny, Mr Hildyard, Lord Melgund, Henry, Charles and Catherine went to see *La Bayadère* or the 'Temple Dancer' on 10 December, the principal part being taken by Maria Taglioni. It was danced 'most enchantingly' and the part of Neptune was taken by Elie, the family's dancing master. Catherine was also greatly impressed by the 'immensely long room called the foyer' where 'everyone who chose could walk about between the acts'. A more serious visit was paid a few days later by Lord Melgund and Mr Hildyard to the Luxembourg Palace to see how the people were behaving since Jules de Polignac, the President of the Council, and other ministers were there for their trial. In July, he had launched four highly controversial ordinances: the first had suspended the freedom of the press; the second dissolved the parliament; the third and fourth modified the code of elections to ensure a majority favourable to the King. Since then de Polignac had been on the run in Normandy. When Lord Melgund and Mr Hildyard arrived they found great crowds around the palace. The windows were barricaded with sheets of iron for fear of any disturbance and a sentinel had been placed at each window; but the people, they said, were 'peaceably inclined'. Sentences of 'perpetual imprisonment' were eventually to be passed on de Polignac and his ministers. He was quietly conveyed to prison at the Château in Ham, not far from Amiens, but he benefited from an amnesty given in 1836 when his sentence was commuted to one of exile, and he was only finally permitted to re-enter France on condition that he did not live in Paris.

Three days before 25 December, the Place Vendôme was filled with National Guards. The new king, Louis Philippe, was expected to pass by but the family waited in the square for nearly two hours without seeing him.[9] They were very sorry to be obliged to come home to dinner. On Christmas day the children followed the traditional pattern with all manner of foods and games, including 'flour mountain' and 'snap-dragon' and the next day, being a Sunday, Catherine went with her mistress to church at the British embassy. When she returned from a visit to Mme Bigarne in the snow on the Monday, there was such a crowd by the Chambre des Députés, and on the Pont de la Concorde, that the fiacre in which she travelled could hardly get through. There was another crowd in the Faubourg St-Honoré, near the British embassy. Catherine wrote that 'they say the people are still very much discontented; that La Fayette has resigned and that several of the Ecole Polytecnique have been arrested'.

On New Year's Eve, the Viaris family joined them for dinner and the children enjoyed games together. They left as soon as tea was over so that the family could dance some reels, and Lady Mary, Fanny, Lizzy, Lord Melgund, Mr Hildyard and Catherine played a game not unlike musical chairs. As midnight struck, the year of 1831 was seen in. The next morning was fine but cold and Catherine went with Lady Minto to the Tuileries, where they saw a hot-air balloon ascend and drove past the colonnade at the Louvre, where the graves of many of those who fell in what had been called yet another 'Three Day Revolution' were spread with garlands of evergreen leaves and everlasting flowers. That evening, the adults went to the Italian opera, where Malibran and Donizelli, the Italian tenor, were singing *Otello*.[10] The artists were applauded so much that they 'had to appear again after the curtain had dropped'.

Three days later, Catherine's wish to see the King in public was granted. Almost everyone had colds and was staying in, but she sallied forth with Lord Melgund and Fanny to an English baker to buy some biscuits. Coming home by the Rue Saint-Honoré, they met the King's carriage with six horses and two outriders in scarlet. Every lady in the vicinity took off her hat. A day or so later, and with Fanny and Lizzy for company, Catherine undertook a number of commissions for the family. She went first to the shop where she had bought a balloon for Blair Adam (who may have been a cousin of the children), then to Petit Dunkerque and on to König, the furrier, to collect a boa for Lady Minto. Calling at the embassy, she left cards for Lady Granville, the ambassador's wife.[11]

Returning home following an afternoon's shopping on 11 January in the Faubourg Saint-Honoré, Catherine was just in time to see Lord and Lady Minto dressed ready to dine with the King and Queen, Louis Philippe and Maria Amalia, at the Palais-Royal. Their daughter Princess Louise Marie was to marry the first ruler of Belgium, Leopold I, two years later. Soon after, Lady Minto took advantage of a ball given by Lady Northland for Lizzy to be launched into society.[12] The boys found several Etonians there and although Lord Minto returned home about 10.30 p.m., Lady Mary, Fanny and Lizzy stayed until 1 a.m. It had been an event about which, understandably, all were highly delighted, Fanny feeling it as much for herself as for her sister.

The countess heard from someone at Minto how Charles X, who had fled to Edinburgh soon after his abdication, had shown the greatest indifference to the fate of de Polignac and his ministers. Lady Minto had been delighted to learn that the day on which news had been expected about their trial, Edinburgh people had been quite disgusted to hear how that the 'horrid, old unfeeling monster' had gone out on a shooting expedition. It was on 21 January that the boys and Mr Hildyard dined at four o'clock before leaving the house an hour later on their way back to Eton. They were to travel in the *malle-poste* this time, which carried three or four people inside and one in front with the courier. It was drawn by four, and sometimes five, horses and was faster than the diligence. However, some described it as a 'little miserable jolting vehicle', inferior to the diligence. They expected to be in London in three days.

Two events at the beginning of February gave pleasure, firstly for the adults and then for the children. On a snowy evening, the family went to hear Rossini's *Barber of Seville*; Malibran sang 'quite delightfully'. Then three days later, Lady Mary went with her papa to a ball given by Lady Granville, the wife of the British ambassador, while the children enjoyed what was called a 'Child's Ball' at the Palais-Royal. There, they galloped and danced quadrilles all the evening and after supper they resumed dancing until midnight. They were very surprised to find the King and Queen 'just like the rest of the world and not sitting on thrones as they had expected'. The King's consort was clearly very fond of children and kept running amongst them all evening, kissing them and patting them, and finding partners for them.

As the weather improved, and temperatures rose to 57 degrees, windows could be opened a little and the children began to enjoy the garden attached to 10 Rue de Courcelles 'without their hats on'.[1] Digging and planting started but the Bois de Boulogne continued to be a frequent place for a drive or walk. One morning, Catherine and the girls met the Queen and two princesses in an open carriage with plain blue and white livery without outriders, to whom 'every lady pulled off their hats'. On one occasion they met Mrs Davenport, and Dr Quin on another. The latter had been called once or twice to Lady Minto when she had been indisposed.

Further disturbances in Paris were sparked off in the middle of February when, during a funeral service for the soul of the Duc de Berri, members of the congregation produced a bust of his son, the Duc de Bordeaux, which they crowned with the title of Henry V. Some of the populace, hearing what was going on, rushed into the church swearing vengeance against the Bourbons and did not leave until they had torn the building apart. Even the poor priest was caught and only saved from being thrown into the Seine by the arrival of the National Guard. Nevertheless, such events did not prevent the family from again going to the opera on 15 February, when Mozart's *Don Giovanni* was performed, with Carlo Zuchelli and Malibran among the singers. Catherine was most enamoured by the bass-baritone playing the part of Leporello, the Don's servant, who 'was very like Gilbert', a reference to her brother. Her verdict was that both the acting and singing were very good and 'the music truly beautiful … there was not one ugly note in it'.

The political scene still remained strained if not tense. Troops bivouacked in the Rue de Courcelles on three consecutive nights and the mob, after stealing many of the crosses in churches, attempted to demolish the fleurs-de-lis on the Arc de Triomphe. Drums beating to arms was an ominous sound. On 22 February, Lord and Lady Minto had been entertained to dinner by the Russian ambassador, Count Pozzo di Borgo, whereupon he reciprocated by calling on the family while they were at tea, a day or so later.[13] He had just come from the Palais-Royal, where he said all the fleurs-de-lis were defaced, a process which had started an evening or so before when the mob in the courtyard attacked his carriage because he had fleurs-de-lis coupled with his own arms. One result of this insult was that he was now using an old travelling carriage. He talked of the late Lord Minto (Gilbert's father) in such an affectionate manner that tears came to Catherine's eyes.

The governess's letter dated 4 March to Gilbert, her brother, was most touching. Catherine had set her heart on them being together in Paris before he had to sail again. Unfortunately, his ship HMS *Belvidera* was required to sail for the Mediterranean and although she was glad to know he was safe and well she never dreamed he would not come to Paris. It was a week later that Count Pozzo di Borgo's fears were realised. Those who were exasperated at what they described as the 'inhuman conduct of the Russians to the Poles' attacked his embassy building, breaking windows and firing guns at random. Lady Minto had seen some of the damage but by then the building was being protected by a detachment from the Duc d'Orléans's regiment. When Catherine and Lady Minto drove into the courtyard at the Russian embassy intending to ask the ambassador whether he would be kind enough to let them use his box at the opera, the mob insisted on peeping at them in the carriage while they awaited an answer. Although everything was quiet and no offence was given, Lady Minto, who seemed very melancholy, said after attending a ball that night that 'it was quite terrible to see how much everyone was cast down, dreading they cannot tell what, shaking their heads and saying *c'est commencé, mais ce n'est pas encore fini*'.

That evening, the family went to hear Malibran singing the part of Ninetta in the *La Gazza Ladra*, an opera they were to hear three times during their stay in Paris. In the company was Faustina Bordoni, whose singing Catherine did not like at all, while Carlo Zuchelli sang the part of Fernando Villabella, Ninetta's father, in a quiet but pleasing manner. The governess, nevertheless, thought that Santini was quite 'incomprehensible' as the wicked magistrate on account of his vulgar acting, but when he opened his mouth 'his voice was beautiful, rich, mellow and of wonderful strength'.

After listening to a 'very good intelligible sermon from the Bishop' at the embassy church on Sunday 13 March, the family drove to the Bois and were walking in the Allée de Longchamp when three royal carriages drove past them and one of the princesses bowed to them, causing all the party to make their 'best curtsies'. Another brief encounter followed the next day when, having walked as far as the end of the Pont de la Concorde, the King passed them in an open carriage drawn by six horses. Behind was another smaller carriage with postillions wearing tricoloured cockades and carrying the young princes. Spring was in the air with almond and peach trees in full blossom, albeit later than the previous year. During another promenade, Lady Minto fortunately met the Russian ambassador again, who told her he would be only too pleased to let the family use his box at the opera at any time. 'Good old thing,' added Catherine in her journal, and 'perhaps we should shout Vivent les Russes!' On 19 March, William's seventeenth birthday, the family, including Clara Viaris, Fanny, Lizzy, Charles and Catherine, went to hear *Otello* in which the Moor was played by Donizelli, and Malibran 'really outdid herself'. Then, four days later, they again heard Malibran, singing the lead in Rossini's *Tancredi* and 'looking well in her armour'.

Where the family was to spend the summer of 1831 depended quite simply on the outcome of the work being done by Lord Durham's committee on electoral reform. 'If it passes,' Catherine wrote in April, 'we return to England to pass the summer in the neighbourhood of London, and if it is thrown out, we set off for Switzerland.' She could only fear that 'we shall all be anti-reformists!' and by the end of the month there was a letter from Lord Minto 'with bad news for us, he gives us no hope of spending this summer in Switzerland'.

Lord Minto, accompanied by his daughter Mary, had paid a second visit to London on 25 February when the reform bill committee was discussing the need for legislation that would survive at least thirty years and reduce the amount of borough-mongering. The owners of those rotten boroughs scheduled for abolition were to be paid no compensation and early in March the speculation about the extent of reform being contemplated was replaced by widespread surprise that as many as 168 constituencies would disappear. Indifferent orator as he was to be all his life, Lord Minto was nevertheless beginning to show some considerable political influence. He spoke on nine occasions in the Lords between 7 and 22 March, his speeches being influenced by events in Paris and elsewhere. At this time he may well have also been testing the water so far as his own preferment was concerned. The bill, however, never reached its third reading and Grey called another general election in April to obtain a clearer verdict from the constituencies on the question of electoral reform.

During the first week of May while the hustings were under way in England, the family in Paris heard from Mr Hildyard. He had taken Lord Melgund back to Eton, leaving Henry behind for several weeks with whooping cough, but he also had been obliged to go to Cambridge to cast his vote for William Cavendish and Viscount Palmerston, the university having two seats. Lord Minto accompanied him. He was rightly fearful that both men might be defeated. Despite reformers virtually sweeping the board in what had been a single-issue election, the university constituencies not only set their face against reform but handed the seats to the Tories for many years to come. The tutor spoke 'very despondingly' of going to Switzerland but, clearly siding with the younger generation, he said that as he passed through London 'he would speak a good word for the poor old Château'.

In her journal, Catherine described how Lady Minto and the girls stayed for a few days in Versailles, partly to see whether a change of air might do Henry's whooping cough some good. On 8 May she too set off in the little carriage to see how the family party was getting on and, exactly a week later, in the middle of the night Lord Minto arrived back at the Rue de Courcelles accompanied by a Mr Fazakerley.[14] The possibility that the Duchesse de Berri might be about to visit several Carlists in France (loyal to the Bourbons) had led to a government order requiring that anyone travelling should show themselves to the *douaniers* at the Custom House, which had been very inconvenient for Lord Minto. Two days later Lord and Lady Minto were to be seen again in the phaeton in the Bois de Boulogne. This seems to have been followed by a celebratory evening visit to the Tivoli Gardens, organised by Lord Minto. He 'took places for us all' and 'three coach loads of us' enjoyed 'all sorts of amusements … skating, ships sailing, Italian singing, dancing, theatres, all kinds of shooting, fortune telling and a very good diorama of the Thames Tunnel' – all among the trees and walks.

Among visitors and guests passing through Paris and the Rue de Courcelles around this time were Mrs Graham, Mr Guthrie (who like Henry had suffered the whooping cough) and Henry Fitzmaurice. Mr Fazakerley called after having dined with the King at Saint-Cloud while there was a good attendance at Lady Granville's grand breakfast on 28 May in honour of William IV's birthday. The ambassador's wife followed this gathering with a ball at the end of the month when there was nearly a duel. Charles Laffitte, nephew of Jacques Laffitte, who had done so much to secure Louis Philippe's accession to the throne, was walking through one of the rooms at the embassy when one of two young French Carlists, seeing that he was wearing the decoration of 30 July 1830, said, loud enough for him to hear, 'I wonder [how] Lord Granville can allow such a person, and in such a dress, to enter his house. I've a good mind to give you a blow.' Lafitte replied he was quite ready. The men agreed to fight with pistols the next morning. Fortunately, Lord Minto seems to have intervened. Madame Apponyi, the Austrian ambassador's wife, gave another breakfast while at the house in the Rue de Courcelles and Catherine recorded the arrival of Mlle Juliette Gordini, another teacher for the children for a trial period. Dr Aitkin, the minister at Minto, also called. They had last seen him at Vevey when he was on his way to Rome. Since then he had been to the top of both Vesuvius and Etna and looked very fat and sunburnt. Catherine could not help recalling the time in 1828 when both of them were staying at Minto while the manse was being rebuilt and she was setting out on her new career.

Evidence could be seen all round the house of the family's impending departure during the first week of June. Five days had been set aside to prepare for the journey. Catherine busied herself all day listing her clothes and books. Sophie, the housemaid, immediately went down with scarlet fever and Clara was sent home in a great hurry. Gibby showed signs of a slight attack of croup but thankfully recovered after a good night's rest. Dr Quin ordered everyone to take belladonna for fear of infection but it soon became clear that the schedule was not going to be met and on Saturday, instead of setting off, there were other impediments. Alice (another servant) came in after a fortnight's absence with a swollen face which Lady Minto thought might be mumps but Dr Sichel thought not and Dr Quin concluded there was little danger of infection. On Sunday, more farewells were said; Mrs Graham came to dinner, and in the evening Count Pozzo and one or two other friends said their adieus. By then, however, it was clear that the family's departure would not be effected until 13 June.

Horses had been ordered for nine o'clock and by 10.30 a.m. the family was on the road for Beauvais, this time with an Italian courier. The following day proved fine and they reached Abbeville a little past six, staying at the Castle Tavern on account of their intended hotel being full. It was quiet and benefited from a garden which sloped down to the River Rance. It was clear, however, that the party was going to make slow progress with all the children now suffering from mumps and Lord Minto decided to go on alone to London, where he was to attend the House of Lords between 20 and 21 June. Those who could went shopping before the journey resumed on Wednesday 15 June. They dined at Montreuil-sur-Mer and arrived in Boulogne from where they decided to sail the following day instead of from Calais as originally intended. Once aboard, Lady Mary and Catherine sat in the carriage during the crossing, both feeling some relief to be nearly in 'Old England' after an absence of almost two years.

As the family landed in Dover on 16 June, young Fanny wrote in her diary that 'everything seems odd here, pokers and leather harness, all the women and girls with bonnets and long petticoats and shawls, and flounces, and comfortable pokey straw bonnets'. The English looked all 'hangy and loose' and the women so different from those in Paris, 'laced so tight they can hardly walk'.[15] Travelling on, Catherine took the children to Canterbury Cathedral, showing them where Thomas Becket had been murdered, en route for Rochester, where they stayed the night. Fanny happily now conceded that English carthorses were beautiful and even beggars looked as if they washed their faces. On 18 June, the party reached London, which 'really looked exceedingly handsome', and they drove into the courtyard at the Admiralty, where Lord and Lady Minto along with Lady Mary got out, the children remaining in their coaches. Crowds of people outside the gates were curious to see who had arrived and the police had to disperse them. Mrs Elliot and the Misses Elliot came over to speak to them. Miss Georgina looked quite beautiful. Soon afterwards Lord Minto drove to Berkeley Square and changed horses in Regent Street, returning as quickly as he could to the family, who then drove to Chelsea, calling on George Wood. The whole party eventually arrived at the Star and Garter Hotel in Richmond about six o'clock.

The whereabouts of Catherine and the family between July and the end of September 1831 is not clear. However, Fanny tells of being at Bognor on 9 October, where 'we were at first all very sorry [at the loss of Lord John Russell's second Reform Bill] but in a little while rather glad because it gives us a chance of Minto'. When Catherine's record resumes at the end of the month, the family was leaving Hatfield for Minto on the morning of 28 October and, having changed horses several times and had the carriage opened up on account of the fine weather, they drove on to Alconbury, where they dined. Having passed Stilton and Stamford with its five churches, it was dark when they reached Newark, 'a nasty murky town', where the landlady was a famous old woman given to wearing a flaxen wig. Having been woken up by Mr Friend, Lizzy was sent to the nursery to see what had happened, only to find that Doddy had been affected by a croupy cough in the night and was still sound asleep. Nevertheless, the party was soon back on the road, dining on roast mutton and redcurrant jelly at Doncaster. When they arrived in Wetherby it was time for plates of muffins, buttered toast and cake – good Yorkshire fare for the last day of October.

It was the second day of November when the Minto party passed the toll between Longtown and Langholm dividing England and Scotland.[16] Fanny wrote ecstatically in her diary how much finer everyone felt, and as the sun shone brighter, the country became far prettier. They were surprised by a loud cheer from some men and boys at the roadside as they drove into Langholm, and the whole town crowded round the carriages while the horses were being changed. That evening 'the house ... looked beautiful' and Fanny wrote that 'we feel as if we had never left Minto'.[7]

That Lord Minto was eager to do all he could to promote electoral reform was demonstrated, not only by the close contact he kept with friends in London but by his willingness to support public meetings where the many issues could be aired. One such gathering took place on 12 December in Roxburghshire. Invited to address a crowded meeting by the ex-governor of New South Wales, astronomer Sir Thomas Brisbane, Earl Minto complimented the audience on their willingness to declare that early reform in the representation of the people was a necessity, not something that people should look upon indifferently. Loud cheering echoed when he assured the audience that the King was with them, and he was 'far from believing that we shall have against us now any great portion of the House of Lords'.

# 4

# DIPLOMACY IN BERLIN
# (1832)

It had been touch and go for the Reform Bill in 1832. Lord Minto's Roxburgh speech at the end of the previous year had expressed an optimism that he must have known, if the truth be told, was wholly unrealistic. Fanatical Tories continued to mutilate the bill and, having attempted unsuccessfully to negotiate with a group of moderate Tory peers known as the 'waverers', Lord Grey realised that the outcome now depended heavily on the second reading debate in the Lords on 9 April.

When the bill passed by a meagre nine votes, the prospect looked gloomy. Furthermore, after a wrecking amendment was put down on 7 May and carried by thirty-five votes, the cabinet decided to resign unless the King agreed to the creation of more peers. William IV, who recoiled at creating so many new peerages, chose to accept Grey's resignation and asked Wellington to form an administration. Rioting spread across the country during the 'Days of May' (9 to 15 May) and with Peel refusing to join the government, Wellington was forced to admit failure despite his promises of moderate reform. The King had no option other than to recall Lord Grey. He then withdrew his followers from the Lords and the bill passed without the need for additional peers. What became known as the Great Reform Act received the royal assent on 7 June, but not before the King had written to Tory peers encouraging them to desist from further opposition.[1]

Lord Minto's attendance in the Lords on some fifty-five occasions between 23 March and 16 August had been exemplary. He seems to have dutifully attended numerous less controversial and more mundane debates in the Lords, sitting through, for example, the discussion on reciprocity duties with France in July. The President of the Board of Trade, the Earl of Auckland (the son of William Eden and Eleanor Elliot), had been successful in achieving a lowering of French tonnage duties on British exports, but Lord Strangford pointed out that 'this country had every reason to complain of France, whose reduced tonnage duty of 1s. 3d., was 50% more than was levied on French goods in English ports, and who for six years enjoyed, by tacit permission of England, advantages which cost the British merchant some £200,000'.[2] After the President of the Board of Trade had denied the charge, the house turned its attention to the third reading of the Anatomy Bill. This specified that no one could practise anatomy without a licence, and provided for the needs of physicians, surgeons and students by giving them legal access to corpses for research that were unclaimed after death. Earl Minto moved the order of the day.

Efforts by two members of the Anatomical Society had led to the bill being brought forward but there had been public revulsion against it, including opposition from the College of Surgeons and the Archbishop of Canterbury, William Howley, until the arrival in 1831 of a group of bodysnatchers called the London Burkers (after Burke and Hare) who murdered their victims to sell to anatomists. Perhaps recalling his lectures at Edinburgh University thirty years before, Earl Minto held that the principle of the bill had 'been tried on the Continent and in America, and had been found eminently successful in putting an end to all illegal traffic in subjects'. For him, the question resolved into whether or not the dissection of a dead body was essential to the prosecution of medical science. To cheers in the peer's chamber, he went on to ask, 'Whom would the general improvement of medical men most benefit?' and 'Was it not the poor who could not command, like the rich, the services of the more accomplished physician?' Lord Minto clearly felt strongly that there were serious weaknesses in the bill but, when the vote was taken, it quickly showed a majority of twenty for the third reading and passed into law.

A week earlier, Lord Minto had written an important personal note to Henry Temple, third Viscount Palmerston, from 19 Lower Grosvenor Street. He said he had called at the Foreign Secretay's house that morning on his way into town in the hope of catching him before he went out, to express his readiness to undertake the mission his old friend had 'so kindly proposed' to him. Minto admitted that it was a little late in life for him to begin to 'buckle on the harness' but he undertook to do his best to justify both the confidence being placed in him and 'the good opinion of [his] friends'. In conclusion, he asked Palmerston to give him five minutes of his time before his name was formally mentioned to the King.[3] The family would undoubtedly have been greatly pleased with the news that Lord Minto was to become envoy extraordinary and minister plenipotentiary to Prussia in Berlin. Two years on the Continent had refreshed him and high-level if informal discussions in Paris with various members of the diplomatic corps had probably encouraged him to look for such a progression in a career that had come to a halt. At that time Berlin was not a capital with significant dignity to entitle it to an embassy, but it was as good a place as anywhere to begin a diplomatic career. He was sworn as a member of the Privy Council on 15 August.

The task which Minto had been given required him to undertake a thorough review of the difficult situation then prevailing in the Low Countries and win the support of Prussia for a lasting peace. The peace which had existed after the battle of Waterloo had received a jolt in 1830. Holland and Belgium had been joined into an unnatural union called the 'Kingdom of the Netherlands' by the Treaty of Vienna after the Napoleonic Wars and placed under the House of Orange, the old Stadtholders of the United Provinces. But the Belgians much disliked the arrangement. They were divided by religion from their northern kinsfolk and had little sympathy with them, or loyalty to their Dutch king. In 1830 they rose in arms and declared their independence. While the sixty-year-old King William I was endeavouring to subdue them a conference in London of the leading powers in Europe was discussing the status of Greece. The crisis was taken up by the conference and an armistice ordered. Two treaties based on the separation of Belgium from the Netherlands were drafted but they failed to resolve the situation: the first was rejected by the Belgians and the second led to hostilities between the two sides in June 1831. If Prussia had chosen to support the Netherlands, both then and later, there was every likelihood of a major war breaking out. It was not to be until late 1832 when an Anglo-French intervention, or more particularly French land forces, were able to drive the Dutch out of Belgium. International recognition of the new state followed, and although an indefinite armistice came into effect in 1833, the treaty recognising the two countries (and Belgium's neutrality) was not finally agreed until 1839. In the interim, Leopold of Saxe-Coburg and Gotha, had become 'King of the Belgians' on 26 June 1831.[4]

It was clear that Whitehall had a tight timetable in mind for when the new British envoy to Berlin would be in post. To meet this, the peace of Roehampton House, where the family had been staying, would undoubtedly need to be disturbed. The first Earl Minto had acquired it in 1797 and when possible the family spent some time there most years. Besides the property's own conspicuous merit, the locality had a peculiar charm for them. The place was associated with early memories and was in the immediate neighbourhood of their most intimate friends. As Lady Minto recalled, 'within no great distance were the villas of Lord Malmesbury at Park Place, of Lord Palmerston at East Sheen, and of Mr and Mrs Legge at Fulham'.[5]

By the time Catherine's journal resumed at the end of August 1832, the family had already set off from Roehampton and, after changing horses at Shooter's Hill and Rochester, they reached Sittingbourne soon after six o'clock on the 27 August.[6] Lord Minto had been obliged to attend a number of meetings in London and could not travel with the family that morning and Lady Minto took Catherine's place in the coach as they travelled through Kent; Catherine travelled in the chariot. They reached Dover the next day, where Catherine found letters awaiting her from Gilbert and her mother. After waiting a few days there for favourable weather, and with Lord Minto returned, the party embarked for Calais on the steam packet *Ferret* at noon on 31 August. They were all seasick except Fanny, but dishes of coffee soon revived everyone. Once ensconced in a comfortable and 'richly furnished' hotel, Catherine had time to comment how much shorter French soldiers looked; she was taller than they were. The following two nights were spent at Mount Cassel and Tournai en route for Brussels, which was reached on 3 September. It was while they were at the hilltop town of Cassel that Catherine gave something of an inventory of the coaches and who was travelling with whom. First in order was the fourgon (a covered wagon for carrying baggage), then the coach containing Lady Mary, Fanny and Lizzy, Miss Georgina Drinkwater (Lady Minto's companion) and Catherine herself, with Henry in the dicky. Third in order was the chariot with Betty, Josephine, Charlotte, Gibby and Harriet, with Georgette and Goodison on the dicky along with two kittens in a basket in front of them. The fourth vehicle carried Lord and Lady Minto with Helen and George behind. The phaeton brought up the rear with Dr Wilson, Mrs Gurbs, William and a coachman.

Driving across the Grand Place in Brussels, they alighted at the Hotel Bellevue in the Place Royale. No sooner had Catherine and the children breakfasted the next morning than they were visiting the cathedral and walking in the gardens nearby while their parents were getting ready to dine with King Leopold and Louise Marie d'Orléans, his queen.[7] Writing to Palmerston from Brussels two days later, Lord Minto referred to the long conversation he had had with the King 'in which he did not appear to be himself'. He expressed strong objections about the customs duties being levied on those using the

River Scheldt, a longstanding controversy, but Minto thought him 'prepared not perhaps quite to agree to, but to submit to a low duty' such as the figure Palmerston had told him about. He concluded by telling his minister that 'we proceed on our journey tomorrow but I find that we shall be detained by a four-day quarantine on the frontier'.[8]

Three days later when the Minto party had got as far as Spa, he was writing again to the Foreign Secretary to say that he had found the Prussian quarantine regulations a much more serious obstruction than he had expected. In Brussels he had been told he might proceed to Aix-la-Chapelle without too much difficulty but, in the event, the family had to take refuge at Spa 'for five whole days' and Lord Minto had to apologise profusely for not being able to dispatch either his report on German affairs or the draft of the Belgian treaty. He had missed the departure of the Foreign Office's messenger.[9] It was Thursday 13 September, soon after they left Spa, that they heard that cholera had broken out at Aix-la-Chapelle, causing fifteen deaths in one night. Catherine's journal, however, told of a beautiful drive to Verviers, where the horses were changed, and an easy check at the border: the Prussian customs officers only examined their papers. Once through Aix, and another change of horses, their postillions were dressed in green and orange coats; each carried bugle horns slung over their shoulders. At Julich, where they spent the night, they were fed on cutlets by an old landlady. Early next morning they left in cold, rather cloudy weather and drove first through Köln and then Bonn on their way to Remagen. Lord Minto had told Palmerston that he would endeavour to spend a half day in Frankfurt if at all possible.

It was around three o'clock in the afternoon of Sunday 16 September when Lord Minto's party reached Frankfurt am Main after travelling through Koblenz and across the Mosel. Their horses had been changed at Boppard, where they lunched in the postmaster's house. The Rhine had looked 'broad and beautiful'; the castled crag of the ruined Drachenfels, and the hills covered with woods and vineyards, made it captivating. The streets of Frankfurt looked broad and the houses magnificent and when they drove into the Hotel de Prussia they were shown to very nice rooms not dissimilar to those of Madame Marchand in Paris. Mr Cartwright, the British minister, who was to brief Lord Minto, came to greet them.[10] Before leaving for Hanau the next day the family visited the fair which was taking place in the city and saw the King and Queen of Bavaria, who were buying something from one of the stalls as the Minto party passed.[11] They had found the colourful scene particularly gay and charming. Lord and Lady Minto were temporarily left behind so that they could arrange matters 'at the bankers'. Arriving at the border, a long speech in German by a soldier was only brought to a halt by Lady Mary whispering the words 'British ambassador'. He immediately walked forward, bowed, and having glanced at one passport, smiled at the party and let them pass. About five miles further on they passed Auguste, Duchess of Cambridge,[12] and two other royal carriages and by late afternoon arrived in Hanau. There they were reunited with Lord and Lady Minto and together the family walked by the riverside as a Rhine steamer came in. They left the town early on 18 September and stayed the night at the Swan Inn at Neuhof, a few miles south-west of Fulda, where they had an excellent tea 'with omelettes, cutlets, and all sorts of bread'. Catherine managed to speak a few words of German and was much surprised at being understood.

Travelling via Eisenach and Weimar, where Catherine had a large room to herself, they dined at Naumburg, where their journey was not helped by inspections of their travel documents at several barriers and the threat that they could be put in quarantine for having travelled through Aix-la-Chapelle. They were to stay two days in Leipzig which they reached on 21 September, the day – as Catherine reminded readers of her journal – that Sir Walter Scott died at Abbotsford. The city was also about to begin its fair, and the main street was full of good-natured people and their carriages. The family had intended staying at the Grossen Blumenberg Hotel but it was full and a commercial hotel in a narrow street, the Hotel de Pologne, had to suffice. After wandering around several bookshops where there were many English books 'temptingly cheap', Catherine and the children went to the theatre in the evening where they saw what she described as *Der Geschafthuber* ('The Busybody'), a sort of *Paul Pry*, the plot of which Catherine understood but very little.[13] It was a small establishment where there were few women in a very scant audience and half the boxes were empty. The following day the family remained in Leipzig until mid-afternoon when it was accepted that there was no post from London for Lord Minto. Leaving, they soon reached Bitterfeld and horses were replaced at Delitzsch. Once the party was in Prussia, they found a large inn in which to stay as the sun was setting across the countryside.

On Monday 24 September the family reached Potsdam just as the sun was setting, having changed horses at Treuenbrietzen and Beelitz, 'a long village very like Stevenage'. Overnight accommodation was found at the 'most deserted-looking' Einsiedler Hotel, where Catherine and the children had fun making up their own beds with nothing more than one sheet below and a feather duvet above. Next morning the earl and countess left for Berlin, leaving the rest of the family to follow later. Meanwhile, Catherine took her charges to the palace, where they were shown Frederick the Great's rooms. The young were especially intrigued by a table which was so contrived that by touching a spring with the foot the middle of it descended through the floor to the kitchen, where it was replenished. Somewhat disappointed with Potsdam, the family left the town the following afternoon. The road as far as Zenlendorf was forested on both sides but thereafter 'it was a complete desert to Berlin, or rather Charlottenburg, which was outside the gates'. They had no directions where the Minto accommodation might be except that it was in the Linden, to which the postillions drove them. After wandering about for a while a footman pointed it out on the opposite side of the road where Robert, now apparently the family's senior footman, was standing in the courtyard. Not as magnificent as they had anticipated, it was 'very large' but fell far short of their Paris houses. Catherine thought that the morrow might show things in a different light.

On 26 September, the family spent the morning arranging their rooms and after lunch they inspected the gardens of the new houses at the west corner of the Linden to which Lord Minto was obviously more attracted.[14] Lady Minto on the other hand, who according to Agatha Russell had fallen dangerously ill soon after their arrival, seemed to like the house of another British resident but Catherine thought it 'looked low and dismal outside'.[15] The Brandenburg Gate did, however, live up to expectations being 'magnificent, handsome and simple' and the figure of Victory in a chariot being drawn by four horses equally so. Her walk with the children had started in what Catherine regarded as some poor woodland but eventually they discovered a prettier and wilder part of the wood and a piece of water which made them all feel much better. Once back, they had just sat down to dine about five o'clock when Lord Minto came home.

The new plenipotentiary and envoy had presented his credentials during an audience with the King, Frederick William III. Catherine commented favourably on how well he looked in his dark blue and gold uniform, cocked hat and sword. The family's next visitor was Mr Ralph Abercromby, who came in while Lady Minto and Catherine were in the drawing room arranging some newspapers. His father, James Abercromby, who was to become Speaker of the Commons in 1835, had buttonholed Palmerston on his son's behalf soon after he had been appointed Foreign Secretary in 1830. Ralph had been appointed to Berlin as secretary of legation the following year.[16]

Later that day Lord Minto wrote a lengthy and introductory letter to Palmerston telling him that he had been received graciously by the sixty-five-year-old Prussian foreign minister, Johann Peter Ancillon,[17] furthermore that the presence of another diplomat in Berlin, Lord Dunthorne, was proving very useful, something of comfort to him on his 'debut'. His reception had been helped by a letter written to Ancillon by Count Pozzo di Borgo, the Russia ambassador the family had met in Paris. The foreign minister maintained that Holland was now desirous of having the territorial issues in the Low Countries settled but he and the King of Prussia were much alarmed at the prospect of the consequences of further delay. Minto told Palmerston how Ancillon had 'jumped at the idea of mulcting, or fining, the Dutch for the arrears of debt as a first measure'. In short, it appeared he would do anything to prevent a military or naval demonstration, and promised to write the next day to Holland in very peremptory terms.[18]

An optimistic Lord Minto wrote to Lord Palmerston twice at the end of September. His second and more substantial missive concentrated on the character of the Prussian minister. He told Palmerston that Ancillon was 'frightened out of his wits; he sees we are in earnest, and both he and the king evidently think that the King of Holland is bent on dragging them into a conflict, and mad enough to run all risks'. On the other hand, it was Minto's view that France was in haste to resort to violent measures by land, and he hoped Palmerston could exert his influence to restrain her. He went on to explain that the tone of his own language in Berlin had been to reassure everyone that England wanted to procure everything by the mildest course; also that she was not insensible to the danger of military operations. Any further delay in bringing the Belgian question to a close posed the greatest problem.

Although Lord Minto said that he did not think Prussia would ever employ force against Holland, it was important that the Dutch did not misinterpret the situation. Rather forcefully he told Palmerston that his 'business should now be to press the matter forward as far as you can before the alarm has subsided here'. Then, he added, if he was minded to wipe off the arrears of debt, 'it might be useful to have some previous understanding with Leopold'. At the end of his letter Minto explained how Ancillon continued to overpower him with 'expressions of confidence and esteem'. He had established 'an easy footing which promises well'.

The extent to which Lord Minto already felt he had got the measure of Johann Peter Ancillon, and understood his own brief, was illustrated by a letter he wrote to Lord Granville, the British ambassador in Paris.[19] He thought 'he could venture to assure him' that all the influence and authority of the Prussian government would now be energetically exerted in Holland to induce the Dutch to accept England's terms. He told him that Ancillon would be writing immediately to satisfy the King of the

Netherlands that 'he can look for no support or protection from this quarter, and that Prussia will as little consent to any hostile aggression upon Belgium which Holland might undertake in retaliation for our maritime operations, as she would tolerate the invasion of Holland by France or Belgium'.[20]

On Saturday morning 6 October, the family went out in the carriage to a nursery garden to buy flowers for the house and a 'nosegay'. There was a good variety of very beautiful plants, and a collection of orange and lemon trees covered with fruit. Walking back part of the way, they passed over a 'very handsome' bridge on which was an equestrian statue, doubtless that of General von Scharnhorst, which set Catherine thinking about how large blocks of granite used for this and other monuments reached Berlin. She could only assume that they would have come by river after being quarried in the mountains of Silesia and been given a fine polish, quite equal to that of marble, once they reached their destination. The following day when Catherine went down to the drawing room in the evening, she heard that what she thought had been the Prussian monarch and his entourage. It turned out to have been Charles X, who was then living in Prague but who had been visiting Prince Augustus at Schloss Bellevue. Later, Colonel Merx, the Belgian minister in Berlin, called; Catherine described him as 'a funny looking old thing' who had none of the charm of Count Bresson, the French minister.

Sunday 7 October was an especially long day for his Lordship. It seems that the Foreign Office messenger had delivered two letters from Palmerston and the draft of a protocol late on Saturday night, but Lord Minto and Count Bresson had not been able to see Ancillon until Sunday afternoon. The earl particularly wanted Palmerston to know that the Prussian minister had shown he was convinced Holland only persisted in her policies in the hope that they would divide the French from the English. However, when the two emissaries eventually achieved their meeting with Ancillon, he 'behaved as ill as possible, and seemed much disposed to recede from assurances he had previously given us of his readiness to accede to any coercive measures'.[21] Later Count Bresson gave the family an account of Berlin society, explaining hat they cared very little for gaiety and did not mix together in society, being fond of their own *foyers*. Lady Minto asked him how they employed their time at home, to which his answer was '*Les femmes tricotent, les hommes ferment*'.[22] Foreign ministers were only invited to court once a year. They were looked on as spies and were avoided as much as possible by the royal family. He told how, while preparing to go to a large dinner party, he received a message saying that one of the princes was to be there – so he need not come! Catherine added her own measure of Berlin society by recalling in her journal 'a ball the other night at which there were six ladies and twenty-four gentlemen'.

The following day – while Gibby was being given a ride on 'Blot', his horse, down the Linden, where everybody turned round to look at them – Lord Minto was busy writing to London. He was not without hope that a letter Ancillon had sent to The Hague might have some effect but he remained astonished at the latter's inconsistency and dishonesty. Telling Palmerston, if he needed to be told, that 'we are a little out of humour here at the moment', Minto said he was grateful for a caution he had been given by Mr George Chad, a man of considerable experience.[23] When Minto had anything to report involving Ancillon, he would show him his dispatch before he sent it.[24]

On Tuesday 9 October, Lizzy and Catherine had been in the Tiergarten when Lord Minto and ten-year-old George rode up behind and frightened them. In the evening, they were just about to begin reading in the drawing room when Count Clam-Martinitz,[25] Prince Schwarzenberg, and Monsieur Perier came to the house and stayed until tea came in. Catherine described the prince, who was the Austrian minister in Berlin, as 'a horrid man; the same with whom Lady Ellenborough ran away the first winter we were in Paris; he has left her and I believe used her horribly'.[26] Monsieur Perier on the other hand, was the French secretary and the nephew of Casimir Pierre Perier, the French statesman who had died of a violent fever in Paris a few months before after visiting hospitals in company with the Duc d'Orléans.

Next day it was Catherine and the children's turn to be introduced to a Norwegian gentleman, a Mr Löwenskiold. He was the Swedish secretary of legation and chargé d'affaires when his minister in Berlin was on leave. He was to become the Minto household's 'own little Swede', and Catherine 'could not help loving him'.[27] They had driven past Prince Albert's 'really very handsome' house and were walking in the Tiergarten when the secretary rode up and returned with them down the Linden. Meanwhile, Lord Minto was writing to Lord Palmerston but in a surprisingly light-hearted manner. He admitted to having sent the diplomatic messenger off to London without his dispatch and he had therefore imposed a fine upon himself to teach himself 'more vigilance in future'. He could only excuse his oversight as being due to 'the exhaustion and head-ache of a long and laborious day when he was otherwise far from well'.[28] Not content with this communication, Minto picked up his pen again that day, this time determined to tell his chief that he had 'employed every argument in his power' to induce Ancillon to reconsider his rejection of Palmerston's dispatch on German affairs, but he 'had failed in making the slightest impression upon him'.[29]

Lord Minto was steadily learning the art of diplomacy but he seems to have often placed undue weight on orderly arguments, paying attention more to the mind than the heart of his opponent. Ancillon would never have expected anything from him approaching the spirit and resolution, to say nothing of the abrasiveness, for which Palmerston was later to become known. It also seems probable that there were times during his difficult discussions in Berlin when the apprentice diplomat did not fully appreciate the strength of support Prussia was prepared to give the King of the Netherlands. Open war in the Low Countries was never far away. The northern powers, including Prussia and Russia, faced France and Britain if they openly supported Holland, while Britain would be at war with France if the latter sought to annex Belgium. It was therefore of paramount importance that the balance of power across Europe was kept, that France and Prussia saw such a balance as in their interest, and that the independence of Belgium was preserved.

Lady Mary took to riding out on her horse 'Mina' although she and the children also walked as far as the Tiergarten while Fanny often rode 'Blot'. The flow of evening visitors to see Lord Minto increased, new among them being the Bavarian minister and his wife, the Count and Countess of Luxembourg. The thirty-year-old Mr Abercromby came to tea and told the family something of an affair, or rather an entanglement, he had become involved in. They all felt exceedingly sorry for him as he was so good and gentle. Catherine and the little ones laughed a great deal at not being able to speak to the people they met in the street but weekend cultural visits to museums to admire pictures and statues continued to be the order of the day. Prayers were usually said in the morning on Sundays with the evening becoming one of the times in the week when his Lordship wrote to Palmerston.

Two weeks into October, and after Bresson had read Ancillon a 'long lecture on the affairs of Germany', Lord Minto opened his letter to London with the news that 'we are all friends again, as regards Belgium'. He reported having congratulated Ancillon that day 'on seeing Prussia in her place at the head of Austria and Russia in the conference instead of being tied to Matuszewic's tail' – one of the two Russian delegates, the other being Prince Lieven.[30] The ratification procedure of the London conference to which he referred was to last until May 1833.

Minto saw Ancillon again on 16 October. The Prussian minister spoke to him about a proposal from the French government to the King, who was at Teplitz, south of Dresden (now Teplice in Czech Republic), and would remain there until 21 October. It suggested that Venlo and parts of Luxembourg should be occupied by Prussia upon the 'reduction' (or destruction) of Antwerp by the French. Belgium, Luxembourg and Limburg in the Netherlands mattered much to the protagonists since they were part of a system of barriers erected after 1815 to contain France. Given Ancillon's tone, Minto was inclined to think that Ancillon had advised the King to accede to it and that, if he did agree to the measure, it should be proposed to the Conference by France. Despite the absence of any indication of the King's likely reaction, Minto told his chief that he had mentioned the matter to Count Bresson, who was about to set off for Paris, where the formation of a new French administration under Marshal Soult, the Duc de Dalmatie, pleased Berlin. Minto thought that 'there would be every disposition to support it'. He, nevertheless, awaited with some anxiety Palmerston's approval of his language in affirming that 'an invasion of Holland by France would not be tolerated by England'.[1] The Austrian chargé d'affaires had asked him if he had the authority of his government to make such a statement, to which he had replied 'certainly not', and explained that he thought he knew enough of the government's sentiments to make it with confidence.[31]

Lord Minto heard from Ancillon the following day. He saw only one difficulty supposing the King were to agree to the French proposal, and that could be overcome.[32] In the circumstances, Minto wrote again to Palmerston. The week had been 'one of great uneasiness and anxiety to Ancillon as well as to the ministers of Austria and Russia' in Berlin. The latter feared that the British Foreign Secretary would decide irrevocably on the proposed measures with France without appreciating how far Austria and Russia were prepared to go in support of the proposal. This, wrote Minto, 'has enabled me to familiarise them with the idea that we were resolved to do the job without delay'. He suggested that the conference might try to buy off any opposition but if this proved ineffective it should be followed by the reduction of Antwerp. So far as Prussia was concerned, Minto advised Palmerston that 'they would stop us if they could, but rather than see us walk alone, they will take our arm and accompany us'.[33]

Two days before the twenty-seventh anniversary of Nelson's victory at Trafalgar, Fanny, Lady Mary, Lizzy and Catherine went shopping for china at a shop in the Wilhelmstrasse, and visited a painting exhibition for the second time – enjoying some of the work by the Düsseldorf School. Among the pictures she mentioned were 'Jews weeping by Babel's stream' and 'An old warrior and child', a man in a coat of mail and a child playing with his mustachios, but the artists were not named. On 21 October, Lord Minto wrote to Palmerston explaining that he had not received any correspondence from England, probably because 'the packet [boat] had been detained at the mouth of the Elbe till it was too late for her to catch the post'. With some movement in the Anglo-Prussian dialogue now expected, Minto told his chief that evening that, if speed became especially important, Bresson had promised to allow his messenger to go by Brussels from whence it would go to London with Sir Robert Adair.[34] The King was expected to return to Potsdam that evening, and would come on to Berlin the following morning when Ancillon would see him. He added that he had received a few lines from Sir Robert confirming that London was resolved to 'have the Dutch out of Antwerp' before the meeting of the French parliament, and that he had mentioned this circumstance to Ancillon with whom he had dined, but without being able to tell him whether or not Palmerston contemplated using pecuniary measures before actually resorting to maritime operations. Just as Lord Minto was finishing his report he received an account of the King of Holland's opening speech to the parliament. If it was correct, Minto told Palmerston, 'it is quite obvious that he is resolved to yield to nothing but superior force, and if such be the case, the earlier the reduction of Antwerp can be effected, the less mischief will he be able to do by an invasion of Belgium'.[35]

After a walk along a canal with the children the following morning, Catherine had a visit in her room from Lady Minto, who invited her to go to a French play with them in the evening. Although she found the plot rather stupid, she did see His Majesty Frederick William III 'peeping from behind a curtain'. She returned home with Fanny and Lord Minto only to find a communication waiting for him from Palmerston, delivered by the messenger of the Prussian minister in London, Baron Bülow. Minto decided to call on Ancillon in order to ascertain, if possible, whether 'he had made up his mind to let Prussia appear directly or indirectly as a party to military operations in settling the Belgian question'. Telling Palmerston about the family's visit to the theatre, he also referred to 'the first thing I saw on entering my box was the king in person just opposite'. The incident showed what sort of man Minto was dealing with. Ancillon had said the King was still in Potsdam, and that no one could have an audience with him when, as the incident in the theatre showed, he was in Berlin.[36]

It was 15 November when the situation in the Low Countries changed quite fundamentally. The diplomatic fog of the last two months did not lift, however, nor were the actions of the French wholly what Lord Minto had been led to expect. Instead, the real fog of war arrived with a ferocious military campaign and a thirty-day siege of the citadel at Antwerp began. Facing 5,000 Dutch troops under the command of General David Hendrik Chassé, who had been left behind in the fortress when the Dutch withdrew from Belgium in 1831, was Maréchal Gérard and the French Armée du Nord which comprised some 50,000 troops. Ten days previously Lord Minto had ventured to detain messenger Hunter for a couple of days on the off chance that he might be needed to deliver initial Prussian reactions about the French siege to London, if operations against Antwerp started. Now he 'was without any tidings of Maréchal Gérard having broken ground' and wished he was better informed about what was happening in Belgium.[37] Ancillon had been made aware of the Allies' intent but his understanding had been that Gerard's advance into Belgium, when it came, would be undertaken simultaneously with a Prussian occupation of Venlo and Limburg, something which had not happened. Nevertheless, Minto was able to tell Palmerston that Prussia was 'acting fairly and cordially' with Britain at this time.[38]

Just before French forces entered Belgium there was a flood of correspondence for Lady Minto, with one letter for Catherine from Charlie telling her that 'he was going to the Scheldt'. The Mintos' third son, who had joined the Navy in May, was being posted to Sir Pulteney Malcolm's fleet blockading the Scheldt estuary.[39] Dr Aitkin wrote from Minto with news that cholera had broken out at Hawick, Denholm and Kelso, and a similar message came from Lord Minto's sister, Lady Catherine, who had heard from Paris that several family friends were 'all dead of cholera'. On 16 November Lord Minto celebrated his fiftieth birthday and later that day, to everyone's surprise, Captain George Elliot's eldest son, George Augustus Elliot, arrived.[40] His ship was at Trieste waiting for Prince Otto of Bavaria, who was going to Greece. With time on his hands after visiting Munich he had come on to Berlin. A few days later the twenty-year-old sailor told Catherine and the girls about 'his chum Paddy Christian, a nice warm-hearted red-haired Irish fellow about his size, only stouter, very ugly – only the ladies invariably fall in love with him', going on to describe something of life aboard HMS *Madagascar*.

Prayers were said at home on Sunday 18 November, both in the morning and evening and Lord Minto was 'in a state of doubt' about the war since no English mail had arrived. Although still 'anxious' about the way the talks in Berlin were going, he would have liked to gratify Prussia's 'amour propre', which had been hurt by France and England. At a meeting on the evening of 20 November, both Minto and Bresson found Ancillon 'a good deal out of humour'. He said that as the Allies could not put Prussia in possession of Venlo before the reduction of Antwerp – it ceased to have any value so far as he was concerned – but he confessed to not having 'taken the King's orders'.[41] Four days later, the two envoys told Ancillon that they felt themselves called upon, in vindication of the work they had done, to make a full report to their respective governments. Lord Minto brought with him a dispatch which he described as harsh, and read it out to him. It had 'an excellent effect and produced explanations', producing quite ludicrous expressions of distress and dismay. Ancillon begged that Minto might adopt Count Bresson's milder representation. In closing, Minto admitted how ashamed he felt having expressed himself in such 'unceremonious and homely' terms, but 'it was quite necessary that we should teach him a little good manners'. He also enclosed an extract from Bresson's report to the Duc de Broglie, the new French foreign minister who had been appointed the previous month.[42]

Meanwhile the newspapers were filled with speculation about who could have fired a shot at Louis Philippe in France. Catherine was full of pity for 'the poor Queen'. The next day Catherine received a letter from her mother written from Minto, enclosing one from Gilbert dated 'Malta, 26 September' which told of him being about to sail for Tripoli. He was well and happy. In the evening the family went to the opera to hear another *Tancredi* with a particularly good German singer in the title part. Catherine concluded that the woman who sang the part of Amenaide was particularly good and free of all affectation. Mr Abercromby, who was sitting in a box opposite, was a 'picture of misery'.

Lord Minto wrote two letters to Viscount Palmerston on 1 December. He was relieved that London now intended to offer Venlo and Limburg to the Dutch; it greatly simplified the matter. He went on to speak about the possibility that Prussia might begin to be a 'little more attentive to Austria' while admitting that he could not perceive any symptoms of much Russian influence. Fortunately, the Russian minister in Berlin was not likely 'to promote it either by his talents or his popularity'. In his opinion England very much overrated the influence of Russia in Germany, where the minister was bitterly disliked from one end of the country to the other. Russia's Turkish and Polish campaigns had also taught Germany to rate her military prowess very lowly.[43] Lord Minto's second letter that day informed Palmerston that neither Ancillon nor the Austrians 'conceal their dissatisfaction with the King of Holland. They do not say a word in vindication of his conduct in the wanton sacrifice of life at Antwerp, and in playing the hero by proxy.'[44] The tone assumed by the Dutch towards Prussia, and the harassment Graf von Maltzahn, the Prussian envoy extraordinary, had received in The Hague, gave great dissatisfaction in Berlin, such that Minto now wished the Belgians were out of Luxembourg.[45] Responding to the panic in Berlin, Lord Minto briefed London about the fear of France which was uppermost in some people's minds when they saw its army assembling to enter Belgium. It made them fly off to Austria or Russia for protection. Nevertheless, by 7 December, he was able to say that the operations against Antwerp were by then being quietly received in Berlin, and 'the public was much less alive to the subject than it was two days ago'.[46]

Catherine wrote in her journal how there had been false rumours about Maréchal Gérard and how his engineer, Baron François Benoît, would reduce the citadel in little more than three weeks. She was very concerned for the French – 'Oh how I pity them'. There had been a large and happy gathering at the house, where Catherine had danced the first contredanse with Mr Abercromby, and the next with Concha, a Spaniard who told her he had received his education in England. The cotillion, which had all sorts of figures and lasted 'all the evening', she gave to a Mr Annerley, an Irishman and the son of Lord Annerley, who had been in Prussian service for eight years. When it came to her turn to choose a gentleman, she chose the Löwen, as Adam Löwenskiold had come to be known. On 10 December, and with the siege still going on, Catherine said that the Duc d'Orléans and the Duc de Nemours were both at the head of their regiments. Among the visitors was Joseph, Count von Trauttmannsdorff, the Austrian minister in Berlin and Monsieur Perier, who spoke most amusingly about architecture and of his first ball when he didn't dance because he didn't know what people said to their partners. He waltzed and danced a mazurka with Fanny and was exceedingly agreeable. It is such a treat, Catherine wrote, to hear a real Frenchman speak.

Soon afterwards there was news of Charlie on his thirteenth birthday. According to Catherine, HMS *Castor* had returned to Deal from the Scheldt and there was 'a diplomatic dinner' in the middle of the day at which his health was drunk.[47] No one left the house as Henry was expected home from Eton but it was five o'clock in the morning next day before he was standing by Catherine's bedside, with 'everybody laughing and staring at her in their night things'. At breakfast he told her that he had brought her a spaniel which was being looked after temporarily by Mr Lettsom from the embassy. When the dog arrived she thought at first to call him Castor but then settled on Carlow. Henry's elder brother, Lord Melgund, also gave Catherine an early morning surprise when he arrived home on Sunday 16 December having travelled straight to Berlin from Calais with only one stop at Aix-la-Chapelle.

While Henry would return to Eton and not go up to Trinity College, Cambridge, until 1835, Lord Melgund had been given rooms in King's Court (now New Court) at the start of the Michaelmas term.

Meanwhile, Ancillon was holding on to his desire to see Britain's terms modified in favour of Holland. Lord Minto felt it was equally important that the siege of Antwerp should proceed expeditiously as 'it now begins to produce much passion and intrigue here'. However, a week before Christmas, it was Venlo that was again on Ancillon's agenda and the earl told his chief that he had, as directed, suggested to him that 'it might be desirable to furnish Baron Bülow with instructions [pertaining to] the Belgian evacuation of Venlo'. In the first of two letters to Palmerston, Minto was at pains to describe the artificial game of chess which Prussia insisted on playing and the 'unnecessary invitations to coercion' that were behind so many of Ancillon's moves. 'When,' he said, 'the Belgians are in possession of their own territory, and what belongs to Holland is offered to the Dutch, we may safely leave all the other conditions of the treaty to the certain operation of time'. He thought it was now perfectly understood in Berlin that England would not consent to any addition to the Scheldt duty or the transit charges in the roads.[48] Then on 18 December, Lord Minto asked his chief to inspect the seal of the letter he was sending him as it had been written as much for Ancillon to open, as for Palmerston to read. Bresson and he agreed that it would be good to know that it had been read in Prussia. However, Ancillon was not behaving like the man he had shown himself to be a few weeks previously and Minto felt he was not likely to retain his present office much longer – he was certainly unfit for it. In closing his missive to London, Minto could only say how sorry he was to see the slow progress being made at Antwerp.[49]

During that week there had been a concert given by Herr Senden and Herr Witzleben, who sang Swiss 'airs' for the family, and a 'great party' chez Ribeaupierre, with all the gentlemen in uniform. Prince Schwarzenberg, who had commanded the main Prussian army in the victories of the allies in 1813 and 1814, was very handsome, as was Count Clam, who was in white coat, red trousers and top boots. On Wednesday, Catherine had gone out with Mlle Gronau to look for an evening gown, and although she saw several pretty things, everything was excessively dear. A fair which lasted up to Christmas was gay and she looked hard for something to take home but her eyes had become so familiar with foreign things that she could find none which were the least special. There were a great many trees full of fittings for the candles Germans burn on Christmas Eve. Catherine and Lizzy then went to Asher & Co., a bookshop, where they bought several books. There had been several Englishmen in the shop as well as an English-speaking Russian prince. As they were leaving, Mr Aaron Asher, who came from a well-known Jewish family which also had a shop in London, commented to Catherine that 'Russians wish to have everything, and pay for nothing'.

Lord Minto was not to know of the compliment Viscount Palmerston paid him just before Christmas. The Foreign Secretary had written in the Whitehall dispatch book how the endeavours he had made to prevail on the Prussian government, and which Minto had been instructed to communicate to Ancillon, had been successful and 'you have thus been enabled to execute completely the instructions which were given you on the subject'. He then added that 'the satisfactory adjustment of this unpleasant affair cannot fail to improve the friendly relations between the two governments'. The outcome was a little surprising since his habit of making his subordinates nervous, such that they rarely sought his approbation, was well known. For his part Palmerston was never reluctant to seek accolades for his own patient work through many subsequent arduous successful negotiations.[50] In his letter to Palmerston immediately after Christmas, Lord Minto took the opportunity of congratulating him in a reference to the first general election result after the Reform Bill, in which he had been returned for South Hampshire on the 15th of the month.[51]

On Christmas Eve, Georgina Drinkwater and Catherine went out in the carriage with Lady Minto and also after prayers on Christmas Day when the weather was 'uncommonly fine'. All the family went to the Tiergarten, which was 'quite crowded' with people in their finery, and they all dined together in the evening. Lord Minto's last communication with London that year was written three days later and reflected what had emerged from the previous evening when he had 'a very large party at my house and had the opportunity of observing the extreme mortification with which the Prussians heard of the success of ... French arms'. Minto now hoped that there would be a prompt retreat by the French army, and during the next day or so he would attempt to judge what effect the reduction of the citadel of Antwerp might have had on Ancillon's fickle mind.[52] In some ways the last month of 1832 was as much a turning point for Lord Palmerston as it was for Lord Minto. The former began to see success for his policy of playing off rival powers against one another, and the latter had within six months of his appointment not only gained in confidence but satisfied himself that, as a diplomat, he had perhaps chosen the right career. What neither he nor the family could have anticipated was the serious illness which Lady Minto was to endure during the following year.

Celebrations to usher in the new year followed a brief shopping excursion to 'Gropius', a store from where Catherine bought a china figurine and a paperweight for Lady Mary. It was to be a very enjoyable eve of 1833 with all manner of happy distractions aimed at entertaining the children. Mr Abercromby, Mr Fitzgerald and Mr Lettsom helped organise the games which began with the last-named gentleman showing how 'capital he was at "Snapdragon" and the "Wolf and the Lamb"'. Mr Fitzgerald introduced 'Flour Mountain' which was won by Lady Mary. Mr Lettsom then 'changed himself into all sorts of people at a fair; a man showing pictures; then the inside of a diligence in which were a fat man, a lean man, a proud man, a discontented old woman, and a young lady who wished to enter the army'. Everybody agreed how good he was at such mimicry. A game of 'Jack's Alive' took the party up to midnight and after the clock had struck twelve they danced reels and waltzed until about 2 a.m. Tears were in everybody's eyes as they all shook hands and thought of Charlie aboard ship somewhere. For her part, Catherine had to admit that all those dear to her were 'far, far away' and she was in a 'foreign land'. Berlin was a cold and lonely place in which to live and she was very homesick.

# 5

# FAMILY PLANS DISRUPTED
# (1833-1834)

As the arduous and frustrating negotiations with Prussia continued into 1833, the family faced up to more of the intensely prosaic social life in and out of the Prussian court. Catherine seems to have found a diversion through an interest in the life of the Jews living in Berlin at that time. She had enjoyed a long talk with a man of Polish origin who told her that he came from a Jewish family, although he had been educated among Christians and 'believed the same as we do'. He said that so long as he was in Prussia, he would remain a Jew since he could not bear the idea of receiving the sum of money which the King gave to all converted Jews, nor attending the subsequent ceremony with its public avowal. He was prepared to do nothing for the present as his mother was old, and a firm Jewess. Were she to hear that he had changed his faith, it would break her heart.[1]

At the end of the first week of the new year the servants had a supper and dance. Catherine went down and danced a reel with them and drank the health of Captain George Elliot, Lord Minto's brother, who had been successfully elected Member of Parliament for Roxburghshire on Christmas Day, with a majority of ninety-two votes.[2] Afterwards some of the maids sat in the nursery while the dancing continued downstairs. On 10 January she was kept awake during the first part of the night by an alarm of fire, with trumpets blowing, drums beating and bells ringing. The fire was later shown to have been outside the Leipziger Tor, where it destroyed three houses. The next day, Lord Melgund set off to skate to Potsdam during the morning, returning in time for dinner at 4 p.m. The distance was some 50 miles, rather more than that between Minto and Edinburgh, and he had done it in five hours without being in the least tired. Soon afterwards the family went to the River Spree to see the skating. William undertook to 'sledge' her and a servant helped her take two turns on the ice but Catherine did not stay long as she was rather afraid of the cold – it being the first time that year she had been out.

On 21 January, Lady Minto felt rather unwell and did not go out. She went to bed the next day and was bled for a fever, feeling much better by the evening. Betty, a nursery maid, sat in Lady Minto's room all night, where her mistress slept very well and was much better in the morning. Catherine stayed with her while the family was at dinner. Later that week she was much better but there was a slight return of the fever and the next day Dr Wilson sat beside her briefly. On the last Sunday of the month, Miss Drinkwater, who had become Lady Minto's companion, read the prayers at the family service and Catherine the sermon. Lady Minto was better but 'her eye looked wandering at times' and by the following evening she had a return of the fever. As Catherine sat by her bedside on the last evening in January, her mistress asked her to tell her if it was true that Lord Melgund had shown an inclination for gambling at Cambridge, a gauche remark in the circumstances. Her knee troubled her a good deal for several days and, after her fainting again, it was leeched on the first day of February, a treatment which appears to have contributed to her soon feeling better.

It was nine days into the new year before Lord Minto could tell London that Prussian troops forming the corps of observation on the Meuse had received orders to return to their usual barracks in Westphalia. The Prussian Foreign Office in Berlin, however, was less quiescent and by 22 January Ancillon was finding fault with England and France for making a proposal to Holland as if it came from them alone. Lord Minto could only answer him by saying that the Allies only wished to give Holland an opportunity of relieving herself from the burdens they had imposed on her. Nothing stood in the way of a final treaty; there were no loose ends to be discussed since all negotiations had closed. Ancillon replied that it was his wish that Her Majesty's government should endeavour to induce the King of the Netherlands to accept the conference which Lord Minto urged. The difficulty was that Prussia would not join it without Russia, and Russia would not do so while the embargo existed.[3] In February, the Prussian minister told Minto that he had written to The Hague to recommend that 'the navigation of the Scheldt should be declared absolutely free to the vessels of all nations, thus even admitting the Belgians provided the embargo and other hostile operations ceased'. While Ancillon denied 'the right of the King of Holland to levy duties on the Scheldt, also the right of a French army should it return for the support of the Belgians to direct its operations against any Dutch forts which levied those duties', he expressed a wish that England and France should endeavour to settle with Holland the conditions of a final arrangement which might afterwards be embodied in a formal treaty.[4]

On 12 March Lord Palmerston wrote an unusually long dispatch to Minto in which he pointed out that 'it would probably be easier to settle the few points remaining in dispute, that belong to the final agreement, than to come to an agreement upon such a preliminary convention'. Furthermore, it was 'extremely important [that he should] endeavour to come to an understanding with the Dutch plenipotentiary upon these points so that they might be settled at the same time that a preliminary convention was signed'.[5] Unfortunately for Minto, it was clear five days later that Ancillon was personally only interested in the adoption of a preliminary convention and Lord Minto's endeavours to convince him of the injury he would be inflicting on Holland by encouraging her to stand up against a final arrangement with England were doomed, despite the fact that Russia had already pronounced herself on the subject and Austria entertained the same sentiments.[6] Soon afterwards, Sir Henry Howard (1809–1898), the new attaché, arrived from Münich to help Lord Minto. He had started his diplomatic career there as secretary of legation the previous year.

Lady Minto was able to get up for an hour on one or two evenings at the start of March and Catherine, who was occasionally unwell, cheered up somewhat when a letter arrived from Charlie enclosing a sketch which had been drawn by the mate of HMS *Castor*. On 21 March, the countess's knee burst and 'nearly a pint of matter' was taken from it. This gave her great relief, and the doctor said that if she had the strength to bear such discharges, he hoped to see her better soon, but for the present he could say nothing. That 'she was going on uncommonly well' was the message a day or so later, and she had a good appetite as well as being in good spirits. However, by the end of the month, Lady Minto, who had just passed her forty-seventh birthday, was again feverish. A Dr Becker was called, who concluded that her good constitution should bring her through. Catherine considered him a very cold person and was relieved when Lord Minto promised to see Dr Wilson, and to send for another doctor if necessary. The patient passed a very bad night and both the doctor and Lord Minto were in her room all night until four in the morning, when she eventually slept. Catherine saw Dr Wilson after breakfast and he reiterated the very dangerous state she was in, begging Catherine to let the boys and children know. She thought it better to speak only to Lizzy. Soon afterwards a Dr Hüfland arrived. He seemed almost blind and was in his fiftieth year of practice but he concluded that everything possible had been done.

At the beginning of April there were several more days of concern about Lady Minto and her husband slept on the couch in his room to be near her. Around midnight on 3 April, Lord Minto summoned up the energy to write to Palmerston what he called 'an imperfect outline' of the commercial treaty which had been signed two days previously between Prussia, Bavaria, Hesse-Darmstadt, Württemberg and Hesse-Kassel.[7] Saxony's initial hesitation about joining the *Zollverein* or customs union was overcome at the end of March and the accession of the smaller principalities was to follow in May, thereby making an association of about 22.5 million people. Where imports of cotton twist from England were necessary for the manufactures of Bavaria, the import duty had been reduced to a mere trifle. His Lordship did not doubt that 'any facilities England might be disposed to offer to the importation of the timber, grain, wool or other productions of Germany would be eagerly invited by ... our industry'. Once received and logged, the Foreign Office summarised his Lordship's dispatch, adding that 'Lord Minto notices the immense improvement in German manufactures'.[8]

The doctors had been divided about Lady Minto's condition, the two old ones being convinced that she was improving, while Drs Wilson and Becker thought she was not. By the time Good Friday dawned on 5 April there had been another worrisome night. About 1.30 a.m. Lord Melgund came to Catherine's room to say he was giving up sleeping on the sofa and going to his own bed as the doctor was going to sit up with his patient all night. Apparently Lady Minto's knee had again burst just as the family was going to bed. The doctors did not even know that it had been gathering fluid again and it seemed to give her instant relief. She fell asleep about 2 a.m. and slept until about 10.30 next morning when she awoke, quite sensible, had her breakfast and then went to sleep again. The doctors came about 11 and, as her knee had to be re-dressed, they were obliged to wake her. On the following day both Dr Becker and Dr Wilson admitted that in all their practices they had never seen a more wonderful or more sudden recovery. Had they 'read of it or been told of it, they'd not have believed it'. There was relief all round and Lady Mary asked her father whether he had noticed how relaxed their governess's face was. Later, after Lord Minto brought the little ones up to

Catherine's room she wrote in her journal that 'he looked better, poor man; what a wretched time he had had'.

Easter Morning had been fine and sunny but there was a biting wind. Lady Minto passed another good night which allowed the family to go out for a drive after dinner. Two days later, while Catherine was in the Tiergarten with the children, there was a sign that Lord Minto had found enough strength to resume his diplomatic duties. When she returned he was deep in conversation with Count Bresson. With hindsight, their friendship might have occasionally blurred Minto's judgement and although the extent to which his Lordship appreciated that France was as much a rival as she was a collaborator with Britain is difficult to assess; his knowledge of the ideological component of the antagonism between Britain and France on one side and the conservative 'eastern' powers on the other was not great. A day or so later he managed to write a few words to London, adding to his original outline report of 3 April. He explained that a fundamental principle of the commercial union which some saw as a threat was wholly wrong since import duties would in no case exceed 10 per cent on the value of the goods, and that Frankfurt-on-Oder and Leipzig were to retain their privilege as free entrepôts for foreign merchandise.[9]

Catherine went out in the little carriage to the top of the Linden with Miss Drinkwater, Fanny, Lizzy and Gibby on 10 April. Electing to walk home, she found there was a letter from George addressed to his mama (Eliza Ness) from Napoli di Romania (Nauplia, Greece), where the sailor was with King Otto I and his suite, enjoying a busy social life following his coronation. There had been dancing for fifty gentlemen and twelve ladies from 8 to 12 almost every night while he was on board his ship, a favourite activity of the new king. In Berlin, those able to went to the theatre. Lord Melgund, Miss Drinkwater, Henry, George, Mr Fitzgerald and Mr Lettsom enjoyed several short humorous plays presented by a master of ceremonies called 'Francisque' who kept the house roaring with laughter at his jokes and riddles. Catherine told of some of his riddles. One asked what the difference was between a woman and a looking glass. Answer – one reflects without speaking, the other speaks without reflecting. A second asked the difference between a watch and a woman. Answer – a watch reminds us of the time and a woman makes us forget it.

By the middle of May Lord Minto was telling London that both Ancillon and the Bavarian minister in Berlin were of the opinion that the delay in ratifying the commercial treaty had arisen solely from the dissatisfaction expressed by the King of Bavaria about small details. Ancillon assured Minto that the only measure adopted at the Diet in Frankfurt was the instigation of a judicial enquiry into disturbances in that city conducted by a commission of members from the different states.[10] Six months earlier, Palmerston had given Minto his reaction to resolutions passed by the Diet. The Foreign Secretary opined to his envoy how many of the states of which Germany was composed were small and incapable of defending themselves against a powerful enemy. Furthermore, he judged it expedient to see the whole of Germany united in a general confederation, while stressing that such a league was intended to secure the independence of its component members. In what was a long and public expression of his personal hope that Europe would achieve greater liberalism, without recourse to war, Palmerston had requested that 'the Prussian government should always employ its influence in restraining the inconsiderate zeal of the Diet'.[11]

For a while Dr Wilson seemed to think that there was another abscess forming in Lady Minto's knee. After he leeched it on 16 May, Catherine went to see her and 'was very much surprised to find her looking so well', but the knee was still very tender. The following day Lady Minto went out at about 6.30 in the evening, being placed in the carriage 'with the greatest of ease'. It was four months since she had last been out. Two days later Catherine went to the Zeughaus, the old arsenal of Berlin, in the company of the four attachés and was much impressed by the arrangement of banners and weapons of all sorts. The former were almost all taken from the French during the time of the republic. The coat of mail and complete armour worn by Napoleon as First Consul had been fitted to a figure on horseback, and the bronze figure of Blücher was very handsome. After sitting for a while on some cannons in the courtyard, the party drove home, where Catherine found Lady Minto sitting on the sofa in the little drawing room. A day or so later she was strong enough to play the family several Scottish airs on the piano and moves could now be made to find a house for the family to rent during the summer. Lord Melgund and Mr Abercromby visited the town of Bad Freienwalde in the Markisch-Oderland district of Brandenburg, riding the 35 miles north-east of Berlin, and when Miss Drinkwater and Catherine met that evening she told her that they were well pleased with their search.

Lord Minto, accompanied by his two eldest children, soon went off to see Bad Freienwalde for themselves but when they returned his Lordship said that although they had taken the house, and it would have to suffice, he thought it only good enough as a place of refuge. On 29 May, and with fewer distractions impairing his role as envoy, Lord Minto reported to London that two of Lord Palmerston's dispatches had been communicated to Ancillon. Nevertheless, he had to express regret that 'provocations under the authority of the Diet, and the hostile tone of the Prussian government' had furnished grounds for fresh irritation in Belgium. Minto said that Ancillon attributed whatever misunderstanding had arisen to the refusal of the Belgians to evacuate the German part of Luxembourg.[12] It was fairly clear that his Lordship had at last realised that although Ancillon appeared to possess few diplomatic talents, he was not simply the King's mouthpiece. The Prussian minister had much personal influence at court and his behaviour was to have a lasting effect on the character of the King. Lord Minto was coming to see that Prussia, Austria and Russia would only reluctantly consent to the outcome of any popular rising. Writing to London in the middle of the following month, he reported having mentioned to Mr Bresson that, in his opinion, Prussia was no longer an independent power but one subject to the guidance of Austria.

It was at the beginning of June that Catherine and Georgina Drinkwater had a long talk about leaving the Minto family's service and going home. They thought it might be a good idea if they went together. Georgina and her brother were known to be leaving in July and Catherine felt her mother might be in need of her company by the time next winter arrived. A decision rather depended on whether the family did or did not leave Berlin. The conversation continued the following day when the two ladies went shopping in the Königstrasse and in the evening when they joined Fanny, Henry and Mr Fitzgerald at the German opera to hear *Don Juan*. Catherine said 'the music was beautiful but the performance [was] not to be compared [with] the Italian opera in Paris'. Afterwards, Senden, Löwenskiold and two other diplomats came and they all danced mazurkas, cotillions and waltzes. Catherine could not help thinking 'it was my last trip in Berlin, and when the Löwen said he expected to dance a mazurka with me this winter, I felt as if real tears might have come had the conversation been prolonged'.

Later Catherine found that it would cost her more to go home from Berlin than she had imagined; furthermore, the original plan would probably have meant that she would 'never see … them all again' – perhaps a reference to the loss of her position in the household. On 4 June a waterbed arrived from London for Lady Minto, who fortunately now had no need for it. It was like a deep trough, narrower at the bottom than the top, covered with an Indian rubber cover. Catherine concluded that it had originally been meant for someone with a broken leg as it was impossible to move in it. Two days later there was a letter from Charlie in which he said that Gilbert's ship, the 42-gun HMS *Belvidera*, under the command of Richard Dundas, the second son of Robert Dundas, was expected soon in England, almost a year earlier than the time Catherine had been told it would return to home waters. Naturally worried that she would not be in England to meet him, she was already fearing that he would be posted away again without her having the opportunity to see him. When Herr Senden heard she might be going to England alone, he kindly offered to accompany her to either Hamburg or Calais.

Lord Minto's dispatch to London the following day dealt with the suspicious mission being undertaken by Baron von Binder, an unaccredited agent of the Austrian foreign ministry, which was beginning to give a good deal of offence at the Prussian court. His Lordship reminded Palmerston that while Prussia was very familiar with Prince Metternich's system of 'an ostensible and a secret diplomacy', this time 'too little pains [had] been taken to put a decent disguise upon it'. Almost avowedly Binder seemed to be superseding the functions of Count Trauttmannsdorff, the Austrian minister in Berlin, and the situation was not made easier by the continued residence in the capital of Count Clam-Martinitz despite the winding up of the military mission to the German Confederation.[13] The influence he was known to have acquired with Ancillon had alarmed neighbouring states. There were also members of the Prussian government who insinuated that Mettemich sought to encourage suspicions with the view of creating a distrust of Prussia. This might explain, argued Minto, the haste of Ancillon and others to proclaim their dislike of Binder's mission and the cold reception the King had given him. He could not ascertain that Binder had been given any special instructions but there was no doubt that he was 'thoroughly in the confidence of Metternich'.[14]

The first family party to leave for the summer break at Bad Freienwalde on 14 June included Lady Mary, Miss Drinkwater, Lizzy and Catherine in what was called locally the 'britska' carriage, with Doddy and Harry behind.[15] The weather was particularly fine and most of the road was very pretty. They changed horses in the village of Werneuchen, where the second party that was following them, comprising Lord and Lady Minto, Fanny and Lotty, was to dine. When they reached the Freienwalde forest they got out and walked. In a valley surrounded by wooded hills, it was good to be among the trees again and see things that were higher than themselves. The house was 'by no means pretty' but the rooms were 'exceedingly clean and airy'. They had just finished a light lunch of eggs and cutlets when the second family coach and the phaeton arrived with Lord Melgund, Dr Wilson, Mrs Gurbs the cook, and Carlow the dog.

The following day, Lady Minto, Lady Mary and Catherine drove through the town in the britska and enjoyed a pleasant day without the noise of carriages but Lord Minto felt obliged to be back in Berlin for a short while, where on 16 June he seems to have had a difficult meeting with Ancillon. It arose as the result of remarks Count Bresson had made to him about Prussia being subject to Austrian influence. The Prussian minister had been mortified and said that common action between the three powers only arose from the necessity of securing themselves against the effects of the French revolution of 1830. Ancillon also spoke 'with much dissatisfaction' about Baron Binder's mission and said that the King, when he was presented to him, had told him to mark his sentiments upon the subject. He had presumed that Binder's stay would not have exceeded a few days. Three days later, Minto repeated to Ancillon Lord Palmerston's desire that diplomatic relations should now be established between Prussia and Belgium which the Prussian minister agreed, saying that a Belgian envoy would be able to establish himself at Berlin towards the end of July.[16]

London received a dispatch from Minto on 26 June which 'did not consider Ancillon's language very sanguine as to a very speedy termination of negotiations' and his Lordship did not see anything in it which indicated any intention by Prussia of supporting the King of the Netherlands in demands beyond present proposals.[17] Such work as Lord Minto had been able to complete in Berlin before he could hand over responsibility for the post to Mr Abercromby included a note to London on 7 July in which he said he did not hold out any hope that the proposal of Prince Metternich as to the Belgian question, much desired in the Prussian capital, would be agreed to. He considered it would put England at a disadvantage and make it difficult for her to enforce her decisions. Continuing, Lord Minto reported that Mr Ribeaupierre was about to visit the spa town of Karlsbad in Bohemia so as to be in the neighbourhood of Teplitz (spelt archaically as Töplitz), where the meeting of the governments of Austria and Prussia was to take place, the latter town being the King's summer retreat.[18] A fortnight later, Abercromby told the Foreign Office that he had heard about instructions having been sent to the French ministers in Berlin and Vienna 'to repair to Teplitz should Lord Minto be there'. His Prussian Majesty left Potsdam for Teplitz on 24 July.

At the end of the first week in July the family were at a little theatre in Freienwalde where some strolling players were entertaining holidaymakers when, to Catherine's great surprise, she turned round to see Mr Ribeaupierre, his wife and their children coming in. Seeing both the pleasure and the obvious usefulness of getting to know the Ribeaupierres better, Lady Minto invited them to dinner the following day. A few days later, in what was by then the start of the holiday season across Europe, there was news that Dr Aitkin had been at Cambridge and the Admiralty, while William and Henry, 'her silly boys' as Catherine described them, had lost some of their luggage during a visit to Copenhagen. Meanwhile, Mr Hildyard was on his way to Dresden. Last but not least, a missive arrived from London recalling Lord Minto to London for ten days. His Lordship set off for England on 12 July telling the family that he did not expect to return for a month.

Ten days later Catherine and the three little ones were the first to leave Freienwalde for Teplitz, south of Dresden, travelling in the chariot with two servants behind. The coach was next with Lady Minto, Lady Mary, Fanny and Miss Drinkwater aboard, and two more servants in the dicky. In the phaeton were Betty, Lizzy, Dr Wilson and Mrs Gurbs while August and Helen travelled in the drosky with the Minto's own horses. Doddy and the cook went on ahead to prepare dinner for them all at Werneuchen and arrange for a change of horses, as they had done when coming from Berlin. Having got there at six in the evening, the family stayed the night, enjoying the size and grandeur of the rooms at the hotel.

When the family reached the Linden, there was news of an engagement off Cape St Vincent which helped Catherine understand why her brother's warship had been sent to Oporto. Peter I had abdicated his throne in Brazil two years previously and come to Britain, where he was joined by exiled Portuguese liberals in his fight against his brother Miguel. As the news reports had said in June while the liberals were themselves besieged at Oporto, they sent another force under the Duke of Terceira to the Algarve which was supported by Carlos de Ponza, the alias of Admiral (later Sir) Charles Napier. On 5 July, Napier had destroyed the much larger Miguelite fleet off St Vincent and Peter I made him an admiral in the Portuguese navy five days later. Whether Catherine had become aware of the cholera that began to sweep through Napier's fleet after the liberals' capture of Lisbon is not recorded.

This period would have been one when the future course of the twenty-seven-year-old governess's life was in considerable doubt. The boys were now too old to be helped much further and her chances of finding a suitable husband were narrowing. If Lady Minto chose to recognise her service with the offer of alternative employment at Minto House, Catherine's acceptance would in all likelihood restrict her future. Catherine had been well blessed but some four years of travel – the pleasure and mental stimulus of social life in Paris, Switzerland and Berlin in the bosom of the family – might nevertheless have produced some understandably over-optimistic hopes about the future.

They left Berlin in the britska and dined in Potsdam in their 'old dismal-looking room'. The Havel river looked more like a collection of lakes at this point. Horses were changed at Beelitz and they arrived at Treuenbrietzen about seven o'clock. It was nearly midday on the following day when Lady Minto walked to the coach on her crutches. Once away, they went towards Herzberg, a town on the Schwarze Elster, a tributary of the River Elbe. Horses were changed at Juterbog and they dined at Hartmannsdorf, where Lady Minto found a seat in a field where everyone was soon gathering flowers. The road afterwards was prettier and there was evidence of bumper crops of wheat, barley and oats despite buckwheat and millet being the principal grain. After arriving at Herzberg they went out of the house a little way among meadows by the side of the Black Elster and found some very pretty water plants, but with a shower coming on they all soon 'galloped' home to avoid a ducking. The house where they were staying was said to have been where the King always slept on his way to Teplitz. It was very nice and clean, and the landlady in her sixties was 'so smart and really very handsome'.

They left Herzberg on 28 July after the landlord in morning dress had come to the door to see them off. Horses were changed at Bad Liebenwerda and as soon as they had dined at Elsterwerda, they found the countryside less uniform. There was a fine Château by the river on leaving town and the fields looked 'so like parts of Richmond Park'. Recognising the green and white posts along the road, instead of the black and white ones of Prussia, they knew they had come into Saxony. The coach was much jolted as they came through the archway at the entrance of Grossenhain, their overnight stopping place, but Lady Minto said it had not hurt her knee. The rooms there were large but very dirty-looking. Outside there was a large *platz* and to the right the town house, but it had a dull and uninteresting appearance. Before leaving the next day 'they wept to see the Protestant Church, which in comparison to the town is immense'. During the war 6,000 Prussian soldiers had been quartered in it. Both Catherine and Miss Drinkwater took the opportunity of playing the organ at the church. They walked round the triple ramparts, now quite in ruins, before leaving for Dresden.

Who should they meet in the middle of the Dresden but Mr Hildyard, who was then lodging at the Hotel de Saxe where the family was also to stay. He left them while they had dinner, returning for tea and staying all the evening. At breakfast, the boys' tutor was joined by Lord Henry Fitzmaurice, third Marquess of Lansdowne, who was then Lord President of the Council. Lord and Lady Minto had called on him at the Hotel de Londres when they were in Paris three years previously. The two men were anxious to take them to see the engravings and sketches by Paul Veronese, Leonardo da Vinci, Michaelangelo, Raphael and Guido, and later walked in a circular garden with 'loads of orange trees' and a fine old building round it. Mr Hildyard came to dinner and then drove out with Lady Minto and Fanny. Catherine walked all round the town, beginning and ending at the bridge. It was a public walk, very pretty and crowded with 'gay' people, such a contrast to the dullness of Berlin. They saw soldiers with scarlet coats like at home but they did not look so nice as the Prussian military.

There was still considerable uncertainty about when Catherine and Miss Drinkwater would leave. Nothing had been said by their employer, which left both of them wondering what was happening. Three days of August passed before the family set off for Teplitz leaving Lady Minto and Lady Mary to follow. Lord Minto was still in London. As the convoy moved out of Dresden, they saw the tomb of Napoleon's general, Jean Moreau, to the right near three small trees. The Elbe was very muddy from the recent rain but the country was very rich and well cultivated. To the left of the river were hills covered with woods and houses here and there. Having changed horses at Pirna they dined at Peterswalde and were soon at Arbesan, where the hills were high enough to provide a fine view into Bohemia, and where their horses were changed. Nearby was a black marble monument erected in memory of those who gave their lives at the battle of Kulm (Chlumec) which was fought in 1813 between 32,000 French and 54,000 Austrian, Russian and Prussian troops. Descending through thick woods the party glimpsed Teplitz surrounded by its own ring of hills. Several Bohemian mountaineers wearing heavy brown coats coming down to the knees, breeches, large deep-looking shoes, immense buckles and with their hair so long that it hung about their shoulders, made 'foreign and picturesque figures'. The town seemed large, and what they were told was the best house, which was their target, was opposite a large fountain. Facing it, or rather a little to the right when seen from the windows of their accommodation, was the palace too. Dr Wilson had apparently been concerned about Lady Minto's pulse and when her coach drove in from Dresden he was relieved when she expressed herself very pleased with the arrangement of the rooms. A pleasant evening followed with Catherine delighted that her mistress looked so well and that nothing untoward had happened on the road. Captain Drinkwater's appearance after dinner on the following day made his sister particularly happy but it brought home to Catherine how near was her departure.

The spa resort of Teplitz caught the imagination of the whole party. The fashionable time of day was between midday and 1 p.m. when the King of Prussia walked in the gardens. While living there he was always known as the Graf von Preussen. Catherine and the children were anxious to meet him so that they could 'scold him for not having a garden like this in Berlin'. They waved to him in his carriage on 8 August but he appeared to disregard them. In the evening there was a letter from Lord Melgund and Henry, who had reached Christiania and were delighted with their journey so far. While in the Norwegian capital they had gone to see 'old Löwenskiold whom they seemed to have liked although his first question [had been] "what is your object in coming here?"'

News soon came that Lord Minto was expected back in Teplitz, and the next day, after Catherine had been out for a drive with Lady Minto and Fanny despite the rather cold air, there he was. After dealing with two visitors, a Mr Humboldt, probably Wilhelm von Humboldt – a retired diplomat – and Prince William of Radziwill, his Lordship read a few of his dispatches from Palmerston.[19] A relieved Lady Minto 'crutched an immense way' around the garden and to and from her carriage. Fanny, Lizzy, Mlle Gronau, Captain Drinkwater and Catherine took to 'dawdling' across a stubble field and up a little hill from where there was a bird's eye view of Teplitz. At dinner, the family had the company of Bresson and Monsieur Roger, the French *chargé d'affairs* in Dresden, the 'very quintessence of a Frenchman', and in the evening, Bresson and Humboldt returned to talk to Lord Minto, along with Ancillon.

Teplitz became a Mecca of curiosity, intrigue and entertainment as the diplomatic clans and minor royalty continued to assemble, some in a relaxed mood and others delicately ferreting out the possibilities of new alliances. The formality of the court at Berlin was replaced by a new informality. Lord Minto would have been particularly pleased to welcome the Maréchal Maison, the French ambassador in Vienna, to dinner during the second week, along with Count Bresson, who was becoming a regular visitor at all their meals. The ambassador had signed the capitulation of Paris when the Allies entered in 1815 and had accompanied Charles X out of France in 1830. The following day Catherine had a long talk with Miss Drinkwater about their return home but she now 'hated the thought of it'. They fixed 27 August for their departure.

One of the international entertainers at Teplitz that year was Alexandre Vattemare, a ventriloquist, whom the family went to see. 'Monsieur Alexandre', his stage name, did not use a dummy in his act, preferring to present plays in which he played all the characters. The quickness with which he changed, said Catherine, was 'quite incredible and he was very much applauded'. Just as Queen Victoria and the Czar of Russia were to enjoy his performances in French, German and English, the party that evening included the King of Prussia, the Crown Prince and General Job von Witzleben, who was to become Minister of War in October 1833. Returning to their accommodation, the family heard the band of the Austrian regiment stationed in Teplitz.

At the end of August, Catherine set off for England accompanied by Captain Drinkwater and Georgina his sister. A few days before, she had been with Edward to look for a carriage that would take them comfortably to Calais; a britska, built in Warsaw and worth about £50, caught their eye. With the trees beginning to change colour, Catherine enjoyed a few last drives to see the local countryside and its volcanic lava rock while presents of white and blue Bohemian glass were being exchanged by those staying as well as those going away. Among visitors to their holiday home was Prince Schwarzenberg, 'an awful man' wrote Catherine, and a Tyrolean salesman who did a good trade when he was selling silk handkerchiefs. Captain Drinkwater bought Catherine a beautiful red crepe fichu and Dr Wilson got her a scarf. On 26 August, the day before their departure, both ladies sat a long time with Lady Minto saying their farewells. As Catherine said, 'she kissed us both and held us so long close to her'. Their mistress was still in bed the next morning as they were leaving and she made them promise to always call Minto their home.

Once on the road there were changes of horses at Arbesan, then Peterswalda and Pirna. The three travellers only got out to walk on coming into Kulm, where there was a steep hill. What was called Swiss Saxony looked clear and attractive with the mountain of Lilienstein, round which the Elbe flowed, raising its flat head above the rest. Reaching the Hotel de Saxe in Dresden they had tea with Mr Hildyard and Mr Lettsom but, being tired after the journey, both soon went to their rooms. Catherine slept on the floor 'for fear of the bugs'. Up earlier the following morning they went out to buy yet more gloves and books to send back to Teplitz with Mr Lettsom. Having written a few lines to Fanny while Mr Hildyard and Captain Drinkwater went to the art gallery, Catherine sought out a Mr Forbes to question him about their passports. They dined together and Mr Hildyard helped them to understand the German play they were to go to that evening. They had been able to get a box at the front as it was very thinly attended. There was a long journey ahead on the morrow when they hoped to reach Leipzig.

After they obtained fresh horses at Meissen and Klappendorf, the ostler at Oschatz at first said that there were no horses available and asked them whether they wanted a *vierspanner* (a four-tension adjuster) only later to come up with two horses. Such assistance was obviously not quite what they wanted since a third change was made at Luppa, only about 8 miles from Oschatz. They eventually reached Wurzen at ten in the evening having been nearly fourteen hours on the road and took the decision to press on to Leipzig with the aid of a full moon. The fine old streets of the city, with the gable ends of the house roofs of different shapes and sizes, looked beautiful in the moonlight. When they arrived at the Hotel de Pologne, an establishment where James Fenimore Cooper had stayed three years before, they had a cup of tea and were soon in bed 'really dead tired, sleepy and stupid'.

The next day's destination was Weimar and again they had an early start, taking their last look at the River Elster in which, Catherine said, Poniatowsky was drowned. Fresh horses were supplied at Lützen, where Gustavus Adolphus had been mortally wounded and carried to Weissenfels to die. The area around for several miles was a complete plain, and looked as if it had been created for battle. Lead seals which had been put on their trunks at Lutzen were taken off at Eckartsberga and, to Catherine's delight, they exchanged their Saxon postillion, with his yellow and blue coat, for 'one of [their] own Prussians' with blue coat turned up with orange and the Prussian eagle. He turned out to be very civil and, seeing them trying to button the leather curtain to the carriage, he got down and did it for them. The meal that evening was made up of good veal cutlets and potatoes. The leg of their journey between Weimar and Eisenach took a tiring nine hours whereupon they climbed up to look at the castle of Wartburg, where Luther had taken refuge for eleven months. They were shown the room in which he both lived and translated the Bible. Evidently now relaxed, they thought that if the Duke of Weimar would let the castle it 'would be such a nice house for the Mintos', with an excellent view from its windows and the Thuringerwald lying at its feet. It was, Catherine concluded, 'a dear little town'.

The first day of September was very cloudy and it rained all day on the way to Fulda, where they were given the same room that Lady Minto had enjoyed previously. In the town, they found the Bishop's Palace and cathedral, which they had seen previously but it was quite a wretched and very cold day. At tea, they met twelve shoemakers who were also on their way to Frankfurt. The party travelled the next day with one side of the carriage buttoned up. At Hanau, they looked up at their old quarters as they passed and arrived at Frankfurt about half past eight, only to find they could not get into the Hotel de Prussia as it was quite full. They drove to a charming *Gasthof* after a few moments of nervous hesitation. Next morning there was an opportunity for them to wander a little through the streets and enjoy the sight of Frankfurt again preparing for another fair. Notices in shop windows told people coming from all over the world where to buy this or that. Repairs to the carriage took until late in the afternoon when they were able to set forth again. In pouring rain they changed horses at Hattersheim and, packed tightly together, 'a little too much squeezed' as Catherine wrote, they found they could not get into another hostelry, the Hotel Frankfurt in Mainz. By then it was 9 p.m. and they were fortunate to find other accommodation nearby, but 'not until the postillion had hauled us dear knows where!'

Having got up before dawn, the party had some coffee and walked down to the steamboat, which left at 6 a.m. on 4 September. Arriving at Köln they crossed a bridge of boats and found themselves in very narrow and dirty streets where the language was 'execrable'. They did not, however, have much time and were unable to visit the cathedral. The next morning they left a little later than on the previous day and received fresh horses at Berkheim, Jülich and Aachen, where they sent a young girl for bread and the postmaster advised them to avoid the road via Battice and Liege which was in a very bad state. When they reached the customs post it was quite dark and they had to get down and go into a small house while their carriage was examined. The two chaise seats were opened and duty paid on the Bohemian glass. This examination resulted in their reaching Verviers very late indeed but they were given rooms, one within another and with Captain Drinkwater on the outside, and were soon fast asleep.

They left Verviers for Brussels next morning 'in no small hurry' only to encounter 'horrid roads', very bumpy and uncomfortable. After changing horses at four stops which included Liege and Thirlemont, they decided to stop and stay the night at Louvain, where they arrived about nine o'clock, almost shaken 'to a jelly'. Catherine said that she had sense enough left to take in the fact that the town was 'lighted by gas'. The two young ladies had a large room together and after tea, a little brandy and water – and a bowl of hot water for their feet – sleep came quickly. They did not leave Louvain until after ten o'clock next morning but once in Brussels and the Hotel de l'Europe they immediately 'gave their things to the washer-woman'. Captain Drinkwater and Georgina left to have a rest while Catherine did some shopping. In the evening they went to the Théâtre Français and saw *La Cheminée* with Mlle Dèjaset playing the part of 'Vert-vert', but Catherine felt she 'was almost too disgusting in her short petticoats'. Being a Sunday, the following morning was allowed to start slowly. They walked in the park, dined at four and saw many more 'fine people' than could be seen in a whole year in Berlin.

Driving across the Grand Place on Monday, en route for Lille, they were amused to see advertisements placed by a British company, Hays & Landen. After crossing the Franco-Belgian frontier, customs men took their trunks off the carriage and, having examined them, pulled 'the chaise seats about'. Captain Drinkwater was on the front dicky and when it came to the piece by piece examination of the German glass, one irritated customs officer mistook Catherine for a maid. Their hotel in Lille was almost full as there was another trade fair going on but they were well satisfied with their rooms. However, very early on 10 September, when they were about to leave it was discovered that the carriage needed repair. As the result of this delay it was several hours before they got away. Stops that day were at Armentières, Bailleul and Cassel, the last being where they received a bow from a guide who had helped the family the previous year. Walking up the hill of the town they encountered an extraordinary travelling party with ladies dressed in riding habits. To Catherine's delight the pavé ceased once they reached St Omer and they slept the rest of the way to Calais.

After resting that night at the Hotel Bourbon-Condé, they found that the wind was too strong for a comfortable crossing to Dover. Early the next morning Captain Drinkwater went out to see whether the weather had improved but it was still 'excessively windy' and they settled back in bed for another two hours, after which they all went down to the pier to see for themselves what the sea was like. They could hardly walk against the wind; it was 'a blow' such as they had not enjoyed for a year. A perfectly delightful old French sailor asked if they were not afraid the wind would get under their clothes and 'raise them like a balloon'. He promised them fine weather for the morrow. That evening they went to a performance of Auber's comic opera *Fra Diavolo*, where they met several English in the same box, and one very talkative Frenchman. The performers were 'wretched' but they were much amused at the proceedings.

Catherine decided to write up her journal early the next day (13 September) but she was interrupted, first by Captain Drinkwater, who rushed in to wish her happy returns of the day, and then by Miss Georgina, who did the same. She had totally forgotten that it was her birthday and the sixth anniversary of her leaving home. When she sat down to breakfast she found a beautiful box of bonbons on her plate. Walking down to the boat they were delighted to find this time that they were to repeat their crossing of the previous August, with Captain Hamilton in command of the *Ferrat*, and be looked after by their 'dear steward, Georges' whom they saw working his way through the crowd towards them. He made them comfortable and never left them during the whole passage. As they left the harbour they did, however, go aground momentarily. On arrival in Dover, they encountered a number of Elliots meeting folk from Boulogne, and Catherine heard that Captain Robert Elliot had married 'a very gay girl' after a short acquaintance.

Leaving a very cold Dover in the afternoon, they 'crept very close together in the carriage' and were delighted to find a good fire blazing in the sitting room of their hotel at Sittingbourne after a journey of four hours. The trunks were taken inside as they wanted a change of clothing before proceeding further. Next day they left for London and taking the Tonbridge road out of Maidstone they were soon at Barming, where Mrs Elliot met them at the door looking fat and rosy. Going inside they found Mrs Brydone in bed but looking better than she did when they last saw her at Roehampton. She generally did everything for herself, Catherine was pleased to learn. The garden was full of flowers and the most delicious peaches and nectarines. Catherine promised to pay them a visit again, if possible.

By the time they got to London it was nearly seven o'clock, where a servant met them as they reached the end of Fitzroy Square to tell them to go round by the mews as Mrs Drinkwater was very unwell. It was a sad reception for Miss Georgina. Colonel Drinkwater met them in the passage and told them that his wife 'had been seized in the street with violent pains in the head and giddiness, and had been carried home almost insensible'. Nevertheless, after a while, they were able to go up and see her. Although the doctor thought Mrs Drinkwater better the next morning, Catherine said she thought her 'very low and nervous' and suggested that Miss Georgina should be allowed to sit with her, to which he consented.

Among visitors to the Drinkwater household during the following week was Mrs Elliot, and arrangements were made for Catherine to go down to Barming to stay for a while. On 20 September, the day after Georgina's twenty-seventh birthday, Colonel Drinkwater drove Catherine in the carriage to the Ship Inn at Charing Cross. Around one o'clock, he put her into a Maidstone coach from which she alighted at six in the evening to be greeted by the Rev Gilbert Elliot and his wife. That evening they talked a great deal about Teplitz and after breakfast the next day Catherine walked out with the children and saw the hops drying in the oast houses locally. After luncheon, the Elliots, Mrs Brydone and Catherine drove out in a pony chaise to view the country. She went to church twice the next day with Mrs Elliot, where Mr Elliot read prayers. He had become rector at Barming in 1832 and was to stay there until 1834.[20] Returning to London three days later Catherine found a carriage waiting to take her back to the Drinkwaters, where there was a letter from her mother.

At Fitzroy Square Catherine was still waiting for tidings of a missing trunk, and she passed the time looking at books of manuscript music composed by some of the Drinkwater family, copying out those she rather liked. She also went shopping for furniture, exploring a store called the Pantechnicon in the hope of finding a secretaire or bureau. She saw only one and none so light and pretty as those seen abroad. With Mrs Drinkwater now much better, Catherine and Edward were able to take her for a walk through the Soho Bazaar and at the end of the week she went to church with the family but felt unwell, and Edward had to bring her home. The doctor was called and she spent a day in bed having been given a draught. The first day of October was so very foggy that it prevented a drive in Hyde Park so Catherine and Georgina turned round and went to the Foreign Office in Downing Street to look for Colonel Drinkwater, who took them home via a furniture shop. Two days later, and after what Catherine described as 'an immense way off', Edward and she set off for the Customs House – and there were all their boxes! On their way home she was able to catch a glance of Newgate, the Tower, the Monument and St Paul's, and during the evening the trunks were delivered. Other boxes, including those containing the china which Catherine had bought, were going by sea to Scotland.

Ten days into October the governess shared the first part of her journey as far as Leamington with Mrs Elliot, Georgina and her brother. Subsequently her route to Scotland took her to Warrington and the south-west borders. It seems, however, that at this time Catherine was particularly worried that she might have done something 'wrong or taken too great a liberty' with Lady Minto, in respect of money matters. Writing from Elstree to her ex-mistress, who was still in Teplitz , soon after the party had left London, she reminded her that 'as you had given me in charge to Captain Drinkwater, and desired him to give me what money I wanted, he wished to know if I had enough to take me to Scotland, or if I knew whether you meant to pay that for me'.[21] She now told him that she did not have enough money to get her to Scotland, a situation which he remedied. Nevertheless Catherine felt that she could not expect her mistress to pay all her journey expenses, for they 'must be something enormous' and she asked Lady Minto to 'tell his Lordship to do whatever he thought proper as all her money was in Lord Minto's hands'. Fortunately, by the end of the month, the matter was settled amicably.

Catherine was genuinely very warmly received by the community when she reached Minto, but a few weeks later she again wrote to Lady Minto. Although now living with her mother at Lanton, she was not becoming reconciled easily to her altered circumstances. Her desire that the family at Minto House should take 'no further notice of her' was an obvious untruth and her reference to parties and invitations from all manner of folk only revealed how much she had lost and was not to regain. She longed to maintain her ties with Lady Minto and the children while still caring for her mother. By the spring of 1834 she still hoped to be her Ladyship's correspondent, albeit at long intervals, and desired that Lady Minto would 'make the others write to her'.[22]

In September 1834 Catherine told of a visit she and a friend, Elizabeth Wilson, had made to the farm at Minto, where they learned that Lord and Lady Minto were expected home in six weeks. She wrote to Lady Minto from the farm in exultant mood about the news. She was 'confused and mad with joy' – time would not pass fast enough. Having given the news to Mrs Fraser, the cook, she ran up to Minto House where she found Ephraim Selby, who had taken over some of the duties of estate factor, and who was equally pleased to have had had a letter of his own from Lord Minto.[23] Catherine delivered Lady Minto's request about putting out the seats around the garden to Ephraim, who passed it on to Andrew Kerr, his assistant. She looked forward to seeing her ex-mistress without crutches and said that she wanted to throw her arms round them all, ending her letter with the words, 'goodbye, my own dearest Lady Minto, believe me your most affectionate, happiest and maddest of creatures – Catherine Rutherford'.[24]

# 6

# LORD MINTO BECOMES FIRST LORD AND HIS BROTHER AN ADMIRAL (1834-1847)

In April 1833, there had been an attempt to seize Frankfurt as the climax to a revolutionary plot in Germany, and Palmerston's response was to try again to separate Prussia from Austria and the 'Metternich System'.[1] He hoped that the *Zollverein* in Vienna would encourage Austria to take more interest in commerce while Prussia placed herself at the head of the German states as their protector. Writing to Lord Melbourne on 18 June, Palmerston asked, 'can or will Austria do nothing about the commercial question; and is she prepared to submit to the encroachments of Prussia? That is the nail to drive.' He wanted to see Prussia take the middle ground and encourage economic improvement as well as address serious grievances among the people.

There followed a series of secret meetings at Münchengrätz in Bohemia and Berlin between September and October that year when King Frederick William III finally succumbed to Metternich and joined the other eastern monarchs in a reaffirmation of the old commitment to mutual aid against revolution.[2] All that Metternich seems to have suggested was an initial meeting between the Emperor of Austria and the Prussian monarch, to be followed by a meeting with the Czar at St Petersburg. He had hoped the next step would be a gathering of the three monarchs at Troppau, then in Austrian Silesia, but unfavourable weather in the Baltic forced Czar Nicholas to travel by land, giving the other two leaders an excuse to abort the meeting. Neither King Frederick William, nor any of his responsible ministers, accompanied the Czar to Münchengrätz and although the Crown Prince was allowed to go he was not given any powers to sign anything. Such agreements or treaties as were signed at Münchengrätz were secret at the insistence of Russia and rumours about their contents unreliable. In broad terms, the agreement signed by Prussia, Austria and Russia established an alliance to 'support conservative causes'.

In 1834, Britain, France, Spain and Portugal were to sign a Quadruple Treaty to counter the earlier agreement in April, so establishing two opposing power blocs in European politics. There was little that the eastern bloc could do to frustrate an Anglo-French solution to the Belgian question but both allies grew increasingly impatient at the Dutch king's obstinacy and in Germany Palmerston failed in his attempt to check the progress of Prussia's *Zollverein*. When the Diet sent their forces into Frankfurt in May, his failure was all too apparent and his protests noted only 'for the record, and lest he be attacked in the House of Commons'.[3]

Meanwhile, Ralph Abercromby had held the fort in Berlin until Lord Minto returned from Teplitz in the autumn of 1833, and on 11 September the ambitious secretary of legation used the opportunity to impress John Backhouse, a civil servant at the Foreign Office, with his response to a request to transmit information about the administration of relief for the poor in Prussia.[4] He reported how funds were raised largely by private charities since there was no direct provision for government funding. Sometimes relief was provided through the use of funds earmarked for public buildings or the construction of roads. Each town had a society for the poor and benefited from regular donations from house owners, in proportion to the size of their property.[5] Another message from the Foreign Office, this time for Lord Minto, explained that the new British consul in Warsaw, Colonel Barnett, would now report to him, and with a change of tempo apparent in diplomatic activity, he was commanded to request a special audience with King Frederick William, for the purpose of delivering a letter from His Majesty William IV, the British monarch. Some days afterwards Ancillon informed him that it was 'contrary to the etiquette of the Prussian court for any letter to be presented to His Prussian Majesty but through his minister'. Rather naturally, Minto sought further instructions from London and on 27 September Palmerston, realising his mistake, authorised him to present His Majesty's letter 'in any manner which the rules established at the Court of Berlin may prescribe'.[6]

Those closely engaged in the tug-of-war in the Low Countries then found that Prince Felix of Schwarzenberg, an Austrian diplomat and protégé of Metternich, was to be the bearer of declarations to the King of Holland which Ancillon was convinced 'must have a good effect'. The mission's objectives were to encourage Holland to agree to a station for Belgian pilots at Flushing, the levying of a duty at Antwerp as well as similar arrangements lower down the river, and the right of fishing for the Belgians. Both Minto and Bresson raised the issue with the Prussian minister, explaining that most of the points in question had already been agreed and were included in articles of the proposed treaty.[7] On 15 October Lord Minto reported that the German congress was certain to meet at Linz, where, although the subject to be discussed was to be of a purely domestic nature, he could see nothing but 'increased agitation' being the result. He did, however, think that if the congress was 'strongly pronounced against' it might be stopped.[8]

On 10 December, Lord Minto sent London a printed copy of the proceedings of the Frankfurt conference that had taken place between 15 July and 15 November. Meetings of the states had been at once controversial and lengthy but as the Foreign Office paraphrase of Minto's dispatch sent to London eight days later said, the new commercial union seemed likely to be conducive to peace, and to wean Prussia from the influence of Austria.[9] Then in one of his last messages to Lord Minto that year, Palmerston wrote on 17 December to say that it was quite manifest that the King of the Netherlands 'systematically and deliberately' thought it in his interest to avoid a definitive treaty. As the result, the Foreign Secretary thought there was no use in Britain entering into discussions which could not lead to any result. What remained to be settled was so little but it had to wait until the Diet and the Duke of Nassau, the Duchy of Luxembourg's ruler, signified their consents.[10]

Although 1834 opened in much the same way as 1833 had ended, differences in the Diet were soon forgotten when the highly significant German *Zollverein* was at last established under Prussian tutelage, but other problems remained. Initially, it was Palmerston's instruction of 2 January that kept his Lordship busy. He was asked to 'point out to Ancillon how little the Prussian minister at the Diet seemed to share the anxiety expressed by the Prussian government for an early settlement', in conformity with the pledge by the three courts in their instructions to Prince Schwarzenberg. By mid-January, however, affairs in Turkey became of concern. Lord Minto spoke to Count Bernstorff without, as the Foreign Office put it, the 'knowledge of the views of HM government upon the subject'.[11] This Prussian diplomat, who was to be sent to Vienna in 1848 and later became Prussia's foreign minister, agreed with Minto when he said 'he did not see how Russia could be brought to renounce the advantages she had obtained in that country or how England could submit to her retaining them'. It was Lord Minto's view that 'war must ensue'.[12]

Minto admitted to being at a loss to account for the change in the tone of Prince Metternich's comments about the Turkish question when he spoke to the French and Russian ambassadors on 22 January. After talking again to the French ambassador he concluded that Metternich was either wishing to restrain Russia by a 'little display of vigour' or to do away with the unfavourable impression the French government had of Austrian oriental policy. Minto told London he was convinced that Prussia would not offer Russia any assistance in its encroachments.[13] Several weeks later, Minto reported that Prince Soutzo had spoken openly to the Bavarian minister of his fear that the interference of France and England in the affairs of Greece gave 'a handle to complaints from St Petersburg'.[14] It appeared that the Russian government had refused to guarantee the third part of the Greek loan except upon condition that Russian influence be established. Prince Caradja, his brother-in-law, considered Soutzo to be a Russian agent.[15]

Early in February, and at the request of Prince Esterhazy, the Austrian ambassador in London, Palmerston assembled a meeting of the representatives of five powers in the Foreign Secretary's office in Whitehall. It seems from the record Palmerston sent Lord Minto that the representatives had been instructed to propose a resumption of the negotiations with the Dutch and Belgian governments so as to settle all the points which remained in dispute. The Prussian, Russian and Austrian governments expressed themselves 'to the same effect' but as Palmerston soon discovered, the King of the Netherlands had not obtained the assent of either the Diet or the agnates to enable his government to sign the requisite articles. Furthermore, the King was no more disposed to conclude a treaty with Belgium than hitherto.[16]

Meanwhile that day in Berlin during a meeting with Ancillon, Lord Minto met another impediment. In response to his reminder that the annexation of Limburg to Holland formed no part of the treaty, Ancillon refused to listen to any proposal which 'did not annex that equivalent to Holland'. In reply, Lord Minto could only hope that 'as the British government did all they could to restrain the indiscretion of the Belgians, the Prussian government would act a like part towards the Dutch'.[17] A week later, after Frankfurt had been occupied by troops from the Confederation, Mr Ancillon was assuring Minto that Prussia 'neither has attempted nor will attempt to induce the state of Frankfurt to violate its treaty with England', and that Prussia was 'not desirous' of joining the commercial union.[18] However, on 26 March, a Dutch contact informed Minto that the King of Holland approved of Ancillon's suggestion that the treaty should be concluded and executed, leaving the question of rights, as regards the German Confederation, for future determination.[19]

The dialogue of the deaf rolled on into May and although Palmerston wrote a long and careful personal note to Minto which reiterated the phases of the talks, and the causes of the various suspensions which usually followed, and asked him to bring them to Ancillon's attention again, this too proved useless.[20] Meanwhile, the nineteen-year-old Fanny was revealing her own views in her diary when she wrote, not without considerable truth, how she had been at a 'stupid dinner of old men', On 17 May, Minto told London that he had heard about fresh instructions being sent to Biberich, south of Wiesbaden.[21] These, he assumed, were in connection with a projected treaty, and which proposed that Limburg should be permanently annexed to Holland. A few days later Ancillon returned to Berlin from Vienna, pleased with his reception there and with 'the sentiments manifested in the congress generally'. Minto, for his part, had to wait until 21 May to hear from Metternich what had been included in the final protocol of the meeting. It seemed that a monetary indemnity had been offered by the King of Holland to the Duke of Nassau. On the first day of June, Lord Minto still thought, quite wrongly it has to be said, that some good effect on the measures being taken by the Diet had been produced by the representations France and Britain had made.[22]

It was not until July that outgoing dispatches from Lord Minto contained any mention of Ancillon's important collaboration with Metternich in what came to be known as the Vienna Final Act of 12 June 1834. Between 2 and 20 July he had been absent from Berlin and Mr Abercromby had been in charge. Lady Agatha Russell states that on 16 July Lord Minto was at Marienbad in Bohemia (now Mariánské Lázné in the Czech Republic), the same day that Lord Grey resigned as Prime Minister in favour of Lord Melbourne.[23] By the time he returned, however, it must have been clear that the futility of many of his efforts to encourage Ancillon towards a greater understanding of Palmerston's approach had hardly been compensated by the occasional success. Nevertheless, he would have disputed Alsager Vian's conclusion that 'the tenure of his office was uneventful',[24] and argued that the quality of his diplomacy contributed to his being given subsequent posts in government, but the Foreign Secretary and his envoy had been outwitted by both Austria and Prussia. Lord Minto told the Foreign Office on 22 July that Ancillon was under the impression that 'there was no treaty signed at Münchengrätz'.[25] He had been kept in the dark about events in Bohemia.

On 3 September, the honour of an Austrian order was conferred on the 'Court parson', as August Gneisenau had once contemptuously called Ancillon. Largely unknown to the Prussian public, their foreign secretary had convinced himself that the Prussian system of rigid class distinction was the ideal foundation of a state, and that his collaboration with Metternich in the Vienna Final Act had helped bring Austria and Prussia together. Then, some fourteen days later, an announcement was made in London of Lord Minto's award of the Knight Grand Cross of the Order of the Bath. For our envoy at least, the unending procrastination of all the parties could now continue without his intervention. He had played a part in thwarting French ambitions in the Low Countries, and Belgian independence would be established without bloodshed. On 2 October Minto had 'an audience of leave' with King Frederick William, followed by a 'gracious reception' by the royal family.[26] The new ambassador,

Lord George William Russell, would not arrive in Berlin until the end of 1835, and in the interim Ralph Abercromby would be the chargé d'affaires.[27]

News soon reached Catherine Rutherford and the tenants at Minto that Lord and Lady Minto would soon be home but, in the event, they spent the last three months of 1834 in London, and did not to reach Minto until Christmas day. Fanny told something of their journey and said that as soon as they entered Hawick they were surrounded by an immense crowd. Bells rang, there were flags hung all along the street, and fine shouting as they set off again. Unknown to the girls at the time, Lord Minto had to make a little speech, and contradict a shameful report of his having taken office in the Peel administration. A few minutes on the Minto side of Hawick the party met the two boys, Lord Melgund and Henry, accompanied by Robert the footman, riding to meet them. The country looked beautiful and Rubers Law (a 424-metre-high hill) seemed to have grown higher. The trees looked large and fine – in short, everything was perfect. To the delight of all, there followed a wonderful Christmas.

Leaving Berlin, the family feared that Quebec might be their next destination as there had been vague and inaccurate rumours of Lord Minto being offered the governorship of Canada, a post which Lord Durham was to fill. With Lord Grey in retirement in Northumberland, the King invited Peel and Melbourne to 'coalesce' and form what could only be an impracticable administration. Lord Melbourne was seen as the most acceptable replacement but he had little enthusiasm for the job, and when William IV found himself facing a set of Whig reform proposals, he dismissed him in the November. The Duke of Wellington advised the King to send for Peel, who had gone to Italy with his family, and a Mr Hudson, later Sir James, was sent to search for him. Peel was back in London by 9 December, and kissed hands the same day, but his ministry was to be short-lived and Lord Melbourne's second government came to power in April.

At the start of 1835, the outlook for Lord Minto had been uncertain, and in many ways he was fortunate that the break in his career would be so short. There seems to have been much lobbying and frequent attendance at Bowood Park, Lord Lansdowne's country house in Wiltshire, as well as occasional lunches with the Holland House set at Lord and Lady Holland's mansion at Kensington where all the great Whig families were frequent guests. It would not have been a surprise if Palmerston had had some say in his being summoned to the Admiralty, having himself started his career as a lord of the Admiralty in 1807, and knowing how Minto could little afford to be without employment for long, given his large family and estate responsibilities. George Eden, Earl of Auckland, had been a success as head of the Admiralty but when Melbourne decided to replace Lord William Bentinck as governor-general of India, he chose Auckland, and on 19 September 1835 he offered Minto the Admiralty portfolio in his cabinet.

The Board of Admiralty was made up of a number of Lords Commissioners, a mixture of admirals known as naval or sea lords, and civil lords who could be politicians. The president of the Board was known as the First Lord of the Admiralty and became a member of the cabinet. In addition to a salary of £4,500, he was entitled to a residence, along with several other lords of the Admiralty, in the complex of buildings between Whitehall, Horse Guards Parade and The Mall. The Ripley Building, then known as The Admiralty, was designed and built by Thomas Ripley and completed in

1726. Admiralty House, a moderately proportioned mansion built in the late eighteenth century to the south of the Ripley Building, was built specifically as the residence of the First Lord. The surveyor's office, on the other hand, was located in Somerset Place.

Not long before his Lordship's appointment, it had been generally established that apart from the First Lord, there would be four naval lords and one civil lord. Most senior of Lord Minto's colleagues was Admiral Sir Charles Adam (1780–1853), first naval lord, who had become Lady Minto's brother-in-law after marrying Patrick Brydone's daughter Elizabeth. He had gone to sea at an early age and had served during the Napoleonic Wars aboard HMS *Victorious*, *Sybille* and *Chiffonne*, and between 1811 and 1814 had commanded HMS *Invincible* (74 guns) and, for a short time, HMS *Impregnable*. With the war over, he was made a rear admiral in 1825, and six years later he sat first as MP for Kinross (1831–32) and then for Clackmannan and Kinross (1833–41). Sir Charles had three periods of service during his seven years as the premier sea lord, working closely not only with Lord Minto but also Lord Palmerston, who had a good opinion of him.[28]

The second lord, Admiral Sir William Parker (1781–1866), had joined the Navy as a captain's servant in 1793 and became acting captain of HMS *Volage* (24 guns) six years later. After spending most of the wars against Napoleon at sea, Captain Parker led the life of a Staffordshire country gentleman until 1828 when he went back to sea in the Mediterranean and was promoted rear-admiral in July 1830. A year later he became second in command of the Channel squadron under Sir Edward Codrington. While at the Admiralty he was to be largely responsible for ordering many of the ships designed by Captain (Sir) William Symonds (1782–1856), who had been appointed Surveyor of the Navy in June 1832.

The third naval lord, Captain George Elliot (1784–1863), Lord Minto's brother, had gone to sea in 1794. Nelson considered him as one of the best officers in the Navy, and he served in the Mediterranean and the East Indies until 1813 in his frigate HMS *Maidstone*. After three years in command of *Victory*, the guardship at Portsmouth, he became MP for Roxburghshire between 1832 and 1835, being also a political secretary at the Admiralty.[29] He was advanced from captain to flag rank in 1837. Admiral George married Eliza Ness, the daughter of James Ness from Osgodby in Yorkshire, in 1810. They had four daughters and five sons, the eldest of whom, George Augustus, born in 1813, was also to become an admiral.[30]

The fourth naval lord was Admiral Sir Edward Troubridge (*c.* 1787–1852), whose career had started on another guardship, HMS *Cambridge*, at Plymouth in 1797.[31] Between 1831 and 1832 he was commander-in-chief at Cork, flying a broad pennant aboard HMS *Stag*. During his service at the Admiralty between 1835 and 1841, Admiral Troubridge had responsibility for the selection of officers for posts afloat. The only civil lord to serve at the Admiralty between April 1835 and August 1841 was Archibald Primrose, Lord Dalmeny (1809–1851), the eldest son of the Earl of Roseberry and MP for the Stirling burghs until 1847.

Senior among the executive naval staff was William Symonds. He had been appointed Surveyor of the Navy three years before Lord Minto's arrival, having spent the Napoleonic Wars aboard HMS *London*. The years that followed saw him designing and building usually experimental, wide-beamed vessels which needed careful handling with their huge spread of sail. Sailing trials, where speed became an obsession, enthused the Lord High Admiral, the Duke of Clarence, and in 1831 Symonds was charged with designing a large 50-gun frigate, HMS *Vernon*, named after a wealthy yachtsman for whom he had worked ten years before and who had introduced Symonds to the Duke of Portland. The latter had served in the cabinets of George Canning and Viscount Goderich in 1827–28, and continued his study of both shipbuilding and naval design when he retired from politics. Captain Symonds, or Sir William Symonds as he was to become by 1836, was not to be the favourite of those young naval architects who were endeavouring to establish themselves in their profession, many of whom saw that his work reflected an uneven knowledge of shipbuilding. Others were to dislike his autocratic behaviour and the way he imposed his designs on the Navy, which occasionally involved him in opposing the virtues of steam and propellers. Rarely disposed to do anything that would broaden the work of the Surveyor's office, his assistant, Captain John Eyde, was often treated as little more than the chief clerk he had been, and paid accordingly. It was fortunate that the Surveyor's assistant possessed the diligence, imagination and experience to contribute as much as he did to the construction and economy of the fleet over a period of twenty years.[32]

Symonds was not, however, the only naval officer to design ships for the Royal Navy. Captain John Hayes had started as a shipwright in the Deptford yard and in 1827 his new design of sloop was entered in that year's trials. When Symonds officially took office in 1832 he was building the 36-gun frigate *Inconstant* at Portsmouth. Lord Minto's brother, George, had also conceived the design for a 18-gun sloop, naming her *Modeste* after a ship he had commanded of that name, and which was launched in 1837 following an argument with Symonds, whose ships George believed were not only too deep but whose qualities could be reproduced more simply. The Board of the Admiralty supported Admiral George's proposal to build a vessel with one-tenth less draught than any Symonds ship of the same class. Much was to be written about her.

Some insight into the more mundane of Minto's new duties was given by the *Hampshire Telegraph* which reported the arrival of members of the Board of Admiralty in Portsmouth on 12 October, aboard HMS *Firebrand*, a steam vessel that was usually based at Devonport. After a salute from the flagship of the Commander-in-chief, they proceeded at eleven o'clock to inspect the *Excellent*, from which ship they went to the *Vanguard*, and thence to the *Brisk*. That evening they dined with Admiral Sir Thomas Williams, who had established the Naval Female School for daughters of naval officers (later the Royal School), and the following day they inspected various branches of the dockyard. Two more days of inspection followed and Minto held a levee at the George Hotel which was attended by upwards of 120 naval officers, followed in the evening by a sumptuous dinner for the heads of departments.[33]

Life in London meant considerable readjustment, not just for the earl but for Lady Minto, whose responsibility it was to ensure the smooth running and success of important social events in a naval context. The older children too had their part to play. Fanny, in particular, seemed overwhelmed by the constant social life, being often happy and depressed in succession. She was slow to cope with events at which her attendance was unavoidable, and the satisfaction of balls and great dinner parties depended on those she met. There were to be thirty-seven dinners given at the Admiralty during Minto's period of office. In the last two months of 1835 alone, there were no fewer than seven dinners for guests of the First Lord. Leaving aside the commissioners themselves, their guests in November included Sir John Barrow, a promoter of expeditions with a wide knowledge of the Navy, and founder of the Royal Geographical Society; Lord and Lady Holland; the Russian ambassador; Lord Melbourne; Lord Lansdowne and Captain George Augustus Elliot; Lord and Lady Howick; Lord and Lady John Russell; and Thomas Spring Rice, a politician.[34]

In January 1836, the Admiralty hosted the cabinet dinner, and at the beginning of the following month the family was introduced to one of the great days in the London calendar with the opening of Parliament. The ladies of the Minto household made themselves 'great figures with feathers and finery' after breakfast as they prepared to go to the House of Lords. The King did not arrive until two o'clock so that the family had plenty of time to see 'all the old lords assembling'. Their robes looked very handsome although Fanny thought His Majesty was the least dignified-looking person in the house. There was 'nothing impressive' but it was amusing. The 'poor old man could not see to read his speech, and after he had stammered half through it Lord Melbourne was obliged to hold a candle for him, and he read it over again'.[35] After the debate, several of Lord Minto's friends came back to Admiralty House to dine.

Soon afterwards the First Lord was elected a member of the Royal Society, which was then housed in Somerset House, and the following month he took the chair as Friends of the Seamen's Hospital dined at the London Tavern in Bishopsgate. The company included Lord Byron, Admiral Codrington and Sheriff Salomons, the City banker. The Seamen's Hospital, which afforded assistance 'to every sailor presenting himself for relief', had helped 25,552 distressed sailors in the fifteen years of its existence. Its utility was not marred by any prejudice on the part of sailors for its establishment being on board the *Dreadnought*, moored off Greenwich. *The Times* listed among those subscribing to this charity as His Majesty (£100), the Queen (£10), the Duchess of Kent and Princess Victoria (£50) and Lord Minto (£21); there were also other sums from the Honourable East India Company, the Corporation of Trinity House and the Merchant Elder Brethren.[36] Then at the end of June, the family attended a breakfast given by the Duchess of Buccleuch which only increased Fanny's 'horror of breakfasts'. The day was perfect, the sight and sound of the music 'pretty', but she 'scarcely ever disliked people more, or felt more beaten down by shyness. She wished nobody would speak to her'.[37]

The following month, when young Henry Elliot was nineteen years old and still at Trinity College, it was agreed that he should accept the post of aide-de-camp and private secretary to Sir John Franklin, the naval officer and Arctic explorer who in April had been appointed lieutenant-governor of the penal colony of Van Diemen's Land (later called Tasmania).[38] They sailed on 21 August and were to find a small community torn by the unsuccessful social reforms of Sir George Arthur, his predecessor, little support for Franklin's own fervent efforts to improve conditions among the convicts at Hobart, and a situation which was soon worsened by Lady Franklin's insensitive and overzealous dealings with other government officials. It seems that when Henry returned to England after four years away he had gained a little in confidence although his career was as uncertain as ever. It was only the result of talking to one of his Cambridge friends, who was about to resign as a précis writer at the Foreign Office, that he persuaded his father to go to Lord Palmerston, who agreed to him having the job. He was to enter the Diplomatic Service in 1841.

Lord Minto shared Lord Palmerston's belief that, on the continent of Europe, Britain had most to fear from Russia, and it was only our relationship with France that prevented the latent bellicosity of St Petersburg, Berlin and Vienna from becoming a reality. The natural tendency of a new First Lord of the Admiralty would have been to ensure that British naval resources could provide a strong and effective deterrent while at the same time protecting the country's commerce. Surprisingly in Minto's case he needed some cajoling in his first year not to reduce the size of the fleet and he only reluctantly commissioned one or two new vessels. He did, however, manage to oversee decisions which resulted in six battleships being posted to the Mediterranean and another three to Lisbon, leaving eight in home waters along with three 'first-rate' guard ships.[39] Nevertheless, no sooner had the fitting out of the few battleships he had commissioned got under way, than the inadequacy of the Admiralty's budget became only too clear. Admiral Sir Charles Adam wrote to him in September 1836 suggesting that the long-term shipbuilding programme would have to be reduced and work on repairs increased.[40]

To its credit, the Melbourne cabinet which relied on much 'political shuffling' had passed the Irish Tithe Act in 1834 but there were those who demanded the repeal of all tithes and others constantly pressing for home rule, both of whom were able to embarrass and manipulate an administration in London. The death of King William IV in June 1837 at Windsor Castle led to the dissolution of Parliament and the general election which took place between 24 July and 18 August. Melbourne's majority had been reduced but the election was won by the Whigs with 344 MPs and the Tories with 314. As the King had hoped, he survived long enough to allow his niece, Princess Victoria of Kent, to reach the age of eighteen, thereby avoiding a regency.

The general election had barely got under way when Lord Minto was able to tell his brother that he had found him a post as commander-in-chief at the Cape. Not unexpectedly, Rear-Admiral George had felt much uneasiness about his career. His defeat as MP for Roxburghshire in 1835 had left him with time on his hands and, at his brother's suggestion, he lived much of the time at Minto and continued to work for the Whig cause whenever possible. However, although living on about £2,500 per annum at most, it became 'a necessity' for him to find what he called 'a job'. He enjoyed his time at the Admiralty and did not want to give up his profession but he had to recognise that a command abroad would probably take him away from his wife Eliza and family.[41] After consulting the second sea lord, the admiral said how happy he would be to accept the appointment so long as he did not have to depart immediately. In the meantime, there had been family celebrations in Roxburghshire following the victory there of John Edmund Elliot, Lord Minto and George's brother, at the general election.[42] However, celebrations were to be short-lived when Lady Minto was called to the deathbed of her eighty-five-year-old mother, Mrs Brydone, on 15 August.[43]

When Lord Minto and Admiral Sir Charles Adam came to examine the Navy's 1837 construction estimates they would have found that the figure was approximately £4.9 million, a meagre £200,000 more than the previous year. The manpower forecast was 34,000 while there were some twenty ships of the line in commission, with eleven of them in home waters, six in the Mediterranean and three at Lisbon. The reduction in the annual naval provisions from almost £23 million to around £6 million had been necessary following the government's abolition of income tax at the end of the Napoleonic Wars, and despite the Admiralty's success in achieving more funds from the government during the 1820s, its peacetime resources were never enough.

Admiralty policy was to concentrate on a programme of repairing ships rather than constructing new ones, and the government ordered them 'to take every step in their power to reduce the public expenditure in their Lordships' department to the utmost possible extent … the voted estimates were not to be exceeded'. Admiral George had left a legacy of 'keeping a careful watch on costs' and by June 1837 Lord Minto had produced a paper in which he called for repair rather than new construction and the removal of men from large ships in favour of steamers and sixth-rate vessels.[44] Such a policy could, however, have benefited from more teamwork and the recognition that a surveyor's department of eight people was inadequate. Mr Wood, the Secretary, who had assessed the capabilities of the dockyards soon after Minto became first lord, and who been on the visit to Portsmouth dockyard the previous year, pressed the case with Symonds that repairs were more economic than construction.[45] He could see merit in the surveyor's ideas – for example, his plan to increase the number of shipwrights available by re-rating former skilled men who had been acting as yard carpenters and boat builders – but overall there was a lack of any well-conceived work programme, and although steps began to be taken towards matching the number of people to the tasks to be done, progress was often piecemeal.

A 'steam department' was established in 1837 and an 'engineering branch afloat' followed but it was not until 1843 that royal dockyards were to set up schools for 'engineering boys' or dockyard apprentices. The use of steam was to increase financial pressures on the Admiralty. Four years before, Sir Pulteney Malcolm had rated his own armed steamer 'more useful to him than another 74' and by 1837 there were twenty-four available. Paddle steamers which were unable to fire a broadside tended to mount guns as large as 32-pounders and they became the standard armament in the Navy despite the view of some seamen gunners that they were, at best, supplements to conventional armaments. As the reader may recall, the American ambassador had been surprised to find there was not a single steamboat on Lake Geneva in 1822, and it was not until 1837 that the Swedish inventor John Ericsson demonstrated his steam launch – and two years later when Francis Petit-Smith, an ex-Romney Marsh farmer, had the 200-ton, propeller-driven *Archimedes* built and trialled successfully against HMS *Vulcan* in September 1839. During this period Symonds had taken the view that while a propeller could propel a ship, it also made steering more difficult.

Admiral George seems not to have left for the Cape as had been intended as he was at Portsmouth in December. Symond's objections to razeeing HMS *Warspite*, or cutting down a vessel's number of decks, were the subject of a board decision following Admiral George's inspection over the Christmas period. Having 'been all over *Warspite* with Mr Blake', he said, there appeared 'no doubt of her being quite worth repairing'. As far as they had been able to examine, she was 'by no means in a state of great decay' and what there was, appeared to be caused by 'the old system of placing a quantity of diagonal timber from the keel to the lower deck beams with longitudinal pieces of the same size in the angles'. To the admiral, 'a more mischievous waste of timber could hardly be devised'.[46]

By the spring of 1838 Lord Minto's nineteen-year-old son Charlie, who had last been heard of at the Scheldt, was serving aboard HMS *Modeste*, the 562-ton sloop which had been launched at Woolwich dockyard the previous October. He had a 'very good set of messmates' and altogether, they lived comfortably on board.[47] The description Charles gave his uncle of the trials of the *Modeste*, *Lily* and *Pantaloon* between 20 and 30 April specifically mentioned the 'the extreme weight ... in the shape of ballast' which the *Modeste* had received, and which he felt confident would beat anything going to windward, particularly in fresh breezes. After a six-hour trial, on the first day the vessels came out, there had been a continuous series of experimental sailings but, as Charlie reported on 23 April, the 'success of *Modeste* stirred up the bile of the Symonites' to such an extent that he was afraid her captain and first lieutenant would be unfairly criticised. The 'origin of the whole thing', in Charlie's opinion, was Mr Eyde, who being a good Symonite had done everything in his power to pick a hole in the behaviour of her officers.[48] A report on the *Modeste*, issued by Commander H. A. Murray at the end of April, concluded that the vessel appeared to do very well against a head sea, tacked freely, steered easily but did not appear to hold a very good wind. He thought that the *Modeste* could scarcely be brought to her intended depth without iron ballast and inclined to the view that she would sail best on an even keel and, confirming Charlie's conclusion, she appeared to do better than both *Lily* and *Pantaloon* 'in strong breezes at sea'.[49] Unfortunately, the *Modeste* had become something of an affair. It rumbled on through the summer into the autumn, and in October it was Sir John Barrow who, at the behest of the Lords Commissioners of the Admiralty, ordered the captain of the *Pique* to cause further trials of the two sloops to be made in such manner as he thought proper.[50] Their Lordships desired a full report on the trials and the effect of any alterations made to the ship's performance.[51]

Just before the trials had begun at Portsmouth the family had taken up temporary residence in Eastbourne, an arrangement which seems to have permitted Lord Minto to leave the Admiralty for several weekends and join the countess and the children there. Four or five weeks later the family went to a concert at the Palace to listen to 'all the good singers' and on 28 June Princess Victoria was crowned queen. Fanny's diary recorded that the young were up at six in the morning and Lizzy, Charlotte and Fanny, who were going to Westminster Abbey, were soon dressed in all their grandeur. The ceremony, she wrote, was 'much what I expected, but less solemn and impressive from the mixture of religion with worldly vanities and distinctions. The sight was far more brilliant and beautiful than I had supposed it would be.' They walked home in their fine gowns through the crowds and found the stand at the Admiralty well filled and were quite in time to see the procession pass. There was great cheering when the carriage of Maréchal Soult, the French ambassador, passed and even more for the Duchess of Kent and the Queen.[52]

On 18 September, almost imperceptibly, the courtship of Lady Mary by Mr Ralph Abercromby ended happily with their marriage. He had become minister resident to the Grand Duke of Tuscany in November 1835. It must have seemed a lifetime away from the days in 1832 when Mary and Catherine Rutherford had occasion to comfort this sensitive and gentle diplomat and son of the Speaker of the House of Commons.[53]

When Admiral George wrote in August 1838 from the naval base at Simon's Town in South Africa, he described his new posting as commander-in-chief 'Cape of Good Hope and Coast of Africa'. He was to be especially conscious of how many of the family were at sea at this time in addition to Lord Minto's Charlie. In the case of his eldest son, George Augustus Elliot, he was 'most exceedingly pleased' with the appointment Lord Minto had arranged for him as commander of the brig HMS *Columbine*, a 'delightful vessel' designed by Symonds.[54] In the case of Frederick, however, the admiral's twelve-year-old son, the family had been in a 'state of anxiety' for three days. He and a friend had been playing with a powder flask when it blew up, taking with it his left thumb and damaging his shoulder. The two doctors who attended him were surprised at the boy's fortitude and composure. When it was over Freddy, as he was to become known, requested the doctors not to scold the boy who had given him the gunpowder for 'it was all my fault'.

Turning to a conversation the commander-in-chief had had with Sir George Thomas Napier, the newly arrived governor of Cape Province, Admiral George reported the occasional slaughter that was occurring on the frontier to Lord Minto. The boundary was 'all bush and underwood' and the last governor had decided to go back to the old boundary, a decision which the admiral (and presumably Napier) thought to be a mistake. Although he feared his brother did 'not care two pins for this subject', George went on to say that 'the late governor had discretionary powers given him which … he ought to have acted on, at least till further orders came, and that proper explanations would have prevented those orders'. There was 'a wish to do justice and protect the Kaffirs' although in the admiral's view it may have been an Irish way of doing them a good turn, to 'rob them of a large district of a country'.[55]

By February 1839, the commander-in-chief was performing his duties in the region of Accra, which was described at the time as one of the most insalubrious localities on the Gold Coast, over which England, Holland and Denmark exercised jurisdiction. Admiral George's mind was, however, still on the *Modeste*. He felt disappointed that both his brother and Admiral Parker had 'lost sight of the experiment proposed by him and approved of by the board when they ordered the vessel to be built. He thought he had worded his proposal in such a way that if it was adhered to, no mistake could take place' and now found that 'in the daily hurry and load of business at the Admiralty', details of her trim and loading had become misplaced and misunderstood.[56]

It was in November that Lord Minto's brother was able to examine a report by Edward Boxer, the captain of HMS *Pique*, about sea trials that had been conducted in respect of *Modeste* and *Rover*. He had been posted to the North America and West Indies station in August 1837, and as the admiral turned the pages of his report, he was inclined to bite his lip for fear of unduly criticising Boxer's work. He had no option but to tell Lord Minto that it was 'full of errors, unfair and incorrect' and 'not borne out by the facts'.[57] However, as luck would have it, Admiral George would soon be able to see for himself how well HMS *Modeste* sailed.

The family spent the winter of 1840 between the Admiralty and Putney House which Lord Minto rented. Fanny described the Thames at night, undisturbed except now and then by a slow barge, gliding 'so smoothly along as hardly to make a ripple'. The young had taken some time to be reconciled to staying in London and waited impatiently to return to Minto, where there were 'guns and dogs, a heathery moor, and a blue Scotch heaven above' and it was not until August that year that the family got away from London. One of the compensations had been the way the countess had, despite the obligations she had as her husband's hostess, organised so many of the children's activities. Their raids on Lord Minto's dressing room, where on one occasion they 'each ate two or three of his compressed luncheon tablets', did 'rather disturb' Lady Minto but there were also delightful theatricals at the Admiralty, where Lotty and Harriet sang their parts in one little operetta called *William and Susan*, written by the countess.[58]

When Lord Minto received his brother's letter at the Admiralty in April 1840 he probably anticipated that the admiral had left the Cape for China, where he was to be commander-in-chief and joint plenipotentiary with Captain Charles Elliot, or that he was either already there or at Bombay. However, 'every exertion' had had to be made to get the fleet ready. The weather had been very severe – gales of wind and much rain – and in the dockyard there was an outbreak of smallpox. The 72-gun *Blenheim* and 20-gun corvette *Nimrod* were probably 'to the northward with these winds' but George could not so easily account for *Columbine*. His son's sloop had two officers besides her captain on board and, since she had been watching slavers, the vessel might have had to run with them to Sierra Leone. Surprisingly, George's son was to be left at the Cape while the *Columbine* sailed to China under the command of Thomas Clarke. For his part, the admiral had thought it most probable that Minto had assumed he had already gone to India without waiting for specific orders after the death at sea of Sir Frederick Lewis Maitland, the previous commander-in-chief.[59]

In fact the admiral's fleet arrived in Bombay on 28 June. In addition to HMS *Melville*, his 74-gun flagship, the 42-gun frigate *Blonde*, and the 18-gun sloop *Pylades*, there was the *Modeste* about whom he 'had no private feeling whatever … but her peculiarities made her so valuable in such an undertaking that [he] could not hesitate to do so'.[60] They were to join up with a British force comprising *Alligator*, *Madagascar*, *Atalanta*, *Wellesley* and the *Lame* which was assembling around the islands of Macao and Hong Kong, and a land army of 5,000 men drawn from regiments stationed in India. These forces were joining what was to be called the First Opium War (1839–42), a one-sided affair which was to greatly enhance Palmerston's reputation. It was, however, not very popular in England since many 'could not divest their minds of the erroneous idea that it was undertaken to enforce upon the Chinese the continuance of a traffic whose morals were of the most pernicious kind, and that it was a domineering and disgraceful attempt to compel the importation of an article strictly forbidden by their own laws'.[61]

There were two Elliots in China at this time, or three, if George Augustus Elliot was included, HMS *Volage's* captain from June 1840. In addition to Admiral George, Charles Elliot, the son of the first Lord Minto's brother, Hugh Elliot, had arrived in 1834 and become chief superintendent in charge of trade affairs in China, succeeding the late Lord Napier. Admiral George arrived off the island of Macao in HMS *Melville* on 5 July and, hearing the report of firearms, he pressed his flagship through the difficult passage by which the inner harbour was at that time entered, but unfortunately when in tow from the steamer HMS *Atalanta* she hit a sharp peak of rock. The damage caused Elliot to shift his flag into the *Wellesley* and leave the *Blenheim* to help the *Melville*. Just as a squadron of vessels was leaving, including HMS *Modeste*, Admiral George dispatched a messenger in a steamer to the mouth of the Ningpo River to deliver to the authorities in that place a letter addressed by Palmerston to the Emperor's chief advisers. It was received by a mandarin and the steamer returned to Chusan harbour.[62]

At the heart of the so-called war was the threat the Chinese posed to British merchants selling them opium imported from India. Any seizure immediately attracted a response against the Chinese authorities. Captain Elliot, as he was known locally, found it useful to encourage the merchants to put together a flotilla of armed boats from among merchant shipping lying in or around Whampoa. In March 1840 the chief superintendent chose Canton as a target and, having established himself at the British factory, he successfully achieved the surrender of some 20,000 chests of opium by the end of May, whereupon he moved on to Macao. The following October saw Elliot asking a Captain Smith for the help of the corvettes *Volage* and *Hyacinth* when the Chinese admiral and twenty-nine war junks threatened the area. A battle ensued and the Chinese were defeated.

The two Elliots reached Peking on 10 August and a series of friendly meetings with the Chinese followed. Even a number of short cruises were made by HMS *Modeste* and *Blonde*, while the *Wellesley*, *Pylades* and *Volage* visited some of the islands to the south. However, when the absence of an official at a planned meeting threw up the suspicion that hostilities might be about to restart, the light squadron set sail to inspect the forts. *Modeste* had to be lightened to be able to cross the bar. In the event the Chinese agreed to a meeting on land and, with Captain Elliot so engaged, Admiral George cruised in a steamer to a point where the Great Wall of China could be seen in the distance. By November another truce had to be negotiated when HMS *Queen* was fired on and forced to rejoin Admiral George in the *Melville* at Macao. Local opinion considered the commander-in-chief should have punished the wrongdoers promptly and severely, and took the view that both Elliots had shown regrettable weakness. Their criticism led to a petition condemning Captain Elliot being presented at Westminster.

It may have been with some sense of relief that the same merchants received a circular from Charles Elliot on 29 November announcing that the 'Rear-Admiral of the Blue had resigned the command of the fleet into the hands of Commodore Sir Gordon Bremer, sudden and severe illness having incapacitated him from its duties'. A month or so before, the admiral had told Lord Minto how he had been 'very languid' and unwell, with a pain in his chest and being only able to lie on his back.[63] He sailed from Chusan with his son in command of the *Volage* on 7 December 1840 after only four months in Chinese waters and returned to England. Captain Elliot was left at Lintin, supported by a fleet which had been augmented by the arrival of the East India Company iron steamer *Nemesis*.[64] One of Lord Minto's naval lords at the time, Rear-Admiral Sir William Parker, was to become commander-in-chief in August 1841 and defeat the Chinese army at Nanking.[65]

It was a little before three o'clock on 7 June 1841 when Admiral George called at the Admiralty in London hoping to have a word with his brother. It seems that in addition to ill health, he was somewhat depressed. With Lord Minto away on account of Fanny's forthcoming wedding, he wrote Gilbert a letter instead telling him that he had been led to suppose that the state of his health was such as to make any return to office 'quite out of the question'.[66] He admitted to having been out of his depth in China and may have become aware of Palmerston's criticism of the way he had handled himself, described by the Foreign Secretary as 'irresolute and ineffective'.[67]

In September, Sir Robert Peel's second government came to power and the Prime Minister appointed the Earl of Haddington to the Admiralty in place of Minto. On his last day at work the earl decided to put on record the opinions he and his colleagues had formed, and the views they entertained about the Navy before he retired from the Board, and which 'may possibly not be unwelcome to our successors'. He hoped that the nominal establishment of the Navy, excluding those used for harbour service, would be some 100 ships of the line. The 'most perfect arrangement' would be to have seventy in the water, ten on the stocks ready for launching, and another ten not laid down but having their frames converted and ready to replace 'such as might be launched'. The departing politician recognised that for some considerable time the Navy would be compelled to keep more ships in the water than was necessary but so many were old and, if the Navy was to compare favourably with the fleets of other nations, 'a rapid succession of new ships' was called for. During his six years' service he had learned that if Britain's trade and possessions were to be protected, the Navy had to remain 'master of the sea'.

About the building and repair of vessels in HM dockyards, Lord Minto's minute directed his successors to consider the constant operation of decay. It was impossible to increase the building of large ships quickly. About steamers, he wrote that 'next, if not equal in importance to the building of ships of the line is the creation of a powerful steam navy'. It had received 'anxious attention' but it would be two or three years longer in Minto's opinion before that branch of the Navy would be complete. Then, turning to the dockyards, he warned that the use of private dockyards threatened the livelihood of shipwrights in royal yards. Labour relations had never been good, and although the proportion of apprentices in the dockyards had increased, Lord Minto had wanted the wages of instructors and apprentices to be increased. There was also a plan for schools to be established in the dockyards for the education of young men. The police force in the yards had received some attention but its efficacy depended much on the character and energy of individual Captain Superintendents, the result being that Minto had wanted to put the policing of the dockyards under the management of the Metropolitan Commissioners of Police.

Other matters raised by the retiring First Lord included the armament of the fleet and the composition of the Board. Notwithstanding the increase in armament established for all classes of ship, Lord Minto considered this 'but a step towards a still more perfect system under which our ships of the line and 4th rates should carry a very much larger proportion of the 8" guns'. So far as his opinion of the existing Constitution of the Admiralty was concerned, it was a subject requiring more time than he had available but he thought there was no doubt that the Board was 'too weak and underhanded [undermanned] to carry out that principle with effect'. He believed it would be greatly to the Admiralty's advantage 'were another professional Lord, unconnected with Parliament to be added to the Board, on whom might devolve the superintendence of the dockyards and the Department of the Surveyor of the Navy, and of some portion of the Stores'. The transfer of this department to the superintendence of the second member of the Board could, in Minto's opinion, be 'a much better arrangement.'[68]

The family had returned to Roxburghshire before the general election result had been declared, leaving Lord Minto in London. When the earl stepped down from his position of power he seems to have encountered something of the black void that erstwhile ministers and MPs sometimes experience in similar circumstances. Admiral

George, whose health and spirits had improved, went to live initially at a house near Horndean, north of Portsmouth, and by the end of the year at Blendworth, not far away. It seems that just before the election he had successfully sold to the Admiralty his idea of designing a small but fast frigate with the aid of Mr Eyde, the second vessel to be called the *Eurydice*. The second hurdle was to establish when there might be a vacancy in the shipyard and on 28 March 1842, while watching another vessel go down the shipway, he hoped *Eurydice* would soon follow.[69] Discussions with Mr Blake, the master shipwright at Portsmouth, and Isaac Watts, the assistant surveyor, followed and later in April, the new vessel was launched. By June there were as many as sixty men working on *Eurydice* but half of them had to be taken away to undertake work on HMS *Firebrand* and HMS *Frolic*. George was nevertheless, pleased to say that 'her frame is all up … except the stem'.[70]

In August, the admiral's son, George Augustus, married Hersey Susan Sidney, 'an amiable and sweet girl', the only daughter of Colonel Wauchope of Niddrie in Midlothian. The only difficulties that had been in the way of the marriage had been the couple's lack of means. They would have to live on £800 a year. Although the admiral had been aware of the Wauchopes all his life, he knew very little about them – but 'we must hope for the best'.[71] The following month, after Admiral George had seen 'above one hundred shipwrights' at work on *Eurydice*, and that she was 'planked up to the top', he turned his attention to finding the most effective way of ensuring that young George was given command of the vessel. His intention was to ask Lord Haddington 'in good time to let [him] command *Eurydice* not merely for the first trial but for her first period of service, during which her character must be established'.[72]

In November, there was the announcement of yet another marriage. The wedding was to be between Georgiana Maria Elliot (one of the Admiral's four daughters) and William Hopetoun Carnegie, the eighth Earl of Northesk, who was 'a most amiable and unaffected person with very good sense and good temper'. The family at Blendworth had been relieved to find that Carnegie was much better off than they had thought and was someone most likely 'to make Georgiana happy'. George had been in the middle of arranging a passage for Georgiana's eighteen-year-old brother, Alexander, who was about to start a successful career in the Army.[73] Content, and in a satisfied mood, the Admiral was fortunately able to concentrate on the potentially serious news of 'a scrape' which Lord Minto's son Charlie, now the young captain of HMS *Spartan* serving off the coast of Newfoundland, had got into.

In August 1842, Mr Delacey Gleig, a fourteen-year-old midshipman aboard *Spartan* had been punished with a rope by the ship's boatswain. This had resulted in the boy's father, the Reverend Mr Gleig, whom Admiral George described as 'one of those virulent Tory ornaments of our Church who preach meekness and forgiveness but in practice [never] lose an opportunity of having a slap at a Whig captain', threatened to bring a charge of 'scandalous, cruel and oppressive conduct' against Charlie, one that carried with it the possible disgrace and dismissal from the Navy.[74] As matters turned out, the outcome of the affair had to wait until April 1843 when Admiral George was staying at the Earl of Northesk's house at Longwood. Much had been written in the newspapers and 'some members of the Carlton Club', as George described all Tories, tried to pervert the evidence during the three-day naval court-martial which was held on board HMS *Imaum* at Port Royal, Jamaica; but Admiral George was able to tell his brother on 8 April that 'it was the most complete triumph for Charles that could be'.[75] Sir John Barrow was to agree later about the impropriety of the case.

As time went by and the admiral had still not heard anything from the Admiralty about young George being given command of *Eurydice*, he became increasingly concerned. However, at the end of May when a note was received from Lord Haddington containing 'no promises … and so forth', the admiral was more convinced than ever that he intended to give his son the *Eurydice*. To his relief, Admiral George heard from Sir William Gage at the Admiralty that George Augustus was to become a supernumerary lieutenant in Admiral Sir Charles Adam's flagship, the 36-gun *Inconstant*, in the West Indies. It was September, however, while the Elliot family was preparing to leave Blendworth for good and live for a while on the Continent, before George Augustus and *Eurydice* could be formally introduced to each other.

Queen Victoria and her consort were the guests of Louis Philippe in September 1843 at the Château d'Eu, his country residence close to Le Tréport, thus allowing the small fleet of ships that habitually accompanied the Royal Yacht to exercise and trial before they were due back in Brighton (from where Her Majesty had sailed). It was calm when *Eurydice* was towed out on 6 September but, as Admiral George reported, 'a slight breeze sprung up as we rounded the spit. We made sail and stood over towards Ryde' and tried out the vessel as far as they could. According to one commentator at the time, *Eurydice* was derisively called a 'jackass frigate' on account of her small size (921 tons). George reported that she seemed to 'keep a very good wind'. There had been a lot of talk about a race from Brighton to Portsmouth between *Eurydice* and the 50-gun *Warspite* before the two vessels sailed to the West Indies. Now commander of *Eurydice*, George Augustus had 'great expectations of running *Warspite* hard'.

Meanwhile, the admiral's daughters Georgiana and Catherine left the now cleared house at Blendworth, and George and Eliza made a few last calls in the town 'to dentists and other torments'.[76] After finding that Grove's Hotel, in Albermarle Street could not receive them, the family stayed a short time at the United Services Club before leaving for Italy. They reached Rome in the third week of November, where George was able to report his pleasure at having kept his expenses 'as nearly as possible' to what he had expected. All had gone smoothly and they 'had seen a good deal, both pictures as well as country and people'. George was soon relaxed and lyrical in his praise for Italy, and in the spring of 1844 the family moved into a villa at Naples surrounded by a garden on the top of Piazza Falcone looking onto the sea if not at Vesuvius. It was 'quite as cool as Capo di Monte or any of the other retreats' and in that part of town built on a high rock opposite Castel Nuovo. So far as his daughters Eliza, Catherine and Cecilia were concerned, they remained 'constant' to the attractions of Rome and did not see 'so much beauty in this bay as we had at Simons Bay … and the mountains on a very much larger scale' at the Cape.

Rome was pretty full at the end of 1844 and 'the gaiety and riot' had begun and although there was snow on the mountains the weather did not promise to be quite so severe as during the previous winter. Answering Lord Minto's questions about their future plans, George explained that he did not want to be so far off as Italy on Frederick's account, but he did not think they could live comfortably on their present means in England.[77] Nevertheless, after leaving Rome, and spending much of the winter in Turin, the family travelled over the St Gotthard pass in late June to Lucerne en route for Geneva, where

George had arranged to meet up with Frederick, who was to spend his school vacation with them there.[78] The latter part of their holiday together was spent in Paris, where they took apartments facing south in the Champs-Élysées for 'at least five months'.

As the numerous members of the Elliot family returned to England, there were two items of news, one which came as a relief, the other bringing great sadness to all. On the first day of October 1845 they heard that the Admiral's son, Gilbert John, was on his way home from Australia. He had not found the 'bush life' there to his liking and now wanted to go into the Church for which, as Admiral George told Lord Minto, he 'was originally intended and, I believe, most fit for'.[79] Then, three weeks later, the admiral wrote to his brother from Paris about the death of his son, Lieutenant Horatio Foley Elliot, RN. Rather extraordinarily, a friend who had read about it in a Paris newspaper broke the news to him when he came out of a dentist's surgery. The admiral admitted to always being prepared for such an event; he knew the dangers they were exposed to in their careers. George Augustus endured the hot season in the Gulf of Mexico, Alexander was soldiering in the midst of cholera in India, where even the surgeon of his regiment had died, while Horatio often served in the vicinity of Freetown and Annobon, a Spanish island in the Gulf of Guinea. He explained to Lord Minto how 'Horatio was taken ill five days after the fever broke out (and nine days after leaving Annobon) and died on the last day of June'. He reminded his brother that 'nobody could have any idea of the risks, the anxiety and the suffering which officers and men undergo in carrying slaves to Sierra Leone and in regaining their ships, but those that have been on that dreadful coast'.[80]

In the spring of 1846 George acted as his brother's house agent, inspecting properties around Belgrave Square before Minto committed himself to the purchase later that year of 48 Eaton Square, at the corner of Eaton Place and Chesham Place. Although Lord John Russell had become Prime Minister, both Lord Minto and the admiral had fallen out of favour with the Lansdowne faction, who wanted to reduce Elliot influence over Russell. In November, George 'received a very kind note' from Lord Auckland, who had become First Lord of the Admiralty in the new administration, offering him command of Devonport dockyard, a post he declined on account of its pay and also as he had his eye on 'a foreign command'.[81] Unfortunately, he was not to hold another seagoing command.

George became a vice-admiral in May the following year and, notwithstanding his earlier decision, accepted the appointment as commander-in-chief at the Nore at Sheerness in 1848, telling his brother that 'all feeling of languor and weakness' had left him.[82] Having become a vice-admiral in course of seniority, and an admiral in 1853, he transferred to the reserved half-pay list two years later and he was made a KCB in 1862. He died at Princes Terrace, Kensington, after a lengthy illness the following year.

# 7

# LIFE ON THE MINTO ESTATE
# (1830-1835)

It was on 4 January 1830, when the family was living in Paris at 12 Rue de Monsieur in 'uncomfortable low temperatures', that Robert Selby, Lord Minto's factor or estate manager, wrote to him about offers he had received for the property known as Standhill near Ancrum on the Minto estate. Two weeks later, having considered the three highest offers, he wrote again recommending Thomas Halden and Andrew his brother to his Lordship as tenants.[1]

At this time Robert Selby was married to Helen Ritchie, whose father had farmed the land over which the battle of Prestonpans had been fought, and he was coming to the end of his factorship. Among the papers sent to Paris was the Minto estate annual rental statement which showed the total of rent and arrears due ($£2,877$ 19$s$ 3$d$), along with the amount of cash received at Candlemas and paid into the Bank of Scotland. He considered all the arrears 'good', or likely to be paid. Among the tenancy changes on the estate was Shielswood which had been let to Mr Thomas Scott, the brother of the tenant of Todshawhaugh, near Harden, and so far as those tenants in temporary need were concerned two payments of 14 and 12 guineas had been made to Mary Donald and Mary Friend respectively, as 'they were greatly in need of money'. He added that 'the price of every sort of farm produce has not only been, but still is, ruinously low'.

Repairs to the church, the overseeing of which Robert Selby was also responsible for, were proceeding well. The 'slating was finished about a month ago and the interior is all lathed and ready for plastering. The tower is the height of the ridging of the church.' In regard to the north approach to Minto House, it was nearly ready for the metal. The old fences on the west side of the road had been cleared away between the stables and the entrance into the chicken yard which was a very great improvement. Turning to the effect of heavy rains on the crops, and disease which affected many stock farmers in the neighbourhood, he could only warn of greater distress, particularly among the poor. The ground had been covered with snow for eight weeks and the thaw had only started three days previously, with the result that farm work in the forthcoming spring would be much behind.[2]

It was usually left to the tenants to raise the question of the habitability of their houses; to do otherwise would invite them to present lengthy lists of renovation or maintenance and could be seen as interference in their affairs. At the beginning of April 1830, Robert Selby told his employer that he had sent Andrew Kerr and John Kennedy to inspect New Mill, the home of John Hope, which he had said was in such a state as to be uninhabitable. They had found the roof to be completely decayed but the walls were good, considering they were built with clay. The tenant was of the opinion that, in addition to a new roof, two more rooms were needed for the convenience of the family; furthermore, that should nothing be done to the property that summer he would have to consider taking a house in Jedburgh. Reminding Lord Minto that it was 'a small thatched cottage, very old', Selby added that should his Lordship be inclined to do anything, he could scarcely advise putting a new roof on old clay walls. A small 'neat house erected new from the ground' would be more convenient and perhaps cheaper in the end. Closing his letter to the French capital, he added that 'old Lizzy Sharp' had died some three weeks before, along with Henry Elliot, the shepherd.[3]

Aware that his master was about to leave Paris, or perhaps had already done so, Robert Selby wrote to Lord Minto on 12 May at Messrs Coutts & Co., bankers, London. He hoped that his Lordship might have an opportunity of speaking to the Duke of Buccleuch. Apparently when the third payment for construction work undertaken on the church became due, and the duke was asked for his contribution of £300, nothing had happened, causing Selby to write to Major William Riddell on the subject, but again without reply. If Lord Minto was in contact with the duke, Selby felt sure the matter would be settled given 'the manner in which he acted regarding the manse'. The church was due to be finished in a few weeks when the fourth and last instalment would have to be paid, and this amounted to nearly £600. Selby was determined to make the payment and told his Lordship that he might take it upon himself to write to him.[4]

In July, when the family were in Switzerland, Selby reported having received the schedules for the return of his Lordship's establishment from 24 May 1829 to the same day in 1830. In order to estimate Lord Minto's taxes, he needed to know the number of male servants, four-wheel carriages, carriage or saddle horses, and servants using hair powder that might have been in England after the first date.[5] Additionally, Selby 'begged to trouble' his Lordship for an answer he could give to a question raised by the tax inspector. The latter wanted to know the date of 'the demise of the Countess Dowager of Minto', the first Earl Minto's wife, Anna Maria, having died in March 1829.

By the middle of October it was becoming clear to Robert Selby that poverty among the tenants was on the increase and, with the exception of Mr James Brodie of Deanfoot, no rents had been paid on time. The poor state of agriculture meant that his Lordship would have to accept delayed rental payments. Payments due to Lord Minto's architect, Mr William Playfair, also preoccupied the factor. He had received 'two or three pressing letters' from him in respect of the plans drawn up for the manse and the church which together amounted to £220 and, having supposed his charge to be at the rate of 5 per cent of the outlay, he had been surprised to receive a bill for £35 more than he had expected.[6] Selby could not see the church costing Lord Minto less than £2,000.[7]

In the middle of November, a member of an earlier factor's family, Archibald Turnbull, was pleased to offer Robert Selby the sum of £104 as the yearly rent of Townhead Farm which he possessed, and the sum of £48 a year for the three West Hillend fields, in the occupation of Mr Reid. He also told the factor that he would require a mews stable for 'fine horses' and the conversion of the present stable adjoining his house into a kitchen.[8] His predecessor, Thomas Turnbull (1706–1774), became factor to Sir Gilbert Elliot, later the first Earl of Minto in 1738. He married twice, first to Nellie Thomson of Reedwater and later to Esther Douglas by whom he had two daughters and a son, born between 1754 and 1758. Just as Robert's responsibilities took in matters of economic and social concern to the community at large, so with Thomas. In the middle of the eighteenth century he had a hand in setting up a carpet factory at Hawick which became the start of the tweed trade in the area. He not only acquired the leases of several properties, including Burnfoot and West Buccleuch, but played the role of banker, lending money at a time when there were no banks outside Edinburgh.

The factor had clearly been taken to task by Lord Minto following the observations he had made about the poor industry being shown by some tenants on the estate. In his reply at the beginning of December, Selby pointed out that 'it was entirely in consequence of the decline in value of farm produce that they were now short of capital'. Tenants, he continued, 'generally take farms in extent according to the amount of their capital, and when the farms produce nothing more than pays the rents, they cannot afford to purchase foreign manure or make any improvements whatever'. He maintained that land had been let at too high a price in past years. The only means of valuing a farm was by the prices of grain and stock for an average of the preceding years and these had been gradually declining in recent years.[9]

On the first day of 1831 Robert Selby was able to tell his master that he had offered Mr Brockie a grain rent for Hassendeanbank, as suggested by his Lordship and, considering that Townhead Farm was also all arable land, he had made the same proposition to Archibald Turnbull. Both tenants agreed to convert their offers into grain at the average of the fiars (or prices set by the sheriff) for that and the four preceding years.[10] Nevertheless, the factor wished to take up another matter with Lord Minto. He could not agree that farms should be let upon leases of fourteen or fifteen years and begged his Lordship's pardon for expressing a contrary opinion. All the farms out of lease were 'susceptible to great improvements' and no tenant would embark on such work without much longer leases. Only 'tenants of capital' could, he wrote, make improvements and they would be deterred from accepting leases of under nineteen years; furthermore, both Brockie and Turnbull 'wish their farms for that period'.[11]

Three weeks later it became clear to Selby that the money rents offered for the farms of Hassendeanbank and Townhead were considerably better than the grain rents, and in March a prospective tenant wrote to Lord Minto from Jedburgh asking whether he had any objection to him having a lease on the estate as he had heard that there might be the possibility of Hassendeanbank being available at Whit Monday. He had not written to Mr Selby due to the fact that the property had not been advertised. The very next day, John Brockie, the existing lessee, wrote to Robert Selby to say that he had found it impossible to agree to a new rent based on the assumed prices of wheat, barley and oats and he much preferred a straight money rent of £370 a year. Archibald Turnbull, on the other hand, accepted a deal based on half money and half grain.[12]

Four days later, it was the wet state of Mr William Reid's property at Kaims that occupied the factor. The previous two seasons had been exceedingly wet and very 'hurtful to that sort of land'. The pasture had been completely overgrown for want of surface draining and the consequence was that Mr Reid had sustained a very serious loss among his sheep stock by the rot, a disease which the factor had never known to exist on that farm. Since it was a farm capable of great improvement, he suggested to Lord Minto, in a letter addressed to him at the Admiralty, that the tenant should have the farm for a few years, even at a reduced rent, and that he should be allowed to employ the Minto labourers to drain the farm whenever they could be spared during its occupation by Mr Reid. The more expeditiously this was done, Selby was sure the sheep rot would be beaten. When Selby eventually sent his Lordship a statement about Mr Reid's reduced rent for two years, he hoped he would give him 'credit for having made the most advantageous bargain he could under existing circumstances'. The pasture fields at Minto, all those outside the policy, were also in need of attention.

Meanwhile a plasterer from Jedburgh had examined the manse in regard to taking off the plaster from the walls and strapping, and plastering it anew. The woodwork

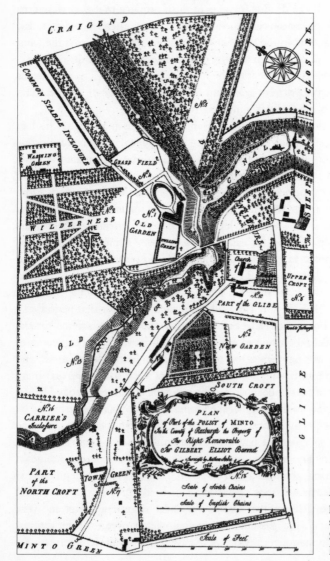

A plan of part of the policy of Minto, as surveyed by Mathew Stobie in 1766. (National Library of Scotland)

and cornice would all have to be taken down where the new work had been done and he estimated the whole expense at between £30 and £40. The walls were now drying very fast, Selby told Lord Minto, and by the end of June he thought they would be perfectly dry. Considering that the whole of the walls were so very wet for 7 feet up, it was surprising how dry they now were especially since the fires had not been regularly kept during the winter, except in the kitchen. One month now would do more than three during the winter. The plasterer thought that once dry the property would not be damp again.[13]

Robert Selby continued to advertise Hassendeanbank farm until Whit Sunday and one offer was received from a Mr William Hall, who farmed in Berwickshire. In money, his bid amounted to £213 or with grain a total of £403, and considering the excellent character he had received of him as an industrious man and good agriculturalist, Selby concluded a bargain with him. By mid-June he was in possession of the farm and he rightly assumed that his Lordship would be satisfied with this action. However, he had to report that the tenant at Dryden had failed to fulfil his promise in respect of security for his arrears and rent. As the result, Selby caused all his effects to be sequestrated and advertised. This action did the trick and he and his brother came to the factor the day before the sale and paid £251 10*s*, the amount due. The settlement was conditional, however, on them being given an abatement of rent and allowed to give up the farm on the next Whit Sunday if they thought proper.[14]

Writing to Lord Minto at Ham Common in July, the factor had to again raise the question of the Minto tax return. His Lordship had been in England 'once or twice' in the course of the previous year, and Selby needed to know whether a return was to be made for any carriages or servants taken south. Then, anticipating his master's return to Minto, he was pleased to report that the two four-year-old colts, and the three-year-old colt, had been broken and turned out to grass. There was, however, a change of plan when the earl's rheumatism returned and the family went to Bognor for some sea bathing. By early September there was clearly some improvement but at Minto, where harvesting had just finished, the crop was generally light and below average. Total rents at Lammas showed a figure of a little more than £3,000, only half of which had been paid on time.[15]

In the spring of 1832 James Brodie explained to Lord Minto that heavy repair costs and other severe losses threatened his ability to 'go on with the farm and pay the rent' of Deanfoot and he asked the earl whether he would allow him £50 for the remaining years of his lease with which to purchase manure. 'With this assistance,' he wrote, 'I am in hopes that it will enable me to go on with the farm.'[16] Without such an abatement the estate might lose what was its second largest rent. Two or three months later Mr Brodie explained to Selby, for obvious onward transmission to Lord Minto, that his request for an allowance of £50 a year was 'not from want of capital to carry on the farm' but because 'he was considerably reduced and sooner than give up a part of the farm, he would quit it altogether'. Meanwhile, having been forced to borrow sums with which to pay the Land Tax and the county Rate Assessment, the factor now required an order on Lord Minto's account to the extent of £400.[17]

The electoral Reform Bill finally received the royal assent on 7 June 1832 and, with the prospect of a general election being called later that year, Selby was soon counselling his Lordship on how important it was for Captain George Elliot to conduct 'a vigorous and spirited canvas' if he were to be the successful candidate in Roxburghshire. He strenuously urged him to appear in the county in person for a few days, and 'to wait upon all the voters, or as many as his time would permit, and assist in directing the committee'. His presence would stimulate their questions; indeed, 'if he does not come down at starting' he could not think his presence would be of much service afterwards. Selby also wanted to see the Whig candidate showing himself to those who 'might be induced to acquaint' their tenants with Captain Elliot's virtues. The factor was convinced that 'the sooner an active canvas' was started the better.[18] It was to prove one of several vociferous actions which put life into the campaign, which was to be won by Captain Elliot in December.

In July 1832, while the family was in London at 19 Lower Grosvenor Street, Lord Minto had to tell Robert Selby how his appointment as envoy and plenipotentiary to the Prussian court would quite definitely prevent him from visiting Minto that summer. Acknowledging what was frustrating news, the factor gave some thought to how he could help his Lordship on his travels, explaining that 'the three blood horses have been taken up from grass. The filly is thriving ... but still very thin in condition ... and unfit for the journey'. He recommended that Lord Minto should take the younger of the two grey ponies in her stead. Captain Elliot had been using both the greys but he was returning to London.[19] Selby was to include the horse which Robert Selby's son, Ephraim, had been using among those being sent to Prussia for Lord Minto's use since it was 'perfectly sound, notwithstanding having been ridden almost daily'. He had been valued at 80 guineas. Selby had found someone accustomed to taking charge of horses at sea and engaged him and a stable lad to travel with them.[20] They were to embark first for Leith and the captain of the packet expected to reach Hamburg in eight to ten days. The factor's only regret was that he had bought a considerable quantity of very good hay at half the previous year's price 'not being aware that there was any prospect of [his] Lordship going abroad'.[21]

By early November, Selby had received three letters from his Lordship in Berlin but his own correspondence dwindled during the winter. As so often it was a time of year when the oldest among the tenants thought deeply about whether or not they could continue farming, and while those with sufficient resources looked around for bargains. Mr Archibald Turnbull died at the end of the year and an offer from another branch of the Turnbull family was made for Kaims Farm but it looked uncompetitive, and the factor felt they had insufficient capital to make a success of the property. Mr John Hope of New Mill was inclined to buy Woodend Farm which had been put up for sale by trustees after the death of Ninian Douglas. Selby could only advise his Lordship to let him have it since he was a very excellent tenant and could farm it along with the Mill cheaper than any other person. Knowing that the children 'had been poorly left', Selby suggested an allowance of £20 a year be paid during the lease if the trustees would give it up. He was very much afraid that the children would make bad tenants.[22]

The rental statement for the Minto estate at Lammas, 1 August 1833, showed a total of nearly £3,000 which included some £1,478 of arrears and illustrated the changing pattern of tenancies due to deaths and retirements.[23] Individual tenants and the names of their properties were as follows:

| Tenant | Property | Rent to nearest £ |
| --- | --- | --- |
| James Brodie | Deanfoot | £444 |
| Andrew Hall | Hassendeanbank | £177 |
| Thomas Usher | Newlands | £35 |
| Widow Turnbull | Town Head | £96 |
| Borthwick Riddell | Dryden | £85 |
| George Thomson | Rapelaw | £347 |
| Thomas Halden | Standhill | £90 |
| John Brockie | Mounthooly | £563 |
| Heirs of Ninian Douglas | Woodend | £102 |
| John Hope | New Mill | £93 |
| Robert Leydon | Roundhaugh | £67 |
| John Tennant | Easter Essinside | £164 |
| Walter Tod | Langhope | £100 |
| Hugh Goodfellow | Headshaw | £160 |
| Thomas Scott | Halewood | £90 |
| Thomas Scott | Muirfield | £37 |
| William Reid | Kaims | £210 |
| Archibald Henderson | Lanton Hall | £55 |
| Alexander Robertson | Temple Croft | £8 |
| Feu duty on | Kirklands | £4 |

What his Lordship thought of the estate's finances at this time is not known but Selby had clearly done a lot of good work and had every hope that the bulk of the arrears would eventually be paid. In the following spring, the factor, instead of transferring income to his Lordship's bank account, explained that he had opened a deposit account in his own name and paid sufficient cash to enable him to pay accounts that were due, including stipends, the Land Tax and Assessed Taxes. He also had to report some unexpected news for the British envoy in Berlin. He suspected that the roof of Minto House required urgent renewal. The ceilings of all the upper rooms were constantly being drenched with water, and the kitchen roof was 'all but rotten'. He recommended the appointment of a properly qualified person to inspect and report, and had more confidence in Messrs Smith of Darnick than any of the inspectors Mr Playfair had so far employed at Minto. The 'insufficiency of the manse' was also becoming more apparent every day and part of the dining room ceiling had already tumbled down; Selby asked whether Lord Minto wished to have the ceiling re-plastered at his own expense.[24]

Just how widely it was known that Lord Minto had agreed to Robert Selby's son Ephraim, then in his early thirties, succeeding him as factor or exactly when it took effect, can only be surmised. It seems to have been by mutual agreement with age playing a part. At this time many of Robert Selby's letters were being written by Ephraim and only being signed by his father. His only request to his employer was that he would value his intervention to prevent him losing the factorship of the Ednam estate which Lord Minto had allowed him when the Earl of Dudley originally purchased it.[25] So far as Ephraim was concerned, he began his apprenticeship by carrying out several valuations, including one for another

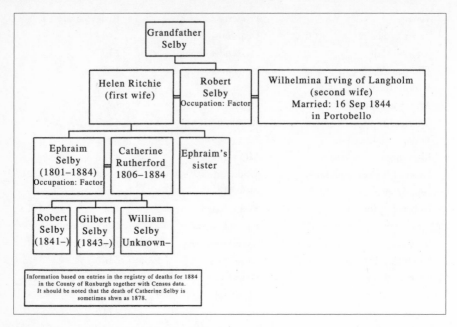

Family tree of Ephraim Selby's grandfather.

Roxburghshire estate and there was soon evidence of the younger man's demeanour and careful approach in dealing with estate matters. However, by July 1835, Ephraim Selby was telling Lord Minto that the person most likely to 'get the management of Ednam [was] a tenant of Sir John Pringle's and one of Lord John Scott's committee'. Tory electoral magnanimity was at work and Ephraim could only say that his father had had 'much trouble with that estate' and conclude that the appointment of a new factor was outside both Lord Minto and his father's hands.

On the face of things Robert Selby's long service had been marred by few errors of judgement, but in June 1834 Ephraim had written a lengthy and deeply heartfelt letter to Captain George, his employer's brother, revealing a different side of his father's behaviour. What he had managed to keep separate from his business affairs for a long time was the suffering which the Selby family had endured from his father's persistent bullying and harassment. Ephraim's letter told him about his father's treatment 'of every one of us' and how he had resolved to put up with it in order to be near his mother and in the hope that his father's conduct might become 'more prudent'. This had not occurred and he could no longer 'see his mother [Helen] used in a cruel manner'. On one occasion, Ephraim had gone into a room when his father was in a rage and using abusive language and, on another, his mother had come into his room in tears having just been begging a 'small pittance' to enable her to live alone. Ephraim had nevertheless no wish to see his father punished in any way; he had been too long 'a zealous servant' for that, and he assumed he would retire as soon as he found a habitable new house.[26]

As matters turned out, it seems that Robert Selby soon withdrew from the scene, leaving his son to grow into his full responsibilities at Minto. On the other hand, old

Selby was not a man to be held down for long, and in September 1844 the Rev John Clark conducted a marriage ceremony at Portobello for one Robert Selby of Samiston and Mina Irving, the eldest daughter of the late William Irving of Langholm in Dumfriesshire.[27] His first wife, Helen, had died in Aberdeen on 21 January that year.

Catherine Rutherford had kept a close eye on events at Minto after leaving Lady Minto's service and going to live with her mother at Lanton in 1834. During the autumn of that year it was fairly evident that one of her closest informants had been Ephraim Selby, she having visited him occasionally at the farm. Her mother seems to have kept well, with only her grandfather's health giving serious concern. Writing to Lady Minto from Teviot Bridge four years later, where she was staying temporarily, Catherine listed those in the Elliot family she longed to see, including Charlie, who was at Minto for a short visit. As usual she was full of sentiment, blaming a 'spell' that prevented her making contact with the family, and mentioning names in a manner which Lady Minto must have found irritating. The governess was very glad, for her ex-mistress's sake, that Lady Adam, the countess's sister, was with her, and anticipated that the marriage of Lady Mary, the Elliot's eldest daughter, had 'every prospect of happiness'. She had heard that all the ladies looked beautiful, and that Charlotte and 'Baby' (Harriet) had grown very much recently. Then, as if in desperation, Catherine expressed the hope that the children would come to visit her if her own stay at Minto could not be arranged. At least, she said, 'write to me'.[28]

When the children did come to see Catherine a month later, they found her suffering from a bad back which prevented her from paying them a reciprocal visit. She wanted to be well again before the winter set in. In a second letter to Lady Minto, her loneliness and feelings of homesickness for the place of her birth became more apparent. She gave the impression of being a sad and rather lost individual, somewhat morbid and unduly self-conscious, exaggerating her fears. She insisted that the countess could have no idea how cold the house was in cold weather. She had tried splashing cold water every morning on her back, and she was about to use hot water before going to bed. In terms more appropriate for those wealthy enough to afford them, she told Lady Minto, 'I ought to go somewhere and take warm baths but, meanwhile, I shall try all I can at home first for I know the back must not be trifled with.' She had begun to think her back would never be strong again.

Catherine was especially vexed to hear that some of the children fancied she did not care for them as she used to. She pleaded that Lady Minto would never suspect her of not caring for her or the children; her heart was 'as warm' to her as ever. She admitted to being 'low-spirited' and asked that the children be allowed to ride down now and then to see her despite the typhus fever that had broken out in Hawick. She also asked for access to the library as she could not get books of any kind at Teviot Bridge and reading prevented her from thinking of herself.[29]

Exactly how or when Catherine and Ephraim came to marry is not known but the wedding probably took place sometime in 1840. She was about thirty-four years old and he some five years older. Both had been unhappy and it was a most appropriate remedy for each of them. The census for 1841 shows that the household at Cleughead in the parish of Minto was made up of eight people. In addition to Catherine and Ephraim and their first child, Robert, who was then six months old, there was Helen Selby, Ephraim's mother, then seventy-five years old and Catherine's mother Alice Rutherford, along with her twenty-five-year-old brother Gilbert, home from the Navy. There were also two servants.

The couple lived at Cleughead for more than twenty years, during which time Lady Minto was to die in 1853, and her husband in 1859. The latter's death accounted for a visit to Minto in September by 'Doddy' or George Francis Stewart, the Mintos' lawyer son, on behalf of his brother William, now the third Earl, and who was busy in London. Having stayed at Abergeldie Castle by Ballater, the Highland retreat of Sir Thomas Myddleton Biddulph (an equerry to the Queen) for a few days' fishing, he went on to Minto House to establish why there had been some inaccuracies in the accounts. Had he known what a commotion his arrival would make, he said 'I should certainly have had the few things I wanted sent after me instead of going to pick them up'. Apparently the caretaker of the house had given everything over to Ephraim and Catherine with whom all the keys were deposited, and the consternation of the household was great when an unexpected guest appeared, George's letter having gone astray. Selby and he were quite satisfied with the state in which they found the house and all in it. George thought it would be good idea to appoint a new housekeeper in order to start things afresh, and he hoped that both William and Nina, his wife, would be there when she was installed.[30]

In 1861, their household comprised Catherine and Ephraim, together with their sons Robert, described by the census that year as a farmer with 434 acres, and Gilbert, then eighteen years old. Their servants included a kitchen maid, housemaid and groom. Early that year, however, George Elliot had news that his brother William had decided on a successor to Ephraim. It was a case of the new earl shaking off more of his father's old regime. Writing from London, George's only doubt about the new man was that his experience had been limited to the management of a home farm and woods. From what his brother had told him he seemed to George rather a rough diamond, and 'he would not be above what was required of him'.[31]

It was now the family's ex-governess, as William would have best remembered Catherine, who picked up her pen. Addressing a long letter on 10 April 1861 to the fourth Earl, she insisted that her sole wish in writing was to beg him to tell her how her husband had offended him. She was certain that Ephraim 'was above doing anything he knew to be wrong and would willingly suffer loss himself than have his Lordship lose 'a farthing by him'. Catherine thought it 'cruel and unkind' that her husband, then sixty years old, should be treated so badly after his long service and 'his real love for you all'. What seems to have happened was that when his Lordship decided to dispense with his factor he also promised the family the house at Hassendean for his retirement. Unfortunately, building work to prepare it for their habitation had fallen behind and William, who had said he would give the couple twelve months' notice, and when they left his service they would have 'a comfortable house' ready for them to go into, seems to have let them down. It did not help that Catherine discovered how one or two of Tod & Romanes' clerks who had been in the neighbourhood had besmirched Ephraim's character by 'letting it be known what had been going on in their office', insinuating that there were other reasons for his retirement.[32]

Catherine went on to demonstrate something of her own legal mind and the persuasive diplomacy she could bring to bear. Admitting that the couple had been given twelve months' 'warning to leave' she reminded Lord Minto that the work on their new home had not been done 'owing to the workpeople at Hassendean Bank not being able to be spared from the harvest'; furthermore, 'you, my Lord',[1] she wrote, 'consented that it should be put off'. Catherine argued that it was unreasonably hard to be forced to move from Minto into a house which was not even ready for their furniture to be put into it. She had 'enquired in every direction' about a house in which they could stay temporarily but 'there was not one to be had'. She begged Lord Minto to let them remain until the house at Hassendean Bank was 'fit to put our things into'. Although 'truly grateful' for his 'handsome yearly allowance', Catherine had become convinced that there was some mystery in his Lordship's change of feeling and behaviour towards them and that 'some evil-speakers had given a wrong motive to something Selby had done'.[33]

Lord Minto replied to Catherine's *cri de coeur* on the same night that he received it. He was 'sensible' of the pain she was feeling about quitting Minto but then rather strangely, and in a manner which must have puzzled Catherine, went on to bemoan the lack of charity Catherine had expressed in her letter. Although glad to do what he could to arrange for their remaining at Cleughead until November, he feared he 'would not be doing any good' if he discussed with her 'the unfortunate events' which had led to the disagreement between Ephraim and himself. There had been nothing 'resembling an agreement or lease, or even an authenticated memorandum'. The transaction, whatever it was, had been 'peculiar in more ways than one' and very perplexing to him. Solicitor George had apparently advised him 'not to volunteer any further explanation'.[34] Fortunately, there was news from 31 Dover Street some week or so later, that Lord Minto had completed all the necessary arrangements for Catherine to remain in occupation of the house at Cleughead until November as she had requested.[35]

Twelve months later, Ephraim, Catherine and their two boys were settled at Hassendean Bank but relations with the third Earl and Mr Mitchell, who had become Selby's replacement as factor, continued to be strained. In April 1862, after there had been a clash between Ephraim's son and the factor, Catherine wrote to his Lordship apologising for the actions to which objection had been taken and reminding him that Robert, their son, had been the 'most truthful of men' despite the 'disagreeable taunting' to which he had been exposed.[36] By July, Catherine's contact with Lord Minto had been reduced to a simple request that he might allow her to tell the factor when it would be convenient 'for the painters to come and paint the woodwork of [their] house'. Dr Aitkin, the minister, had told Catherine that Lady Minto was in Brighton. She wished them both 'all the happiness in the world'.[37]

Ephraim Selby died in March 1884 aged eighty-three. Catherine followed in October the same year. As will have been evident, the life of a factor or land agent was neither easy nor one without its hazards. Finding, evicting and dealing generally with tenants, establishing and recommending rent levels and co-ordinating home repair and maintenance, were all important aspects of a factor's work, especially where an employer lived elsewhere for long stretches at a time and he was unable to attend personally to such details. Arranging for the care of animals, the harvesting of agricultural products, and the sale or removal of timber, gravel and minerals, called for a wide knowledge. Quite apart from dealing with tax matters requiring the closest scrutiny, he had to depend on the trustworthiness of numerous contractors, many of whom during Victoria's reign were neither licensed nor always professional in their behaviour. The particular headache of controlling costs and maintaining a steady cash flow, seen in the case of both Selbys, was critical to the survival of the Minto estate – a battle which was to be lost in the twentieth century.

Ephraim and Catherine lived in a class-bound society and their relationship would have been marked by their different backgrounds. He was a man of his time who may never have been outside Scotland, whereas Catherine had been brought up at Minto and her subsequent travels with the family had greatly broadened her mind. She had seen the social and educational grooming of the Elliot girls at first hand, their learning of French and German, sewing and embroidery, along with music and dance. She grew into something of a campaigner, somebody who in later years might have become a socialist or member of the Fabian Society, but she never lost her intense sentimentality which, like others of her generation, could ignore extreme squalor and hardship, even opium wars for the sake of the country. Her factor husband probably welcomed the way she showed herself incapable of being the stereotypical fragile woman, and stood up to all who threatened to run roughshod over her egalitarian or moral views.

The hierarchy of those who served the family inside the house and outside on the estate was distinct. Whether they were companions, housekeepers, maids, butlers, footmen, grooms, lawyers, Presbyterian ministers, skilled tradesmen or factors, all were servants, each with a place clearly prescribed. Even an ex-employee had a place in this society, something that Catherine took a long time to appreciate. She had been valued as an employee for five years but it took many more years for her to realise that an ex-employee carried no status.

# 8
# FANNY MARRIES LORD JOHN RUSSELL
# (1840-1847)

During the summer of 1840, Fanny Elliot was beginning to see more of Lord John Russell, not just at 'rather solemn dinner parties' or when he called on Lord Minto in London, and occasionally at Minto. She knew the middle-aged politician well enough to feel a good deal of sympathy for him on the death of his wife Adelaide in 1838. A dozen or so years before, she had married Thomas Lister, second Baron Ribblesdale, and they had had a son (Thomas) and three daughters (Adelaide, Isabel and Elizabeth). After Lister's death, Lady Ribblesdale married Lord John Russell, and spent three and a half happy years with him until sadly she died having given birth to their second daughter, Victoria, sister to two-year-old Georgiana.

At this time, the Elliot family was dividing its time between work at the Admiralty and Putney House. Lord John, who had become known as 'Finality Jack' when he was at the Home Office after refusing to consider more electoral reform, refused to contemplate legislation against the Chartist leaders In May 1839, the senior civil servant at the Home Office wrote how 'Lord John in his quiet way, without parade, but with a steady decided hand, and a most undisturbed temper' had avoided a major crisis.[1] Becoming Secretary of State for War and the Colonies later that year, he spoke frequently in the Commons until the summer recess on such diverse subjects as Municipal Corporations in Ireland, Turkish affairs, sugar duties, the Canadian Clergy Bill and the transportation of convicts.

In June, Fanny wrote in her diary that Lord John and Harriet Lister, the sister of Lord John's first wife, came 'to spend the afternoon and dine' at Putney House, together with 'all the little Listers'. All was very merry and Lord John 'played with us and the children at trap-ball'. The next time she met him had been at the Admiralty, where, according to Agatha Russell, he spent until bedtime talking to Palmerston about war with France, something about which Fanny hoped her father had told 'the truth as to its improbability'. Dining at Lord Russell's house at 30 Wilton Crescent the following evening, she found herself sitting next to the Bishop of Durham, Montague Villiers.

In September 1840, two years after his first wife's death, the leader of the Whigs, Lord John Russell, was to propose to Fanny Elliot. There had been two places to spare in the carriage from London when it left for Minto on 13 August and these were taken by Lord John and Tom, his stepson, the third Lord Ribblesdale. The party made excellent time, arriving on the second day, and from Hawick they had 'the most lovely moonlight, making the river silver and the fields like snow'. At the end of the month many eyes were turned on Lord John when he and the family went to church. He was especially amused at a remark by one old man who said he was 'a silly-looking man [meaning in Scottish that he was a 'delicate-looking' man] but he's smart too!'

With Lord John having to return to London during the first week of September, a decision about his proposal took on some urgency. As her diary for 30 August recorded, 'I lay awake, wondering, feeling sure, and doubting again.' They visited Melrose Abbey and Abbotsford on the last day of his stay but doubts and certainties oscillated in her mind. After dinner, Fanny wrote, 'Miss Lister asked me so many questions chiefly relating to marrying, that I began to believe such that Lord John's great kindness to us all, but especially to me, meant something more than I wished.' Lord John had left by the time her mother gave her the note which he had left, and Fanny immediately answered it. She had dreamed about him all night and wrote the following morning, 'begging him not to come back'. On 4 September Lord John wrote accepting that he had deceived himself, not from any fault of hers, but from a deep sense of unhappiness and a foolish notion that she might throw herself away on 'a person of broken spirits and worn out by time and trouble'. Fanny was to describe it as a 'very, very, sad note … so kind, but oh so kind'.[2]

In the new year, the family were back in London and there was a surprising number of visitors at the Admiralty, 'one very alarming, no less than Lord John – and I saw him', wrote Fanny in her diary. During the second week of March, Fanny wrote at length to her sister Lady Mary in Italy, explaining how she had not been able to put her thoughts into words for a long time. She admitted how grateful she was that her parents had left her free to sort matters out for herself. Meanwhile, the young Miss Adelaide Lister, who 'positively worshipped' Lord John, and who wanted the match, was begging Fanny to see him and allow herself to know him better. Fanny could only say that if they were together at a dinner she hoped not to sit next to him. Then, after a dinner at Lady Holland's when he 'was all the evening by me' Fanny felt she '*must* speak' and realised how wrong it was becoming to let matters go on as they were. She was convinced that Lord John would only blame himself if she said it must stop and reproached herself bitterly for her hardness. She clearly wondered whether her refusal of him at Minto House had been a rash decision.[3] Fortunately for Fanny, Lord John 'had a long conversation with Mama', who 'liked him better' when he called at the Admiralty the following day. Lady Minto went on to tell her eldest daughter how sensibly Fanny had spoken to her about her feelings and 'if he had been a younger man she would have decided a long time ago'.[4]

In Parliament, where Lord Russell had first held the portfolio of Home Secretary until 1835, becoming thereafter Secretary of State for War and the Colonies, he was endeavouring to move the political agenda away from Irish issues, bringing in a fixed duty on corn and his speech about sugar at the beginning of May was described by Greville as 'an extraordinarily good one'. The Chancellor of the Exchequer had proposed to lower the duty on imported sugar. Lord Sydenham, the governor-in-chief of British North America, spoke of it 'with feelings of admiration and pleasure'. In the absence of orators among the Free Traders, Sydenham said, Russell had hammered away at the facts and figures, elevating the subject and exciting 'the feelings of the people'. However, before details could be announced, Peel defeated the government and at the beginning of June won a motion of no confidence by one vote. Lord Melbourne dissolved Parliament ahead of a general election.

Four days after the Prime Minister had woken Lord John with the sad words 'beaten by one', Fanny and he were engaged. Lord John visited the Admiralty in the morning from his home in Wilton Crescent.⁵ After he proposed, she was left in 'a strange dream all that day' and no sooner had he left than Lady Minto comforted and congratulated her, followed by Lord Minto and her brothers and sisters. She never saw William 'so overcome'. On 10 June, her husband-to-be presented her with an emerald ring after which all his children, except for Victoria, joined the Elliot children for tea. Writing to Lady Mary, the countess had to admit that Fanny's 'happy face' told of her pride about the position she had put herself in, and 'how it delights her to think of the son-in-law she has given to your father'. She reminded Lady Mary how an ordinary person would not have suited her while it was evident how fully Lord John appreciated 'the singular beauty of her character'.⁶

26 June was nomination day for the general election in the City of London, where Lord John had been invited to stand as one of its four members. Lady Minto, who attended, said 'he looked calm amid the uproar' but, despite a show of hands 'greatly in his favour' and being returned, he came fourth when the result was announced at the end of the month. Meanwhile, Fanny was approved of by the Holland House set, Lady Holland describing her as 'good tempered and sensible', and telling Lord John that the knowledge she had of his admirable bride made her feel confident that all her wishes would be realised – 'God bless you both'. The family then left London for Minto, leaving Lord John to follow.⁷

When Lord John arrived in Roxburghshire for the wedding he had earlier requested should be 'the quieter the better', he found all the children in awe of him except for fifteen-year-old Gilbert. Writing to Lady Mary, Fanny said they were 'much too respectful to Lord John, not to me, for they take their revenge on me, and I am unsparingly laughed at'. The couple spent much of the day before the event out of doors; as Fanny wrote, 'He and I sat in the Moss House. Never saw the glen more beautiful; the birch glittering in the sun and waving its feathery boughs; the burn murmuring more gently than usual; the wood pigeons answering one another from tree to tree.'⁸

The wedding finally took place in the drawing room of Minto House on Tuesday 20 July 1841. It was a small gathering, solemnised by the Rev Gilbert Elliot on whom Catherine Rutherford had called at Barming in 1832. Absent were Lady Ribblesdale's six children with whom the couple started their married life. They appear to have been staying in Ramsgate, Kent, at the time. Later that day, the couple set off for Bowhill House near Selkirk which had been lent to them by the Duke of Buccleuch for their honeymoon. It was, Fanny said, 'a most charming house' where the surrounding walks were beautiful and nothing was wanting 'but a little fine weather'. She hardly knew how to begin her journal again having written the last page as Fanny Elliot, only to become Fanny Russell. Her mother was also delighted and content, writing in a 'Border Ballad' of her own how Lord Russell had proved not to be 'the robber that cam' o'er the border to steal bonny Fanny away'.⁹ The couple came back to Minto for a brief stay after a grand reception at Selkirk where her husband was given the freedom of the burgh.

Back in London by the second week of August, and beginning to make her own home at Wilton Crescent, Fanny had to get used to being called 'Mama' by Georgiana (known as Georgy) and Victoria. She was also much relieved when Lord John mentioned their mother. She felt a weight had been lifted from her and 'the greatest bar to perfect confidence' between them had been removed.[10] On the evening of 28 August Lord John dined at Lansdowne House, at what was the cabinet's last dinner together, since by the 30th of the month Peel and the Tories were in power. Fanny was overcome for a moment to see a letter from the Queen to her husband, regretting the loss of 'a faithful adviser'. It was already a very different life, one to which she adjusted fairly quickly but not one that she was ever fully to enjoy.

Peel's administration proved to be forceful given the eighty or so majority the Tories held and, in addition to his revival of income tax and a thorough revision of the tariff, the new Foreign Secretary, Lord Aberdeen, showed skill in bringing about a new *entente cordiale* with France, much to the annoyance of Palmerston. In October, Lord John was to hear from Lord Minto's erstwhile mentor that what he had been saying about O'Connell in Ireland had his support. Lord John had no intention of giving in to the nationalist leader and Palmerston wanted to preserve in opposition nearly the same relations he had when in office. It was now a period of relative inactivity in Lord John's political life, a fact demonstrated by a letter he wrote to Lady Holland in which he said:

> I have been reading several of Mr Fox's great speeches lately. They are beyond compari-
> son the best ever spoken in Parliament but I am almost as much struck by his want of
> prudence in conducting opposition as by his genius and eloquence. Pitt's are astonish-
> ingly meagre and commonplace; but he speaks some practical sense, which in this country
> goes a long way.[11]

In September, and as a break from the formality of Woburn, the Russells went down to Endsleigh, a cottage orné and estate near Tavistock in Devon, designed by Humphrey Repton and built in 1811 for the sixth Duke of Bedford, where he shot pheasant and the duchess fished. The duke had placed the property at Lord John's disposal and both of them were to retain happy memories of it. Lord John was able to begin editing the fourth Duke's correspondence while Fanny spoke of a 'long delightful shooting walk' with her husband despite 'the horror that I and all women must have of it'. More poetically, she described the 'snow-white mist over all except the garden below my eyes'. In November they went together to the school at Milton Abbot, where his Lordship gave the prizes and made a speech in praise of the masters and boys which made her far more nervous than when she heard him in Parliament. Writing to Lady Minto, Lord John described their visit to Endsleigh as 'the most fortunate thing for us all', a means of 'fitting and cementing' Fanny and his earlier family together.

Fanny's husband was not the only one adjusting to the absence of formal employment. Her father and the family had vacated the Admiralty in the autumn of 1841 just before the arrival of Lord Minto's successor, Thomas Haddington, ninth Earl of Haddington, after he had declined Peel's offer of the governor-generalship of India. Having established himself temporarily 'almost next door' to the Russells, in accommodation at 48 Eaton Square, where Fanny seemed to 'govern her establishment very handily', Lord Minto probably went to the beginning of the Corn Law debate in mid-February 1842. Lord John spoke unsuccessfully on his amendment against 'the absurdity of any corn laws to make [the country] independent of foreign countries'.[12] In March, Lord Russell admitted that he felt opposition to Peel's 'miserable' Corn Bill was the best course open but had he been in the House of Lords he would have been disposed 'to vote for the second reading as any bill of the kind must come from the House of Commons, and the present bill makes some little improvement on the existing system, leaving the trade, however, still a gambling trade'. Out of office, he conceded that had they proposed their own scheme of reform in the Commons: 'we should all have been fighting one another'.[13] It seems that Lord John expected the Tories to disintegrate and, writing to Lady Holland, he told her so.

Being less beholden to the political world, at least temporarily, and now resident at 37 Chesham Place which had been built for him, Lord John would have been delighted to hear from Lady Minto in March that year. She was looking forward to seeing her Fanny again, telling her son-in-law that he had 'not lived with her five and twenty years, and therefore memory has no place in your affection for her ... but you can well comprehend the extent of my pleasure in reading her letters which breathe happiness in every line'. Her mother's only fear was that her cares and occupations would weigh at times too heavily upon her.[14] Just before the countess's letter, Lord Minto had himself written to their eldest daughter in Italy explaining that living almost next door to the Russells had its advantages, but not knowing how much Lady Mary knew about Lord John, he was at pains to tell her about there being 'a simplicity and gentleness and purity in his character which is quite delightful, and it chimes in very fortunately with Fanny's.[15]

The tenth day of December 1842 was marked by the birth of the Russells' firstborn son, John, afterwards Lord Amberley.[16] Fanny suffered several miscarriages and was often laid up for months at a time. Early February the following year there were signs of growing pressure on Fanny and writing to Lady Mary she spoke of being completely worn out in both mind and body 'at the end of a common day'. She said that only those who had become 'in one moment, mother of six children, wife of the Leader of the House of Commons [or more correctly Leader of the Whigs], and mistress of a house in London' could imagine her situation and she blamed 'hateful London' for much. She doubted her capacity for 'everything except making husband and children happy' but delighted in her father's reactions when 'darling baby' was brought in to be seen in his christening dress – a gift from Mama, who was in Roxburghshire. Anxious not to have exaggerated her fears, she wrote in July hoping to convince her mother that 'the seclusion of Belgravia, though great, is not like that of Kamchatka' – enclosing thirty names of friends she had met in one week.[17]

Parliament was prorogued at the end of August and the whole Russell family moved down to Endsleigh, where Lady Georgiana, the elder of Lord John's daughters by Lady Ribblesdale, soon fell ill with a grave fever. A weakened Fanny caught the infection, the family putting it down to the fact that 'she had been living up to the limit of her energies'. It was to be the last time they used Endsleigh.

Meanwhile, as summer drifted into autumn, there was news from Minto, where Harriet Gertrude, the youngest of the Elliot clan, resumed her journal. Acting rather like a social secretary, she was to tell the absorbing tale of a year in the life of a teenage young woman who was never well in body and who would die aged only twenty-eight years old. Lord Minto, together with her uncle John (John Edmund Elliot) and aunt Anna Maria, who had been widowed two years before, had been hunting on a very cold day at Bedrule.[18] At church that week Mr Aitkin preached, while Harriet and her older sister Charlotte (Bob'm) went down to Kirklands by Ancrum, the property Sir Walter Scott had suggested John Richardson should buy and where he spent the autumn months each year.[19] Harriet's diplomat brother, Henry, was expected from Russia soon and Fanny and Lord Russell were to stay until just before Christmas.[20]

Two days later Lord Minto went to Edinburgh to look for horses, with snow and ice everywhere. Dinner that evening was taken by an exceptionally small group, comprising Mama, Bob'm, Lizzy and Harriet, who was soon able to report that the Abercrombys, Ralph and her eldest sister, Mary, would be coming on to Minto after their stay at Colinton, the home of his parents. Ten days later Henry arrived 'looking well and very merry' and no sooner had he settled in than Lord John, Fanny and Johnny, their eleven-month-old son, were at the door. Henry and Uncle John 'beagled' on the first of November and 'good old fat Doddy', as Harriet described her brother George, came the next day. Two days later, the Abercrombys left after their short visit, intending to stay a week in London before going to Paris while Harriet's daily routine of a short walk or a drive with her mother continued. On 9 November, there was a shooting party made up of Henry, Doddy, Uncle John, Lord John Russell and Mr Congreve, a 'new county man', after which the day was finished off with Fanny and Lizzy playing duets. After Halloween, 'heaps of letters arrived from Gibby', who was with his regiment and William, having come up from London, soon joined the foxhunting party. Aunt Anna Maria left them for a short time and Captain George Augustus's wife, Hersey, and her baby arrived. The baby was 'a nice little thing' and Johnny had 'excellent fun with her'. At the beginning of December, Charles Bethune arrived, bringing with him poor Russell Eliott, the youngest son of Sir William Eliott of Stobs. It was the first time he had been at Minto since his wife's death in August that year.

Fanny and Lord John left Minto on 14 December soon after 8 a.m., together with Gee, Victoria and Johnny, en route for London via Althorp, the Spencer family seat in Northamptonshire, and Woburn. Harriet wrote in her journal the previous day that she did not know what they would do now that Johnny had 'grown so dear, and says so many words, we shall miss him sadly'. With fewer in the house, William, Henry and Lord Minto were able to go down to Lees for a few days to hunt with Lord Elcho (Francis Wemyss Charteris), MP and landowner, who had married Lady Ann Anson in August, and two days before Christmas Admiral George's sailor son George Augustus arrived. He was to stay in accommodation near the house on account of the size of the party. Aunt Anna Maria dined with the family but also went home at night. It had been a happy day, followed in the evening with songs and games, and the following day Lord and Lady Minto along with Lizzy and Bob'm went to Bowhill House at Selkirk for a couple of days. Harriet told of a 'very old merry party' being left behind comprising Helen, Jemima, Miss Lister, Maggy, William, Henry and Freddy (Admiral George's youngest son, who would have been seventeen years old) whom she liked very much. He had quite changed, she said, and 'was immensely improved, and talks very nicely and sensibly'.

The week after Christmas Harriet tells of the two eldest Elliot boys enjoying much hunting while sleeping at Linthill House, about five miles from Melrose and not far from Lilliesleaf, rather than returning to Minto. When she went down to Kirklands with Helen and Jemima on the morning of 27 December, in whose charge she seems to have been left, the house was 'left completely empty'. That afternoon, the three went for a walk to meet Mr Richardson and Lord Cockburn from Edinburgh, now and then driving in Harry's cart.[21] When the party sat down to dinner Harriet 'expected to be in a great fright' but she sat next to Sir William Scott, who 'talked enough'. Others present were his wife Lady Scott, Freddy, Mrs Wauchope and Hersey. A game of letters and anagrams followed, with Lord Cockburn being 'very amusing'.

With the return of the Mintos from Bowhill House, and Hogmany approaching, there were numerous comings and goings. Bob'm and Lizzy joined Henry, who had moved into Kirklands, and Russell Eliott and Charles Bethune arrived again – the latter being described as 'a very odd boy'. The ground was quite white on 31 December when a Sir John Hacket, a 'merry and pleasant' friend from Lees, joined the family hoping for some hunting. It was cold on the first day of 1844, and with Freddy moving back to the house, Henry and William promptly went back to Linthill House with Sir John Hacket only to find that the snow had unfortunately prevented their sport. Good news arrived the following day with a letter from Gilbert giving an account of an adventure that he, Major Beckwith and three other officers had had in Albania. With Augustus still at Minto, Harriet and the young danced in the evening and followed the exercise with 'a new kind of dumb crambo', the original being a game where players try to guess a word through mime.

Two weeks into January, William hurriedly set off for London leaving Harriet and the other young to draw the happy conclusion that 'he has settled it suddenly and we are terribly afraid Nina must be his greatest reason though he has never mentioned her'. He was to be married to Emma Hislop, always known as Nina.[22] On 21 January, a Sunday, the morning post brought two letters from London, one from William, the other from lawyer Doddy, saying that all was decided. William had proposed to Nina, though Lady Hislop would not call it 'fixed', and said much about it 'not taking place for a year or two'. In her quiet and usually shrewd manner, Harriet added that, 'in short, there is an immense quantity to be said for, and very little against, the marriage' and there was 'no fear of them not being happy together'.

At the end of the month Lord Minto went to London and Fanny's brother Henry heard from the embassy in St Petersburg that his attaché colleague there was not well and he might have to leave for Russia earlier than planned. At Minto, all the villagers were delighted with the news about William. A week or so later the family heard that Henry did not now have to return to his post early and that Willy (William Brownrigg Elliot), the second of Uncle John's four sons, had arrived in London from India and when he arrived at Minto 'he looked quite unchanged, not even blacker with the Indian sun'. On 12 February, there was a servant's dance at which a fiddler played, and with deep snow still on the ground the young continued to enjoy the sledge. Papa and William had been expected from London but they did not arrive for another six days and, even then, on foot from Denholm Bridge as they had been forced to send the carriage round due to a flood they could not ford.

The twenty-eighth day of March was Harriet's seventeenth birthday, and she enjoyed a walk with Bob'm. Two weeks later there was a major meet of the hunt at Hassendean and she sat in the carriage to watch, accompanied by Lady Minto and Bob'm, the rest of the family being among the 140 or so riders, not very many of whom wore red coats. It was an attractive sight and 'a lovely day for it'. Very soon afterwards the family was made aware that their sojourn in London for William and Nina's wedding was to be at 34 Chesham Place and on 22 April servants from Minto began to move south, followed a week later by Lady Minto, Henry, Lizzy and Bob'm. Lord Minto and Harriet had been left alone as he had a meeting that required his attendance at Jedburgh. It was May Day when the two set off for London via Darlington, Derby and York and three days later their arrival at 34 Chesham Place took Fanny, who was there fortuitously, Lizzy, Bob'm and Doddy by surprise.

Rented by the family for two months, the property turned out to be 'terribly small and uncomfortable' although it was conveniently close to Fanny and Lord John. Harriet took some time to adjust to London life but a series of visits to important buildings was soon in train. After seeing Lansdowne House and the National Gallery, Lizzy and Bob'm went to hear Lord John speak at Exeter Hall on the north side of the Strand, after which he came to dinner.[23] Walks in Kensington Gardens and along the Serpentine provided some compensation for the loss of Roxburghshire countryside. Preparations for the wedding occupied everyone; repeated visits to dressmakers' rooms, the trying on of frocks, the ordering and collection of presents, details of the church service, and writing invitations, all had to be fitted in. Lady Minto drove down to Whitchurch with William and the Hislops to look at the house where the couple were to spend their honeymoon.

Quite apart from dining at the Hislop's home in Wilton Crescent, Lord and Lady Minto with Lizzy and Bob'm went to a large party at Devonshire House, and on 12 May the earl and countess dined with the Palmerstons. With accommodation in short supply, William and Doddy took lodgings, the latter living in Jermyn Street. Returning from a visit to Fanny a few days before the wedding, Harriet found Ama, Caroline (Carry) and Agnes Boileau at Chesham Place,[24] and when William decided he wanted to buy a boat, he took Henry and Bob'm down to Windsor and Eton. Then, calling on Mrs Wauchope, Harriet obtained 'a kind promise of an opera box from her'. At the Russell home, on the evening before the wedding, where William was staying with Fanny, Harriet met up with Miss Lister and Mr Tufnell. He looked happy and felt that the time had 'really almost come'.

Nina and William were married on 20 May at St George's church, Hanover Square, on 20 May 1844, becoming known as Lord and Lady Melgund. It was an impressive affair with between thirty-five and forty sitting down at the breakfast. In the evening, there was a ball at the home of Madame de Salis attended by Lady Minto, Lizzy, Bob'm and Henry. Four days later Harriet spent a long time with Fanny at 30 Wilton Crescent, talking over the events of the wedding. On 25 May, Lady Minto, Lizzy, Bob'm, Henry and Doddy went to the opera, leaving Lord Minto and Harriet behind; whether they used the box promised by Mrs Wauchope, Harriet did not record. The following Sunday, after a 'great deal of beautiful singing' in St Paul's Cathedral, several of those who had been at the wedding visited the Elliot household at Chesham Place. The following day, Gina, Admiral

George's daughter, called with her baby on 27 May. She had married the eighth Lord Northesk the previous year.

On 19 June, Lady Minto and Harriet went to see Fanny and Johnny at the Russells, and later attended a breakfast at the London home of the Duchess of Bedford in Campden Hill, but the highlight of the month came ten days later when, having dined with her aunt Catherine, Harriet went to the opera for the first time. The party included Sir John Boileau, Ama and Carry but not Henry, whose last night it was and who had to leave for Copenhagen on his way back to St Petersburg. The principal singer in a production of Donizetti's tragedy, *Lucia di Lammermoor*, was the Italian coloratura soprano Fanny Tacchinardi-Persiani, whose voice was 'pretty but not to be compared with that of Guilia Grisi. The Italian tenor, Napoleone Moriani, was 'delightful' but very different from Luciano Fornasari, the bass whom Charles Dickens was to hear in December that year. Among the arias Harriet particularly liked was a comic one sung by Lahlache, a basso-buffo. She was also impressed by the four ballet dancers: Fanny Cerrito, the Frenchman Arthur Saint-Léon, Jules Perrot and Fanny Elssler, the Austrian ballerina. Harriet's only conclusion was to record in her journal how 'having once been there makes one only long the more to go again'.

After a month with the family, Fanny and the children, with the exception of Adelaide, left at the beginning of July for Unsted Wood, a property near Godalming which Lord John had rented. Two days later, a plan that had probably been hatched when the Boileau and Minto families met for William's marriage was revealed. Instead of spending another two weeks at Chesham Place and returning to Minto from there, it had been agreed that Harriet should stay with her aunt Catherine, Lord Minto's sister, and her husband Sir John Boileau for a fortnight and be picked up by the rest of the family on their way to Scotland. The Boileaus, who had four sons and five daughters, lived at Ketteringham Hall in Norfolk between Wymondham and Norwich.[25] Three years before, the family had moved into the impressive gothic property which had been built to Sir John's orders. He was a county magistrate and became high sheriff of Norfolk that year.

Having said goodbye to friends on 5 July, and finding herself unexpectedly sorry to be leaving London, Harriet regretted that she would not see the Melgunds, Fanny or Doddy 'for ages', but the next morning she set off for Norfolk directly after breakfast. She was to give the reader of her journal an especially good account of rail travel and a journey off the beaten track at this period. Generally speaking, rail travel was dependable, fast and cheap. Having joined up with Sir John she went through the 'miserable streets of Shoreditch' to where the railway began. The station was situated on a viaduct and was the new London terminus of the Eastern Counties Railway Company for the 51- mile journey to Colchester.[26] At Shoreditch, they met Gina and her baby, who were also going to Ketteringham; Lord Northesk was seeing them off safely.[27] She stayed in her own railway carriage, that of Harriet and Sir John being full but with 'no bad people, very quiet and not talkative'. Some trains had separate ladies' compartments but the pair would have travelled first class with reasonably comfortable seats and probably an interior aisle as well as doors leading out to the platform. It was usual for maids or servants to be accommodated in a second-class carriage elsewhere on the train. Third class might be an open goods wagon, even without seats, such that the Railway Regulation Act of that year was to require that third-class passengers be provided with seats and the running of at least one train a day with such accommodation. When the train eventually reached Colchester, Harriet caught sight of Gina and her baby 'getting their dinner' but she had to leave her as she was travelling in a separate carriage, a britzka.

Harriet described the country as 'prettier than it really was'. The fields had 'immense crops and the luxuriance of the foliage and leaves' was great. The hedges were beautiful and full of flowers, 'convolvuluses climbing all over them' and they travelled along many 'nice English-looking lanes' but, she wrote, it did not 'do to look far, for this all gets tiresome when there is no pretty country to look at beyond'. The village churches, farms and cottages 'with their whitewashed walls and thatched roofs' which she would have seen as she passed through Suffolk to Diss were 'pretty, old-fashioned buildings' but in Norfolk there was 'not much fine wood and a good deal of horrid pollards'.

She arrived at Ketteringham Hall in time for dinner, and well ahead of Gina. Her immediate reaction to the house was how rather pretty it was outside and the drawing room very comfortable. Sir John had lived at Tacolneston, a village five miles south of Wymondham in the mid-1830s, taking his title from the property in 1838 as first Baronet Boileau of Tacolneston Hall. Commenting on the journey in her journal, she concluded that Sir John had been 'rather less disagreeable as a travelling companion than as anything else'. He had long been known as a hot-tempered and paternalistic squire whom one historian of Ketteringham was to describe as a bull-headed character who might have stepped out of the pages of Trollope. Aunt Catherine and the children had arrived the day before and Harriet soon found that 'the quiet, along with the sweet smell and freshness of the country air' hardly allowed her to regret leaving a 'murky town'.

The next day, being a Sunday, the family went to the church, probably St Peter's on the estate, which was quite small and close to the house, and in the afternoon Gina, Ama and Harriet took a long walk. Two of the Boileau's boys spent the day with them, Eddy aged thirteen and Charlie four years younger, taking a walk with them in the park surrounding the house in the evening. Harriet thought both 'seemed nice but terribly afraid of Sir John who was very disagreeable in his manner to them'. The next day Harriet went to see the school which Ama Boileau looked after, where the children were 'disorderly and sang out of tune'. There followed a visit to some of the estate cottages, all of which were 'very tidy and clean, with bright beautiful gardens'. They returned to write and have lunch, and later the three met up with Lady Boileau, who was gardening in an old gravel pit which had been planted with shrubs and plants sloping down to what the family called a burn. In the evening, when Sir John was not well, and 'happily' Harriet saw little of him, Gina and Harriet tried playing and singing some duets with Ama.

Visits to a variety of buildings within a carriage ride followed. The spire and carvings in the cathedral at Norwich were admired along with the Bishop's Palace and garden, a 'rather nice old-fashioned place'. The streets in the town on the other hand were horridly narrow, badly paved and noisy so that two carriages could not pass. Drives to Hallan, an 'old place with a farmhouse' belonging to Sir John, and to Hethel Hall, ten miles south of Norwich, where Eddy and Charlie were described as being at school 'with the clergyman', were followed by a visit to Wymondham church, where they inspected the carved ceilings and tombs before going up to the organ loft and having the working of the organ explained to them.

News came from Lady Minto on 14 July explaining that she would not be coming to Ketteringham to pick her up her youngest daughter as Fanny had become unwell and she had to be with her at Unsted Wood. The change of plan meant that Uncle George would be responsible for taking Harriet from Ketteringham to London. That afternoon Harriet – now unsettled and 'anxious to be away' – and the others took a walk to look at the beginning of a railway line which was under construction at the back of Ketteringham village. Harriet thought it would do less harm there 'than in most places in the country'.

Five days later and after a 40-mile drive to the 'railroad', and an hour's journey by train to a terminus she did not know, Harriet and her uncle had 'a long drive through the city' which she rather liked. Once at Chesham Place Harriet found herself deserted. Lord Minto, who was dining out, had taken Lizzy and Bob'm to a ball, Addy was out of town and her mother was with Fanny. She did, however, have the company of Doddy, who told her that the family would be leaving 34 Chesham Place in three or four days as the lease had to be surrendered. The next morning Harriet and Bob'm called on Lady Hislop, brother William's mother-in-law, and later met Uncle George's son Freddy, who was going to Italy with his father. Having dined, Lord Minto, Bob'm, and Harriet took a train of the London & South Western Railway from the terminus and locomotive works at Nine Elms to Woking. From there the drive to Unsted Wood took an hour. The house stood on a hill with a lawn and trees and shrubbery stretching down in front. She was glad to see her mother and surprised how dreadfully ill her sister had been, much worse than she 'ever fancied' and so weak that when Lizzy went in to see her 'she hardly heard her voice and cannot expect to be recovered for many months'.

Harriet attended church at Godalming on 21 July along with Addy and Lizzy on what was a baking hot day but the next day, Lord John, Lord Minto and Lizzy went back to town having settled that Harriet would start for Minto in six or seven days. Lady Minto and Lizzy would follow when Fanny was well enough to be left. With the temperature in the seventies, Addy and Harriet explored the possibility of having a bath, going down to the farm, where they found a bath of 'a good size' in a large barn with a boarded floor round about it so that they could run in and out as they pleased. The water was like ice, too cold for them to stay in longer than a plunge or two at a time.

There was news that Henry had arrived safely at St Petersburg after a passage of eight days and Harriet managed to take another bath while Fanny was being wheeled about the house into whichever rooms were the coolest. Towards the end of the week the invalid was able to go out in the pony carriage and Lord Minto came for two nights 'looking better' but plainly 'having had enough of London'. But the weekend came and went with continued uncertainty about Harriet's journey to Minto. There was also a visit from Tommy, the young third Baron Ribblesdale, 'such a nice merry boy', who came by coach from Eton and was met by Lord Minto. On the last day of July, Lord John went back to town for a few days, taking Bob'm with him so that she could go to a concert and ball at Apsley House.

On 1 August, Harriet's last day at Unsted Wood, she described a conversation between Fanny and Lady Minto which she hoped would 'do real good' in the future.

Her married sister admitted that she felt the burden of so many children was 'more than her health can bear'. As the result, the countess wrote to Lord John in strong terms about the need for a separate establishment for the Listers, maintaining that 'something must be settled'. Throughout Fanny's illness Russell's conduct had been 'more than odd'. He had treated Lady Minto like 'a slave' and was 'quite unfit to take charge of Fanny'. Harriet wrote that he meant well but he acted 'without sense or consideration of other people'.

Without the lease of 34 Gresham Place, accommodation for the family during Fanny's illness was becoming tighter. Lady Minto and Harriet drove to Lady Hislop's house at 36 Wilton Crescent on 20 July where she kindly agreed the family could be crammed in temporarily. With plans for another establishment 'talked of but none settled', after an early dinner Lord and Lady Minto set off with Bob'm and Lizzy back to Unsted Wood, where Lady Minto and Bob'm were to stay until they left it for good. The next day, and with no one to walk with, Harriet went to church in the morning and greeted her father and Lizzy when they came back to Wilton Crescent from Unsted bringing an excellent report on Fanny, who had walked a little.

On 5 August, Lord Minto spoke in the House during an amendment debate on the Railways Bill, and 'the state of the Navy'. Harriet feared that a war with France was 'not unlikely'. Two days later, Lord Minto, Lizzy, Harriet and a servant set out for Derby leaving Lady Minto and Bob'm to follow them in a week's time. The train arrived at eleven in the evening and the party transferred to a 'good inn by the station'. Next day, they discovered that the railroad was open all the way to Newcastle 'but very badly managed from Darlington, with constant delays'. They found the inn they wanted full and had to be content with 'a very bad one'. Despite a delay about horses the party set off early, going over Whitelee moor, where they 'walked and polka-ed' into Scotland. They were at the Cheviots and Carter Bar, and 'fairly over the top' before the carriages caught up with them. The drive down the River Rule struck them as 'far more beautiful than ever; the whole place and rocks looked so well'. As usual a brace broke at the bottom of Lodge Hill and they walked up. Harriet described the pleasure of being home as so very great that she could not understand 'ever wishing to leaving it'.

In February 1845 Fanny and her husband were together in London but as soon as Parliament rose they decided to go to Minto, but when Fanny's health again deteriorated they were forced to move into Edinburgh, where access to medical advice was better. It was while there that Lord John – without consulting other Whig leaders and the party, except his father-in-law and Andrew Rutherfurd, who had been Solicitor-General for Scotland – wrote a letter announcing his conversion to complete free trade. In the Commons in June that year he had challenged ministers to deny that 'the present Corn Law is intended to, and does in the opinion of political economists, add to the rent of the landlords'.[28] He now urged his constituents in London 'to unite to put an end to a system which has proved to be the blight of commerce, the bane of agriculture, the source of bitter divisions among classes, the cause of penury, fever, mortality, and crime among the people'.[29]

Hardly had Lord John returned to Edinburgh from London, where he had been required to attend Lady Holland's funeral, than an alarmed and embarrassed Peel was calling a cabinet meeting to consider the repeal of the Corn Laws. He faced the strong dissent of several ministers including Lord Stanley, Secretary for War, and having failed to carry his cabinet he resigned on 6 December.

Two days later there had been 'utter consternation' in Edinburgh. As Lord John wrote in his journal, when he was 'sitting in the evening with my family at Douglas's Hotel, a waiter informed me that a person wished to speak to me who had come a long distance. I declined to see him and desired he would write. Upon which the waiter brought me a letter with G. E. Anson on the outside, enclosing one from the Queen, in which Her Majesty desired that I should attend her at Osborne House on the Isle of Wight, upon affairs of great public importance'. The following day, Lord John set off at ten in the morning after seeing Dr Simpson. He went in a carriage and four post-horses to Newcastle, which he reached at half past eleven at night. On Wednesday 10 December, he 'went by express train to London where I arrived before nine o'clock. I wrote a letter to Sir James Graham asking him the best passage to Osborne House, and also proposing to see him on my return. He replied, expressing his readiness to see me on my return, and giving me the information I required.' The final leg of Russell's journey was completed on 11 December when he went by an early train to Southampton and, after waiting there an hour, went by the ordinary steamer to Cowes. He reached Osborne House before four o'clock and soon afterwards, and in the presence of Prince Albert, had an audience with the Queen. She said at once, 'I suppose you know why I have sent for you; it is to form a government,' to which he replied that he had gathered from the newspapers that Sir Robert Peel had resigned but that Her Majesty must remember that he was the leader only of a minority and thus not in a condition to form a ministry. Whereupon the Queen put a letter she had received from Sir Robert Peel into his hand and asked him to read it.

The letter stated that on 1 November Peel had proposed to his colleagues a plan for the immediate suspension of the Corn Law duties, either by Order in Council, or by Act of Parliament; in either case Parliament was to be immediately summoned. There was also a plan to gradually diminish duties on corn with a view to their total repeal 'in the spirit of caution and forbearance', accompanied by measures for the diminution of burdens on hand. Lord John then explained that although 'the difficulties were certainly diminished by this communication' he could not at present accept the commission to form a government and asked if Her Majesty would permit him to consult such of his friends as were within reach, and for that purpose he would set off for London early the next morning. The Queen was graciously pleased to consent.

On Friday morning, 12 December, after staying the night at Osborne, Lord John recorded that

> while I was at breakfast Prince Albert came into the room. His chief topic was the importance of retaining the services of the Duke of Wellington to the Queen and Country as Commander-in-Chief. I entirely agreed with him and suggested that Her Majesty should write to the Duke of Wellington expressing her personal wish that he should remain Commander-in-Chief in case I should become Minister. This was done and the Queen afterwards informed the Duke that I had fully concurred in the wish expressed by Her Majesty.

He arrived back in town at two o'clock and Lords Lansdowne, Clarendon and Cottenham, the Lord Chancellor, and afterwards Thomas Macaulay, whom his nephew was to call 'a staunch and vehement Whig', joined him. They were of the opinion that he should ascertain more about the detail in Peel's plan, whereupon Lord John asked Sir James Graham, the Home Secretary, to come to him, which he did at half past five but could not inform Russell more particularly of Sir Robert's plan. On Saturday 13 December there was another meeting at which Francis Baring was present, and it was agreed that Lord John should draw up the heads or an outline of a plan to be put to Peel and communicated to Her Majesty.[30] By Tuesday 16 December, when Russell had spoken to Lord Grey and Edward Ellice, his brother-in-law, he and his advisors proceeded to discuss the Corn Law and agreed that a simple repeal of all duties was the best course. Peel was informed and asked whether he had any insuperable objection. On Wednesday, the Queen asked Lord John and Lord Lansdowne to come to dinner at Windsor, or after dinner if more convenient, whereupon the two men dined at Eden Lodge, the home of George Eden, Earl of Auckland and then went to Windsor Castle, where they attended the Queen and Prince Albert in the Queen's sitting room. Her Majesty showed Lord John the reply Peel had sent her in respect of his plan; both the Queen and the Prince 'were of the opinion that we might depend on [his] support'.

The next meeting was held on the following day at Lord Russell's home in Chesham Place, where to the list of those consulted earlier were added the names of Lord Monteagle, Lord Palmerston, Sir John Hobhouse, Mr Labouchere, Sir George Grey and the Duke of Bedford. After Sir Robert Peel's letter was read, all but five of the group agreed that it gave sufficient foundation upon which to form a ministry and thought 'it was their duty to do so'. On Friday 19 December, at half past eleven in the morning, Lord John saw Palmerston, who wished to make it clear that the only office in which he would be useful was the Foreign Office and if he came into the ministry he would take no other. Having reminded him of the impression he gave as being 'a warlike politician' and asking him whether there were any circumstances where he might accept the Colonial Office – to which he said no – Russell agreed to offer him the Foreign Office. This meeting had taken half an hour and there was a small gathering waiting to consider other business. Once over, Lord Grey was asked to speak to Lord John alone, who proposed that he might take the Colonial Office. Grey would not give a reply until he knew how the ministry was to be constituted but he hoped he would see Lord Palmerston at the Colonial Office and himself as a colleague. When he learned that Palmerston would be offered the Foreign Office, he was quite ready to be left out of any administration. Immediately, Russell called on Lord Auckland and, as his record shows, 'asked if they would go on in the House of Lords without Lord Grey. He said he thought not. I sent for Ellice or Ellice came to me [he could not remember which]. I desired him to go and speak to Grey, saying I would not go on without him. He came back and said Lord Grey would not change.'[31]

While Peel had been forced to abandon Corn Law repeal on 6 December due to the dissent of Lord Stanley and others, Lord John and the Whigs had to abandon their first attempt to form a government some two weeks later due to Grey's 'insuperable objections'.

Fanny's own account of the evening in Edinburgh when the affair started shows her concerned more by young Johnny's health and being forced to call for Dr Davidson (not Dr Simpson as Lord John recalled) than by the Queen's message requiring her husband's presence at Osborne House many hundreds of miles away in England. It was not until 13 December, when she acknowledged her husband's letters of 10 and 11 December, that she learned that he had spent the night at Newcastle and met John Bright, the anti-corn-law agitator 'at one of the stations' the following day. Having reached the Isle of Wight after what Fanny called 'his dreary and anxious journey', only to find that the Queen thought he might have completed the journey more quickly, he was invited to form a new ministry. The same day, Lord John asked Fanny rhetorically, 'can I do so wild a thing?', recognising that he had to consult his friends given his minority in Parliament. Her reply, written on 14 December, assured her husband that becoming Prime Minister was not a 'wild thing'. It was 'a great duty which you will nobly perform', one which she hoped 'no timid friend will dissuade you from'.[32]

The same day, Fanny had told her sister in Italy how convinced she was that Lord John should aim at being Prime Minister 'unless the difficulties are much greater than I have wisdom to see'. The prospect of witnessing Lord John repealing the Corn Laws and pacifying Ireland were political benefits which repaid much private regret. He had, however, left Edinburgh 'looking so miserable himself that she was longing to hear from somebody else how he looked now. It had been 'a thunderbolt' to them both. They were 'reading aloud about an hour before bedtime when the messenger was announced – and he brought the Queen's fatal letter'. He had not been able

> to conceal either from himself or me how entire the sacrifice must be of private hap-
> piness to public duty, of which this parting was the first sample; and he writes of the
> desolation of domestic prospects in so sad a way that I am obliged to write like a
> Spartan to him.[33]

There followed another week of dual indecision during which Macaulay described the scene to his sister. Lord John, he wrote,

> has not consented to form a ministry. He has only told the Queen that he would con-
> sult his friends and see what could be done. We are all most unwilling to take office,
> and so is he. I have never seen his natural audacity of spirit so much tempered by dis-
> cretion, and by a sense of responsibility, as on this occasion. The question of the Corn
> Laws throws all other questions into the shade. Yet, even if that question were out of
> the way, there would be matters enough to perplex us. Ireland, we fear, is on the brink
> of something like civil war – the effect, not of Repeal agitation, but of severe distress
> endured by the peasantry. Foreign politics look dark. An augmentation of the Army will
> be necessary. Pretty legacies to leave to a ministry which will be in a minority in both
> Houses ... Nevertheless, our opinion is that, if we have reasonable hope of being able to
> settle the all-important question of the Corn Laws in a satisfactory way, we ought, at
> whatever sacrifice of quiet and comfort, to take office, though only for a few weeks.[34]

There was some suspicion among Lord John's colleagues that they might be walking into a trap. They thought Peel an artful and insincere man. Writing to Fanny from Chesham Place on 14 December, Lord John said, 'All my friends agreed with me that, unless I could have a very good prospect of carrying a grand measure about corn, I had better decline the Queen's Commission.' There was to be a meeting, he told her, of 'all the old Cabinet men' at his home to ascertain the extent of support there was in favour of acceptance but Lord John felt that despite his knowledge of public affairs, it 'was as if [he] knew nothing about them and was quite incompetent to so great an office – to rule over such vast concerns, with such parties. With so many great things and so many little things to decide it is quite appalling'.[35] Three days later he told her he 'wanted a security that I shall be able to carry a total repeal of the Corn Laws without delay, and that security must consist in an assurance of Sir Robert Peel's support. Unless I get this, I give up the task.'[36]

In a third letter to his wife on 21 December, Lord John could only rejoice at his escape 'a thousand times more' than he would have done had he had to spend 'every moment of [his] time' in details of appointments when his thoughts were with her.[37] At Minto, Fanny was in suspense. Her thoughts were not for Russell as a statesman but as her husband, and for her country rather than herself. She hoped that her 'low and gloomy fits' and the probable consequences of her ill health would not disgrace him.[38] She explained to Lady Mary that Russell could perhaps have gone on successfully to carry the repeal of the Corn Laws if the cabinet had been united but, in his opinion, they 'would have only carried that and then gone out'.[39]

Peel reconstituted his cabinet after Lord John's failure to form a ministry, replacing Lord Stanley with Gladstone. He then set about preparing the bill to abolish the Corn Laws which envisaged a three-year period during which the sliding scale would be used until repeal became absolute. By the first day of February 1846, Lord John was convinced that the Tories 'would carry their corn measure' but would 'hardly last a month after it'. Eight days later, he was in the House 'on an important night for corn' but very nervous as he intended to speak, and wanted to take care 'not to join in the bitterness of the Tories and … avoid the praise of the Ministry'. By 16 February, Russell was telling Fanny how remarkable the affair had become. There had been

> no move, no agitation in the counties but wherever a contest [local election] is announced, the Protection party carry it hollow. In London they have created in a fortnight a very strong and compact party … thus we are threatened with a revival of the real old Tory party … How things may turn out no one can say.

Then, a few days later, he turned twice to the 'thorny point' of Ireland which now vexed him more than the Corn Laws.

Fanny had returned to Edinburgh in January on account of her 'varying and wearying state of health' but by the start of February she was back at Minto and telling her husband that she thought he was quite right in his intention of voting for Sir Robert Peel's measure as it was, since any amendment might delay or scupper any settlement. She liked the way politics were discussed in Edinburgh and had to come to this conclusion not because she was 'heart and soul a free trader'. Doing all she could to become a good wife, she was glad to think that though one wife was far from him, his other wife, the House of Commons, left him little time to spend in pining for her. She had also learned that when private happiness clashed with public duty, it was always the latter that won.[40]

A dozen days into February, Lord George William Russell, Lord John's brother who had succeeded Lord Minto as ambassador in Berlin until Peel's return to power, wrote to Fanny from Genoa, where, as he said, 'I am domiciled with your brother and sister, under the same roof, dine daily at their hospitable table, sit over the fire and cose and prose with them.' Fanny had said it would have been unworthy of John to pine for office, to which the now unwell and retired diplomat had replied how grateful the country should be to any man who would take on the job of Prime Minister. He was full of gratitude to Peel for having sacrificed his ease and enjoyment so as 'to enable us to sit in the shade under our own fig trees'.[41] He was to die in July that year.

Fanny wrote to Lady Mary in Italy at the beginning of March, telling her how being the wife of Lord John meant that she had become separated from the real world: without a permanent residence 'one does not become really acquainted with poor people' in their adversity or their prosperity. She realised that in her position 'one only does a desultory, unsatisfactory, sort of good'. A letter which Lord John wrote to Fanny from London two days later contained some evidence that he had not only underestimated the seriousness of his wife's recent illnesses but blinded himself to a miscarriage she may have experienced. She had obviously not told her husband the whole story. He was contrite, admitting that his hopes were often extravagant, and that the interest of a great crisis, and the best company of London' could not make him even tolerably patient 'under the misfortune of [her] being away'.[42]

In Ireland, the violence and sedition feared by Macaulay were threatening life and property, and Lord John was much occupied in persuading Lansdowne to speak out against the harsh Insurrection Act – 'ordinary medicine' for the Irish, as those supporting coercion said. Lord John knew that Bessborough, who had been less active politically, and whom he considered the best authority on Ireland the Whigs had, thought that such coercive legislation would tend to stop crime – particularly murder. Fanny had earlier registered how much special police powers and additional power for the executive frightened her, and she did not trust 'any Englishman on the subject' except her husband.[43] She wrote to him from Edinburgh in March and concluded after reading all the speeches in favour of the Coercion Bill that 'nothing … would do the slightest good'.[44] Always prepared to listen to both sides of extreme arguments, Lord John replied by saying he would 'be loath to throw out a bill which may have [the] good effect' of reducing murder, but he promised to 'move a resolution which will pledge the House to measures of remedy and conciliation'.[45]

Later that month Fanny appears to have been strong enough to drive to Portobello Sands from where she walked for an hour admiring Inchkeith, the island in the Firth of Forth, with the opposite coast in front of her and a snowy Arthur's Seat behind. In her letter to her husband she could only say with affection that 'even if we could have foreseen four years ago all the various anxieties and trials that awaited us, we should have married all the same'.[46] Replying a few days later, Russell thanked her for what had been a 'precious letter' and referred to the good news that she was hoping 'to get away on the second' of April. As a later note from Lord John made clear, the plan for her to 'be a companion' to him during his political trials on London was too ambitious. It was his turn to say, 'in sickness and in sorrow, so in joy and prosperity, we must rely on each other and let no discouraging apprehensions shake our courage'.[47]

Throughout May, Lord John endeavoured to steady the party both in and out of Westminster. Peel's bill to repeal the Corn Laws (the Importation Act 1846) had its third reading in the Commons on 15 May and to the annoyance of the protectionists there was a majority of ninety-eight for repeal. By June, however, it was clear that Lord Bessborough and Lord John had changed their minds about the value of a Coercion Bill; they were both against it – although for reasons which differed in each case. On the 25th of the month, the Tories had the satisfaction of seeing the repeal bill pass through all its stages in the House of Lords with Whig support. Then, in the Commons, during the early hours of 26 June, it was the turn of those Tories who had been in favour of duties on corn to ally themselves with the Whigs and bring down the administration by voting against Peel's Coercion Bill. Charles Wood said later that the vote had been 'a bad return to Peel for all he has done in carrying our measures, especially the corn bill'. Sir Robert resigned the next day. The laying to rest of the Corn Laws, and the vote on the Coercion Bill, which Prince Albert called the 'factious combination', fractured the Tory party and put the Whigs in power with short intervals for the next twenty years.

On 28 June 1846, Queen Victoria sent for Lord John a second time; this time both parties had their minds made up. He was to become the 'minister of necessity', as one biographer described him. Nevertheless, while he was at Osborne House, he received a note from Charles Wood, who was to become his Chancellor of the Exchequer, and which he thought he should have had before he left the Isle of Wight. Wood had heard that Earl Grey was prepared to waive his objections to Palmerston being appointed Foreign Secretary and would accept the post of Secretary for War and Colonies in the Russell administration.[48] With relations between the two men clarified, Lord John could proceed with forming his administration, albeit that he had little room to manoeuvre or few candidates from which to choose. In the event, his first cabinet was made up of eight members from each house. They were:

- Lord Cottenham (Lord Chancellor)
- Marquess of Lansdowne (Lord President of the Council)
- Sir Charles Wood (Chancellor of the Exchequer)
- Sir George Grey (Secretary of State at the Home Office)
- Viscount Palmerston (Foreign Secretary)
- Earl Grey (Secretary for War and Colonies)
- Earl of Auckland (First Lord of the Admiralty)
- Earl of Clarendon (President of the Board of Trade)
- Sir John Hobhouse (President of the Board of Control)
- Lord Campbell of St Andrews (Chancellor of the Duchy of Lancaster)
- Henry Labouchere (Chief Secretary for Ireland)
- Thomas Babington Macaulay (Paymaster-General)
- Viscount Morpeth (First Commissioner of Woods and Forests)
- Marquess of Clanricarde (Postmaster-General)

Lord Minto completed the tally as Lord Privy Seal, a post which was the fifth of the great offices of state, ranking just below the Lord President of the Council. Being without a portfolio, the occupant was free to undertake special assignments.

Russell's immediate problem was the second year of famine in Ireland. There were to be none of the expensive purchases of maize which Peel had made and which Lady Agatha called 'more pauperising than almsgiving'.[49] After some discussion in July, the cabinet decided against calling a general election, choosing to carry on with the 1841 Parliament. The following month, Lord John introduced his Labour Rate Act (lasting for one year until 15 August 1847) which was to employ the destitute on public works and relief measures, and distributed a total of £10 million from the Treasury. Landowners were compelled to employ the starving or see that they were employed, and that they were paid sufficient wages to enable them to buy food for their families. Destitute cotters had the opportunity to become waged labourers and the cash distribution contributed to the beginning a new class of shopkeepers. When Parliament met in January 1847 the Poor Law was modified to enable out-relief to be given to the able-bodied in Ireland, while the sale of encumbered estates was made easier and emigration could be assisted.

At the end of December, Lord John and Fanny withdrew to Chorley Wood, the country house near Rickmansworth which the Prime Minister had bought some months before, little thinking that the Queen would soon offer him an out-of-town property. Celebrations for the New Year included a 'grand ball for children and servants' which was, as Fanny's diary recorded, 'All very merry. John danced a great deal, and I not a little. Darling Johnny danced the first country dance holding his Papa's hand and mine.' But a month later Fanny once again became dangerously ill and was cared for by Dr Rigby, not only 'the skilful doctor, but the kindest friend'.[50]

In March 1847, the Queen offered Pembroke Lodge in Richmond Park to the Russells for life. Its former occupant had been the Earl of Erroll, the husband of a natural daughter of William IV. As Lady Agatha wrote, it was the 'perfect home for a statesman' and had 'an air of cheerful seclusion and homely eighteenth-century dignity'. It became much loved by Fanny and the children, the young only staying in London in the busy season between the opening of Parliament and Easter. The couple slept there on Wednesdays, Saturdays and Sundays 'with as much regularity as other engagements allowed' and although regretting the loss of society, they gave up most dinner engagements in London.[51] They were to spend the short Whitsuntide holiday at Pembroke Lodge settling in.

When the mandate of the Parliament of 1841 expired, and the results of the August 1847 general election became known, it was clear that the Tories outnumbered the Whigs, but the latter would be able to remain in power, if not able to command a regular majority, on account of divisions within the Tory party. Lord John himself had been returned by the City of London at the head of the poll. The election was barely over, however, when the country faced a financial crisis and in Ireland the famine continued into another year. Meanwhile, the Foreign Secretary was determined to exploit the liberal tide which was already starting to flow across Europe and which, in the case of Italy, looked to Metternich like 'gratuitous interference'. Palmerston had written to Lord John suggesting they followed up Cardinal Wiseman's suggestion that a special and temporary mission should be sent to Rome. In 1847, while president of Oscott College near Birmingham, the cardinal had been commissioned by the English bishops to visit Rome in order to propose the restoration of a Catholic hierarchy in England in place of a government by vicars apostolic established a century before. He reported the growing understanding between Anglicans and Catholics, and other advances being made in England and Wales, to Pope Pius IX, who was persuaded by his arguments. However, he cut short his visit short when the Pope asked him to return to London and explain to Palmerston the nature of the increasingly difficult situation that faced the Holy See, caused by the presence of Austrian troops in the Papal States to counter the movement of Italian unification.[52]

The person the Foreign Secretary wished to entrust with the mission was Fanny's father, Lord Minto,[53] whom he thought 'particularly well-qualified for it' and who was apparently about to go to southern Germany on private matters.[54] The Queen sanctioned his being given the mission since it seemed difficult 'to find a person of inferior rank and position than Lord Minto and of equal weight, but on the understanding that the object of it would be communicated beforehand to the Courts in Vienna and Paris, and that both these governments would be made fully acquainted with the position England thought herself bound to take with regard to the Italian controversy.[55] Such opposition from Victoria, who had her own conception of how foreign policy should be conducted, was to impede many of the efforts made by Palmerston on behalf of the Italians. Prince Albert even stated that a mission to the Vatican would be a 'most hostile step towards our old and natural ally, Austria'. He was, however, prepared to admit that by adopting such a policy, England would be morally bound to uphold the independence of the Italian States and Lord Minto's projected mission would not commit the country to interfere on their behalf.[56]

# 9

# Lord Minto Goes to Rome and Revolutionary Sicily as Special Envoy (1847-1852)

Ralph Abercromby, the British minister in Turin, told the Prime Minister at the end of August 1847 that the post was expecting the arrival of Lord and Lady Minto, and that he was ready to brief him on the political situation within an Italy which had become the home of a number of sovereign dynastic and ecclesiastical states. Their existence had been the result of Papal pressure aimed at ensuring that no large state would rival its power and influence. Lady Mary Elliot's husband was particularly concerned about the need for dialogue with the individual governments in an attempt to establish a national identity. On 20 September, Lord John received a letter from Lord Minto written from Bern, where he said his party was about to proceed south.

Lord Minto had been instructed to take note of the situation in Switzerland which pointed increasingly towards the possibility of a bloody civil war. Palmerston hoped Minto would 'warn the Diet against violent acts' which would have given France or Austria the pretext to interfere in the country by force of arms.[1] Once in the Swiss capital, Minto lost no time in contacting Ulrich Ochsenbein, whom he found was reasonable to deal with, but whose election to the post of president of the Federal Diet had greatly upset the Catholics.[2] Misleadingly, he assured the British envoy that if the Jesuits who constituted the chief obstacle to a peaceful settlement could be removed, 'all danger of war would disappear'.[3] Protestant liberals, seeking a stronger central government and greater freedom of worship, had tried to impose their views on the Swiss Confederation as a whole ,which caused the seven Catholic cantons to form a defensive alliance called the 'Separatist League'. By the time the Mintos reached Bern, both sides were openly preparing for war and on 29 October the Swiss Diet was to pass a measure requiring the league to be dissolved, whereupon the Catholic deputies formally left the Federal Diet. Fortunately, when the civil war broke out in November, it was short and bloodless.

At the end of September and while still in Turin, Lord Minto could see little reason to expect 'any extensive or serious movements for Italian unity'. He concluded that 'Austria, by her hasty menace and the hostile attitude of her army' had given Italians a rational objective, and his initial impression was that a good deal would depend on the position taken by the governments in both Turin and further south. He certainly did not have any mandate to encourage the movement in favour of Italian unity or do anything that might deprive the Emperor of his Italian possessions. It did nevertheless seem to him that Lord John had a right to ask Austria distinctly what her intentions were. The force she was collecting on the frontier (including Croatian troops) was 'quite sufficient to justify the demand for explanation'. He also reminded Lord John that despite his 'undiplomatic prejudice in favour of the truth and plain dealing', he did not think the Italians would trust him the less because he did not profess to participate in all their passions.[4] A couple of days before Lord Minto moved on to Genoa and Rome, he reported 'a little check … in the happy progress of affairs' due to some distrust on the part of the public and, after discovering there was an intention of receiving him with a grand *ovation*, he soon put an end to it. He had been well received in Turin and heard that he was being 'looked for with impatience' further south.[5]

On 7 November, Minto told Lord John that he had been introduced to Cardinal Ferretti ahead of an audience with Pope Pius IX. A distinguished cardinal who had commanded part of Gregory XVI's army during the revolution of 1831, Ferretti was a cousin of the Pope and Secretary of State at the Papal Court. Writing home, Lord Minto described the Pope as 'a most amiable, agreeable, and honest man and sincerely pious to boot … but he is not made to drive the State coach'. In preparation for his audience, and rather belatedly, Minto raised one or two important issues with the Prime Minister and then answered them for himself, trusting that their views were not dissimilar. He assumed that any British minister appointed to Rome would 'invariably' be a Protestant, and that should the Pio Nono desire to establish a mission in London his representative must be 'a layman' unless told otherwise. Then there was the question of the Irish Colleges. Lord Minto, who was not sufficiently master of the question to discuss it with advantage, indicated that since he would not be able to say much beyond vague assurances about England's desire to do her best for the Roman Catholics, he asked to 'be enlightened'. Palmerston wanted him to request the Pope to make the Irish priesthood keep out of politics and through the Congregation of the Faith the pontiff did reprove the clergy for political activities. He sent a solemn exhortation to some of the Irish bishops, reminding them that the Church was a place of prayer not a meeting place for politicians and requiring them to assess the importance of the damnatory reports.[6]

A week later, Minto described the Pope and Cardinal Ferretti as being 'such plain-dealing men that one may talk to them with little reserve and with the assurance of being understood'. He was, however, too ready to draw conclusions on a modicum of evidence, telling his son-in-law that he thought the two princes of the church were 'quite ready to do justice to our motives', and that they knew only too well how much they owed to British support. Minto wanted them to understand that the administration was anxious to do the best it could for the Irish Catholics. He told the pontiff that Lord John had 'every disposition to make such arrangements respecting the Irish Colleges as ought to be satisfactory to the Catholics'. Furthermore, there had been no difference of opinion on either side regarding the eventual appointment of an Archbishop of Westminster and Minto told the Prime Minister that 'the influence of the English name is now so great in Italy that they look as much for my assistance in tempering the views of their own public as in averting danger from without'. Minto concluded that every day brought fresh proofs of the confidence with which Britain was regarded.[7]

The opening deliberations of the Consulta di Stato got under way in November and Lord Minto reported them as 'a great political event'. The Pope had announced his intention to establish such an advisory council in April that year, composed of laymen from the various provinces of papal territory, and it was to be followed in December by the creation of a cabinet council. Writing to Lord John, Minto explained that members of the advisory council were 'contending for the publicity, not of their discussions, but of their proceedings' which upset the Pope, and his Lordship was uncertain whether or not Pius IX would give way or speak out against the council. Again, and too optimistically, he added that he had 'learnt to rely strongly on Italian moderation and good sense'.[8]

By the second day of 1848, just eight weeks after his arrival in Rome, Lord Minto had concluded that his task had been completed. He felt confident enough to ask Lord John what his wishes were about his return to London, reminding the Prime Minister that the crisis which brought him out to Italy 'was over, and especially all danger from without'. If, on the other hand, he was not wanted at home, he suggested his presence there 'might be serviceable' pending the eventual appointment of a minister in Rome.[9] Palmerston agreed with the Prime Minister that it would be best if Minto stayed on at Rome perhaps until Easter. It was already clear to the Foreign Secretary, if not Minto, that the opening of a mission in Rome would be a blow to 'the influence of McHale and Co. with the Papal authorities'. Three years before, John MacHale, the stormy Archbishop of Tuam in Galway, had rallied opposition against Peel's Colleges Bill which provided non-denominational education for Catholics and Presbyterians, and Palmerston wanted to avoid the English Catholics making MacHale 'a sort of chief of their clan'.[10] Accordingly, Lord Minto continued to press the necessity for liberal measures and the appointment of respectable ministers upon the Pope and Cardinal Ferretti. Austria was the 'greatest bugbear to all Italians' and although it was not expected she would invade at once, local opinion was that the forces which she had assembled could hardly be purely defensive.[11]

However, by the 18th of the month, the 'fat was in the fire to the southward' following the start of the Sicilian revolution of independence which had been timed to coincide with the birthday of Ferdinand II of the Two Sicilies. It was a distraction to Minto's task and not long before he was telling Lord John how it gave him 'great uneasiness'. Having spoken to the Pope, his Lordship reported that the pontiff did not 'apprehend any danger' since the Sicilians were only recovering what they could claim as their right. This 'satisfactory conversation' also included news of a lecture the Pope was to give his ministers assembled in the new Council, about which he laughed and said, 'there are really some good men amongst them now, though they may not all be very efficient'.[12]

During the first week of February a street riot in Rome extracted the promise of a lay ministry from the Pope and a month later he was to be obliged to grant a constitution to the Consulta di Stato. The riot happened when Lord Minto was 'within a quarter of an hour of starting for Naples'. Expressing his sympathies with the Sicilians to Lord John, he feared that the Bourbon King Ferdinand II would not consent to the terms the Sicilians wanted: a separate Parliament of their own. He went on to ask Lord John to give him his views as to the degree of protection to be given to the Sicilians, and 'what to say if Austria advance[d] to Naples'.[13] Having arrived in the south, the envoy must have envisioned Italy as a tinderbox with fires breaking out everywhere. The accounts he received from Rome spoke of an unpleasant situation where the Pope had put off many liberal measures, and Russia was pressing the Pope to accept a French force for his protection. Fortunately, this was peremptorily declined.[14]

In London, on the other hand, it was France that was catching and holding the headlines. News reached the House of Commons on 26 February that Louis Philippe had been deposed and that the country was on the cusp of a Bonapartist revival. Lord John and Fanny dined at the palace and found the Queen and Prince Albert, the Duchess of Kent, and the Duke and Duchess of Saxe Coburg full of indignation against the French nation and François Guizot, its prime minister. Lady Fanny sat next to the Duke of Coburg, who showed 'very little reasoning' and did 'not care whether Guizot lost his head'. The Queen, she said, spoke with 'much good sense and good feeling, if not with perfect impartiality'.[15] The dethronement of Louis Philippe had proved as severe a shock to Victoria as any that she had yet suffered.[16] It wounded her tenderest feelings and despite her recent differences with him she thought only of the distress of a fellow sovereign. 'If it were not for the generosity of the Queen of England,' Louis remarked shortly afterwards at Claremont House near Esher which had been put at their disposal, 'I should not have either this house to cover my head, or the plate or anything which is on the table'.[17]

At Palermo, the capital of Sicily, a circular had been distributed in January, calling on a population of approximately 2 million people to rise up against the exactions of the Naples government. The police arrested a dozen or so revolutionaries but it was not long before people in the poorest part of the town were being killed as the result of clashes with authority. A moderate local politician, Giuseppe La Masa, formed a committee to take charge of the rising and was soon supported by Rosolino Pilo, an aristocrat. The poorly armed rebels were vastly outnumbered by some 6,000 troops belonging to Ferdinand II who decided to shell Palermo from the fortress of Castelmare. Substantial Royalist reinforcements were landed on 15 January but the rebels were able to hold on to the town and, having seen his offer of autonomy rejected, Ferdinand was forced to withdraw his forces from Palermo towards the end of the month. He then appointed a more liberal ministry led by Nicola Maresca, the Duke of Serracapriola, who sought the mediation of Britain.

During February Lord Minto was ensconced at Naples, where he thought the bulk of his work would be done, advising King Ferdinand's government to offer Sicily a modification of its 1812 constitution. It soon, however, became clear that the French Revolution had turned the heads of the Palermitans, who now wanted the King's abdication. On 19 February, Vice-Admiral Sir William Parker, previously Lord Minto's second naval lord at the Admiralty, wrote to his Lordship from HMS *Hibernia*, his 2,500-ton, 110-gun flagship, then moored in Palermo Harbour. He had just finished five hours of discussion with Lord Mount Edgcumbe, who was a resident on the island at the time,[18] together with the president and secretary of the insurgents' General Committee. Ruggiero Settimo, the president, was a retired admiral now past seventy years of age. Two days before, he had issued an inspirational handbill which started with the words, 'We have won with the weapons; arbitrary power is fallen, a social structure is being built.' The secretary, Signor Mariano Stabile, was 'in fact the sole director and adviser of their measures' and 'by far the most able and discreet member of their body'. Admiral Parker had encouraged him to put down on paper more of his thoughts about the concessions offered by Ferdinand's government.

Understanding the sensitive nature of the burgeoning democratic process in a distant island on the southern extremity of Europe took time to seep into the British mind. Emperor Frederick II's so-called 'parliament' had been held at Messina in 1234, and a parliament in 1541 contained three Marquises, ten counts, two viscounts and sixty-two barons. Few diplomats or naval officers would have been conversant with the three houses of Sicily's parliament, the 'clerical' chamber, the 'feudal' chamber which included peers, and the 'demesnial' which was made up of land-owning representatives from the principal cities, all of which had emerged in the eighteenth century. Meanwhile in Palermo there was violent feeling against the French according to Mount Edgcumbe. In the *Indipendenza e Lega* to which many leading members of the committee contributed, Guizot and General Vial, the French minister in Malta, were 'classed together'. However, the town was slowly resuming an appearance of tranquillity.[19]

Waiting in Naples, Lord Minto heard that Parker proposed to detach HMS *Hecate* and *Porcupine* to Baia, and Mount Edgcumbe reported having explained to Stabile the difficulties Minto had encountered in getting the government to consent to the non-admittance of Neapolitan or foreign troops without the consent of parliament. He had declared that it 'must be considered a *sine qua non*'. Stabile had also been reminded about a proposition put forward in earlier talks, where the dispatch to Sicily of the Sicilian Regiment in the King's service might help, albeit 'with proper officers'. So far as Lord Minto's accommodation on the island was concerned, Mount Edgcumbe told his Lordship that the National Guard commander, Baron Pietro Riso, intended to offer him the use of his 'most magnificent palace'. The alternative would be 'a very comfortable hotel on the Marina' next to the house he occupied himself.[20]

In March, the Neapolitan government offered to legalise the Sicilian parliament, subject to changes in the constitution and the recognition of Ferdinand as king. It was proposed that Ruggiero Settimo should be recognised as viceroy, and Sicily would have a separate foreign ministry. Uncertain about Bourbon promises, the revolutionaries rejected the proposal and demanded the immediate withdrawal of Neapolitan troops from Sicily. The Sicilians, well aware of how little the government could be relied upon, 'justly feared that should Ferdinand's troops again occupy the strongholds from which they had so recently driven them, they would have no security against the restoration of an absolute government'. Many of the Sicilians in Naples refused to take the oath to the new constitution promulgated by Ferdinand. Minto was disappointed that the promised constitution did not prove such as he had been led to expect. It allowed only one general parliament for both kingdoms and, as the result, held out little hope for the Sicilians.

Travelling aboard HMS *Hibernia*, commanded by Edward Codd, Lord Minto told Lord John on 10 March that 'we are within twenty miles of Palermo'. He intended to 'assume a high tone with them and to refuse to land, or treat at all with the Committee' if they still wanted the King's abdication. He had little doubt he would find them tractable once they saw that he was in earnest. So far as Naples was concerned, Minto told the Prime Minister that 'it was a toss up how things go'. He wanted to settle the situation in Sicily and 'face northwards again' in order to be of more use in Rome, and still more towards home lest Ireland 'should catch fire from France'. Then, with Admiral Parker's presence nearby and his own memories of life in Whitehall having an obvious effect, he added, 'I heartily wish we had two or three more *big ships* in the

Mediterranean ... in such times as the present it is surely madness to run the risk of starting at a disadvantage.'[21]

Soon after the party landed, Lord Minto presented the King's concessions to the provisional government which were answered by an official bulletin published in Palermo declaring 'any concession to be contrary to the Constitution of 1812, and therefore null and void'. He next suggested that the Sicilians should put their own terms to the King but 'he earnestly exhorted them to maintain the crown of both kingdoms on one head, and to resign their right to absolute separation', which they claimed by the 1812 constitution. The Sicilians yielded to his advice, stipulating, however, as an express condition, that royal troops should within eight days evacuate the only two fortresses remaining in their hands on the island. Minto assured them he would obtain the King's consent to this within two days.[22]

A report sent to Lord John Russell on 14 March opened with the news that Minto had had 'some difficulty preventing the Sicilians from deposing the King. 'Unless he accepts the conditions now required,' the envoy wrote, 'this will inevitably be voted on the assembling of parliament which meets on the twenty fifth.'[23] The day before, Captain Codrington of HMS *Thetis* had told Lord Minto about the failure of the authorities in Messina to achieve any armistice between the sides after hostilities had been resumed following the conference aboard his ship. The captain had spoken to President Piraino, whom he hoped he had 'smoothed down' but the fact was, as he said, that Palermo was now 'the decision point'. Everything hung on what the *Comitato* agreed to.

Writing to Lord Minto from Naples two days later, Lord Napier, then our chargé d'affaires, told him that as soon as his letters had arrived they had been delivered to Gaetano Scovazzo, who had been appointed Minister for Sicilian Affairs by Ferdinand II.[24] Napier had read him Minto's long narrative addressed to Lord Palmerston, together with a letter from Mr Erskine, a young diplomat who had travelled to the scene aboard HMS *Bulldog*. These 'he studied and understood every point in his patient, careful way. It had been agreed that he should go and inform the king in the morning.'When he met His Majesty, Scovazzo said he was convinced of the necessity for an immediate resolution of the situation, also asking His Majesty to see Lord Minto. He replied that 'he would gladly do so at a later period but he must first consult the Council'. Informed that the *Porcupine* had orders to return instantly, and that the decision of the Council must be conveyed by a Neapolitan steam vessel, the King agreed. It had not, however, been a successful meeting, and in closing his letter Napier hoped Minto 'would not be disappointed with the absence of a result'.[25]

Writing the same day from the legation in Naples, Napier sent a copy of the ultimatum of the General Committee to Prince Cariate at the palace, along with his own opinion of the course which the Neapolitan government ought to pursue. He advised the prince that 'should the Council resolve to send a plenipotentiary to Palermo', a good choice would be Count Ferretti, who was neither Neapolitan nor Sicilian, yet naturalised in the kingdom, and 'intimate with Lord Minto'. With the meeting of the Sicilian parliament scheduled to meet on 25 March, there was little time left.[26] As the pot came to the boil, Napier was faced with other problems. He told Minto that since he had left for Palermo there had been a period of uncertainty and agitation.

Just how sensitive were the players charged with settling Sicilian affairs for the benefit of the population was revealed when Scovazzo expressed his fear to Lord Napier that he might incur 'an undeserved unpopularity' by having accepted and retained the office of Sicilian minister at Naples. He had, Napier told Minto, to have explained to him 'how patriotic were his motives' in accepting the task, but he still spoke of 'instant resignation should the king not accede to the demands of the Sicilians'.[27]

Meanwhile Napier told Erskine, who was with Lord Minto at Palermo, that Ferdinand had 'partly recovered from his terror and depression' and he drove out as usual in his phaeton. The people were beginning to take some interest in the elections and, in Napier's opinion, he thought that 'the monarchy will last until the first of May'.[28] The chargé d'affaires was forced to tell Minto the next day that individual articles in the Sicilian memorandum had been discussed 'one by one' and a 'laboured report was in the course of preparation'. The deliberation followed its dilatory course 'as if the matters in discussion were an every day routine business'. When Scorazzo saw the King, wrote Napier, 'he appears quite alive to the pressing nature of the emergency, but he refers everything to the Council in whose hands the affair will be drawn out until it be too late, and Sicily is lost'. Continuing his report he said, 'I attack Cariate every night, and Cariate attacks the Sicilians, never hearing the name of Stabile ... or mention of the *Squadri* without "*avec quatre bons battaillons*".' He declared 'a general war to be inevitable'.

The situation in Naples had improved. The Riot Act worked and an ordinance for the suppression of the old-guard force of gendarmes had given satisfaction. They were to be incorporated into the regular army and a new body of paid and mounted National Guard was to be organised for the rural districts. One result was that public attention was being turned more and more to the elections. Minto learned from Napier that everything had 'the worst complexion' in the north of Italy but the Pope's new constitution gave great satisfaction.[29] Palmerston was to tell Minto that London had just heard of the entry of Sardinian troops into Lombardy to help the Milanese. 'If the Italian sovereigns,' he wrote, 'had not been urged by you to move on, while their impatient subjects were kept back, there would by this time have been nothing but Republics from the Alps to Sicily.' 'North Italy,' he said, 'will henceforward be Italian, and the Austrian frontier will be at the Tyrol ... Of course Parma and Modena will follow the example, and in this way the king, will become a sovereign of some importance in Europe. This will make a league between him and the other Italian rulers still more desirable.'[30] Such an assessment would have helped Minto put his work into some sort of perspective.

However, on 22 March, Napier sent a letter addressed to him by His Excellency Prince Cariate to Lord Minto in Palermo. It contained a formal refusal of the terms offered to the Neapolitan government by the committee in Palermo in the memorandum that had been forwarded by Lord Minto.[31] Three days later the Sicilian parliament voted in a provisional government and elected Ruggiero Settimo president (or regent) of the kingdom. Minto wrote to his son-in-law trusting that Lord John did not think he 'had too easily relinquished the hope of attaching Sicily to the Crown of Naples'. He reminded the Prime Minister that no one could 'understand the intense hatred with which all classes from the Prince to the peasant regard the king, and every member of his family' without going Sicily. When 'the last answer from Naples arrived to release [their leaders] from this engagement it was joyfully received, though the people knew that they should again have to fight for their independence'. Although it was true, wrote Minto, that 'the king is individually the first object of their aversion, they also remember that their interests have always been sacrificed to those of Naples, and any connection with that country is most distasteful to them'. In the envoy's opinion, the government was likely to be well composed. The regent was a temperate and high-minded old man, and there were also some able men in the Council.[32]

Four days into April, Lord Minto was back in Naples, having left Palermo on the first of the month, and was preparing for his departure for London. He could not help telling his son-in-law that 'rogues and fools and cowards formed the whole stock-in-trade of that country'. In contrast, he described 'his' Sicilians to Lord John as 'trembling in the balance between Monarchy and Republic' and felt that the former might still be secured. He was going to speak to King Ferdinand on the subject, and 'make it plain to him in courteous terms that he is individually too odious to every Sicilian – man, woman or child – to be himself now accepted as their sovereign'. The envoy had met Ferdinand but he doubted that the King would 'make up his mind in time to give the Sicilians one of his children as their king'.[33] A few days before, Francis Napier had reported, 'all was going to pieces' in Naples.[34]

On 6 April, Minto wrote to the Foreign Office, this time to give the Prime Minister another *tour d'horizon*. He was convinced that Ferdinand's 'folly, insincerity and dishonesty' was the greatest difficulty. The people were bad enough but he was the 'master demon'. He hoped that Lord John was 'seriously preparing for a considerable increase' in the size of the British naval force off Italy as a French fleet, equal if not superior to Parker's squadron, was already at sea. 'You must remember,' he wrote, 'that at a first start they can bring forward a few fresh ships faster than we can do, though in the end we outrun them.' Minto was glad to see that the French government desired to keep in well with Britain but he had no confidence in its power 'nor in the honesty or discretion of its agents or officers'. Understandably, in this many-fronted crisis, the envoy wanted to hear what had been the Prime Minister's 'tone with regard to all that was passing in Lombardy'. When he had been obliged to say anything Lord Minto said he usually condemned the aggressive measures of the King Charles Albert of Piedmont-Sardinia and other Italian governments 'who invade Austrian territory', making it clear in good diplomatic language that 'we may not be disposed to take part in the quarrel'.[35]

On his way home, Minto hoped to stay as few days as possible in Rome. When he wrote to William, his concern was whether there would be enough post-horses in Piedmont and Lombardy, if not on the other side of the Alps. His best estimate of the time they would be on the road between Turin and London was fifteen days, arriving back at Eaton Square by the second week in May.[36] Lady Minto contemplated appointing a cook, and the earl himself spoke of recruiting an under-butler and a footman – but nobody 'out of any of the great houses'. He probably anticipated an end to his involvement with Sicilian affairs, but as the situation in the Mediterranean got worse, he found that in the eyes of London-based Sicilians his experience as a special envoy qualified him as a helpmate in their cause.[37]

The revolutionary government in Sicily was to repudiate both Ferdinand and the Bourbons while at the same time retaining the monarchy. The crown was offered to the Duke of Genoa, the second son of King Charles Albert, who declined it. In the interim, a moderate ministry had been formed in Naples by Carlo Troya, described by Napier as 'a fat, infirm and learned historian'. Rumours that there might be a monarchical coup led to a clash between rebels from the Neapolitan countryside and the King's troops. Fighting on 15 May only lasted a few hours and after the insurgents had been overwhelmed Ferdinand dissolved the lower house of parliament and the national guard.[38]

In London, Fanny was telling her elder sister Lady Mary about the preparations being made to reduce the threat of rebellion. To her mind, there was a 'new revolution' somewhere every hour. On 14 April, Queen Victoria approved the ordering of a form of prayer for 'the present time of tumult and trouble'. Her Majesty admitted that a thanksgiving for the failure of the most recent Chartist meeting would not have been thought judicious. It was unlike giving thanks for preservation from a foreign war. It would, however, be quite in order to pray for 'peace and quiet *generally*'.[39] Fanny might have taken an interest in the words used in such a prayer had she not given birth that day to her second son, George Gilbert William. Dr James Simpson, who had attended her when she had been in Edinburgh earlier in the year, had written to her in March in anticipation of her second child's birth saying that he had once made a pledge that he 'would gladly leave all to watch and guard over' her safety if she so desired. He had reminded her that, like almost all 'his medical brethren' in Edinburgh, he also now used chloroform 'in all cases'.[40] She had, however, not needed his assistance and both her boys – John, now a little over five years old, and George – were well.

Resuming his duties as Lord Privy Seal and a member of Lord Russell's cabinet, Lord Minto called on Prince Metternich in London on 21 May, intending his visit to be only one of civility. The Vienna mob had clamoured for his resignation as Chancellor, and when it was accepted by the Emperor on 18 March he and his family left for England, where he lived in retirement at Brighton and London until October the following year. No sooner had he made Minto sit down beside him than he sought to give his views on the state of Germany and Italy and vindicate his own policy at great length in much detail. He was at pains to point out that he had only been able to advise and propose, not command. Furthermore, if his design for a separate Lombardy–Venetian kingdom presided over by an arch-duke had been pursued and it had been given the character of an Italian kingdom, though subject to a German sovereign, there would have been no disaffection such as had been witnessed in Lombardy. Minto accepted that the prince was acquainted with most of the leading characters in Italy but he could not believe he knew 'how much the moderation manifested in the early progress of reform was the consequence of their influence and exertions'. He also supposed the Pope 'to have been more of a political liberal in spirit' than was really in his character.[41] For his part, Palmerston was to put too much emphasis on the usefulness of conventional diplomacy and trying to achieve permanent solutions through his envoys, with the result that closer relations with the Papacy were never achieved.

When news arrived in London that Messina had fallen in September after a military attack by 20,000 troops belonging to Ferdinand, and shelling for eight hours by a naval flotilla, Minto feared that Sicily might become 'the scene of a very savage war'. Writing to his son-in-law, he thought other coastal towns might share the same fate if attacked with the 'superior force of ships and field artillery' the Neapolitans possessed. Beyond this, the envoy suspected, they would not make much impression and he looked upon the conquest of the island as 'quite impossible'. Minto had seen the Prime Minister's note to Palmerston on this subject just before the Russells had left town and it gave him 'great pleasure' although he feared the most valuable part of it was lost sight of in the dispatch the Foreign Secretary had written – the intimation that Britain could not suffer Sicily to be ravaged by war. He told Lord John that Palmerston had thought the Sicilians might be induced to take back Ferdinand II if he gave them good terms, something which he certainly did not. Minto hoped that after the shelling of Messina, Palmerston had come round to agreeing with him. Letters Minto had received from Ruggiero Settimo (now president) and others deprecated any urging on them to accept the King or any member of his family, or the House of Bourbon. Rounding off this unusually forceful letter to his son-in-law, Minto spoke of the distress and mortification he felt both as a minister and an Englishman that the invasion had been allowed to take place. He hoped it was not yet too late to stop further bloodshed.[42]

It seems that at the end of September Lord Minto's name had been put up as an alternative to that of Normanby, the British ambassador in Paris, to mediate between Austria and the Italians, both being 'unexceptionable'. The plan was to hold a conference in Rome, Bologna or Pisa, and invite the parties which had met at conferences on the subject of Belgium, namely Prussian and Russia, should they wish it. Lord John had, however, to tell the Foreign Secretary that Minto would 'be very unwilling to undertake a mission to which he [could] not see a prospect of favourable results either to England or to Europe'. As a result, he was inclined to urge the nomination of Normanby. If, however, the Queen objected, he suggested Palmerston should name Lord Minto to her.[43]

The government of Pope Pius IX was overthrown on 16 November by a revolutionary mob which demanded a democratic government, social reforms and a declaration of war against Austria. The following night, the ambassadors of Bavaria and France aided the Pope's escape from the Quirinal to the fortress of Gaeta, 50 miles from Naples in the Kingdom of the Two Sicilies, disguised as an ordinary priest. Ralph Abercromby described the murder of Rossi, the Pope's prime minister, on his way to the Legislative Assembly as a 'horrible crime'.[44] A few days later, Louis Philippe paid a visit to Pembroke Lodge and the Prime Minister and Fanny listened while he spoke much of France and how he hoped that Louis Napoleon Bonaparte rather than General Cavaignac would become president. Lord John expressed some fear of war if this happened but the deposed monarch discounted such an event since 'France had neither the means nor the inclination for war'.[45]

It was not long before Fanny was telling Lady Mary that 'the great question of the French Presidency' was decided, whether for good or evil to other countries none could foresee. After intensive campaigning Bonaparte had been the only candidate voted for, whereupon he had sent French legions to help the Pope reconquer Rome while subduing workers at home with stern brutality. Lady John could only say Louis Philippe was a disgrace to his country, and a man 'known only by a foolish attempt to disturb France'. How strange it was, she said

> to see this great King, this busy plotter of the glory of his own family and the degradation of England, taking refuge in that very England, and sitting in the house of one of those very ministers whom he had been so proud of outwitting, giving the history of 'ma chute'.[46]

In January 1849, and without a government, the citizens of Rome held elections much against the Pope's wishes, and in which the voters expressed their preferences for individuals, not parties. The Constitutional Assembly was convened on 8 February 1849 and the proclamation of the Roman Republic followed at midnight the next day. One of its first acts was to declare the right of the Pope to continue his role as head of the Roman Church, but runaway inflation, the threat of an external attack, and the call by the Pope for military help to crush the revolutionaries, were to contribute to the overthrow of the Republic. Under great pressure from French Catholics, the newly elected President of France, Louis Napoleon, chose to send an army to restore the Pope.

Nine thousand troops landed at Civitavecchia on 25 April under the command of General Charles Oudinot while Spain sent 4,000 men to Gaeta, where the Pope had found refuge. The French sent a staff officer to tell the guiding spirit of the Republic, and Genoese founder of the newspaper *La Giovine Italia*, Guiseppe Mazzini, that the Pope would be restored to power. Although not expecting that it would come to a fight, the resolve of the Republican government was greatly stiffened by the arrival in Rome two days later of Guiseppe Garibaldi, who had been able to form his 'Italian Legion' from soldiers who had been at the battle of Novara a month before. There, the Austrians under General Radetzky overcame the army of Charles Albert, a victory which led directly to the King of Sardinia's abdication and his death soon after. Similar support was drawn from the entry into Rome of the Lombard *Bersaglieri*, who had been successful in battles against the Austrians in the streets of Milan. Both sides clashed at the end of April and to the surprise of the Republican forces the French were beaten back to the sea, whereupon Oudinot regrouped and awaited reinforcements. The siege of Rome began in earnest on 1 June and this time the French were successful. The French army entered Rome on 3 July after a truce during which Garibaldi withdrew from the city with 4,000 troops. The Roman Republic had lasted four short months. Louis Napoleon now wanted to be seen re-establishing the Vatican's temporal power and bringing about a reformed liberal state, both matters which the Pope felt were more properly his responsibility. His fear of French meddling in his affairs led to him to postpone his return to Rome itself until April 1850.

Also at the beginning of 1849 a disagreement surfaced between Lord Minto and Lord John Russell on the question of Sicily. His pro-Italian sentiments and hostility towards Austria was to bring him near to resignation. In his journal for 9 January he described how he had written to the Prime Minister a few days earlier telling him that he felt unequal to any employment at the Admiralty, where there was a vacancy as the result of Lord Auckland's sudden death, adding that he was ready to put his own seat in the cabinet at Lord John's disposal. The cause of this breach appears to have been the orders the Prime Minister had sent to Sir William Parker 'to abandon the Sicilians to their fate', which meant that the admiral could no longer oppose Neapolitan operations against Sicily. Minto did not wish to be 'a party to so foul a blot on our national honour'. When the two men met there was 'an unpleasant conversation' which irritated Minto, not least on account of the way Lord John appeared to be acting unnecessarily in his defence. The offer of another post was declined, leaving him content to remain in the cabinet but out of ministerial office.[47]

With affairs going ill in Italy, Lord Minto was of the opinion that Charles Albert, the King of Piedmont-Sardinia, would 'not renounce his views of aggrandisement and war in Lombardy' and was concerned that the Pope, who had even refused to receive any communication from Rome, was calling for an invasion by a foreign army 'as the only mode of his restoration to which he will consent'. Minto hoped that Charles Albert might somehow be induced to resume his help to Leopold II, the Grand Duke, and the restoration of his authority in Tuscany. This was supported at the cabinet meeting in London at the beginning of March. Lord Minto thought 'something of the kind' would be attempted but he doubted 'if we shall manifest such determination as to give our influence much effect for our present temper is strongly passive'. He subsequently spoke of this 'dangerous weakness of purpose and action' to Palmerston, who felt about it as Minto did. Even Lord John agreed that there was 'some unaccountable spell on his conduct'.[48]

Having heard that a question was likely to be raised in Parliament about guns in British ordnance stores being supplied to the Sicilians, Minto went to both Russell and Palmerston on 6 March, telling them that if this led to any discussion of the Sicilian question, he would speak his mind about it. After a meeting of the cabinet four days later, it seems the government sent an apology to Naples, an action which greatly upset Minto. Then, on 12 March, three gentlemen, Signori Granatelli, Luigi Scalia and Baron Friddiani, who was 'not so judicious', and who was returning to Paris the next day, called on the Lord Privy Seal. They informed Lord Minto that one of the steamers bought for their government in Sicily (the *Vectis*[49]) had sailed without interruption from Liverpool, and the other (the *Bombay*) was in the Thames about to leave unless means were found by Prince Castelcicala, the Neapolitan minister, to detain it. Four days later when he was in his office, Minto was again joined by Granatelli and Scalia, who were 'a good deal out of spirits' as the result of the disgraceful terms which Britain had consented to in Sicily. They also told him that their steamer, 'unarmed and unequipped for war' and belonging to the Peninsular & Oriental Steam Navigation Company, and with a British crew, had been stopped by authority of the Customs House at the moment when about to sail. It was to take some time before the *Bombay* was to be released.[50]

After taking a law degree in Sicily, Luigi Scalia (1806–1888) had become one of the twelve chief citizens of Palermo who signed the constitution of a free Sicily in 1848, along with Ruggiero Settimo, the Marchese Torrearsa, Mariano Stabile and Prince Butera.[51] He and his colleague were subsequently appointed to treat with England, who with France acted as intermediaries between the Sicilians and Ferdinand II. Although 'a man of culture, with real legislative abilities', Prince Franco Maccagnone Granatelli seems to have cut a somewhat ignoble figure in London society, into which he and Scalia were launched. Countless stories were told of his 'amazing behaviour'. At an important semi-official dinner he stirred his coffee at the end of the meal with his little finger in place of a spoon. On another occasion, at a soirée given by Lady Belcher (the wife of Sir Edward Belcher, who lived separately from her admiral husband) he clapped his hostess after she had sung by 'beating his open palm violently upon his side in such a way as to attract all eyes towards him'. Nevertheless, during the twelve years that the two men spent in London they made many friends.[52]

Luigi Scalia's labours were apparent from his notebook, from which Tina Whitaker quotes how often 'everything went wrong'. 'Palmerston was out,' she wrote on one occasion. Then again: he 'called on Minto. Lady Minto received us as he was out; she was most sympathetic and full of condolences for the fall of Syracuse. Lord Minto returned before we left; he gives us no encouragement.' On another day, Scalia reported having 'dined at Lord Minto's; he said the rising in Ireland had done a great deal of harm to the Sicilian cause; it has frightened the timid. Until July and even until August the English government were determined to help you.' The two men met Nina, Lady Melgund, who was 'most amiable and pretty, and most sympathetic to the sad story of Sicily'.[53]

Lord Minto received a letter from Ralph Abercromby on 19 March telling him that war was about to start in Italy. Written in cypher, the British minister in Turin reported that the Duke of Genoa was about to sail from Nice to Sicily.[54] Simultaneously, the two Sicilian envoys visited Minto with similar news; they had heard that Admirals Parker and Baudin were at Palermo. The former had written to the Sicilian government urging acceptance of the terms offered by the King, though 'not pretending to regard them as satisfactory', a phrase which Minto disliked as it dwelt on Ferdinand's 'gracious benevolence'. The mood in Palermo was strongly in favour of rejection of the King's terms. The populace had made up its mind to 'perish in the ruins of their country rather than submit to Neapolitan tyranny. Both French and English ships saluted the Sicilian flag, and members of the government visiting the admirals were received with salutes and all honours. So far as the Lord Privy Seal was concerned, it now remained to be seen 'What our course will be. We have engaged to recognise the Duke of Genoa who was elected by our advice. Can we abandon him and the Sicilians after every attempt to obtain fair terms from the King of Naples has failed.' He was not very sanguine about London departing from its 'wretched neutrality' but he was prepared to make another effort to induce Lord John to do so. As matters stood, he noted, 'the national honour has been made a sacrifice to the interest of the administration'.[55]

A long letter from Palermo written by Sir William Parker reached Minto on 2 April. In it he described 'the excitement and enthusiasm of all classes in Sicily' but he did not think the population was 'in a condition to make a successful stand against the overwhelming force of the king'. The following morning he spent some time with his son-in-law, whom he thought had come some way towards his views on Italy, and after a short meeting of the cabinet Palmerston spoke to Minto of 'his wish that we should write to the King of Naples' and 'insist upon his giving them a free, separate, representative government'. Minto naturally agreed with him but he wanted him to go further. However, he recognised that with Charles Wood, the Chancellor, and other members of the cabinet 'riding the non-interference hobby so roughly', Lord John's patience was being sorely tried. That evening he attended a debate in the House of Lords and called on Signor Granatelli on his way home.[56]

The next day, 4 April, the earl and countess accompanied by Captain Charles, their thirty-year-old son who was without a ship, left for the Netherlands, where they were to visit their older son Henry and his wife Annie at the embassy in The Hague. A break from his exertions in Naples and Sicily was called for. While at Blackwall docks, Lord Minto saw the *Bombay* detained, as he wrote, under a very 'forced construction of the Foreign Enlistment Act' by the authority of the Treasury. They then embarked for Rotterdam aboard the *Giraffe*, a 'singularly slow steamer, under-powered with only two 60 hp engines, but very steady'.[57] Arriving in the afternoon of the following day, they took a train for the three quarters of an hour journey to The Hague, where they dined with Henry 'in his very comfortable house' but found Annie weak. Having settled in, his father first went to the palace, where his eye was caught by several 'goodish Italian pictures and a good Murillo'. At Haarlem, he inspected the Dutch system of polders. Visits to major art galleries and the King's Library with Lady Minto followed, and during a second meeting with the Queen, Minto learned about her extensive correspondence. Writing in his journal he said, 'she would gladly take an active part in public affairs were she permitted to do so, but she has no influence with the king'. There was none of what Minto called the 'vulgar stiffness which is so offensive at our court'.

In the second week of April they moved on to Antwerp, where the church of St Jacques, the cathedral and the city's many galleries showed them many of the best works by Rubens and Van Dyck which Minto admitted to having underestimated. In Brussels they stayed at the Hotel Bellevue, where Baron Howard de Walden, the minister plenipotentiary, arranged a preliminary meeting with the King's confidential secretary so that he could learn something of Leopold's interest in the affairs of Italy. Surprisingly, the secretary explained that Leopold entertained 'an intense hatred of Palmerston, even forgetting his habitual prudence and reserve in the terms in which he sometimes expresses his dislike of him'. When Minto had his audience with the King it lasted three quarters of an hour. He found him in better spirits than their previous meeting and anxious to talk about German as well as Italian affairs. Austria, he thought, was not disposed to interfere by force in Central Italy but he spoke very complacently about his own policies and government. Lord Howard arranged a dinner for Minto later that day so that he could meet many of the King's ministers before he and Lady Minto left for Calais but this was complicated by the party taking the wrong train and spending an unnecessary night at the Hotel de l'Europe in Lille, where there was snow on the ground.[58]

The railway carriage used by Lord and Lady Minto for the onward journey to Calais on 18 April was 'very luxurious and well-warmed by hot water cases'. It had snowed all night and the snow was lying in the fields inches deep. They reached Calais in the middle of the day intending to sail at ten that night but that would have brought them into Dover at low water in the middle of the night and the ladies would have had to land on the beach from boats. Lord Minto thought it 'better not to expose Mary to that operation' and they decided to await the next morning's packet. With time to spare, Charles and his father went over a French screw steam packet which was to take over the night mail. She was 'the sharpest sea-going vessel', and said to be one of the fastest. Minto noticed that her engines were facsimiles of those in HMS *Fairy*, tender to the *Victoria and Albert*, the Royal Yacht.[59]

After embarking at five o'clock in the morning, the family had a difficult passage to Dover in rain, wind and snow. Everyone except Lord and Lady Minto was sick. They came up to town by the ten o'clock train and went straight to see Fanny. That evening his Lordship was in the House listening to a question put to Lansdowne by Lord Stanley, the Tory leader. The following morning he saw both Granatelli and Scalia, who told him that it was the Attorney-General's opinion that the detention of the *Bombay* was 'justified on the ground of an affidavit sworn by Mr Aubrey who declares that soldiers recruited by him for the Sicilian service were to embark in her'. This falsehood was, Minto concluded, the reason for the vessel's delayed sailing. According to his Lordship, Aubrey was an 'adventurer originally introduced to the notice of the Sicilian government by a Mr Farley who had taken service there and subsequently been expelled from the island'. Aubrey called himself a lieutenant colonel and claimed to be a friend of Colonel Bouverie, a member of Prince Albert's household.[60] According to Lord Minto's journal he had while in Sicily 'undertaken to raise a force of 2000 Irish for the Sicilian service and to have received some money to defray his expenses to England'.[61]

Before attending a cabinet meeting on 21 April which was to sit very late discussing foreign affairs, Lord Minto had gone to the Privy Council office with Lord Melgund, now in the Commons as the Member for Greenock, to consult the secretary-architect about a school he was promoting at Lochgelly in Fife. That evening he attended 'an august diplomatic and ministerial dinner' given by the French Admiral Cécile. Among those present were Lords Lansdowne, Clanricarde and Palmerston; Lionel Rothschild, a member of the eminent Reventlow family; and Graf von Colloredo-Wallsee, the Austrian ambassador in London. The admiral's niece was 'a pretty little woman' and the only lady of the party. Minto sat next to the admiral and 'got a good deal of information from him respecting the system, regulations and administration of the French navy'. Returning to Eaton Square, where Anna Maria and Catherine Elliot were staying, he found another letter from Sir William Parker with an account of the new atrocities committed by the Neapolitans in Sicily.[62]

Two days later Minto paid another visit to Granatelli, whom he had now taken to calling 'Prince', and Scalia, both of whom were anxious to have the attention of Parliament called to Sicilian affairs. It was, they thought, something that had to be done 'without waiting'.[63] However, on 25 April, he visited both Lord John and Palmerston to urge that Britain and France should protect Piedmont from 'the excessive and unjustifiable demands made by Austria', a view which his cabinet colleagues were 'much-inclined to'. He hoped this could be achieved despite 'the far niente section' of the cabinet. In the case of Sicily, the King of Naples should at least be told that Britain wanted the island to have a free constitution, and not 'insincere and artificial terms'. So far as the *Bombay* was concerned, Palmerston told Minto she was to be released although, mysteriously, 'no damages or compensation for her detention were to be demanded!'[64]

On 26 April, the Lord Privy Seal met the Marquis of Sauli, the Sardinian minister in London, at Eaton Square during the afternoon and spent the evening with Fanny. The following day, Sicilian affairs were being discussed in both Houses of Parliament. Speaking in the Commons, Disraeli asked Lord John whether he had any intention of assisting the provisional Sicilian government by releasing the *Bombay*, or whether it was their intention to let the case be adjudicated upon by the courts in the usual way. The Prime Minister said there had been reason to believe that the ship's detention by the Board of Admiralty came under the provisions of the Foreign Enlistment Act but the opinion of the Crown's law officers was still awaited.[65] After a long cabinet meeting on 28 April, Lord Minto said he thought the time had come for him to speak 'without reserve' when the subject of Sicily was next mooted in Parliament. He had 'no wish to force any change of opinion upon the majority of the cabinet' with whom he differed, but wanted to protect his 'public honour', his catch-all defence at that time. He could not 'suffer his name to go down to posterity'. He concluded by writing in his journal that 'we shall see what happens when I have spoken out in public'. In the meantime, he thought that his disagreement was leading to 'more effective and energetic' action to secure fairer terms for the Sicilians.[66]

The Mintos attended numerous social occasions during the first week in May. Sir Edmund Antrobus, Henry's father-in-law, held a large party. There was a dinner at the Royal Academy, then the cabinet dinner at the Lansdownes, followed a day or so later by another at the Lansdownes which the earl described as 'a senile party'. At the weekend, Lord Minto rode to Richmond to visit the Russells and the Melgunds, who were living in the neighbourhood. A day or so later, Signor Carpi from Rome called on Minto with an introduction from Lord Beaumont, and left the impression of being an 'intelligent and well-informed man'. He was known to Minto as a representative of a small republican faction but he went on to explain that there was 'something approaching unanimity in the demands for a complete separation of the Civil and Ecclesiastical power in the country'. Whereupon, Minto asked him if this extended to the absolute rejection of the temporal sovereignty of the Pope, to which he replied that 'if it was possible to have the Pope on the same footing as the Queen of England' and exercising 'no power or authority except through ministers responsible to the nation', the Pope's sovereignty 'might be borne'.[67]

Lord Minto continued to ride as much as possible and paid several visits to Pembroke Lodge with his sailor son. At the end of May Charlie encountered his father talking to a Mr Pasini, a gentleman on a mission from Venice, a few days before the family enjoyed a concert at court. There the earl met Baron Bunsen, the envoy extraordinary of Frederick William IV, King of Prussia, who was 'quietly elated by his monarch's proclamation of a constitution for Germany' although it had as yet only been accepted by a few of the smaller states. It excluded Austria from the union, admitting her simply as an ally.[68]

The late minister of foreign affairs at Rome called at Eaton Square the next day. Signor Rusconi was in London to solicit British intervention but Minto had to explain that he believed the state of public opinion prevented the government from thinking it could 'make itself a party in the discussions of Italy and other powers'. Roman emissaries met with no success either politically or financially. Palmerston had been willing to give good advice but he would not move a finger officially. He had given his opinion to another Italian in clear terms ten days before when he told him to 'advise those who govern the republic to treat with France, immediately and with frankness'. It was not long before disheartening news was arriving for the Triumvirs in Rome from several quarters.[69]

As temperatures rose steadily across southern Europe there was a flurry of letters from Sir William Parker, Captain Pelham (who commanded the steam-paddle frigate HMS *Odin*), and Captain Richard Dundas of HMS *Powerful*, the latter two being both in the Mediterranean, describing final arrangements for the possible evacuation of Palermo. The last lap was at hand and the naval men involved were 'much gratified'. French officers, on the other hand, were 'mortified and displeased' that the town should have been saved by English intervention sought by the Sicilians, who refused to confide in them.[70] A few days later, Lord Minto received a short letter from Captain Astley Key of HMS *Bulldog*, then at Civitavecchia, the port for Rome. He had learned that General Oudinot had just received orders from Paris 'to proceed with the attack on Rome immediately'. The Pope had been overthrown by the revolutionary republicans, causing Louis Napoleon to send a task force to mediate between the Papal and Republican sides in Rome. The Roman Republic resented the French intrusion and attacked the task force, whereupon Louis Napoleon increased the French presence. When Minto received the captain's news, the siege of Rome was about to start, the result of which being that Rome was recaptured and the Pope reinstated.[71]

In the summer of 1849, the Neapolitan government opened a campaign of persecution against Granatelli and Luigi Scalia through its representative at the Court of St James's, Prince Castelcicala. On two previous occasions he had failed to prove embezzlement on the part of the two envoys. Money had been voted for the purchase of two ships in England, with technical assistance for the two political envoys being provided by Benedetto Castiglia, who 'spared no effort to obtain the best possible vessels' for the amount of money at their disposal.[72] Messrs Allen and Brodie Wilcox, the latter being the son of one of the directors of the Peninsular & Oriental Steam Navigation Company, gave their advice and guaranteed the ships chosen.[73] Castelcicala now saw an opportunity to bring an action against them 'for manning a ship on British territory' and engaging men to fight against the King of Naples. They were, wrote Tina Whitaker, 'entirely innocent of the charge, which could not be proved'. The trial took place on 6 July 1849. Sir Fitzroy Kelly spoke for nearly three hours in defence of the two Sicilians, who were found not guilty. Lord Palmerston, who had given evidence in their favour, would not even bow to the Neapolitan government's representative as he left the court. Born in England, at Richmond, Castelcicala's father had been minister for the Two Sicilies before him. He was afterwards sent to Palermo as governor, probably as a reward for his zeal.[74]

It soon became the turn of many in Hungary to express their dream of self-determination. Increasing unrest grew among minorities, particularly Magyars, Czechs and Slovaks within the kingdom of Hungary; discontent even spread to the middle classes in Austria, who began to see in the bureaucracy and secret police other unwelcome aspects of the society in which they lived. Palmerston took the view that Italy had the right to be free of dynastic autocracies, but in the case of Hungary a constitutional government was probably the appropriate form of democracy for Magyar malcontents. Unlike Queen Victoria, he took the view that revolutions should be judged on their merits. Budapest wanted complete independence, not more autonomy under the Emperor acting as King of Hungary, so provoking the Austrian government into an open declaration of war. Britain showed no interest in confederacies along the Danube of the kind formulated by Lajos Kossuth, the radical Hungarian politician. There had been some support for South Slavs, Czechs, Slovacs and Romanians which helped a British consciousness to grow but Kossuth's two-year war of independence while Austria was fighting on the plains of Lombardy was ultimately crushed at Világos (now Siria) in August 1849 with aid from the Czar, who sent his armies across the Carpathians to assist the Emperor.

Despite his sympathy for Hungary, Palmerston made no protest to Czar Nicholas about his part in its suppression, simply expressing the hope that her troops would be withdrawn quickly. Austria on the other hand seemed to him 'a European necessity'. However, in September when the Russians were about to leave, a joint Austro-Russian declaration was promulgated demanding the extradition of Kossuth and other rebels then in the safety of Turkey. When it became known that the Porte had been persuaded by the British and French ambassadors, Stratford Canning and General Aupick, to refuse their surrender, the Russell government supported the action, 'if possible in cooperation with France'.[75]

At the beginning of October Minto wrote to Lord John saying how refreshing it was to see that 'our sense of honour [was] not extinct'. He hoped that Russia would 'pause in her course' when she found Britain was in earnest. Then, leaning again on his experience at the Admiralty and the interest he had continued to take in all things maritime, he advised his son-in-law that to co-operate with the Porte in the event of a threatened attack, the British fleet should pass the Dardanelles. It would also 'be well to slip out two or three ships of the line very quietly to reinforce Parker with a few additional steamers'. Minto was of the opinion that the Russians could muster about twelve sail of the line in the Black Sea and hoped that there would be no need of fighting.[76]

Admiral Parker was ordered to Besika Bay not far from the entrance to the Dardanelles in case Turkey needed help and a French squadron was sent to Smyrna. Moving his flag to HMS *Queen*, he began his second consecutive term as commander-in-chief Mediterranean but two weeks after his last letter to Lord John, Minto still wanted an increase in Parker's fleet, warning that 'time may be of the utmost importance and the game lost in waiting for reinforcements'. If the movement of Russian troops and naval activity at Sevastopol had a threatening aspect, he thought Parker ought 'to be at hand, with authority to pass through the Dardanelles'.[77] Palmerston on the other hand wrote to the Prime Minister a week later to say that 'as long as our ships are in the Mediterranean Russia cannot say that their movements are aimed at her'. He had also pointed out to Baron Brunnow, the Russian ambassador in London, that this arrangement was no threat to Russia.[78]

During that summer Fanny's third son, Francis Albert Rollo, had been born at Pembroke Lodge and, on 10 July, the Russells opened a village school at nearby Petersham. It was to be an enterprise in which Fanny took particular interest and one that was soon able to refute the forecast of an old gentleman that a school 'would ruin the aristocratic character of the village'. Then, after the Prime Minister's visit to the Queen at Balmoral in September, where 'no hostess could [have been] more charming or more easy … or more kind and agreeable than the Prince', Lord John returned to London with a rather surprising plan in mind, to extend the suffrage.[79] When he outlined his thoughts to the cabinet on 9 October, 'all looked grave. Sir Charles Wood and Lord Lansdowne expressed some alarm' according to the entry in Fanny's diary. Enlarging on what she had been told by her husband, she wrote that

> to grant [more] weight to the people of this country when revolutions are taking place on all sides, when a timid Ministry would rather seek to diminish that which they already have, is to show a noble trust of them.[80]

It was, however, to be some time before he could bring the matter to the House, and then only as a way of maintaining support for his administration. Reform had been stimulated in Parliament in June and July 1848 when Joseph Hume backed the Chartists and put forward a 'Little Charter' for household suffrage, secret ballots, triennial parliaments and more equal electoral districts only to find that Lord John was against it, believing as he did that the Great Reform Act of 1832 had been in effect a 'final' settlement.

At the start of 1850 yet another action brought by Ferdinand II in the High Court of Chancery in London finally closed a chapter in Anglo-Sicilian affairs. The King sought to establish the extent to which the purchase of the *Vectis* and the *Bombay* had involved fraud or illegality, and since both Prince Granatelli and Luigi Scalia had been signatories to the contract of purchase there was considerable concern about the outcome of the case. However, after hearings on 28 and 29 January, and 8 February, it was decided that as the members of the revolutionary government of Sicily had entrusted the two London envoys 'with monies with which they had purchased the steamships', they were not made parties to the suit.[81]

Back in London, Fanny wrote two longish letters in November 1850 to her sister Mary in Italy describing the events which had followed the Pope's decision in September to divide England into twelve sees. Bigoted outcries started by the Papal Bull were not helped by an intemperate letter written by Lord John to his friend the Bishop of Durham in which he denounced the Pope's 'aggression' as 'insolent and insidious'. He also chastised 'the unworthy sons of the Church of England' who indulged in 'mummeries of superstition'. This lost him the confidence of Irish Members and Peelites, and his support for toleration, so highly regarded by Fanny, had been seriously compromised. The Prime Minister had acted without consulting his colleagues in cabinet about any aspect of the 'Durham Letter'.

In the first of her letters to Italy, Fanny expressed her pleasure that the Abercrombys 'had liked John's letter to the Bishop of Durham' but she had not expected Roman Catholics, whose 'claims to toleration and equality of civil rights' he had defended all his life, to 'take offence because he [declared] himself a despiser of the superstitious imitation of Roman Catholic ceremonies by clergymen of the Church of England'. Ireland, she wrote, had 'taken fire at the whole letter, and most of all at the word "mummeries"'. Then giving herself some comfort that 'no amount of dislike to any creed' could shake her own conviction for a moment, Fanny went on to say that 'complete toleration to every creed and conviction [was] the only right and safe rule … at all times and on all occasions'. The Papal Bull had been 'wrong, but not quite inexcusable' in Fanny's opinion and the 'signal for double-dealing and ingratitude among his spiritual subjects – and consequently for anger and intolerance among Protestants'.[82]

Resuming the argument a week later, Lady John found the change of vicars-apostolic into bishops and archbishops something 'impotent for evil to Protestants' but she assured Mary that her husband had only written as he did after Samuel Hinds, the Bishop of Norwich, had asked him for 'some expression of opinion on the part of the government'. He had then calmly surveyed the state of religion throughout the country, and 'thought he saw that it was in his power to prevent the ruin of the Church of England'. The letter was 'a Protestant one, and could not give great satisfaction to Roman Catholics', written at 'a moment in which he had to choose between a temporary offence to part of their body and the deserved loss of the confidence of the Protestant body, to which he heart and soul' belonged. That Lady Mary had required some assurance, and differed in her opinion from her younger sister, seems certain – with the result she ended her letter by begging Lady

Mary 'not to confound John's letter with the bigotry and intolerance of many speeches at many meetings'.[83]

Queen Victoria opened Parliament In February 1851 to cries of 'no popery' but the immediate issue was one of electoral reform in which the government had little interest, and defeats and resignations followed. Lord John declined to accept a radical electoral reform motion, and when he was defeated by its supporters he promptly resigned. The Queen first sent for the Tory leader, who declined to accept the office. On the 22nd she consulted Lord Aberdeen with a view to encouraging a fusion between Whigs and Peelites but she recalled Lord Russell when this failed. He consented with some hesitation and managed to get through the rest of the session in safety. Meanwhile, Palmerston was disturbing both the Prime Minister and the Queen's equanimity. Kossuth, the leader of the Hungarian revolution, had just arrived in Britain and when the cabinet ordered Palmerston not to meet him, he received a radical deputation instead, and refused to rebuke them for making violently hostile references to the Austrian and Russian emperors.

There was, however, some relief at hand. On 2 December, Louis Napoleon made himself the absolute head of the French government by a coup d'état, with the intention of re-establishing the imperial Napoleonic dynasty. In a casual conversation with the French ambassador, Palmerston expressed his approbation of the new form of government. This friendly recognition was exactly opposite to the feelings of both Lord John and the Queen. The Prime Minister asked for Palmerston's resignation and offered him another office, which he declined, and the seals of the Foreign Office were transferred to Lord Granville. Predictably, Russell's administration was in a state of some confusion as Palmerston devoted his energies to bringing down the government. In February 1852, the ex-minister condemned the government's Militia Bill and carried an amendment against it. Recognising that the feeling of Parliament was hostile to the government, Lord John straightway resigned. Within two months of his own dismissal Palmerston had driven his colleagues from office; one of his biographers reported him as saying, 'I have had my tit-for-tat with John Russell and turned him out.'[84] The Queen asked Lord Derby to form a new administration, and he nominated Disraeli as Chancellor of the Exchequer and Leader of the Commons. Five months later, after a general election, Derby's Home Secretary, Viscount Palmerston, was to form his first government.[85]

Lord Minto's service as Lord Privy Seal had started with his mission to Rome in 1847 and moved through several phases, not the least of which had been his support for Sicily and his uneasy relationship with his son-in-law. It was now over, he was in his seventies and would not return to office or play any further part in politics despite continuing to sit and vote in the Lords. Lord John, on the other hand, was to occupy himself with editing and writing several literary works, including a life of Charles James Fox and the memoirs of his friend Tom Moore, the poet. During the summer of 1852 correspondence between Lord Aberdeen, the Duke of Newcastle, Sir James Graham and Gladstone developed earlier ideas of an alliance between Whigs and Peelites to the point where a fusion or the creation of a new political party might have been possible. This influenced the make-up of Aberdeen's cabinet, formed after the general election of December, and which surprisingly included Lord John as Foreign Secretary for two months until February the following year. Then the Earl of Clarendon succeeded him and Fanny's husband became Leader of the House of Commons and Minister without Portfolio until June 1854. Lord John had been hesitant about joining Aberdeen's administration and it was the Queen, anxious to avoid calling on Palmerston, who persuaded him to accept the post. Her Majesty thought the moment had arrived for a government to be formed by the 'sincere and united efforts of all parties professing Conservative and Liberal opinion' and trusted that Lord John would give 'his valuable and powerful assistance to the realisation of this object'.[86]

During this period it seems that Lady Minto had gone to stay with her eldest daughter at Nervi on the coast south of Genoa on account of her health. Then sixty-seven years old, and described as 'alarmingly ill', she may have had a recurrence of the fever and swollen limbs that had so affected her during the first half of 1833. Writing from Downing Street on Christmas Eve, Fanny sought to reassure Lady Mary that her thoughts were with their Mama but there was still much 'to dread'. Her own news – or her 'painful *public* anxiety' – turned on how odious she had always thought it would be were Lord John to take office under Lord Aberdeen. Continuing in what she called her 'grumpy' mood, she complained about the 'want of high motives and aims' which she found in 'the buzzers who hover round the house while the honest and pure and upright keep away and are silent'.[87]

Lady Minto was well enough to write 'a bright and happy letter of congratulation' to Fanny on the birth of her granddaughter, Mary Agatha, which occurred on 28 March 1853 but four months later she was dead (21 July). The funeral took place in August at Minto, where, as Lord John said, it was 'very sorrowful to see Lord Minto and so many of his sons and daughters assembled to perform the last duties to her who was the life and comfort of them all'. The house and estate looked beautiful and Lady Minto's garden 'never so lovely' wrote Lord John to his wife, who had been required to remain at Pembroke Lodge. It was, however, 'pleasant in all these sorrows and trials to see a family so united in affection, and so totally without feelings or objects that partake of selfishness or ill-will'.[88]

The countess had married her husband when she was twenty years old, and the couple had enjoyed forty-seven years of happy marriage. Together whenever the exigencies of the earl's work allowed, and devoted to the upbringing and happiness of their ten children, there had been times when financial crises threatened the very existence of the home and estate in Roxburghshire. She became the society hostess her diplomat husband's position required, and on numerous occasions helped him interpret the worrying behaviour of foreign dignitaries who did not like, and had to be brought round to respect, the British view of the world. She had been the exact partner for the son of a barrister, whose adventurous and successful diplomatic career had been crowned by becoming governor-general of India. Her husband possessed considerable political influence, but it was Lady Minto who taught him how to use it.

# 10

# WILLIAM – SCOTTISH POLITICIAN AND SOCIAL REFORMER (1837-1891)

William Hugh Elliot, Viscount Melgund, the eldest of the family's five boys, was born on 19 March 1814. After leaving Eton he went up to Trinity College, Cambridge, where he stayed until 1836, and was awarded an MA degree. He entered as a Pensioner but was soon upgraded to a Nobleman. His tutors included Wlliam Whewell, who was to become Master of Trinity in 1841[1] and Connop Thirlwall.[2] Lord Melgund came sixth out of a class of nine in his first year and had been excused the examination in his second year. He took his third-year examination in 1835.

He showed little propensity to follow his father's profession as a diplomat while the family were in Prussia. Instead, and while only twenty, he seems to have entertained the thought of standing for the Roxburghshire seat, where local Whigs, Liberals and freeholders would have 'zealously attended' him. In November 1835, his father wrote him a congratulatory note after taking his final examination, adding somewhat irately that he had seen a newspaper report that he had joined 'an unhallowed set', the University Pitt Club, which had been formed by undergraduates that year for the avowed purpose of influencing borough elections in favour of Tory candidates. Lord Minto wanted his son to keep himself apart from such a set.[3]

The following month when William had returned to Minto, Lady Minto said she hoped he would remain there 'even if you are alone; it is a comfort to me to think that the poor old place is not entirely deserted'. She could hardly imagine anyone wishing to leave it who could remain. Both she and her husband had only taken up residence at the Admiralty in London three months before when he became the First Lord and she was already longing to walk round her 'own dear garden' at Minto. Parties, which his mother enjoyed, and which she knew William would have hated – even two with Fanny and Lord Russell at Pembroke Lodge – had been part of his father's responsibilities, and they were to stay at Bowood for a short time before Christmas.[4]

It was May 1837 when William, then aged twenty-three, became the Member of Parliament for Hythe but he never gained the universal support of the constituency and in June 1841 his father took a deliberate hand in matters, suggesting a number of alternative constituencies where he might stand, including Rochester, but he left the decision too late. In August 1842, William went to Russia to visit his younger brother Henry, who had been appointed a paid attaché at St Petersburg. The junior diplomat thought that if he could obtain some leave he might return to England with William but his brother had plans to go as far as Moscow in the company of a friend, one Studholm Brownrigg. They planned to follow the River Volga some distance, 'cut across to Odessa and then steam up the Danube to Vienna and so home'. The two brothers did, however, find time for a shooting expedition in Finland which, as Henry told his father, was 'altogether very pleasant and almost entirely without drawbacks … except some in the shape of fleas and bugs but even these were less formidable than [they] had expected'. Before they started, neither could find anyone who could tell them 'anything whatever about the country, not even those parts within a couple of hundred miles of St Petersburg'.[5]

His father rarely lost an opportunity of telling William the political news of the day, or how important it was for him as his father's heir to keep in touch with all members of the family. One such occasion occurred on 24 November 1842 when Lord Minto wrote to William about the 'unexpected vexation' inflicted on the family 'in the shape of a most malicious complaint' against his sailor brother Charlie by Mr Gleig, the father of one of his midshipmen – already described in Chapter 6. At the Admiralty, Lord Minto said there was every disposition 'to deal fairly and favourably with the case' but both Lord Haddington and Lord Cockburn were always 'troublingly afraid of attacks from the Press or in Parliament' and their timidity made them shrink from acting on their own views and responsibility. They had therefore resolved to refer the case to a court-martial. He thought this might ultimately be the best course for Charles as it would enable him to disprove every imputation against himself in public. Since a ship was going out almost immediately with orders for the court-martial there was 'time for you to write by her'.[6]

Three days later, the Admiralty was 'half inclined to order HMS *Spartan* home' so that Charles could be tried in England but his father protested against this. The *United Services Gazette* published a scurrilous article full of incorrect statements and, writing from Brooks's Club, William's father could see that it would be soon copied into the *Kelso Mail*. He advised William to let the local press know the case as far as it had been reported and also told him that no statement would be made to newspapers.[7] Over the following days, Admiral George, William's uncle, was able to confirm that the court-martial would take place on the station, and although his father's fears about its outcome subsided, he wrote 'volumes' to Charlie 'by the West India mail'.

In July the following year, Lady Minto wrote from Roxburghshire, her letter being addressed in the first instance to her brother-in-law, Vice Admiral Sir Charles Adam, at Admiralty House, Halifax, Nova Scotia. William was in Jamaica, the southerly extreme of the West Indies and North Atlantic station, having left England to be with Charlie at the conclusion of his court-martial. She told William and Charlie that their brother Gibby had joined the Rifle Brigade with a little help from his father, having seen 'letter after letter from half the tailors in London' arriving for 'the Hon. Gilbert Elliot, Rifle Brigade'. He was

all life and energy, working hard with Mr Smith and with Lizzy, brushing up French and German, reading military books and practising with the rifle – a beautiful one Lord Minto has given him – very zealously; in short, he is as nice a boy … amazingly like Henry in many ways.

Gilbert was to join the regiment at once in Corfu, and not its depot in Ireland. The family at Minto were to go to Edinburgh to have him measured and get part of his outfit, something which saved a journey and longish stay in London.

Just how the thirty-year-old William came to meet and marry Emma Eleanor Elizabeth Hislop (and known as Nina) is not clear. The Hislops lived at 36 Wilton Crescent, her father being General Sir Thomas Hislop, who had died the previous year. Her mother was a daughter of Hugh Elliot, making her a distant cousin of her husband. Never strong in health, Nina had the spirit of a soldier and wherever she went, according to John Buchan, she 'radiated an atmosphere of gentleness, mirth and courage'. The young couple were married on 20 May 1844 and were to have four sons: Gilbert John, who became the fourth Earl Minto; Arthur Ralph Douglas, who at the age of four had to have a leg amputated but who climbed, rode, shot and swam throughout his life; Hugh Frederick; and Lt-Col. William Fitzwilliam.[8]

As Harriet's journal recorded, on the morning of William and Nina's wedding she got up and dressed before breakfast and drove to the church with Ama Boileau. Carry Boileau went with Lady Minto, Lizzy and Bob'm, reaching the church at 11.30 a.m. She found the vestry nearly full. Nina, who was 'very prettily dressed and looked really pretty', was given away by Frederick Elliot. William looked 'beautiful'. Harriet described how they followed Nina, two by two, the bridesmaids being Lizzy and Lady Lucy Pelham, Bob'm and Harriet, Ama and Miss Ross, Addy (Adelaide Lister) and Harriet Elliot. The service was read by Uncle Gilbert and 'his impressive voice made it most excellent'. Lady Hislop and all 'behaved well'. Then, having assembled again in the vestry, they drove to Wilton Crescent, where they 'were talking and busy downstairs' until the breakfast was ready. The inner drawing room had a long table where sat Lord and Lady Minto, Henry, Fanny, Lord John, Gina and Lord Northesk, Hersey and Mrs Wauchope, Sir Frederick and Lady Nicholson, Frederick Elliot, Uncle Gilbert, Mrs Plumridge, George Eden (Lord Auckland), Miss Eden, Mrs and Miss Vansittart, Mr James Colvile, Mr Arthur Drummond, Mr and Mrs R. Eden, Mr Richardson, Lady Buckinghamshire,[9] Lady Mary Pelham, Miss Elphinstone, and William and Nina – who 'talked, ate and laughed as much as possible'. Lady Hislop sat at a small side table with Mr Henry Elliot, Jemima, Freddy, Carry, Little Hughy and Gibby, while in the outer room the bridesmaids had a table at which also sat Doddy, Augustus, Willy Adam (the son of Admiral Sir Charles Adam[10]), Mr George Fitzwilliam and Captain Stewart, who made 'many jokes'. In the evening of the great day Henry and Doddy joined the Mintos for dinner, after which Lady Minto, Henry, Lizzy and Bob'm went to a ball at the home of Madame de Salis.[11]

William's marriage reawakened his desire to become a Scottish MP and he took to examining all manner of infrastructure plans, including those for railways, and matters specifically affecting Scottish trade. It greatly pleased his father to see that he had been to a meeting about the Fife Railroad. Developers contended that the line should go through Kinross, although his father thought it would be better going east of Lochleven, but it was a question that ought to be decided after careful survey and consideration of the accommodation afforded by each option.[12]

During the summer of 1845, however, William decided to undertake a protracted journey on the Continent with Nina and baby Gilbert, who had been born in July. Their carriage was especially fitted with a shelf to serve as the baby's crib while the entourage included a courier, nurse, and lady's maid. Lord Minto had seen an account given by Nina of the proposed travelling arrangements and could not resist giving William 'the result of my experience in such matters'. As regards comfort and convenience, he said, 'there is nothing like an English chariot for the number of people it is calculated to carry – and its stowage – but on the other hand you must lay your account to its requiring certainly not less than from £70–100 of refit after its travels on the continent'. His father warned him that he was pretty sure that he would find his allowance insufficient for such a party and 'it would annoy me seriously if I found you had any scruples about drawing for two or three hundred pounds on Coutts where needful'.[13]

It was the second day of 1846 as the party was travelling up the Rhine to Switzerland and over the St Gotthard Pass into Italy when Lord Minto wrote to William. Appreciating that William had probably followed the London news through reading Galignani's *Messenger*, his father explained that Lockhart Elliot would be the Duke of Roxburghe's candidate. He would of course be elected, but the 'patriots' of Hawick and Selkirk had resolved to have a contest. It was his belief that a very few years more would 'suffice to recover that county out of the Duke's hands'. He intended to quarter himself with Lord John at Richmond for a few days before going up to a meeting of Parliament.[14]

Returning to Minto between debates at Westminster, his father kept William abreast of such hunting as had been possible, always a subject of great interest between them. By February, however, Lord Minto indicated that he would be writing on William's behalf to Lord John and Henry Tufnell, who had been his private secretary when he was at the Admiralty, 'begging them to give you a better notion than I can ... of the period at which your presence [in London] may be desirable'. Dissolution was in the air and an election could be William's opportunity to return to Westminster. In the meantime, if William and Nina found themselves in Naples, his father asked to be 'remembered to Salvadore Madonna ... if he is still alive and officiates in doing the honours of the crater'.[15]

Near the end of March there was some doubt about how long William and Nina's 'Roman Holiday' would last. Lord Minto heard that Willy Gibson Craig, the MP for Midlothian, had suggested William might like to stand for the Haddington burghs which were about to be vacated by the conservative James Maitland Balfour of Whittinghame. His confidential note suggested that he should proceed with a canvass immediately but Lord Minto held back, leaving the matter for William to decide. Nevertheless, he seems to have 'taken measures to obtain accurate information as to the state and real strength of parties in the five Burghs' and at the beginning of April he was in touch with Sir James Gibson Craig, Willy's father, well known in Edinburgh for his integrity and kindness. He assured him about William's readiness to become a candidate. By then other constituencies were being mentioned, one being in Fife, where he might be a welcome candidate for the Liberals on account of Francis Wemyss-Douglas's retirement, although Lord Minto thought it would be 'rather a formidable undertaking'.[16]

These and other ideas were sent to Naples but William had not given his father a reply, which annoyed him somewhat, especially as the fate of Peel's government was about to be decided. Furthermore, 'having decided to emigrate in the autumn', Lord Minto's arrangements were 'thwarted by the apprehension of being involved in any ministerial change that may be at hand'. Both father and son were at a crossroads in their political lives. He told William that he and his mother had taken a house next to Farrance's Hotel in Belgrave Street and intended 'to employ two or three months in the contraction of debt before we fly to the continent from our creditors'.[7] Correspondence with William the following month stressed the need for him to be back in England. The important second reading of the Irish Coercion Bill was expected in the House of Commons on the 26th. The upshot was, however, that Minto felt there would probably be no need for William to hurry on so long as he and Nina could reach Lucerne. From there, 'steam and railroads' would bring them towards London without much delay. William asked that any later news his father had should be addressed to Lyon *poste restante*.[18]

Writing to William the following spring, when he had been attending the House of Lords and was about to help push through Lord John's Irish Poor Law Bill, Lord Minto advised his son on a number of matters about which any prospective Member of Parliament could expect to be questioned. If he was to be an effective Scottish parliamentarian he had to study at least some of the differences between English law and that north of the border. One issue was the question of civil registration of births, deaths and marriages which had begun in England in 1837, but a scheme for Scotland which would have tackled the problem of irregular marriages – for example, those carried out by a blacksmith at Gretna Green – was thrown out. The expense of registration was understandably objected to by the poor and there was a long-standing dispute about who should keep the new registers. His father promised William he should have the text of the Registration and Marriage Bills as amended – and parts of a proposed bill for madhouses in Scotland for him to read. 'You will find the law of marriage in Scotland sufficiently explained in Erskine's Institutes,' he said, and 'the importance of an accurate registration of births, deaths and marriages is sufficiently obvious'. The want of it had long been the subject of popular complaint in Scotland.

Lord Minto went on to say how much he felt it desirable to leave the law unaltered. Marriage was a civil contract and evidence of such contracts should be clear and precise, and be of such a nature as to indicate due deliberation. There were, he said, three old acts on the statute book against clandestine marriages, or those now called 'irregular marriages' which could not be solemnised by the established clergy. He now supposed that the sanction to be given by the bill to marriages before the Registrar without ecclesiastical intervention would take them out of the category of 'irregular marriage' but there would be a penalty on the non-registration of a birth, death or marriage. So far as he could see, this did not exist in the English Act and although some were lobbying for similar terms, the registrar-general for England stated that 'the want of it to be a great and injurious defect' in the English legislation, so much so that an amendment was already under consideration.[19] A month later Lord Minto referred to the fact that 'our Registration and Marriage Bills have been condemned by the General Assembly'.[20]

Having also touched on legislation affecting the manner of disposing of pauper lunatics in Scotland, as part of William's apprenticeship on 3 May his Lordship turned to the question of parish schools. In a speech in Parliament, Lord John had expressed the belief that 'you never could effectually raise education in this country till you raised the condition and prospects of the schoolmaster'. He suggested that all the schoolmaster's stipend, beyond the minimum required by law, might be considered as a voluntary contribution as well as all the house accommodation beyond what was prescribed by statute. Schools also needed to be inspected, and conducted so as 'not necessarily to exclude the children of any persuasion'. It was also 'of the utmost importance that provision should be made for the removal of bad or inefficient schoolmasters and for the superannuation of the old and infirm'. Lord Minto mentioned that the Prime Minister, Lord John, proposed to allow pensions for teachers with fifteen years' service.[21]

Towards the end of May, Henry, who was home on leave, wrote to his father from Edinburgh, apologising for not telling him 'what had been going on about Greenock'. William had decided to return to the parliamentary scene, allowing his name to go forward as a candidate for the Greenock constituency whereas Lord John Hay, having become superintendent of Woolwich Dockyard, chose to represent Windsor instead. His lawyer brother was convinced that 'if the thing goes right it will have many advantages over Haddington', the smallest of them being 'its cheapness'. The previous election against a Walter Baine had cost £250.[22] Writing from Glasgow on 31 May, Henry told his father that he had met a deputation from Greenock comprising one Tory, one Free Churchman and a Roman Catholic, who gave a 'very flourishing' account of affairs. He had also seen 'a vague sort of address' which William had written out and shown to the men in the deputation.[23] At the end of the first day's canvass, the agents declared there were fewer defections of people who had promised their votes to Lord John than they expected.[24] The following day Lord Minto was sent the first of several abstracts which included the best estimates of votes in the five wards of the constituency, both for and against William. Other reports showed no evidence of bribery, particularly in those wards which were 'remarkably respectable' and by the afternoon of the third day's canvass, results were 'particularly good'. The canvassers were also to 'dine with one of the great Free Kirk men' in the hope that it might have a good effect, while the opposition candidate, Alexander Dunlop, was putting about his wish to have a public meeting where he and William were to be pitted against each other.[25] Henry told his father that he would 'not be sorry when this work is over for it is rather severe in the heat which one has to be out in all day'.[26] Having concluded by the end of the month that William had little more to do than 'get through some visits of civility to his chief supporters', Henry returned to Minto, catching a late train from Glasgow.[27]

It took some time for Lord Minto to appreciate how much work had been put in at Greenock but by the beginning of June he acknowledged the effect that William and Henry's letters had had on him, telling the candidate 'they have put me in good heart and I have made up my mind that your spirit in coming forward is to be rewarded with success'. He had spoken at length with Lord Russell, who, despite the need to show neutrality in such matters, was 'most eager and anxious' for William's success. Privately, the Prime Minister had received conflicting reports about his prospects.[28] Lord Minto was convinced that Greenock was likely to make a more grateful constituency than a small district of burghs and admitted candidly that what had been achieved had been done by William without 'further interference' from him. 'I will not conceal,' he said, 'that I look with pride and satisfaction upon the spirit and decision and independence of your course on this occasion.'[29] A report in a Greenock newspaper applauded at least one of William's speeches greatly. By 25 June, Minto hoped to be able to tell him the probable date on which Parliament would be prorogued but it was 'impossible to speak confidently' and his best estimate was about 20 July, with the election in the first week of August.[30]

In fact, the household at Eaton Square attended the obsequies of Parliament and wished Godspeed to the new writs on 23 July but neither activity prevented William's father sending some of the evidence taken before the Criminal Law Committee of the House of Lords to William in Scotland. The earl had enjoyed a 'little breeze' in

Parliament the previous evening when the Earl of Derby, Edward Stanley, and the Bishop of London condemned any relaxation over religious instruction given in schools while he, Lansdowne and Grey 'contended for the utmost latitude of religious liberty'. Meanwhile, it had been decided that Lord Minto would leave town towards the end of the following week but without Lady Minto. She wanted to wait in London for accounts of Lady Mary's confinement.[31]

Election meetings in Greenock only encouraged Lord Minto to continue his commentary on the education system. This time he wanted to remind William that it was a question 'full of practical difficulties not actually involved in it, but arising out of sectarian jealousy and animosities'. As a member of the Privy Council's committee on education, he was 'not at liberty to say anything more on that subject' save to give the reassurance that 'it was the government's desire to render education acceptable to all classes without distinction of sects'. But the question regarding Catholics was not quite so simple as some people imagined, there 'being amongst them in some quarters a desire to exact conditions which could be objected to'. If the country should pronounce itself in favour of purely secular education from the state, the 'measure would be relieved of much of its difficulty', he argued, but 'we are very far from anything like such a public opinion at present'. 'You are in a community,' he told William, 'where the tide seems to be setting in that direction but in a great part of the country, it runs the other way' and 'you are not quite right in thinking that Scotland has ground of complaint that her Parish Schools are not to the full extent of their endowment by the heritors made partakers of the educational grants'. He ended by saying that he did not like the measure much himself as he would rather have seen the money going to pay poor working parsons.[32]

Amid all the electoral panic, William heard from his father at the end of July that his brother Henry's marriage to Miss Anne Antrobus had been 'happily arranged'. The Antrobus party were about to leave for Ems in Germany for a previously planned visit while Henry was available to join William and Charlie in Scotland 'with a light heart', intending afterwards to follow his in-laws-to-be to the Rhine.[33] However, the news of William's 'triumph', his victory over Dunlop, came on the first day of August. He had won the seat with a majority of eighty-three, being greatly helped by a particularly good speech by Walter Baine, the former MP. The family drank tea together in celebration at Pembroke Lodge and found Lord John eager to read out from Nina's letters what had happened at Greenock. Once Lord Minto felt strong enough, he and Lizzy proposed to go northward and stay in Scotland at Douglas's Hotel.[34]

On the last day of August, however, Lord Minto wrote to William in confidence to tell him that he had agreed to undertake 'a special embassy on the affairs of Italy' to Rome, Turin and Florence which would occupy him until the meeting of the new parliament. The object, he wrote, was 'important and if I am able to do any good in the cause of liberal government, I shall not grudge the labour'. The reader will recall from the previous chapter how his father's mission as Lord Privy Seal turned out.

William was to move into his father's house in Eaton Square, and as the first session of the new parliament would only be a short one, it was decided that Nina and the bairns should remain at Minto. As his father came to understand the timetable of his Italian mission, and that he would not be back until the following spring, he suggested that the younger Elliots might like to 'lodge' themselves in another house with more room. His own income would not suffice now that he was in Parliament and his father said he 'must of course have help' from him. A quiet eve of Christmas in Rome had given Lord Minto the opportunity of thinking these matters through and it seems that the family had been greatly amused by his visit to the Pope a day or so before, wearing 'a morning coat and Scotch trousers'.[35]

While about to respond to Lord Napier's call for his assistance from Naples, the Lord Privy Seal had time to say to William that he not only expected but 'wished him to help himself out of his pocket at Coutts Bank'. 'You cannot,' he wrote, 'make your present income do while in parliament, and I must be saving enough at present to enable me easily to supply you.'[36] Although preoccupied with 'the disgraceful conduct of the Neapolitan ministers', Minto still found time to write to William about Scottish parliamentary business. He had 'great doubts about the practicality of disconnecting our Parish schools altogether from the establishment' and did 'not despair of seeing them practically thrown open, by the abolition of every test, or by bringing them under the direction of a public board which should leave to the church little more than a nominal visitorial right'. William had written about the new government's legislative programme and his father agreed that a Scotch Entail Bill was much wanted.[37] By the time April came, and with his parents requiring Eaton Square again, they hoped that William and Nina would have found somewhere to lodge nearby.[38]

No sooner had 1849 started than *The Times* published what the Lord Privy Seal described as another falsehood. The charge related to earlier promotions and appointments bestowed by him on relations, the favoured targets being Charlie and young George, two sailors named Plumridge[39] and Charles Bethune,[40] Admiral George (his brother) and Charles Adam. It was said that the last had exchanged their seats at the Board of Admiralty for commands which they considered almost the right of the naval lords when they wished it. His father wanted William to appreciate the inaccuracies of the claims. Of the twelve Elliots whose names were in the Navy list only five were related to the family, and of these, he said, 'three only got anything from me – including your Uncle George'. Minto said he had asked Henry Tufnell, who had been his private secretary at the Admiralty, to have his memorandum on the subject conveyed to John Delane, the editor of *The Times*. He thought it right, Minto told William, to put Delane 'in possession of the truth' although he did not suppose that *The Times*, which 'is as infallible as the Pope', would at once acknowledge its error, but like the Pope it might 'possibly seek an opportunity of unsaying in substance what it has written, by publishing the truth'.[41]

Quarrels between the churches in Scotland halfway through the nineteenth century held back the development of a national system of education for more than twenty years. Each had their political influence, the Kirk being identified with conservatism, and liberals with the United Presbyterians and the Free Church. Both were able to organise protests, petitions and public meetings to express their deeply held and different views, and Members of Parliament such as William were often frustrated in their efforts to see learning opportunities for children broadened. Three years before the formation of the National Education Association (NEA), and as part of his almost daily briefings on parliamentary matters, Lord Minto discussed the question of education grants with William, reminding him that they had existed since 1839 – and 'it would have been quite impossible in the present temper of the public to make any progress if we had overstepped the limits hitherto recognised'. So far as Roman Catholics were concerned, he said they had a strong objection to submitting their schools to visitorial inspection under the authority of the Privy Council, and his father was convinced that the whole system was 'extremely imperfect and unsatisfactory', although it might gradually lead to a more liberal provision for national education.[42]

In 1850, the NEA and other reformers saw a school rate and a school committee elected by the ratepayers as a step in the right direction. Local committees could represent the needs of the area, promote the absorption of existing denominational schools into the system and found new schools where needed. Parish schools might continue as a distinctive type but their sectarian character would be ended by the abolition of church supervision and the religious test imposed on schoolmasters. It was thought that separate subsidies from the state would not be needed once denominational schools had been absorbed into the system. For his part, William seems to have been attracted to the secularist programme of the NEA and on 19 June he introduced the second reading of the School Establishments (Scotland) Bill. After providing the House with a historical résumé of legislation in Scotland from an Act of 1494 down to one in 1803 which had not worked as had been intended, he turned to an assessment of the actual condition of education in Scotland, using evidence from the Prison Report of 1846 and a clause in the later Police Act. There were, he said, 883 parish schools with an average attendance of 84 pupils at each, making 74,300 scholars in all. There were 200 supplemental parish schools with an attendance of 16,800 and 125 General Assembly Schools, making a total of 106,000 scholars in attendance in schools of the Established Church. Connected to the Free Church were 626 schools, with 55,000 scholars, where the masters received gratuities. Of non-salaried schools there were 190 with 10,000 scholars. There was, he said, a total of 321,000 children in school and another 180,000 'quite uneducated'.

Lord Melgund's proposed legislation was based on the abolition of all tests. Fifty or sixty teachers had been expelled from parochial schools in recent years for no other reason than they attended the Free Church. He wanted local taxation to continue but for it to be supported by grants from the government. Clauses included one to grant pensions to superannuated schoolmasters and another requiring a strict examination of all schoolmasters prior to their appointment. The estimated total cost of his proposals was, he said, about £125,000 a year, compared with £40,000 for the existing system. Unfortunately when the question was put to the House, the 'Ayes' had ninety-four votes and the 'Noes' a hundred; he had lost by six votes.[43] He was to bring in a second bill the following year, but without success.

As the family left in September 1852 for what was to be an extended stay at the Abercromby's much-loved home at Nervi near Genoa, Lord Minto chose to write a serious and important note to William about the finances of the Minto estate. He clearly had in mind how difficult it might be for the family to go on living a life of relative luxury both in London and Roxburghshire. His father said he 'felt it absolutely necessary to clear off some debt' in the medium term, and a year or so spent in Italy had the advantage of being cheaper than living in London. It was also likely to be a help to Lady Minto's health. Just how concerned Lord Minto had become was demonstrated when he told William that

when you are my age you will discover that the condition of those whom you leave behind is a subject of far more anxiety than any present interest of your own but, as you will only have four paupers instead of ten, these thoughts may sit lighter on your mind in the year 1884 than they do on mine at present.

In truth, he feared that William's position would be anything but pleasant – with 'high rank, a great intensive place [Minto], a very considerable estate at rental, and a very small income for your station'.[44]

The result of the general election of December 1852 did not lessen William's worries. Not only had Lord Derby been defeated but he had failed to be re-elected for Greenock and he would be out of the House of Commons until 1857.

Genoa became Lord and Lady Minto's 'first place of refuge' and William's daily diary for the year 1853 demonstrated how much effort his parents put in to reduce their expenses. Although the Grahams dined with them at the beginning of January, and there were outings from Nervi to Genoa with Charlie, who arrived from Sardinia on the 25th, and donkey rides for Nina and young Gilbert, it was a prosaic existence – at least in winter. Carriage rides to Genoa and walks in the hills were sprinkled with the occasional visit from English visitors staying in Liguria.[45] In March, Lord Minto asked George to settle some small unpaid bills, most of which were of London rather than Scottish origin, along with the cost of binding such of his parliamentary papers as Frazer, the Long Acre bookbinder, had been asked to undertake. If George was to come out to Nervi, Lord Minto asked him 'to bring a couple of dozen compound rhubarb pills and a two pound canister of snuff from Fribourg & Pontet in Pall Mall'. He was also asked to check whether the Foreign Office might not be glad to entrust him with dispatches for James Hudson, the minister of legation at Turin, since they no longer sent a regular messenger there. Lord Minto said he was doing all in his power 'to preach prudence and forbearance' and that there was 'a disposition in general to listen' to him. Hudson was

> doing remarkably well and has much of the confidence of the government at Turin. It is fortunate we have so good a man there instead of such animals as we employ in some other missions but to enable him to do any real good, his hands must be strengthened by assurance of support at home and by evidence that we shall support the independence of Piedmont.[46]

Turning to what Lord Minto described as 'the more important question' of lawyer George's proposed visit, he said,

> we are all I think for different reasons rather of the opinion that you would do better to defer it until the summer as there is nothing pressing in the state of your mother's health. The last attack has passed off with much less injury than I had apprehended and though a distressing check in the progress of recovery, I think no ground has been lost by it and she is now going on particularly well and again picking up a little flesh.

He was certainly not so sanguine as Dr Bertani, their physician, in believing that they might escape a recurrence of these attacks, but the fine weather and open air always proved such good restoratives that he was willing to hope that the improvement would be less uninterrupted than it had been.[47] Lord Minto had little doubt of their being obliged to pass the summer in Nervi, in which case George could pay them a longer and more useful visit.

William had written to warn George that 'we are a sufficiently large party already to make it not very essential on her account for you to take a step which might be very disadvantageous to you in some respects', but George arrived for dinner at Nervi on 22 May, going for a visit to Genoa the next day with Nina and Lotty.[48] Soon afterwards, it seems that a decision was taken whereby William, Nina and the children would holiday in Switzerland and leave Lady Minto to be cared for by other members of the family. After spending two nights in Turin according to William's diary, Nina, Lady Hislop and he reached Vevey on Lac Léman on the first Sunday in July. A short stay at St-Gingolph followed and on Gilbert's birthday, 9 July, they were in the region of Bouches du Rhône. Five days later they were 'on a tour' much as William had enjoyed in 1830, staying at Bern, Thun, Interlaken and Grindelwald, and while they were at the last resort news came of Lady Minto's death on 21 July 1853. The party returned to Vevey a week later, where the news of her death caught up with the family. Leaving Nina and Lady Hislop behind, it seems that William and his father were in Genoa on 2 August, and left the next day for Minto, where the funeral was to be, travelling via Geneva, Dijon, Paris, Boulogne and London, which was reached on 6 August.

William left Minto House for the Continent soon after the countess had been buried at Minto House, reaching Folkestone on 17 August. Meanwhile, his father wrote to George from Roxburghshire telling him that his sailor brother Charlie and his wife Louisa had arrived on their way to Bonjedward House, a little north of Jedburgh, to 'see how things go on in that quarter'.[49] Lord Minto thought they would probably return there for good early in September – braving the scarlet fever which had hung around Jedburgh for months.[50]

By the start of September 1853 William's diary recounts how he, Nina, Lady Hislop, Lotty and the children had visited Lausanne with John Boileau. George appears to have joined the party later that month and the three men climbed the Dents du Midi together. Further expeditions followed and at the end of the month his diary recorded him having dinner in Vevey with his father, who had delayed his departure a little. As the colder weather of early October arrived, Lord Minto and his party left for Florence while William and a none-too-well Nina set off homeward on 11 October. The route then took them via Karlsruhe to Frankfurt and onward to The Hague, which they reached eight days later. A week's stay with Henry and Anne was passed by William shooting snipe and partridge with Henry and visits to the library, the palace and Delft. After a night at Ghent, the party arrived in Dover and London at the end of the month, where they stayed some six weeks.

William found a couple of occasions to visit George at his chambers in Lincoln's Inn and with Nina dined with Lady Mary and Ralph, who were shopping in London before returning to Holland. On the last day of November, William and Nina were entertained by Lord Palmerston, and at the beginning of December they themselves gave a dinner for aunt Anna Maria and John Boileau before going down by train to Bowood for four or five nights. They eventually reached Minto for Christmas and Hogmany was celebrated by a short stay with Lord Murray in Edinburgh. They returned to Minto by the late train on the night of 31 December 1853.[51]

In January of the new year William gave his father in Florence a report of a meeting in Kelso at which he had spoken. Lord Minto, who supposed that the country was by then at war with Russia, liked his son's speech 'extremely' and thought him quite wrong in being dissatisfied with it. So far as the Crimean War was concerned, the widowed earl could only describe it as 'a very formidable adventure and one likely to lead to greater consequences' than anything that had occurred during William's lifetime. He hoped the country would have the 'constancy to support the sacrifices it must make'.[52] At the end of the month, Lord Minto told William, who was at Minto busily engaged in sorting out some of his father's affairs, that he need not worry about his vote in Parliament. He had sent 'a couple' of proxies to Lord John some time ago and 'he has promised to have some regard for my opinions in the use to be made of it'.[53]

A month or so later, Lord Minto asked William what his expectations were in respect of the Scotch Schools Bill which was intended to establish a national and less sectarian system of elementary education. It had been debated in the Commons on 23 February. The Lord Advocate had introduced it in a speech which seemed to his father better in many respects than he had expected. What most offended him was the provision made not only for existing but new denominational schools. This reminded him about Lochgelly School which William had helped start and which was now thriving. His father much appreciated a suggestion made by Lord Murray that William should replace Lord Minto as vice-president of the United Industrial School. This 'ragged' school at South Gray's Close in Edinburgh had been set up as a non-sectarian institution where religious and secular instruction were separated, and as a rival to that established by the Rev Thomas Guthrie, a leading figure in the Free Church in 1847.[54]

A week before Christmas 1854, young Harriet and her father were at The Hague, where Henry was preparing to take up a new diplomatic appointment. News was also awaited about Gibby, who was hoping that he would see the fall of Sevastopol in the Crimea. His father told William that 'should we learn nothing to alter our intentions, we may proceed sometime before the end of next week to Marseilles and wait there, or in the neighbourhood, for further information on which to determine our further movements'. He now considered that 'there would be some convenience in a halt of eight or nine days at Marseilles as it would enable me to send [a servant] to collect our goods and chattels from Genoa and Florence'.

Towards the end of 1854 Lord Minto seems to have wished that William would find more occasions to discuss public affairs with Lord Russell. Writing from The Hague he said 'it would 'be good for him and I am sure he would like it'. But with war much on his mind Minto described the Dutch and other continental politicians as being 'in great dismay at the bellicose tone of all parties in England', and with the offer of peace terms to Russia much in people's thoughts he had also been forced to hear what others thought of society in Britain. The health of William's brother, Gilbert, also lay heavily on Lord Minto's mind as will become apparent in Chapter 12. He asked William to make sure that everyone who wrote to Gibby should advise him to leave his regiment.[55] Unfortunately, on 9 February 1855, there was news of the sad death of young Harriet. It seems that her father had hoped to take her to Constantinople after leaving The Hague but they only got as far as Paris. She had probably been born in 1827, the last of the Minto children and a year after Gilbert.

By April 1855, the gentle bliss of Camelot had returned, but those around the family table faced the future with some trepidation. Change was in the air. Obediently, Gilbert was home and about to be decorated by the Queen, and Lord Minto was living at Eaton Square. William had received an increase in his allowance. Originally calculated on the assumption that he would be in fairly constant residence with his father at Minto, it was now 'wholly inadequate'.[56] On the advice of Mr Tod, the family's Edinburgh solicitor, his father had, among numerous settlements, also arranged for William's debts of £4,300 to be paid off, one effect of which was to strengthen his annual income now that the four boys had reached 'a more expensive age'. The best provision for their education Lord Minto now thought would be to employ an intelligent tutor for them. In the case of William's London house, his father did not want him to part with it given that he would not easily find one to suit him so well, if and when he returned to Parliament.[57]

Two years later Lord Minto went to Florence and enjoyed the end of a warm winter with Henry, Anne and little Gertrude, then nearly two years old. In the event that a change of government provided William with a chance of resuming his career in politics, his father wanted him to understand from the outset that he might need to forget a constituency where the electors were farmers and lairds. He wanted him to know that while it was wholly his decision where he stood, he would do all he could to help him and he suggested that if William had anything important to say in haste about his electoral prospects in Glasgow or anywhere, he should telegraph him in French.[58] In the event, he identified and then won the seat of Clackmannanshire and Kinross-shire from James Johnstone. He was to hold it until May 1859 when his cousin William Adam took it, also serving as the chairman of the General Board of Lunacy for Scotland during these two years.[59]

In February 1858, William turned his attention to the Conspiracy Bill.[60] A public meeting at Hawick had been called to consider the condition of the unemployed and measures that might mitigate distress in the district, which included the establishment of a soup kitchen, where a bowl of broth and bread could be provided for one penny. Another proposal involved the distribution of a quantity of coals, and the supply of oatmeal, both being funded from subscriptions paid by gentlemen in the town and surrounding area. A week or so later, William was sent a petition against the amendment of the Conspiracy Bill based on resolutions carried at the public meeting and which the inhabitants of Hawick wanted him to present to the House of Commons.[61]

During the winter there had been much curling on the ice at Minto and frost persisting into March. Writing to William on 4 April 1858, Lord Minto acknowledged the comfort he drew from his son's letter, with its news about the family. He had been especially concerned about the trouble Bertie, William and Nina's youngest son, had been having with his throat.[62] Lord Minto had been on the look out for a pony for the nine-year-old boy, who was now expected to go to Eton the following year. George had been out frequently with the hounds. Unfortunately, on 17 April when Ralph Abercromby, Lady Mary's husband, was expected to visit them, his father, the former Speaker of the House of Commons and first Baron Dunfermline, died at Colinton House in Midlothian. Drawing his letter to a conclusion, Lord Minto wrote that the nearer the time for his leaving Minto came, 'the more I dislike the thought of giving up my quiet life here'.[63]

It was a little more than a year later when the second Earl of Minto died. Aged seventy-seven, he was at Eaton Square on the last day of July 1859 and had been ailing for about a month. The poet and novelist Sir Walter Scott was to describe Lord

Minto as 'a very agreeable, well-informed, and sensible man' but one without the high breeding, ease of manner or the eloquence of his father.[64]

William was forty-five years old when he became the third Earl of Minto. *The Times* immediately published an obituary notice which combined debatable and ill-judged comments about his father's person, character and career, while William found himself having to deal not only with letters of condolence but dozens of pleas from friends who objected to the horrid and distressful falsehoods. An elderly friend of the family, Dr John Waldie, raised the question with William as to how his father's name was to be rescued from such calumny.[65] The notice described Lord Minto in the following terms:

> He was one of the heavy weights of the Legislature who did his duty unrewarded by the great public ... he was a poor speaker and of small public account ... and enjoyed not a little influence as a sort of chamber counsel to the old Whigs ... his weight in the counsil's [sic] of the nation was such that he must naturally excite the public curiosity ... He entered Parliament in the eventful session of 1806, as member for the borough of Ashburton ... and, it is said, had been trained for the diplomatic service but he obtained no employment until 1832 when he reached the mature age of 50. He was then sent as Ambassador to Berlin where he remained until in 1835 he was recalled in order to assist Lord Melbourne in the responsibilities of a cabinet. He who previously had not the slightest acquaintance with office, and probably had but very little notion of any business whatsoever, was at once appointed First Lord of the Admiralty. The appointment proves either that in those days the Admiralty was not supposed to require an experienced and capable Minister, or else in the judgement of his friends Lord Minto was a man of extraordinary ability, whose business faculty more than counterbalanced any deficiency of experience ... Lord Minto held this important office until the overthrow of Lord Melbourne's administration in 1841, and the only thing for which the rule of the Admiralty is distinguished is the outcry which it excited on account of the number of Elliots who crowded the naval service. Lord Minto was a good family man. He stuck to his friends; otherwise he made so little impression on the public in the capacity of First Lord that most of our readers have quite forgotten the fact ... When Lord John Russell came into power in 1846, his father-in-law was intrusted [sic] with no office that entailed the necessity of work – he was made Lord Privy Seal, and retained that post until the Ministry was overthrown.
>
> If Lord Minto had no very important duties to perform as Lord Privy Seal, he had quite enough to do in a different capacity. Towards the close of 1847 he was sent on a special mission to Italy ... The Italian tour was the only very important part which Lord Minto played in public, and it was a failure. He never afterwards had anything ostensible to do in the management of English affairs. He retired into the bosom of the family, and after a long illness, expired at his house in Eaton Square on Sunday morning last, leaving his title and estates to his eldest son, Lord Melgund.[66]

Now that William was in the House of Lords, which he did not regularly attend, and no longer the representative for the counties of Clackmannanshire and Kinross-shire, the responsibility for Minto House and estate fell to him. It has to be admitted, however, that the second half of William's life, divided as it was between London and Minto, was neither exciting nor of great public interest. When the 1861 census was taken in April that year it showed William and Nina at Minto House accompanied by the four boys; Alexander Walker, aged twenty-four, their tutor; and four male servants who lived in, including a butler, footman, under-footman and a cook. The youngest of their sons, William Fitzwilliam, was not quite in his teens while Hugh Frederick and Arthur Ralph, who was to go to Edinburgh University two years later, were thirteen and fifteen years old respectively. Sixteen-year-old Gilbert John, their eldest, had been at Eton and would go to Trinity College, Cambridge, in 1867. After university his father purchased a commission for him in the Scots Guards but with little to do other than hunt, row and follow horse racing when his ceremonial duties allowed, he and a friend established the Machell stables at Limber Magna in Lincolnshire. Racing under the name of Mr Rolly, his most notable success was in 1874 at Auteuil, where their horse won the French Grand National. Unfortunately his father had died before Gilbert John became governor-general of Canada (1898–1904) and viceroy of India (1905–1910). He was to marry Mary Grey, the daughter of Queen Victoria's private secretary – a charming and intelligent twenty-five-year-old with good connections about the court.

When in London, William and Nina seem to have lived at 31 Dover Street and only moved into the family house in Eaton Square later. Towards the end of the decade, William's work took him to the House of Lords, where he built up a reputation as a sound workhorse. He became chairman of a select committee on the Scottish police system and suggested the use of 'a detective constable' of police to investigate crimes rather than officers of the procurator fiscal.[67] When the Salmon Fisheries (Scotland) Bill came before the House in 1868 William complained of the stringency of clauses in the bill that related to mills and other manufacturing along rivers since there was

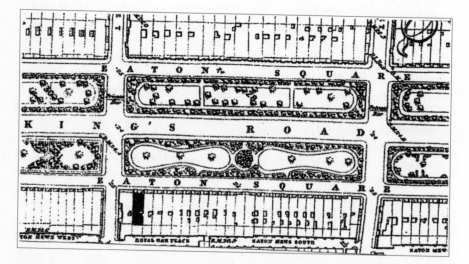

Eaton Square, the London home of the Minto family. The second property on the southerly side of the square (marked in black), and next to the corner house on the east side of Elizabeth Street was No. 48 Eaton Square. The houses were much the same size 'with three rooms on the dining room floor and four on everyone above – with, of course, the extra bedroom floor, double coach-house and four-stall stable'. (Plan supplied by City of Westminster Archives Centre)

nothing more demoralising than to draw up clauses which the government had not police enough to enforce.[68]

The following year William was congratulated for a 'highly commendable step' when he brought forward a motion in the House of Lords relating to the duties and position of procurators fiscal. With a few exceptions, there were no procurators fiscal in Scotland who were permitted or chose to act as agents in civil matters. The friend from Glasgow who briefed William on the subject said that anything which allowed the public to suspect the even-handedness of justice was to be avoided.[69] In May 1869, the House of Lords discussed sudden and accidental deaths in Scotland. William was soon on his feet to thank Lord Kinnaird for bringing this matter to their Lordships' attention. The first steps of criminal proceedings in Scotland were, he said, taken in secret and 'his firm conviction was, if the matter were thoroughly investigated, great advantage would be found in the system of publicity'. There would be 'much less abuse if those proceedings took place before the eyes of the public'. He recalled the evidence taken the previous year by his committee but 'as it was felt they were getting rather beyond the fair scope of their enquiry, it was not thought proper to pursue the investigation'. William accepted that

> the principle of having public prosecutors in Scotland was most admirable but the office of Procurator Fiscal was one not only of importance but of great delicacy. It was to be regretted that with the exception of Edinburgh, Glasgow, Dundee and four other places in Scotland, these officers were allowed to accept private agencies and acted as legal advisers in their capacity as lawyers.[70]

There is no evidence to link William's appointment to the Order of the Thistle on 13 May 1870 with any representations or influence exerted on his behalf. Appointments were a matter of the sovereign's own personal choice and not publicly declared. He would, however, have drawn some satisfaction from the progress made with one of the most momentous of Gladstone's domestic reforms after two days of debate the following week. Forster's Education Act, which was to provide sufficient school accommodation for the whole infant population of the country and make the attendance of all children at school compulsory, was being hammered out in both Houses. In the House of Lords, Lord Stratheden brought in a bill to bring about compulsory and rate-supported education; but in reply to Lord Russell, Earl Granville said the government had not yet received the report of the Royal Commissioners in Ireland which would not be available until June. Although further proposals and amendments followed, the royal assent was forthcoming on 9 August.

The 1871 census showed the household at 48 Eaton Square as including William and Nina along with their son Hugh, who was then twenty-three years old and a clerk at the House of Commons, and Margaret Elliot, a first cousin and forty years old. The eleven servants included two butlers, two footmen, two lady's and two house maids, a cook and two kitchen maids.

William received two pleas for his support of women's causes in April 1871. The first came from Mary McCombie, a member of the well-known Aberdeen family whose head became the editor of the *Aberdeen Gazette* until his death locally at 9 Broadford Place in May 1870. She wished Earl Minto to lay a petition 'praying for the removal of the electoral disabilities of women' before the House of Lords, and speak up for the claims of female householders to the franchise. Three days later a second petition signed by 1,927 people, this time from Cupar in Fife, arrived. Its formal text of Mr Robert Maconachie's petition referred to measures known as the 'Contagious Diseases Acts' which in providing 'for the police and medical surveillance of prostitution, are both unjust in themselves, and dangerous to the public health, and to public morality'. It went on to say that

> these measures, designed specially for the protection of men from the consequences of their own vices, are demoralizing to the men who profit by them, degrading and cruel to the women who suffer under them, dangerous to the liberties of all women, and worthless for the permanent prevention or even mitigation of disease.

On this occasion, the petitioners wanted the repeal of the existing legislation and hoped that the Lords would consider the best methods of dealing with the 'causes of immorality amongst our people'.[71]

After the death of Lord Minto, William's wife Nina had turned her attention to writing a biography of her grandfather, the Rt Hon. Hugh Elliot. When the book was eventually published in 1868 she spoke in its preface about how many lively family letters there had been to work with, quite apart from political records. She was unlikely to have been motivated by thinking that her earnings from publishing a number of articles or even the memoir about Hugh Elliot could do much to help the family's finances. However, by 1873 Nina was ready to give the Edinburgh publishers Edmonton & Douglas her three-volume *Life and Letters of Sir Gilbert Elliot, First Earl of Minto from 1751 to 1806*. She had put together several volumes of notes in preparation for this work and much enjoyed her research and the help she had received from Lord Russell. Her readers were to come not only from a wide field of Minto family friends but also included many women with whom she had not had previous contact. At the beginning of April 1874, 'notices' about her biography began to appear in the press. With the exception of the *Standard*, critics were generally complimentary and one friend said that she had 'certainly tuned more critics to one song of praise' than was 'usual amongst gentlemen with such discordant voices'.[72] She was especially pleased to see how her sons, Arthur and Hugh, both very much young men of their generation, showed interest in her work.

While Nina and William were staying at Brighton in February 1874 they received a letter from John Hill Burton and initially neither of them could decide who would answer it. Burton had been the impoverished secretary to the Scottish prison board, and although he had written several works on Scottish law it was not until he produced his life of Hume that his financial situation improved. He would at this time have been working on the first volume of his Register of the Privy Council. It was Lady Minto who eventually took on the job of replying to him. 'I assure you,' she wrote, 'that whether it be he or I in possession of the pen it makes no difference in ... the gratification your approbation of my book has given us both.' Particularly satisfying for the author was his approval of the way she had arranged the book.[73]

Writing from Ridgeway, the house at Shere, Surrey, in which she died four years later, Harriet Grote sent Nina her comments about *Sir Gilbert* early in July.[74] Although she

*Above left*: 1. Gilbert Elliot, first Earl of Minto, by W. Joseph Edwards, James S. Virtue and George Chinnery. (National Portrait Gallery, London)

*Above right*: 2. A mezzotint portrait of Gilbert Elliot Murray Kynynmound, second Earl of Minto, by G. Zobel (after Sir Francis Grant, 1842). (National Portrait Gallery, London)

*Above left*: 3. Admiral Sir George Elliot (1784–1863), an 1834 portrait by Sir George Hayter. After serving with Nelson at Trafalgar he became a Lord Commissioner at the Admiralty in 1835. (National Portrait Gallery, London)

*Above right*: 4. Admiral Sir George, the second Earl Minto's brother, in his old age. (National Library of Scotland)

*Above left*: 5. Catherine Selby, née Rutherford (1806–1878), a signed miniature by Mme Bigarne. (National Library of Scotland)

*Above right*: 6. Ephraim Selby, factor and Catherine's husband, by R. S. Lauder, RSA. He has a gun under his arm, powder flasks on a belt and is dressed in a dark-green shooting jacket. (National Library of Scotland)

*Above left*: 7. Fanny Elliot, Lady John Russell, with her eldest son, from a miniature by Thorburn, 1844.

*Above right*: 8. The second Countess of Minto, from a miniature by Sir William Ross, 1851.

*Above left*: 9. Maria Felicia Malibran (1808–1836), the French opera singer, as Desdemona in Rossini's *Otello*. Portrait by Henri Decaisne.

*Above right*: 10. Maria Taglione (1804–1884), the famous Italian/Swedish ballerina whom the family saw dance *La Bayadère* in Paris. Lithograph by Josef Kriehuber, 1839.

11. Minto House, Roxburghshire, towards the end of the nineteenth century. (Royal Commission on the Ancient and Historical Monuments of Scotland)

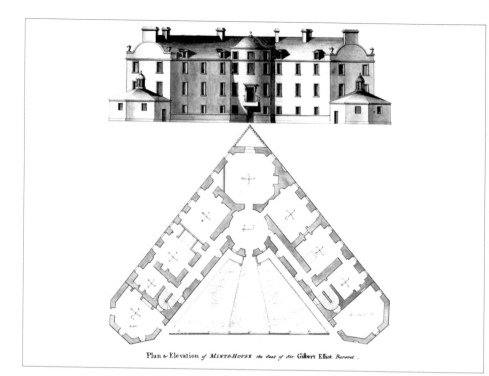

*Above*: 12. Plan and elevation of Minto House for Sir Gilbert Elliot. (Bodleian Library, Oxford)

*Left*: 13. The Klosterstrasse in Berlin in 1830 by Eduard Gaertner (1801–1877).

*Below left*: 14. A watercolour by Eduard Gaertner (1801–1877) of General Gerhard von Scharnhorst's statue by Christian Rauch, erected by Frederick William III in 1822 on Unter den Linden, Berlin. (Stadmuseum Berlin)

*Above left*: 15. Portrait of Johann Peter Friedrich Ancillon (1767–1837), with whom Lord Minto negotiated in the early 1830s, by Adolf Rinck. (Nationalgalerie, Staatliche Museen zu Berlin)

*Above right*: 16. King Frederick William III of Prussia (1770–1840).

*Above left*: 17. Portrait of Charles Grey (1764–1845) by Sir Thomas Lawrence in 1828. (The Paul Mellon Centre for Studies in British Art)

*Above right*: 18. Portrait of Henry John Temple (1784–1865), third Viscount Palmerston, by Graham Vivian, 1858. (National Portrait Gallery, London)

*Above left*: 19. Sir John Barrow, first Baronet (1764–1848), a founder of the Royal Geographical Society. Mezzotint by George Thomas Payne, published 1847. (National Portrait Gallery, London)

*Above right*: 20. Sir John Franklin, naval officer and Arctic explorer, who took Lord Minto's son, Henry, to Tasmania as his aide-de-camp in 1836. (National Portrait Gallery, London)

*Above left*: 21. Henry Tufnell (1805–1854), politician and Lord Minto's private secretary at the Admiralty. Stipple engraving by William Holl, Jr. (National Portrait Gallery, London)

*Above right*: 22. Sir William Symonds (1782–1856), surveyor of the Navy. Lithograph by Edward Morton, published in 1850. (National Portrait Gallery, London)

*Above*: 23. Pembroke Lodge, in Richmond Park, was granted by Queen Victoria to Lord John Russell and Fanny in 1847 for their lifetime occupation. Fanny's sitting room and bedroom were on the first floor, whilst her drawing room and the bow room were at ground level.

*Right*: 24. Lord John Russell (1792–1878), Fanny's husband, painted by Francis Grant in 1853. (National Portrait Gallery, London)

*Above left*: 25. Portrait of William Henry Playfair (1790–1857), Lord Minto's architect. Stipple portrait by J. B. Smyth. (National Portrait Gallery, London)

*Above middle*: 26. John William Ward, Earl of Dudley, who was to be a long-standing friend of Lord Minto. Portrait by Day and Haghe, after Edward Berens. (National Portrait Gallery, London)

*Above right*: 27. Sir John Peter Boileau (1794–1869), Lord Minto's brother-in-law, who lived at Ketteringham, Norfolk. Portrait by Thomas Herbert Maguire. (National Portrait Gallery, London)

*Far left*: 28. A photograph by J. Watkins of John Russell, Viscount Amberley (1842–1876), the eldest of Lord John Russell and Fanny Elliot's four children. (National Portrait Gallery, London)

*Left*: 29. Fanny Tacchinardi-Persiani (1812–1867), who sang the part of Lucia in Donizetti's *Lucia di Lammermoor* when Harriet went to the opera in 1844, had also been in a performance given in 1838 at Her Majesty's Theatre.

*Above*: 30. An artist's impression of an Eastern Counties Railway train not dissimilar to that which would have run on the company's line between Shoreditch and Colchester in the 1840s, and on which Sir John Boileau and Harriet would have travelled.

*Above left*: 31. Giovanni Maria Mastai-Ferretti reigned as Pope Pius IX for thirty-one years from 16 June 1846. Lord Minto was charged with assisting him to carry out his reforms.

*Above middle*: 32. Painting by Alessandro Capalti of John McHale (1791–1881), Roman Catholic Archbishop of Tuam in Ireland. (National Gallery of Ireland)

*Above right*: 33. Ferdinand II (1810–1859), King of Naples, nicknamed 'bomba' as the result of his bombardment of Messina during the 1848 unrest.

*Above left*: 34. Ruggiero Settimo (1778–1863), Sicilian patriot and politician who became head of the revolutionary government in 1848.

*Above right*: 35. The start of the unrest in Sicily. Revolutionaries outside Messina Cathedral during the second week of January 1848.

*Above left*: 36. Lajos Kossuth (1802–1894), leader of the Hungarian war of independence, and visitor to London in the autumn of 1851.

*Above right*: 37. Francis Napier, tenth Lord Napier of Merchistoun (1819–1898), secretary of legation at Naples between 1848 and 1849. (Scottish National Portrait Gallery)

*Above left*: 38. William Hugh Elliot (1814–1891), third Earl of Minto, MP between 1847 and 1859 and active in the House of Lords after his father's death in 1859. (National Library of Scotland)

*Above right*: 39. The Rt Hon. Sir Henry George Elliot (1817–1907), Lord Minto's second son, who married Anne Antrobus in December 1847.

*Above left*: 40. Gilbert, fourth Earl Minto (1845–1914) governor-general of Canada. (McCord Museum, McGill University, Canada)

*Above right*: 41. Mary Caroline Grey (1858–1940), daughter of General Sir Charles Grey, married the fourth Earl Minto in July 1883. (McCord Museum, McGill University, Canada)

*Top left*: 42. Russian defences under attack at the siege of Sevastopol, 1855. Painting by Grigoryi Shukaev.

*Top right*: 43. Maréchal François Canrobert (1809–1895) discussed the prowess of the Rifle Brigade with Lord Raglan in Captain Elliot's presence on 21 November 1854.

*Right*: 44. General Sir James Simpson, GCB, who replaced Lord Raglan as commander-in-chief in the Crimea.

*Below left, middle and right*: 45. Lieutenant Colonel Gilbert Elliot (1826–1865) of the Rifles, towards the end of his life. (National Library of Scotland)

*Above left*: 46. A portrait of Ernst, fourth Prince of Leiningen, captain of HMS *Magicienne* (and his cousin Prince Victor), whom Admiral Charles Elliot met in the Mediterranean. (Royal Collection)

*Above middle*: 47. Lieutenant (later Colonel) William James Montgomery Cuninghame (1834–1897), a fellow Rifleman of Gilbert Elliot and recipient of the Victoria Cross in the Crimean War.

*Above right*: 48. Portrait of Sir Henry Knight Storks (1811–1874), the last High Commissioner of the Ionian Islands, whose hospitality Admiral Charles Elliot enjoyed in 1863.

*Above left*: 49. Francisco Solano López (1827–1870), the dictator of Paraguay responsible for the War of the Triple Alliance.

*Above right*: 50. Joaquim Marques Lisboa or the Marquis of Tamandaré (1807–1897), who was the admiral in charge of the Brazilian fleet for most of the War of the Triple Alliance.

51. The city of Montevideo, capital of Uruguay. The drawing, published by *Harper's Weekly* on 8 April 1865, shows the headland facing the sea not far from Admiral Charles Elliot's quinta, where he and his first wife lived during the siege of the city that year.

*Above left*: 52. Emperor Pedro II of Brazil (1825–1891), who reigned for nearly fifty-nine years, a 'wise, benevolent, austere and honest ruler'.

*Above right*: 53. Watercolour published by *Vanity Fair* in 1866 of Sir Edward Thornton (1817–1906), British minister in Buenos Aries and later envoy at Rio de Janeiro. (National Portrait Gallery, London)

*Above:* 54. Bonjedward House, at Jedburgh in the Scottish Borders, where Admiral Charles Elliot, Louisa and the family lived after returning from Montevideo in the late 1860s.

*Left:* 55. Matfen Hall, Stamfordham, near Newcastle, the home of Sir Edward Blackett, the sixth Baronet of Newcastle, and Admiral Charles Elliot's first wife, Louisa.

*Bottom left:* 56. Ravensworth Castle, near Gateshead, was the home of Sir Henry Liddell where Admiral Charles and his son, Bertram, stayed at Christmas 1873.

*BIARRITZ. — Arrivée du Tramway de Bayonne*

*Above left*: 57. Prince Alfred (1844–1900), Duke of Edinburgh and second son of Queen Victoria, who embarked at Devonport during the period of Admiral Charles Elliot's command, and whom the Elliots later entertained, along with Alfred's duchess, Marie Alexandrovna of Russia.

*Above right*: 58. After a small steam tramway system had been inaugurated in 1877, Baron Emplain, a wealthy Belgian engineer, came up with the plan for the Bayonne-Lycée-Biarritz tramway using 0–6–0 locomotives over the 5-mile route. This opened in October 1888 and ran from Bayonne to the casino in Biarritz.

*Below left*: 59. The third earl Minto's son, Arthur Ralph Douglas Elliot (1846–1923), whose parliamentary campaign in 1880 was helped by his lawyer uncle, George Elliot. (National Portrait Gallery, London)

*Below middle*: 60. Hugh Culling Eardley Childers (1827–1896), who was appointed First Lord of the Admiralty in 1868 and Secretary for War in Gladstone's second administration after having married Colonel Gilbert Elliot's widow in 1879. (National Portrait Gallery, London)

*Below right*: 61. King Oscar II of Sweden (1829–1907) in the uniform of an admiral rather as Charles and Har would have seen him at Devonport.

*Right:* 62. Sir Walter Elliot (1803–1887) of Wolfelee, one of the small army of antiquarians who helped George Elliot to obtain and check information for *The Border Elliots*, published in 1897.

*Far right:* 63. Sir William Fraser (1816–1898), a lawyer who successfully commercialised genealogy and established a format which attracted customers from across the Scottish aristocracy – and with whom George Elliot worked between 1867 and the publication of his family history.

*Middle:* 64. HMS *Eurydice*, a fast 908-ton, 24-gun frigate designed by Admiral George Elliot in 1841, which was refitted in 1877 for seagoing service as a training ship, only to be sunk in a heavy snow storm off the Isle of Wight in 1878 with the loss of 376 lives. Both lawyer George and Admiral Charles were among those horrified by the news.

*Below:* 65. A photograph taken in 1890 at 'Monen' in Norway. Mr William Warren Vernon and his wife are seated to the left, with lawyer George (and a stick) at the end of the row on the right.

was still reading only the first volume, Harriet said that she felt her 'old reviewing faculty kindled to a degree'. She had special praise for the first Earl's wife, saying, 'What a capital woman.' The 'single drawback' to Harriet's pleasure was what she called Elliot's unfair dealing with Mr Pitt's character. So far as printing and publication were concerned, she disliked the miserably pale ink Mr William Spottiswoode persisted in using since it 'precludes one from reading you by candlelight'.[75] Next among those singing her praise was Alexander William Kinglake, a historian who witnessed the battle of Alma and who had taken dinner with Lord Raglan after the battle in 1854. Writing from 28 Hyde Park Place, he said Nina's book was doing well 'in a way that perhaps she had hardly foreseen ... by carrying down the tradition of statesmanship to this the present generation which had all but lost the treasure', having being drowned in newspapers.[76] Then Thomas Emerson Headlam, a retired MP who like William had been at Trinity College, wrote from Gilmonby Hall near Darlington. He thought Nina's books would live as long as there was anyone interested in history.[77]

It was 'how well and cleverly' Nina had arranged her book that caught the attention of Louisa Beresford, the Marchioness of Waterford. She wrote from Northumberland in October although her praise was offset by one complaint. Nina had, she said, dismissed her grandfather with one mention of his name as 'General Stuart' and 'from your notice it might be imagined he did nothing in Corsica'.[78] The well-known editor of the *Edinburgh Review*, Henry Reeve, then wrote to Lady Minto from Abington in October requesting a baggage cart to meet his 'large family party' at Hassendean railway station. They were to stay with Nina and William at Minto.[79] The following month, Reeve confirmed that the couple would again be pleased to come to dinner – this time in London – and went on to tell Nina that he had 'sat up until an undue hour to read your first chapters which have now reached me'. He acted as literary adviser to Longman, who were to publish Nina's *Lord Minto in India* in 1880, and went on to say that he did not know ' a fresher or more graceful and genuine thing anywhere than the introductory chapter ... it is delightful'.[80]

As Nina became better known through her writing, she began to be invited to support women's movements. She also gained greatly in confidence. In March 1875, she received an invitation from Henrietta Stanley, a Canadian-born political hostess and campaigner for women's education, to join her in her work. Lady Stanley became an energetic member of the National Union for the Improvement of Women's Education and also found a useful role among those engaged in building Girton College, Cambridge, where she provided several Exhibitions for students who were then at Hitchen as well as donating £1,000 towards the library that bears her name.[81]

The year 1877 had started with Gladstone winning a majority of the votes cast in the general election but with victory going to Disraeli and the Conservatives, who had won a majority of the seats. North of the border, the neglect of Scottish legislation by Westminster led to William experiencing another period of being pushed and pulled by people wanting his help. In February he was pressed by the Convention of Royal Burghs to attend a meeting, and in April the Edinburgh West End Liberal Association hired the Music Hall for a demonstration in favour of the disestablishment and disendowment of state churches – at which they hoped for Lord Minto's presence. In September, some Jedburgh citizens who met to form a Liberal association in the town invited his Lordship to preside at its inaugural meeting in the Corn Exchange.

This he gave, but not before several letters had been exchanged, and he had received an assurance that 'nothing of a political kind' would be brought before the meeting.[82]

The following year, the 'Eastern Question' sparked numerous public meetings, including one at Denholm under the chairmanship of Thomas Riddell, a Glasgow reformer and a good friend of William. He wrote asking him to present their petition to the House of Lords. To restore order in the Balkans in the wake of the Russo-Turkish War, the German Chancellor, Bismarck, hosted a meeting of the great powers in Berlin in 1878 to balance the interests of Britain, Russia and Austria-Hungary. Among the British delegates was Odo Russell, Baron Ampthill, the nephew of Fanny's husband who had died in May that year at Pembroke Lodge. Peace was on the mind of many and, writing to Riddell, William said he 'yielded to no one ... in an anxious desire for the maintenance of peace, and for the adoption by the government of such a course as may be most likely (with a due regard to general and national interests) to lead to that end'.[83]

Among items of family news at this time were two weddings. Hugh Frederick married Mary Euphemia Long in July 1879, and Elizabeth Fanny Rutherford became William Fitzwilliam's wife in the first quarter of 1880. Both were to have children. In the spring that year the Mintos chose to have a holiday in the Mediterranean and were in Algiers when their son Arthur was about to stand for the Roxburghshire parliamentary seat. Nina had apparently been deeply affected by the deaths in quick sequence of Admiral George's youngest son Frederick and his wife Lady Charlotte. It had been a 'sad tragedy'. William and Nina continued to enjoy their stay and, having been impervious to George's inducements to 'head homewards earlier', George was left with the duty of commenting on Arthur's public utterances during the election campaign.[84] On their way home they were to stay at Baveno in Italy.

At the start of the 1881 winter, however, Nina left Roxburghshire for Eaglescliffe at Bournemouth. She had apparently not enjoyed the best of health for three years and the doctors had accordingly recommended a more congenial climate. When his mother's health assumed an alarming aspect, Gilbert John was summoned south, to be present at her deathbed on 21 April 1882. He subsequently brought the body back to Minto House by train for burial. The report published in *The Scotsman* four days later spoke of how much of her time Lady Minto had devoted to literary pursuits, and how her published works were of considerable historical importance. The newspaper said that 'in conversation she had few equals, and many of the foremost men of the time, both in letters and politics, were frequent guests at Minto House. The poor on the estate and elsewhere found in her a generous friend and many will miss her kindly visits and seasonable gifts'. Her remains were subsequently laid in the private vault at Minto.[85]

In 1884 the lives of two of the family's old servants came to an end. Ephraim Selby, the retired Minto estate factor, died on 16 March 1884 aged eighty-three and Catherine his wife, who had helped tutor most of the children, died at Denholm aged seventy-six on 11 October 1884. Poor health prevented William leaving Minto in May 1886. He wrote to Lord Morley of Blackburn saying that much as he would have liked to, he could not undertake to go to London to support his Lordship's candidature for deputy speakership in the House of Lords. 'Unless,' said William, 'the spirit of Toryism has recently been exorcised ... I fear your chances of success are little likely to be practically prejudiced by the failure of my one vote – but I regret much losing the opportunity of recording it for you all the same.'[86] Ten days later, William was writing to Mr Gladstone to say that he could not have the honour of dining with him at the end of the month to celebrate Her Majesty's birthday.[87] Nevertheless, he would undoubtedly have been very proud of the fact that two of his sons had followed him into politics. Arthur Ralph Elliot had been elected Liberal MP for Roxburghshire at both the 1880 and 1886 general elections despite his physical handicap. He married Madeline Ryan in February 1888, the daughter of Sir Charles Lister Ryan, who had been sometime comptroller and auditor-general. For his part, Hugh Frederick won the seat of Ayrshire North in 1885 as a Liberal. He opposed Gladstone's Home Rule policy and, while he was re-elected as a Liberal Unionist a year later, he continued to represent the constituency until 1895.

William walked to Teviotbank on a fine and frosty New Year's Day in 1889. The ice was hard enough for curling, or so he was told. He was to have lunch with Lady Florence Dixie, a thirty-three-year-old author and traveller who had published *Across Patagonia* in 1880.[88] Two days later, his eldest son Arthur arrived from Burley Beeches in Hampshire and went to a ball arranged by the Dixies at Teviotdale the following evening. William stayed for a few days at the New Club in Edinburgh later that month and visited Colinton, where the Abercrombys' only daughter was probably living on her own.

Financial considerations continued to occupy William's attention, not least so far as the lease and expenses associated with 48 Eaton Square were concerned. It was an expensive property, and although the lease from the Duke of Westminster would not expire until 1924, ground rent and other charges were substantial. Among smaller items, Tods, Murray & Jamieson, as his Edinburgh solicitor had become, were asked to remit an extra £100 to Fitz, his youngest son in the army, for removal expenses, and an extra allowance of £200 to Lord Melgund.[89] Having watched a meet of hounds on Innocents' Day, William and his eldest son were soon riding out together to inspect the line of the run taken by the fox three or four days previously.[90] Going up to London for a week at the end of January, William stayed at the Pulteney Hotel, being principally concerned to see the building works on 2 Portman Square, a property he had leased. He managed to have dinner on one evening with Arthur, eating on other occasions at his clubs, the Travellers' and Brooks's.

The Melgunds returned to Minto in February for a short visit and skated on the curling pond and a month later William went by train to Pembroke Lodge, where he found Fanny well but Agatha pale from influenza. He dined with George at Brooks's one evening and had lunch with Henry the following day before returning to Minto. The shortest of possible visits to Lochgelly was paid by Gilbert and his father in April and on the 16th there was a point-to-point from Horslihill round the Minto Hills to Teviot Bank, a distance of about 7 miles, which was won by Gilbert on 'Polecat'. On the following day, one Gideon Pott came to lunch after which the Melgunds left for a short visit to Viceregal Lodge, Dublin.[91]

Back in London during May 1890 for a short stay, William drove with Henry on a strangely foggy morning to Pembroke Lodge, where he met a prospective MP and his wife. Improvement works at 2 Portman Square continued and he slept there for 'the first time since purchase of it', and paid another bill amounting to £326. In June, he came down from Minto in the hope of seeing more of Fanny at Pembroke Lodge. Both took a walk round by Ham Common and back by the Park. When he left it was to go by train the 12 miles to Weybridge and down to Laverstoke to see Lotty and her husband. The second day saw the two men sitting on the lawn after a walk together. Katie and Alaric, two of the Portals' children, were there, the latter being 'much out of health and depressed'. After reaching Surbiton on the return journey by train, William took a carriage back to Richmond.

In the late autumn that year, and after a stream of visitors had left Minto, the Melgunds received the news that Lady Caroline Grey, Gilbert John's mother-in-law, who had been one of the Queen's Ladies of the Bedchamber, was seriously ill in London. He promptly left to be with her, but she died on 4 November at St James's Palace, where the couple had been married. With Arthur also departing for London a few days later, William had time to consider how the collapse of the family's fight to save Minto and the estate was becoming a reality despite all his and his father's efforts to sustain the heritage. Gilbert John had reacted badly to his failure to win a seat at Hexham in 1886, and the tedium of his county responsibilities as deputy lord lieutenant led to his seeking alternative interests such that by 1898 he was campaigning to achieve the position of governor-general of Canada with the assistance of his wife's court influence. Meanwhile all William could do was to ride out on the first day of the season. He found the hounds running near Newlands. On 21 November, the earl was pleased to note in his diary that *The Scotsman* had published his letter on 'the Scotch Church'. The rest of the day seems to have been spent pheasant shooting with Hugh, Gilbert, Mr Pott and Mr Scott of Sinton, near Selkirk.[92]

William died on 17 March 1891 aged seventy-six. His death drew a careful and considered letter from Lord Moncreiff to the editor of *The Scotsman*, which particularly recognised his 'eminent qualities as a public man'.[93] What was in effect an obituary went on to say how 'his temperament was unassuming as his manners were courteous and unobtrusive, but he was eminently and essentially a man having a pervading interest and influence in public affairs'. There were few public questions affecting Scotland, said Lord Moncreiff, on which he had not left 'the mark of his vigorous thought'. His course in the House of Commons was not unchequered, but 'he never ceased to lend his aid to the great political principles he had at heart'. He had many qualifications and some advantages, including membership of 'the fraternity of Scottish members in the House of Commons'. In these councils, Moncreiff wrote, Lord Melgund, as he was then, was always 'an important and weighty element. Calm, always open to conviction, always anxious to come to the right conclusion, yet very tenacious of his opinions when he felt he was right; he was a very safe and valuable adviser'. Moncrieff referred to William's exertions and public usefulness in Scotland saying that he

> was one of the first, if not the first, of our public men to remark [on] and proclaim the growing defects of our educational system, and to endeavour to apply a legislative remedy. He very early in his public life introduced into Parliament a bill on the subject of education in Scotland and never ceased to take a warm interest in the questions which the subject raised.[94]

In his memoir about the fourth Lord Minto, John Buchan described William as someone who had always taken an alert interest in public affairs while at the same time leading a quiet country life. 'His nature was rare and fine; his extreme modesty, his complete indifference to his own advancement, and his dread of ostentation inclined him to conceal, even from those nearest to him, his public and private services.' Buchan said it was only those who actually worked with him, such as Lord Moncreiff, who knew his quality.[95]

At William's funeral in Minto parish church, the Rev A. Galloway gave a lengthy but incisive appraisal of his Lordship's life. Among those who followed the coffin from Minto House to the churchyard were Gilbert John, who had become the fourth Earl; his three brothers, Arthur Elliot MP, Hugh Elliot MP, Lt-Col. William Fitzwilliam Elliot; George Elliot; Mr William Elliot of Brownrigg; Lt-Col. Trotter; the Earl of Dalkeith; Lord Polwarth; Hon. Cospatrick Hume; Mr Maxwell of Teviot Bank; Captain Maxwell; Mr E. Maxwell; Mr Pott of Knowesouth; Mr Scott of Sinton; Captain Eliott Lockhart; Mr Haddon; Dr Blair of Jedburgh; Mr Purdom of Hawick; Mr Anderson of Shaws; and many others. The Minto minister maintained that William had

> native talents of mind far beyond the common order, and but for his innate defect of shyness or backwardness, from which he greatly suffered, he was pre-eminently fitted as few men are for occupying a high place among the councils of the nation ... for he had a clear-headed, keen-sighted sagacity which, on the one hand, was tempered by a patient gentleness of dealing, while on the other, it was strengthened by an unyielding and firm decision of character. Lord Minto was no obscure or menial waverer. He had the rare virtue of being able to say 'No', as well as 'Yes'; and beneath an exceptionally modest and quiet exterior, there was in him a strong moral backbone which in these days is a positive relief and pleasure to see in our public men. He was, moreover, no mean authority in almost all matters of public and national importance, especially those relating to education and the Church. Lord Minto's whole object was quiet reformation, cautious and timely reconstruction, but not destruction.

In conclusion, the Rev Galloway expressed the hope that 'the fragrance of his gentle life' would remain with his family and friends, and that 'they may love to recall his simplicity of character, his fearless straightforwardness and his unaffected benevolence'.[96]

# 11

# ST PETERSBURG TO CONSTANTINOPLE – HENRY'S DIPLOMATIC CAREER (1841–1877)

It was 'by the merest chance' that Henry, the second of Earl Minto's sons, came to enter the diplomatic corps, and about the last career that would have been deliberately chosen for him. Before going to Cambridge, his father had evaded his son's questions about what he might do with his life by saying that 'the army was a wretched profession and diplomacy worse'. At Trinity, Henry admitted to no 'dissipation' but to being thoroughly idle, and quite content to live '*au jour le jour*', as he put it. Then, after about eighteen months at the university, and in the middle of the long vacation of 1836, Lord Minto had packed him off to Van Diemen's Land, where he 'could not fail to do well' with Sir John Franklin. Fortunately for Henry, he was to experience something embodying 'real work' under 'one of the finest characters that ever lived'. When he returned after four years he met an old college friend about to resign from the lowly job as a précis writer at the Foreign Office, and who inspired him to join the diplomatic service. His father spoke on Henry's behalf to Palmerston, who soon arranged for him to be given the same lowly role, and before leaving office at the Admiralty he saw him appointed as a paid attaché at the British Embassy in St Petersburg.[1]

It was a twenty-five-year-old gentleman – whose father had sent him 'a good-looking weapon' for shooting game, and to whom he would soon turn to for 'a couple of trout rods' as replacements for those recently broken – who now settled to the task of attaché at St Petersburg. He was to remain there for the next six years. Having told Lord Minto what he had learned about the Czar's latest *ukase* (or proclamation), Henry mentioned the death of the Russian minister in Stockholm, Count Matuszewic, whom he thought his father might have known.[2] Two months or so later, he was airing his 'prospects of advancement' with his father, recognising that early promotion was 'completely out of the question', except perhaps to first instead of second attaché. He maintained, however, that the corps was 'certainly not entirely composed of Solomons' and that he might be able to make himself 'more useful than the majority of them'. So far as Henry's expenses were concerned, he believed he 'should live for less at home than I am here obliged to spend above my salary' and he hoped to get home on leave. It depended on whether the ambassador who had just gone home, Charles Stuart, Baron de Rothesay, was able to return to St Petersburg. The Russian chancellor, Count Nesselrode, was to call him *un cadavre ambulant*.

The Russian winter was almost upon him when Henry learned that his application for leave had been turned down. Naively, he instantly wrote to his father about a decision which he considered both outrageous and a deliberate rap over the knuckles, especially as 'there was nothing [for him] to do' in St Petersburg.[3] He had yet to learn the meaning of paid inactivity. Far from being able to live on his government salary, Henry was soon writing to his father about money. He reminded him that when he left Minto the previous year 'you gave me a credit upon Coutts for £500 which, together with my pay, has now very nearly disappeared, the expense of the year from having to set up in furs and furniture being about £750'. St Petersburg was 'not a reasonable place' and he desired his father to pay in a regular sum to Coutts – either quarterly or monthly. His pay as an attaché was not much more than £250 and he was looking for another £350 from Lord Minto.[4]

At the beginning of May 1843, there was 'absolutely nothing to say', Henry told his father. It was, he explained, really 'quite a comfort' to have the Russian dispute with Turkey going on. Negotiations to settle boundaries in the region of the Shatt al Arab River kept the embassy busy although it was a subject about which England 'kept herself entirely quiet'. Henry told his father that he hoped to make another attempt to get leave in the autumn to catch his sister Lady Mary during her stay in England. There was still plenty of time to settle these matters. Ice on the River Neva was thick enough for anyone to walk across it and he looked forward to the end of what was usually a seven-month winter. The formalities associated with the opening and closing of the river were the 'Derby and St Leger of Russia' on which innumerable bets were made. Another great event acknowledged by Henry was the arrival of his allowance, which was 'very ample as I live a quiet life'.[5]

In the autumn of 1844, a note from Ralph Abercromby about other promotions failed to placate Henry, who could only think of those whom he could approach about his position. He had written to the private secretary of Lord Aberdeen, Sir Robert Peel's Foreign Secretary, and asked his father to approach him if he thought it 'worthwhile'. To soften the tone of his appeal Henry was ready to sympathise with his father, who had got 'out of London at last' and he supposed him to be thinking of 'brushing up [his] spurs and top boots'. He wanted accounts of 'Musulman's wind and Fanatic's legs' – two of Lord Minto's horses which Henry had ridden when last at home in Roxburghshire.[6]

Henry was soon telling his father about a vacancy he had heard of from the Foreign Office for a paid 'first attaché-ship' at Constantinople. The change would most certainly not be for the better, he said, 'for I should move from about the best to one of the most awkward chiefs in the line', a reference to Sir Stratford Canning. Henry could see, however, that so long as Edwardes was the paid first attaché in St Petersburg, he himself was not eligible for promotion, whereas if he were the first attaché at Constantinople he might be made secretary of legation any day. On this occasion, he did not want his father to intervene on his behalf, believing himself 'well-backed up' in London by Edmund Hammond, then a clerk at the Foreign Office, who had alerted him to the possible vacancy at Constantinople. He wanted to be chosen as 'the proper person' for the job.[7]

Henry, whose grasp of economic matters was improving, believed that those who thought that there could be a greater outlet for Russian grain if there was free trade in England were mistaken. Merchants 'would find themselves unable to bring any great additional supply to their ports without so much being spent on inland carriage as to consume most of the profits'. Throughout the previous year bread was selling in St Petersburg 'as nearly as possible at the same price as it was in London, though certainly from the price of wheat it ought', he said, 'to be much cheaper'. There was still the most dreadful distress in Livonia and Estonia, where proprietors were reporting between three and six weeks' supply of grain for their peasants, after which there would be nothing 'to put in their mouths'. 'So much,' concluded the attaché, 'for the advantage of trusting entirely to yourselves for your supply of grain.'

In March 1846 he turned his attention to affairs in Poland. In spite of expressing a sympathy for that country, he still found it impossible to feel anything for the late insurrection which, he said, 'was evidently got up by schemers at a distance where they have remained safe and out of harm's way while the poor dupes they misled are taking the consequences of what everyone could have foreseen must turn out a failure'. The worst part of the business in his view was that Russian provinces had remained tolerably quiet while Galicia and Poland have been disturbed, giving weight to the arguments the Czar was always using to Austria and Prussia to treat their Poles 'with the same severity he does his'. Henry was at pains to tell his father that the Austrian and Prussian Poles in reality had little to complain of. It was a different story in many parts of Russia where there was much misery and starvation. He reported a fearful fever which was 'carrying off the people faster than the cholera ever did'. Recently, mortality in St Petersburg was considered to be about 800 a day, which was 'enormous for a town of under half a million people' but it was confined, Henry said, 'in the most wonderful way to the lower classes and it is a curious thing that our doctor who is almost worked off his legs has not lost a single patient of the higher orders'. The fever was not forecast to diminish until the ice on the Neva broke up. Personally, the attaché was in good health and had clearly enjoyed much riding despite having taken a few falls, one of which had damaged his thumb.[8]

Henry's correspondence to his father at this time was being directed to Brooks's Club in London, where Lord Minto had been listening to the debates on the Coercion Bill. The young diplomat felt certain 'you must have been against it, for I do not think that in all the speeches either in the House of Lords or Commons, a single argument has been used to show that it is the right remedy for the lamentable state of Ireland'. The attaché maintained that if Czar Nicholas was to embody a coercion bill with a *ukase* against Poland, all Europe would point it out 'as a wonderful stretch of granny'. Henry wrote that the Czar had just set off for Warsaw, where he was unlikely to show much sympathy for the poor wretches who had been implicated in the late disturbances, but he did not want to say too much against the Emperor just at that moment, as he had acted 'very handsomely' to a great friend of his, one Colonel Betancourt, an aide-de-camp of the Czar.[9]

Writing to his mother in July 1846, Henry spoke of a 'vast commotion' involving the Czar, a consul's nightmare. All 'the bigwigs of the court' had been aboard a steamer going to inspect the fleet when there was a collision with an English brig which carried away the steamer's funnel and paddle box, and 'damaged her beauty considerably'. By good luck 'it happened that all the blame was on the part of the steamer; the brig being close hauled beating up, was bound to keep her course which she did'. The Czar, considering it *infra dig* to go astern of her, tried to cross her bows and momentarily 'near got scranched'. Although imprisoned for a day or so, the captain of the brig was, said Henry, 'now going to bring a claim against the government for the damage he sustained'.[10]

Henry had been very much tempted, not for any pleasure it would give him but as 'a kind of duty', to make a tour of the interior of Russia and he was looking around for a good companion. It seemed a shame, he said, to know nothing of a country where he had lived for four years except what he had seen in the capital, but he could see how much of a serious undertaking it would be. The distances to be covered and the few subjects of interest were not small problems. It did, however, depend on him finding a companion for such a trip. He finished his letter by suggesting that if the family was going to Italy for the winter one or two might like to consider joining him, particularly if it coincided with the end of his tour in Russia, but he felt like 'the Charity School boy and his alphabet' – it was a great deal to go through for so little.[11]

It was about this time that Lord Palmerston, then Foreign Secretary, approached Henry's father for the third time, about a new job for Henry, but Lord Minto turned it down without talking it over with his son. Henry later realised how 'exceedingly kind' it had been of the Foreign Secretary to suggest that he might become either his private secretary or a précis writer at the Foreign Office, particularly when he had been so 'slow and spooney' when he worked there for a short time in 1841. Writing home in August 1846 Henry had concluded, however, that 'his very kindness in offering is about the best reason for not taking it up as it shows so much goodwill that I may look forward with some confidence to an early Secretaryship of Legation'. Henry seems to have missed the notice on 6 July about Lord Minto's appointment to the post of Lord Privy Seal, and was sorry that his father was not going to Vienna as ambassador, as 'he had a sort of tenderness' for such a place. He could only suppose that much of his father's time would now be spent in London and that there would be no visits to Minto that year. So far as his own leave was concerned, he expected to be on his way to England during the next few weeks, where he hoped to meet up with Gibby.[12]

Henry arrived back in London towards the end of September only to find he was the last man left in town. George had gone to France and Gibby to St Leonards-on-Sea, and his parents were on their way to Switzerland and Italy at Palmerston's behest. Henry had intended to travel to Buxton but this was put off after he experienced some trouble with his throat. A few days later Henry wrote to his mother from a hotel in Paris telling her that he had just arrived after visiting Brussels, accompanied as it would seem by his wife-to-be. 'We have been here now for four or five days, all of which have been diligently employed in the great object of our journey.' The couple's stay was expected to last a further ten or twelve days, 'some of which will probably be better spent than in continual shopping'. A Mr Edmund had joined the couple at Brussels and would be staying with them in Paris until 8 October when he had to be back in London. This was too soon for Henry so that 'we shall let him go alone'.[13] Henry's temper had not improved when he told his mother on 9 November that 'the day after tomorrow ought naturally to have been our wedding day but now the earliest that is talked of is a month, and I do not feel the least sure of it being then'.[14]

There was a flurry of letters between father and son in November 1847 and Henry was finally able to say, 'I believe at last we really are to be married.'[15] Anne, the eldest daughter of Sir Edmund Antrobus, was to become his wife on 9 December but she had been 'most provokingly weak and unfit for anything' and doctors suggested she might be 'better in a month'. In the event all went to plan and their honeymoon was spent at Pembroke Lodge which was 'borrowed' for the purpose. Henry apologised to his parents for not writing after 'the eventful ninth' but, as he said, 'a honeymoon spent in writing would have been so unorthodox that such a thing was not to be thought of'.[16] Anne wrote to her mother-in-law the following day, promising to make Henry as good a wife as he deserved but there were unspoken regrets about the absence of Lord and Lady Minto from the church. Fanny and Lord John also had been unable to attend the ceremony. Anne and Henry now planned to spend a few days at Cheam before going north to Minto.[17]

Little is recorded about Henry's service at The Hague, where he first became secretary of legation on 26 June 1848. He undertook the duties of a chargé d'affaires on five separate occasions between 1850 and 1853 and it may be assumed that he had been quite content not to be sent to Constantinople at this stage in his career. Nevertheless, he often looked back over his time at St Petersburg with pleasure and Gertrude Elliot, his daughter, maintained that he never lost interest in Russia. She said that he read every book that was published about the country, frequently remarking that 'a revolution would come there, though not in his lifetime, and that when it came the horrors would surpass anything previously known in history. The French revolution would be a joke compared to it.'[18] When Annie, as she became known, wrote to Lady Minto in July 1849 she told her that Henry was in good spirits and had 'lately become a member of a rifle club which gave him a walk every Wednesday afternoon besides being an opportunity of meeting some of his colleagues'. Their house in The Hague was especially pleasant, with most of the trees in front of it being limes. The 'perfume in the morning and evening was most sweet'.[19]

Henry and Anne's first child, Francis, was born at The Hague in March 1851. His vigour and strength were the wonder and admiration of all who saw him. Henry, of course, considered him 'quite a phenomenon' and told his mother that Anne and he allowed themselves to be flattered by all those who 'tell us it is an unheard of thing to find an animal of 18 months old knowing his letters'. His chief accomplishment latterly had been to speak the last word in each line of his nursery rhymes. So far as 'Mimi', his mother-in-law, was concerned, Henry said the child had 'a very great admiration for her but their hours are too different and the difference in their ages too great for them to be of great use to each other yet'.[20]

Six days before Christmas 1852, 'such a good merry letter' arrived at The Hague from his mother at Nervi, where he supposed she was about to be joined by the Melgunds. After telling her of his disappointment that their son Arthur's leg 'had not yet quite healed' and of his hopes that 'the warm climate of Nervi' would have a good effect upon him, Henry turned to the political life, knowing how it always held an interest for his mother. He explained that everyone was still quite in ignorance about what government was likely to be formed and the two options were for 'a fair half and half mixture or a Peel government with one or two Whig ingredients'.[21] On Christmas Eve, Fanny wrote to her sister Mary Abercromby from London, praying that God might grant the continuance of the 'present good accounts' of their mother's health although it was clear that she was alarmingly ill. She said that 'whenever my thoughts are not with Mama, they are wearying themselves to no purpose in threading the maze of ravelled politics, or rather political arrangements, in which we are living'.[22] Lady Minto was well enough at the end of the following March to write a happy and bright letter of congratulation to Fanny, who had given birth to Mary Agatha at Pembroke Lodge.[23]

Henry had told his mother that Annie would be writing her a long letter and it was duly sent from The Hague at the end of February 1853, addressed to 'Dearest Lady Minto'. She was at pains to thank her mother-in-law for sending her an exceedingly pretty pelisse which she had made for Francis and in which she expected him to look 'very magnificent'. She was, nevertheless, concerned that he had a set of warm admirers who would certainly turn his head about 'his charms of face and manners if he were a little older'. He had become rather less studious than formerly when he cared for nothing but his books and liked going to Ralph's house, as he called the adjacent premises. When she had asked him what he would like to send his grandmother for her pretty pelisse, he said 'a gingerbread', that being 'the thing … he likes best'. Describing the routine of her own life in which she had gained some liberty by insisting on perfectly quiet mornings, she now felt gay and able to do much more than she used to. As well as dining out she went to the opera frequently. Henry, on the other hand, never came away from a court ball 'without a bad headache' because, in Anne's view, he had to stay too long at such events. Ralph Abercromby looked infinitely better than when he arrived the previous year.[24] His colour was much better and cough less frequent, and Anne hoped that when the two new rooms which were being built in their house were completed they would find themselves more comfortable, and that Ralph would become reconciled to his new abode. There were also plans for them to give some parties. Finally, Anne said her adieus and asked Lady Minto to give her love to Nina and those with her in Italy.[25]

Ten days into March after a 'disagreeable' winter, Henry and Anne were hoping that the Italian weather was at least having a beneficial effect on Lady Minto. So far as the adjacent Dutch households were concerned, 'it was melancholy' he said, 'how little Mary and Annie have ever seen of each other, Mary having been shut up with her colds and Annie, after several weeks of apparent progress having fallen back' and missed a ball given by the King (William III) at the palace. As Henry put it, 'Mary was no more fit for a party that evening than for a walk to the top of the peak of Tenerife'. Among other news was a letter written by Nina to Lotty which told them that William and Nina's five-year-old son Arthur, who had hurt his leg quite seriously, was at last 'quite healed'. It had been amputated. Gibby, who was fighting in the Crimean War, had had his name 'mentioned in the General's despatch' which was 'as good as a letter in all essentials' and would no doubt, as Henry put it, make 'the young soldier very happy'.[26]

Two weeks later, the family received good accounts of Fanny and Mary Agatha but Henry had heard that his mother had again been unwell. He and Anne had made up their minds to pass three weeks in England in May and then migrate to Switzerland on account of the need to find a high and relaxing place where Anne's health might benefit, leaving the Abercrombys at The Hague.[27] Lady Minto approved of Henry's determination to 'try and get a dram of some stronger air' for Annie, but her own health prevented any thought of them joining the family there. Henry thought it would not be wise for his wife to undertake any long drives even if the immediate application of leeches subdued her attacks. Referring to what he called his 'vagabond profession', there was some prospect of him being transferred to 'a more active and important place' after five years at The Hague, and he hoped the new Foreign Secretary, Lord Clarendon, who had taken over from Lord John in Aberdeen's coalition government, was of the same mind.[28]

Three weeks later, the family's plan had changed. Their home visit would take place but they now intended to return to The Hague again 'for a bit'. Ralph Abercromby wanted to pay his father and mother a visit in Scotland, and though he was sure Clarendon would allow a colleague to be the chargé d'affaires during the three weeks he would be absent, Henry had 'too strong an aversion to being away' from the post at that time. The result was, as Henry said, 'to put the Swiss part of our plan rather far back'. Meanwhile, rumours were circulating that he was to be posted to Vienna and with obvious pride he told his mother that 'it would be an immense advantage to me to be at one of the great courts from which I should be pretty sure of promotion sooner or later, and in spite of the drawbacks at present, it is one of the posts I should best like'.[29]

Writing from 146 Piccadilly, ten days later, Henry told his mother that Annie had 'stood the bustle and racket' of the journey to London so well that they meant to remain in town instead of going to Cheam. She was to be seen by the medical professor who had examined her the previous year – and after his visit he declared her to be stronger and recommended that she should try 'a flattering process' of rubbing the arms and feet with hot olive oil which was being produced by a manufacturer in Galashiels. Despite the additional and routine prescription of what 'a good warm winter would do to her mucous membrane', it was clear that the plan to visit Switzerland was at an end. They would go back to The Hague in two weeks' time and remain there until the autumn 'and then ask for leave for the winter'. Henry had not been able to learn anything of an intention to move him to a more active post but he supposed himself 'a poor creature if one did not allow a certain quantity of the noble fire of ambition to run through one's veins'.[30]

Mary, Countess of Minto, died aged sixty-seven at Nervi on 21 July 1853. Unread, as it would have been, Henry's last epistle to his mother, written two days after her death, showed him trying to comfort her with news of his wife and expressing some repentance for his admitted neglect. 'You always used to abuse the atmosphere of London, and I begin to believe,' he wrote, 'that besides its physical impurities it must contain qualities very deleterious to the morals for I believe I neglected you most shamefully during the whole time we were there.' He had heard from Lotty that the weather in Italy was 'far too hot for enjoyment' and that the accounts of his mother were 'capital', but he did confess he was 'always rather afraid of hearing of you're [sic] being so well as to tempt an increase in your very spare diet'. Again, rather too optimistically, and almost as if he was unaware of the seriousness of her condition, he asked her to imagine 'how anxious we shall be to know what is decided for your winter plans'.[31]

It was at the beginning of August that Fanny wrote in her diary that

the world is changed for me ever since I last wrote. My dear, dear Mama has left it, and I shall never again see the face so long and deeply loved … Thursday, July 21st was the day her angel spirit was summoned to that happy home where tears are wiped from all eyes.[32]

Ten days later, those of the family who could, assembled at Minto House from where Lord John Russell wrote to Fanny, who had been left at Pembroke Lodge to care for five-month-old Agatha. Describing the scene, he said how sorrowful it was to see Lord Minto and so many of his sons and daughters assembled to perform the last duties to her who was the life and comfort of them all. The place was looking beautiful, and 'your mother's garden was never so lovely. It is pleasant in all these sorrows and trials to see a family so united in affection, and so totally without feelings or objects that partake of selfishness or ill-will.'[33]

Lady Minto had been the strong anchor and undoubted centre of deep affection so essential in the upbringing of all her ten children. Until her health deteriorated she shared many of the children's activities with enthusiasm and enjoyment, and continued to take great interest in the detail of their lives. She had always been conscious of how tightly her husband had been forced to control the family's finances. They were far from poor but the needs of the estate and the necessary size of the household called for constant care and a careful balance of the resources which were available – lessons which had to be passed on to the two eldest boys in particular, neither of whom had any entrepreneurial flair or interest in commerce.

By the end of the year Henry was still at The Hague though his transfer to Vienna was no longer 'only a probability'. He had not yet been gazetted but Lord Clarendon had given him the news he wanted. His appointment was to date from 23 December, and he expected to set out eastward in three or four weeks' time. His first letter as the new secretary of legation in Vienna arrived in April 1854, a month after the French and British declaration of war against Russia and the start of the Crimean War. Ralph Abercromby had always favoured the Austrian appointment rather than one to Constantinople and now, writing to his father, Henry said he thought it probably the more interesting of the two cities. Meanwhile, following the death of his wife, Lord Minto had turned to his sister, Anna Maria, for mutual comfort, she herself being within a year of death. Henry knew 'the sentiment you and Aunt Anna Maria kept for the place'.[34] Despite the dark war clouds close at hand, Henry was full of plans for visits to the Tyrol and other places to which he would be free to go without 'having to ask leave from home'. From the Netherlands there was a report that Ralph, who was always frail and prone to the cold, had become depressed on account of there being little or no political interest to occupy him. Unfortunately he did not care about 'commercial matters'.[35]

Henry was soon telling his father how he often discovered more from the English newspapers in Vienna about what was happening to the east than was known at the embassy. Newspaper correspondents were on the spot. As one commentator said, the Crimean War 'took longer to get itself declared than any war in history' and throughout its duration was a war of diplomats as well as the military. Temperatures had risen between the powers although the immediate cause was soon forgotten as Czar Nicholas I moved two army corps along the Danube and Allied troops landed in the Crimea. By October the city of Sevastopol, the home of Russia's Black Sea fleet was under siege. According to Henry, the intentions of the Russians in crossing the Danube were still unknown but the

> general opinion seemed to be that they will push on to Varna which would not be able to resist them, but others on the contrary imagine that all they mean for the present

to do is to occupy the line of Trajan's Wall from about Rassova to Kutschendji until
the season is far enough advanced for them to attempt to cross the Balkan [River] and
march upon Adrianople [Edirne].

Then, knowing how much his father always wanted to hear of things naval, he passed
on his fear that both the English fleets in the Baltic as well as in the Black Sea
might be commanded by the wrong men for this type of service. Accounts from
Constantinople said that Whitley Dundas, commander-in-chief Mediterranean,
was extremely unpopular but that Sir Edmund Lyons was quite the reverse, and 'our
officers do not like Dundas's fancy in denying them to have as little as possible to do
with the French officers'. The latter situation had, Henry said, probably been caused
by Dundas being afraid of quarrels. In Henry's view Sevastopol was 'not to be taken by a
fleet'. Adding that relations with the Turks could occasionally be strained, Henry told
of some 'middies' playing leapfrog over the devotedly prostrate bodies of Turkish
'Musselmen at prayer'.

Soon after Christmas 1854 the secretary of legation wrote to his father at
Farrance's Hotel in Upper Belgrave Street telling him that he had written to Trieste
about the non-receipt of letters from London. Both men were concerned about the
whereabouts and health of Gilbert, Henry's youngest brother, who had arrived in
the Crimea with two battalions of the Rifle Brigade after serving for three years in
South Africa. The first battalion of the brigade was to lead the advance across the
Alma River at Inkerman and fight at Sevastopol. The embassy had been sending large
supplies of warm clothing of all descriptions from Vienna but the bulk of them took
considerable time to be dispatched from Trieste. It was a poor consolation to know
that the sufferings of the Russians 'were in all respects much greater than those of our
own troops'. Describing himself as 'our own correspondent', Henry told how after the

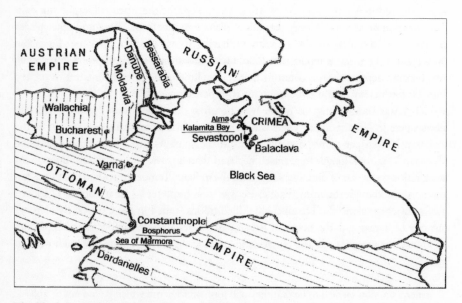

The Black Sea and the Crimean peninsula, 1853 to 1856.

battle of Alma in September 1854 he had asked to see one of Lord Raglan's staff only to be kept in the dark and regarded with the usual 'official reserve and aristocratic hauteur'.[36]

As the reader will already be aware, Lord Minto and Harriet, the youngest of the Minto daughters, had it seems planned to go to Constantinople from The Hague. Henry and Anne had been disappointed that the earl had elected to travel by the Marseilles route but they could not deny that it was likely to be an easier land journey, which 'on Harriet's account, is I am afraid, a great object'. In December 1854 Henry still had hopes that in the summer there would be no excuse for them not calling at Vienna on their way north.[37]

On 14 January 1855, two weeks after his first letter, Henry received a second, much-delayed communication from his father in Paris, which by then the pair had reached. It said nothing new about Harriet's health but 'it took away the hope that [the family] had that Sir Joseph Olliffe's opinion might not be confirmed by other doctors'.[38] Henry could only reiterate that the utmost thought had to be given to the probable effects of fatigue and cold during a long journey at that time of year. It was far from obvious that the 'advantage to be expected from a southern climate' would 'counterbalance' such effects. For his part, Lord Minto seems to have regarded his son's work in Vienna with 'a great deal of distrust', something that did not surprise Henry despite his view that the post deserved rather more credit than his father was inclined to allow. Circumstances required that a sharp lookout be kept so as to avoid being drawn into 'unmeaning negotiations'.[39]

Lord Minto and Harriet were still in Paris ten days later staying at the Hotel Bristol. Henry was 'exceedingly glad' to learn that George (Doddy) was to make the journey south with them, and that they would have the company of a doctor. He agreed with his father that Malta seemed 'a good point for you to make for, with the very great chance there now is that Gilbert will have to come away from the Crimea'.[40] However, the proposed expedition was not to be and Harriet died on 5 February. He had heard nothing about Gilbert other than the probability of him being moved away from the war zone.

Meanwhile, a few weeks before, Lord Aberdeen's coalition government had been brought down as a direct result of its incompetent management of the war. The former Home Secretary, Lord Palmerston, then formed his first government, with much popular support. Lord John was given the task of representing Britain at a conference in Vienna which would either lead to a negotiated peace or to Austria entering the war on the side of the Allies. France was represented by François Adolphe Bourqueney (1799–1869) while Turkey sent Aarif Effendi. Later the negotiators were reinforced by the arrival of the French foreign minister and Turkey sent another representative.

Preliminary talks had been held between the parties at Lord Westmorland's house in Vienna on 1 January 1855 at which Prince Gortschakoff, one of the Russian commanders, and Count Buol, the Austrian foreign minister, had been present.[41] Although the talks gave the impression that negotiations were going on, this was not so. Westmoreland had been ill and unable to go out to the Austrian Foreign Office building. Gortschakoff declared he had full powers to treat for peace on the basis of the 'four points'.[42] This made it necessary, Henry explained to his father, that England, Austria and France should ascertain that they interpreted them strictly in the same manner, and that the meeting was for the purpose of coming to a complete understanding with respect to them. When this was done Gortschakoff was called in and informed of the sense in which they were taken by the three Allied Powers.

He admitted he might have said more than he should, adding that he thought it had been unfortunate that the meeting had taken place at the ambassador's residence.[43]

In February, Lord John, the specially appointed British plenipotentiary, set out for Vienna with lawyer George as his private secretary, calling at Paris, Brussels and Berlin to brief himself en route. He told Fanny that 'the country is in great difficulty and every personal consideration ought to be waived'.[44] Fanny joined him at the beginning of March. On his way to the Austrian capital he was offered, and he accepted, the post of Secretary of State for the Colonies. His instructions had been to insist on a limit to the number of Russian warships in the Black Sea but by the time Lord John arrived, and unknown to him, the French and British governments had shifted their approach in favour of the neutralisation of the Black Sea. This was to occasion severe criticism of him by both newspapers and Parliament.

Henry told his father that he at least had 'no right to complain of these negotiations for they have given us a very pleasant visit from Fanny, George and Lord John at a time we were likely to be longer than usual without seeing our own people'. It had been especially timely as Annie was expecting a child in August and he anticipated that she would take a considerable time to recover after the confinement, making a visit to England the following winter impossible. Gertrude, their second and last child, was born on 13 August.[45]

Writing in her diary on the last day of March, Fanny concentrated on the Viennese negotiations, referring to private letters which Lord John had received from Lord Clarendon and Lord Lansdowne (Minister without Portfolio) which 'were full of distrust and disapprobation of the proceedings'. Lord Clarendon's were more especially warlike, the very reverse of every letter he had written in the days of Lord Aberdeen. Lady John's appreciation of political affairs had matured over the years. She had learned what it meant to be the wife of a Prime Minister and now, after a period out of office, her diary was less frequently the domain of fantasies and more a record of political reality. More letters and dispatches arriving in the Austrian capital made 'John's position still worse; representing him as ready to consent to unworthy terms', and Fanny worried as Lord John talked of 'giving up the mission and the Colonies' – 'his reputation cannot afford a fresh storm, and he must show that he did not lightly consent to belong to a Ministry of which he knew the materials so well'.[46]

During May and June in London, however, it became clear that Lord John had put himself in a false position believing as he did that the Austrian terms were good enough to be accepted. Henry saw how 'from the beginning of the affair a year and a half ago up to the present we have been going on the principle of patting Austria on the back and trying to coax her on when a more decided course would have been much better'.[47] During the debate on Disraeli's motion of censure at the end of May, Lord John accepted that the limit put on the number of Russian ships in the Black Sea did not guarantee the safety of Turkey, and when questioned he had to admit he had himself been in favour of exactly such a compromise. In effect, he had criticised the terms to which he had agreed. With both the French and British governments changing their war aims to the neutralisation of the Black Sea, the British press fell on him for being servile to the Russians and misleading the House of Commons. He resigned on 13 July 1855 while Fanny was 'thinking of my dear and noble husband, doomed to suffer so much for no great fault than having committed himself so far without consultation with his colleagues'.[48]

In June, Henry had told Lord Minto that 'we shall have all the discussions over again as to the manner of accomplishing an impossibility which I think this must be as long as one party is as weak as Turkey and the other as strong as Russia'. Just how long the ambassador, Lord Westmorland, intended to be away from Vienna, Henry had not a 'notion' but he knew he was going to London and had taken both his riding and carriage horses with him. Meanwhile, the warm summer in Vienna and temperatures in the higher 80s prompted him to wish similar weather on his father, who was about to leave for Minto. All his carefully laid plans for a visit to Constantinople were now forgotten. An immobile and expectant Annie sat in the embassy garden.[49] At the start of September it was the thought of Lotty's prospective marriage to Melville, the thirty-six-year-old son of John Portal, of Freefolk Priors and Laverstoke in Hampshire, that took centre stage.[50] Henry suspected that his father would miss Lotty's company despite the pleasure he might take in seeing her well settled. Certainly, 'she was a great deal too good [to be] an old maid'. The wedding took place on 9 October.

Writing to Lord Minto just as he reached London for Lotty's wedding, Henry had news of his brother Charlie, who was in the Far East. He was especially irritated 'at the provoking way in which the Russian fleet have slipped through our fingers on the coast of China'. The previous year an Allied squadron had laid siege to Petropavlovsk on the south-eastern end of the Kamchatka peninsula. British and French forces far outnumbered the Russians and as the 60-gun *Pallas* retreated up the Amur River to avoid being a target the remaining Russian ships took refuge in Petropavlovsk harbour, the town itself being lightly defended by some 1,000 troops. Unexpectedly, a naval brigade of 700 British and French seamen and marines was ambushed and forced to retreat, leaving behind 208 dead. Despite the Allied withdrawal and fearful that they might again be attacked, Muravyov, the governor-general, evacuated the Russian garrison under the cover of snow in April 1855.

His wife's brother who was in Hong Kong, Robert Crawfurd Antrobus, was the authority for the story that Henry then told his father, using the version which was 'believed at Canton'. It seemed that Charlie, commodore aboard HMS *Sybille*, was in company with *Hornet* and *Bittern* when they discovered the Russian fleet at anchor in a bay. Mustering only 90 or so guns against a Russian force of 114 guns, including those of 'our old friend' the *Aurora*, the commodore decided not to attack. Instead he sent a native vessel to let the admiral know his position. This was the 'bad part of the story'. The admiral apparently received Charlie's letter in five days but then waited another fourteen days in the hope that some French ships might return from a cruise. At last, after thirty days had elapsed, he gave up on the French and joined the commodore. Of course, the Russians had slipped out. He greatly sympathised with Charlie, who must have been 'terribly disappointed for with a little activity there might have been a chance of getting hold of the Russian Fleet' which included transports with the garrison of Petropavlovsk on board. Even supposing the admiral to have been right 'in wishing to have a greater force with him', Henry said he could have left word for the French ships and 'hurried up himself to the place where he was wanted'.[51]

At the embassy in Vienna there was no little depression in November and a growing concern about the Allies' failure to win the war. Sir G. Hamilton Seymour arrived as envoy extraordinary, so providing the negotiating team with still greater experience and was very well received, particularly by Count Buol, and 'old Metternich', then eighty-six years old. Henry described the situation as one where he was on the point of 'hauling down' his broad pennant.[52] Sevastopol had fallen on 8 September while a successful Anglo-French naval campaign in the Sea of Azov had come to an end and the siege of Kars had been lifted ten days before. Henry admitted that the political atmosphere much improved after the taking of Sevastopol but the Austrians were on the worst possible terms with the more Russian of the German states, and with Russia herself. It was 'a holy alliance between neighbours who hate each other so cordially'. For Henry this had 'at least a certain advantage'.[53]

More family news reached Vienna at the beginning of 1856. Lord Minto gave Henry an 'excellent account' of Lotty, her husband and her home. He had seen her 'fairly established' in December when he had been in London for the state visit of Victor Emmanuel II, the King of Sardinia. Then, having read 'the very hard measure' of comment his father had dealt out to 'poor Austria', Henry went on to defend his approach to the continuing dialogue about peace. It had been a great mistake, he wrote, 'to call what has been going on here a negotiation, for it really has been nothing of the kind'. He thought his father underestimated the importance of a rupture of diplomatic relations between Russia and Austria. Henry went on to tell his father that he had received a very good account of Gibby, who was being treated near Scutari on the eastern side of the Bosphorus, where 'he was most comfortably housed'.[54]

It would appear that George and Lord John returned to London by different routes. Henry's brother had decided to make an expedition to Bulgaria to see something of the Turkish lines at Shumla, one of the six districts into which the army was organised and where Omar Pasha had his headquarters. He seems to have stayed a few days at Bucharest in March 1856 to allow the frost and snow to pass away before he began the rough part of the journey. In Vienna, Henry met a man who had come up that way and who declared that all the stories of the difficulties and hardships were a 'great nonsense'. Beyond 'two or three days hard riding' there would be for him nothing to complain of but he hoped that George had been wise enough to lay in a supply of diacodum as he had not had much riding lately. Only one mention was made of George's companion, his 'devout friend Waldegrave'.[55] The latter, however, seemed 'much too soft to be a desirable companion on a rough journey'.[56]

The end of war was in sight when Russia accepted preliminary peace terms in February 1856 after Austria threatened to join the Allies, and a final settlement, the Treaty of Paris, was signed on 30 March. One important result was that Austria, having sided with the Allies, lost the support of Russia in Central European affairs and became dependent on Britain and France. In May, Lord Minto paid a brief visit to The Hague, telling Ralph and Lady Mary while he was there that he had a 'half-formed project' about spending the 1856/57 winter in Italy. Henry and Anne discussed the possibility of their joining him but there were too many people they needed to visit in England,

and long journeys took up much of his leave. Such a proposition was also beyond the reach of both their purse and of Annie's strength. Turning to his work, Henry told his father how surprised he had been to find him 'so favourable and indulgent to the peace'; he had not expected him to like it. It had also taken people in Austria off their guard, many of whom considered it 'a rash act on the part of the Imperial government. The Russians were furious with it' – more so, said Henry, than they 'would be if they were themselves quite convinced they had become permanently the innocent lambs they profess themselves'.[57]

During an excessively hot Viennese summer even Henry, who was usually impervious to the weather, found travelling the 4 miles between his home and the Chancery heavy going. A doctor who was consulted about the advisability of Annie travelling to Italy agreed it was 'much the best thing she could try'. Rome would be 'decidedly bad for her' but Nice and then Florence were 'strongly' recommended. Having made up his mind that 'no inconvenience must stand in the way of what doctors say', he also contemplated her taking the waters at Franzensbad near Carlsbad. As the year went on, the family decided to 'guide its movements' so far as possible by those of Lord Minto, but this proved far from easy. They heard that it was likely that the Russells would go to Nice instead of Florence but, in the event, Lady John and the children went first to The Hague, and after joining Lord John at Antwerp went on to 'a villa beautifully situated above the Lake of Geneva' in September. The early part of the winter was spent in Italy, where Lord Russell came into contact with Cavour and other Italian patriots whose cause he strongly supported.[58] Nobody had dropped any 'hint' to Henry about whether or not the change in the Russells' holiday arrangements affected his father's 'winter projects' and this made him think he might be better going 'straight to Paris to see whether [they] might not find some doctor there' who could do Annie some good. In Vienna the medical profession had done 'absolutely nothing' and he feared he ought to be concentrating on his wife's health instead of contemplating 'the effect of a little Italian air'.

Henry had a dread that the plans for the family to meet up together would be upset by his being sent by the Foreign Office to replace Francis Napier as the secretary of legation at Constantinople. Other appointments he anticipated, wrongly as matters turned out, included James Hudson to succeed Sir William Temple, the minister at Naples. Although Britain was not bound to look for a man who would please King Ferdinand, his nomination 'would not delight Bomba'. As a result Henry was afraid that

> we may be tempted to show displeasure and ill-humour by not naming anyone for the present but if we intend to withdraw the Mission as a hint that a more serious move was contemplated, it would be far better that we should have a minister there to give relief to the withdrawal, and to make the king feel that we were really in earnest.[59]

Early in September, Henry wrote to Lord Minto, who was at the Hotel de l'Univers in Lyon telling him that he hoped to see him in Florence sometime in October or November, but before he could leave for Tuscany there were works on his house that he had to supervise. It was not a property which could be heated in winter. Back at Minto there was a similar story with 'fresh paint and new carpets' on order, but the greatest change had been work to repair the library chimney which 'seemed to have established a vested right to remain as it was'. He had heard several months before that his father had also carried out the removal of 'the fence under the rocks' during his short autumn visit – a 'special eyesore' for William and Nina.[60]

In the meantime, Fanny was in Frankfurt with Lord Russell also en route for Florence, where they were to spend the early part of the winter at the Villa Capponi with many of the Minto family nearby. Built in the fourteenth century and purchased by the Capponi family in 1572, the villa and its garden terraces below were especially attractive. It had been touch and go whether they made it, according to Lady Mary, since they 'had nearly determined on doctor's advice to abandon Florence for Nice'. In Lord John's case, he had been on the verge of a breakdown after being forced from office. The villa also became a meeting place for liberals in Tuscany, and despite the annoyance to the Tuscan government Lord John was able to enjoy a brief meeting with Cavour. By December, the ex-Prime Minister was able to tell Nina, Lady Melgund, that the party had passed the time at the villa 'very agreeably' and in clear skies and bright sun there had been several visits to galleries and churches. Besides the Florentines and 'their acute sagacity' they had entertained 'many of those whose wits were too bright or their hearts too warm to bear the governments of Naples and Rome'.[61]

It was a great happiness for Lord Minto to have Henry, Anne and their children living with him in what he called their 'colony' in Florence, not too far from the Russells, who were about a half a mile out of town. His friend, James Lacaita, a scholar and politician had accompanied him on the journey.[62] He had found in the literary, scientific and political society 'more resource and interest than he expected'. Florence was, the earl said, 'very full of English of whom we see nothing and very well stocked with natives of all the States of Italy of whom we see a great deal'. There were even convicts under sentences of death, the galleys, or exile, who were allowed to reside there by the 'comparatively mild government of Tuscany while the 'barbarous despotism' of the dominions of the King of Naples and the Pope continued to be anathema to Minto.[63]

Henry and the family returned to London on leave at the end of March 1857, staying a few days at 146 Piccadilly. He told his father (who was again in Lyon) that Annie had stood the journey from Vienna very well but Gertrude had been unwell. Referring to the results of the general election, he gave him the news that Lord John had retained his seat for the City of London constituency much against the odds. William, he thought, had not been opposed in Scotland. On the other hand, opposition to Melville Portal in North Hampshire had been 'a great vexation to Lotty'; her husband had been obliged to make room for another candidate and was to lose the seat.[64] Knowing her father's interest in the City of London election, Fanny wrote to him from 'Pemmy' Lodge, saying,

> I thought my days of caring for popular applause were over but there was something so much higher than usual in the meaning of the cheers that greeted Lord John whenever he showed himself, that I was not ashamed of being quite delighted. There was obviously a strong feeling among the electors and non-electors in Guildhall and in the streets that John had been unfairly and ungratefully set aside.

He survived, however, an attempt to oust him.[65] Even Charles Dickens, who was an admirer, had put off a visit to Fanny. He had 'abstained', knowing that she 'would be overwhelmed with congratulations'.[66]

It was Charlie who was now looking for more excitement. In June, Sir Henry Keppel, commodore and second-in-command on the China station, led an attack on a fleet of Chinese war junks. Having successfully sunk about seventy of them, he was complimented by the commander-in-chief and subsequently promoted admiral. Writing to his father that month, Henry said that he could not help hoping that circumstances would allow Charlie to 'have something to do with the gunboats' although he anticipated that any real action would have to wait until there were troops available to fight the Chinese. Furthermore, it seemed to him that 'what we have now most to dread would be the complete success of Lord Elgin's mission'. With his usual circumlocution and even a touch of eastern delicacy, Henry suggested that were the Chinese Emperor to 'turn out thoroughly moderate and accede to all demands, we shall be left without a shadow of excuse for occupying Canton'. To threaten Canton and finish without occupying it, meant in Henry's mind that 'we should lose in their estimation the respect we want to gain'. What actually happened was that James Bruce, the eighth Earl of Elgin, moved against Canton after failing to gain any concessions from the governor during two days of talks in December, whereupon he moved on to Shanghai. There he endeavoured to negotiate with the government in Peking, and after months of seemingly tedious talks during which Lord Elgin played the part of an 'uncontrollably fierce barbarian', a Treaty of Tientsin was eventually signed in June the following year.

At the beginning of summer, Henry and the family had arrived back in Austria, where they were able to enjoy occasional short breaks at their new country house. They no longer regretted the loss of the holiday home they had lived in during the previous three years, and although Annie had to be brought out into the garden in a bath chair, she enjoyed 'this comparative liberty'. Lord Minto would have been delighted to know how much of an impression he had made on Gertrude, the two-year-old, during their stay together in Florence. Henry told him how 'she continues faithful to you and constantly talks of you'. Then, recalling the political discussions they had enjoyed in Italy, Henry told his father that he was pleased to see the improved relations across Europe. All the amnesties and restorations of property 'appear to be real and fully carried out'. In Italy, he believed no application 'had been refused to a single refugee who has applied for it'. In Hungary, such applications would only be refused to Lajos Kossuth, the radical politician, and one or two of his associates.[67]

A more cheerful letter from Charlie arrived three months later. It described him as being greatly relieved at 'having an opportunity of doing something' and 'getting credit from the public in China'. It had been brought by a steamer carrying the Indian mails which had docked at a bustling Trieste. According to Henry, it was 'a very advancing place and the people there who are enterprising enough, imagine they are now to grow still more rapidly', albeit that they were greatly displeased with Palmerston's declaration against the Suez Canal.[68] The port scarcely knew whether 'it stood on its head or its heels' since all the world was there for the opening of the railway which completed the line from Vienna to the Adriatic. The journey could be accomplished 'between morning and night'. The new link prompted Henry to suggest to Lord Minto that he might make use of it if he meant to go to Italy that year. He would have a special welcome from Gertrude and enjoy the facilities of a 'most capital house' he had obtained for the winter period.[69]

In September there was another 'most excellent piece of news' about Charlie, who was coming home after five years in the Far East. The Second Anglo-Chinese war had produced one reward for the family at least. The commodore's part in operations in the Canton River had been recognised by his award of the Companion of the Bath, and he would be made an aide-de-camp to the Queen later that year. 'After all the annoyance and vexation he has had,' wrote Henry to his father, 'it will be a real satisfaction to him to end his commission with a public mark of approval like this.' The newspapers were full of the Indian mutiny which had started in March but Henry reminded his father that there was yet another piece of good fortune. A Royal Commission had been examining the Army's system of purchasing promotion and Gibby had been awarded 'his majority' without his father having to purchase it.[70] 'If it excuses him,' wrote Henry, 'and I suppose it does, from having to go to India for some time it is a very fortunate thing for I should not imagine him to be in a state to stand hard work in a hot climate without much risk'.[71]

The new year came and went uneventfully and Henry could only suppose in February 1858 that Doddy and Lord Minto 'were keeping house alone at Minto'. He hoped they were 'not freezing in their solitude' as Anne and he had been in Vienna. Fortunately, the new house had proved itself 'more than perfect' and given Annie 'quite a different existence', so much so that she had 'been out to several great balls and other places of dissipation'. The first steps she had taken while they had been in Florence had helped her prevent the monotony to which she had long been condemned. She 'astonished the world' wrote Henry, at a ball at court where for the first time the wives of 'subordinates' were admitted – a change of such 'portentous magnitude' as to be a revolution in the eyes of the Austrian aristocracy. They had also heard from numerous friends they had made during the winter in Florence.[72]

In the spring, when he had almost become reconciled to the absence of any immediate promotion, and the family was at last appreciating some of Vienna's social delights, Henry received some quite unexpected news. Having spent six years at St Petersburg, followed by a long period at The Hague and four years in Austria, both as secretary to legation, he was to become British minister at Copenhagen. As he wrote after his eventual retirement, 'it was a complete surprise to me when Lord Malmesbury, on becoming Foreign Secretary, at once appointed me minister to Denmark'.[73] Henry was, however, not destined to remain there long, and a little more than a year later when he was home on a short leave of absence, he called at the Foreign Office to say goodbye to Lord Malmesbury, who told him that he had just heard of the death of Ferdinand, King of the Two Sicilies, and that he wanted him to go at once to Naples to congratulate Francis II on his accession, and to re-establish the diplomatic relations which France and England had broken off three years before, when '[King] Bomba had snapped his fingers at our remonstrances against his misgovernment'. The assignment was not intended to last more than a few weeks but the change of government, whereby Palmerston became Prime Minister and Lord John Foreign Secretary, put an end, as Henry described it, to that arrangement.

After one or two hiccups caused by the Prime Minister and the Foreign Secretary's diametrically opposite views on Italian politics, Henry left England for Naples in May 1859. As he wrote later, 'it was the most enviable post in the whole diplomatic service, and which, thanks to Garibaldi, was also soon to become the one most full of interest and excitement', but the war of France and Sardinia against Austria had just begun.[74] By the time he arrived three weeks later it had been brought to a close. Two ferocious battles in Northern Italy had cost some 6,000 Austrian and French-Piedmontese lives and ended Austrian power in Italy.

As these events and the change in Henry's career were unfolding, Lord Minto died at Eaton Square on 31 July. Agatha Russell's shortest of short acknowledgements of the event referred to the fact that his 'keen interest in public questions continued to the end, with a firm belief in the ultimate triumph of good. "Magna est Veritas et prevalebit" (Truth is mighty and it shall prevail) were almost the last words he spoke on his deathbed.'[75] For the forty-two-year-old Henry it was a particularly sad loss. Both men had represented their country and fought disappointing battles in revolutionary circumstances. Now in Naples, the Foreign Secretary's brother-in-law was encouraging Francis II to abandon the arbitrary methods of his father and introduce constitutional reform. Henry hoped there would be at least some relaxation of the previous system and some disposition to govern with a little regard for the law, but again success was illusory. Early in 1860, Garibaldi and his thousand 'red shirts' seized Sicily in the name of King Victor Emmanuel and, on Lord John's instructions, Henry had an interview with him in the cabin of Admiral Munday on board HMS *Hannibal*, then in the bay at Naples.[76] London had decided on a policy of non-intervention and he managed to dissuade Garibaldi from attacking Venice; but after a plebiscite in October, Sicily was annexed and integrated into the Kingdom of Italy. This left the British legation with no *raison d'être* and Henry returned home.

Greece became the target for two special and rather secret assignments by Henry in the early 1860s. He had been at home since his return from Naples. In April 1862 Lord John, who had been created Earl Russell the year before, appointed Henry as the British minister at Athens on the death of the previous incumbent. His task was to encourage the emergence of a more liberal administration in Greece, where discontent against King Otto had led to a coup against him and his exile in Bavaria. It meant negotiating with the provisional government to agree terms whereby the second son of King Christian of Denmark, Prince William, could become the new Greek monarch. On his first audience with King Otto he found him 'standing in the centre of a large room in an attitude of attention and it became evident that, instead of talking things over, it was expected that I should make a sort of harangue; so I set off at the top of my voice [the King being deaf] and was rather well-pleased with myself for the number of disagreeable things I was able to say'.[77] At breakfast on 30 March 1863, Henry received a telegram announcing the King of Denmark's consent and before two o'clock Prince William was acclaimed by the National Assembly and elected King of Greece under the name of King George I.[78] Although only seventeen years old, he learned Greek quickly and met his future wife Olga Constantinovna, a cousin of the Czar, on a visit to Russia in 1867.

Rhetorically, Henry asked whether there had been 'such a diplomatic shuttlecock' as himself. In September 1863, he was off again, this time to replace Sir James Hudson as minister in Turin, then the seat of the Italian government.[79] It was an appointment which lasted nigh on four years and was to generate offensive imputations in the newspapers of job-fixing by Lord John on Henry's behalf, a story which his brother George was to tell after Hudson's death in 1886. It was nevertheless some six months into his posting before a major agitation occurred. Pope Pius IX's health was such that his death was expected and, with Rome still occupied by a French army under an emperor whose designs were always inscrutable, a serious dilemma was emerging. The location of Italy's capital was also being debated. In September 1864 Henry had the first of numerous meetings with Marco Minghetti, the prime minister, who told him that a convention in Paris had initially agreed to Rome becoming the country's capital, but after further negotiations, and no little rioting and firing by soldiers in Turin, the Emperor agreed to withdraw his troops while the King of Italy would respect Papal territory and move his capital to Florence.[80]

In the spring of 1865 the British minister, Anne and the family moved from Turin to Florence. In October, Palmerston, the Prime Minister, died of pneumonia two days before his eighty-first birthday and was buried in Westminster Abbey. The Queen had wisely sent Lord Russell a note at Pembroke Lodge informing him that in the event of Palmerston's death it would be her intention to ask Russell to carry on the government. A month later, with him again Prime Minister and Lord Clarendon his replacement at the Foreign Office, Fanny was happy and 'so full of reality – the hours of work so cheerfully got through, the hours of leisure so delightful'. Lord Russell and Lord Derby, the leaders of their respective parties, were, however, 'no longer the principal men on either side' in Parliament. Gladstone and Disraeli became the contestants most watched.[81]

Lord Derby became Prime Minister for the third time in June 1866 and Fanny's husband in his seventies was never again to bear the responsibilities of office. Once he had finished writing his *Life and Times of Charles James Fox* the previous year, and following a stay with Fanny in Venice, the couple visited Henry and Anne at Florence in November that year. It was two months or so after the 'Seven Weeks' War' in which Austria had declared war on Prussia and Italy and entered it as a Prussian ally, only to be defeated on land at Custozza and at sea near Lissa in the Adriatic. The Russells viewed the 'magnificent' entry of Victor Emmanuel into the city as king of all Italy, an 'impressive sight' as Agatha was to say. Henry's sister was full of support for 'poor Italy'. The retired Prime Minister described the people as having their hearts full rather than their voices loud 'when the Italian flag was first raised none of the crowd could cheer for weeping and sobbing'. He was also struck by the fine pictures and 'the magnificent colouring and the large conceptions of the Venetian painters'.[82]

The Russell party returned to England early in 1867 and in July Henry finally achieved the post he had avoided twenty years before when he thought there were 'more interesting' capitals. Not only had he been appointed British ambassador to the Sublime Ottoman Porte in Constantinople, but before he left London he was sworn a Privy Counsellor, which attracted the title of the 'Right Honourable' Henry Elliot. He later recalled how his appointment had been just before Sultan Abdulaziz had visited France and England, a visit memorable for being the first that a Turkish sultan ever paid to a foreign monarch, and which occasioned him being made a Knight of the Garter by Queen Victoria. When Henry succeeded Lord Lyons, the previous ambassador, Turkey was quiet and prosperous except for Crete, where a serious rebellion had broken out. In August, however, the Greek government announced its determination of declaring war against the Porte should hostilities against Christians on the island not be ended. Instead, Turkey and Greece severed diplomatic relations. The rebellion led to the loss of many lives and the destruction of the Arkadi Monastery, matters with which Henry was called to deal.

In the winter of 1869, the ambassador was sent to Egypt to represent Britain at the 'solemn opening' of the Suez Canal. Around him were more exalted representatives such as Empress Eugenie for France, the Emperor Franz Joseph for Austria-Hungary, and Prince Henry of the Netherlands for Holland. Palmerston's ill-judged opposition to the canal had only encouraged the French to build it. As Henry said, 'newspaper correspondents were there in shoals … as well as innumerable private visitors who were the recipients of … splendid hospitality'. A fleet of steamers was assembled to carry representatives and guests through the canal with the long procession preceded by Empress Eugénie in the 'beautiful' yacht *L'Aigle*. They halted for the night at Ismailia, where a ball was given, while the next day they arrived at Suez and then proceeded to Cairo for further festivities. 'Old Lesseps was in his glory,'[83] wrote Henry, a few days before he and Anne left Egypt on leave for England, where he was made a Knight Grand Cross of the Bath.[84]

The Rt Hon. Sir Henry Elliot, GCB, had hardly returned to duty when on 6 June 1870 the embassy house in the Pera district of Constantinople, which had been built by William James Smith with advice from Charles Barry in 1842–54, was almost completely destroyed by fire. Government archives and much of the furniture in the state rooms were saved but it had been a close shave for Lady Elliot and her daughter, and all Henry's private property was destroyed. In a letter to Edmund Hammond, the under-secretary at the Foreign Office, Henry described how 'Lady Elliot, our little girl, her governess and the maids were on the bedroom floor, and after filling every bath, jug and basin kept on the look out that the insidious enemy should not slip in unawares'.[85] The following year, John Lessels Jr, an architect born at Dawyek, Peeblesshire, was selected to rebuild the property and survey the other embassy house at Therapia.

During the Franco-Prussian war of 1870–71, Britain stood on the sidelines; it was said to be of little significance. Russia, on the other hand, used the conflict as an opportunity to abrogate a clause in the Treaty of Paris which required the neutrality of the Black Sea; and with Prussia providing tacit support for Russia, there was little Lord Granville, the Foreign Secretary, could do other than call a conference in London to examine the situation.[86] In the event, it cancelled the Black Sea clauses but strengthened Turkey's control over the Dardanelles. Meanwhile, Mahmoud Nedim Pasha, the Grand Vizier, who was a poor administrator but much in favour with Sultan Abdulaziz, fell under the influence of General Ignatieff, the forceful Russian ambassador. He shared the Czar's plans for the direct liberation of Orthodox Christian states and the dream that one day Russia might own Constantinople. Sir Henry was faced with almost daily Russian intrigues both in and out of the sultan's court and Russophobes in England said unfairly that he was no match for Russian ambition.

Henry was returning to Constantinople from leave in May 1874 when in the train between Vienna and Pest he received a telegram asking him to dine that evening with

Bulgaria after the Conference of Constantinople, 1876–77.

Emperor Franz Josef at the palace of Buda. His purpose was to convince Henry of his friendly feelings towards Turkey. After dinner, Count Andrássy, the foreign minister, took the ambassador to his own rooms and explained his policy at some length. At this point Henry said that 'we were all ready to support him in urging the redress of grievances upon the Porte but we all knew perfectly well that it was not the redress … but an entire separation from the Turkish empire that the discontented were aiming at'.[87]

In 1875 insurrections broke out in the Balkans against the brutalities of Turkish rule and the continued disregard of the Orthodox tradition of autonomous churches, to be followed the next year by two events, the first being called the 'Salonika Massacre' in which the French and German consuls were murdered. A young Bulgarian girl had a Turkish lover and one day while visiting his home she declared she had converted to Islam but the family refused to keep her until her conversion had been legally registered. In order to go through this formality she was sent to Salonika by rail. The Greeks waiting for her at the station tried to prevent her from being taken to Government House to make the official declaration, but after a scuffle the police seized her and took her to the American vice-consulate. The ire of the Turks was now thoroughly aroused. About the same time M. Moulin, the French consul, and Mr Henry Abbot, the German consul, were seen going to the Turkish quarter whereupon the mob hustled them into a mosque, where the governor, having been called, found them huddled in a room. A little later the mob broke in and slaughtered both consuls. The Porte at once promised a prompt and severe example would be made of six of the murderers. Henry insisted on having a member of his staff associated with the proceedings and nominated Mr Blunt in that capacity. Altogether twelve people were sentenced to death and another twenty to penal servitude. At a second trial held in Constantinople, the governor received a sentence of degradation and imprisonment.[88]

On the last day of May 1876, Henry sent a telegram of 'an urgent private nature' to London which read, 'The doctors have found it necessary to bleed poor Jane. Grandmama is with her and cousin John has taken charge of the business.' Sultan Abdulaziz (or Jane) had been deposed (bled), and the Valide, his mother (Grandmama), and Sultan Murad V (cousin John) had taken charge.[89] Henry told the Foreign Office that 'none regretted his fall except the immediate dependants of the palace ... and the Russian party'. On 4 June it was announced that Abdulaziz had committed suicide by opening the veins of his arms with a pair of scissors but, as Henry wrote, 'there was not a person who doubted, anymore than I did myself, that he had in reality been the victim of an assassination'.[90] Three months later, with Abdulhamid II on the throne following the demise of Mehmed Murad, the increasing impatience of the people was quietened by the issue of a general scheme of reform for the whole of the Ottoman Empire. It promised a senate and a representative assembly to vote the budget and taxes.

In the second half of 1876, the insurrections that had started the previous year in the Balkans against the brutalities of Turkish rule were followed by a second event, the 'Bulgarian Atrocities'. Henry said nothing 'ever caused a sensation compared with that produced by the Turkish excesses'. The 'almost official assistance given by Russia to the insurgents in Bosnia and Herzegovina through its consul-general together with the scarcely less open encouragement of the Austrian Slav generals in Dalmatia, had effectively prevented the suppression of the insurrection in these provinces', and during the winter of 1875/76 'Russian agents, directed by the Slav committees of Moscow and Odessa, in close alliance with General Ignatieff were busy organizing a rising in Bulgaria'.[91]

Henry received a dispatch from the vice-consul at Adrianople giving the report of a Polish gentleman who had witnessed an incident at Otlakeui not far from Philippopolis, where a post of Turkish *zaptiehs* (a police post) had been fallen upon and murdered by a party of Bulgarians led by Servians (Serbia was then spelt Servia) who subsequently burnt some twenty small villages including Sarambey. Turkish volunteers called *bashibazouks* suppressed the revolt, but not before some 15,000 Bulgarians were massacred and more than fifty villages and monasteries destroyed. In June, Serbia declared war on Turkey and by the end of the month sensational details of Turkish atrocities started to appear in the European press.

It was June before anything about the Turkish response to the Bulgarian atrocities reached Henry or his colleagues in Constantinople. A dispatch from the vice-consul at Adrianople arrived which in the ordinary routine of the service ought at once to have been communicated to Henry but it was 'improperly withheld' from him and given to Edwin Pears, a lawyer and part-time journalist in Constantinople for the *Daily News*. He sent a number of letters to his newspaper which subsequently printed Henry's dispatch. Antonio Galenga, the *Times* correspondent in the Turkish capital, reported 25,000 Bulgarians massacred, over 100 villages destroyed and about 10,000 arrested and tortured. As Henry was to say, 'the public thus got from a newspaper much that the government would have learned from me if it had not been for this unjustifiable proceeding, of which I remained in ignorance for two years and when the officer who had so misconducted himself was already dead'. He soon found himself notorious and the central target of the campaign against the atrocities. Disraeli, the

Prime Minister and now Lord Beaconsfield, considered he had been ill informed and in his correspondence at the time frequently alluded to 'Sir Henry's lamentable want of energy, and deficiency'. He felt that 'Elliot's stupidity … nearly brought us to great peril. If he had acted with promptitude, or even kept himself informed, these atrocities might have been checked.

Writing later, Henry told how Gladstone too did not scruple to declare that, without the letter in the *Daily News*,

> we might have been left in the dark, and he had no hesitation in concealing from the public their real action at Constantinople. Every scrap of information that reached me was at once sent home and my published dispatches of 28 May and the eighth and tenth of June reported the repeated protests I had been making against the employment of bashibazouks who, I said, had been acting with cruelty and brutality.

Henry admitted, however, that the original report from the vice-consul at Adrianople had brought to light outrages of all kinds and on a scale of which the embassy 'had not the slightest conception'.[92]

Inevitably, Beaconsfield, the Prime Minister, asked his Foreign Secretary to conduct an investigation into the troubles in which Henry had got himself. Under orders from Lord Derby, Henry sent Walter Baring, the second secretary at the embassy, to conduct an investigation as the government's official commissioner, but he did not speak Bulgarian and the Bulgarian community in Constantinople feared he would not obtain the full facts – the result being they asked Eugene Schuyler, the American consul, to conduct his own investigation. Baring's report came to be cited at every indignation meeting held in England. It stated that 'a conspiracy on a very large scale had been hatching for many months'. Henry was to say that 'the insurrection had been planned and fomented by Russian agents who went about persuading deluded peasants that, as soon as they rose, they would be supported by a Russian army'. Little was heard, wrote Henry, when 'the victims were Turks and the misdoers, Christians; our so-called humanitarians had not a word of pity for the first, or blame for the latter'.[93] Schuyler's report, on the other hand, which had been put together after he and a secretary from the Russian embassy had spent three weeks documenting the atrocities, came to the conclusion that 15,000 Bulgarians had lost their lives. When it was published in the British press it caused a sensation.

Henry was not recalled; instead he assisted Robert Cecil, third Marquess of Salisbury, whom Beaconsfield appointed as plenipotentiary to a conference between December 1876 and January 1877 convened by Britain at Constantinople. It aimed to forestall any Russian military pressure on the Turks but the place chosen for it was a mistake and it foundered on the Turk's refusal to be coerced, thinking as they did that they could depend on British support in any crisis. Seventeen years later, Henry called this 'ill-starred conference', one which directly paved the way for the Russo-Turkish War'. It was a subject on which he had no disposition to dwell. By the summer of 1876, tranquillity had been restored in Bulgaria, but no progress was being made towards repressing the insurrection in Bosnia while Serbia and Montenegro were still at war with Turkey.[94]

Lord Salisbury's appointment gave Henry 'unmixed pleasure'. He anticipated the presence of a cabinet minister of his eminence would give weight to the talks. However, almost immediately, he found him to be 'a docile instrument in the hands of the Russian ambassador' . Salisbury knew nothing of Turkish affairs or of the people with whom he was to work. Henry soon concluded that 'it was very possible that Lord Salisbury might obtain a promise of all that he was empowered ... to ask for' and still fail to protect British interests. The two men were not at one with their thinking. When the delegates from Russia, Austria-Hungary, Germany, Italy, France and Britain met in December at a preliminary meeting, General Ignatieff made a speech announcing that he was going to lay before them resolutions that had been drawn up by Lord Salisbury and Henry, but what Britain had pledged was to be treated as a fiction. The resolutions he put forward certainly did not address the question of how the Bosnian insurrection was to be halted.[95]

Having failed to move Lord Salisbury in his direction, Henry decided to express his views to Lord Derby, sending his colleague a draft before its dispatch. When Salisbury advised him against such a move, Henry, rather weakly, kept it back. His lengthy draft, dated 17 December 1876, referred initially to the conference's aim of averting war between Turkey and Russia and how the preliminary meetings of the plenipotentiaries had given little expectation of it being realised. The ambassador explained that the proposals the delegates seemed about to agree were, in his view, in excess of anything to which the Porte was likely to agree. He also wanted a system of local administrative autonomy in the provinces to give the population some control over their own affairs. So far as Bulgaria was concerned, he urged the creation of a Christian militia. He could hardly imagine 'a measure more fraught with danger than the establishment of a militia drawn exclusively from that class of the population in which the disaffection exists'. The introduction of Christians into the gendarmerie or police, or measures for their gradual incorporation into the army, were, in Henry's view, points to be insisted upon.[96]

Nine formal meetings of the representatives – a conference in all but name – were held at the Russian embassy without the participation of the Turks, who were incensed at finding that in their own capital an elaborate scheme for the administration of their own provinces was being prepared by their arch-enemy, General Ignatieff, so wrote Henry in his book of recollections. At the last meeting the general produced what he called 'the irreducible minimum of demands', the acceptance of which he felt sure all the Christian representatives would consider themselves bound in honour to impose on the Turks. As Henry recorded, there was to be no question of negotiation. The scheme as framed 'was to be flung before the Porte to be swallowed by it in full'. A meeting the following day considered any objections to the 'irreducible minimum' put forward by the Turkish delegation. And Henry made an attempt to obtain a more conciliatory course of action. This failed, his speech being 'little to the taste of General Ignatieff', who looked 'very glum' as he spoke.[97]

Thinking that Henry might have more influence at the Porte, and seeing failure staring him in the face, Lord Salisbury asked him to speak to the Grand Vizier, Midhat Pasha. The ambassador had a promising meeting and the only important point upon which difficulty seemed likely related to the nomination of the governors-general and the international commissions, and these were not insuperable. Patience, however, was 'not one of the virtues of the Conference', as Henry said, nor was 'negotiation its mode of proceeding'. The ninth meeting of the Conference took place on 20 January when Safet Pasha, the Minister of Foreign Affairs made a speech listing all the demands the Porte was ready to accede to, but the difficulties outlined by the Grand Vizier prevented agreement. Then, two days before the final meeting, the Porte, according to custom, convoked a Grand Council made up of some 200 important personages of the empire. As Henry reported later, 'it was afterwards pretended by the Russian party that the Grand Vizier had laid the question before the Council in such a way as to ensure its rejection', but he was convinced the reverse was more likely to have been the truth.[98] It was said that the Turkish rejection of the plan at the last moment had been done with the secret support of Britain.

Our embattled ambassador had been unwell for much of 1876, and as soon as the Conference was over in January 1877 Henry came home. To his surprise, three months later, when the Foreign Office decided the embassy ought not to be left under a chargé d'affaires, Lord Derby asked him whether he felt well enough to resume his duties in Constantinople. It was something he personally wished although there was a section of the cabinet which objected. As Henry was to say 'nothing could possibly be handsomer than the support he was ready to give me'. Derby so fully recognised Henry's right to go back if he wished that he pledged his own resignation would follow if he did not carry the point. It was ultimately arranged that Sir A. H. Layard, an ambassador near retirement, should be sent on a special and temporary assignment to Constantinople while Henry continued to hold the post of permanent ambassador to the Porte, the 'duties of which', Henry wrote, 'my health made me hardly fit to resume'.

When Henry left Constantinople in January 1877 a 'representative deputation' presented him with an address in which they alluded to his 'life and character, as they had known them for ten years'. It had been signed by 'all the responsible British residents without exception' and included 'some of the principal men of the native Christians, Greek and Armenian' whose welfare he had represented. Then, towards the end of the year he was appointed to Vienna again, as ambassador. His brother-in-law, Lord Russell, died in May the following year and was buried at Chenies in Buckinghamshire. In 1880 when Gladstone became Prime Minister, Henry would not have been surprised if he had been recalled as Gladstone had 'been loud in his blame' of his behaviour, but it was not to be. He remained in Vienna for another three years before retiring on a pension at the end of 1883.[99] Happily he was to see the diplomatic gene in the Minto blood pass to his son, Sir Francis Edmund Hugh Elliot, who became the British agent and consul-general in Bulgaria between 1895 and 1903 and then minister at Athens until the middle of the Great War.

Sir Henry's last years were spent between London and Ardington House, a charming property in Oxfordshire lent to him and Lady Elliot by Lord and Lady Wantage, with whom they were on most friendly terms – Henry's mother-in-law being a Lindsay. The parents of Baron Wantage had lived there until 1884, when Mrs

Lindsay died. Soon afterwards the Elliots and daughter Gertrude moved in. Henry assiduously performed his duties on the local bench and regularly hunted into his eighties when his sight began to fail. Anne died in December 1899 and Henry followed on 30 March 1907.

# 12

# GILBERT – THE YOUNG SOLDIER (1842-1865)

Gilbert Elliot, or 'Gibby' as he was known in the family, was born on 23 May 1826. Little is known about the schooling he enjoyed after Catherine Rutherford had ended her period as governess in 1834. Eight years later, when he was sixteen years old, the family appear to have made considerable efforts to secure him a place in one of the Guards' regiments. When these failed, Lord Minto used such influence as he had to find a good, if second-best, offer of a commission in the Rifle Brigade. This brought some relief to his father since the soldier's personal expenses would be lower than those of an eligible Guards officer.

Part of the 1st Battalion of the Rifle Brigade embarked aboard the *Boyne*, a troop ship, at Malta on 2 March 1843 and landed at Corfu on the 6th; the other followed a day later. Gibby was to catch up with his battalion soon after. British regiments and detachments stationed on the Ionian Islands regularly moved to and from Malta, and a number of civilians also spent time in both places. Gilbert was to endure four years of 'parades, inspections and exercises' but the young subaltern, like his 'fellows', nevertheless found Corfu 'the best place out of England, next to Canada'.

In the ancient town of Corfu many of its military buildings were housed in both the old and new fortress buildings. The British governor's residence was part of the palace of St Michael and St George which had been designed by a British architect in 1823. Gilbert kept a journal about life on the island from September 1845 which reflected something of the routine life officers were obliged or chose to follow. A morning bath was followed by inspection of the guard and his horse had a short gallop before breakfast; later in the day he might go up to the citadel for a game of rackets, dining in the guard room or the mess. General parades and drill were sometimes performed in the town's lower square. There was some sailing and fishing. Church parades at the Anglican church of St George, which had been built in 1840 within the old fort, were well attended although sometimes, when there was no formal parade on a Sunday, the colonel read prayers with the men. After walks along the esplanade it was possible to listen to the band in the afternoon, although it did not always play well.

Gilbert often rode to the town's race course, where he would gallop round to exercise his and others' horses, and occasionally he swam over to Vido, a small island opposite Corfu and important enough to the town's defence to have a detachment of riflemen there, taking little more than 30 minutes each way. Occasionally, there was an opportunity to attend a performance of Italian opera which the Corfiotes, as the local population was known, much appreciated, or enjoy more formal regimental dinners as well as several balls held at the palace. Among other duties with which he was charged was the administration of a savings bank for his fellow junior officers, and when public horse races were announced he often ran a book for other subalterns. Cricket matches, usually men versus officers, and mess billiards were other diversions but there was no mention of female company in his journal at this time save for a 'Linda' with whom he went to the opera. The arrival of the steamship with English newspapers and post was always keenly awaited. He had only been in Corfu for three months when he heard of the death of Horatio Elliot, the twenty-five-year-old son of Admiral George and Eliza Ness.[1]

Gilbert left Corfu in something of a hurry in June 1846, travelling homeward aboard the *Emperor* having 'got a shakedown in the saloon'. He arrived at Trieste two days later, where he jumped overboard for a bathe both morning and evening. The next day he 'got ashore at eight, had breakfast and set out with three other fellows for Mestre' just north of Venice.[2] His leave in Britain seems to have lasted until April 1847 when he received orders from the War Office while staying in Oxford, requiring him to embark at Portsmouth.[3] He resumed his journal the following month and was soon halfway across the Northern Atlantic, sailing towards Canada, and in receipt of 'a very undue allowance of foul winds' and a 'best run of 140 miles in 24 hours'. He was very proud and fancied himself 'a great sailor, not having been sick once'.[4] After calling at Halifax, HMS *Belleisle* seems to have gone, firstly to St John, where Gilbert's name was among arrivals listed by the New Brunswick *Courier* of 26 June at the St John Hotel, and then to Montreal, where his regiment was to be quartered during the remainder of the year.[5]

Writing from Toronto to his youngest sister Harriet, in the middle of December 1847, Gibby reported that 'Toronto is certainly the gayest place that I ever saw, and I have myself been dissipating at a great rate during the last fortnight, at balls, tea-fights, dinners and breakfasts'. Only the winter weather occasioned some complaint, it being necessary to dress in 'furs and greatcoats and long boots', all of which cost a lot of money for 'unfortunate officers'.[6] In the following year military life saw him taking men on to the common and keeping them 'at light drill for an hour' as he feared they would not 'show to advantage at the General's inspection'.[7] Life in the garrison was particularly harsh and desertion across the nearby border with America an exceptional temptation for some on account of the deserter being safe from pursuit. Army pay was poor, food often bad, and discipline prone to brutality. He told his sister about the desertion of some bandsmen from his regiment and the great efforts being made to get them back. Gilbert was by then adjutant and responsible for the day-to-day-running of the battalion so that when a fire threatened to destroy the city hall, cathedral and many private houses in February 1848, he called the troops out in support of the firemen and their pumps, whereupon, as Gilbert was to say, the latter men disappeared and 'left our men to do all the work'.[8] Firefighting seems to have become an unofficial and unpaid duty of the battalion which greatly displeased him. It was, however, a different sort of aid in support of the civil power that the battalion was to become involved in later.

The Rebellion Losses Bill, modelled on similar legislation in Upper Canada, was introduced in February 1849 to compensate Lower Canadians whose property had been damaged during rebellions ten or so years before. Lord Elgin, the governor-in-chief, was caught in a dilemma when he discovered the bill gave both the Tories (or loyalists) and the Reformists (or radicals) grounds for complaint, and at the end of April he was forced by a mob to retreat to Monklands, his residence outside Montreal. The city's library and parliament buildings were burned down, the two factions facing each other's cannons, muskets and pistols. In Toronto, there was no obvious public target to be attacked, and although he had feared more serious rebellion was likely, events were confined to mass demonstrations. Writing to his mother, he said, 'We [the battalion] have been called out two or three times, but have never had to act, and I hope we never shall, as it is the most unpleasant duty soldiers can be put to.'[9] To Lotty, he said, 'I must say the most alarming thing that I have seen was an effigy of Lord Elgin burned by a mob of 7000 or 8000 men who behaved very quietly indeed.'[10] In the end, Gilbert's fears proved groundless, Tory opposition to the controversial legislation fell away and peace was restored, so permitting the winter round of balls, concerts and formal dinners to be followed by summer picnics and excursions.

Gibby had met a Miss Jane Fitzgerald at a concert and he was soon seen with her at dances, balls and occasionally church. Writing to his mother in August 1848, he said 'I do not know how the time passes, which it certainly does in a very pleasant way. In a week more we shall have been a year in Toronto and it has gone past so very quickly that I shall be very glad to spend another in it.' Lady Minto was by then beginning to be concerned about his affair with Jane Fitzgerald.[11] The family, both in England and Italy, was convinced that Gilbert would soon be writing to tell them of his impending marriage and put unremitting pressure on him. He had earlier admitted to Charlotte that the ladies of Toronto were very charming and that she should not be afraid of his getting married for he was 'not so green'.[12] Lady Minto's advice about young ladies stealing the hearts of young officers had brought protestations from Gilbert, but he was soon very close to announcing his engagement. Writing to Lady Mary, Harriet described the thought of marriage as more than foolish and very wrong. Moreover, she had never seen Lord Minto 'more vexed'.[13]

While at a ball given by a Toronto family at the end of 1849, Gibby met Miss Fitzgerald again after a gap of some four or five months. There seems little doubt that she was probably an accomplished, kind girl about twenty-six years old, the daughter of an army officer, now dead, who had settled in Canada. However, at the end of April 1850 when Gilbert was in Boston, his journal carried the news that 'I was accepted by Miss F about two minutes ago and have spent part of that time most delightfully with her'. It nevertheless went on to describe how his father would not consent to the marriage on the grounds that he could not afford to marry on a lieutenant's pay, nor could the Fitzgeralds offer a dowry.[14] Lord Minto immediately obtained the agreement of the War Office to Gilbert being given six months' leave, and the Duke of Wellington notified Gilbert's colonel that the boy was expected to leave for England immediately. Meanwhile, Captain Charlie had gone out to Canada to report on the situation – where he found the Fitzgeralds 'a good specimen of colonist' – and bring his brother home. While waiting for a ship at Boston in April, Gilbert said he was on his way home in the hopes that 'I will be able to obtain my father's consent on condition of waiting a little time. I shall never forget my parting with poor Jane. I thought her heart would have broken. I have promised to be back in July.'[15]

After a short stay in Britain, Gilbert gathered up his sister Charlotte, Bob'm, and left London on 29 June, arriving the following day in the Netherlands, where they found Henry and Anne 'very comfortable ... and apparently very happy'. He passed four days with his brother, who admitted that the diplomatic world was better than he had expected. It was his journal, however, that spoke of Gilbert's continued heart-searching. There was

> no chance of my returning to Toronto this month – not having the means of paying my passage to America. My father and all my people have represented to me the impossibility of my marrying, and I fear my father imagines I have given up all hopes of doing so.

Gilbert hoped that time would be on his side and that the family would see how bent he was on marrying 'as soon as I can do so without the risk of involving poor Jane in poverty and misery'. He was waiting in great anxiety to see what Mrs Fitzgerald's answer would be to a letter he knew his father had sent her, and also in the 'terrible position' of either giving up Jane or 'I must distress my poor parents'.[16]

At The Hague, Henry was convinced that Gilbert was 'well out of his troubles' and encouraged him to think of other matters. The family went to the opera and heard three acts of Donizetti's *Lucia di Lammermoor* which 'was pretty good on the whole'. The soldier, on the other hand, saw his hopes fading fast when a few days later he received two letters – one from 'poor Jane', the other from his mother. Mrs Fitzgerald had also written 'an excellent and very decided letter' to Lord Minto which Gilbert had not seen, and by which he supposed she had said 'that as I cannot have my father's sanction to my marriage, the engagement must be considered as off'. But the letter from Jane herself contained a promise to continue to be faithful and begged him to write regularly in the hope that the time might come 'when we may be made happy'.

Once again, Gilbert did not know what to do. Should he go out again to Canada as soon as possible and see 'them all' or leave with the 1st Battalion. He knew he could not marry, but they would be able to see each other if he was in Toronto. Another possibility was for him to stay the winter at Minto, which would enable him to save some money for a passage in the spring. Concluding his journal for that year, he maintained that 'at all events, I will do my best for the next few years, if necessary, to live as cheaply as I can'.[17] However, in November 1850, Gilbert was writing to Jane from Minto telling her that he had been persuaded to break off the engagement, and he wrote in in his journal, 'Poor thing, how will she bear it? It is the severest trial I have ever had, and a hard battle have I fought with myself.'[18]

Meanwhile, reports were being received in London from South Africa that there had been a fresh outbreak of what were called the Kaffir Wars and that reinforcements were needed in the colony. During 1851, the 1st Battalion of the Rifle Brigade in which Gilbert served had been stationed at the Western Heights in Dover while the 2nd remained at Kingston in Upper Canada. The uncomfortable HMS *Magaera* transported Captain Gilbert Elliot (as he had become) and his regiment from the Downs to Algoa Bay, some 400 miles east of the Cape of Good Hope, between January and March 1852. The Riflemen were promptly then marched by companies to Port Elizabeth, where they camped and two or three days later they were again on the march, travelling through Quagga Flats and Sidbury to reach Grahamstown. Finding widespread evidence of Kaffir (or Bantu) depredation, the battalion was kept busy for the rest of the year with clashes in the Waterkloof valley, Fort Beaufort, Mundell's Krantz, Sabella and Balotta. In addition to restocking posts and keeping up patrols, there were roads and housing to be built.[19]

General Cathcart, who had succeeded Sir Harry Smith as governor and commander-in-chief, summoned the first Cape parliament as soon as he arrived in South Africa in January 1852. He then determined to push towards the north-eastern frontier in November and demand satisfaction from, or to punish, Moshesh the First, chief of the Basuto tribe, for his incursions and depredations on the settlers near the Orange River. He had intended to take four companies of Riflemen with him but this was reduced to one when Kaffirs and Hottentots showed themselves in force near Fort Beaufort. Rooper's company was in line for duty but, given his lack of knowledge of the colony, command devolved on Lieutenant the Hon. Leicester Curzon. The men were ordered rather unexpectedly late in the evening of 17 November to march at daylight the following morning. The rest of the troops had left about a week before under Colonel Eyre, and General Cathcart was to overtake them at Burgersdorp, about 160 miles from Fort Beaufort. Once there, the whole force was inspected and divided into brigades, the Riflemen being placed under the command of Colonel Eyre. On 1 December, after a hot march, they forded the Orange River without much difficulty, it being lower than it had been for many years. Two days later they crossed the Caledon River at Commissie Drift, remaining there until the 8th and arrived on the 13th at Platburg, where they camped near the Wesleyan Missionary Station.[20]

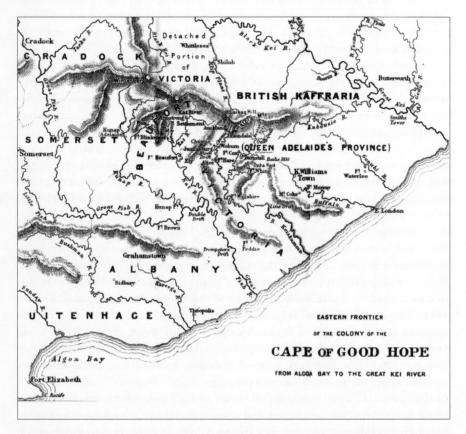

Sketch map of the eastern frontier of Cape Province during the Kaffir Wars, from the Autobiography of Lieutenant General Sir Harry Smith.

Gilbert had marched about 600 miles and, while he and the men rested, the governor arranged matters with Moshesh and his chiefs. The Basuto chief was given three days to pay a fine of cattle, imposed on him for certain thefts committed by his people on the inhabitants of the Orange River Sovereignty; but by the end of the three days only one-third of the fine had been paid and the governor decided to march against him the next day and help himself. Accordingly, Gilbert and his men marched to the banks of the Caledon River on 19 December and 'formed a flying camp having left about eight or nine men in the standing camp at Platburg'. The following day they crossed the river and marched towards a long flat-topped mountain (the Berea Plateau) upon which Gilbert knew Moshesh was keeping his cattle.

Colonel Sir William Eyre, who had been a successful commander in the Cape Frontier War of 1847, and 'a highly accomplished bush fighter', was ordered to take his infantry brigade up the north side of the mountain, while Colonel Napier with the cavalry was to march round the east side. The subsequent battle was not easily resolved. So far as Gilbert could judge there were some 6,000 Kaffirs, all mounted, while the Rifles totalled 400 men. Writing to his brother George at Eaton Square after the battle, Gilbert said that 'considering the force opposed to us' he thought their losses 'wonderfully small'. It was, he said,

> beautiful to see our troops in skirmishing order jump up and charge these uncounted men who would always turn tail and gallop off to the nearest hollow as hard as they could. What the enemy's losses were we, of course, can't say as the Kaffirs pick up and carry off the bodies whenever they have a chance, but from what has been heard since from Moshesh, and by the calculations of the different officers, I should think it must be between two and three hundred.[21]

In another letter to George again in April 1853, this time from King William's Town, Gilbert was beginning to think he might at last manage to be in England by the end of the year, but all he could do was to wait for the arrival of the next steamer with further information.[22] Grahamstown had become 'quiet and uninteresting' although they had paid a visit to Fort Beaufort and Blinkwater. A bored and restless Gilbert did not know 'one single recommendation the country has beyond its climate – and that is much too hot for my taste'.[23] In May, he contemplated resigning his appointment and returning home. Cricket and some horse racing, a 'different-looking thing from Epsom', occupied men and officers' time. In the evenings, the men had the pleasure of 'handing the ladies by dozens in and out of their ox wagons' after 'beauty and fashion' had seen the sport. The only other news was that General Alexander Russell, son of John Russell, sixth Duke of Bedford, had 'passed through' on his way to England the previous week.[24]

The following month Gilbert was comforted by his lawyer brother, who had just returned to Pont Street after visiting the countess at Nervi, and he quietly determined to 'bide his time' in the Army until the governor went home, for which there was not long to wait.[25] There was still no news regarding which regiments had been selected to return to England. Gilbert said, 'What I should like best would be to go home with the battalion or the governor but if I cannot do either of these pretty soon, I must apply to join the depot, provided government will give me a passage.' He had been in Fort Beaufort on a few days' leave and had attended the races there. He did not care 'a fig about racing' and, with amusement so very hard to find, he said 'it was however, pleasant to travel about the country with two or three fellows and one pack horse' instead of riding along with the governor at about four miles an hour and with a train of mule wagons in the rear.

The governor published a minute showing the state of the colony when he first came to it, and what had been done since, which Gilbert thought might make him more popular among the colonists. Colonial newspapers were, he said, 'the most infernal publications in the world; they almost invariably abuse the government and as all the colonists read and believe everything they say, it must be a hard thing for a governor to make himself popular'. Sir John Clark, a diplomat, was to go up to Bloemfontein immediately to settle the sovereignty question after which, according to some, he was to succeed General Cathcart as governor. Gilbert thought this unlikely.[26]

In early September the Rifle Brigade received orders to hold itself in readiness to embark for home, and by the 12th of the month they were awaiting the arrival of ships. Gilbert was to be left behind in 'this detestable country' and he could only assume that the governor might yet manage to get away about the end of the year or the beginning of the next, and also take him with him. Sir John Clark had announced the government's intention of giving up the Orange River Territory and, as was expected, 'the whole colony was crying out about it'. Two infantry and cavalry regiments came under orders to sail for India so that altogether the reduction of the military force was considerable.

There was a welcome surprise that month when, as Gilbert put it, he discovered he might 'get a look at Charlie and his ship'. His brother wrote to say that HMS *Sybille*, his command, was at the Cape en route for the Far East. Circumstances were, however, to be against such a meeting. The length of leave that would be necessary was much longer than Gilbert could ask for, and it was a good 600 miles to Cape Town. It was just possible that His Excellency might have to go there himself soon, but this was far from certain. So, concluding that they would probably not meet, and anticipating his next posting, Gilbert's thoughts turned to politics. He was convinced, he told Doddy, that Britain had been behaving 'shabbily' towards Turkey, first 'patting her on the back and getting her into a scrape, and now wishing to sneak out of the way. I suppose it is all right but really our behaviour does not appear half so dignified as one would wish. Russia is twice as straightforward.'[27]

General Order No. 238 was issued from Headquarters, Grahamstown, on 10 October 1853. It was one of a series which had the effect of bustling Gilbert and a large part of the British Army twice across two continents in little more than six months. The Rifle Brigade was required to march to Port Elizabeth for embarkation aboard HMS *Simoom*. Accompanied by many of the local population from Fort Beaufort, the battalion under Lt-Col. Horsford passed through Grahamstown and Sidbury, reaching the coast at the end of October only to find that the *Simoom* had not arrived. With Colonel Buller back in command, the battalion eventually embarked, sailing from Algoa Bay and then Table Bay, and finally for England in mid-November. The service companies of the 1st Battalion arrived in Cowes Roads on 7 January and disembarked three days later at Portsmouth, proceeding direct by the South Coast and South Eastern Railways to Dover, where they joined the depot companies and occupied Western Heights. Three months later they were again moved by train to Clarence barracks at Portsmouth.

The Crimean War started at the end of March 1854. Already one hundred men of the 1st Battalion had readily volunteered to be transferred to the 2nd Battalion, which was then under orders to embark for Turkey. Many of these were veterans who had served through the Kaffir Wars. Their replacements, however, were made up by a hundred volunteers from the 60th and other regiments, the majority being very young soldiers. With both battalions duly inspected, and armed with the Enfield Minié rather than the Brunswick rifle, they were ready to join Lord Raglan's army. The first, commanded by Lt-Col. Beckwith, sailed from Portsmouth on the *Orinoco* on 14 July. The second, under Lt-Col. Lawrence, had left Southampton three months before aboard HMS *Vulcan* and HMS *Himalaya*. Both were to arrive at Malta and, after several mishaps, sail on through the Bosphorus to the Black Sea port of Varna. To the great gratification of the Riflemen, the 1st Battalion was placed in General Torren's brigade and attached to the 4th Division, which was commanded by Sir George Cathcart from South Africa. The 2nd Battalion, which lost thirty men from cholera during July and August, was not so fortunate, being broken up into seven companies, each of which sailed in separate vessels before making their rendezvous in Kalamita Bay off the west coast of the Crimean peninsula, where both battalions landed – bivouacking on the beach without tents in the rain.[28] Lord Raglan had predicted that it would take twelve days to capture Sevastopol.

On the last day of August 1854, Gilbert was aboard the troopship *Harbinger* which had also called at Malta on its way from England.[29] They were in the Sea of Marmora expecting to reach Constantinople the following day. Writing to Bob'm, he said,

> although the wind has been against us ... there was so much to interest one in coming up the Dardanelles today, both in the scenery which is pretty, and in the ships, dozens of which we passed loaded with wild-looking Turkish troops. We passed Gallipoli in the afternoon where we saw a large camp apparently of French cavalry and some artillery. Why such a force should be kept down there I can't make out. You have no idea what an exciting thing it is to pass a number of towns and ships as we have done today and yet not to get a word of news; in short, to be as ignorant as we were a thousand miles from our journey's end. We are, I believe to go to Beikos [Beykos] Bay, halfway up the Bosphorus after touching at Constantinople for orders. Sir George's Division has not all arrived yet, indeed I dare say, some of the regiment have not yet left England but I trust they will let him go on with what he can collect and not keep him down at Beikos Bay until he gets his whole force together.[30]

As expected, and after returning from the shore, where he had been sent for news, the soldier was able to tell his sister that 'the troops will be at Varna tomorrow and the general embarkation for the Crimea will take place next day. About 30,000 English and about 25,000 French are to form the expedition. We sail immediately for Varna so I must stop.'[31]

It was two weeks or so later when Gilbert found time to write, on this occasion to George from Kalamita Bay. He was happy to say that they were safe on shore in the Crimea about 15 miles to the south of Eupatoria (Yevpatorya), and about 26 miles from Sevastopol. 'The Russians,' he said, 'had been kind enough to allow us to disembark without the slightest opposition.' His horses arrived, which was a relief to his mind, and he wrote that 'they will be a great relief to my legs which are getting a little stiff from doing the duty of my chargers'. The whole of his division (the 4th) was in excellent health and spirits, and everyone who could be spared was employed in hunting up wagons and bullocks. They found the inhabitants most civil and ready to furnish anything in their power. The French had landed about 2 miles on his right and had apparently marched into a little village which in a short time they had sacked and plundered of everything, shooting pigs, oxen etc., carrying off whatever came in their way. 'Our men, on the other hand,' he wrote, 'have behaved very well and I think the Crimeans are beginning to find out the difference between French and English already.'

Gibby went on to tell his lawyer brother on 17 September that 'there are different reports about, as to the strength of the Russians'. One said they were entrenched some 12 miles away and that 'we shall have to fight two battles before we get to Sevastopol' while another was certain that all troops had already been withdrawn to within the town. One report, which Gilbert was much inclined to believe, based on dispatches found in a captured Russian ship, suggested that Russian forces were suffering much from sickness and there were 'not as many as 30,000 men at Sevastopol'. All in all, he could only recognise that 'we people in these parts know very little about the war we are engaged in'. He also asked his readers in the family to 'make allowances for our being at present pretty hard at work; moreover, the position one is obliged to adopt to write – without table or chair – is not comfortable'.[32]

It seems from Cope's *History* that during the advance one flank was covered by Riflemen in skirmishing order with another line of their skirmishers protecting the rear. The 1st Battalion reached the river on 19 September and camped for the night. The following day, and provided with three day's rations, the 1st Battalion advanced, covering the left and rear of the army. On approaching the River Alma, a large force of Russian cavalry was observed and Sir George Cathcart answered its movements by continually throwing out skirmishers which kept the Cossacks in check during the engagement. Being repulsed at every point, the enemy retired along with their cavalry. The Riflemen then forded the Alma and ascended the heights on its south side, the enemy being in full retreat. Two men had been wounded but the battalion had hardly been engaged. It was the 2nd Battalion who on the 20th began to descend from the long slope of the ridge to the Alma, two companies in skirmishing order and two in support. As they drew near to the village of Búrliúk, they were surprised to see it burst into flames. They were sharply plied with grape from the batteries on the opposite slope and musketry from the village.[33]

At daylight on 21 September, the 1st Battalion ascended the heights and halted on the ground which had been occupied by the enemy's right. There they spent two days burying the dead and carrying the wounded to the field hospitals. The 2nd Battalion was similarly employed until both groups of Riflemen left the heights and advanced to Katchka, passing through the vineyards and a village.[34]

With Gilbert bivouacked along the Alma River, it was again Bob'm's turn to hear that he was alive and well 'after a severe but most successful battle' which had taken place the previous day.

I cannot possibly give you anything like a detailed account of the affair as I have neither time nor power to describe one thousandth part of what took place – but t'was

a glorious victory. Yesterday morning we marched at daylight from a small burn 12 miles from where we landed, and towards the afternoon we saw the Russian army on the opposite side of the River Alma and it was evident that they intended to prevent our crossing.'

With the French on their right and when they were about a half a mile from the bank of the river, Gilbert and those around him deployed into line. Once at the river, they crossed it in the face of a most dreadful fire but, as he told his sister, there was

hardly a waver to be seen in our ranks and the infantry advanced up the hill and took all the entrenchments though opposed by a most terrific fire of musketry and artillery. They drove the Russians right over the hill on the left bank of the river and then followed them across a valley and on to another hill about two miles further on; in short gained a most complete victory.

Gilbert's division had not been in the thick of it, being in the rear of the Duke of Cambridge's division, and its casualties were very few. He wished he could tell Bob'm that the rest of the army had suffered similarly but he thought about 1,000 or 1,200 had been killed or wounded. Gibby was pleased the Russians were in full retreat upon Sevastopol, having given up their position on the only river Allied forces would have to cross before getting there. He thought them completely cowed and unlikely to stand up in front of them again. 'It was perfectly splendid to see the way the redoubts were taken,' he wrote. Then, turning to the dead and wounded, Gilbert said he had 'been much phased to see how very kind our men are to the wounded Russians, giving them water and making them as comfortable as possible – poor fellows, there are many of them still lying about'. They had been hard up for food and water since they landed but he was able to report towards the end of September that ships were landing stores at last. Lord Raglan was said to be in very good spirits and health, and most popular among both French and English armies.[35]

Captain Gilbert had written to his sister under the stars and without the need of a tent. The next evening his correspondent was Doddy, with whom he shared reports about the 'most severe' casualties and the 'good many ill with cholera'.[36] A week or so later he sent him another letter, this time from the 'Heights above Sevastopol', where the Rifles had taken up position on the south side of Sevastopol. 'We are,' he wrote, 'about one and a half miles from the town and, as we are considerably above it, have a pretty good view of what is going on inside. The Russians are all very busy throwing up works in different plains but as yet I have not seen anything that looks very formidable.' That morning a good many very well-directed shells had found their way into the middle of Gilbert's division but without doing them much damage. They were waiting for the arrival of their siege train which had been landed at Balaclava and they hoped to begin work on the hillside in a day or two. Sir George Cathcart had been much disgusted with the delays caused by waiting for the battery train and was 'for going in and taking the place with the bayonet'. Telling his brother that 'we have lost men enough already both by battle and disease', Gibby added that he thought their generals were right in trying 'the safest though the slowest means of taking the place' but when he saw the progress the Russians had made in their works during the last few days he regretted that 'we did not march down on the place and take it three days ago'.[37]

The heading of Gilbert's next letter to Doddy was shown as 'before Sevastopol'. Anticipation was the name of the game. There was still nothing to suggest the scale of death and horrors yet to come. He explained that

> we have not yet fired a single cannon shot at the town. It is most trying to have to remain in our place to be shot at all day long and yet not having the means of returning the compliment. I must say, however, that considering the number of shot and shell the Russians have expended upon us, they have done us wonderfully little harm – only a few men of our division have been killed. It is nevertheless very unpleasant to have a big shell bursting in the camp every now and then. We have opened one or two trenches and are going to work again tonight so that by the fourteenth [of October], I trust, we may be able to begin pounding.

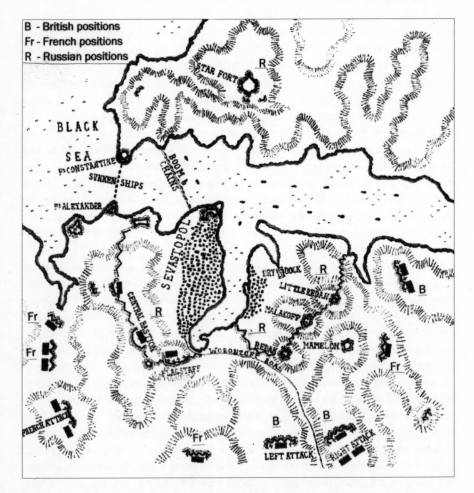

The latter phase of the long siege of Sevastopol – October 1854 to September 1855. See also the map of the Black Sea and the Crimean peninsula on page 206.

The previous two days had been most bitterly cold and there was the prospect of a good deal of snow. If so, Gilbert reported, 'it will be very bad for us on the top of these hills with a scanty supply of wood'.

The captain was very ready to admit to his lawyer brother that

> I certainly never knew till I came to this country what it was to be really hard worked, or the feeling of getting up very hungry after dinner. I used on the march to be in the saddle from an hour before sunrise to after dark, galloping all about and with nothing to eat but a little bit of biscuit … Luckily the weather was fine and we did not feel the want of tents so much as we might have done. I have now got a tent with four other inhabitants besides myself, and a great luxury it is in this cold weather. Sir George Cathcart is enough to shame anyone from knocking up [wearing out or becoming exhausted] as I really think he works harder, and sleeps less than anyone in the camp. There has been a terrible amount of cholera in the army but thanks to the cold weather I really think it is going away at last.

The following night more trenches were opened nearer Sevastopol and Gilbert hoped it would soon be possible to get some guns in position. He had worked all night and felt 'stupid' as well as 'sleepy and dirty' which was not to be wondered at. He confessed to Doddy that 'I've only had my clothes off once since we marched from our landing place'.[38]

Responding to the 'lots of letters' she had sent him, Gilbert told young Harriet that until Sevastopol had been captured he did not know where his winter quarters would be or whether there was to be any chance of getting leave; this would depend wholly on success in the war. Meanwhile, the fleet and the first steamer-of-the-line with screw propulsion, HMS *Agamemnon*, in which Sir Edmund Lyons was flying his flag, had hammered the batteries for some time without doing much good.[39] Giving news of the war to George on the same day, Gilbert described how the climate of optimism had changed:

> The fact is we have now learned that the Russian works are by no means made of gingerbread, and our guns by no means such very wonderful things as the gunners made them out to be. I must, however, in fairness to the artillery say that a Russian Martello tower was destroyed in less time than an hour and a half. Almost all the other works are of earth like our own and stand very well, though we have knocked them about pretty well in some places.

Going on to mention reports that said the streets of Sevastopol were 'full of dead', Gibby told of him paying occasional visits to the trenches which was 'sometimes warm enough work, but as we generally go at night when the firing is slack, we have had not much to go through. Once in the trenches and you are pretty safe but it is the going to and coming from them that many men get knocked over.'[40]

A week passed before Gilbert wrote to George again. On 10 October they were still in the same position on the heights above Sevastopol, and although British guns were keeping up a continual fire on Russian defensive works there was little evidence that they were making any impression. Gilbert noted towards the end of

October that the Russians were 'constructing batteries inside the town to the rear of their original ones' and concluded that they intended falling back on them. The French, who had 'pretty level ground to work upon', had made their approaches to about 5 yards of the most advanced of the Russian works. He was convinced they did not have such formidable batteries against them. Apparently, Gilbert and some of his men had been sent for in a hurry two days before to go to the aid of Balaclava, which had been attacked by the Russians. It was the first of two efforts made by Prince Menshikov, the Russian commander-in-chief, to relieve the siege of Sevastopol. 'We marched about five miles,' wrote Gilbert, 'and found that the rascally Turkish soldiers had bolted from the earthworks we had erected for the defence of the place, and had allowed the Russians … to carry off some of our guns.' The Russians kept possession of the works for some time but General James Yorke Scarlett (and the Heavy Brigade) 'charged in most splendid style and sent them flying with considerable loss'.

The Russians then retired and halted in a plain, whereupon Lord Cardigan made his gallant but most disastrous charge with the Light Brigade. Having advanced on the enemy with 800 men, Cardigan was reported by Gilbert to have returned with half that number, some 113 men having being killed. When many eventually turned up, he corrected his arithmetic to a total loss of 400 killed, wounded or missing. 'All this,' Gilbert said, 'was occasioned by an ADC giving Lord Cardigan a wrong order. He was the first that was shot and a written order which he had never delivered was found in his pocket. I am very glad for Lord Cardigan's sake as it will quite clear him of any charge of rashness and show that he only obeyed the order he received.'

Just after the Charge of the Light Brigade, Gilbert's division took up a position near one of their own works. About a dozen of the Rifle Brigade crept up to about a hundred yards from the Russian guns and in about ten minutes the enemy gunners 'found it too hot to load with Minié bullets [conical .702 calibre] going about and got under cover as soon as they could'. Despite this, Gilbert was forced to say that 'altogether it was anything but a good day's work what with the Turks running away and their guns being lost' and he admitted that 'on the whole we got the worst of it, though the Russians certainly suffered much and were far superior to us as numbers were concerned'. They were evidently still bent upon retaking Balaclava. Something to offset the bad news was obviously called for and Gilbert could only tell his brother something about a 'beautiful little engagement'. Although his division had not been engaged and remained in reserve, he rode forward with the general and saw some of the affair very well. 'During the earlier part I was at a very safe distance indeed, looking through a very big telescope. Our loss, I believe, was not more than 12 killed and about 50 wounded – that of the Russians is supposed to be about 300.' Gilbert was later to confirm that upwards of 100 Russians had been buried. He again apologised for 'writing in a very cold-blooded way about these poor fellows'.[41]

A most fierce engagement took place on the heights at Balaclava on 5 November. The harsh Crimean War deeply affected armies unprepared for the conditions and many soldiers fell victim to cholera and dysentery, so outraging the public back home. Gilbert took no part in the action at all, 'having been sent down' from the Heights 'some days before'. The weather, he later said, had 'brought on a regular attack' of his lung infection and a camp at Balaclava had done him some good although he was 'still very weak'. Writing to Doddy, he said,

Our division, as you will see by the newspapers, has suffered terribly in officers. Amongst others our poor, kind, old general was shot dead.[42] Both his brigadiers were hit and one has since died. Colonel Seymour, the assistant adjutant-general, the best and kindest friend I ever had was shot and stabbed to death, and Major Maitland, the D A A-G [or deputy acting adjutant-general] badly wounded.

The division had held its ground until other forces came up, after which the fighting lasted for many hours and only ended when the enemy made a hasty retreat down the hill having suffered miserably. Their force, Gilbert explained, was

supposed to have consisted of about 40,000 besides very many guns, and we had, including a division of French, not more than 25,000 to oppose them. Though their loss was much greater in this action than ours, they can better spare 1000 than we 100 men, and I think our victory is not one over which we can rejoice much.

He expected to be well enough soon to go up to the camp again and take command of his company, but winter was ahead and he could not see how they could leave the Crimea even when Sevastopol was taken.[43] On the following day Bob'm was told about the previous battle in which the Light Brigade had been involved:

The poor Guards suffered much – among others, young Disbrowe whom you remember at The Hague is killed.[44] I ought to have told you before ... I was not in the action ... and I felt as if I should go mad when I thought of them all fighting away on the heights, and I as it were, chained by the leg down here. I should like to have been with our dear old general when he fell. I cannot tell you what an awfully dead, heavy feeling has been hanging over me since that battle. He had been to me on many occasions a kind friend, and was one to whom I always applied for advice being quite sure that what he advised would be right and honourable.[45]

While hoping in a few days' time 'to go on board the *Sans Pareil* (commanded by Acting Captain Leopold Heath) for a little time to pick up some strength', Gilbert wrote a short note to Fanny. Now reconciled to wintering outside Sevastopol and anticipating a sufficiently reinforced attack in 1855, he told her 'what a shame it was of the papers to get up the report that Sevastopol had fallen just after Alma' knowing how much of her life at Pembroke Lodge was taken up reading the newspapers and how concerned she always was with 'feelings and duty'. He said *The Times* in particular had 'more false reports and lies than any other and it makes one quite angry to read them. It has behaved very badly to the 4th Division and both in the battle of Alma and everything else, has put us in the wrong place. The 4th Division never got the credit of covering the rear of the French and English armies against the whole of Menshikov's army when on our march to Balaclava.'[46]

It was 20 November when Gilbert was able to tell his lawyer brother about the hurricane he had experienced while on board HMS *Sans Pareil*. Nearly thirty vessels were wrecked along with their precious cargoes of food, medical supplies and clothing. In the generally sheltered harbour at Balaclava 'the jamming and knocking about of the ships was terrible. Just outside the harbour eight or nine ships were lost and a great number of men drowned.' He had gone to the top of the hill soon after and there was 'a more melancholy sight' than he had ever seen. 'There were some ships still at anchor but hardly a mast amongst them. As for those that had gone on shore there was nothing to be seen but broken spars and bits of wood that looked no bigger than chips. In the camps hardly a tent remained standing, and in one position on a high hill almost everything the men had was blown away. They had nothing but the wet clothes they stood in.' It had been an extremely rare occurrence but heavy rain in the early winter was a great threat to the well-being of the troop. With roads spoiled or swept away it would be hard for food and fuel to be brought up to the army's positions.

Continuing his letter to George the following day, Gilbert reported how 'last night our fellows went out and did a very gallant thing – but I am sorry to say that out of the 200 that were sent out, we lost an officer and seven killed and had 13 men wounded'. Some Russian riflemen, having taken up a position about 300 yards from a small advanced trench had been annoying both English and French soldiers. Men from Gilbert's regiment were ordered down, half being left in an advanced trench as a support while the remaining one hundred crept on and got within about 30 yards of the Russians before they were seen, the night being very dark. As soon as the Russians opened fire 'our fellows gave a cheer and turned them out at the point of a bayonet' but the enemy had support at hand and fell back on it. They then opened a heavy fire on Gilbert's men, who had not much cover, situated as they were in an old Russian position. Support was brought up after a half an hour and, as Gilbert said, 'we drove them clean away'.

The following morning, the commander of the French army, General Canrobert (later Maréchal) called at Lord Raglan's headquarters to ask which regiment had done what he called 'the most gallant thing he had ever known'. He proposed to issue a complimentary order about it. Gibby told George that 'our party was commanded by Tryon', a subaltern whom Gilbert had been surprised to hear was to take a party of 200 men on such a service. He also reminded the adjutant that beside himself there were two other captains available but the colonel had decided that Henry Tryon was to go, being first on the roster. The lieutenant was the only one who had ever seen the place he was to attack which, at night in particular, was a great advantage. In the event, poor Tryon did his work in a most gallant manner but he was killed just after taking the Russian position. Gilbert could not help telling his brother that 'we have lost in him one of the very best officers the Regiment ever had'. For his own part, Gilbert felt that a young officer had done the real work of a soldier while he had remained useless. He wrote how 'I feel I must admit that my complaint annoys me more than I have ever yet said, not that I am really very ill, indeed I am far from it, but I constantly get pains which come on without a moment's notice though I may have felt well for hours before, and as long as the pain lasts I feel totally unfit for anything ... I can't go on doing half-duty, and in this country I have no chance of shaking off this most horrid complaint.'[47]

Writing to his father on 27 November 1854, Gibby said,

I cannot say I think the end of the siege looks a bit nearer than it did a month ago. We have certainly got one or two trenches a good deal nearer the Russian works than we had at that time but we can put no guns in them, and consequently they are of little use to us further than to prevent the enemy from encroaching on our batteries. We lose men daily in these advanced works, the approaches to which are very much exposed to the enemy's fire; a single man showing himself being sufficient to bring down a shower of grape and rifle bullets.

He went on to say that 'the men have a terribly hard time of it now being nearly every other night in the trenches. When they come back they find a little bit of meat and some biscuit, and then have to go a long way for firewood to cook it with.'

Gilbert was prepared to say that everybody had great confidence in Lord Raglan, and did not doubt that he and Canrobert probably had some good plans in their heads, but the troops knew nothing about them. In his own case he was 'doing nothing but camp duty and ingloriously getting off trench work'. Other poor fellows were ready to pay almost any sum for shirts and socks, or any kind of warm clothing that was to be obtained, but Gilbert wanted to get them a whole commissariat wagon-load of 'vegetables or meat as among other diseases, scurvy has occasionally made its appearance'. He had himself just asked his servant what he was to have for dinner and received the unsatisfactory answer of 'no meat today'. So far as conveyances were concerned, the men were very badly off except for the sick and wounded who had 'good comfortable carts, very far superior to anything the French have got'. He admitted that 'the papers would not believe in the possibility of anything English being good or well-managed'.[48] There were those who thought that Sevastopol would be captured before Christmas, but it was not to be.

Given his father's special interest, Gilbert told him how two Russians vessels had avoided the vigilance of the fleets:

> two steamers quietly went out of the harbour of Sevastopol, and after going for about a mile towards Cape Khersonese set to work and shelled the French from a position which must have enabled them to enfilade most of their works. They fired away for about an hour when some of our steamers went out and drove them back. From this position we could not of course, see what damage was done to the French and I dare say it was trifling as the ships had to fire upon the heights but it is surely strange that with such a strong fleet as we have here something is not always kept to watch the mouth of the harbour.[49]

Doubtless remembering his diplomat brother's favourite outdoor apparel when serving at St Petersburg, Gilbert started a letter to Henry on 16 December by saying

> a snow storm last night made me think what a nice thing a fur cloak would be, and then I ... remembered that I had had two letters from you, one of them telling me that you were sending me the above-mentioned desirable article ... I do thank you very much and I am looking forward anxiously for the arrival of the cloak as it is hard to keep oneself warm in such weather as we have at present.

He had been forced to leave his own tent to write letters as his fingers became frozen and 'would not do their duty'. He went on to tell Henry how his battalion had been reduced to not much more than 300 fighting men. The previous July it had been 945 strong. He was not at all pleased to hear that 'his brother's Austrians' had at last declared war. 'I really think it is high time that Austria should declare decidedly one way or another.' Wrapping up his letter, Gilbert expressed the pleasure Lord Minto's projected winter stay at Constantinople gave him, although he recognised that it would not be possible for a serving officer to visit him and miss another engagement.[50]

There had been a heavy fall of snow on the night of 15 December and Gilbert's fire would not burn on the following morning as the wind was in the wrong quarter. His letter to George was short, mentioning only the hardships faced by the men and his own health which 'goes on in the old way, sometimes better and sometimes worse'. Someone, however, had taken a decision about his further treatment and he was to be moved by ship to the Army's medical base at Scutari facing Constantinople in Turkey. The following month, the adjutant-general was to record some 11,290 admissions – one in five men sent to the Crimea died there. Writing to his father from Pera, part of Constantinople, on 15 January 1855, Gilbert said there was now little chance of their meeting though he still thought he may be able to join him at Nice or Marseilles if he visited either place.

> I have improved a little during the last two days ... I went over to Scutari yesterday to see the doctors and was told I must remain in here a little longer ... as they know nothing of my case and I am looking well-enough. They recommend me to remain at the Inn here, rather than go into the hospital at Scutari where I would be put into the same room with two or three sick officers, and where one sees a good many sights that are not likely to do one much good. I am fortunate in having found the surgeon of the 8th Hussars who is an old friend of mine living close by and I have the benefit of his attendance.

Gilbert added that:

> The inns here are without exception the most expensive places people ever were pushed into, and if I am condemned to remain where I am, I fear I may have to take advantage of your permission to draw on your account but if I can get off within a fortnight I shall not have any occasion to do so ... The only letters I have received since I came here were those that had come through Lord Napier, all the others having being sent on to the Crimea. If I am ordered to England I fear I shall have to go round by sea on account of my poor black servant who has had both his feet frozen but if I can get him into good hands on board ship I may after all manage to go by Marseilles.[51]

Two weeks later Gilbert was able to tell Bob'm that he was finally going to take up quarters at Scutari, where he

> would be within reach of the doctors who appear to forget all about one unless one keeps perpetually jogging their memories. I have been getting better and stronger lately, and I think in ten days or so I may be able to decide whether I had better go back to camp or get further from it; what the doctors will decide is quite another thing but I must abide by their decision whatever it may be.[52]

He felt a little better a week later although whenever he passed through the hospital wards on the way to his room, Gilbert said,

> I feel ashamed at looking plump and well in the middle of the poor skeletons round about me. I can assure you I think it hard though that my healthy appearance should be the cause of my passing months here ... God knows I have never had any reason for wishing to go home but that I know, and the doctors who know me say it is the best thing I can do, and that if I go to camp half-cured I shall have to be sent away again directly.

His sole wish was to get back to work as soon as he felt able to do it properly and much as he sometimes felt inclined to declare himself well, and go back to camp, in his soberer moments he recognised his duty was to go to England if I he could. Having taken 'the great step of coming so far on a medical certificate', he was annoyed at not being able to do what he knew would be the best thing. He wanted 'if possible to be all right again and in camp by the beginning of spring when we may set actively to work again'.[53]

How long Gilbert was at Scutari is unclear but by July 1855 Major Elliot was back at Sevastopol having been in England, where he received the Crimean medal from the Queen on Horse Guards Parade on 18 May 1855. He was subsequently presented with the Ottoman Order of the Medjidie as a reward for distinguished service and shown at that time in the records as a lieutenant colonel.[54] He had missed important changes in command (especially that of the 1st Battalion), the Russian attack in March over the whole length of the Allied line, and the first assault on the redan (or V-shaped fortification). But there was much war left to be fought and it would not be until September before Allied troops entered an abandoned Sevastopol. Gilbert told Bob'm that he had come up to the camp two days before and that he was now re-established in his old place as deputy assistant adjutant-general to the 4th Division. 'Things were very different indeed,' he said, 'from what they were when I left. The camp looks twice as big, and the men and horses are looking twice as well. It is very hot but I have a tent to sit in to do my writing work so that you can see that I at all events am not to be pitied.' News of the family included the transfer of a 'desperately wounded' Charlie Boileau aboard the *Great Tasmania* which was about to sail for England. It seems that when the ship reached Malta, Sir John's youngest son was lodged in the palace built for Napoleon I.[55] He was to die on 1 August.

Gilbert seems to have taken his lawyer brother's advice and decided to use the form of a journal rather than writing full letters to each of his correspondents. In the middle of July he recorded 'nine of our division killed and wounded yesterday and last night awfully hot again, ninety-two degrees' in his tent. Although he feared his black horse had an incurable disease, he had ridden it to visit Captain E. W. Blackett, who was going along well after being wounded but who complained very much of severe pains in his leg. He was to be decorated with the French award of Knight, Légion d'Honneur, and in 1862 was to gain the rank of major before becoming a lieutenant colonel in 1870 and an aide-de-camp to the Queen eight years later. Readers will meet his sister Louisa in the next chapter. Meanwhile, Sir George Cathcart's tombstone, which had been paid for by subscriptions, had been 'finished, set up and looked very well'. Below the English inscription there was one in Russian giving an account both of his and his father's service in Russia early in the century.

Gilbert also remarked that the number of ships in the harbour at Sevastopol appeared to have increased since he had been in England. They were now 'in a more conspicuous place just under the north side'. It was supposed to be the Navy's last move and, as he tried to explain, as soon as 'the French have erected a new battery near Mount Sassone, it will be a case of check-mate to the *Twelve Apostles* [or the *Dvienadtsat Apostlov*] and four or five others'. His rather obscure ecclesiastical reference was to the presence of the Russian 120-gun battleship and her frigate escort, all later scuttled. Then, finishing his note, Gilbert said he was happy to say that 'I have just been ordered off to Balaclava to do some work which will most likely keep me till late tonight'.[56]

On 19 July Gilbert noted that 'General [Sir James] Simpson is confirmed in his place as Commander-in-Chief and I must say I hope he is, as I am sure there is no better man. Lord Raglan is a very great loss.'[57] Three days later on a hot day, men from Gilbert's division fired on the enemy from the quarries without receiving a shot in return. In two English attacks there were to be about 22,000 rounds of small arms ammunition fired each day. The following day after sunset there was very heavy gun and musket fire from the French whereupon Gilbert went to the ridge of his hill, where he saw that an assault had commenced on the Mamelon Vert. 'We watched,' said Gilbert, 'for about a half an hour without being able in the least to make out whether French or Russians were getting the best of it … and to judge from the tremendous fire the French kept up on them, they must have lost very many men.' On 23 July, Gilbert and Major Smith, 'an excellent fellow' under whom Gilbert was working, helped transfer those who were called 'convalescents' to their camps so that they could be evacuated from Balaclava. He had been impressed with the ships that took them to Scutari. They were well fitted up and 'every man soon after he is put on board is put into a bath, if he is well-enough to stand it, and then into clean clothes'. Nevertheless, the morning returns showed a decrease in the number of those in the division with cholera. He thought that there were only twelve cases under treatment and they had only lost one man in the last few days.[58]

Gilbert's whereabouts between August and October can only be surmised but in all probability he did not take an active part in the final part of the siege at Sevastopol. The French commander, Maréchal Aimable-Jean-Jacques Pelissier, had been moving his trench works forward and by September the Allied lines were within 100 yards of the Russian defences. Constant pounding reduced the Malakoff Battery and the little redan to ruins. The attack which started on 8 September began with no flare or trumpet signal to alert the Russians, who barely noticed the French soldiers charging them until the attackers were in the fortifications. Some 57,000 men were engaged in the assault and, seeing his men in control of the Malakoff, Pelissier signalled the British to commence their attack on the great redan. The Russian counter-attack, however, beat the French back temporarily and the British suffered a similar fate. It was not until three o'clock in the afternoon that the French flag was seen flying from the captured tower and the Russian General Gortschakoff signalled the garrison to evacuate Sevastopol.[59] The abandoned city was occupied on 10 September after a 322-day siege but this was not the end of the war. The task of making peace was to take place in Paris the following year. Representatives of the great powers came together in February 1856 when Russia accepted the initial set of peace terms after Austria threatened to enter the war on the side of the Allies. The final terms of a settlement were completed and signed on 30 March.

Gibby told Charlotte a month after the end of the siege that 'we are still in doubt here as to whether we are to remain where we are, or to embark for Kaffa', on the south-east coast of Crimea (now Theodosia). The first brigade was still on board ship, never having landed since its return from Kinburn, on the south shore of the Dnieper estuary, where the English and French navies had shelled forts on 17 October. It was waiting for orders to come from England to say whether, in Gilbert's words, 'the expedition is to take place or not. If we are to go, the sooner the better as it is impossible to calculate to any kind of certainty about the weather now.'[60]

There was little excitement on account of soldiers having been 'converted into navvies and labourers' until the afternoon of 15 November when the 'most awful explosion' took place in the French siege train park. 'It was really a most fearful sight,' Gibby wrote; 'at first there was the great explosion then the whole of the Light Division's camp appeared full of shells which kept bursting in all directions and showering down upon the huts and tents. The wonder is that more lives were not lost. The French had 251 killed and wounded and the English 145'.[61] Anxious to reassure his sister, he wrote again on 24 December, telling her not to make herself unhappy by thinking they were all being frozen as they were last winter:

> Tonight I am going to the play, and tomorrow night I am to eat my Christmas dinner with my regiment. I have not got the bill of fare or I would have sent it to you. Leicester Curzon and another fellow are coming to dine with me today to go to the play afterwards, so you see our Christmas week is pretty full of gaieties. You people at home appear to think there is some prospect of peace, though the last accounts we have do not make it appear so certain.[62]

It was not long before the 4th Division had to contemplate becoming 'ornamental instead of fighting soldiers'. As the pendulum swung more in favour of peace at the end of January 1856, Gilbert admitted to his sister that 'I am not going to pretend that I like fighting, and I don't believe anyone really does like it till it is over, and he can talk about it'.[63] The second week in February was 'a gay week with us', he told Bob'm:

> the theatre having been re-opened on a larger scale, the consequence is that we have to give dinners to our friends who come from other parts of the army to see the play. Last night we had guests to dinner and went to the play ... you know one must do the honours of one's house or division.[64]

Gilbert had taken to riding across the ruins of Sevastopol. It was 'a very melancholy sight, there was not a house that is not a complete ruin and if ever the Russians do come back to it', he told Bob'm in March, 'they will have to begin all over again if they want to make a respectable-looking town of Sevastopol. We are, of course, awaiting the result of the Paris Conference.'[65]

With both belligerents without a purpose, two strange encounters were organised. There were to be athletic races between them on a piece of ground near the Tshernaya River, and an inspection of Allied forces by a Russian general. In a tone that reflected some amazement, Gilbert explained that 'the Russians are not only going to be asked to attend but there will also be a purse of English money to be run for by them. Of course, we shall be very civil to each other, having been fighting for nearly two years, and perhaps going to fight again in a fortnight.'[66] The races turned out to be 'fun' and not without military significance. They helped Gilbert familiarise himself with the land on the other side of the river, an area he took to riding over regularly. He also inspected the McKenzie Heights, where he did not think 'the defences are so strong'. Then, on 17 April, the Russian General Lüders 'came over and had a look at the French Army in the morning and ours in the afternoon.[67] We turned out about 36,000 men, and the French about the same.' As memories of the panorama of armies on parade and an enemy general faded, Gilbert found a moment to tell his sister about reports of the different times regiments were expected to leave the war zone. 'I now think,' he said, 'I may calculate on being out of the Crimea by the middle of next month. I shall then most likely have the pleasure of being sent off at once to Aldershot on my arrival in England.'[68]

By the middle of May, Gilbert was losing patience, telling Bob'm that 'it is too bad that we, with the fleet of which we are so proud, have allowed the French to remove 53,000 men in the same time it took us to remove about 15,000'.[69] However, on 24 May, the two battalions of the regiment were marched to Balaclava to celebrate the Queen's birthday and medals granted by the French Emperor were distributed. Two days later, and in his last letter to his sister at this time, Gilbert expressed the hope that when the Army got home 'the country will not object to a good many officers and men getting a little leave of absence to go and see their friends and tell them all the stories of the campaign, instead of playing at soldiers at Aldershot'.[70]

It was four days into June at eight in the morning that the 1st Battalion of the Rifles marched to Balaclava and embarked immediately in HMS *Apollo*. After calling at Scutari, Malta, Algiers and Gibraltar, she anchored on the 27th off Corunna, where the soldiers were visited by Spanish generals, their ladies and soldiers. They reached Portsmouth on 7 July and were reviewed by Queen Victoria the following day. The 2nd Battalion embarked in the sailing transport *King Philip* on 8 June and arrived at Portsmouth on 11 July and proceeded by rail to Aldershot.[71] The two heroes of the engagement called 'The Ovens' the previous November, Lieutenant Claude Bouchier (by then Brevet-Major) and Captain William Cunninghame, reached England before the rest of their battalion. They were presented with the Victoria Cross on 26 June 1857 in Hyde Park along with Brevet-Major the Hon. Henry Clifford, Lieutenant John Knox and four privates of the 2nd Battalion.[72] The Queen had founded the order the year before, and it was her first investiture. There were sixty-two recipients of the Victoria Cross. At this time there was no precedent for posthumous awards, with the result that Lieutenant Tryon who Gilbert thought so worthy of it could not be given the Victoria Cross.

The next chapter of Gilbert Elliot's life opened on 17 August 1858 when the thirty-two-year-old officer married Katherine Ann Gilbert, the sixth daughter of the Rt Rev Dr Gilbert at Chichester.[73] His father-in-law had been elected principal of Brasenose College, Oxford, in 1822, the same year as he married the only daughter of the vicar of Culham. He was consecrated Bishop of Chichester at Lambeth Palace in 1842. In the summer of 1859, Gilbert, Kate and his regiment were in Malta, where the main island served as the 'Nurse of the Mediterranean', a hospital base for the wounded from the Crimean War. A few months before the war began, the *Malta Times* had told its readers about 'orders from England to prepare quarters for 10,000 men'. Several localities were fitted up, among them the Lazzaretto and adjoining Plague Hospital, where it was said there was room for a thousand men, and the dockyard lofts where as many men could be housed. 'Convents will be used if absolutely required.' The first wounded soldiers had arrived in November 1854.

On 4 June 1859, and with a half an hour available before he was required at the barracks, Gilbert started a letter to lawyer George and thanked him for news of their father and his failing health. On Malta, the couple were finding the pleasantest time of day was between 6 and 8 p.m., and that day Gilbert said they would be dining 'with the General at six-thirty'. Major-General Sir William Reid served as governor and commander-in-chief of Malta from 1851 to 1858. His replacement, whom they were readying themselves to meet, was Lt-Gen. Sir John Le Marchant. Gilbert understood that 'we are to play with the little prince and some other children after dinner'. Another social contact at this time was the widow of Sir Peregrine Maitland, who had been governor of Cape Province. Regretfully, Gilbert told George that

> Lady Sarah Maitland with her daughter and son go off for England today.[74] They will be a great loss to us, more especially to Kate who used to get many drives in their carriage. They are very jolly people and if you come across them I hope you will make friends.

Gilbert related that 'the admiral was still in harbour but most of his ships were cruising about within sight of the island'. He had hoped that Charlie's ship, HMS *Cressy*, which was then leaving Portland for the Mediterranean, would soon join the fleet. From what had been said there was a chance that Admiral Fanshawe, would be 'very glad to get Charlie under him' and Gilbert thought Charlie would like him as his commander-in-chief. He was 'a very kind, good-natured old man' who would be good to serve under in peace time but 'almost too mild for a war admiral'. The soldier was especially pleased to hear that orders had been given for all the regiments on Malta to be instructed in the working of big guns. In a 'place like this, every man ought to be a gunner!'[75]

In January 1860, Gilbert would have been aware that Henry was in Italy, where another conflict was about to start. The thought of war in Italy, and the changing character of the way in which discipline and authority were exercised in both the Army and the Navy, seem to have been much on his mind. What Gilbert found disturbing was the 'very common sort of animal' to be found all over the United Kingdom which called itself a rifleman, not from the Rifle Brigade. They were 'to be seen in full fig on the top of buses and smoking, and in full fig at ceremonies, drunk'. He maintained that it was time to change both uniform and name as even a London Rifle Brigade now existed. 'Higher authorities truckled to them instead of supporting the officers' even when the officers were in the wrong. Discipline was being seriously undermined. So far as flogging in both the Army and the Navy was concerned, Gilbert felt that HRH Prince Albert was right in thinking it should not be inflicted except in certain cases.

Among visitors expected in Malta were Kate's brother, who had lately obtained a fellowship at Trinity after 'very hard work', along with one of her sisters. He was going to 'knock about the world a little' before taking up his university place. Another prospective visitor was Sir John Boileau, who was to die at Torquay nine years later and whom Gilbert had last heard of in Canada. He had been disappointed when his doctors would not allow him to go to Australia, only as far as Malta. Gilbert had been 'very virtuous and begged him not to come' as all the doctors agreed that the islands were a very bad place for chest complaints but he could not help thinking it might do him some good.[76]

At the end of April at least one of Gilbert's duties became clear when he undertook some invigilating at a Board of Examination – or as he put it, 'doing nothing' while the victim was at his lessons. Outside the Sirocco wind was blowing away 'a sprinkling of mosquitoes'. Charlie and his ship had arrived and were 'looking smart and are both very useful … in many ways'. His sailor brother had been busy sitting on a court of enquiry in respect of Captain Edward Codd and HMS *James Watt* where the petty officers were not inclined to come forward and point out any particular men as having taken part in the affair. He feared there would be insufficient evidence against anyone to enable the authorities to make an example of the captain. No doubt reflecting Charlie's conclusions, Gilbert told George that 'these constant disturbances on board our ships are getting most serious and it is impossible to say how they will end'. Charlie had been very unhappy about discipline in the Navy, and had said how impossible it was for any captain of a ship to feel safe as the smallest thing may 'set the crew to create a disturbance'. Personally, he was keen 'to go to sea for a little bit' to give his men more training. Gilbert was 'sure that the whole fleet ought to be kept much more at sea' than it was as 'all these rows appear to take place in port'.

Our soldier had done nothing about leave but he intended to ask for six months and 'be selfish and not to take [his] leave out of the four worst months of the year in order to please others'. Then, as he brought his letter to a close, Gilbert supposed George knew that Henry was 'by far the greatest man in Naples, much feared and … much hated by the Neapolitan ministers though he says he can see no change in this manner towards him since the publication of his dispatches'. Pride in his brother's diplomatic career was obvious. Malta's 'respected' governor, Sir John Le Marchant, was about to go on leave in England but, wrote Gilbert, 'I suppose you will see him; I don't think you will admire him much.'[77]

Kate and Gilbert were lost for words when they received an especial gift from George in May. Fifty pounds was 'a very big sum, and a very nice thing' to them. Speaking about 'the spending of it', the couple were in doubt whether it was to go to increase their 'very small stock of spoons' or 'be invested in a small trap [or light carriage] to be drawn by [Gilbert's] chargers'. They recognised that both possibilities would be 'good investments' but they did not yet know enough about the price of small traps to be able to decide. The trap 'would certainly be a very great convenience and would also save us a certain amount of money'. He was in hopes that 'we may be able to find one to suit us, and have something over for a few spoons as well'.

It was pretty well settled that the couple were to apply for four months leave from the beginning of July, and Gilbert not only knew he would get it but also have an extra month tacked on to it by the War Office. It meant they would be in England until the end of November. So far as Charlie was concerned, he was still at sea, and Gilbert suspected he had asked to be allowed to remain out so as to give his crew 'a little drill'. He met the captain of the fleet, Admiral Sir Sidney Dacres, on the evening of 10 May, who explained that 'the *Cressy* ought to be with other ships for a little time as her men were rather backward in their exercises and a little competition would do them good'. Captain James John Stopford of HMS *Exmouth* had gone home, leaving Charlie as the senior captain on the station, with the worst ship. There were, nevertheless, reports that *Cressy* was going home and of the captain getting 'something better'.[78]

It seems that the soldier and his wife managed to spend much of the second half of 1860 in Britain albeit that they had returned to Malta by February the following year, where the island had been visited by 'earthquakes and robbers'. The first natural shock had come at 12.30 a.m. just as they reached home after a ball. The whole house had rattled under them and there was a sound like a heavy wagon rolling along a road. It did not last long but there were two after-shocks in the morning – sufficient to spoil the ball for those who stayed to dance. They were broken into for a second time a little afterwards, this time while they were out at a dinner party. Gilbert concluded that the thief had got onto the roof and entered the house along the upper veranda and in through the dining room. His servant was in the house and, on hearing steps, went to investigate but 'being rather frightened he did not look behind the curtains'. While he was calling a policeman it appears that the thief walked out of the house when he found he could not get into the locked cupboard in the pantry. Gilbert's dog, Rose, was in the drawing room all the time and Gilbert, who noticed that she seemed very drowsy and was later sick, was in no doubt that she had been drugged.[79]

When Kate and Gilbert finally left Malta is not clear but the handwriting used by the soldier in his last letter did not have the precision and clarity so evident when he was in the Crimea. By April 1864 they had arrived in Ireland, he having accepted a quiet posting on account of his continued physical weakness. The couple had settled down at 'Castleview', a pleasant house with a cheerful outlook, surrounded by grass and trees, in the garrison town of Buttevant, County Cork. He told his brother that they were both 'well-pleased with the place' and saw no reason why they 'should not be very jolly' there, and that he was a good deal better than he had been ten days previously, but he could still not get rid of 'pains and aches'. The couple had been to a flower show at Mallow, a country town to the south, and 'already found one or two acquaintances'. The mayor's wife was something of a busybody, which was 'lucky for Kate', and there was the possibility that they would meet Lord and Lady Doneraile – a member of whose family had devised the St Leger horse race at Doncaster – 'when they come back'.[80]

By the end of May, Gilbert was thanking his brother for having recommended that they visited Killarney and Buttevant, also asking him whether he might choose to pay them a visit. They had found the house very convenient for the lakes and could easily put him up. He explained that it took two or three hours to get to Killarney at this time of year and 'there is no difficulty about getting hotels'. Rivers were very low in the dry weather so that there had not been any salmon fishing and he had had hardly any pain for three days. But being in 'a most sporting neighbourhood' and with the ground 'hard as flint', there were steeplechases going on all round the county. Gilbert had gone to see a 'punching match' but arrived too late. One of the two men backed himself to punch the other or ride him to a standstill in three hours. There was a large attendance to see 'necks and bones broken', but everyone was disappointed when one of the horses 'wisely and positively' refused the second fence. Gilbert was impressed with the quite wonderful things that people managed to get over in these 'pounding matches' (or steeplechases).[81]

There was still hope that summer that George might yet pay them a visit to Killarney although Gilbert had no knowledge about his brother's plans in August. He hoped for his sake that he was on the moors in Scotland as by all accounts there were lots of birds. Grouse shooting in Ireland did not start until the 20th but it was 'never very good'. The couple were hoping for a passing visit from the Russells at the end of September after Fanny and Lord John's stay at Berwick.[82] Meanwhile, Gilbert had not been offered any military appointment and told his brother that he would have declined it as he 'was hardly up to it yet'. Temperatures of between 74 and 77 degrees were not welcome to him.[83]

On the last day of January 1865 Gilbert was at least prepared to say that he was altogether much better than when the couple had left London ten months before. Despite this, one of his concerns was an incident involving his brother's ship HMS _Bombay_ and the subsequent court-martial (explained in the next chapter), and the break-up of the 46th depot and its departure for Templemore in County Tipperary. Pay lists for the battalion would not be closed until the end of March. Gilbert told George that 'it would be absurd for me to remain and I shall ask to be allowed to go a week after the leaving of the last depot. I have heard nothing about myself yet.' Then, to these last words, he added his thoughts about 'Shamrock', his horse, whom he had had to blister. The vet had assured him that the leg would be better than ever. It had been something of a bore as the frost at Buttevant had 'broken up' and hunting was beginning again.[84]

It was not long, however, before Gilbert's uncertain health drove the couple from Ireland. In March 1865, Kate was looking after her husband in rented accommodation at 1 Robertson Terrace, Hastings.[85] An Army friend, Col. Hugh Smith, had helped him settle in after a short stay in a hotel. Kate went out to make a few purchases, including a pack of cards with which they could play écarté. It seems that no sooner had he arrived on the south coast than his cough had worsened and once the news reached the Elliot family, Nina and George set off for Hastings and took hotel rooms nearby. Kate's notebook records the almost daily visits of doctors, initially Mr Ticehurst and then Dr Aidey, following episodes when Gilbert was spitting blood. Treatment included much rest, lead pills, drops of spirit of turpentine and mustard poultices on the patient's chest. Kate's own loving ministrations were continuous, prompting Nina to advise her more than once to rest more and take some exercise; even Gilbert begged Mr Ticehurst to prescribe a glass of wine for her. Days went by slowly with Nina buying him a present of a backgammon board while Kate read to him every day.

Although there was a return of Gilbert's haemorrhage on Monday 3 April and the expectoration very quickly lost any brighter tinges, Kate persuaded herself that Gilbert was becoming stronger. He 'was able to be lifted on to the sofa, and enjoyed the little change, and being able to see what was going on'. On one occasion he asked Kate to clean the pair of opera glasses he was using. Nina and others in the family very much wished to have Dr Blakiston's opinion 'as his ear was said to be so very good'. Hitherto, both Dr Ticehurst and Dr Aidey had hoped that his lungs, if affected, were only slightly so, as they said that haemorrhage usually came either at the beginning or in a very advanced stage of the disease and that from all that they could gather, the disease could not have been in a very advanced state with him. They also thought a good deal of the opinion given by William Stokes, the eminent specialist in diseases of the heart and lungs who had examined him in December 1864. He had published _A Treatise on the_

*Diagnosis and Treatment of Diseases of the Chest* when only thirty-three years old and, in Gilbert's case, he pronounced his lungs sound; but all the doctors had to admit that so long as the lungs were so full of blood, an opinion was almost impossible.

On Wednesday 12 April, Dr Blakiston came and made an examination. He asked a great many questions about Gilbert's former state of health and, having seen George and Nina, he told Kate that there was extensive disease of the left lung but he did not feel sure about the right one. He had nevertheless known worse cases recover – or at least be arrested. Kate recalled how weak she had often seen Gilbert in Malta and how wonderfully he had rallied. On Good Friday, Lotty, who had arrived a few days before, sat with him and on Easter Sunday, 16 April, Kate went to the public service while Gilbert read the order of service privately to himself. Lotty had been to the early communion service. The following week, Kate's father came over from the episcopal palace in Chichester but he did not see Gilbert on his first visit as he was asleep. The doctors began to think that 'something ought to be said to Gilbert about his profession' or seeking formal retirement from the Army, but Kate would have none of it. Lotty took Kate for several drives and used these times together to talk about her life if Gilbert were to die.

It had apparently been decided that Gilbert was to be moved to 10 Robertson Terrace in Hastings, a Regency property not far from the sea, and on 26 April he was carried downstairs and wheeled along the street. Wearing a blue veil, he found the little breath of air beneficial and when the party arrived Lotty was waiting in the dining room to receive them. Mr Ticehurst seemed quite pleased with the way in which his patient had borne the move. With Gilbert installed in an armchair lent him by Lady Waldegrave, a clergyman's daughter and a well-known if somewhat overbearing philanthropist in the town, Mr Ticehurst threw the windows open for a little while and in the afternoon Kate took a short walk on the beach. William was the next visitor and there was even talk of Gilbert possibly going to Minto during the course of the summer, especially since Hastings might prove too hot for him. Meanwhile, Gilbert repeatedly asked whether any fly (or light horse-drawn carriage) he saw in the street below his room had contained Fanny, his sister. She was to stay nearby for a week, coming to see him several times. For his part, Gilbert gained enough strength to go out and he begged to be introduced to Lady Susan Harcourt, the daughter of the second Earl of Sheffield, who had been very kind to him.

On Wednesday 17 May, Kate's notebook told of her being in the company of one of her sisters and reading various verses to Gilbert, including some from Psalm 103 which he repeated after her. Similar readings took place on Friday the 19th when they seemed to quieten him, but on 25 May 1865 Lt-Col. Gilbert Elliot died aged thirty-nine years. In 1879 his widow remarried in Paris the Rt. Hon. Hugh Culling Eardley Childers, whom Gladstone would appoint as Secretary of State for War. Kate was to die in May 1895.

# 13

# CAPTAIN CHARLES ELLIOT'S
# LATER YEARS (1845-1895)

Captain Charles Gilbert Elliot's ship, HMS *Cressy*, an 80-gun, screw-driven, steam-powered battleship, had sailed out of harbour at Sheerness to join the Channel fleet in May 1859. The vessel had been one of three depot ships of the steam fleet in reserve. A fortnight later, the forty-year-old seafarer, his 3,700-ton ship and its crew of 750 men arrived at Portland, 4 miles from Weymouth. There, ships' companies were 'organized and exercised', something much required in the case of HMS *Cressy*, which had been the guard-ship at Sheerness and had 'got into harbour ways of skiving'. Telling his brother George that if members of the family wished to visit him, Charles explained that there were steamers four or five times a day from Weymouth and a number of inns situated near the breakwater at Portland where they could stay. He said 'immense works' were going on at Portland, where the breakwater provided one of the finest anchorages possible, 'large enough for any fleet Britain was likely to muster'.[1]

As recorded in the previous chapter, Charlie sailed from England soon after, calling at Gibraltar, where the newspapers helped him keep up with the news, and from a homeward-bound packet he learned the names of Palmerston's new cabinet in which Lord Russell had become Foreign Secretary. By the morning of 15 July, Gozo was in sight and that evening they reached Valetta, where they docked and heard something of the great and especially gruelling battle of Solferino which had been fought on 24 June. Some 100,000 Austrian troops had been defeated for a second time after fighting 118,000 French and Piedmontese-Sardinian forces. 'We hear,' wrote Charlie, 'that the armistice has been concluded.' Napoleon III, moved by the losses, had decided to put an end to the war with the Armistice of Villafranca on 12 July. The journey to Malta had been accompanied by generally light airs and calms which allowed the *Cressy* to carry out more exercises and target practice than would have been possible had war been declared and she had been required 'to throw away coals in steaming' so as to reach Malta more quickly. 'There is no doubt,' said Charlie, 'that our men know well how to fire. They have not yet had trials in rough waters which is the next practice I shall try to have.' He was, however, not satisfied with the ship's sailing qualities and was beginning to think that his ship might be '*the* dull sailor of the fleet, particularly in the smooth water of the Mediterranean'.[2]

Without question Charlie must have been hugely pleased to be at sea again and no sooner was some gunnery practice completed and he had fulfilled his responsibilities as a member of a court-martial than he was away with others of the fleet. His stay in Malta was short-lived. He took HMS *Cressy* to Alexandria, where all went well except that the ship had proved herself 'the greatest tub' he had ever sailed in. A fresh sea breeze and a strong sea seems to have forced the squadron to remain off Africa for some six days and many of the crew had gone to Cairo. Personally he hoped to see the pyramids but whether he achieved a visit to Giza is not recorded and HMS *Cressy* soon returned to Malta.³ On 5 September she finally left Valetta, anchoring in the Bay of Naples around the 11th of the month.

Writing to Doddy on 17 September 1859, Charlie explained that he had come across the bay and was staying the night in Castellamare, where *Cressy* would have the advantage of being close to the British minister, his brother Henry, and also take in the target practice which would not be possible at Naples. He fully expected that some ship would have to remain there but it was a bad winter anchorage. It seemed impossible to Charlie that 'Italy should quiet down'. France and Austria were likely to dictate to her and Britain would not wish to be without a ship there. Later in the month *The Times* newspaper described the distribution of the Mediterranean fleet at Malta. The flagship of Vice-Admiral Arthur Fanshawe, the 131-gun *Marlborough*, had left for Gibraltar and *Hannibal*, flagship of Rear-Admiral Munday, was off the coast of Sicily. Most movements were towards Gibraltar but *Exmouth* was at Naples. Vessels other than screw steamships of the line included the *Terrible*, a steam frigate also at Naples, while steam corvettes were at Corfu, the Pireus, Constantinople and Venice.

Having heard of an unfortunate repulse in China, his old stamping ground, Charlie was anxious to know what Palmerston's government would say about the matter. He was afraid that although there was no want of gallantry 'there may have been a want of a plan of attack' and he knew what defences paddy fields and swamps were. There had been a lamentable event and a rebuff to British arms. In June the *Chesapeake*, flying Sir James Hope's flag, had anchored in the River Peiho, but a reconnoitre showed the passage blocked and the Allied ambassadors requested him to clear a way through. The Chinese fought fiercely and Hope failed in his efforts although it had been forced successfully by Sir Michael Seymour only the year before, a man who, in Charlie's opinion, deserved great credit for the manner in which he had planned and executed his attacks when he had been in charge of the China station. Three ships had been sunk, 89 men had been killed and 345 wounded, including Hope, who was seriously wounded. 'If it is true,' wrote Charlie, 'that the Emperor of China disclaims having anything to do with it, and as he has beheaded the mandarin who did them I suppose we shall have to accept the apology but the mischief done will still be immense in having let them know their strength.' He went on to say that he believed Hope to be a most gallant and fine fellow and he hoped he would not be condemned out of hand.⁴

The instructions given to Charlie's diplomat brother were to dissuade Francis II of the Two Sicilies from allying himself with Victor Emmanuel, King of Sardinia, and when the two men met at this juncture Henry was endeavouring to persuade Francis to start constitutional reform. The brothers' contact was, however, infrequent due to their respective responsibilities. Charlie wrote home on 12 November after a lengthy gap to say that he was expecting to remain near Naples for another month but the admiral's intention seemed to be to relieve him. He admitted he had no right to complain having had 'a pleasant autumn here' and they did manage a day amongst the snipe later in one of the royal family's reserves and shot a couple of woodcock into the bargain. The newspapers were reporting what they had reported before, namely, that the 4th Battalion of the Rifle Brigade was going to China. Charlie hoped this was not true as he did not think Gilbert would be fit for 'eastern heats'. Surprisingly, he had 'a great mind' himself to offer his services 'for the China business'.[5]

A few days before Christmas 1859, the Bay of Naples experienced a dose of winter. Strong wind was accompanied by rain and hail, and snow on Vesuvius was nearly down to the level of the sea. Charlie had decided to set up a subscription for a library on board his ship and now wanted George 'to get and send any catalogues of cheap editions such as Routledge' (the publishing house) so that his sailors might 'choose the books'. In the meantime, he wanted to make a start by a small donation from himself of books for the library. He enclosed a list of a dozen or so volumes he thought would do, leaving it to George 'to get such as have bindings of some sort. Routledge advertises a Shakespeare in four volumes for 10 shillings with the same in calf 21 shillings. Half calf would probably be best for a book of that sort.' Included were volumes by William Hickling Prescott and Sir Edward Bulwer, and he especially asked George to obtain a copy of Lord Elgin's *Mission to China* when it was published.[6]

As the year turned, Charlie began to worry quite seriously about the state of the ship's provisions and he estimated they only had enough food and drink for four weeks. It was a question of either going to Malta for re-provisioning or having a supply sent to him. Thinking about the political situation, Charlie wanted to be in Italian waters for a few months longer since, as he wrote, 'things can't remain as they are, and even Naples will have to adapt its government to the times or be prepared for revolution'. It was not until the first days of February when he supposed the admiral was on his way to Malta from Gibraltar, and he was about to send a telegraph to Valetta describing the state of his ship's provisions, that orders came for him to return to Malta.

Keeping his ship adequately victualled was not the captain's only concern. His own future in the Navy and the well-being of his crew were also on his mind. Promotion to admiral rather than continued cruising with the squadron into the following year would 'suit' him best. Charlie was convinced that the Navy had 'some young enough admirals' but there were too many old gentlemen on the admirals' or captains' lists. With Naples hardly as salubrious as he had anticipated in the winter months and fevers rather common on land and afloat, the captain had to keep a watchful eye open for the health of his officers and crew. A member of Henry's staff at the legation in Naples by the name of Phipps had been very ill and George Burgess, one of *Cressy's* officers, had also been laid up.[7] It was the end of February when Charlie sailed to Malta, which was 'not a bad place to be at for a short time to see or hear what goes on in the naval world'.[8]

Writing to Doddy at the end of May, the captain told him about a letter he was expecting from Sir Richard Dundas, a previous second-in-command of the Mediterranean fleet and a quiet and undemonstrative reformer quite unlike the popular image of an officer. Charlie wanted his views on the possible transfer of the ship's company to a more suitable vessel, one able to compete with newer ships, including those of the French fleet. He appreciated only too well that the Admiralty did not like being spoken to plainly regarding a matter of that kind, with the result, he wrote, that 'I may very likely get snubbed'. Nevertheless, he continued,

there seems to be an excellent feeling amongst men and officers on board *Cressy* and discipline is satisfactorily kept up but nowadays one has no right to feel oneself secure from outbreaks [of indiscipline] when one sees some accidental or injudicious behaviour on the part of an officer create a mutinous outbreak among the ship's company previously apparently contented and well conducted.

Charlie said he was quite disposed to adopt very different measures for keeping up discipline than what used to be the practice, saying that 'we do treat men more like rational beings than we used to but if they behave in a manner to oblige one to resort to strong remedies they must be carried out as formerly'.[9]

The captain had been writing his commentary while trying to prepare a list of those members of the crew who were to go home for a change of climate. Both activities were brought to a halt when there was news that Sir William Fanshawe Martin, 'our new Admiral has come, and I go to meet him at dinner'.[10] It seems that he soon persuaded the Admiralty that the appointment of Charlie to a larger ship had virtue. A 5,500-ton, 101-gun, screw-driven battleship, HMS *St Jean d'Acre*, which had been built in 1853 and which was in the Baltic during the Crimean War was to be his new command. Navy records show that Charlie became her captain on 26 September 1860, the same day that Captain Thomas Harvey took command of *Cressy*. Having sailed to Gibraltar aboard the *St Jean d'Acre* in June 1861, Charlie explained to George now his orders to return to Malta had been cancelled and the following day he was instructed to take his ship across to Tangier and be ready to accompany John Drummond-Hay, the British resident minister, on a mission to the Moorish court.[11]

Having asked for change, he received it in spades, describing his new duties as likely to be 'an interesting expedition' and one which would 'not be a bad way to wind up my Mediterranean service'. Drummond-Hay had negotiated a treaty of friendship and trade with Morocco at the end of 1856 but on this occasion it seems he felt the need to reinforce his position by having Captain Charles and his ship to hand. So far as the sailor could make out, the two men were to travel to Meknès, a journey of about six days and an absence of about three weeks. The opportunity of a visit to Fez might present itself although he did not look forward to being smothered in dust as they rode with their escorts or around their camp sites.[12] Charlie was soon to find himself working with a diplomat of the highest order and engaged in delicate negotiations under the desert sun of North Africa. Spain had declared war on Morocco in October 1859 and an early skirmish resulted in 400 Spanish dead when the Moors attempted to take a newly built redoubt at Ceuta. In November, Captain-General Leopoldo O'Donnell reversed the outcome and in the new year Tetuan was occupied. The Moors were forced to sue for peace at the end of March when casualties had amounted to 6,000 Moroccan dead and wounded and some 4,000 Spanish.

From what George was told by his brother, Charlie thought it was pretty clear that the Spaniards had been playing false with the English to prevent any good being done by the Drummond-Hay mission. Furthermore, it looked to Charlie as if the Moors also had sound reasons to doubt the good faith of the Spaniards. The new Sultan, Mului Abbas, said that the Moorish government declared it would not carry out the various articles of the treaty until Tetuan was evacuated. Charlie learned privately through a Swedish colleague that the Spaniards intended to keep Tetuan, information the Swede reported to his government at the time.[13] Soon afterwards, Charlie went to see Hay, who was about to send his private secretary, Mr Green, with dispatches to the British minister at Madrid, suggesting that he might enlighten the Foreign Office.[14]

By July 1861 there was no end of telegrams to and from the Foreign Office, one of which ordered Hay to Meknès if he thought he could be useful but he decided to await the outcome of the dispatches he had sent to London via Madrid. Charlie wrote to George saying that

> I dare say the impression at home may be that we ought to be off at once but it must
> be remembered that the announcement about Tetuan is not calculated to assure the
> Moors of the intention of the Spaniards to give it up if the indemnity is paid.

Ready to undergo 'the excessive baking' he had been warned about, Charlie thought a run among the Moors of Africa would not make him anxious for the somewhat fresher air of the moors of Scotland. The distance to Meknès 'as the crow flies is not great', he said, 'but we are evidently not crows and cannot hold their straight course or go their pace, so we are to take 8 days to do it. Three weeks away is the very least we can be … and I suspect [that] as the places for our halts are settled by the Moroccan authorities we take a little longer than necessary.'[15]

Writing to Nina on 2 July after they reached Meknès, the sailor told her that the reception and treatment given to the Hay mission by the Sultan was particularly flattering and calculated to show the good feeling which existed towards England. The Vizier himself, al-Tayyib ben al-Yamani, called on Hay soon after they arrived, quite an unusual if not unprecedented condescension. In a long conversation which Hay relayed to Charlie, the Vizier showed himself reasonable and peaceably inclined despite the difficult position the Moorish government found itself in. In a letter to George the following day, Charlie told him that 'Hay has apparently convinced him that whether they offer the terms we recommend or not, I believe the Vizier wilt do all he can with the Sultan'. In a private interview with the Sultan the same day, Hay spoke about the disadvantages of going to war and recommended that he should accept the opening now afforded him.

Morocco and the war with Spain, 1859–60.

Throughout these transactions Charlie had been impressed by the way Hay had shown him his correspondence, and discussed proceedings with him.

> I confess I think he is doing well to attain the end in view. The Moors, Sultan included, respect him as their true friend and honest adviser. He certainly has much influence with them but they feel and say that Spain has been faithless and harsh in her conduct towards Morocco and they mistrust her. The fact of the English government declaring its belief that Spain will accept in good faith the terms or overtures from the Moorish government is alone what gives fair hope of an amicable arrangement.

Charlie thought every exertion ought to be made to get the Spaniards to agree to a reasonable settlement at Tetuan. The Moors had raised part of the indemnity and were making such arrangements as they could for the eventual payment of the remainder. The Sultan eventually paid Spain 20 million pesetas and, with it safely in the bank, the Spanish army evacuated Tetuan.[16]

With the Hay mission coming to its close, it seems that Charlie had heard from John Moore, secretary to the First Lord of the Admiralty, who made it clear that he would not be relieved of his command other than to be made an admiral. Naval records show that he became a rear-admiral on 5 August 1861 and he relinquished command of *HMS St Jean d'Acre* on 13 September when she was paid off at Plymouth. Charles's next command was not to be until April 1864.

Towards the end of January 1863, the admiral was in the Ionian Islands at Santa Maura, an island separated by a sand bar from the Greek mainland, south east of Paxoi, and 6 miles south of Corfu. He had left Henry in Athens and spent a week in the vicinity of Patras, where he enjoyed the company of a party aboard HMS *Icarus*, an 868-ton sloop, made up of the vice-consul Mr Wood and a Greek friend of his, together with her commander Nowell Salmon. The last was then only twenty-eight years old and the proud possessor of the Victoria Cross which he had won in 1857 for conspicuous gallantry in India. In five days they 'bagged' 219 woodcock and some hare, snipe and duck. It was 'very pretty sport' but the country on Santa Maura, with its barren-looking plains and hills, was very different from anything over which they had been shooting around Patras.

Commenting on the political scene, the admiral said there was 'a terrible feeling of insecurity in these parts. The people are nearly all going about armed, and robberies and murders are very common'.[17] It was not until May the following year, after the Treaty of London had been signed between Britain and Greece, that the Ionian Islands, which had been under British protection since 1815, were handed over to Greece. Although he anticipated that Corfu would not provide much in the way of sport, on 29 January Charlie found passage from Santa Maura to Corfu in a small 20-ton yacht. It was rather a smaller craft than he was used to but 'it made a very good run northward', first anchoring in a small bay. He enjoyed the hospitality of Sir Henry Knight Storks, who had been the Lord High Commissioner since 1859 and who was to hand over to Count Dimitrios Karousos the next year and later become governor of Malta. The plan had been to stay a few days but the captain of HMS *Magicienne*, Ernest Leiningen, offered to take Charlie to Messina in Sicily if he could sail almost immediately. Thereafter the admiral hoped to go to Naples and probably homeward via Rome.[18]

Once at Messina in Sicily, Charlie had time to recall his passage with Captain Leiningen and explain to Doddy how the easy-going seafarer had come to remark that no one would 'catch me going there' when they were discussing Greece's constant plight. Charlie had heard of Leiningen's name having been put forward as a potential king of Greece. He was a step-nephew of Queen Victoria and, after a career in the British Navy since 1849, he was about to become captain of the Royal Yacht *Victoria and Albert*, a 2,500-ton paddle yacht in May 1863.[19]

Writing to Doddy from Messina on 9 February, the admiral continued to be concerned about Henry, who was occupied with the election of the King of Greece, and whom he assumed would be 'very ready to return home when [he had] done with him there'. The admiral was revisiting old haunts and friends during a pleasant week's break in Sicily but he told his lawyer brother that he was 'now ready to be moved homewards' which he intended to do either via Marseilles or Genoa and Mt Cenis. It would depend on the weather. The previous day, he had seen Prince Alfred, or 'Young Alfie' as Charlie called him, on board the 120-gun battleship HMS *St George* and joked with him and told him 'he had better not show himself in Greece if he wanted to get away again'.[20] The twenty-year-old son of Queen Victoria was anticipating going home to England the following week overland from Marseilles but these plans were to fall through. A correspondent of *The Times* wrote from Malta on 21 February that 'arrangements for Prince Alfred going home have been unavoidably altered owing to the unexpected illness of the young Prince who has been suffering from a severe attack of cold and fever'. For his part, Charles hoped to be in London towards the middle of March, staying a few days en route in Paris at the Hotel Mirabeau in the Rue de la Paix. His London accommodation was less easy to determine and although he had written to a Mrs McManus to ask whether she had lodgings for him, he asked Doddy to call at Motcomb Street at the rear of Belgrave Square 'to hear whether they are full'. Another alternative he suggested were the lodgings opposite his lawyer brother's house in Pont Street. Just how Charlie's plans worked out once he got back to London, and probably Minto, is not clear, but he would undoubtedly have lobbied hard with their Lordships at the Admiralty for a posting suitable for a rear-admiral.

To the delight of his brothers and sisters, 6 December 1863 saw Charlie's marriage to Louisa Blackett at Matfen, Stamfordham, west of Newcastle; she was the sister of a Rifleman with whom Charlie's brother Gilbert had fought in the Crimea. The Blacketts had been part of a mine-owning family from the Pennines, and with estates 'twixt Tyne and Tweed' since the seventeenth century. Louisa was the eldest daughter of Sir Edward Blackett, the sixth Baronet of Newcastle, and the late Julia Monck, his first wife. Sir Edward had been educated at Eton and Christ Church, Oxford, and after service in the First Life Guards he held the office of deputy lieutenant and justice of the peace. Charles and Louisa would have four sons born to them between February 1865 and March 1870.

Charles's life changed substantially during the spring of 1864; he was confirmed as commander-in-chief, south-east coast of America station, and it was anticipated he would sail aboard his flagship HMS *Bombay* the following month. Originally constructed in the East Indies this 2,783-ton, 91-gun warship had been in dry dock undergoing major reconstruction and was commissioned at Chatham dockyard by

Captain Colin Campbell, her captain-to-be, on 24 March. She had been lengthened forward and additional cabins and offices erected for the admiral and his suite. In early April she was moved to Folly Point at the entrance of Chatham harbour. Having been armed and prepared for trials the ship eventually sailed the measured mile off Maplin Sands on the last day in the month. With a final adjustment to her compasses, *Bombay* left for Plymouth on Tuesday 10 May.[21] Meanwhile, Louisa and Charlie were staying at Admiralty House in Devonport with Admiral Sir Charles Fremantle, who had been responsible for the Channel squadron until 1860 and who was now commander-in-chief. Their sailing was somewhat delayed, apparently on account of a man's carelessness in dropping an important brass fitting overboard, which annoyed the admiral, but HMS *Bombay* eventually left Plymouth Sound on the evening of Friday 13 May.[22]

Twelve days later, the ship was in the harbour at Funchal in Madeira, and Charlie and Louisa were able to enjoy riding together in pleasant weather on the nearby hills. The voyage had not been a rapid one and Louisa had been horridly seasick due to a great deal of swell. She did, however, recover when the sea went down much better than Charlie had expected. The admiral continued to find matters he had omitted to deal with before he sailed and Doddy was to receive a lengthy list of commissions soon after they arrived at Rio de Janiero, the admiral's station. He found himself short of a number of servants and those available attracted wages he could not afford. Charlie asked him

> to look out one for me … I want a man to work under the steward and wait at table and perhaps do valet's work sometimes. His pay from Government as an 'Admiral's domestic' would be … £28 17s 11d and I would make it up to £40. He would have board and lodging but must find his own clothes.[23]

The dinner uniform for the admiral's servants included a white jacket and waistcoat, and white tie in hot weather and a tailcoat instead of the white jacket in cold weather.

HMS *Bombay* had made a slow passage to Brazil, arriving on 28 June. The journey had taken forty-nine days from Plymouth, exactly the time Charlie had taken aboard the old *Goldfinch* packet when he came out to join the *Actaeon* early in his career.[24] They had remarkably light winds both before and after getting to Madeira: 'even the trades deceived us, being very light indeed until we neared the coast of Brazil when they became foul, holding more than usually from the south'. He had expected to better this time aboard a steamer. In other respects, he said, 'all has gone well and even the long passage was more of an inconvenience to Warren than to me'. Charlie had felt in no desperate hurry to relieve Rear-Admiral Richard Laird Warren in Rio. So far as he could judge,

> the *Bombay* seems to steam well, and to sail pretty well too in light winds but she is very frank and on a wind when the breeze freshens heels over so much that she gets her great bluff bow buried in the water on the lee side and will not move at all. She appears to be a handy ship notwithstanding.

He was still somewhat concerned about Louisa's general health and the way she had lost quite a lot of weight, but she was able to enjoy 'the delightful climate' and some drives in 'the near neighbourhood', and 'very fine' they were. The couple took up temporary quarters for a few days at a hotel kept by an Englishman in a pleasant position on the bay, a couple of miles out of town.

Admitting that he had yet to find the time to make acquaintances in Rio, Charlie told George that there seemed to be no want of civility within the government. He felt he was in a better position to succeed than Henry had been when he succeeded Hudson in Turin, where popularity with the public placed anybody coming after him at a disadvantage. His predecessor, Rear-Admiral Warren, 'certainly was not popular and I don't think he had the knack of smoothing out difficulties'.[25]

George had used the French mail boat for his last letter to Charlie. Our friends, the admiral told him, counted on the monthly service from Southampton and his letter was all the more welcome. 'We shall be anxious for the next mail,' he wrote, 'to learn what the failure of the conference brings about. I hope to hear we shall not throw over Denmark altogether.' His brother had been working as Lord Russell's private secretary and had become involved in discussions during the spring of 1864 arising from the Second Schleswig War between Denmark and Austro-Prussian forces which had invaded Jutland in February. The admiral 'fully counted upon hearing of a determined attack upon our government, and particularly upon Lord John, by the opposition in England'.[26]

In London, the House of Commons debated the conduct of the Brazilian government on 12 July when Palmerston, the Prime Minister, was asked whether it had fulfilled its obligations to Africans liberated by British naval cruisers given that Earl Russell had said 'some thousands of negroes entitled to freedom' were still held in bondage in violation of treaty engagements. Palmerston was obliged to say that the conduct of the Brazilian government 'had been marked by great neglect'. Britain had asked in vain for lists of those set free and there were some twenty individual requirements to be met, which his Lordship listed, before negroes could obtain their emancipation. He believed that at least the slave trade had been 'for the time' put to an end and took personal credit for achieving this. Towards the end of the debate, Sir John Hay, a naval officer turned MP, referred to the efforts being made to put down the slave trade on the west coast of Africa. Referring to the naval squadron of eighteen steam vessels there, only one of them, HMS *Rattlesnake*, was capable of going more than 8½ knots an hour. A general order had been issued as the result by the commanding officer stating that the speed of slave steamers on the coast was now so great in comparison with British cruisers that it was useless to follow them. Her Majesty's ships were directed to remain at anchor on the coast on any part of the coast where it was likely that slavers destined for Brazil might be embarked.[27]

So far as politics across South America were concerned, Charlie supposed his lawyer brother had seen reports of the failure of negotiations which had been conducted with the Uruguayan government in Montevideo. In 1863, General Venancio Flores,[28] a member of the Uruguayan Colorado Party, had organised an armed rising against the Blanco Party President, Bernardo Berro. Flores won backing from Brazil while Berro made an alliance with the Paraguayan leader

South America at the time of the war in the 1860s between Argentina, Brazil and Uruguay on the one hand, and Paraguay on the other.

Francisco Solano López. The admiral did not know what the consequences of this action would be but, he wrote,

> they are accustomed to a state of revolution in that country and all being quiet at Montevideo, I do not at present see much probability of my having to go down to the River Plate before October … when the heat here will make one very ready for a move into a cooler climate. Nothing could be more agreeable than the weather we have as yet had here.

Charlie had no particular desire to leave Rio just then as he wanted to get to know the station more thoroughly and had it in mind to pay a visit to Bahia (Salvador) and Pernambuco (Recife) in the course of August. He was afraid this would entail deserting Louisa, leaving her in Rio, or at Petropolis which Emperor Pedro II had founded in 1843 and where he had built his summer palace, but 'she may just as well remain in a fair climate as undergo the discomforts of a good deal of seawork'. They had only stayed on shore for a week and had since been living comfortably on board *Bombay* where it was cooler. A change of diet or contaminated water had given Louisa what first-comers were apt to get in Rio, 'a derangement of the stomach', as Charlie called it. It weakened her just at the time she had begun to pick up strength. Although the local population showed every disposition to be civil, notwithstanding 'our troubles' as the admiral said, he appreciated that Louisa found it a little difficult to make acquaintances and there were few ladies she would be likely to see excepting those among the *corps diplomatique*.[29]

Writing to George in August, Charlie hoped his letter would not find him at the Foreign Office but rather 'refreshing himself on the moors'. There were none in the neighbourhood of Rio, he wrote, 'but we have hill air within easy reach and we can invigorate ourselves'. It had been pleasantly cool though latterly with more rain than desirable. Louisa was stronger than she had been and, although picking up steadily, she was not yet ready for long excursions. Charlie was sorry to say that he would have to leave his wife for about a month while he made acquaintance with the northern parts of the station, but he told George that he might only go to Bahia on this occasion and not beyond.

So far as the political scene was concerned, the admiral had heard that proposals suggested by Portugal for bringing about a reconciliation between Brazil and Britain had been sent out by the French packet, then altered, and sent back. Charlie did not think there was much chance of any quick progress on that front although it was said that the Emperor was anxious to see a settlement. He hoped that there would soon be a new British minister in Rio before the marriages of the Emperor's two daughters took place. A curious fact caught Doddy's imagination when he discovered that despite the weddings being scheduled for October it was not yet known who the bridegrooms were.[30] It gave the admiral great pleasure that he was 'happily free from all attendance at court'. That night there was to be ball at the Grand Casino (a club), where the Emperor was to attend but the admiral declined to go since he had not been presented at court.[31]

It was two months before Charlie was able to express his gratitude to Doddy for 'his successful exertions about servants'. He had arranged for some to be sent out from England by the *Dromedary*, a storeship. They would help 'when we set up house'. There was also news of 'a good man coming as Consul' at Montevideo. Charles had told Lord John that, in his opinion, old Mr Morgan was not fit for the place, that 'he and his family were far too Brazilian in their attitude'. He had also fulfilled his planned programme of inspection, visiting both Bahia and Pernambuco. Louisa had stayed at a hotel in Rio enjoying generally cool weather except for one week of real heat. When he returned they spent a few days together at her hotel before going up to Petropolis which was very pleasant. He told George that 'we had nothing to envy you for your Italian mountains though ours were of a very different kind'. In the quiet surroundings of Petropolis they enjoyed the company of the Russian minister, who was an agreeable man with a well-informed daughter, and General James Watson Webb, an ex-newspaper publisher who had just become US minister to Brazil. Notwithstanding what Charlie called his 'coarse writing and blustering Americanisms', he was 'a kind hearted man and not a bad companion for a short time'.

During his absence from Rio, the political climate in Uruguay had worsened. The civil war had led to Venancio Flores laying siege to Montevideo, a situation which Charlie judged now required his and HMS *Bombay*'s presence in the River Plate. The town was hardly in a state where they could expect to stay for six months and the admiral could only hope that 'things will not become so bad in that unhappy country of revolutions as to render it inadvisable to remain there'. With many people wanting shelter in Montevideo he feared that it would not be easy to find a house and a high rent was to be expected.

As things turned out, Charles and Louisa had a good passage down to the River Plate. It took little more than seven days, with only light winds and smooth water for the first days when they made use of steam, and a strong nor'wester subsequently. He had thought there was little chance of Louisa making the journey without undergoing the discomforts of seasickness, but he was proved wrong. The couple were glad to be 'getting away from Rio before the great heats came on', but Uruguay was 'in a wretched state of revolution'.[32] According to Charlie's account,

> Flores, with his so-called army, which I hear is amounted to 1500 men, or perhaps a little more, showed himself on the heights a few miles from the town and everyone expected an attack but by 22 October when I got here, he was off again having done no more than fire four or five round shot into the outskirts of the town.

It seemed to him that the Brazilians, if they were not at war, were approaching one when their forces marched across the frontier. Charlie had heard that 'they have now declared towns up the river Uruguay [Paysandú and Salto] blockaded. It is a complicated affair and I think the best chances of getting through it would be if Flores succeeds in ousting the present government.' The admiral told George that he was going to Buenos Aires the next day as he was anxious to see Mr Thornton, the minister plenipotentiary, who had said he would like to talk over matters with him.[33] He also wanted to meet the Brazilian admiral, Baron Tamandaré, who had put off his departure up the Uruguay in order to see him.

Having told George about the arrival of the servants back in Rio, and how he had dismissed his cook, Charlie painted a picture of the couple's domestic circumstances in Uruguay.

> The disturbances were very fatal to our househunting, for quintas a few miles into the country are deserted, not being considered safe to settle in at present when any day they may have an army of vagabonds in the vicinity. We are comfortably off at our hotel, or rather at a house opposite a hotel and under its management, where we have a quiet suite of small rooms to ourselves. Louisa got through the voyage very satisfactorily and was seasick the last day in roughish weather when we were steaming but was not much upset until then. She comes with me tomorrow in HMS *Satellite* to Buenos Aires.[34]

Pressure to find a house of their own increased as Louisa was expecting their first child, and by the middle of November the admiral was telling George about the quintas they had inspected. There were plenty to be had but in the country there was the possibility of the surrounding neighbourhood being occupied by undisciplined troops who could be unpleasant neighbours. In the event of warlike operations being undertaken they might find themselves compelled to move, although there were many proprietors who were glad to have their property occupied by an English admiral as the best way of securing it from pillage. The couple spent some eight days with Edward and Mary Thornton in Buenos Aires, where Louisa would have greatly appreciated the opportunity of sharing her hopes and fears with a sympathetic mother. Charlie told his brother that 'we like them both and they were most kind and civil to us. It was a comfort for Louisa to meet with a lady in whom she felt she could confide and be on really friendly terms'. However, it seems they had taken against dusty Buenos Aires. 'Argentinian country,' he said, 'looks very tame after feasting on the rich scenery of Rio but I think better of Montevideo, and of its neighbourhood, since seeing Buenos Aires than I did before. There, all is on a dead flat.'[35]

Drawing a comparison between British diplomatic representation in Argentina with that in Uruguay, the admiral said,

> [We] are not so well off here. [Mr W. G.] Lettsom may be an honest straightforward Englishman but he seems to be a mighty rough one. I have not seen much of him yet but I cannot say I think he takes any clear view of things. When I arrived here he had just got into what seemed to me an unnecessarily long correspondence with the Brazilian admiral Baron Tamandaré about the intention of the said admiral of stopping warlike supplies being carried to the ports or forces of the Oriental [or Eastern] Government up the River Uruguay.

Whether the sailor was aware that the Lettsom with whom he had to deal had been the entertainer of his brothers and sisters when Lord Minto was serving in Berlin some thirty years before is not known. Charlie wanted the representatives of the foreign governments in Uruguay to act together as their interests were generally the same. In his view, diplomats were far too much inclined to 'dip their fingers into the political pie' of the country, 'a nasty pie and not likely to be much improved by their sauce'. So long as Uruguay became more settled, Charlie did not think it mattered whether Flores or the present party was in power.[36]

Meanwhile, HMS *Bombay* was anchored some 2 miles offshore and about to lose Commander John Wilson on account of his poor health. He had served under Captain Colin Campbell. A week or so later, Charlie and Louisa's plans had prospered to the point that the keys of their quinta were handed over to them. Describing the property to George, the admiral said, 'it is a very small house rather further from the town than I like and unfortunately not commanding the bay from the windows but far as it is from the town it is not so far from the ships'. It had the advantage of being furnished, a rare occurrence saving them both trouble and expense. 'It is in a good neighbourhood', he added, 'clean and more comfortable-looking than any quinta I have seen. It is a two-storied house built by an Englishman, perfectly ugly and you may think it rather small for us and some of the staff, when I tell you that on the ground floor there are only four rooms.' Two of them had been used as drawing room and dining room, the other two as kitchen and pantry or servant's room. Upstairs there were four bedrooms with some small rooms in the outhouses. There was a garden with some shade and at least some fresh air to be found. 'That of itself is of great value to Louisa,' he said.

More news was forthcoming when Charles reported that 'Flores was close to Salto [one of the towns blockaded by the Brazilians] and that he has applied to the Brazilian commander to assist him with his gunboats to take the towns, and that the commander has referred it to his admiral at Buenos Aires for instructions on that point'. Charles did not know how far the Brazilians would be inclined to act with Flores since they wanted to establish themselves and hold all the country lying north of the Rio Negro until they had obtained satisfaction for the injuries they claimed to have received. Such considerations, he thought, might prejudice their willingness to act with Flores. Then, breaking off writing on account of the arrival of the carriage which was to drive them to their quinta, Charles wrote,

I don't care if you at the foreign office decide that they shall be told to keep within their own boundaries but I am not disposed to follow up the declaration of the 'diplomatic body' at Montevideo by offering to stop by force the pounding of the Brazilians.[37]

It was on 14 December 1864, little more than five months after their arrival in Brazil and some three weeks after the Elliots' first visit to their quinta, that tragedy struck. Charles immediately sent the following dispatch addressed to Lord Clarence Paget, the first secretary to the Admiralty. It said:

Admiral Elliot reports the total loss of Her Majesty's ship *Bombay* by fire, at Montevideo on the 14th of December. Mr Smallhorn, assistant-surgeon, of the officers alone is missing; but 93 of the crew are supposed to be lost. Lieutenant Starling, bearer of the despatches, proceeds by French packet to Bordeaux today.

Three or four days before Christmas the admiral had time to give his brother George a hurried account of events. The only other letter he had been able to write to the family had been to Lady Blackett assuring her that Louisa 'was well notwithstanding the excitement of last week'. He had had little inclination to write and no intention at all of communicating with the Admiralty in any detail at this stage since 'in all probability they would publish it', thereby possibly prejudicing the investigation which would soon take place or any court-marshal. He did, however, want to say that 'nothing could have been finer than the general behaviour of all on board. Poor Campbell seems very much cut up, and no wonder. I feel it deeply enough myself ... as if I ought myself to be tried with them being so entirely connected with the ship.' He touched on one reason he thought so many had lost their lives, namely that some had not stripped themselves of their clothes while marines and idlers could in general not swim.

The day HMS *Bombay* was destroyed had been the first occasion on which she had left the harbour since her arrival and Charlie recalled that he had planned to sail in her that day towards Maldonado, near the mouth of the River Plate. He happened to be close to the signal post at a landing place not far from the Elliots' quinta when a signal was made by HMS *Stromboli* and HMS *Triton*, both 1,000-ton, paddle-driven sloops, that *Bombay* was on fire. A signal was immediately sent to the squadron to get up steam, and Charlie called up his gig from the *Triton*, whose steam was up when he reached her but, as the admiral told George, 'it was all too late'. The first positive intelligence of the ship being on fire was taken to the captain of the Port Office about 5 p.m. and the magazine blew up 'when we were but little more than halfway in the *Triton*, the whole distance being 15 miles'.[38]

Among things Charlie had lost in the *Bombay* were his silver plate and a side-saddle. For the moment, the latter would not be wanted but, by and by, he hoped Louisa would be able to ride about the country. He asked George to send him out a side-saddle at the first chance he had, by packet if nothing was going immediately. The previous one had been bought in Bond Street but he did not care where it came from and had no objection to its being second-hand. Horses in Uruguay were very narrow animals and the Bond Street supplier sent numbers of narrow saddles to Montevideo. Charlie also wanted a bridle. Other items lost included clothes but these were insignificant. His tally of things for which the Admiralty would not reimburse him was longer, amounting to as much as £1,000, with a great deal of that being in wine, although as he said to his brother, 'I was lucky in having sent part of my stocks to the *Egmont* receiving ship [or storeship] at Rio till I required it.' He had lost a good many books too.

Once into 1865, the town of Paysandú fell to a joint attack by Flores and Brazilian forces after gallant resistance. Forthcoming pressure on Montevideo seems to have triggered no mean amount of panic on the part of the British diplomat Mr Lettsom. While the weak and unpopular government in Montevideo was making a few preparations to resist an attack by land or sea, Lettsom attacked it for exposing the whole town to danger by accumulating an enormous quantity of gunpowder, and storing it in very unsafe magazines. The admiral described him as 'rather mad on the subject and does not see that we must be neutral'. Lettsom next wrote to Charles asking him to estimate the probable damage of so large a quantity of gunpowder on the town while the government requested that some marines be put ashore to protect the banks. At this point Charles told George, 'I must be off. A row in the town may take place any day and we must do what we can to protect our own people by maintaining order, but the less we meddle the better.'[39]

The admiral now had his flag in HMS *Satellite*, a 2,100-ton corvette under the command of Captain Stephen Crofton. Writing to George, who was exchanging a holiday life in Italy for the interests of the Foreign Office, he explained that

we are still in an uncomfortable state of revolution and … hear that at a meeting between the Brazilian chiefs [Admiral Tamandaré and the many Paranhos] and Flores, it has been arranged that this country shall pay the expenses of the war and give proper satisfaction for the original complaints brought against it. Flores is to be president … for five years, Brazil keeping 7000 troops in the country till it becomes settled.

Charlie felt Brazil and Flores ought to be able to bring such a force against the town as to make resistance useless. The men who comprised the present government, he said, were

by all accounts a bad lot, and it is wonderful how the people here tolerate them so long. Their days are numbered but the Blanco Party which they represent are numerous, and Flores has probably lost popularity in the country by associating with the Brazilians, so how all is to end is more than I can say.

It was particularly inconvenient for Charles to have the prospect of a siege on his hands just when he wanted Louisa to have a quiet time ahead of her confinement. He thought it quite possible that he might have to take her to Buenos Aires 'to be away from warlike troubles', but he sincerely hoped not as he could not remain there with her. The couple had to decide matters in the course of a week or two. 'Louisa is very well,' he wrote on 14 January, saying that 'we are neither of us inclined to be driven out of our quinta if we can help it'.[40]

A week later, however, and with the chance of an attack on the town coming just at the time Louisa needed 'perfect quiet and no excitement', the couple embarked on board the *Satellite* for safety, leaving their quinta virtually an outpost of government troops, with supporters of Flores showing themselves nearby. The next day skirmishing went on there with two or three men being knocked off their horses by musket balls on the road close to the house, the sort of thing Charles did not want Louisa to see. When he next returned there he found the Colorados in possession of the neighbourhood but their quinta had been perfectly respected by all parties. The Colorados, who the night before had bivouacked just outside the grounds, were fraternising and showing great goodwill to Charlie's coxswain and the servants who had been left in the house.

Under more normal circumstances, the admiral told George he would have remained on board ship, returning with Louisa when it became quiet enough but

> that would not do just now and I sent her off to Buenos Aires yesterday. The Thorntons have most kindly offered to take her in. It is accepting a great deal from them but I am too glad to have her in such excellent keeping to hesitate a moment about it … I cannot get away from Montevideo just now.

His only worry was that she might encounter some of the hot days which were so much worse in Buenos Aires than in Uruguay. Had the Brazilians been a little more energetic in their movements Charlie thought they might have been there long ago, and though the government at Montevideo declared it would still fight to the last to defend the town, he had hopes that when the pinch came, Atanasio Aguirre, the acting president of Uruguay, and his colleagues would be found to have cut and run. In the meantime people were flocking out of Montevideo by the thousand. The town was perfectly open to attack from the sea. When the Brazilian squadron was still not in sight, Charlie had more requests for George to obtain replacements for items lost in the *Bombay*. He was to purchase half a dozen toothbrushes for him without ivory handles from Floris in Jermyn Street along with 'a pocket comb, and bath sponge'.[41]

In London that day, a letter had been sent to the editor of *The Times* by someone calling themselves 'Voyageur'. Ever since the loss of HMS *Bombay*, naval officers and others had begged the press to stay its judgement until the inevitable court-martial had done its work. The correspondent had two points to make, one being the position and construction of the spirit room, the other being the size, number and condition of the lifeboats belonging to the ship at the time of the conflagration. It was not easy to conceive, he said, if the spirit room was, as it should have been, a watertight iron compartment, accessible only for ordinary purposes by a small scuttle from above and lighted from without by means of glass bull's eyes, how fire could be communicated from it to the rest of the ship. With respect to the boats, it was, he wrote, of the utmost importance to the public to know whether they were sufficient in number and capacity to save the lives of those on board. Ninety-three lives had been lost in fine weather, in sight of shore, with only one boat swamped. It pointed to some grievous error.

Next month the newspaper reported that the remainder of the officers and crew of the *Bombay* were expected to arrive at Portsmouth by special train from Liverpool. The *Herschel* steamship in which they returned to England from Montevideo had been ordered by the authorities to Liverpool from Lisbon, her last port of call. On arrival at Portsmouth, the officers and men were to be temporarily berthed on board the *Duke of*

*Wellington* training ship under the command of Captain John Seccombe, pending the result of the court-martial which was to assemble on board HMS *Victory*, Nelson's flagship, about 6 February.

Charlie was able to tell the family that Louisa had given birth to Gilbert Edward Elliot on the second day of February – 'Louisa and the baby were going on capitally'. A note had been sent to Fanny by the Liverpool steamer; and in a letter to George, Charlie explained that the confinement had taken place in his absence, he being tied down in Uruguay 'by the miserable wars going on'. He had only managed to pay a day's visit to Buenos Aires since the event but, as he wrote,

> the Thorntons are such excellent people for Louisa to be with that I am perfectly easy
> in mind as to every care being taken of her. She could not possibly have been more
> attentively watched and nursed than she has been with them and Mrs Thornton has
> been of the greatest use and comfort to her. They took to each other on our first visit to
> Buenos Aires and it has been a great windfall to find such good quarters to fly to on being
> driven out of our own quiet quinta.[42]

Edward Thornton married Mary, the daughter of John Maitland, while serving as consul-general at Montevideo in 1854, moving on five years later to Buenos Aires, where he was minister plenipotentiary to the Argentine Confederation. When Charlie and Louisa met up with them, he was living in Buenos Aires and also accredited to the Republic of Paraguay. They had two daughters and one son, also named Edward, who also became a diplomat after leaving Trinity College, Cambridge, in 1878, serving as ambassador at Constantinople and St Petersburg in 1886 and 1889 respectively.

Meanwhile, Montevideo was still in the hands of the Blancos but an end was in sight to the conflict. The lengthy account he wrote from the *Triton* on 14 February, as much to the Foreign Office as to his brother personally, may have been to protect himself as he dealt with the delicate political situation. There were hopes that a change of government would take place very soon and that overtures to Flores would be made immediately by the new ministry. The incumbent President Aguirre, or rather president of the Senate upon whom the duties devolved, was expected to retire the next day. An attempt to elect a successor had been made but the senators failed to assemble. 'Whether Aguirre will give up tomorrow,' Charlie supposed that by the following evening 'the town will be summoned and a certain time given for the answer'. Baron Tamandaré assured Charlie that if they had to attack the place he would confine the fire of his ships' guns to the line of defence, and not fire into the town itself unless first fired upon. Charlie took the view that neutral men-of-war like his squadron should not be required to land their men for the protection of neutral property. He thought that the wretched local government had been unnecessarily buoyed up by the belief which some diplomats encouraged that, come what may, the neutrals would not allow the town to be attacked. He and his French colleague, Admiral Chaigneau, a 'clear-headed sensible man', were, he said, prepared to land their people if they could do so usefully and without placing their men in the position of antagonists to either party. Such was the delicate and precise language called for. In the case of Flores and the Brazilians, Charles thought the first difficulty would probably be to establish order and prevent pillage. In such a case, Admiral Tamandaré would probably be one of the first to ask for his assistance in the case of disorder.

Fortunately, three days later, news arrived that Aguirre was on board the French packet and Charlie thought it likely enough that he would escape in her. The minister of war, a very violent man, quite mad according to Lettsom, had been dismissed and the minister for foreign affairs had resigned. The admiral was pleased to report that 'a peace policy now prevails and we shall probably get through our difficulties without any fighting beyond what one has a right to expect in enmities of the present kind'.[43]

Back in England on Tuesday 14 February, the deputy judge-advocate read the finding of the court-martial after a five-day investigation. The court was of the opinion that no evidence had been given by which the origin of the fire could be traced, and that Captain Campbell, the other officers and the crew of the *Bombay* were not to blame. The court was also of the opinion that after the fire was discovered all possible efforts were made to subdue it, but they proved unavailing as a consequence of the way the ship's ventilation had allowed the fire to gain ground with extraordinary rapidity. It also concluded that the ship was not abandoned until all hopes of saving her were at an end, and the officers and crew were forced over board by the flames; also that the steadiness and discipline displayed were a credit to the captain, officers and ship's company. The saving of such a large number of the ship's company was mainly due to the promptitude with which the boats were hoisted out and the court therefore acquitted the captain, officers and crew of all blame. The president of the court, Rear-Admiral S. C. Dacres, then handed the officers back their swords and declared the court dissolved.

It had been an anxious time for all those concerned and the proceedings had been watched by Rear-Admiral George Augustus Elliot, the eldest son of Admiral Sir George Elliot, who had appeared as the prisoner's friend by permission from the court.[44] Proceedings had started on 8 February with the reading of Charlie's original order to Captain Campbell to take HMS *Bombay* 'on a cruise for target practice, and to make the cruise as much as possible under sail'. Campbell went on to tell the court how he had attempted to go below but had been driven back by the smoke. His long and careful evidence, particularly on the question of how the fire might have started, was followed by Captain Scott, who testified that 'no junk or tarpaulins were stowed in the after-hold'. Next to be examined was the lieutenant who had been supervising the passing up of shells for practice firing. When the fire bell went off he handed over to another lieutenant and went to his fire station on the upper deck, where he had sight of the whole drama until he went overboard by a rope's end hitched in the bowsprit shroud. Enquiries as to the cause of the fire produced little firm evidence, and Robert Jasper Hay, the ship's chief engineer, could only report having overseen the working of the hand pumps and minutes later finding the sea-cocks would not open.

The court-martial's third sitting took evidence from a Mr Spriddle, the ship's steward's boy, who said that when going to the after-hold he was called by one of the men who had been lost with the ship to ask the lamp-trimmer to come and trim the lights in the light room. He was walking to the light-room door, and in the act of opening it, when someone shouted 'fire'. The door was sufficiently open for him to see four lights. One was out, the other three were burning. He saw a small piece of something lying on the floor, about 2 inches from the lamp socket, like a piece of candlewick just extinguished. Questioned by one of the members of the court, he explained that the lamplighter was in the habit of getting a light from the bread-room and going down below at quarters to light the lamps. The captain of the ship's hold said he had never had cause to complain about anyone throwing oil rags or tow about the hold. A private marine, Owen M'Caffery, told the court that on the afternoon of the fire, he was on sentry in the after cockpit, his orders being to allow no naked lights in the cockpit and to see that no one entered the spirit room during quarters. Five or six more witnesses from the crew were called and completed that day's hearing.

Having reassembled on Saturday morning, 11 February, much of the evidence only corroborated what the court had already heard. The only exception was part of the evidence given by a sub-lieutenant who had commanded the jollyboat during her gallant duty of rescuing part of the crew. He described the appearance and condition of the ship and how he had watched what he thought had been a mail ship, a Brazilian steamer with officers in uniform on deck, pass within an hour's sail from the burning wreck but it offered no assistance. The fifth and final sitting of the court on board *Victory* took place on Monday 13 February and in bringing to an end a lengthy, final speech to the court, Captain Campbell desired that his thanks be conveyed to Admiral Chaigneau and the French ship-of-war *Astrea*, and to Commodore Martini and the Italian ships-of-war *Fulminante* and *Ercole* for timely assistance rendered at the time of the burning of the *Bombay*, and the kindness and sympathy shown by them to her officers and ship's company on being taken on board the French and Italian ships after the fire.[45]

Charlie did not hear the outcome of the court-martial until the beginning of March and it was to be the end of the month before he was able to tell George something of Louisa and baby Gilbert's progress, the safe arrival of Louisa's saddle 'just when she was up to riding again', and several political developments. The Paraguayans, he wrote, 'are believed to have declared war against the Argentine Republic which seems to me a suicidal act on their part'.[46] He thought President López counted on having the support of General Justo José de Urquiza at the San José Palace in the province of Entre Rios; it was said the latter had assured the Argentinian government of his fidelity and his determination to work with them. Failing the support of Urquiza, the Paraguayans now had single-handedly to contend with Brazil, the Argentine and Uruguay. Charles thought the blockade of the Paraguay River, or of the ports along it, would not effect British trade greatly.[47]

Two weeks later Charles was able to tell his brother more about Paraguay's undeclared war with Argentina. Paraguay began it, he wrote, 'by sending five government war steamers down the River Paraná to Corrientes, where two Argentinian steamers were easily captured and taken back up the river. The next day, Corrientes was occupied by a force of 7,500 Paraguayan troops. Charles was convinced that without support from other quarters President López 'ought soon to be smashed'.[48] Nevertheless the advent of a new antagonist and theatre of war prompted the admiral to undertake some reading on Anglo-Parguayan relations in case his role at sea was again extended to land-based diplomacy. He wanted to know what the Foreign Office had meant by issuing him with an instruction to see that the privileges granted to Great Britain by a treaty with Paraguay dated 4 March 1853 were not infringed. According to his reading of Article XVI of that treaty, Charles concluded, 'it must have expired by 4 March 1863'. He told George that he naturally accepted the superior judgement of the diplomats but he had asked London whether the treaty had ever been renewed. So far as Thornton and he could make out, Britain had no treaty rights with Paraguay.[49]

In June HMS *Narcissus* arrived at Montevideo. Following his clearance by the court-martial, Captain Colin Campbell had taken command of this 3,500-ton, 51-gun, screw-driven frigate after her commissioning at Devonport. It was to be Charlie's new flagship. News from England told of brother Gilbert's death the previous month, prompting the admiral to ask George in the absence of any will to make some financial provision for his widow, Kate, from his own resources. By the middle of July and after a short visit to Buenos Aires to see the Thorntons, the decision had been taken to keep on their house outside Montevideo and sail for Rio, hopefully making part of the passage in fine weather.[50]

In September the admiral was aboard HMS *Narcissus* and writing to George from Rio. On the Uruguay River, Flores had had 'a very decided victory over a small body of some 4,000 Paraguayans' and, so far as Charles could judge, the check to their advance was important. Other successes were, he wrote, 'now likely to follow in that quarter and it is of much importance for the sake of peace that they should'. He thought there was good reason to fear that the successful advance of the Paraguayans would encourage discontented spirits in the provinces they had invaded. On the Paraná, Charles explained that the Brazilians had allowed their flotilla to get into a mess and for a third time they had allowed the Paraguayans to erect batteries below where the Brazilian squadron was lying. This time, in retreating down the river past the newly erected batteries, the vessels had suffered severe and unnecessary losses.

> These Brazilians [the admiral wrote] are the slowest people I have ever had to deal with. I don't know that one has a right to expect much from a cross between degenerate Portuguese and niggers, or hot-climate Indians. They and their allies must show a little more life in [the] movement of their army or the Paraguayans may give much trouble yet.

The mail also brought notice of Edward Thornton's mission to re-establish diplomatic relations with Brazil. As the Emperor, Pedro II, and one of his ministers were in Rio Grande do Sul (which had also been invaded) it was assumed that Thornton would endeavour to see him there instead of going to Rio first, as form required. HMS *Stromboli*, a paddle-driven sloop of 1,280 tons, was 'ready at Montevideo to take him to whatever port he likes', wrote Charlie, adding that 'I have offered to send *Narcissus* to bring him and his party up here if he wishes it. We can receive him here and see him landed with due honours.' The couple now expected to be in Rio for at least the next month or six weeks, Charlie having given up thought of a visit to Bahia. There were several places they wanted to visit, including Tujica and Petropolis for a second time. They stayed at the latter with a Scottish doctor by the name of Gunning who had been a professor of anatomy in Edinburgh and who had come out to Brazil some fifteen years before. Charles and Louise had been asked to stay with him in a house he had built in a very pretty situation amongst the hills close to the new railway line which, the Scot did not doubt, would 'make his property valuable by and by'. The air was expected to refresh them all. Charles wrote, 'I do like to breathe a little hill air myself and Louisa and the baby will, I take it, be all the better for it too.'[51]

Having duly achieved his interview with the Emperor at Uruguayana in Rio Grande, the new British envoy arrived back in Rio, where he went on shore 'under a cloud of smoke from our guns, and with the guns manned so that the natives may see him treated with proper respect'. A few days later, the officers of *Narcissus* gave a ball which was very successful, the Brazilians being well pleased with their reception. After consulting Thornton, Charles decided it would be better for him to remain in Rio until the Emperor returned towards the middle of November. He anticipated having formal meetings with government officials. The admiral had hoped to have got away to Montevideo and the Falkland Islands but those visits would have to wait. Louisa and baby were very well but, as Charles told George, 'the poor Thorntons had a miserable passage [from Buenos Aires]. They had embarked on board the French mail steamer where they were very comfortable ... but at Montevideo where they had gone ashore, a boiler which had been employed as a donkey engine in coaling, burst, killing seven people on the spot and injuring many others.' The vessel was so badly damaged as to be unable to proceed on her voyage and many passengers came on to Rio in a Liverpool steamer, the *Newton*. Although HMS *Stromboli* was still at Montevideo and immediately placed at the envoy's disposal, Thornton had declined the offer.[52]

Pedro II, who was Emperor of Brazil for forty-nine years, presided over thirty or more provincial legislatures across the country and was continually away from Rio. While waiting for the opportunity to meet him formally, Charlie and Louisa had gone to stay for a few days with the Thorntons at Petropolis, where they were settling in for the summer months. The envoy passed Charlie a dispatch from the Foreign Office requesting him to send a vessel up the Paraná. It asked him to give any gunboat orders to go up to Asunción if she could do so. The Brazilians, he said, 'will I believe, make no difficulties in allowing her to pass any blockade which exists'. Rumours had it that the Paraguayans were retreating to their own country and the Argentinians were said to be so bloodthirsty against López that his best option might be to find his way aboard a foreign ship if he wanted to make an escape.[53]

The Elliots were back in Montevideo early in December and were soon busy getting their house in order. Writing to George, who had changed his address to Downing Street, Charlie said,

> It is very much of a home to us and is snug and comfortable, small as the rooms and house are. I mean to be off within a week to visit the Falkland Islands leaving Louisa here. The cruise will occupy at least a month and it is not in general an agreeable one. Gales of wind and dirty weather in those seas are too frequent to be pleasant even during summer.

They had enjoyed a pleasant passage from Rio visiting several places en route, Ilha Grande (with its fair anchorages), San Sebastian, Santos and Santa Catarina but no town of any size. Santos was a low, unhealthy-looking town a few miles up a river which the *Narcissus* could go up if necessary but it would be a pinch. There was a good deal of trade there and the country about São Paulo was said to be fair. The island of Santa Catarina was fair but larger ships did not go near the town, some 12 miles off. Charlie described it as 'a sort of watering place for the Brazilians', who went there even from Rio in the summer months.

The war was not going on as briskly as the admiral had hoped. López had returned within his own frontiers, and large as the Brazilian force against him was, Charles had no faith in it making much headway. The Brazilians had been slow enough when there was little or nothing to stop their advance and he did not think it would be an easy task for anyone to increase their ardour.[54] By February 1866, the admiral was able to report to George that 'his gallant colleague', the Brazilian admiral Tamandaré, was still at Buenos Aires. Charles said that the latter had never 'yet been up to Corrientes to see what he can do, and the press and people in general are abusing him for his tardiness'.

A month later, Charles admitted something of the quiet life he and Louisa were living. The Paraguayan war, he wrote, 'does not affect us much here except that it prevents the country improving as it would do in time of peace. We might then expect to find a road passable even after rains between our quinta and the town. We have not suffered from rain however this season.' Charles was beginning to think that if something didn't happen which would 'bring some work for the English Naval Commander-in-Chief', his official life will be 'monotonous and unimportant'.[55] At the end of March, and following a visit to Maldonado, Charlie found that neither Louisa nor Gilbert were in a flourishing state, the former having a cold which she had since shaken off and the boy having been really unwell and much troubled with teething. He had been an enthusiastic young rider, enjoying his rides as much as his parents did theirs. The only inconvenience around the quinta were dust storms not unlike those he had encountered in Morocco in the early 1860s. There was also a shortage of books, which prompted Charlie to ask his brother to see what 'you or Nina, or other reading people' could find to send them.[56]

It was the middle of May when the mail brought tidings of Charlie's promotion. His move from rear- to vice-admiral, which had been published by the Admiralty in London on 6 April, led immediately to a discussion about when would be the best time to leave South America. 'If my pecuniary interests,' he wrote to George, 'were the only consideration it would have been best for me to complete my three years on the station.' He had written to Sir Frederick Grey in Whitehall saying that he would prefer getting away from Rio not later than September. He thought that this would coincide with the time his successor, Rear-Admiral George Ramsay, previously captain superintendent at Pembroke dockyard, would arrive in Brazil.[57] At the end of the month there was still no communication from the Admiralty, but Charlie reported 'we are beginning our preparations for a move home by moving into Montevideo where we intend to take up our quarters in a few days but probably only to remain there till the middle of June when I mean to sail for Rio should nothing occur to keep me here'. They were clearly very sorry to give up their comfortable quinta and Charlie didn't 'like giving up our horses which [were] going to be shown to possible purchasers'.

In Paraguay, fighting continued and there was news of a battle. The admiral told George that 'López attacked the Allies intending to surprise them at night, but a deserter from his army gave information of the impending attack. Bartolomé Mitre [the president of Argentina and supreme commander of the Allied troops] being prepared had gained a victory. We have no details … but it is to be hoped López has been defeated.' The slowness of the Brazilian army and navy was 'astonishing' to Charlie After the Allied army successfully crossed the Paraná it lay inactive for a month in a swampy, unhealthy position being steadily reduced by sickness. It seemed that the navy had been reluctant to come within the range of the guns of Humaitá, a town in southern Paraguay which was to be home to 26,000 troops between 1866 and August 1868.[58] It was not until December that year that the three new commanders of the Triple Alliance's forces felt able to ask for López's surrender. Asunción fell in January 1869 and, after organising resistance in the mountains for over a year, Solano López was fatally injured while trying to escape from the Brazilian Emperor's son-in-law, Count d'Eu, who had led the last campaign of this long and bloody war in March 1870.

The Elliot family sailed for Rio de Janeiro in the *Narcissus* on 15 June 1866. Although it was to be a speedy passage, there had been a heavy sea, one that Louisa had been far from proof against. Although no one knew when Admiral Ramsay would arrive or be ready to hoist his flag in the *Narcissus* it was a relief for the admiral, who could now look forward to 'the prospect of dropping into a more humble position as a poor, half-pay officer'. Much as he was for ever wanting his life to be sliced into shortish periods, he could not say whether he would 'be content to remain long in that position'.[59] Monetary worries were not far from his mind. The Admiralty accounts department had informed him that they had a balance of £420 in his name and Charlie prayed some of this would find its way back to him. They also had a power of attorney, and although there was no suspicion of any dishonesty he did not know whether the money he had invested in Foreign and Colonial Securities was safe or whether it had been meddled with.

It was July when the admiral's party embarked at Rio. The Royal Mail Steam Packet Company had expanded its services in 1850, originally serving only West Indian routes. Travelling via Lisbon the family arrived in Southampton early the following month. Louisa had been carrying their second child, and no sooner were they safely ashore than they seem to have headed for Scotland, where Walter Charles Elliot was born on 8 December 1866 at 6.30 p.m. The address shown on the birth certificate was 6 St Colme Street, Edinburgh. Earlier that year when Charlie was still in Montevideo he had asked his lawyer brother to find a 'small establishment' to rent or purchase near Minto. The property George had found turned out to be Bonjedward House, the Dower House of the Dowager Marchioness of Lothian in the village of the same name, 2 miles north of Jedburgh.[60]

Sadly, however, no sooner had the Elliots moved into Bonjedward House on 29 January 1867 than baby Walter died on 19 February after barely two months of life. Then on 5 December Bertram Charles Elliot, their third child, was born at 7.45 p.m. when Charles was present at the bedside once again. This third son was to be the only one of their children to reach adulthood and live into his sixties. During the next three years the family seems to have spent a happy time together, entertaining numerous visitors. A Miss Abercromby stayed for ten days in April 1868 followed by Mrs Beaumont for a week in May. During the summer of 1869 the list included Fanny Blackett, Sir Edward's second wife, along with Mr and Mrs Stirling[61] and Mr Carr. The Misses Richardson and Charles Cooke followed in October. Then at the end of the month, Charles and Louisa went to Matfen Hall, the Blacketts' home, for a week but Louisa was again expecting and would have been relieved to reach home before winter set in.[62]

With Hogmanay over, the family left for a week at Minto House; and later in January, Gilbert Elliot's widow, Kate, came to see Charlie and Louisa. It was a little after one o'clock in the morning on 8 March 1870 that Julian Arthur Elliot was born. The next event in what could easily have been described as an *annus horribilis* was the death on 23 June of young Gilbert, the happy, pony-riding youngster who had been born in Montevideo. His mother, whom it would seem had been greatly weakened by Julian's birth, sadly died on 17 July, at least ignorant of the baby's subsequent death on 18 October. Louisa's own death came just sixteen days after the Admiralty announced Charlie's appointments as administrator of the fleet and commander-in-chief at the Nore.

In August 1870, the widowed and lonely vice-admiral was in the dockyard at Sheerness reading a dispatch from the Falkland Islands, which he had never been able to visit. The governor suggested the transfer of the Naval Stores Depot in Rio de Janeiro to Port Stanley.[63] His work, and that of his officers at the Nore, extended over a wide area relating to the inspection of reserve and drill ships, the regular checking of moorings, the inspection of barracks, alterations in the crewing of gun vessels and the overseeing of courts of enquiry. Other responsibilities included clarifying when corporal punishment was permitted, improving the design of naval uniforms, identifying the steps that might be taken to reduce the number of non-seamen on ships, hiring cooks and servants, and introducing Presbyterian services in the dockyard chapel. Keeping naval discipline throughout the dockyard and maintaining the seaworthiness of HMS *Pembroke* were continuous concerns.

The admiral would have been pleased to leave this very bureaucratic appointment in February 1873; his life on the Thames had not been inspiring. Towards the end of the year, William offered his brother the use of Minto House only to find that preliminary plans had already been made for him and Bertram, now six years old, to stay at Kirklands at Ancrum.[64] There was, however, a change of plan when Charlie and Bertram were invited to Ravensworth Castle for Christmas, the home at Gateshead of Sir Henry Thomas Liddell (first Earl of Ravensworth) and Isabella Seymour, his late wife who had died in 1856. Writing to William, the admiral said that 'unless the house turns out to be dull, we shall probably be there to see the New Year'.[65] He did not know the earl but he had apparently met Lady Harriette when visiting his first wife's family at Matfen. Then thirty-nine years old, and one of the Liddells' seven daughters (there were also two sons), she was known as 'Har'. She made great friends with Bertram on this occasion, and was to become his stepmother when she married Charlie in February the following year. They were to have two daughters: Sybil was born in London in May 1875, and Rachel followed in June 1876.

As winter approached Charlie decided to take his family to Biarritz. Staying at a house called *Maison Dumont* and sitting near an open window, they looked out at 'a quiet sea and a clear horizon'. The temperature at breakfast had been 58 degrees and people had been complaining of the heat. Along with an eleven-year-old Bertram, they had been out for several drives in an open carriage 'with great-coats discarded'. Seated, they had followed a meet of foxhounds at the lighthouse where many of the Biarritz 'gay world' assembled. Charlie had not yet had a mount but he was hoping to go out on one of the country ponies, not one of the horses let for hunting, to 'keep the liver in order by a more agreeable way than by physic'. He thought the appearance of the hounds and huntsmen had improved from what it had been previously. They dined with the Hamptons at Christmas,[66] only giving a small dinner party themselves as their 'cook was inferior'. With the new school term due to start at the end of January 1878, Bertram returned home in the charge of one Victor Williamson, who had brought him out.[67]

Charlie was posted to Devonport in January 1880, becoming commander-in-chief. The couple were still establishing themselves at Admiralty House in Stoke-Demerel when Admiral Charles Hope, the admiral superintendent, died, casting a gloom over the beginning of their time at Plymouth.[68] Charlie knew him very well and had been fortunate in finding him as a colleague at Devonport. They had seen a great deal of him and his family and Charlie much regretted that 'the widow will have very little besides whatever small pension will be granted to live upon and bring up eight young children'. The four youngest of them, all boys, had been staying with Charlie and Har. Only a little before, Har's uncle also died. Sir Hamilton Seymour had been a Privy Counsellor and diplomat, and someone of whom she had been very fond.

The city of Algiers, where William and Nina had moved for the winter, was 'not in all respects perfect' despite its ideal weather. In England on the other hand, the West Country was cold, clear and frosty, which made Charlie wonder how the climate would suit Har. She had organised a dinner party for twenty people and a large programme of dinners was in the offing. In regard to the admiral's work, winter was a quiet time – there were few ships in port. The reverse was true in the summer and Charlie anticipated being 'again occupied with professional work'. Har was looking 'forward immensely to water excursions' when the weather improved. She admitted to liking boating and yachting but as yet, as Charlie told his brother, 'she has never gone on any water expedition except pulling about the harbour in the galley'. The new commander-in-chief was already using the admiral's steam launch – which was 'a capital boat' – when visiting ships in Plymouth Sound or going up the River Tamar. Charlie's military opposite number, General Leicester Smythe of the Rifle Brigade, was 'a very pleasant man' who had been a great friend of Gibby's during the Crimean War, but he was about to be replaced.[69]

News of the 1880 election campaign poured in upon Charles every day in March but on the morning of the 26th, Charles, Har and Bertram left their family guests to breakfast alone while they went off 'to offer civilities to the Empress Eugenie who arrived in the Sound at an early hour'. Her steamer called at Plymouth for the mails on the way from Southampton to the Cape and Zululand.[70] As Charlie wrote, 'the poor Empress was on deck and received us there'. He was glad that Har had come with him, 'her sister [Lady Maria Liddell], Sir David Wood's wife, having been very intimate with her when at Woolwich' where he had been general-commandant of Woolwich garrison from 1869 to 1874.

Charles admitted that Devonport did not attract the amount of royalty, or ex-royalty, that Portsmouth was honoured with, which was some relief but he knew they would not get off without occasional visits. When the Duke of Edinburgh, Prince Alfred, second son of Queen Victoria, passed through, embarking in his yacht for Ireland, Charlie 'offered to put him up for the night or give him dinner' only to find that 'he wanted to push on and sail at once'. Charlie concluded that there was 'interesting work in this command occasionally' and he hoped 'some day' William would be able to pay them a visit.[71]

As the number of the Elliot's friends and acquaintances increased, so did the amount of entertaining they were called on to do, and Charlie had no doubt that 'the emoluments of the office will be more than swallowed up'. Unfortunately, what must have seemed like a continuous flow of deaths at sea continued with the loss of the training ship HMS *Atalanta* and Louisa's brother, Lieutenant Blackett, in a storm between Bermuda and Falmouth in 1880.[72] Nevertheless, during the next eighteen months, Admiral Charles was able to enjoy a full life with Har and their daughters. There was a steady flow of visitors, one being the Duke of Edinburgh again and Marie Alexandrovna, his duchess, with whom they had had 'a perfectly easy, quiet dinner' aboard ship before they took them to Weir Head by steam launch the following day. Soon afterwards, Oscar II, the King of Sweden, found relief from political debates in the Riksdag by sailing into Plymouth. What pleased Charles most in the late spring of 1881 was that he was to be awarded a KCB. Lord Northbrook, an ex-viceroy of India and First Lord of the Admiralty after the Liberal election victory of 1880, had submitted his name to the Queen. He 'never felt the least desire to have the "Sir" … I had always felt that I would not care for getting it if it was bestowed when I was not serving … when it would appear to be given from seniority or rank rather than as a reward for service'. Charlie felt he could accept the knighthood without any such feeling, as 'a valued honour bestowed by Her Majesty for past services'.[73]

It was the end of 1881 when Sir Charles left Devonport and was appointed Admiral of the Fleet, a post he was to hold until he retired from the Navy at the end of 1888.

In the summer of 1886, the Elliots decided to make their way home in slow stages from Aix-les-Bains and the Hotel de l'Europe, where the admiral had been receiving treatment for rheumatism, and visit friends who lived close to the Château de Varennes, near Angers. On their return, they stayed at Kirklands and Bonjedward House before moving to 'Brydone' (his mother's maiden name), a house at Bitterne, near Southampton. Charles wrote to William at Minto in December, whom he thought 'must be very solitary and cold in that big house all alone', Nina having died in 1882. The two men exchanged thoughts about income generation from selling garden produce. At 'Brydone', Charles said he kept two men, a gardener at 24 shillings a week, and a man at 16 shillings, and grew potatoes 'enough for the house; we never buy'.[74]

The year after Sir Charles's retirement the family decided to return to their favoured resort, Biarritz, for the winter. Even Rachel, the younger of the two girls, 'their delicate one just now', had been none the worse for the journey. Instead of travelling by night from Paris, they had taken the day train to Bordeaux which involved staying there overnight and 'getting up at an early hour next morning to go on by the 7.15 a.m. train which brought us to Biarritz soon after 11 o'clock'. Once established at the Maison Berhouet in Rue Gambetta, a new holiday house for them, Charlie played some golf, it being as much exercise as he cared for. The course near the cream-coloured lighthouse had only been opened that year and been played by Willie Dunn, the Scottish professional, and already William K. Vanderbilt had contemplated playing *dix-huit* holes, so publicising the numerous attractions of Biarritz.

In the autumn of 1890 Charles brought young Bertram and his tutor, a 'bookworm and wonderful linguist', back to 'Brydone' temporarily from Wiesbaden, where he had been learning German and some Spanish. Earlier that year Bertram had been put up for a clerkship examination at the Foreign Office but he seems to have been advised to try again later, with the result he was to return to Germany after enjoying the company of 'some of his Blackett belongings' (i.e. relatives). The hopeful diplomat nevertheless ventured to ask the eighty-seven-year-old third Earl Minto whether he would care 'to house such a dull member of society for a couple of nights'.[75] Whether he paid this visit to his uncle before his death the following year is not known. On the way back to Southampton Charlie and Har stayed two days at Laverstoke, where Lotty was going to Dunrozel, near Haslemere, the home of Fanny's son, Rollo.[76] The family enjoyed pleasant weather and, with their governess away, the two girls 'spent their days in the open air'. Writing to William in December, the old admiral hoped that he too would be 'energetic enough' to find his way to Biarritz. He would be sure to meet some people he knew among the numerous English, and 'some of the right kind you would not object to associate with'. In going so far as to suggest he stayed in a hotel facing the sea, it seems Charlie was unaware how near to death his brother was.

Early in 1891 both Charlie and Har were unwell. A cold had turned into what the admiral called 'rinderpest' (an acute viral disease of cattle) but in Har's case she suffered great pain during a nasty attack of shingles, for which the French doctor had given her several subcutaneous injections of morphia. Among his other prescriptions were champagne and good claret 'in considerable quantities twice a day'. Before this happened they had enjoyed using 'two little pony carriages for our party of five' from which to watch the hunt.[77] The following year they were living at Maison Berhouet and such was their concern for William that both Charles and Har wrote deeply felt letters to him, even seeking his understanding of the fact that it would not be possible for them to join the family at Minto for his eventual funeral.[78]

Charles was seventy-seven years old when he died at 'Brydone' on 21 May 1895. His wife outlived him by seventeen years, dying just a year before the start of the Great War. He had been a typical man of his time, staunchly patriotic and always zealous in the service he gave his country for nearly sixty years, not only as a sailor but as a diplomat.

# GEORGE FRANCIS ELLIOT – A BROTHERLY LAWYER (1847-1901)

George Francis Stewart Elliot, known in the family as 'Doddy', was born in Scotland on 9 October 1822 and, as the reader will recall, his early schooling was largely in the hands of Catherine Rutherford. Early in 1832 after his two elder brothers, William and Henry, had returned to Eton, George would have been found at Minto ruling straight lines across a sheet of paper in preparation for writing a letter he was about to send. Later that year the family left for Prussia and in October he celebrated his tenth birthday in Berlin. However, the decision of his governess to leave the family's service during the summer of the following year, when Lord Minto was about to return at the end of his duty, presented them with a problem. He may have been taught for a period by someone else but eighteen months was to pass before a firm decision was taken about his further education.

George entered Rugby School at Easter 1835, where he boarded in School House under Dr Thomas Arnold, the headmaster who during the previous four or five years had endeavoured to replace the harsh discipline and low moral standards he had inherited. He had increased the salaries of assistant masters, and any with church livings were required to relinquish them so that they could devote themselves entirely to teaching. Reforms to the curriculum followed and regular reports were given to parents. At the age of seventeen, and after four years at Rugby, George was admitted as a pensioner (an undergraduate without financial support or a scholarship) at Trinity College, Cambridge, in May 1839. He was assigned to Professor William Whewell, who had taught William and who was responsible for all his studies. Having matriculated at Michaelmas, George became a fellow-commoner (an undergraduate permitted to dine with the Fellows) on 14 October.

During his holidays from Cambridge he enjoyed some good sport at Minto riding his horse 'Fanny' with both the foxhounds and the beagles. She carried him well and 'flew the leaps in fine style'. Early in 1840 it had been his uncle John's turn (John Edmund Elliot, George's father's brother) to take the beagles out, but with so much frosty weather the ground was 'as hard as rock with just the top a little greasy'.[1] In term time his studies were relieved by skating on the Cam when the ice was thick enough, as seems to have happened in 1840. In good undergraduate style, he asked his brother William to speak to 'paternity' about the possibility of him paying in 'a little money' to his Cambridge bank as he had no more credit there. He had been unable to pay several bills, one of which was for his share in a horse.[2] Back at Minto, soon after the season had started, Doddy was again writing to 'dear Bill'. He had been riding with Lizzy but this time his mare had 'got such a bad over-reach' that she would not be able to go out for a little.[3]

George passed the Mathematical Tripos in 1843 as a senior optime (i.e. in the second class), and obtained the degree of MA the same year, since as the son of a nobleman he was entitled to the higher degree immediately on taking his first degree. In May, he attended the marriage of William and Nina and was admitted to Lincoln's Inn on 7 June 1843. By the time he was called to the bar in January 1847 he was twenty-four years old and he had received as good an educational grounding as any in the family. Doddy was to practise as an equity draughtsman from chambers at 6 New Square, Lincoln's Inn until 1853 and then at 3 Old Square between 1854 and 1868 – an activity which at last provided a steady if small income. Such draughtsmen and conveyancers were a specialist kind of barrister engaged in the technical business of drafting all the complex written proceedings in a court action in Chancery, and also legal documents concerned with land and trusts within the jurisdiction of the Court of Chancery.

No sooner had he been judged competent to plead in court, George seems to have joined the family party which went to Italy, where his father had become Palmerston's special envoy. He visited Turin and Florence briefly and returned by Switzerland. Back at 36 Jermyn Street by 9 November, he told William that 'we were a jolly travelling party, and what I had seen of Italy was quite enough to make one wish to see a good deal more of it, however, a stern sense of duty called me home'. George had spent a week in Florence visiting galleries and churches and then wrote about it as if he had been there for several months. So far as he could read the situation, his father was 'very well satisfied' with the way things were going with his diplomatic duties. The Grand Duke of Tuscany seemed 'sensible, liberally inclined and not disposed to give way to the Austrians'. The only thing he was uneasy about was the completion of the transfer of Fivizzano in Tuscany to the Duke of Modena. Its inhabitants were determined to resist if force was used against them. Hoping that he had given William a 'full, true and particular account' of the affairs in Italy, George said that unfortunately the old King of Sardinia was falling 'back into bad ways again'; he 'wants someone to be constantly poking him in the ribs to keep him up to the mark'.[4]

In December, George's 'mouth watered and his legs itched to be across a horse again' when he heard that William had been enjoying better than usual weather at Minto and that he had ridden to Hassendean. He had, however, been told by William's mother-in-law, Lady Hislop, who had been in London, to draw the attention of all the hunters at Minto to Lord Inverary's fatal accident, and he used to ride rather well.

As the Crimean War started, the lawyer became increasingly wrapped up in domestic politics and anxious to hear what brother William, the politician, thought of the Education Bill. Having listened to the Lord Advocate's speech and 'not being such an out and out secularist' as his brother, George said that

> the preamble states very fairly the principle to be followed in regard to religion but all the provisions in the bill itself about religious teaching are so vague that it would depend very much upon the way in which they were carried out, and whether the system became a sectarian one or not.

He went on to suggest that it might be wise to have 'a separate school fee for the religious teaching'. This might 'act as a valve for tender consciences'. It was unfortunate that the established Kirk was rather severely used since the bill took 'all her own schools out of her hands' and they were to pay money to all her enemies' schools out of the general rate.

So far as the Reform Bill before Parliament was concerned, George said its postponement had been 'very well taken' in London and it was

> probably wise of Lord John [Russell] to do as he did rather than thrust it down people's throats against the advice of so many but he cannot with credit give it up altogether for it cannot be said that anything more has happened than was anticipated when the measure was introduced at which time we must suppose the government were acting *bona fide* and intended to proceed with it.[6]

The bill had been brought in on 13 February 1854, a 'great day', as Fanny called it when writing to her sister Mary, even though she would have been 'better pleased' if there had been 'more enthusiasm'.[7] Two weeks later she was writing to Lady Romilly (Lizzy) to thank her for her 'most welcome' congratulations on 'all that John had said and done since Parliament met'. Such praise helped protect Lord John from the 'various arts of every variety of politician' who 'urged and pressed, and threatened and coaxed and assailed' in their efforts to induce him to give up reform.[8]

Writing a hurried account of what happened in the House of Commons on the evening of 8 February 1856, George told his father how 'unsatisfactory' it had been. Towards the end of the Crimean War efforts had been made by the Admiralty to indict Commodore Charles Elliot on vague charges that he should have done more to bring the Russian fleet into battle off the Kamchatka peninsula. In the Commons debate, a speech by Charles Baillie, a lawyer and MP, showed that he 'either knew nothing of the case or had been bought off by Stirling's friends [Sir James Stirling, commander-in-chief China and East Indies] for he never alluded to the Admiral's share in the business'. George did not believe that Sir Charles Wood, who was to become First Lord of the Admiralty, meant to be hostile but his statement had been 'shabbiness itself'. In conversation, he had spoken to George in positive terms about Charlie being 'quite right in not attacking' at De Castri Bay in Siberia but in his speech he said 'he was justified in not attempting it', which implied that he would not have been wrong to do so.[9]

Back from his expedition to Bulgaria in the company of his friend Waldegrave, referred to in Chapter 11, George was helping his elderly father keep house at Minto in December 1858. He told William that Lord Minto's 'attacks' had not persisted although their frequent occurrence was 'not encouraging whether brought on by the cold weather or not'. Five days later, his father was much better and out of bed 'but not downstairs'. With time on his hands Doddy then told his politician brother that he had 'just hit on a new way of getting the representation of minorities'. His plan, implemented in the twentieth century, was

> to give each voter one vote more than the number of members to be elected and to allow him to give two of his votes for any candidate he prefers. Thus if two members

are to be elected each voter would have three votes and would have the option of giving two votes as a plumper for one candidate or not voting at all for the others, or of giving two votes for one candidate and one for another.

He particularly praised William for the letter he had sent to *The Scotsman* newspaper. It made a strong case against private schools receiving a grant rather than parish schools, and if sectarianism was to be the ground of attack, George hoped he would 'follow up this onslaught on the Privy Council's system [which had been introduced in England in 1839], either by a bill or a motion for enquiry'.[10]

Writing from 2 Pont Street off Belgrave Square in August 1859, almost a month after his father's death, George illustrated several of the mundane family responsibilities which were increasingly coming his way, explaining to William that he had 'paid all the bills and settled with the servants' at Eaton Square. Mrs Henson, the housekeeper, had not received anything beyond her wages but the others received a month's wages and the present William had 'marked'. The amount exceeded his estimate very considerably, chiefly on account of the bills of Harries & Ward, the chemist and potion maker so beloved by the Victorians, which came to about £100.[11] Some personal reassurance about William's new position as head of the family was also called for, with George explaining that the memorandum left by their father had no evidence of 'any bad feeling' towards William and that his father's intent was that 'you should have an income equal to what he had after deducting all fixed payments to children and others, though of course, with your family your necessary expenses would be greater as his own were during the life of [their] mother'. There was no doubt in George's mind that 'the whole difference' lay in 'whether the expense of maintaining the children' was included in the estimate or not. When he heard of William's idea of selling the Chester Square house, the lawyer could only advise him that letting might prove to be a better arrangement.[12]

Having told William how he had spent Christmas 1859 with the Portal family at Laverstoke House, where he found Melville was 'up to his ears in building plans for schools and cottages as well as alterations in the house', George tried to impress upon his brother how much there was that could be done at Minto 'merely by keeping things as they were intended to be' and seeing that the rules which the second Earl laid down for the management of the estate were properly carried out. Looking at the accounts for the sawmill at Minto, George told William that he had discovered a discrepancy. The estimated value of the wood taken from the estate during the year was in doubt. He thought that if the amount consumed for home purposes could be established from the accounts and, assuming 'all the timber which was not sold by public roup [went] to the sawmill, the quantity sawn ought to show how much had been used for the castle, or sold in planks'. If he was wrong in thinking that an account was kept of the quantity of sawn timber, then an approximation would have to be arrived at by examining the number of days on which sawing took place.[13]

George's duties as private secretary to Lord John Russell, the Foreign Secretary, between 1859 and the middle of 1866 released him somewhat from responding to many of the family's requests although, as seen in the last chapter, not from meeting requests for new toothbrushes. Part of this period, particularly in 1865, saw George visiting his brother Gilbert in Sussex and intervening with the Army authorities in regard to his and Kate's pension.[14]

It was probably some time in 1863 when Walter Elliot came on the scene. The owner of 'Wolfelee' at Hawick, and a scion of the old Border family of the Elliots of Lariston, he had spent forty years of his life as a servant of the East India Company, first as an assistant to the collector in Madras, then to the governor of Bombay at Dharwar. He married Maria Dorothea, the daughter of Sir David Hunter-Blair of Blairquhan, in 1839 and fifteen years later became a member of council at Madras, gaining a reputation as an antiquarian and linguist before retiring in 1860.[15] In January the following year, he wrote to George saying 'how much gratified' he had been by the packet of papers the lawyer had sent him. The retired collector and archaeologist had read a substantial part of the memoir on the Elliots and found that it embodied a great amount of research not only into the records of the name but into the history of the Borders. Walter Elliot's impression was that George 'ought to print it' since it formed 'a valuable and useful compendium of all that had been published on the subject'.

Elliot wrote again to George in both March and June 1865 telling him something of the research he had undertaken on his behalf. He had kept some of the lawyer's papers so that he might refer to them from time to time and 'not take the unnecessary trouble of travelling over the ground' he had already covered. His hunt for relevant old documents proved 'very unsatisfactory' at first. The Duke of Buccleuch did eventually give him access to his charter room, where there were two or three charters of Robert Elliot of Redheugh which he 'hoped shortly to examine more carefully'. Among the family news Walter Elliot passed on to George was the arrival of William Elliot at Stobs, where he 'meant to settle', a branch of the family which was to feature in George's history, *The Border Elliots and the Family of Minto*.[16]

George was at work in the Foreign Office on 23 October 1865 when Earl Russell, his brother-in-law was asked to form his second ministry. Lord Palmerston had died six days earlier and was to be buried in Westminster Abbey. Despite his role as Foreign Secretary, Fanny's husband had been a man of letters for much of the time since 1861. There was, however, 'no hesitation on the part of the Queen as to who she should call upon – indeed she intimated her intention before Lord Palmerston's death had actually taken place'. Continuing his report to William, who was at Minto, George added that

> before the Queen's decision was known to him, Gladstone wrote in the most friendly
> way, opining that Lord Russell would be premier and showing the greatest readiness
> to serve with him ... It is no doubt a pleasure to him to stand once more in the first place
> and also to feel that on home questions his own feelings and opinions may now have
> freer scope.

Unfortunately, this was not to be.

*The Times* was immediately 'overflowing with bile', venting its spite in an article 'prepared with much care' which could damage Lord Russell. George saw how difficult it would be to deal with the venom in every ingredient of it. He also told

William that the new Foreign Secretary, Lord Clarendon, came to the office 'much to the dismay of all the clerks who look forward with no satisfaction to hard work and late hours instead of the easy times they have been enjoying under the present rule'.[17] It was not therefore surprising that George gave up his duties as Lord Russell's private secretary a month after the government resigned in June 1866.

Another of those who were to help George with his genealogical research was William Fraser, later knighted in 1887, who wrote to him from 32 South Castle Street in Edinburgh, the house in which Kenneth Grahame, the author of *The Wind in the Willows*, had been born. Fraser had started life as a solicitor and assistant keeper of Sasines in Edinburgh but, as many titled landowners started to vie with each other to produce volumes of their history, he caught on to the substantial income to be made from giving advice and undertaking the necessary and often very detailed research. He was to chronicle the history of more than twenty noble families while becoming the deputy keeper of records at Register House, Robert Adam's great work – 'a proper repository for the records of Scotland'. At the end of 1867 Fraser reported that the work he had done for George in framing the Elliot pedigree had cost him 'a good deal of trouble' and that he had submitted his sketch to Sir Walter Elliot for whom he had done some work. The enterprising genealogist could not resist mentioning that he had 'in hand several of the Border families' and had noticed references in their charters relating to the Elliots.[18]

George heard from another source of assistance in January 1868 when Dr Aitkin, the old minister at Minto, wrote several letters from Charlotte Square in Edinburgh, where he was living in retirement with his wife Elizabeth, whom he had married in 1836. He had spoken to a friend in Register House who had consulted George Burnett, a lawyer and expert in peerage law who had just published *The Art of Pedigree-Making*. He was 'the best authority on such points'. Aitkin had also called at the Advocate's Library for him despite both he and his wife being 'indifferently well'. The minister was also able to tell George that Mr Walker, who had been tutor to William and Nina's boys, had narrowly missed being awarded the post of Rector to the Normal School in Glasgow. Other items of news included a pleasant visit to Minto by Miss Abercromby, although her father was to die on 2 July that year.[19]

In February 1868 an aging and sick Lord Derby, who had become Prime Minister little more than six months before, handed over the premiership to Disraeli, who was soon bogged down with an Irish policy which few of the public could easily support. With a general election scheduled for November, and the franchise greatly increased by many more male householders being allowed to vote in line with the Reform Act of the previous year, a Liberal government was on the cards. By June, it was clear that George wanted to throw his hat into the parliamentary ring. His proximity to the political world while working at the Foreign Office had encouraged such an ambition and enquiries about a suitable constituency had identified the new one of the three burghs of Hawick (Roxburghshire), Selkirk and Galashiels (both Selkirkshire). Soundings by Mr Haldane, the chief magistrate at Galashiels, suggested that he would be generally well received as a liberal candidate but his brother William obviously had his doubts.[20]

A few days later, William told his brother that Lord Russell had failed in his attempt to discover who had put George's name forward. Fanny shared the family satisfaction that George was going to stand for election and asked him to arrange for the *Kelso Chronicle* to be sent to her.[21] Lady Mary, who was caring for her husband through his long illness at Colinton, wrote him a sympathetic sisterly letter full of genuine praise and acute political sense. She was glad to confirm that George's speech at Hawick 'had been all that the most fastidious – like himself – could desire. We had all agreed that the manner of your opinions was exactly right, the opinions themselves of course, to my mind, excellent – and indeed to the mind of all to whom we have spoken.' As it turned out, Mary thought 'it was uncourteous of the Hawickites to be so ready to invite Mr Trevelyan' and when the provost and his committee decided George (later Sir George) Trevelyan was the better man, the lawyer withdrew, so allowing Trevelyan to be returned unopposed.[22] He was to represent the Hawick district for eighteen years and pursue not only a long political career but become a great historian and scholar. Lizzy was 'provoked beyond measure and disappointed, though in such matters my hopes are never high. It is always the wrong man who succeeds.'[23]

At the start of the new decade George was living at 6 Pont Street in London, continuing his genealogical correspondence within an ever-widening circle of contacts. Sir Walter Elliot wrote to him from Wolfelee about the descendants of the last Elliot of Lariston. He had discovered in 'an inquest before the Sheriff of Roxburghshire' that William Elliot, a general officer in the Bengal Army, had been declared 'heir general and heir in line' to the last laird of Lariston in 1788, and that Robert Elliot who sold Lariston to Mr Oliver of Dinlabyre went to Newcastle after the sale.[24] In June 1872, Walter Riddell-Carre, a topographer who had worked for Messrs Fletcher, Alexander & Co., an East India merchant in London, before inheriting the estate of Cavers Carre in Roxburghshire and retiring as a family sketch writer, sent him a copy of the ballad 'Little Jock Elliot'.[25] Early in 1876 he received seven letters, including a series of simple drawings of branches of the Elliot tree from Ninian Elliot, a clerk in chambers working at Hall Street, Edinburgh.[26]

In the summer of 1876 George heard from Charles Abbott, Lord Tenterden, the permanent under-secretary at the Foreign Office whom he described as 'the busiest Hammond', a reference to his predecessor Edmund Hammond, who had retired in 1873 and recently been on holiday with his wife at the Marine Hotel in Nairn. Tenterden said how sorry he had been to hear about 'the gossiping articles' in the press and how Henry 'had been having a tough time of it' in Constantinople. He had no doubt that he would come out of it with distinction and that the papers about to be laid before Parliament would be a sufficient answer to his critics. Writing to William, George could only remind his brother that Henry's 'nature is not a gushing one and that caution and reserve are his chief characteristics'.[27] The lawyer was about to go down to Laverstoke and was looking forward to meeting Henry in Turkey so that he could reassure him about the rumours circulating in *The Times*.

In early November 1876, William returned to Minto after attending a 'formidable' wedding in London, and George had arrived in a rainy Constantinople to be with Henry after spending some time in Therapia, not far from Constantinople and where the embassy had another property. As the reader may recall from Henry's record of these events in Chapter 11, Lord Salisbury, the British plenipotentiary, had been charged with convening what came to be called the Conference of Ambassadors, attended by representatives from France, Germany, Austria-Hungary, Russia, Italy, Turkey and

Britain, and whose purpose was to look for solutions to yet another crisis in the Ottoman Empire. An uprising in Bulgaria, and of Christians in Bosnia-Herzegovina, had been quelled but only after much blood had been spilt. All the ambassadors were in town by 7 November 1876, except for General Ignatieff, the Russian representative, who it seemed had made no preparations for his stay – expecting to have been back in Russia before then. He had been 'put out and [was] angry' when he discovered the Turks had complied with the terms of an armistice.

George told William that whatever else was happening the ambassadors were 'a long way' from conferring. France accepted the proposal for a conference but only in 'a half-hearted way', Austria had always been against it and Russia had found 'the bullying game' successful in the past and was 'unlikely to drop it'. He found that Henry had been 'uneasy for some time at the prospect' of the conference and 'did not like the idea of having to bring forward and support schemes of autonomy' for individual regions which the government might favour one day and reject the next. HMS *Antelope*, which had some of the British party on board (including Freddy Boileau), was to have made a trip, involving George, to the naval commander-in-chief at Besika Bay, but it was cancelled when Henry 'thought it well' to keep hold on the vessel for the moment. George feared he would leave 'without seeing much of Constantinople beyond its walls – that is, the walls of the chancery'.

Rumours about Henry's conduct were being circulated by *The Times* and an artifice used by the newspaper particularly angered George, who felt it should be shown up. In an edition of 31 October there had been a long letter from their Austrian correspondent dated the day before. The beginning and end of the piece had been written in Vienna, whereas the middle had been unmistakeably written from Therapia by Antonio Gallenga, a brilliant journalist whom *The Times* had appointed in 1859 and who had arrived in Constantinople two years before. George's legal eye had spotted that a date in the Gallenga part did not correspond with that shown at the head of the letter; the day quoted as that when General Ignatieff had his first audience was inaccurate.[28] The lawyer did not like the tone of *The Times*, believing that feelings in the country had not nearly reached the point of calling upon the government to resist Russia by force. He was, however, glad to see that Lord Salisbury's appointment had been made public despite the fact that the other powers did not seem 'disposed to send a second representative'. George told his brother at Minto that Henry was 'pretty well' but 'sadly persecuted by visitors here'.[29]

Writing from Constantinople, a day or so before the opening of the Conference of Ambassadors in the Palais d'Amirante on 23 December 1876, George said that the only noticeable event was a preliminary diplomatic shuffle during which General Ignatieff 'moderated his tone and showed symptoms of uneasiness'. George praised the practical measure adopted by the government in sending out engineer officers to survey and lay out a line of defence for Constantinople extending from the Black Sea to the Sea of Marmora. It had been done 'very quietly but of course could not be kept secret'. During a lull in the preparations for the conference, a rather jittery Henry sometimes winced when he heard his wife Annie talking in 'her rabid fashion' and expressing her 'hopelessly one-sided' point of view, and George could not help wondering about the effect it might be having on Lord Salisbury's negotiating party.[30]

George gathered from what William had told him that 'John Bull' would 'not object to our occupying and defending Constantinople if threatened but he has still got atrocities on the brain, too much to agree to our going further in defence of the Turk, so he will not resent this step'. As it turned out, Lord Salisbury and General Ignatieff agreed on a political constitution for the Bulgarian lands and Bosnia-Herzegovina, and sessions of the conference followed without Turkish officials being present. The Russian plan envisaged a united Bulgarian province but Austria-Hungary's Count Andrássy objected to this, and since Lord Salisbury disliked the idea of a united autonomous Bulgarian province other geographical divisions had to be considered. Unfortunately, all involved Christian or Muslim governors appointed by the Porte and a system of justice based on Ottoman civil law. An international supervisory commission would have had to monitor delicate agreements. When the first day of the conference proper arrived, 23 December, the Turkish chairman of the session unsubtly proclaimed a constitution which rendered the conference and its resolutions pointless and countries started recalling their ambassadors. When the conference failed, Lord Derby did not show his displeasure openly, watering down an order to Henry that he should come to England 'to report on the situation'. It was left to the Russo-Turkish War of 1877–78 to liberate Bulgaria from Turkish rule.

Both the lawyer and the diplomat were back in England when Fanny's beloved husband, Lord John Russell, died at Pembroke Lodge in May 1878. He had taken little direct part in politics during the previous ten years but had completed his *Recollections and Suggestions* and *Essays on the History of the Christian Religion*. He had spent the winters of 1869/70 and 1871/72 in the south of France and six weeks of the summer in 1873 at Dieppe on account of his health. In 1875 Fanny had noted in her diary how her husband had written to *The Times* giving his support to the Herzegovina insurgents, and how he frequently spoke with indignation of the systematic murders contrived by the Turkish government and officials. In September that year, he had received a warm and supportive note from Garibaldi which referred to him pleading 'the cause of the Turkish Rayahs, non-muslim subjects who were then even more unhappy'.[31]

Lord John's last years had been saddened by the illness of his sons Rollo and William, to say nothing of the deaths of Lord and Lady Amberley and their daughter Rachel, his six-year-old granddaughter, who caught the diphtheria that killed her mother. Gladstone had found him 'a noble wreck' who was 'quite ready to die' when he visited him. Queen Victoria wrote to Fanny from Balmoral at the end of May 1878:

> Lord John, as I knew him best, was one of my first and most distinguished ministers, and his departure recalls many eventful times. To you, dear Lady Russell, who were ever one of the most devoted of wives, this must be a terrible blow though you must have for some time been prepared for it.[32]

Nina's letter of condolence at the beginning of July was especially pertinent:

> I rather wished to hear that the Abbey was to have been his resting place but, after all, it matters little since his abiding place is in the pages of English history ... I remember

often going *down* to you when London was full of some political anger against him – when personalities and bitterness were rife – and returning *from* you with the feeling of having been in another world, so entire was the absence of such bitterness, so gentle and peaceful were the impressions I carried away.[33]

Admiral Charles, George's brother then out of a job, and Admiral Augustus Elliot, the retiring commander-in-chief Portsmouth who had been knighted the previous year, would have been horrified to hear about the loss of the late Admiral George's beloved ship HMS *Eurydice* in March that year. The vessel had been doing duty as a training ship and two years before had undergone a routine refit at John White's shipyard at East Cowes and was considered still in top condition after her recommissioning at Portsmouth. The ship had left the West Indies on 6 March 1878 and crossed the Atlantic in only sixteen days, arriving off the Isle of Wight on 22 March. At three in the afternoon, the Bonchurch coastguard station saw her 'moving fast under plain sail, studding sails on fore and main, bonnets and skysails'. Suddenly a great squall bore down on the ship at great speed as she was in Sandown Bay. Heavy clouds were blackened with snow and ice. The captain of the *Emma*, a schooner nearby, reefed his sails but according to witnesses, the *Eurydice* continued at full sail with her gun ports open before disappearing in the midst of the blizzard. Only two of the ship's 378 crew and trainees survived and most of those not carried down with the ship died in the freezing waters. It had been one of the country's worst peacetime naval disasters.

Meanwhile, Sir Walter Elliot had put some more work in hand for George through a Captain Lawrence Archer, and a letter arrived from the pastor of Christ's Church, Newburgh Village, Maine, USA. Addressed a little inaccurately to 'Sir Gilbert Elliot' and passed on by William, George soon discovered that the Rev G. T. Ridlon, who called himself a 'genealogist, herald and antiquary', had been the author of a history of the 'Riddells, Riddles, Ridlons and Ridleys in Britain, France and America', a work which was about to be published. The 'publishing committee' formed in Philadelphia had asked the Rev Ridlon to 'ask the present proprietor of the Minto estate to furnish the names of four females (daughters of Walter Riddell) who sold the place to the Elliots'. The committee also wanted a 'photographic view of the Minto House from which to make a plate for our books' – the latter being likely to cost $380 to $600. George was to spend some time in June preparing a four-page note about Walter Riddell, the 'possessor of Minto' in 1670, but he was forced to scribble on the copy he kept for himself, 'I never received any acknowledgment of my letter and paper from Mr Ridlon.'[34]

Towards the end of the year George heard from one Robert Armstrong of Marsh Cottage, Canonbie, Dumfriesshire, to whom he had lent some genealogical material. His correspondent subsequently went down to London, staying at the Junior Carlton Club on some business for George and the Society of Antiquaries. In December, Armstrong thanked the lawyer for his 'most interesting paper on the origin of the name Elliot and also that on the Border Elliots'. He had just finished reading the treaty entered into by Henry VII in 1491 with Archibald Bell and a lengthy correspondence was to develop.[35]

The new decade of the 1880s was to open with a significant political campaign. Despite the atrocities committed by the Turks, Lord Beaconsfield's administration continued its policy of support for the Ottoman Empire as a bulwark against possible Russian expansion in the area. Gladstone, who four years before had published his pamphlet *The Bulgarian Horrors and the Question of the East* which contained a call for Turkish withdrawal 'bag and baggage', followed it with a campaign against 'Beaconsfieldism'. As he decided not to stand again for Greenwich at the next general election, negotiations were opened with a group of Scottish liberals. The 'Midlothian Campaign', in and around this corrupt country seat between 1879 and the first four months of 1880, set the stage for Gladstone's comeback. Verbatim reports of his speeches appeared across the country in newspapers the next day, but the contest with Lord Dalkeith, the sitting Tory member, was not to be a walkover.

Writing to William in early March from 2 Pont Street, George answered the question he had asked him about the date of the dissolution of Parliament; it had been announced the day before. It had been quite unexpected and George could only assume that 'the scrape the government got into about the Water Companies' Bill' was the cause of their final decision.[36] Arthur Elliot, William and Nina's second son, who was to stand for the Roxburghshire constituency, left London on 10 March.[37] Despite his dislike of public meetings and weeks spent canvassing, George offered to join him there, bearing in mind his disablement and the need for him to use carriages when travelling around the constituency. Arthur had apparently asked his father whether he would be coming home to Minto as it would 'have been a great advantage to have him at his elbow' but with William and Nina in distant Algiers it could not be arranged. There was nothing for it; the candidate and the lawyer would have to do their best without him. Nina had apparently been deeply affected by the deaths in quick sequence of Admiral George's youngest son, Frederick, who was only fifty-four years old, and his wife Lady Charlotte. It had been a 'sad tragedy'.

In the event, George 'made no scruple' about taking up his quarters at Minto and began a series of briefs for the candidate on 'foreign politics', where there had been a great change of tone among Liberal publications. The *Daily News* had reported that the party association at Tynemouth had agreed to accept Eustace Smith as its candidate in spite of his having supported the foreign policy of the government.[38] The newspaper had been pleased to give some latitude to liberals holding independent opinions, a policy it had been following for two years, and to ostracise them on that account would in its opinion be 'suicidal'. According to George the general expectation was that there would be no great change in England but the government would lose a good deal in Scotland, where several of the seats were held by small majorities.[39]

A few days later George had to admit bewailing his brother's absence and the disadvantage in not having the wherewithal for 'a social and political centre' at Minto around which all interested could gather 'at such a time'. Matters were not helped by Mary (née Long), the wife of William's son Hugh, being ill in London so that there was every expectation that her husband would have to leave Minto to care for her.[40] George found he got on well with Arthur and Mrs Smart, the housekeeper. She and 'her maidens' looked after the canvassing party at Minto in a 'most kind and attentive' manner. They were a 'great deal of trouble with the irregular hours' they kept. Dinner time could be anywhere between 8 and 11 p.m. Arthur had spoken at three public meetings and his speeches had been 'very good and very cordially received'. At Galashiels, where he was expected soon, he 'would have to deal with salmon' and, in closing, George humorously told his brother that he would be writing to Fanny to say that 'she could be of no use here'.[41] The poll had been fixed for 8 April and the declaration would follow the next day when George promised to send a telegram to Algiers. After what had been a successful meeting at Galashiels, the largest yet, Arthur was committed to two 'distant' meetings, one at Morebattle and the other at Yetholm, both near Kelso, to which George did not plan to go as he could be 'more usefully employed elsewhere'. With Mary in better health, the Minto team expected Arthur's brother Hugh soon, while there was news that a Jim Elliot had sent out his election address to voters among the Border burghs – concentrating on pollution and poaching, his two great interests.[42]

By the end of March, Arthur's campaign was going well but, as George told William, the 'cold shade of the great aristocrat' was over them, i.e. the preceding MP Sir George Scott-Douglas. Nevertheless, George now thought there was a chance that they could win but there were important meetings yet to be held in Melrose and Hawick.[43] There followed what was being called several 'ovations' and when Denholm turned out 'with torches', it was to drag out the hero of the day. George described how he looked out of one window of a small carriage and Arthur 'popped his head' outside the other. It struck him how much it looked like a Punch and Judy show. At Ancrum the following night there was another 'ovation' got up in the same rather comic style, and with their thoughts so concentrated on local affairs George had to admit that details of the Liberal success across the country, which indicated they would have a majority at Westminster, had passed them by.[44]

When the national results were declared, the Liberal Party had gained 352 seats (a net gain of 110 seats), Conservatives 237 seats (a net loss of 113) and Home Rulers 63 seats (a net gain of 3). In Roxburghshire, as George said, we 'had a narrow squeak ... and I never was more surprised than when the Sheriff read out the numbers – Elliot 859, Douglas 849'. Both sides had been 'very much out' in their calculations and local opinion suggested that the 'delinquent' was Melrose. George had been particularly surprised to encounter one member of the family at the poll who had voted for the Tory candidate, telling William how sad it was to see Elliots 'going over to the enemy'. He reminded him that 'it began in the last generation with Sir William of Stobs, and now we have Wolfelee [his description of Walter Elliot and his son] to say nothing of Admiral George [Augustus] whose ratting luckily [did] not affect our county'. Elliot of Clifton was the only 'set off' the genealogist could recall. The Edinburgh *Courant* stated that after his defeat Sir George Scott-Douglas announced to his committee that he would contest the seat on the next occasion, but George was convinced that his present intention was to retire for good. He felt 'no less confident that when the time [came] he [would] give way to the pressure ... put upon him by his party'. George thought their own best hope was that the franchise might be lowered before the next election and a number of the village people would be brought in who could swell the liberal majority.

So far as the scene nationally was concerned, George had little doubt that

however much the Queen may kick against it, it will end by Gladstone being Prime Minister. There will be preliminary attempts and negotiations but the constitutional and proper course is that he, who has taken the leading part in the overthrow of the government, and who is looked upon by the great liberal majority, now returns to parliament as their true leader ... the person on whom the responsibilities of carrying on a government should be thrown, and this I expect will be followed, whatever the objections felt to him in high quarters and in a portion of the party.

Arthur and George left Minto on 9 April and travelled together as far as Carlisle, where the new member 'branched off to Greystoke for the night', perhaps to stay with one of the Grahams of Cumberland on his way to Manchester, leaving George to resume his normal life and return to his house in Pont Street.[45]

William and Nina had enjoyed their stay in Algiers and, writing to them at Baveno in Italy on their way home, George told them he had not seen Arthur since returning to town. Places in Gladstone's second cabinet had been 'shuffled in an unexpected way'. Nobody, he said, 'had thought of [William Edward] Forster being Irish secretary' and he could not help thinking that 'putting a man of his calibre into the place must portend some big Irish measures about land, or modified home rule in the shape of local representation'. Willy Adam, his cousin who had been one of those who with Lord Rosebery had encouraged Gladstone to stand at Midlothian, was now 'looked upon as having been inadequately rewarded for his work in opposition'. He had been offered no more than his former post as first commissioner of works but there was apparently some kind of understanding that after a time Henry Brand would retire and Adam be made speaker.[46] In the event, before the end of the year Willy accepted the governorship of Madras, and died there in 1881.

George had been sorry to see Lord Granville return to the Foreign Office, where he feared he would act as 'chief clerk' to Gladstone. George Leveson-Gower, second Earl Granville, had long been a target of his sarcasm as exemplified in his note to William:

The best hope is that being Chancellor of the Exchequer, leader of the House of Commons, and engaged with great home measures, his attention may be turned from foreign affairs – but that after all is a faint hope, for his energy and activity and universality increase with years, and if he lives to be a hundred he will be capable of undertaking the duties of every department of the government.

The appointment of the Marquess of Ripon as viceroy of India, after Viscount Goschen had declined it, was, according to George, 'universally condemned'.

The lawyer's letter to William contained a rather bland reference to Hugh Childers, who had become Gladstone's Secretary of State for War, another appointment 'most criticized'.[47] His administration at the Admiralty during Gladstone's first administration had not been a success and the idea of his trying his hand at the sister service was not liked. So far as George was concerned, putting him at the War Office meant 'an intention to reduce strength and retrench expenditure'. Another objection made to him was that he would not be strong enough to control the Horse Guards. He had, however, married Gibby's widow, Katherine, in Paris the previous year, she having devoted many years to nursing the Elliot soldier. On this occasion there was no mention of her. George did not know what to think of him but he was inclined to 'hope better things than the public expect'.[48]

No sooner was the general election over than Robert Armstrong wrote to George from 5 Melville Street, Edinburgh, telling him he was leaving for Norway from Leith, but he was back in Scotland by the middle of August. With the hot dry weather 'hard on men and dogs', Armstrong had been going through manuscripts in the Justiciary Office for him and had come upon a paper dated 1537 in respect of Robert Elwald of Redheugh and his brother Archibald.[49] Then in January the following year, Armstrong wrote to say that he had had an unsuccessful correspondence with Mr William Fraser in an attempt to have a paper withdrawn from before the Society of Antiquaries on the subject of the feud between the Elliots and the Scotts. By May 1881 Fraser was transcribing a portion of the Border Club's transactions and referred to Chapters III and IV as being finished. He intended asking George to look through them and 'point out those [he] thought most useful'. When he next wrote it was to list the various spellings of Elliot since 1541, of which there had been some sixty-seven by his reckoning.[50]

The 1881 census taken in the spring that year showed there had been a change of servants in George's Pont Street household during the previous decade. Elizabeth Merton, his housekeeper, and Nellie Brener, a fourteen-year-old niece, had both been born at Binfield in Berkshire, while Elizabeth's husband John Merton, who came from the neighbouring county of Oxfordshire, was described as a messenger. In April, William wrote from 76A Marine Parade, Brighton, where he had been examining some notes about the origins of the Brydone family. He also wanted his brother to join him in Sussex for the Army review. William's third son 'Fitz' was going into the Army and was 'doing business in London'.[51]

Five years later, William was telling George how he had been occupying himself 'by fits and starts in the business of searching out the contents of the various boxes full of papers' at Minto. He too had been recruited into George's army of researchers and he recognised that 'old receipts and vouchers' were not what his brother really wanted or needed. He passed on one paper by Alexander Jeffrey, an antiquary who had been born in Roxburghshire, which he said might be 'only worthy of the wastepaper basket'. It seems that Jeffrey had concerned himself with the etymology of 'Minto', suggesting that its origin had a lot to do with the crags locally. He had also concluded that the Elliots were originally from Renfrewshire, a John Sempel or Sempie of Elliotstown being sheriff of that county in 1481.[52]

Between 1882 and 1898 George was a regular guest and fishing companion of William Warren Vernon, who owned a property in southern Norway.[53] Returning from Scandinavia in 1884, George found a letter from Sir Walter Elliot, who explained he had not 'been tending to matters genealogical' but rather Indian archaeology and he was 'still immersed in it'. Notwithstanding this, he had reported how the Elliots intermarried so extensively that it was almost impossible to extricate each family in a direct line.

Speaking of others involved in the build-up of family information, Sir Walter also told George that Dumfriesshire-based Robert Armstrong was coming to 'dine and sleep' at Wolfelee and he and his wife were so looking forward to the visit that he hoped the lawyer could also join them.[54]

At the beginning of 1886, Sir James Hudson died. Twenty-three years earlier he had been at the centre of much newspaper speculation which alleged that Lord Russell had retired him prematurely from Turin in order to find a diplomatic post for Henry Elliot. In 1860, Henry been British minister at the court of the King of Naples, while Sir James Hudson held a like post at the court of the King of Sardinia. During the course of that year Garibaldi conquered Naples and added it to the dominions of King Victor Emmanuel, with the result that the mission in Naples was no longer required. At this point, Lord John wrote to Henry on 12 November saying that 'the triumph of Italy is death to your mission … and I think you may as well stay in England for a time when you get home, without looking for a fresh appointment. This I understand is your own wish.' The next day an article in *The Times* claimed that Sir James was being removed to St Petersburg in order that Henry might take his place at Turin.

George now felt it was the appropriate time for him to publish *An Historical Rectification* which would finally put the record straight regarding the Hudson affair and help protect his brother Henry's reputation. Sir James Hudson's death and reviews of his career published in some English and foreign newspapers now revived the original offensive imputations and George concluded that justice could only be done by his publishing a true record of the events about which he had prepared a draft – based on the correspondence of Lord Russell in his possession. In January 1886, Sir Henry Layard, who had been Russell's under-secretary at the Foreign Office, responded to George's request that he read the correspondence before he sent his text to the printers for publication. Having been on the most intimate and confidential terms with Hudson, Layard felt it was his duty to do all in his power to 'remove an unmerited stain upon the reputation of a distinguished English statesman'. He enclosed copies of two letters from Hudson for George to read which he thought sufficiently proved that Hudson had resigned his post at Turin on two grounds. The first was the inadequacy of his salary, which was insufficient for him to live on as British representative at the Italian court without getting seriously into debt. The second was that, with the probability that a Tory government was about to come to power, he would be dismissed by Lord Malmesbury, Lord Russell's probable successor. Layard went on to recall a meeting he had had with Hudson when he was living in a villa on Lake Garda during which he declared he 'had been long waiting for the day when he could claim his pension and retire from diplomacy, of which he was heartily sick'.[55]

When George's slim volume, entitled *Sir James Hudson and Earl Russell: An Historical Rectification*, appeared in print late in 1886, published by William Ridgway of Piccadilly, it contained sixty-five pages and copies of the letters that had crossed in 1863. The lawyer ended it by saying that he left it 'to the candid judgement of anyone who has taken the trouble to read the preceding pages' to deny that Lord Russell and Henry's part in the affair had 'not been marked by fairness, friendliness and honesty'.

In June 1886, George travelled to Norway once again to stay with his 'old pal' William Vernon, a scholar in his fifties, whose house, called 'Monen', was in the small southern coastal town of Mandal not far from Kristiansand. Two months before, Vernon and he had called on Sir James Lacaita, an authority on Dante, at his property, 'Leucaspide', near Taranto in Italy.[56] William had married Agnes Boileau, one of Sir John Boileau's daughters, in 1855 and by 1872 the couple had taken to visiting Norway regularly. Five years later, the Lutheran priest of the parish of Holme told them that permission had been given for them to build a house there on glebe land. 'Monen' was the result, constructed by a local builder, although the real name of the site on the county map was Hegre Moen.[57] Unfortunately Agnes died in 1881, and William Vernon married his second wife Annie, the daughter of Charles Eyre, three years later.

Writing on some of Vernon's headed notepaper (with the family crest *Vernon semper viret*) from what George called his 'fishing box' on the River Mandalselva, where his friend had fished for salmon every year since 1871, George told his elder brother William that his hosts had been delayed on their journey to Norway from Florence. He had spent 'five deadly dull days at Kristiansand waiting for them'. George soon caught his first fish 'although there did not appear to be many in the water yet'. As a result it was the fate of the Irish Government Bill which offered Ireland partial home rule, and news of the 'decision of Chamberlain and his friends', that occupied his mind. Joseph Chamberlain had resigned in April after Gladstone rejected his concept of a legislative assembly in Ireland. He had read in the newspapers how it was generally assumed that there would be an immediate dissolution of Parliament – a line of thinking that made him wonder what might happen in Roxburghshire. He said, 'after the line Arthur has taken, the Tories ought not to attack his seat'. While beside the sea in Norway, he could only promise William that if there was a contest he would be prepared 'to start off at once' but he had 'no desire to cross the North Sea again so soon'.[58]

At the start of 1886 liberals and 'home-rulers' had voted together to defeat Gladstone, who was then allied with Irish Nationalists; but on 30 January, Gladstone received the Queen's commission to form a third government. Then in March, when the Land Bill was being explained to the cabinet both Joseph Chamberlain (president of the Local Government Board) and Sir George Otto Trevelyan (Chancellor of the Duchy of Lancaster) resigned. Further internecine debate ensued and after another confused general election in August, which Gladstone lost, Lord Salisbury formed a second administration which was to last until 1892.

In November 1889, with some visitors having departed and the party at Minto 'reduced to four', including Lady Antrim, who was returning to Ireland, George took to searching the terrace library for William Lecky's *A History of England during the Eighteenth Century* to find only the first four volumes which had been published in 1880. There were several other incomplete sets of books, prompting him to ask his brother to see whether the missing volumes could be elsewhere, in which case 'it would be well to send them down' to Minto. He was glad to know that 'in the opinion of competent authorities', William had made a good purchase of a property in Portman Square, where houses were 'rising in the market' although the noise of traffic was the chief objection found to it. 'Even had it been otherwise,' said George, who seemed not to appreciate that it had been bought to rent out, 'I should have rejoiced at your being well-housed in London.'[59]

In the spring of 1890 George turned his attention to two old seals, one of which had been used by Gilbert of Stobs in the eighteenth century (and reproduced eventually on page 251 of the family history). He asked William to look out for a drawing of either of the seals at Minto. Armstrong had spoken of 'a man at work on the seal for Roxburghshire', explaining that this did not mean that 'the modern one' was actually being engraved. In the middle of March, George was enjoying the company of Henry and Annie, who had come up from their home at Ardington House in Wantage and were staying with him at Pont Street; with Henry's troublesome cough a little better, the couple were thinking of going to the Isle of Wight for a change.[60] In the event, they went to Bonchurch, a small village east of Ventnor for ten days. A week later, after being away himself, George returned to find that William had suggested he looked at Bailey's *Dictionary* which was not, according to George, a dictionary of heraldry.[61]

Referring to that morning's newspaper report and the report of another Irish debate in the House, George told his brother on 27 March that Arthur had again voted against the government but he thought he was 'quite right' to do so, and even on personal grounds it was 'not a bad thing to show that a Liberal Unionist in giving it a hearty support on the one great question does not become a government hack'.[62] William planned to be in London in early June, a date that suited George as he planned be in town until Eton Day and the Derby had been run (and won by the Duke of Westminster's 'Bend Or'), and thereafter at Mandal. There had been exceptionally fine weather both at Minto and in the capital, where Lizzy thought of 'offering herself to Pembroke Lodge' – paying Fanny and her daughter Agatha a visit – before going to Aberdeenshire.[63] There was soon to be news that 'Lizzy and her belongings' were getting over their troubles.

George was to write twice from Norway to William, who was still staying with Fanny. In July he went with William Vernon to the valley of Setesdal which he had been told was 'worth seeing on account of the primitive habits and costumes of the natives having been retained there unchanged'. Annie Vernon was 'laid up' with a miscarriage almost the whole time. They had travelled with their own carrioles (or two-wheeled rickshaws) and horses through fine scenery with a couple of the Vernons' own men to look after them, just as his host had done in 1871 when he first arrived in Norway from Hull. Exploring as far as Valle, some 100 miles from Kristiansand, they stayed at a recently constructed 'Summer Home' of 'good size and very prettily situated'. Norwegian dress amused them, particularly that of the women in short light-coloured petticoats over which they wore another brightly coloured one with large silver buttons at the neck. Vernon, who had a great objection to being ill fed, had taken the precaution of bringing 'tinned meat and soup, and other provisions' without which their fare would have been 'scanty'.

The arrival of a batch of newspapers just before their return to Mandal – which included *The Times*, the *Spectator* and the *Graphic* – brought news of the Barrow election where William Sproston Caine, a well-known advocate of temperance, had been beaten. George was 'immensely interested in the result'. He had taken an active part in organising dissenting liberals into the new party of Liberal Unionists and in the division on the second reading of Gladstone's Home Rule Bill in 1886, Caine was one of the tellers for the ninety-three Liberal Unionists who brought down the government. Home-rulers were to call the new party 'The Brand of Caine'. Caine had then fallen out with his new friends and, standing as an independent liberal, he was defeated – something about which George could only say, 'What a fool he must feel now', although he regretted the loss of the seat to Sir Charles Cayzer, a Conservative.[64]

At the end of July 1890 George wrote to William from Mandal with news of 'the unhappy state of things between Frank and his wife'. Viscount Amberley's eldest son, John Francis (second Earl Russell) had married Edith Mabel Scott in February 1890.[65] Frank and his brother Bertrand had come to live with the Russells at Pembroke Lodge when their father died in 1876. Frank was then ten years old. Telling brother William that whatever the reason may be, George wrote that it 'seems that they cannot get on together' and he felt not only that the fault was on Frank's side but that he would 'never come to any good' in spite of his abilities being above the average. It would be something 'if Mabel is a comfort to Fanny for it is little likely that she will ever derive any comfort from him'.

Meanwhile, the regular course of life with the Vernons had been 'broken in upon' by a visit from a Norwegian couple who had been at 'Monen' for nearly a week, and about whom William Vernon 'was getting a little impatient at their never having hinted at the probable period of their visit'. George was deputed to settle this 'interesting question' and, with his diplomacy successful, he told his brother more about the attractions of the area he was in, saying how when they came back from their Setesdal trip they found that the river had risen considerably, enabling a few fish to be killed. Doddy doubted that William had been in Setesdal, it being 'quite in the southern part of the country' but 'I dare say, there are other districts where the men adopt the fashion of trousers coming up to their necks!'[66] Expecting to find that politics would be at a standstill when he got back to England, the lawyer proposed to be 'one of the population' at Minto by about the end of August if matters worked out as planned. By the afternoon of 25 August, George had returned as far as the Travellers' Club after a 'nasty passage across the North Sea' and would 'not be able to write for a few days to come by reason of a small operation' he was to undergo the following day. Lest William thought too much of it, George added that 'it was only taking out an inflamed cist in the breast'. It had been lanced before he went to Norway and something remained which he wanted to 'get completely rid of … and as it is a case of chloroform and a nurse', he supposed that meant confinement for some days at least.[67]

During the Christmas period Henry paid a visit to the National Portrait Gallery's offices at Great George Street in Westminster in his search for the portraits his brother wanted of the first Lord Minto when he was governor-general of India. Laurence Holland, the assistant director, was subsequently in touch with the curator of the Scottish National Portrait Gallery in Edinburgh on his behalf. The latter explained that the picture had been for a long time wrongly titled but through the assistance of a Colonel Yule it was now accepted as a portrait of Lord Minto, full length and sitting at a table in plain clothes.[68] Mr Holland was himself able to clear up the origin of a small sketch in oils recently presented to the London gallery by Canon Atkinson, who was a son of the artist, James Atkinson, an Army surgeon and oriental scholar. It had been taken from life and not made up from a larger picture. The canon told him that Lord Minto gave his father an appointment in India and was always a great friend to him.[69]

Two days after Christmas 1890, George wrote to William from a London 'only a degree or two above freezing', obviously intent on keeping his brother's mind as active as possible. He wanted him to discover whether or not there was a picture of the rocks at Minto in the billiard room 'somewhat in the same style and with a number of figures'. George could not remember its subject but suggested it might be based on Sir Walter Scott's epic poem *Marmion*. He then asked him how long he was likely to stay at Minto, particularly as the strike which had started on 21 December in the traffic departments of the three leading Scottish railway companies 'looked like continuing some time longer'.[70] In another letter, written on the last day of the year from the Travellers' Club in Pall Mall, George was able to report that the railway strikes were 'beginning to collapse', suggesting that William would be able to 'make out his journey' later that week. Whether he did is not known and William died three months later, aged seventy-six.

In the middle of July 1891 Fanny was writing to her son Rollo, who, having lost his first wife Alice in 1886, a year after their wedding, had married Miss Gertrude Joachim, the niece of the violinist Joseph Joachim, on 28 April 1891. Queen Victoria 'rejoiced to hear' that Rollo was to marry again.[71] George's sister continued to write to her forty-two-year-old son from Pembroke Lodge almost daily with news of her health and visitors, where the household comprised Fanny, Agatha her daughter, and five-year-old Arthur, Rollo's son by his first wife. Soon afterwards, Fanny rented 'The Grange' at Hindhead, which she particularly liked on account of the heather and its similarity to Scotland. Young Bertie was to stay with her there. George's sister had a 'capital long letter' from Rollo in October 1891. Fanny was glad about what he had said about Cambridge – the beautiful 'backs', the singing at King's Chapel, together with the breakfasts and functions with Bertie and his friends. The latter had gone up to Trinity the year before and was to take part one of the Mathematical Tripos in May 1893. It was such a joy, she said, to think of him as 'one of a good set'.[72] Rollo remembered to send his mother a birthday letter the following month but they were no longer sharing 'daily interests'; their lives were growing 'gradually more apart' despite the gratitude she felt for his happy marriage.[73]

'Becolded people' travelling on the train into London might, according to Fanny, have been the cause of Rollo's winter cold in February 1892. His mother was vexed that he had not shown the wisdom of staying even one day in bed. After sixteen years as a clerk in the Civil Service, Rollo had resigned in 1888 and developed his interest in meteorology from Dunrozel, his home.[74] He had been elected a Fellow of the Royal Meteorological Society in 1868 when only nineteen. Between 1870 and 1890 he was especially interested in the London fog and wrote a best-selling pamphlet on the effects of atmospheric pollution. He was to become vice-president of the society in 1893. During the year when Fanny would have confined him to bed, Rollo was working on a considered piece of academic work entitled *Epidemics, Plagues and Health*.

Having spent the summer of 1892 in Denmark, Robert Armstrong moved into a house in Randolph Cliff, Edinburgh, which 'had given endless trouble'; but he hoped George would come over from Minto and examine the work being done on the history of Liddesdale, of which Bothwell had become lord in 1492.[75] In November, the Hon. Colonel Robert Boyle from Sumner Terrace in London's Onslow Square, who was to become a Fellow of the Society of Antiquaries of Scotland four years later, told George he now better understood 'the difficulty and complexity of the problems which all genealogy sets up, and the labour which has been expended on their elucidation'. The colonel, who was a distant Elliot relative, soon came north, staying at the Scottish Conservative Club in Edinburgh, from where he wrote to apologise for drawing conclusions 'a great deal too hastily' about parts of the deed he had been examining.[76]

Towards the end of 1892, George received a cheerful letter from brother William's third son, Hugh Elliot, who lived at 'Corwar' in Newton Stewart with his wife Mary (née Long), whom he had married in 1879. He had won the seat of Ayrshire North in 1885 and was to publish his *Life of the Earl of Godolphin* three years later. Hugh had found some papers which he felt might be of interest. They dealt with the deportation of the Border Grahams to Flushing in the early 1600s and had been bound up with other manuscripts and effectively lost. He had also found the names of some 'special malefactors' in the Borders, one of whom was John Armstrong, who was 'the Jack the Ripper of his age and notorious for many murders'. He went on to tell George that the house they were living in at Newton Stewart was nearly finished but its floors and fittings were yet to be completed. There had been a number of changes since the lawyer's last visit. The 'outside water closet and shed has been knocked down and is now being built up again of granite', wrote Hugh. This will act, he continued, 'as a screen between the lawn and the back court … and is a great improvement'. In conclusion, Hugh asked for his uncle's forgiveness for any mistakes in his letter since Mary was deafening him 'with a march of Wagner's and the uproar is terrible'.[77]

The following year George again travelled to Norway to be with the Vernons at 'Monen', and pressure grew to finalise what was to be his *magnum opus*. The Earl of Home's help was enlisted to identify a seal in an old document, his predecessor in 1616 having disponed land to Gilbert Elliot of Stobs. Armstrong was staying at Arkleton, near Langholm, the home of Mr Scott-Elliot, but still working at the Record Office in Edinburgh, aided occasionally by the Rev Walter Macleod, who was generally to be found there on 'the first four days of the week'.[78] In December, a new contributor to his work wrote to him from Northfield near Bournemouth. Sir Archibald Dunbar suggested that he would find a seal he wanted at the British Museum, where copies could be obtained for a shilling. Anxious to guide George as precisely as he could, he recommended that once through the door where 'you will have to give up your umbrella', he should ask the police inspector if he would show him the way to Mr Ready's door. Ring the bell, he told George, and 'when Mr Ready (father or son) appears, tell him you have an old document with a seal and you wish to have the seal copied'. While he was taking an impression, Dunbar went on, 'he will not let you see him' for fear of 'your betraying his secret'. He also suggested he had it 'photographed and autotyped'.[79]

Fanny was wrapped in what she called 'the dark side of life' in 1894, speaking of the way Lotty and her daughters had had 'their young joy and spirits crushed out of them by their father'. In February, George called on his sister, telling her that he had seen Lotty at her son Raymond's funeral and, although weak she was 'wonderfully calm and able to talk a great deal about Gerald'. As for Melville, Fanny said George was 'simply imperturbably indignant with him' and she could not bear to think what he was like at home – 'why did he ever win the love of such a one as Lotty?'[80] Then, in December, and despite Fanny's initial and violent objections, a twenty-two-year-old Bertie Russell married Alys Whitall, the daughter of an American Quaker from

Philadelphia who had settled in Surrey. However, as time went by, Bertie came to loathe Alys's mother, who lived close to their home at Fernhurst in Sussex.[81] Fanny continued to worry about the absence of news from Laverstoke. In the spring of 1895 she feared that little new light would shine on the problem of Melville Portal, given that he had 'contrived to make home miserable to his wife and daughters, and forced them to feel that even in the deepest sorrow they can expect no sympathy [and] no tenderness from him'.[82]

Another of those whom George kept a loving eye on wrote to him from 27 Rutland Gate in the middle of May. Arthur Elliot, who was then in his late forties, had read a number of the lawyer's draft chapters.[83] It was the following February before he was in a position to return the manuscript. He had made a few pencilled notes in the margins 'but they were of no importance' save for some information about Roxburghshire MPs taken from the parliamentary return. Not long after, while Arthur and his wife Madeleine were staying with Henry at Wantage, he drew George's attention to half a dozen references in John Rae's *Life of Adam Smith* which might put him 'on the scent to discover more'. The couple were about to leave for their cottage on the Isle of Wight.[84]

Later in 1897 both Arthur and Hugh and their wives were on holiday together at Tolland in Somerset. While there, Arthur raised several literary matters, telling George that Professor Sidney Colvin, the art and literary scholar who had been a great collaborator of the late Robert Louis Stevenson, was going to publish 'something about his last border novel'. Arthur explained to Colvin that Hermiston was a real place and later heard that he had seen Sir George Douglas, another authority on Border matters. When it came to the time for their departure there had been concern about Mary (Hugh's wife) who was 'better but certainly still very weak'. She had not walked 20 yards since she arrived at Tolland and 'the long journey to Newton Stewart with the sixteen mile drive at the end of it will be ... a heavy trial'. Arthur, Madeleine and possibly their sons had enjoyed some glorious sunshine and would have preferred to have stayed on until after the Queen's Diamond Jubilee was well over. The police, Arthur wrote to George, 'seemed to be rather nervous about it all as nowadays the railways bring together such vast crowds of people ... The dimensions of mobs have become so gigantic that there may be a difficulty in keeping order.' They had it in mind to go abroad with Hubert, their youngest boy, at the end of July – probably to the Tyrol.[85]

In the event, Arthur seems to have changed his mind. Towards the end of August he told his uncle the family was at Clifton Cottage, Braemar, describing himself as 'a tourist'. He hoped to be in London the following month when he could give George advice about his book and also review another book on the Borders. Turning to political affairs, Arthur told George that he wished 'the government had left the sentence on Jamieson and Co. alone'. To his mind, 'Rhodes, Jameson and Willoughby were three conspirators in a plot, concocted with financial ends in view'.[86] The whole power of the empire was to be used in support of their speculations and worst of all, our national good faith was 'to be trampled underfoot'.

Admiral Charles Elliot's death occurred in May and towards the end of the year. Fanny came up to her eightieth birthday and seems to have invited the Rollo family to stay. Although always fonder of the country than the town, Rollo had decided to move from Surrey into town – probably to 43 Holland Street, Kensington, where he was to die in 1914. His mother maintained that any question of them 'being too many for us' was nonsense. He would be 'nearer everything and everybody' and Gertrude could have a nurse to dress the baby instead of doing a nurse's commonest of duties herself. Fanny suggested her 'dearest children' should 'stay quietly here till you settle in town'.[87] In February 1897 she took pride in seeing that Rollo had read a paper on 'Meteorology and the Atmosphere' to the Royal Meteorological Society.[88]

During the summer of 1897 Fanny became very unwell and Sinclair, her maid and housekeeper, read to her a great deal; but by September she was able to resume her daily letter-writing such that the following month Agatha wrote to Fanny's friend Mrs Isabel Warburton to say how happy she was that Mama had been able to take a perfect drive round the Park again, and as full of pleasure and observation as she ever remembered. She looked so well and fresh in all her interests with her sight and hearing betraying little sign of change. The diary entry for her eighty-second birthday on the 15th talked of a party she gave for seventy happy boys and girls from Petersham village school who came to see a ventriloquist and his acting dolls in the sitting room at Pembroke Lodge, which had been cleared for the occasion.[89]

It was David Douglas of Edinburgh who towards the end of 1897 eventually published 125 copies of George's 570-page work, *The Border Elliots and the Family of Minto*. Fifteen chapters were given over to the Border families from the fifteenth century and a further five lengthy chapters described the Elliot family at Minto, with a number of illustrations. Originally employed by Blackwood & Sons, Douglas had started publishing in 1854. He had been a Fellow of the Royal Society of Antiquaries for thirty years and would have known much about the market for such a publication. Writing to Thomas Craig-Brown, a manufacturer, antiquarian and well-known Selkirk benefactor, in December that year, George invited him to look at his volume as it included 'an account of the Liddesdale Elliots. A few days later a second letter followed, expressing the pleasure Craig-Brown's reply had given him, coming 'from one who has so real an interest in, as well as an exceptional knowledge of Border history and who has been a successful labourer in the same field as myself'. George valued 'the favourable opinion' he expressed and his kindness in having asked that one of the remaining copies of his own work on the history of Selkirkshire should be sent to him.[90]

By December that year numerous members of the family had received copies of George's volume from him and, in giving him their reaction, most also took the opportunity to ask after the lawyer's health, which had been a cause for concern. Samuel Henry Romilly, Lizzy's eldest boy and then in his late fifties, was one of the first. He and 'a regular caravan' were staying at Huntington Park, the family house in Herefordshire.[91] The same day, George heard from 63 Onslow Square, where Margaret Elliot, 'Maggie', was delighted with his 'magnificent book' and so glad that he had 'accomplished this big task'. As an elderly lady she found 'finishing anything the most difficult'.[92] Then, writing from Redbourn House, St Albans, on 5 December, George's niece, Katie Scott, said that her family had been poring over his book 'in a desultory sort of way only, as yet'. She had been surprised 'what an attractive house the old Minto was. It fills me with awe to think what a huge amount of history you must have read before producing a book like this.'[93] Brother Henry received his copy of the 'uncommonly handsome volume' at Wantage and the same day Mimi Trotter wrote to her uncle thanking him for the 'splendid present' over whose cover she had only as yet been 'able to gloat'.[94] She also gave George the news that 'poor Fitz' had made up his mind to move into Edinburgh. She was sorry for him as Lizzy (his wife) was 'worse than she has ever been'. In bidding him goodbye Mimi said she would not be content until George came and wrote her name in her book.[95]

Also dated 5 December 1897, and rather as if the call had gone out for all the family to respond, Rollo Russell was the next to acknowledge receipt of George's book from Dunrozel. He thought the history of the family 'ought to be kept up … it would be interesting to descendants'.[96] Next was a note from William's son 'Fitz' himself, writing from 'Nisbet', his house at Jedburgh. It had been terrible, he said 'to think of you of all people being laid up' and he hoped George was 'getting strong … and fairly happy about yourself'.[97] Fanny followed with thanks for her copy of the 'big, brown, beautiful Border book', at the same time questioning how she was going to be able to read it. So far as George's health was concerned, his sister wondered whether the pain he still felt in his leg was 'the remains of sciatica'.[98] Congratulations followed from Admiral Charlie's widow, Harriette Liddell. Writing from 'Brydone', their home near Southampton, 'Har' spoke of the interest shown by Rachel, her younger daughter – Sybil, the older, being away. She recalled how her own father used to feel after completing each of his literary works.[99]

Lotty wrote to 'Dearest Doddy' from Laverstoke House in Hampshire before she 'took a dip into the noble book'. Her first thought had been how much Nina, William and Lizzy 'would have rejoiced' over it. She immediately wanted to know whether there was any possibility of her seeing her 'dear old Doddy' at Christmas; it 'was a sad part of old age that we cannot get to each other'. It was 18 December when, having 'strayed into Part 2' of his book (subsequent to page 263), Lotty wrote, 'how very proud I am of the first Sir Gilbert and how one regrets there are not more records of such an adventurous and noble life; he seems to have been just the kind of unflinching, brave patriot one admires, and so able withal'. She went on to say that as a Borderer herself she had been pleased to learn that 'even in those very rough days they did not wantonly kill' and she had been mortified 'to find how my knowledge of the whereabouts of places whose names are still so familiar to me, has faded from my memory. You must really miss your work … but I hope the knowledge and delight you have given to so many of us and others gives you some compensation'. Katie (Scott) had been 'so touched and proud' at George giving her a copy. Ending her panegyric, his motherly sister said 'the socks go by the same post as this'. Finally, Lotty could not resist mentioning the political scene, asking her brother whether there was 'anything to equal' Kaiser William II and his brother's speeches at Kiel, where the German Emperor was building a navy to rival that of Britain and France.[100]

Soon after, there was news from Henry and the Boileau family. Sir John's son, Francis G. M. Boileau, who had succeeded to the baronetcy in 1869, and who was a Fellow of both the Royal Society of Literature and the Society of Antiquaries, was very pleased with George's 'splendid volume' which obviously 'involved much labour and midnight oil'.[101] Henry had been 'astounded at finding the amount of labour and investigation' his brother had 'brought to bear'. Although he always knew that the Elliots 'came of a rough stock' he had 'hardly figured [their] forebears as such an utterly lawless lot'. The elderly diplomat had been reading about the life of Sir Stamford Raffles and toying with the scope there might be for a book about Java. Had the first

Earl Minto 'lived till the peace', Henry wrote, 'it would probably not have been given up'.[102]

It was six days after the start of 1898 that Fanny was attacked by influenza which soon turned to bronchitis. Although Dr Anderson did what he could for her, and he sat beside his patient for ten days or so, her illness got worse. She died on 17 January 1898 and was buried four days later with her husband Lord John Russell at Chenies near Amersham in Buckinghamshire. Lotty, the last of the Elliot sisters, was to die in June 1899. A few days later as the flow of letters to George continued, Admiral Sir George Augustus Elliot, the eighty-four-year-old sailor son of the second Earl's brother, wrote from Brant House on Wimbledon Common. He had sent him a copy of his father's memoir along with 'a little book on theology' in exchange for his family history.[103] Soon afterwards, Arthur Elliot, the editor of the *Edinburgh Review*, asked the lawyer to confirm that the draft review he was reading was mistaken in saying that Rousseau had been to Minto. He would have been such 'an incongruous personage in Teviotdale'. He also asked George to send any small alterations he wanted the printer to take account of in future copies to his house, 'Dimbola', on the Isle of Wight.[104]

In April, Francis, Lord Napier of Ettrick, the diplomat who had been at Naples with Lord Minto fifty years before, wrote a lengthy review of George's volume, entitled 'A Scottish Border Clan'.[105] Acknowledging that 'the production of works on these subjects' was often of 'a very beautiful and costly character', he went on to admit that such books constituted 'a considerable and increasing element in the literary recreation of the Scottish people'. In George's case, Napier said it had been 'a labour of love ... cast in the form most congenial to local and family history, a dignified quarto, well-printed, on good paper, enriched with views and portraits, plans and maps, suitable to the text but without ostentation'. He did not treat his subject 'in the narrow spirit of a genealogist'. Two chapters deserved 'the study of all readers of national history'. So far as the second part of George's work was concerned, Napier felt that there was nothing more remarkable in the social history of Scotland than the survival and prosperity of the great Border families, including that at Minto, after the civil disorder in the first half of the seventeenth century and the religious persecution in the reigns of the two last Stuart kings. After touching on the family's circumstances during the Napoleonic wars, the diplomat summarised the life of George's father, describing him as 'a man of natural shrewdness, cool judgement, literary culture and business faculty', noting that he did not inherit 'the gift of eloquence possessed by his father and grandfather, so necessary to impart relief to a figure on the parliamentary scene'. Finally, the old Lord declared that George's history showed his 'warm interest in his forefathers and his country' and provided a recent example of local and family history of 'the most sympathetic type'.

In the meantime, George's friend William Vernon had gifted 'Monen' to the Norwegian church in Holme, receiving the warm thanks of the community and a canteen of silver spoons and forks in a handsome case. The bishop responded to a petition from the inhabitants of the Mandal valley by sending it to King Oscar II, the dual monarch of Norway and Sweden, whom Admiral Charlie had entertained fifteen years or so before, and who conferred on Vernon the dignity of a Knight of St Olaf. In August 1898 the family said their last goodbyes and sailed from Kristiansand in the *Montebello*, a 1,700-ton steamer owned by the Wilson Line from Hull, taking up their residence once again in England at 14 Waterloo Crescent, Dover. During the following summer William Vernon played in the Paters' cricket match at Castlemount School in the town, and finished writing his *Readings on the Paradiso* in August that year.

On 3 January 1901 Field-Marshall Roberts returned victorious from the Second Boer War and was immediately created an earl by the Queen. Two days later, lawyer George dined with the Vernons but, as William Vernon was to say, 'it was for the last time in his life'. It seems that George had taken 18 Clifton Gardens, Folkestone, until May but on 14 February 1901, two weeks after Queen Victoria's funeral, 'poor Doddy died of an attack of influenza while we were out of town. This loss of an old pal was a great grief to me', wrote William Vernon.[106] Only Henry would outlive him.

George Francis Gilbert Elliot had been the family's legal reference point for half a century. It was as if he ran its switchboard, receiving communications from everyone and dispensing advice almost daily. He kept the family in touch with the news and gave comfort. Having been an equity draughtsman at Lincoln's Inn, he took a particular interest in the meaning and intended purpose of all parliamentary paperwork, and was often at work to aid the family's politicians. On numerous occasions he was called on to calculate the odds and determine a project's likelihood of success. 'Dear Doddy' was expected on one day to convey the detail of parliamentary debates to his father as well as his brothers, or shop in St James's for esoteric toiletries requested by siblings whose supplies had run out while they were overseas. On the next day he might be required to give an expert opinion about property, estate management, matrimonial disputes, money matters, and that other ever-present subject of Elliot concern – ships and naval personnel. With the family involved both directly and indirectly with various court-martials – all of which Doddy was called upon to explain or help the family comprehend – George became almost as knowledgeable about naval affairs, and their significance politically, as the family's admirals.

George never married but he enjoyed feminine company and was rarely out of sorts, physically or mentally. He had an even temperament which attracted him to all with whom he came into contact. He was kind, warm-hearted and generous. Doddy's death occurred at a time when his brother's son, Gilbert, the fourth Earl was governor-general of Canada, from where he would return in 1904 before going out to India as viceroy of India in November 1905.

# EPILOGUE

By the turn of the century the heyday of the Elliot family was over, never to return. The Great War which followed the reign of Edward VII was to result in the loss of 700,000 British and Irish lives, with acute pressures both before and after which contributed to the decline of the Elliots and other governing families. What Charles Masterman described as 'the flower of the British aristocracy' in *England after the War* died among the carnage in Belgium. Some 42 of the 225 relatives of Scottish peers who served in the war were killed in action, among whom were three Elliot sons in their twenties, one in 1915 the others in 1917.

Growing debts among landowners, caused by a declining income stream from falling agricultural prices in the last ten years of Victoria's reign, were made harder to bear when in 1894 Sir William Harcourt, Gladstone's Chancellor, introduced a single estate duty which could be charged on all property, real and personal. The imposition of such death duties had been designed to help pay for increased spending on the Navy. Then in 1907, Herbert Asquith brought in an unearned income surcharge which was levied on rental income so occasioning income from land between 1880 and 1910 to fall by some 25 per cent. The result had been the sale of a number of estates owned by such landlords as Lord Kinnoull and the Duke of Queensberry, but what had been a trickle before the Great War soon became a steady stream afterwards, with several estates being broken up as death duties and income tax increased steadily.

In June 1919 the US president, the French prime minister and David Lloyd George met together at Versailles to devise a method by which Germany would pay reparations for the war, Maynard Keynes being against them and in favour of the mutual cancellation of Allied war debts. It led to punitive conditions being put on Germany and that country's hyperinflation. In terms of the Beaufort scale, what appeared to be a 'gentle breeze' blowing through the management of larger estates during the last decade of Victoria's reign became a 'moderate gale' in the Edwardian era, and a 'violent storm' moving towards 'hurricane force' between the wars. By 1922, hyperinflation in Germany meant that wages had to be paid twice a day if workers were to have the chance to spend them before the notes lost their value. In Britain three years later, the overvalued pound, and an attempt to reduce prices and wages, caused the General Strike, and in October 1929 the New York stock market crashed. The slump and tighter credit control followed, and Britain came off the gold standard in 1931. Three years later, with Adolf Hitler the new Chancellor, social turmoil in Germany resulted in mass unemployment.

By 1945 the world had paid for appeasement and the trail of damage included Britain's near bankruptcy. It looked to some as if it was only a matter of time before the landed classes and large estates would disappear for ever. By the end of George VI's reign, the power of the House of Commons had increased and that of the Lords was in decline. The head of the Elliot family no longer ruled from Eaton Square, and the Roxburghshire house and estate, described by Fanny to her father in 1857 as 'that loveliest and dearest of places' and the 'happiest and most perfect home that children ever had', was under threat. The Camelot-like world where Fanny's 'meticulous conscientiousness' (as Bertie described some of her thoughts) and a passionate conviction for justice had ruled, was no more.

The post-war period was an especially difficult one. Debts became bigger, resources smaller and the family's dreams could not be turned into reality. The end of Minto House was in sight. During the war it had been requisitioned and in 1952 the house was leased to a girls' school, being purchased for the sum of £20,000 ten years later. The school closed in 1966, only to be unoccupied for twenty-six years. In 1972, the sixth Earl Minto, who had served in the Malay campaign (1949–51) and in Cyprus before retiring from the Army in 1956, applied for permission to demolish the property. Listed building consent was granted on the grounds that any restoration was impracticable but little happened during the following years. The sixth Earl then became leader of the Borders Regional Council in 1990, continuing as a member of the Planning Committee, when a move was made by Gregory Lauder-Frost, a member of the Monday Club at Westminster, to set up a preservation trust to rebuild and restore Minto House. Lord Minto immediately made it clear that the house was not for sale. In 1991, when the property was roofless, another hare-brained scheme appeared in the press whereby every stone would have been dismantled and shipped to Japan for reassembly. Nevertheless, during the summer of 1992 matters came to a head. In August the dilapidated building was badly damaged when workmen set it alight as a preliminary to demolition the next day. The following month saw last-ditch attempts being made to save part of the house.

The planning history for Minto House shows that in October 1993 the house was demolished and 'top-soiled over'. In August 1994 the erection of the first of four dwellings was approved, followed by a second house in 1998. Two years later approval was given to a third dwelling house together with stables and garages, while in December 2003 a fourth house was approved along with stable and workshop. Nothing now remains of the original house, apart from the Sir Lorimer Garden which had been created in 1906 by the architect Sir Robert Stodart Lorimer.

Unfortunately, marital difficulties in the family were to emerge. In 1952 the sixth Earl of Minto married Lady Caroline Child-Villiers (the daughter of the Earl of Jersey), from whom he obtained a divorce in 1965. Later that year he married Mary Ballantine, the daughter of Peter Ballantine of New Jersey, USA, a marriage which was to last until his wife's death in 1983. It was in 1991 that the sixth Earl, then sixty-three, married for the third time; his bride was Mrs Caroline Larlham (née Godfrey), a thirty-nine-year-old ex-model. This marriage lasted until 2004 when they were divorced, the earl's health at that time having deteriorated to the point where he needed daily treatment.

In 2008 the press reported that the sixth Earl's third wife, then living in a small flat in Italy, was to sue her late husband's executors, Timothy Melgund, now the seventh Earl, and the Edinburgh solicitor Douglas Connell. The dowager countess desired a ruling that some £200,000 of assets transferred by her husband to the family's Minto Trust should be returned to his estate to pay a legacy she was due. The disagreement over the will revealed deep divisions in the family, with Timothy Melgund, chief executive of a greetings cards and stationery company, accusing his stepmother of deserting his father when he became ill some years before his death.

From the long perspective of the nineteenth century, it seems that the Elliot family won its struggle for sustained prosperity, but by the end of the twentieth century it was a shadow of itself. With the exception of several great estates still in hereditary occupation, landowners – historically the governing class – had by and large lost their traditional role to a variety of democratic forces while landownership itself now includes some wealthy foreign purchasers.

The Elliot family motto as published by George Elliot on the cover of The Border Elliots in 1897 – 'He needs not the bow' or 'Elliots are not warlike', probably taken from an ode by Horace.

# Notes and References

The following abbreviations have been used:

BLO     Bodleian Library, Oxford
BL     British Library
EUL     Edinburgh University Library
GUL     Glasgow University Library
NA     National Archives, Kew
NLS     National Library of Scotland
NMM     National Maritime Museum
USHL     University of Southampton, Hartley Library
YBL     Yale University, Beinecke Library

## Introduction

1. *The Times*, 2 August 1859, p. 3, issue 23374, col. A.

2. Carman Miller and Philip Woods, 'Kynynmound, Gilbert John Elliot Murray, fourth Earl of Minto (1845–1914)', *Oxford Dictionary of National Biography*, Oxford University Press, 2004.

3. Melgund and its castle in the county of Angus became an Elliot property when the first Earl's father, Sir Gilbert Elliot, married Agnes Murray Kynynmound, the heiress of Melgund.

4. NLS MS 31057, ff. 22–23, Catherine Rutherford's Journal 1832.

5. *Letters of the First Earl of Minto*, vol. 3, pp. 400–401.

6. H. Taylor, *Autobiography 1800–1875*, 2 vols, 1885.

7. MacCarthy and Russell (eds), *Lady John Russell*, 30 August to 5 September 1840.

8. Born in 1792, Lord John Russell's first marriage in 1835 was to Lady Ribblesdale, who brought with her from her previous marriage (according to MacCarthy and Russell, pp. 48–49) one son, Thomas (to become the third Baron), and three daughters, Adelaide Lister (Mrs Drummond), Isobel Lister (Mrs Warburton), and Elizabeth Lister (Lady Melvill). Lady Ribblesdale died giving birth to the second of the two daughters she gave Lord John, Georgiana (1836) and Victoria (1838).

9. MacCarthy and Russell (eds), *Lady John Russell*, Fanny to Lady Mary, 7 February 1843.

10. G. P. Gooch (ed.), *The Later Correspondence of Lord John Russell 1840–1878*, 2 vols, London, 1925. Lord John Russell's record of the crisis between 8 and 19 December 1845.

11. MacCarthy and Russell (eds), *Lady John Russell*, Fanny to Lord John, 14 December 1840.

12. Ibid., Fanny to Lady Minto, 29 March 1848.

13. Ibid., Fanny to Lady Mary, 10 December 1848.

14. Ibid., Fanny's Journal, 31 March and 5 April 1855.

15. Ibid., Fanny to Lord John, 13 July 1855.

16. Ibid., Lord John Russell's dispatch, 27 October 1860.

17. The Romilly's third son, Hugh (1856–1892) arrived in Fiji in 1879 and remained in the South Pacific until 1890 serving in New Guinea as the Queen's special commissioner. In 1891 he left the colonial service and took charge of a prospecting mission to Mashonaland for the Northumberland Mining Syndicate.

18. *The Times*, 2 August 1887, p. 7, issue 23043, col. E.

19. GUL, Correspondence of James McNeil Whistler with Cyril Rower *c.* 1876.

20. NLS MS 12319, William's Diary for June 1890.

21. In 1892 Gladstone and the Foreign Office were anxious to annex Uganda. Sir Gerald Herbert Portal was sent out as a Commissioner to report on whether the country should remain under British control. He took with him his brother, Captain Melville Raymond Portal, only for him to die on the journey.

22. BLO MS Eng.Lett.e.113, ff. 66–68, Fanny to Rollo, 29 July 1893.

23. BLO MS Eng.Lett.e.113, ff. 72–73, Fanny to Rollo, 3 February 1894.

24. NLS MS 31056, ff. 5–6, Catherine Rutherford's Journal, September 1832.

25. NLS MS 11765A, ff. 21–24, Gilbert Elliot to Harriet, 22 October 1854.

26. NLS MS 12014, Lady Harriet's Journal, 11–13 June 1844.

27. NLS MS 12364, ff. 38–39, Thomas Headlam to Nina, Lady Minto, 17 July 1874.

28. Sir Henry George Elliot, *Some Revolutions and Other Diplomatic Experiences* (ed. Gertrude Elliot, his daughter; John Murray, London, 1922), pp. 4–7.

29. Gertrude Elliot's 'Introduction', pp. ix, in *Some Revolutions and Other Diplomatic Experiences*.

30. NLS MS 11899A, ff. 109–112, Henry Elliot to Lady Minto, 30 March 1853.

31. Henry's only son, Sir Francis Edmund Hugh Elliot (1851–1940) served in the diplomatic service, becoming minister to Greece.

32. NLS MS 13091, ff. 31–32 Gilbert Elliot to George, 12 September 1853.

33. Sir William H. Cope's *History of the Rifle Brigade*, chaps 9 and 10, pp. 296–297 and 298–303 respectively.

34. NLS MS 11765A, ff. 98–99, Gilbert to Lotty, 25 January and 18 April 1856.

35. NLS MS 13090, ff. 173–175, Charles to George, 1 March 1866.

36. NLS MS 12251, ff. 177–183, Charles and Har Elliot to William, 13 December 1890.

37. NLS MS 13090, ff. 195–198, Charles to George, 29 May 1881.

38. NLS MS 12252, ff. 51–54, George to William, 6 September 1859.

39. NLS MS 12252, ff. 76–77, George to William, 30 November 1876.

40. NLS MS 12252, ff. 82–83, George to William, 16 March 1880.

41. NLS MS 12252, ff. 93–96, George to William, 10 April 1880.

42. NLS MS 12252, ff. 108–109 George to William, 2 November 1889.

43. John Francis Stanley Russell's second marriage to Maria Cooke also ended in divorce in 1915. His third marriage to Mary Annette Beauchamp also ended in divorce in 1919.

I

## The First and Second Earls of Minto

1. From *Life and Letters of Sir Gilbert Elliot, First Earl of Minto from 1751 to 1806*, edited by his great-niece, the Countess of Minto, in three volumes, Longmans, Green, and Co., 1874. vol. 1, p. 86. Subsequently abbreviated to *Letters of First Earl of Minto*.

2. *Letters of First Earl of Minto*, vol. 1, pp. 56–72. Harriet, Lady Elliot's sister, married Sir James Harris, who became the ambassador at the court of Catherine in St Petersburg. The couple had lived in Russia for four years but the climate did not suit Harriet.

3. *Letters of First Earl of Minto*, vol. 1, p. 113.

4. Sir Elijah Impey, the Chief Justice in Bengal, had refused a reprieve or a stay of execution in March 1775 for a Brahman called Nandkumar who had charged Warren Hastings with corruption.

5. *Letters of First Earl of Minto*, vol. 2, p. 66.

6. Ibid., vol. 2, p. 153.

7. Ibid., vol. 2, pp. 157–158 and 162–164.

8. Ibid., vol. 2, pp. 209–222.

9. Ibid., vol. 2, pp. 292–3.

10. Ibid., vol. 2, pp. 374–379.

11. Ibid., vol. 3, pp. 1–2.

12. Ibid., vol. 3, pp. 6 and 9.

13. Ibid., vol. 3, p. 115.

14. Ibid., vol. 3, p. 121.

15. Ibid., vol. 3, pp. 191–192.

16. Ibid., vol. 3, pp. 221–223.

17. See Edith Haden-Guest's essays in R. G. Thorne (ed.), *The History of Parliament: The House of Commons 1790–1820*, 5 vols, HMSO, London, 1986, pp. 390–396.

18. Sir George Elliot (1784–1863), the second son of the first Earl of Minto, was a naval officer and politician. He joined the Navy when he was ten years old and was present at Hotham's action off Toulon and at the battles of St Vincent and the Nile. Promoted lieutenant in 1800, he served in the *San Josef* and *St George* under Nelson. He was promoted commander the following year and went to the Mediterranean as a volunteer with Nelson aboard HMS *Victory*. He was to be regarded by Nelson as one of the best officers in the Navy. He took his father to and from India while captain of HMS *Modeste* and HMS *Hussar*. From 1827 to 1830 he commanded HMS *Victory* and in September 1830 he was nominated a Companion of the Bath. He was to be in Parliament until 1835, his subsequent political career forming part of the forthcoming story.

19. Lord Minto writing to his wife from Calcutta, 31 July 1807, from *Lord Minto in India: Life and Letters of Gilbert Elliot, First Earl of Minto from 1807 to 1814*, edited by his great-niece the Countess of Minto, Longmans, Green & Co., London, 1880. Subsequently abbreviated to *Minto India Letters*.

20. *Minto India Letters*, p. 28.

21. Ibid., p. 94, from Lord Minto to his wife, 24 May 1808.

22. Ibid., p. 231.

23. Sir (Thomas) Stamford Bingley Raffles (1781–1826) was the colonial governor and founder of Singapore. With his customary attention to detail, Raffles sent agents to Madura, Bali and Java, and won the support of the Sultan of Palembang. On arriving in Melaka in May 1811, Minto approved Raffles's recommended invasion route. To the disappointment of the expedition's military commander, Colonel Robert Rollo Gillespie, the Dutch capitulated in September 1811 and Raffles was appointed lieutenant-governor.

24. *Minto India Letters*, pp. 302 and 351.

25. Ibid., pp. 323–325, from Lady Catherine Elliot to Lord Minto, 1 May 1811.

26. Ibid., pp. 327–331. Lady Minto's description of 'Harry', Lord Palmerston was to be confirmed later by the second Lord Minto. She said that 'he is doing very well – with a clear head and a good understanding. He will never be a great man because he has no great views; but he is painstaking and gentlemanlike to the highest degree, and will always swim where greater talents might sink.'

27. His son Gilbert adopted the title Viscount Melgund in 1813 as a courtesy title during his minority.

28. *Minto India Letters*, pp. 384–385, Lord Minto to Lady Minto, 19 May 1814.

29. Ibid., pp. 387–389, Lady Minto to Lord Minto, 19 May 1814.

30. Ibid., p. 390, Lord Minto to Lady Minto, 27 May 1814.

31. Ibid., p. 391. Stephen Lee suggests that the disease suffered by Lord Minto had been 'a stranguary' or a urinary disease of some long standing.

32. Ibid., p. 394.

33. *Letters of the First Earl of Minto*, vol. 3, p. 404.

34. Ibid., vol. 3, p. 220.

35. Sir Hugh Inglis (1744–1820) was three times the chairman of the East India Company and the Member of Parliament for Ashburton between 1802 and 1806 along with Walter Palk. The latter maintained his seat in this dual constituency both before and after Minto's election in 1806.

36. Earl Minto's father-in-law, Patrick Brydone (1736–1818), had been a great traveller, publishing an acclaimed account of his visit to Sicily and Malta in 1773. In 1781 he was appointed Controller of the Stamp Office for life, which brought in some £600 per annum. Little is known about his wife and the latter part of his life was spent in 'retirement and almost obscurity'. He died at Lennel House in June 1818.

37. *Letters of the First Earl of Minto*, vol. 3, pp. 400–401.

38. Lady Mary Elizabeth Elliot was Lord and Lady Minto's first child to reach adulthood; she was born in 1811. William Hugh Elliott (Lord Melgund) followed on 19 March 1814 while Lady Minto was at Chamonix. Henry was born when the couple were in Switzerland, at Geneva on 30 June 1817 but when the couple reached Interlaken later that year (26 September 1817) it appears that a son who had been born to the couple on 31 October 1807, a little more than a year after their marriage in 1806, died suddenly aged ten. He had been christened Gilbert Elliot, and conventionally styled Viscount Melgund.

39. MacCarthy and Russell (eds), *Lady John Russell*, p. 2.

40. Born in London, William Henry Playfair (1790–1857) became one of Edinburgh's most enlightened mathematicians and architects. Much travelled in Italy, he beat off eight architects who submitted designs for Edinburgh University's Old College in 1816. His contemporaries praised him for his eclecticism. He died having undertaken over sixty commissions in the region of Edinburgh.

41. NLS MS 11976, ff. 3–4, described as a disbound notebook containing an incomplete journal of Lord Minto's tour in 1808.

42. Lady Edith Haden-Guest's note, p. 692 in Namier and Brooke (eds) *The History of Parliament: The House of Commons 1754–1790*, HMSO, London, 1964.

43. *Minto India Letters*, pp. 386–387.

44. *The Times*, 8 December 1819, p. 3, issue 10796, col. E.

45. *The Times*, 17 November 1820, p. 2, issue 11094, col. D.

46. *The Times*, 31 May 1824, p. 3, issue 12352, col. B.

2

## A Governess's First Year (1829–1830)

1. NLS MS 31051 Catherine's Journal, 1825 to 1829 includes letters to Miss McGilchrist dated 12 October and 5 December 1825.

2. Catherine Stephens was a soprano and actress who became the Countess of Essex in 1838. Watford called her the 'queenly Kitty Stephens' and it was rumoured she earned £5,000 from one tour to Ireland in 1826. She was being paid £5 per week in 1823.

3. Dr Robert Gordon (1786–1853) was an original thinker and eloquent preacher who in 1825 had just been translated from Hope Park to the new North Church in Edinburgh.

4. NLS MS 31052 Catherine's Journal, March 1829 to March 1830, with additions from the (undated) record she gave Miss McGilchrist.

5. The Walcot Place referred to may have been an address of that name in Lambeth. Archie Turnbull's death is recorded in Catherine's journal for 18 October 1832.

6. In *Roundabout Papers*, Thackeray describes a similar rough crossing to Calais and his disinclination to travel further that night on his road to Paris. He knew the Calais hotel as one of the cleanest, one of the dearest, and one of the most comfortable hotels on the continent of Europe.

7. Colonel John Drinkwater Bethune (1762–1844) was an army officer and military historian who had been secretary for the military department and deputy judge-advocate during the occupation of Corsica and the vice-royalty of Sir Gilbert Elliot (first Earl of Minto). In 1829 he would have been comptroller of army accounts, an office he held from 1811 until 1835 when it was abolished. He was to live at Balfour Castle in Fife and become known for the journal he kept during the siege of Gibraltar in 1782. He married Eleanor Congleton of Edinburgh in 1799. In addition to the daughters referred to by Catherine, their eldest son was another John (1801–1851), who was a law member of the governor-general's council in Calcutta. He became known for promoting women's education in India.

8. Felton's *Treatise on Carriages* makes no mention of the name. The family's phrase came from such usages as a 'bang-up cove' (a dashing fellow who spends his money freely), to 'bang up prime' (to bring your horses up in a dashing or fine style) and a 'slap-up gal in a bang-up chariot' as Dickens had it.

9. Maria Louise was the daughter of Francis I, Emperor of Austria, and Princess Theresa of Naples. Of French nationality, she had been born in 1791 and had married Napoleon shortly after his divorce from Josephine. Her son Napoleon II, infant Emperor of France, was born in 1811 and died in 1832. She was to marry morganatically her grand chamberlain in 1834, Charles-René, Count of Bombelles. She died in Vienna in December 1847.

10. The Mintos' visitor, John Peter Boileau (1794–1869) was a learned antiquary and county magistrate in Norfolk who lived at Thursford Hall, near Fakenham until he bought the Ketteringham estate and built Ketteringham Hall, where he resided from 1841. He had married Lady Catherine Sarah Elliot, the third daughter of the first Earl of Minto on 14 November 1825 and was to become a baronet in the coronation honours.

11. College records show that Lord Melgund and Henry George Elliot signed the entry book at Eton on 31 October 1829.

12. Soon after Gilbert Rutherford joined HMS *Winchester*, she sailed for Jamaica.

13. La Muette de Portici was a one-act opera by Daniel Auber. The main character, Fenella, the mute girl, is eventually driven to suicide and Masaniello, her brother, murdered. The character of Fenella was taken from the 1822 Walter Scott novel *Peveril of the Peak*.

14. Maria Malibran was born in Paris, the daughter of a Spanish tenor. She was one of the most famous opera singers of the nineteenth century. The range, power and flexibility of her voice were extraordinary. She became a legend after her early death at the age of twenty-eight.

15. Henry V of France, the disputed King of France, was given the title of Duc de Bordeaux at his birth in 1820, also becoming the Comte de Chambord. He was the younger son of King Charles X by his wife, Princess Caroline Ferdinande Louise, daughter of Francis I of the Two Sicilies.

16. NLS MS 31061 Catherine in Paris (Poems and Drawings).

17. NLS MS 31053 Catherine's Journal, 29 March 1830 to 14 June 1830.

18. When the Whigs returned to power in the following November (1830), the third Marquess of Lansdowne (1780–1863), then in mid-career, turned down the post of Foreign Secretary in Grey's cabinet and settled instead for that of Lord President of the Council.

3
## The Family Returns to Switzerland (1830–1831)

1. This chapter is based principally on Catherine's journals: NLS MS 31053, 27 May to 14 June 1830; NLS MS 31054, 15 June to 14 September 1830, and NLS MS 31055, 25 November 1830 to 29 October 1831.

2. An American diplomat who arrived in Geneva in 1822 was surprised to find that there was not a single steamboat on the lake. He was an enthusiast for such vessels and he personally commissioned the building of a wooden hull from a boatyard in Bordeaux, and boilers and engine from a company in Liverpool. Church's vessel, named the *Guillaume Tell*, came into service in 1823. Its success prompted a new company to build the *Winkelried*, which was capable of carrying 300 passengers. The journey from Geneva to Lausanne then took 4 hours and 40 minutes. Competition increased when the Vaudois decided to commission a boat from the yard of Boulton & Watt in Birmingham. This boat, to be called the *Leman*, was built on the shore of the lake by shipwrights from England and sailed on her maiden voyage in July 1826. She had accommodation for 500 passengers and a speed of 17.5 kph.

3. James Fenimore Cooper's *The Red Rover* had been published in Paris in three volumes in 1827 by Hector Bossange. Another steamboat called the *Red Rover* was the first to service the Hatchie River in Tennessee in 1828. Catherine and the children appear to have called the lake steamer *Leman*, the 'Red Rover'. The captain made them particularly at home on his vessel.

4. The camera lucida was patented by William Hyde Woolaston in 1807. It performed an optical superimposition of the subject which is being viewed upon the surface which the artist is drawing. Being able to see the scene and the surface of the paper simultaneously, the artist was able to duplicate parts of the scene on the drawing surface, thereby helping produce a true perspective.

5. On this occasion Catherine's journal contains no mention of Gilbert's ship calling at Rhode Island on its way to England.

6. Giovanni Antonio Galignani (1757–1821) had been an Italian newspaper publisher until his death in 1821. Thereafter the paper, with its English edition, was carried on by his two sons. It enjoyed a high reputation and followed a policy of encouraging good relations between France and England.

7. The family named their boat *Bawsy* after a character whose name was spelt 'Bawsie' in the fable of 'The Cock and the Fox' by Robert Henryson (died *c.* 1490) in the Denton Fox edition published by the Clarendon Press, Oxford, 1981.

8. Thomas Stamford Raffles (later Sir) went out to Penang with his first wife, Olivia Devenish, in 1805 when the first Lord Minto was governor-general of Bengal. She died suddenly in November 1814. He married his second wife, Sophia Hull (1786–1858), in February 1817. A day before Raffles's forty-fifth birthday in 1826 Sophia found him dead at the bottom of a spiral staircase at their home at Hendon, Middlesex. Faced with financial problems, she resolved to live abroad and during the summer of 1830 visited Bern, Zürich, Einsiedeln and Zug, and spent six weeks at Interlaken before a trek in the mountains on horseback.

9. Louis Philippe of France (1773–1850) came to the throne in August 1830 and his eldest son, as Prince Royal, took the title Duc d'Orléans. In 1832 his daughter, Princess Louise-Marie Thérèse Charlotte Isabelle (1812–1850) became the first Queen of Belgium. He ruled in an unpretentious fashion, was much loved and called the 'Citizen King'. The economic crisis of 1847 led to a reversal in the attitude of the citizenry and when the February 1848 revolution occurred he abdicated. Proposals to continue the Bourbon line failed and he escaped to England and lived at Claremont in Surrey until his death.

10. Domenico Donizelli (1790–1873) was a remarkable Italian tenor who became most famous as Pollione in Bellini's *Norma*.

11. Granville Leveson-Gower, first Earl Granville (1773–1846), was a younger, paternal half-brother of the first Duke of Sutherland. He served as British ambassador to Russia between 1804 and 1807, and to France in 1824–28, 1830–35 and 1835–41. He married Lady Harriet Cavendish (1785–1862), daughter of the fifth Duke of Devonshire. He was created Viscount Granville in 1815 and Earl Granville in 1833.

12. Lady Northland was the wife of Thomas Knox, second Viscount Northland. He was created Earl of Ranfuriy of Duncannon (in the peerage of Ireland) later in 1831.

13. Carlo Andrea, Count Pozzo di Borgo (1764–1842), was a Corsican politician who became a Russian diplomat. During the English protectorate of Corsica between 1794 and 1796 he was president of the council of state under Sir Gilbert Elliot (the second Lord Minto's father). His influence at the Palace of the Tuilleries declined with the accession of Charles X but in the revolution of 1830 he did good service in preventing difficulties with Russia.

14. Possibly John Nicholas Fazakerley (1787–1852), MP, one of whose properties was Burwood House in Surrey.

15. MacCarthy and Russell (eds), *Lady John Russell*, p. 14.

16. The editors of *Lady John Russell* allowed Fanny's misspelling of Langholm (as Langham) on page 15 to go uncorrected.

17. MacCarthy and Russell (eds), *Lady John Russell*, p. 15.

4

## Diplomacy in Berlin (1832)

1. See A. E. Smith's excellent resume of the political life of Charles Grey, *Lord Grey, 1764–1845*, Clarendon Press, Oxford, 1990.

2. Thursday 19 July 1832, reported the following day by *The Times*, p. 2, issue 14909, col. A.

3. USHL MS GC/MI/62, Lord Minto to Palmerston, 12 July 1832.

4. Leopold (1790–1865) was the youngest son of Francis Frederick, Duke of Saxe-Coburg-Saalfeld. He served as a general in the Russian army and married Princess Charlotte, daughter of the Prince Regent (later George IV) in 1816. After her death the following year, Leopold remained in England. In 1830 he rejected the throne of Greece but in 1831 he accepted election as king of the newly formed Belgium. In 1832 he married a daughter of King Louis Philippe of France and subsequently brought about the marriage of his niece Queen Victoria to his nephew Prince Albert.

5. *Letters of the First Earl Minto*, vol. 3, p. 3.

6. So far as the family is concerned, this chapter is based on volumes 5 and 6 of Catherine's Journal (NLS MS 31056, MS 31057 and MS 31057).

7. Louise-Marie (1812–1850) married King Leopold I on 9 August 1832 at Compiègne.

8. USHL MS GC/MI/63, Lord Minto to Palmerston, 5 September 1832.

9. USHL MS GC/MI/64, Lord Minto to Palmerston, 11 September 1832.

10. Sir Thomas Cartwright (1795–1850) was envoy extraordinary and minister plenipotentiary to the German Confederation in Frankfurt from 1830 to 1838. He spent the last twelve years of his life in Stockholm. Lord Minto probably heard from Cartwright about the late resolutions of the Diet in Frankfurt which Palmerston said 'could not fail to attract the serious attention of HMG'. The Foreign Secretary had already sent Minto, ahead of his arrival in Berlin, the same dispatch as that which had gone to the British envoy in Vienna, where the *Zollverein* was meeting.

11. Ludwig I (1786–1868) was King of Bavaria from 1825 until the 1848 revolutions among the German states. In 1810, he married Theresa of Saxe-Hildburghausen (1792–1854). Ludwig supported the Greek fight for independence and his second son, Otto (1815–1867), was to be elected King of Greece that year (1832).

12. Auguste Wilhelmine Luise Prinzessin von Hessen-Kassel (1797–1889) married Adolphus Frederick Hanover, first Duke of Cambridge, son of George III, first at Kassel on 7 May and again later in the month at Buckingham Palace. She is buried in St George's Chapel at Windsor Castle.

13. In 1825, John Liston, the leading comic actor of his time created a farce where the hero, Peter Pry, is consumed with curiosity and unable to mind his own business. Dressed in striped trousers and hessian boots, tail coat and top hat, he became an endearing character that came to be stamped on snuff boxes and all the leading potteries produced figures of him.

14. On 25 May 1833 Catherine writes from 21 Unter den Linden.

15. MacCarthy and Russell (eds), *Lady John Russell*, p. 17.

16. Ralph Abercromby (1803–1868) had been attached to the mission in Frankfurt in 1821, to the embassy at The Hague in February 1824, and at Paris in November 1824. At the age of twenty-four he became a précis writer at the Foreign Office and a year later he was secretary to Viscount Strangford's special mission to Brazil, and to Lord Ponsonby's mission to Brussels in 1830. Ralph became secretary of legation in Berlin on 14 July 1831.

17. Born in Berlin, Johann Peter Friedrich Ancillon (1767–1837) studied theology in Geneva but his reputation as a historical scholar led to an appointment at a military academy. By 1818 he was director of a department in the Prussian Ministry of Foreign Affairs under Count Bernstorff, and in the spring of 1832 he became head of the ministry upon Bernstorff's retirement. Of Huguenot stock and bourgeois origin, he believed that the rigid class distinctions of the Prussian system were the philosophically ideal basis of the state. He had a strong personal influence at the Prussian court on the character of Frederick William III.

18. USHL MS GC/MI/65/67, Lord Minto to Palmerston, 26 and 29 September 1832.

19. Granville Leveson-Gower (1773–1846), first Earl Granville, had been attached to Lord Malmesbury's missions to France in 1796–7 and was envoy to Prussia in 1798. Appointed ambassador to Paris in 1824, he served there until 1828. He was reappointed to Paris by Lord Grey in 1830, where he remained until 1841.

20. USHL MS GC/MI/67, Lord Minto to Lord Granville, 28 September 1832.

21. USHL MS GC/MI/70, Lord Minto to Palmerston, 7 October 1832.

22. NLS MS 31057, ff. 22–23, Catherine Rutherford's Journal 1832.

23. A reference to George William Chad (1784–1849), who had been Minister to Saxony between 1829 and 1830. He subsequently became envoy to Prussia, being replaced by Lord Minto in 1832 after he had fallen out with Count Ancillon and lost the confidence of Lord Palmerston.

24. USHL MS GC/MI/71, Lord Minto to Palmerston, 8 October 1832.

25. Count Clam-Martinitz married Lady Selina Meade, daughter of the second earl of Clanwilliam in 1821 and became aide-de-camp of the Emperor of Austria.

26. Edward Law, first Earl of Ellenborough, married twice. He divorced Lady Jane Digby (1807–1881), his second wife by Act of Parliament in 1830. Jane Digby had numerous affairs, including one with her cousin, one with Ludwig I of Bavaria and one with Prince Felix zu Schwarzenberg (1800–1852).

27. The Swedish envoy and minister in Berlin was Genseric Brandel (1782–1833). He was to die at Berlin on 16 December 1833 when the Norwegian Adam Löwenskiold was made chargé d'affaires, a post he held for more than a year until the next envoy was appointed.

28. USHL MS GC/MI/72, Lord Minto to Palmerston, 10 October 1832.

29. USHL MS GC/MI/73, Lord Minto to Palmerston, 10 October 1832.

30. USHL MS GC/MI/75, Lord Minto to Palmerston, 14 October 1832.

31. USHL MS GC/MI/77, Lord Minto to Palmerston, 17 October 1832.

32. USHL MS GC/MI/78, Lord Minto to Palmerston, 17 October 1832.

33. USHL MS GC/MI/79, Lord Minto to Palmerston, 18 October 1832.

34. Sir Robert Adair (1763–1855) was engaged between August 1831 and July 1835 on a special mission to the newly crowned king of the Belgians, which, along with the efforts of Minto and others, was to help prevent war between Flemish and Dutch troops. He had been appointed GCB (civil) in 1831 (see Oxford *DNB* essay by H. G. C. Matthew).

35. USHL MS GC/MI/80, Lord Minto to Palmerston, 21 October 1832.

36. USHL MS GC/MI/81, Lord Minto to Palmerston, 22 October 1832.

37. Étienne Maurice Gérard, Comte Gérard (1773–1852), had been in command of the Northern French army in 1831 and was successful in driving the Netherlands army out of Belgium in thirteen days. In 1832 he commanded the besieging army in what has been described as the notorious and scientific siege of the citadel of Antwerp. Baron Haxo (1774–1838) was Gérard's renowned engineer.

38. USHL MS GC/MI/94, Lord Minto to Palmerston, 11 November 1832.

39. The Naval Biographical Database at Portsmouth gives the date of Charlie's joining of the Navy as 6 May 1832. It was not until 27 June 1838 that he obtained his seniority as a lieutenant. His first posting as a lieutenant was aboard second-rate HMS *Rodney* in August 1838. Other references to his career are given as they appear in the text.

40. George Augustus Elliot had been born in Calcutta in 1813. He entered the Navy in November 1827, becoming a captain in 1840. He married Hersey Susan Sidney, the only daughter of Lt-Col. Wauchope, in 1842. He was

to captain HMS *Volage* in China and, by 1843, HMS *Eurydice* in North America. During the Crimean War he commanded HMS *James Watt* in the Baltic. In 1874 he became MP for Chatham and was given a KCB in 1877, the year before he retired. He published *A Treatise on Future Naval Battles and How to Fight Them* in 1885 and died in London in December 1901.

41. USHL MS GC/MI/98, Lord Minto to Palmerston, 20 November 1832.

42. USHL MS GC/MI/100, Lord Minto to Palmerston, 24 November 1832.

43. USHL MS GC/MI/104, Lord Minto to Palmerston, 1 December 1832.

44. USHL MS GC/M 1/105, Lord Minto to Palmerston, 1 December 1832.

45. USHL MS GC/M 1/106, Lord Minto to Palmerston, 1 December 1832.

46. USHL MS GC/MI/108, Lord Minto to Palmerston, 7 December 1832.

47. HMS *Castor* (fifth rate) of 26 guns and 1,808 tons was commanded by Captain Lord John Hay between September 1832 and November 1836 and present at the blockade of Dutch ports. After her intervention in the 'Belgian Question', she became involved in the Spanish Civil War, returning to operations on the coast of Syria in 1840.

USHL MS GC/MI/110, Lord Minto to Palmerston, 18 December 1832,

USHL MS GC/MI/111, Lord Minto to Palmerston, 18 December 1832.

50. USHL Add. 48480, f. 57, Viscount Palmerston's entry in the Foreign Office dispatch book.

51. USHL MS GC/MI/114, Lord Minto to Palmerston, 26 December 1832.

52. USHL MS GC/MI/115, Lord Minto to Palmerston, 29 December 1832.

5

## Family Plans Disrupted (1833–1834)

1. So far as the family is concerned, this chapter continues to be based on volume 6 of Catherine's Journal (NLS MS 31057). It moves on to volume 7 (NLS MS 31058) from 25 May 1833.

2. The election was the first since the previous year's Great Reform Act and the number of males who could vote had risen fourteen fold, from 4,500 to 64,447.

3. USHL Add. 48482 ff. 52–53.

4. USHL Add. 48482 ff. 57–59.

5. USHL Add. 48482 ff. 67–69, Viscount Palmerston to Lord Minto, 12 March 1833.

6. USHL Add. 48482 f. 60.

7. Mosslang, Freitag and Wende (eds), *British Envoys to Germany, 1816–1847*, FO 64/189, Minto's Dispatch to Palmerston No. 25.

8. USHL Add. 48482 f. 62, 3 April 1833.

9. USHL Add. 48482 f. 62, 10 April 1833.

10. USHL Add. 48482 f. 67.

11. Mosslang, Freitag and Wende (eds), FO 64/189, Viscount Palmerston to Lord Minto No. 3, draft dated 7 September 1832.

12. USHL Add. 48482 f. 68–69.

13. The military commission had met between September 1831 and December 1832. The main point of the negotiations had been the reorganisation of the Confederation's army and discussion of military measures should France invade across the Rhine.

14. Mosslang, Freitag and Wende (eds), FO 64/189, Minto's Dispatch to Palmerston No. 44.

15. The britska carriage (from the Polish word Bryczka) had a straight body with ogee curves at the front and back, with a single folding hood, and was hung on C springs. It was a distinctive and popular feature among carriages between 1824 and 1840.

16. USHL Add. 48482 f. 72.

17. USHL Add. 48482 f. 73, 26 June 1833.

18. USHL Add. 48482 f. 73, 7 July 1833.

19. Wilhelm von Humboldt (1767–1835) had a younger brother, Friedrich Wilhelm Heinrich von Humboldt (1769–1859), who was the famous naturalist and explorer.

20. Rev Gilbert Elliot was the third son of The Rt Hon. Hugh Elliot (1752–1830) and governor of Madras. He was ordained in 1824 and after serving at Newington Butts, Barming, Kirkby-Thore & Brougham, and Wivenhoe, he became Dean of Bristol and Chaplain to the Archbishop of Canterbury in 1850, a post he was to hold until 1891. He married Williamina, daughter of Patrick Brydone, in 1825 and Frances, daughter of Charles Dickenson, in 1863.

21. NLS MS 11906 ff. 103–6, 10 October 1833.

22. NLS MS 11906 ff. 123–5, 10 March 1834.

23. Lord Minto had written to Ephraim Selby's father from Berlin on the first of March 1834. In his reply Robert Selby had explained that Captain Elliot had spoken to him some time before about his future plans and his wish that Ephraim should succeed him. His Lordship had been pleased to agree to this in consideration of his long service to the family, and because he had much esteem for Ephraim personally.

24. NLS MS 11906 ff. 155–7, 24 September 1834.

6

## Lord Minto Becomes First Lord and His Brother an Admiral (1834–1847)

1. The 'Metternich System' represented Metternich's efforts to maintain the 1815 settlement through an alliance of European monarchies, and by the comprehensive repression of nationalism and liberalism within states.

2. Münchengrätz, a town in Central Bohemia, is now Mnichovo Hradiste in the Czech Republic.

3. See Kenneth Bourne, *Palmerston: The Early Years 1784–1841*, chap. 8.

4. John Backhouse (1784–1845) was the son of a Liverpool merchant. He became a partner in his father's business, where his talents were recognised by the local MP, George Canning, who used him as his private secretary. When Canning moved to the Foreign Office, he asked the Prime Minister to find him a vacancy. This led to his appointment as a commissioner of excise followed by posts at the Foreign Office. As an under-secretary he became responsible for managing affairs in the northern hemisphere until his retirement in 1842.

5. Mosslang, Freitag and Wende (eds), FO 64/190, Ralph Abercromby's Dispatch to John Backhouse, No. 4, 11 September 1833.

6. USHL Add. 48480 f. 77 and 48482 f. 77–78.

7. USHL Add. 48480 f. 79.

8. USHL Add. 48482 f. 82.

9. USHL Add. 48482 f. 90.

10. USHL Add. 48480 ff. 85–86.

11. The Prussian statesman Albrecht, Graf von Bernstorff (1809–1873) was born in Mecklenburg-Schwerin. During the 1848 revolution he was sent to Vienna, where he distinguished himself as an opponent of German unification schemes. His opposition towards the German policy of Austria's prime minister, Prince Felix zu Schwarzenberg led to his recall in 1851. Shortly before the outbreak of the Crimean War he was sent as head of the Prussian embassy to London, where his son Johann-Heinrich was born in 1862. He left this post to become Prussia's foreign minister in 1861 but the following year he was replaced by Otto von Bismarck, later returning to London as ambassador, and in 1871 as the German imperial ambassador until his death in 1873.

12. USHL Add. 48482 f. 93.

13. USHL Add. 48482 f. 94.

14. The Soutzos were a large family. A Prince Michael had been hospodar of Moldavia from 1819 to 1821 and present at a conference in London about Greece in 1830–31. The house of Caradja originated in the Byzantine Empire and Beyzad Constantin (1799–1860), Prince Caradja, married Adele Condo-Dandolo bearing him one son, Prince Jean Constantin (1835–1894).

15. USHL Add. 48482 f. 95.

16. USHL Add. 48480 ff. 89–94.

17. USHL Add. 48482 ff. 95–96.

18. USHL Add. 48482 f. 97.

19. USHL Add. 48482 f. 104.

20. USHL Add. 48480 ff. 109–113.

21. Biberich, and its castle, also spelt Biebrich, was the principal residence of the dukes of Nassau.

22. USHL Add. 48482 f. 108–110.

23. MacCarthy and Russell (eds), *Lady John Russell*, p. 19.

24. Alsager Vian, 'Kynynmound, Gilbert Elliot Murray (1782–1859)', rev. H. C. G. Matthew, *Oxford Dictionary of National Biography*, Oxford University Press, 2004.

25. USHL Add. 48482 f. 115.

26. USHL Add. 48482 ff. 120–121.

27. Lord George William Russell (1790–1846) had been attached to Sir Robert's Adair's mission to Belgium. In 1832 he had been sent on another special mission, to Portugal during the struggle between Don Miguel and Donna Maria and in 1834 he was moved to Stuttgart, becoming ambassador in Berlin on 24 November 1835.

28. See J. K. Laughton's essays, revised by A. D. Lambert, *Oxford Dictionary of National Biography*, Oxford University Press, 2004, from which extracts have been taken in respect of Admiral Sir Charles Adam, Admiral Sir William Parker, Admiral Sir Edward Thomas Troubridge, and Sir William Symonds.

29. While he was at Portsmouth, George Elliot was much praised by the Duke of Clarence, later to be King William IV, and it was as the result of a royal command that he became both a political secretary (1830–34) and third naval lord (1835–37) at the Admiralty.

30. The children born to Eliza and Captain George Elliot and Eliza Ness were: Eliza (died December 1877); Catherine Frances (died April 1914); Georgiana Maria (died February 1874); Cecilia Mary (died January 1894); Admiral Sir George Augustus (1813–1901); Gilbert John (1818–1852); Lieutenant Horatio Foley (c. 1820–1845); Major-General Sir Alexander James Hardy (1825–1909); Frederick Boileau (1826–1880).

31. Admiral Troubridge was appointed lieutenant of HMS *Blenheim* in 1806, which went out to the East Indies as the flagship of his father, Rear-Admiral Sir Thomas Troubridge, and by whom he was appointed to command the brig HMS *Harrier*. After being invalided for a period, he returned to sea in 1813 and served on the North American station where he commanded the naval brigade at the battle of New Orleans.

32. See A. D. Lambert's, *The Last Sailing Battle Fleet: Maintaining Naval Mastery, 1815–1850*, for a full picture of life at the Admiralty at this time.

33. *The Times*, 12 October 1835, p. 3, issue 15918, col. F.

34. Thomas Spring Rice MP (1790–1866) came to the notice of the Marquess of Lansdowne, who became his patron. He succeeded Althorp as Chancellor of the Exchequer after Peel's failed attempt to form a government in April 1835.

35. MacCarthy and Russell (eds), *Lady John Russell*, p. 24.

36. *The Times*, 7 March 1836, p. 5, issue 16044, col. B.

37. MacCarthy and Russell (eds), *Lady John Russell*, p. 25.

38. Sir John Franklin (1786–1847) was to return to England in June 1844 with his confidence undermined by what he regarded as his failure in Van Diemen's Land. It was only the prospect of the Admiralty undertaking an expedition to the Canadian arctic to explore the unknown 300-mile stretch of the route between Barrow Strait and the mainland, that lifted his depression. He was given command of the expedition on 7 February 1845. The *Erebus and Terror* sailed in May 1845. Franklin died in June 1847 and the horrors and mystery of an expedition in which a total of 129 men perished remains only partially accounted for today. (See B. A. Riffenburgh, 'Franklin, Sir John (1786–1847)', *Oxford Dictionary of National Biography*, Oxford University Press, 2004.

39. A ship's 'rate' was decided by the number of guns she carried.

40. NMM Caird Library ELL 221, Sir Charles Adam to Minto, September 1836.

41. NLS MS 11751, ff. 40 and 51–52.

42. John Edmund Elliot (1788–1862) was the third son of the first Earl Minto, who had married Amelia, daughter of James Henry Casamajor in 1809. He also sat for Roxburghshire between 1847 and 1859 and became Joint Secretary to the Board of Control between 1849 and 1852 in Lord John Russell's administration.

43. There is a tablet in the Westmorland church at Brougham to the memory of Mary Brydone, daughter of William Robertson and widow of Patrick Brydone. The memorial was erected by her daughters – Mary, Countess of Minto, and Lady Adam – and William Elliot.

44. NA ADM 222/11.

45. Charles Wood (1800–1885), later first Viscount Halifax.

46. HMS *Warspite* was fitted as a 76-gun ship, and her upper decks would require no alteration, but the system of altering her to a frigate was very expensive.

47. NMM Caird Library ELL 221, Charles Elliot to his uncle, 15 April 1837.

48. Ibid., Charles Elliot to Admiral George Elliot, April 231838.

49. Ibid., Commander Hon. H. A. Murray to Lord Minto, 30 April 1838.

50. Sir John Barrow (1764–1848) had been elected to the Royal Society in 1805 and was a close friend of Sir Joseph Banks, its president. He entered the Admiralty as Second Secretary in 1804, a post he held except for one short period until January 1845. As a writer he was especially known for the *Mutiny on the Bounty*, which he published in 1831. His second son, also John (1808–1898), became the Head of the Admiralty's Record Office in 1844, retiring in 1855. He was the only civilian member of the Arctic Council which had been founded in 1855 to search for Franklin.

51. NMM Caird Library ELL 221, a communication from Sir John Barrow at the Admiralty, 20 October 1838.

52. MacCarthy and Russell (eds), *Lady John* Russell, p. 29.

53. Ralph Abercromby moved from Tuscany in March 1840, becoming envoy extraordinary and minister plenipotentiary to the King of Sardinia. Ralph and Mary's only child was christened Mary Catherine Elizabeth Abercromby.

54. HMS *Columbine*, an 18-gun wooden sloop of 492 tons, was built at Portsmouth in 1826 for the 1827 Experimental Squadron. Admiral Sir Thomas Hardy found that '*Columbine*'s capacity of stowage is much inferior to *Wolf*, *Sattelite* or *Acorn* but her greater breadth of beam and lower bulwarks enable her to stand under her canvas and in general weather, her sailing qualities are very superior to the whole of the squadron.' Between May 1838 and June 1840, she was commanded by George Augustus Elliot (Admiral Sir George Elliot's eldest son).

55. NMM Caird Library ELL 221, Admiral George Elliot to Lord Minto, 25 August 1838.

56. Ibid., Admiral George Elliot to Lord Minto, 21 February 1839.

57. Ibid., Admiral George Elliot to Lord Minto, 12 November 1839.

58. From a letter by Miss Adelaide Lister, Lord John Russell's stepdaughter; see MacCarthy and Russell (eds), *Lady John Russell*, pp. 31–32.

59. NLS MS 11751 ff. 67–68.

60. A postscript to the communication from Sir John Barrow at the Admiralty, 20 October 1838.

61. See John Ouchterlony, *Chinese War: An Account of All the Operations of the British Forces from the Commencement to the Treaty of Nanking*, chap. 3.

62. See Ouchterlony, *Chinese War*, chap. 4

63. NMM Caird Library ELL 221, Admiral George Elliot to Lord Minto, 21 October 1840.

64. William Laird Clowes, *The Royal Navy*, vol. 6, pp. 279–304.

65. Signed on 29 August 1842, the Nanking Treaty meant that the ports of Canton, Amoy, Foo-chow, Ningpo and Shanghai were thrown open to British merchants, the island of Hong Kong was ceded to Britain in perpetuity, and China agree to pay \$21 million 'in the course of the present and three succeeding years'.

66. NMM Caird Library ELL 221, Admiral George Elliot to Lord Minto, 7 June 1841.

67. See J. K. Laughton, 'Elliot, Sir George (1784–1853)', rev. Andrew Lambert, *Oxford Dictionary of National Biography*, Oxford University Press, 2004.

68. NLS MS 12063 ff. 134–156, Lord Minto's final report, summarised in the previous five paragraphs, was probably written before 6 September 1841.

69. NMM Caird Library ELL 221, Admiral George Elliot to Lord Minto, 28 March 1842.

70. Ibid., 8 June 1842.

71. Ibid., 19 June 1842.

72. Ibid., 25 September 1842.

73. Ibid., 24 November 1842 and 18 January 1843.

74. NLS MS 19577 (ii) Substance of the statement by the Rev Mr Gleig upon the case of his son Mr M. Gleig 1843.

75. NMM Caird Library ELL 221, Admiral George Elliot to Lord Minto, 9 April 1843.

76. Ibid., 24 August and 6–10 September 1843.

77. Ibid., 21 December 1844.

78. Ibid., 28 June 1845.

79. Gilbert John Elliot had apparently acted on the advice of Sir George Gipps, who was the governor of New South Wales. The bishop had been 'all kindness to him' as well as the daughter of the Rev Thomas Gore (1767–1834), Isabella, whom he was to marry in November 1849.

80. NLS MS 11751 ff. 93–94, Admiral George Elliot to Lord Minto, 20 October 1845.

81. NLS MS 11747 ff. 109–111, Admiral George Elliot to Lord Minto, 17 April 1846.

82. NLS MS 11751 f. 165, Admiral George Elliot to Lord Minto, 30 October 1848.

7

## Life on the Minto Estate (1830–1835)

1. NLS MS 13190 ff. 1–2, Robert Selby to Lord Minto, 4 January 1830.

2. NLS MS 13190 ff. 3–4, Robert Selby to Lord Minto, 15 February 1830.

3. NLS MS 13190 ff. 7–8, Robert Selby to Lord Minto, 2 April 1830.

4. NLS MS 13190 ff. 11–12, Robert Selby to Lord Minto, 12 May 1830.

5. NLS MS 13190 ff. 13–14. Robert Selby to Lord Minto, 17 July 1830. Where there were taxable items that were in France or Switzerland due to the family's stay abroad, these would have been exempt. The factor needed to provide the Revenue with the number of people and items of transport that remained in Scotland.

6. William Playfair was about to start detailed work on the Royal College of Surgeon's building in Edinburgh.

7. NLS MS 13190, ff. 19–20, Robert Selby to Lord Minto, 10 October 1830.

8. NLS MS 13217, f. 146, Archibald Turnbull to Robert Selby, 15 November 1830.

9. NLS MS 13190, ff. 23–24, Robert Selby to Lord Minto, 3 December 1830.

10. Fiars were the prices of grain legally fixed by the Sheriff of a Scottish county for the current year and used as a basis for certain rates and tenant–landlord negotiations.

11. NLS MS 13190, ff. 25–26, Robert Selby to Lord Minto, 1 January 1831.

12. NLS MS 13190, ff. 25–26, Robert Selby to Lord Minto, 8 March 1831.

13. NLS MS 13190, ff. 35–37, Robert Selby to Lord Minto, 18 March 1831.

14. NLS MS 13190, ff. 46–47, Robert Selby to Lord Minto, 16 June 1831.

15. NLS MS 13190, ff. 48–53, Robert Selby to Lord Minto, 13 July and 20 August 1831.

16. NLS MS 13217, f. 159, James Brodie to Lord Minto, 9 March 1832.

17. NLS MS 13190, f. 60, Robert Selby to Lord Minto, 12 June 1832.

18. NLS MS 13190, ff. 62–63, Robert Selby to Lord Minto, 23 June 1832.

19. NLS MS 13190, f. 69, Robert Selby to Lord Minto, 24 July 1832.

20. NLS MS 13190, f. 72, Robert Selby to Lord Minto, 3 August 1832.

21. NLS MS 13190, f. 73–74, Robert Selby to Lord Minto, 13 August 1832.

22. NLS MS 13190, ff. 88–89, Robert Selby to Lord Minto, 22 February 1832.

23. NLS MS 13190, ff. 102–103, Robert Selby to Lord Minto, 27 August 1833.

24. NLS MS 13190, ff. 106–107, Robert Selby to Lord Minto, 5 March 1834.

25. The Ednam estate, some two miles from Kelso, was bought by John William Ward (1781–1833), who became Earl of Dudley in 1827. The factorship had become an extra source of income for Robert Selby until news reached him in 1832 that Dudley was under restraint in an institution near Surbiton after exhibiting signs of mental derangement. He died there in March 1833 after a series of strokes and Selby feared that William, a second cousin and Dudley's heir, might want to alter the previous arrangement.

26. NLS MS 11750, ff. 138–140, Ephraim Selby to Captain George Elliot, 28 June 1834.

27. Marriage Notice in the *Wigtown Free Press*, September 1844.

28. NLS MS 11907, ff. 113–114, Catherine Rutherford to Lady Minto, 8 September 1838.

29. NLS MS 11907, ff. 126–128, Catherine Rutherford to Lady Minto, 7 October 1838.

30. NLS MS 12252, ff. 51–54, George to William, 6 September 1859.

31. NLS MS 12252, ff. 60–62, George to William, 23 February 1861.

32. Tod & Romanes, the Edinburgh solicitors used by the Minto family.

33. NLS MS 12263, ff. 277–278, Catherine Selby to William, 10 April 1861.

34. NLS MS 12263, ff. 280–281, William to Catherine Selby, 10 April 1861.

35. NLS MS 12263, f. 282, William to Catherine Selby, 10 April 1861.

36. NLS MS 12263, ff. 352–353, Catherine Selby to William, 4 April 1862.

37. NLS MS 12263, ff. 127–128 Catherine Selby to William, 4 July 1862.

# 8

## Fanny Marries Lord John Russell (1840–1847)

1. Samuel March Phillipps (1780–1862), writing from Cumberland Terrace in October 1839.

2. MacCarthy and Russell (eds), *Lady John Russell*, pp. 35–36.

3. Ibid., Fanny to Lady Mary, 16 March 1841.

4. Ibid., Lady Minto to Lady Mary, 18 March 1841.

5. The 1841 census, taken on 8 June, indicates that the household at Wilton Crescent comprised Lord John, five of Lady Ribblesdale's six children (Tom Lister being missing), along with eleven servants and staff.

6. MacCarthy and Russell (eds), *Lady John Russell*, pp. 42–43.

7. Ibid., pp. 45–46.

8. Ibid., Fanny to Lady Mary, 19 July 1841.

9. From 'A Border Ballad', written by Lady Minto in July 1841.

10. MacCarthy and Russell (eds), *Lady John Russell*, p. 60.

11. Gooch (ed.), *The Later Correspondence*, Lord John Russell to Lady Holland, 11 December 1841.

12. MacCarthy and Russell (eds), *Lady John Russell*, pp. 61–63.

13. Gooch (ed.), *The Later Correspondence*, from Lord John Russell to Lord Lansdowne, 11 March 1842.

14. MacCarthy and Russell (eds), *Lady John Russell*, pp. 64–65.

15. MacCarthy and Russell (eds), *Lady John Russell*, Fanny to Lady Mary, 7 February 1843.

16. Fanny and Lord John's four children were John Russell, Viscount Amberley, born 10 December 1842, died 9 January 1876; Hon. George Gilbert William Russell, born 14 April 1848, died 27 January 1933; Hon. Francis Albert Rollo Russell, born 11 July 1849, died 30 March 1914 (he married Alice Godfrey on 21 April 1885 but she died in childbirth in 1886 – Rollo's second marriage was to Gertrude Joachim on 28 April 1891); Mary Agatha Russell, born 1853, died 23 April 1933.

17. MacCarthy and Russell (eds), *Lady John Russell*, pp. 66–68.

18. 'Uncle John', or John Edmund Elliot, had taken to drawing landscapes and village scenes while in India between 1812 and 1813 and benefited from the instruction he received from another, more famous artist, George Chinnery.

19. John Richardson was an eminent Scottish lawyer who lived and practised in London from 1806 until he was eighty. An amateur poet, he lived in literary circles and was a longstanding friend of Thomas Campbell, Sir Walter Scott and Francis Jeffrey, Scott describing him to Joanna Baillie, the playwright and poet, as 'a good honourable kind-hearted little fellow with a pretty taste for poetry which he wisely kept under subjection. He married Elizabeth Hill in 1811 but she died in 1836. At the time of the 1841 census, Richardson was living at Fludyer Street, Westminster, with two of his daughters, Hope and Isabella, who had been born in 1816 and 1821 respectively.

20. Harriet's story at this time is taken from NLS MS 12014, Journal of Harriet A. G. Elliot, October 1843 to July 1844.

21. Possibly Henry (1779–1854) among the many Cockbums.

22. The surname 'Hislop' is used although it was occasionally spelt with the letter 'y'.

23. Exeter Hall, completed in 1831, and the Great Hall, capable of holding 3,000 people, were used by several religious societies and often used for concerts. Haydon painted the *Meeting of Anti-Slavery Delegates in the Great Hall* in 1840.

24. Ama was known throughout the family by this name. She had been christened after her aunt Anna Maria.

25. The Boileau children were Agnes Lucy (died 1881); Ama, but christened Anna Maria (*c.* 1826–1897); Caroline (Carry) Mary (died 1877); Mary Georgina (died 1910); Theressa Anna Catherine (died 1872); John Elliot (1827–1861); Sir Francis George Manningham (1830–1900); Edmund (Eddy) William Pollen (1831–1883); Lieutenant Charles (Charlie) Augustus Penrhyn (1835–1855).

26. Incorporated in 1836 to build a line from Shoreditch to Yarmouth via Ipswich, the company ran its first public trains between Mile End and Romford in June 1839. Shoreditch to Brentwood did not open until 1840 and Colchester was finally reached in 1843. It was left to the Eastern Union Railway to build the line further north.

27. William Carnegie and Georgians (Gina) Elliot had two children: Margaret Mary Adeliza, who died in 1871, and Lieutenant Colonel George John Carnegie, who was born in December 1843 and who died in 1891.

28. Hansard, 3rd series, vol. 81, paragraph 368.

29. MacCarthy and Russell (eds), *Lady John Russell*, p. 70.

30. Francis Thornhill Baring, first Baron Northbrook (1796–1866), had been Chancellor of the Exchequer in 1839 but in 1841 his inept proposal to cut the discriminatory tariff on foreign sugar produced by slave labour was defeated and led to the government's fall on the resulting vote of confidence. He was to refuse the Treasury under Russell in 1846 and became First Lord of the Admiralty in 1849.

31. Gooch (ed.), *The Later Correspondence*, Lord John Russell's record of the crisis between 8 and 19 December 1845.

32. MacCarthy and Russell (eds), *Lady John Russell*, pp. 71–72.

33. Ibid., Fanny to Lady Mary, 14 December 1845. It is hard to think that Fanny knew much about the life led by Spartan women either in simple matters, such as their relaxed dress code and freedom to do as they wished, or the expectation that husbands could agree to wives bringing lovers into their homes and bearing the children of other men for the good of the state.

34. G. O. Trevelyan, *The Life and Letters of Lord Macaulay*, 2 vols, Longmans, Green & Co., London, 1876.

35. MacCarthy and Russell (eds), *Lady John Russell*, pp. 74–75.

36. Ibid., John to Fanny, 14 and 17 December 1845.

37. Ibid., Lord John to Fanny, 21 December 1845.

38. Ibid., Fanny to Lord John, 21 December 1845.

39. Ibid., Fanny to Lady Mary, 24 December 1845.

40. Ibid., Fanny to Lord John, 25 and 26 January and 7 February 1846.

41. Ibid., Lord William Russell to Fanny from Genoa, 12 February 1846.

42. Ibid., Fanny to Lady Mary, 1 March, and Lord John to Lady John, 3 March 1846.

43. Ibid., Fanny to Lord John, 23 February 1846.

44. Ibid., Fanny to Lord John, 12 March, and Lord John to Fanny, 13 March 1846.

45. Ibid., Lord John to Fanny from the House of Commons, March 1846.

46. Ibid., Lord John to Fanny, 19 March 1846.

47. Ibid., Fanny to Lord John, 23 and 25 March, and Lord John to Fanny, 3 April 1846.

48. Gooch (ed.), *The Later Correspondence*, from Charles Wood to Lord John Russell, 30 June 1846.

49. MacCarthy and Russell (eds), *Lady John Russell*, p. 88.

50. Ibid., pp. 90–91.

51. Ibid., pp. 91–93.

52. Pope Pius IX had only succeeded Gregory XVI in June 1846 but his reforms encouraged reactionaries in Rome to look to Austria for support, and a summons from the Vatican for Austria to withdraw troops from Ferrara was ignored. Permitted by treaty to occupy the citadel, they had gone further by occupying the town.

53. Gooch (ed.), *The Later Correspondence*, Lord Palmerston to Lord John Russell, 21 August 1847.

54. H. C. F. Bell, *Lord Palmerston*, vol. 1, p. 413.

55. Gooch (ed.), *The Later Correspondence*, the Queen to Lord John Russell, 4 September 1847.

56. T. Martin, *Life of His Royal Highness the Prince Consort*, vol. 1, pp. 428–423.

9

## Lord Minto Goes to Rome and Revolutionary Sicily as Special Envoy (1847–1852)

1. Bell, *Lord Palmerston*, vol. 1, p. 413.

2. Ulrich Ochsenbein (1811–1890) was a lawyer and from 1835 the leader of the Radicals of Bern, who later became the Free Democratic Party. He was elected to the Federal Council of Switzerland in November 1848, holding office until 1854.

3. J. R. Hall, *England and the Orleans Monarchy*, p. 427.

4 Gooch (ed.), *The Later Correspondence*, vol. 1, chap. 12, Lord Minto to Lord John Russell, 29 September 1847.

5. Ibid., Lord Minto to Lord John Russell, 16 October 1847.

6. Bell, *Lord Palmerston*, vol. 1, pp. 415–416.

7. Gooch (ed.), *The Later Correspondence*, vol. 1, chap. 12, Lord Minto to Lord John Russell, 15 November 1847.

8. Ibid., Lord Minto to Lord John Russell, 18 November 1847.

9. Ibid., Lord Minto to Lord John Russell, 2 January 1848.

10. Ibid., Lord Palmerston to Lord John Russell, 11 January 1848.

11. Ibid., Lord Minto to Lord John Russell, 16 January 1848.

12. Ibid., Lord Minto to Lord John Russell, 18 and 23 January 1848.

13. Ibid., Lord Minto to Lord John Russell, 3 February 1848.

14. Ibid., Lord Minto to Lord John Russell, 15 February 1848.

15. MacCarthy and Russell (eds), *Lady John Russell*, Lady John to Lady Mary, 26 February 1848.

16. While Lamartine was proclaiming the republic in the name of the provisional government, Louis Philippe had slipped across to England from Eu under the pseudonym of 'William Smith'. He was followed two days later by Louis Napoleon Bonaparte travelling in the opposite direction to put himself at the disposal of the republic – only to find that his timing was at fault. As McCarthy and Russell explain, the law banishing the Bonaparte family had yet to be repealed and he returned to England in time to become a special constable at a Chartist meeting.

17. Sidney Lee, *Queen Victoria: A Biography*, p. 186.

18. Ernest Augustus Edgcumbe (1797–1861), the third Earl of Edgcumbe was the second but eldest surviving son of Richard Edgcumbe, a writer on opera and the second Earl, and known as Viscount Valletort between 1818 and 1837. He married Caroline, daughter of Rear-Admiral Charles Fielding, in 1831. He also wrote *Extracts from Journals Kept during the Revolutions at Rome and Palermo*.

19. NLS MS 12077, ff. 13–14, Sicilian Papers, 22 February 1848.

20. NLS MS 12077, ff. 24–26, Sicilian Papers, 24 February 1848.

21. Gooch (ed.), *The Later Correspondence*, vol. l, chap. 12, Lord Minto (aboard HMS *Hlbernia*) to Lord John Russell, 10 March 1848.

22. Susan Horner, *A Century of Despotism*, p. 157.

23. Gooch (ed.), *The Later Correspondence*, vol. l, chap. 12, Lord Minto to Lord John Russell, 14 March 1848.

24. Francis, the tenth Lord Napier of Murchison (1819–1898) was secretary of legation at Naples between 1848 and 1849.

25. NLS MS 12077, ff. 60–62 Sicilian Papers, 16 March 1848.

26. NLS MS 12077, ff. 66–67 Sicilian Papers, 16 March 1848.

27. NLS MS 12077, ff. 77–79 Sicilian Papers, 16 March 1848.

28. NLS MS 12077, f. 83 Sicilian Papers, 20 March 1848.

29. NLS MS 12077, ff. 84–86 Sicilian Papers, 20 March 1848.

30. Evelyn Ashley, *The Life of Henry John Temple, Viscount Palmerston 1846–1865*, pp. 55–57.

31. NLS MS 12077, f. 91 Sicilian Papers, 22 March 1848.

32. Gooch (ed.), *The Later Correspondence*, vol. l, chap. 12, Lord Minto to Lord John Russell, 26 March 1848.

33. Ibid., Lord Minto to Lord John Russell, 4 April 1848.

34. NLS MS 12077, ff. 97–101 Sicilian Papers, 28 March 1848.

35. Gooch (ed.), *The Later Correspondence*, vol. l, chap. 12, Lord Minto to Lord John Russell, 6 April 1848.

36. NLS MS 12079, Sicilian Papers, 16 April 1848.

37. NLS MS 12241, ff. 234–235, Lord Minto to William, 6 April 1848.

38. It was not until June that another ineffectual parliament was elected, and September when Ferdinand sent a force of 20,000 to seize Messina. The Neapolitan army bombarded the city for three days, both the British and the French being appalled by Ferdinand's 'savage barbarity'. After an armistice, yet another offer of a separate Sicilian parliament was rejected. In March 1849, Ferdinand achieved the diplomatic support of Czar Nicholas and, believing he had the support of the French, abolished the parliament in Naples and ordered his forces in Sicily to take the offensive. Although the populace attempted to stop the invasion, the Sicilian government had disintegrated and Baron Riso announced that his forces would not resist the Neapolitan army. The inevitable came about when General Carlo Filangieri occupied Palermo on 15 May, remaining there as governor until 1855.

39. MacCarthy and Russell (eds), *Lady John Russell*, Queen Victoria to Lord John, 14 April 1848.

40. Ibid., Dr James Simpson to Lady John, March 1848.

41. Gooch (ed.), *The Later Correspondence*, vol. l, chap. 13, Lord Minto to Lord John Russell, 21 May 1848.

42. Ibid., Lord Minto to Lord John Russell, 16 September 1848.

43. Ibid., Lord John Russell to Lord Palmerston, 8 October 1848.

44. Ibid., Ralph Abercromby to Lord John Russell, 22 November 1848.

45. MacCarthy and Russell (eds), *Lady John Russell*, p. 102.

46. Ibid., Lady John to Lady Mary, 10 December 1848.

47. NLS MS 11995, Lord Minto's Journal, 2–9 January 1849.

48. Ibid., Lord Minto's Journal, 3 March 1849.

49. The steamship *Vectis* seems to have been built at Cowes (probably by J. Samuel White) and was sold by the Peninsular & Oriental Steam Company to the Sicilian government for £40,000.

50. NLS MS 11995, Lord Minto's Journal, 17 March 1849.

51. T. Whitaker, *Sicily and England: Political and Social Reminiscences 1848–1870*, p. 95.

52. Ibid., pp. 120–122,

53. Ibid., p. 130.

54. Prince Ferdinand, Duke of Genoa (1822–1853), was born in Florence, the second son of Charles Albert, Prince of Carignan, and Maria Teresa of Tuscany. His father was the head of the House of Savoy-Carignan, a cadet branch of the House of Savoy. The senior line of the House became extinct in 1831 and his father succeeded as King of Sardinia. With the ascension of his father he was created Duke of Genoa. As a result of the Sicilian revolution he was a candidate for the throne, being the most acceptable candidate to the British, who informed him that he would be recognised as king as soon as he took possession of the throne. In July 1848 the national assembly of Sicily unanimously voted to offer him the throne.

55. NLS MS 11995, Lord Minto's Journal, 19 March 1849.

56. Ibid., 3 April 1849.

57. The Mintos would have travelled to the docks by the London & Blackwell Railway which had only been opened in 1840. There they would have joined the Rotterdam packet.

58. NLS MS 11995, Lord Minto's Journal, 7 to 16 April 1849.

59. Ibid., 18 April 1849.

60. Possibly a reference to Sir Henry Frederick Bouverie (1783–1852), an Army officer who received a GCMG on leaving Malta in June 1843. He was approached in 1846 to be commander-in-chief in Canada but he declined it on account of his age.

61. NLS MS 11995, Lord Minto's Journal, 20 April 1849.

62. Ibid., 21 and 22 April 1849.

63. Ibid., 24 April 1849.
64. Ibid., 25 April 1849.
65. Hansard HC, 27 April 1849.
66. NLS MS 11995, Lord Minto's Journal, 28 April 1849.
67. Ibid., 11 May 1849.
68. Ibid., 27 May to 1 June 1849.
69. Ibid., 2 June 1849.
70. Ibid., 4 June 1849.
71. Ibid., 7 June 1849.
72. Benedetto Castiglia (1811–1877) and Paolo Morello established the journal *L'Ruota* in January 1840 which soon became known for its pungent reporting.
73. Whitaker, *Sicily and England*, p. 138.
74. Ibid., p. 148; see also the Central Criminal Court hearing before Mr Justice Coltman on 5 to 7 July 1849.
75. Gooch (ed.), *The Later Correspondence*, vol. 2, chap. 14, pp. l–3.
76. Ibid., Lord Minto to Lord John Russell, 3 October 1849.
77. Ibid., Lord Minto to Lord John Russell, 17 October 1849.
78. Ibid., Lord Palmerston to Lord John Russell, 23 October 1849 and to Baron Brunnow on 1 November 1849.
79. MacCarthy and Russell (eds), *Lady John Russell*, Lord John Russell to Lady John, 6 September 1849.
80. Ibid., p. 105.
81. The King of the Two Sicilies *v.* Willcox (1851), 1 Sim NS 301.
82. MacCarthy and Russell (eds), *Lady John Russell*, Lady John Russell to Lady Mary Abercromby, 22 November 1850.
83. Ibid., Lady John Russell to Lady Mary Abercromby, 29 November 1850.
84. See Ashley, *The Life of Henry John Temple, Viscount Palmerston 1846–1865*.
85. MacCarthy and Russell (eds), *Lady John Russell*, pp. 117–118.
86. Ibid., Queen Victoria to Lord John, 19 December 1852.
87. Ibid., Lady John Russell to Lady Mary Abercromby, 24 December 1852.
88. Ibid., Lord John to Lady John Russell, 10 August 1853.

10

## William – Scottish Politician and Social Reformer (1837–1891)

1. William Whewell (1794–1866) entered Cambridge in 1812 as a sub-sizer after which he gained a string of academic successes and graduated as second wrangler in January 1816. He became a fellow the year following. At the time Lord Melgund was at Trinity, Whewell was becoming involved with the British and European scientific and intellectual communities. He wrote on mineralogy in 1832 and electricity and magnetism in 1835, serving as a vice-president of the British Association before accepting the mastership of Trinity, for which Sir Robert Peel had recommended him to the Queen.
2. Connop Thirlwall (1797–1875) was to become Bishop of St David's in 1840 after he had been forced to resign his post as assistant tutor at Trinity College for supporting the admission of dissenters to Cambridge degrees.
3. NLS MS 12240, ff. 4 and 48, Lord Minto to William, 15 November 1835.
4. NLS MS 12240, ff. 68–70, Lady Minto to William, 4 December 1836.
5. NLS MS 11899A, ff. 103–106, Henry Elliot to Lord Minto, 27 August 1842.
6. NLS MS 12240, ff. 98–100, Lord Minto to William, 24 November 1842.
7. NLS MS 12240, ff. 102–103, Lord Minto to William, 27 November 1842.
8. Gilbert John, the first of William and Nina's four sons, was born in July 1845 at the house of his grandmother. Arthur followed in December 1846, Hugh (February 1848) and William (September 1849).
9. Probably Sarah, the daughter of Robert Hobart, fourth Earl of Buckinghamshire, who died in 1816.
10. William Patrick Adam (1823–1881) went on to be the governor of Bombay's private secretary between 1853 and 1858. The following year he contested Clackmannan and Kinross-shire, holding it for the next twenty-one years.
11. NLS MS 12014, Harriet Elliot's Journal, Monday 20 May 1844.
12. NLS MS 12240, ff. 137–140, Lord Minto to William, 21 June 1845.
13. NLS MS 12240, ff. 173–174, Lord Minto to William, 18 August 1845.
14. NLS MS 12240, ff. 191–193, Lord Minto to William, 2 January 1846.
15. NLS MS 12240, ff. 200–201, Lord Minto to William, 20 February 1846.
16. NLS MS 12240, ff. 206–214, Lord Minto to William, 26 and 27 March 1846.
17. NLS MS 12240, ff. 216–218, Lord Minto to William, 4 May 1846.
18. NLS MS 12240, ff. 221–224, Lord Minto to William, 23 and 25 June 1846.
19. NLS MS 12241, ff. 9–10, Lord Minto to William, 26 April 1847.
20. NLS MS 12241, ff. 47–48, Lord Minto to William, 28 May 1847.
21. NLS MS 12241, ff. 19–22, Lord Minto to William, 3 May 1847.
22. NLS MS 11899A, ff. 154–158, Henry Elliot to Lord Minto, 29 May 1847.
23. NLS MS 11899A, ff. 159–160, Henry Elliot to Lord Minto, 31 May 1847.
24. NLS MS 11899A, ff. 161–162, Henry Elliot to Lord Minto, 1 June 1847.

25. Alexander Dunlop (1798–1870), lawyer and politician, was born at Keppoch in Dunbartonshire and educated at Greenock Grammar School and Edinburgh University. He had played a leading role in the Disruption of the Church of Scotland in 1843, subsequently becoming a legal adviser to the Free Church. In 1845 and 1847, he unsuccessfully contested the parliamentary seat of Greenock. With obvious Free Church sympathies he was unable to unite other dissenting voters in the constituency against Mr Walter Baine, a Whig who had received the support of the established Church.

26. NLS MS 11899A, ff. 163–165, Henry Elliot to Lord Minto, 2 June 1847.

27. NLS MS 11899A, ff. 166–168, Henry Elliot to Lord Minto, 7 June 1847.

28. NLS MS 12241, ff. 55–56, Lord Minto to William, 1 June 1847.

29. NLS MS 12241, ff. 110–111, Lord Minto to William, 26 June 1847.

30. NLS MS 12241, ff. 104–107, Lord Minto to William, 25 June 1847.

31. NLS MS 12241, ff. 178–179, Lord Minto to William, 23 July 1847.

32. NLS MS 12241, ff. 180–183, Lord Minto to William, 24 July 1847.

33. NLS MS 12241, ff. 186–187, Lord Minto to William, 27 July 1847.

34. NLS MS 12241, ff. 190–191, Lord Minto to William, 1 August 1847.

35. NLS MS 12241, ff. 218–221, Lord Minto to William, 24 December 1847.

36. NLS MS 12241, ff. 226–227, Lord Minto to William, 3 February 1848.

37. NLS MS 12241, ff. 228–231, Lord Minto to William, 3 March 1848.

38. NLS MS 12241, ff. 234–235, Lord Minto to William, 6 April 1848.

39. Captain (later Admiral) James Hanway Plumridge (1787–1863) had command of *Sappho*, *Magicienne* and *Astraea* between 1820 and the 1840s. His second wife, Harriet Agnes, who died in 1845, was the daughter of the Rt Hon. Hugh Elliot (1752–1830), the father of Charles Elliot, diplomat and governor of the Leeward Islands 1809–13 and governor of Madras between 1814 and 1820.

40. Charles Drinkwater Bethune (b. 1802) captained HMS *Calliope* in Chinese waters between 1840 and 1841 and subsequently on the West Indies station.

41. NLS MS 12241, ff. 240–241, Lord Minto to William, 17 January 1849.

42. NLS MS 12241, ff. 1–2, Lord Minto to William, 20 April 1847.

43. Hansard HC, 19 June 1850.

44. NLS MS 12241, ff. 242–243. Lord Minto to William, 26 September 1852.

45. NLS MS 12272, William's Diary for each day in 1853.

46. NLS MS 19471, ff. 1–2, Lord Minto to George, 17 March 1853.

47. Agostino Bertani (1812–1886), born in Milan, was a physician who took part in the insurrection of 1848 and collaborated with Mazzini and Garibaldi.

48. NLS MS 19471, ff. 5–6, William to George, 18 March 1853.

49. Louisa Blackett was the daughter of Sir Edward Blackett, sixth Baronet, and Julia Monck. She married Charlie on 8 December 1862 and they had four sons.

50. NLS MS 19471, ff. 7–8, Lord Minto to George, 27 August 1853.

51. NLS MS 12272, William's Diary for each day in 1853.

52. NLS MS 12241, ff. 244–245, Lord Minto to William, 26 January 1854.

53. NLS MS 12241, f. 246, Lord Minto to William, 31 January 1854.

54. NLS MS 12241, ff. 252–253, Lord Minto to William, 21 March 1854.

55. NLS MS 12241, ff. 262–263, Lord Minto to William, 15 December 1854.

56. NLS MS 12241, ff. 264–265, Lord Minto to William, 6 April 1855.

57. NLS MS 12241, ff. 266–267, Lord Minto to William, 7 April 1855.

58. NLS MS 12241, ff. 274–275, Lord Minto to William, 12 March 1857.

59. NLS MS 12241, ff. 272–273, Lord Minto to William, 5 March 1857.

60. NLS MS 12358, f. 201, George Rutherford to William, 17 February 1858.

61. NLS MS 12358, ff. 205–206, James Murray to William, 17 February 1858.

62. At this time William Fitzwilliam Elliot was called 'Bertie'. Leaving Eton, he went to Trinity, Cambridge, in 1864.

63. NLS MS 12241, ff. 300–301, Lord Minto to William, 7 April 1858.

64. *The Journal of Sir Walter Scott 1771–1832*, David Douglas, Edinburgh, 1891, p. 61.

65. Dr John Waldie (1781–1865) was a wandering dilettante and a devoted enthusiast of the art galleries, concert halls and theatres of Europe. His family came from Newcastle-upon-Tyne, where they seem to have owned a colliery. Waldie's letter to the third Earl Minto makes many warm references to his friendship with the second Lord Minto, Nina, Lady Mary, Fanny and George.

66. The Late Lord Minto, *The Times*, 2 August 1859.

67. NLS MS 12359, ff. 80–82, Lord Kinnaird to the third Earl Minto, 24 June 1868.

68. NLS MS 19471, ff. 9–10, third Lord Minto to George, 3 July 1868.

69. NLS MS 12359, ff. 125–133, John Alexander to the third Earl Minto, 19 April 1869 and enclosure.

70. Hansard, 11 May 1869.

71. NLS MS 12360, ff. 62–66, Mary McCombie and Robert Maconachie to the third Earl Minto, on 18 and 21 April 1871 respectively.

72. NLS MS 12364, ff. 3–8, to Nina, Lady Minto, 6 April 1874.

73. NLS MS 9140, ff .147–152, Nina, Lady Minto to John Hill Burton, 23 February 1874.

74. A woman of letters, Harriet had married George Grote, a radical politician and historian of Greece who introduced her to a large circle of radical and intellectual friends. She joined the feminist movement during the 1850s and in 1871 wrote *The Personal Life of George Grote* without any allusion in it to her husband's attachment, after forty-four years of marriage, to Susan Durant, the sculptress.

75. NLS MS 12364, ff. 34–35, Harriet Grote to Nina, Lady Minto, 1 July 1874.

76. NLS MS 12364, ff. 36–37, Alexander Kinglake to Nina, Lady Minto, 14 July 1874.

77. NLS MS 12364, ff. 38–39, Thomas Headlam to Nina, Lady Minto, 17 July 1874.

78. NLS MS 12364, ff. 46–48, Louisa Beresford to Nina, Lady Minto, 3 October 1874.

79. NLS MS 12364, ff. 55–56, Henry Reeve to Nina, Lady Minto, 11 October 1874.

80. NLS MS 12364, ff. 59–60, Henry Reeve to Nina, Lady Minto, 12 November 1874.

81. NLS MS 12364, f. 69, Henry Reeve to Nina, Lady Minto, 23 April 1875.

82. NLS MS 12360, ff. 116–117; 124–125; and 133–143, Miscellaneous Political Correspondence of Third Earl Minto.

83. NLS MS 12360, f. 181, third Earl Minto to Thomas Riddell, 27 April 1878.

84. NLS MS 12252, ff .93–98, George to William, 10 and 15 April 1880.

85. *The Scotsman* Digital Archive, death of Nina, Lady Minto, 25 April 1882.

86. BL Add. 48267, f. 63, third Earl of Minto to Lord Morley, 8 May 1886.

87. BL Add. 48267, f. 122, third Earl of Minto to Gladstone, 20 May 1886.

88. Lady Florence Dixie married Sir Alexander Dixie in 1875. Towards the end of the century she became a campaigner for sex equality and argued against blood sports until her death in Dumfriesshire in 1905.

89. Lt-Col. William Fitzwilliam Elliot (1849–1928) had served in the Zulu War of 1879 and married Elizabeth Rutherford in 1880. They had one son and two daughters.

90. NLS MS 12317, concludes William's Diary for 1889.

91. *The Irish Times* for Saturday 19 April 1890 records the appearance of Viscount and Viscountess Melgund at a dinner party given at Viceregal Lodge by their excellencies the Lord Lieutenant and the Countess of Zetland for some thirty guests. A military band played during dinner.

92. NLS MS 12319, concludes William's Diary for 1890.

93. James Wellwood Moncrieff, first Baron Moncrieff (1811–1895), was a lawyer and politician. He first introduced an Education Bill for Scotland in 1854 and in 1861 he was able to carry a small reform whereby parish schools were opened up to teachers from other Presbyterian denominations by abolishing the Church of Scotland's religious test. From 1858 to 1869 he was dean of the Faculty of Advocates. He was awarded honorary degrees from Edinburgh and Glasgow Universities.

94. *The Scotsman* Digital Archive, 14 March 1891, p. 5.

95. John Buchan, *Lord Minto: A Memoir*, pp. 95–96.

96. *The Scotsman* Digital Archive, William's funeral, 24 March 1891.

II

## St Petersburg to Constantinople – Henry's Diplomatic Career (1841–1877)

1. Sir Henry George Elliot, *Some Revolutions and Other Diplomatic Experiences*, pp. 2–4.

2. NLS MS 11899A, ff. 101–102, Henry Elliot to Lord Minto, 4 June 1842.

3. NLS MS 11899A, ff. 107–108, Henry Elliot to Lord Minto, 12 October 1842.

4. NLS MS 11899A, ff. 109–110, Henry Elliot to Lord Minto, 9 November 1842.

5. NLS MS 11899A, ff. 111–114, Henry Elliot to Lord Minto, 2 May 1843.

6. Sir John Crampton, second Baronet (1805–1886), at Eton and Trinity, and entered the diplomatic corps as an unpaid attaché at Turin in 1826. After one year in Switzerland he went on to Washington, where he was particularly successful.

7. NLS MS 11899A, ff. 125–126, Henry Elliot to Lord Minto, 12 July 1845.

8. NLS MS 11899A, ff. 142–144, Henry Elliot to Lord Minto, 31 March 1846.

9. NLS MS 11899A, ff. 146–150, Henry Elliot to Lord Minto, 16 May 1846.

10. NLS MS 11899A, ff. 31–36, Henry Elliot to Lady Minto, 17 July 1846.

11. NLS MS 11899A, ff. 146–151, Henry Elliot to Lord Minto, 16 May 1846.

12. NLS MS 11899A, ff. 152–153, Henry Elliot to Lord Minto, 14 August 1846.

13. NLS MS 11899A, ff. 48–49, Henry Elliot to Lady Minto, 29 September 1847.

14. NLS MS 11899A, ff. 50–53, Henry Elliot to Lady Minto, 9 November 1847.

15. Sir Edmund Antrobus, second Baronet (1792–1870), married Anne Lindsay in October 1817. The couple had ten children. The girls were Jane (d. October 1899), Harriet Coutts (d. 1826), Caroline (d. 1903), Anna Maria (d. January 1898) and Anne (d. December 1899). The five sons were Sir Edmund, third Baronet (1818–1899), Hugh Lindsay (1829–1899), Robert Crawford (1830–1911), John Edward (1831–1845), and Reverend Frederick (1837–1903). Henry George Elliot and Anne Antrobus had two children, Gertrude (1855–1947) and Sir Francis Edmund Hugh (1851–1940), who was to follow closely in his father's footsteps in the diplomatic corps.

16. NLS MS 11899A, ff. 54–59, Henry Elliot to Lady Minto, 15 December 1847.

17. NLS MS 11899A, ff. 60–61, Anne Elliot (née Antrobus) to Lady Minto, 16 December 1847.

18. Sir Henry George Elliot, *Some Revolutions and Other Diplomatic Experiences*, p. x.

19. NLS MS 11899A, ff. 66–70, Anne Elliot (née Antrobus) to Lady Minto, 16 July 1849.

20. NLS MS 11899A, ff .92–95, Henry Elliot to Lady Minto, 4 December 1852.

21. NLS MS 11899A, ff. 96–100, Henry Elliot to Lady Minto, 21 December 1852.

22. MacCarthy and Russell (eds), *Lady John Russell*, Fanny to Lady Mary, 24 December 1852.

23. Ibid., p. 128.

24. Ralph Abercromby had been born in 1803 and after service in France, United States, Brazil, Berlin, and as envoy to the King of Sardinia he retired on a pension in November 1849. He was made a KCB in March 1851 and appointed envoy extraordinary and minister plenipotentiary to the King of the Netherlands in November that year. He succeeded his father as second Baron in April 1858 and resigned finally from the diplomatic service in October 1858, dying ten years later.

25. NLS MS 11899A, ff. 101–103, Anne Elliot to Lady Minto, 26 February 1853.

26. NLS MS 11899A, ff. 104–107, Henry Elliot to Lady Minto, 11 March 1853.

27. NLS MS 11899A, ff. 109–112, Henry Elliot to Lady Minto, 30 March 1853.

28. NLS MS 11899A, ff. 114–115, Henry Elliot to Lady Minto, 16 April 1853.

29. NLS MS 11899A, ff. 117–118, Henry Elliot to Lady Minto, 27 May 1853.

30. NLS MS 11899A, ff. 120–123, Henry Elliot to Lady Minto, 9 June 1853.

31. NLS MS 11899A, ff. 125–128, Henry Elliot to Lady Minto, 23 July 1853.

32. MacCarthy and Russell (eds), *Lady John Russell*, pp. 128–129.

33. Ibid., Lord John to Fanny, 10 August 1853.

34. Anna Maria Elliot was the daughter of the first Earl of Minto. She had married Lt-Gen. Sir Rufane Shaw Donkin in 1832, who died in 1841.

35. NLS MS 11899A, ff. 184–187, Henry Elliot to Lord Minto, 26 December 1853.

36. In fact Gilbert's battalion had moved at daylight on 21 September 1854 and climbed the heights previously occupied by the enemy, where they bivouacked. On that and the following day they buried the dead and conveyed the wounded to the field hospitals. Cholera, which had disappeared from the time the battalion left the Bosphorus, reappeared soon after they landed and the battalion suffered much from it about this time, losing one assistant surgeon (Mr Shorrock), one sergeant and nine privates (Sir William Cope, *History of the Rifle Brigade 1800–1874*, p. 309).

37. NLS MS 11899A, ff. 195–198, Henry Elliot to Lord Minto, 29 December 1854.

38. Sir Joseph Francis Olliffe (1808–1869) was educated in Paris and practised medicine there from 1840, becoming a Fellow of the Paris Medical Society. He was promoted by Napoleon III to the rank of officer of the Légion d'Honneur in 1855. He had been knighted at Buckingham Palace in June 1853 and became a Fellow of the Royal College of Physicians in 1859.

39. NLS MS 11899A, ff. 206–210, Henry Elliot to Lord Minto, 14 January 1855.

40. NLS MS 11899A, ff. 199–202, Henry Elliot to Lord Minto, 1 January 1855.

41. Count Karl Ferdinand von Buol (1797–1865) was an Anglophile who served as Austria's foreign minister between 1852 and 1859. He had not made prime minister on the death of Prince Schwarzenberg, who had held the post of foreign affairs since the young Emperor Franz Joseph was taking an increasing role in the direction of cabinet affairs.

42. The four points were – 1. Russia was to give up its protectorate of the Danubian principalities; 2. She was to abandon any claim granting her the right to act on behalf of Orthodox Christians in Turkey; 3. The Straits Convention signed at London in 1841 was to be revised; and 4. Free access to the River Danube for all.

43. NLS MS 11899A, ff. 203–205, Henry Elliot to Lord Minto, 2 January 1855.

44. MacCarthy and Russell (eds), *Lady John Russell*, Lord John to Fanny, 23 February 1855.

45. NLS MS 11899A, ff. 215–216, Henry Elliot to Lord Minto, 9 April 1855.

46. MacCarthy and Russell (eds), *Lady John Russell*, p. 154.

47. NLS MS 11899A, ff. 217–219, Henry Elliot to Lord Minto, 23 April 1855.

48. MacCarthy and Russell (eds), *Lady John Russell*, pp. 158–159.

49. NLS MS 11899A, ff. 219–222, Henry Elliot to Lord Minto, 20 June 1855.

50. Melville Portal (1819–1904) went to Harrow and Christ Church, Oxford, becoming president of the Oxford Union in 1842. He was called to the bar in 1845 and as a Peelite was elected MP for North Hampshire. He spoke in the House of Commons for the first time in March 1851. The couple were to have three sons and three daughters. In 1863 he became High Sheriff for Hampshire.

51. NLS MS 11899A, ff. 227–230, Henry Elliot to Lord Minto, 3 October 1855.

52. Sir George Hamilton Seymour (1797–1880), a well-established diplomat, had been sent to St Petersburg in April 1851, where he conducted the 'Seymour conversations' with the Czar between January and February 1853. He was recalled just before the outbreak of the Crimean War after the conversations were leaked in the press. Although pensioned in October 1854, he was recalled the following year to participate in the Vienna discussions which ultimately led to the end of the war and the Treaty of Paris in 1856.

53. NLS MS 11899A, ff. 231–233, Henry Elliot to Lord Minto, 29 November 1855.

54. NLS MS 11899A, ff. 234–241, Henry Elliot to Lord Minto, week ending 6 January 1856.

55. Possibly Granville Augustus William Waldegrave (1833–1913), third Baron Radstock, a philanthropist and evangelist who served as an Army officer towards the end of the Crimean War.

56. NLS MS 11899A, ff. 242–243, Henry Elliot to Lord Minto, 31 March 1856.

57. NLS MS 11899A, ff. 246–251, Henry Elliot to Lord Minto, 21 May 1856.

58. MacCarthy and Russell (eds), *Lady John Russell*, pp. 165–166.

59. NLS MS 11899A, ff. 262–265, Henry Elliot to Lord Minto, 26 August 1856.

60. NLS MS 11899A, ff. 266–269, Henry Elliot to Lord Minto, 2 September 1856.

61. MacCarthy and Russell (eds), *Lady John Russell*, Lord John Russell to Lady Melgund, 19 December 1856.

62. Originally named Giacomo Filippe Lacaiti (1814–95), this Italian politician had been arrested in 1851 for having supplied Gladstone with information about Bourbon misrule.

63. YBL Osborn File 10316, Lord Minto to Murray 3 December 1856.

64. NLS MS 11899A, ff. 270–271, Henry Elliot to Lord Minto, 31 March 1857.

65. MacCarthy and Russell (eds), *Lady John Russell*, Fanny to Lord Minto, 4 April 1857.

66. Ibid., Charles Dickens to Lady Russell, 22 May 1857.

67. NLS MS 11899A, ff. 270–271, Henry Elliot to Lord Minto, 30 June 1857.

68. Palmerston did not foresee the potential advantages the canal would bring for British trade and was opposed to the setting up of a powerful company by the French on Egyptian soil.

69. NLS MS 11899A, ff. 277–280, Henry Elliot to Lord Minto, 31 July 1857.

70. A report by the Commissioners on promotion in the Army had pressed for promotion above the rank of lieutenant colonel to be on merit. Promotions to colonel, historically by seniority, might be based on years in active service.

71. NLS MS 11899A, ff. 285–288, Henry Elliot to Lord Minto, 25 September 1857.

72. NLS MS 11899A, ff. 289–292, Henry Elliot to Lord Minto, 17 February 1858.

73. Lord Palmerston's administration was overthrown when his Conspiracy to Murder Bill was defeated in Parliament in February 1858. The Tory leader Lord Derby became Prime Minister briefly and the Earl of Malmesbury Secretary of State for Foreign Affairs.

74. Sir Henry Elliot, *Some Revolutions and Other Diplomatic Experiences*, p. 4.

75. MacCarthy and Russell (eds), *Lady John Russell*, p. 191.

76. Admiral George Rodney Munday (1805–1884) was the grandson of Lord Rodney and at this time he was coming to the end of his career. He was to become commander-in-chief, North America, in 1867 and Portsmouth between 1872 and 1875.

77. Sir Henry Elliot, *Some Revolutions and Other Diplomatic Experiences*, p. 127.

78. Ibid., p. 166.

79. Ibid., p. 169.

80. Ibid., pp. 171–176.

81. MacCarthy and Russell (eds), *Lady John Russell*, pp. 200–203.

82. Ibid., Lord Russell to Lady Minto, 11 November 1866.

83. Ferdinand de Lesseps (1805–1904), who had been vice consul at Alexandria in the 1830s, held numerous diplomatic posts until his retirement in 1851. Three years later, Said Pasha invited him to build the Suez Canal and several schemes were drawn up by two French engineers in the service of the government, Louis de Bellefonds and Mougel Bey. In 1856 their plan was adopted after it had been scrutinised by an international commission of civil engineers.

84. Sir Henry Elliot, *Some Revolutions and Other Diplomatic Experiences*, pp. 191–192.

85. Ibid., pp. 195–196.

86. Granville George Leveson-Gower, the second Earl Granville (1815–1891), moved from the Colonial to the Foreign Office in 1870 on the sudden death of Lord Clarendon.

87. Sir Henry Elliot, *Some Revolutions and Other Diplomatic Experiences*, pp. 203–204.

88. Ibid., pp. 222–226.

89. Mehmed Murad V (1840–1904) became sultan when his uncle Abdulaziz was deposed. He was to reign for ninety-three days before also being deposed on the grounds that he was mentally ill. His successor was Abdulhamid II.

90. Sir Henry Elliot, *Some Revolutions and Other Diplomatic Experiences*, pp. 235–236.

91. Ibid., pp. 255–256.

92. Ibid., pp. 260–263.

93. Ibid., pp. 267–269.

94. Ibid., p. 274.

95. Ibid., pp. 276–280.

96. Ibid., pp. 281–282.

97. Ibid., p. 286.

98. Ibid., pp. 288–290.

99. Ibid., pp. 293–295.

## 12
## Gilbert – The Young Soldier (1842–1865)

1. NLS MS 12016, ff. 1–11, Gilbert's Journal, September to November 1845.
2. NLS MS 12016, f. 12, Gilbert's Journal, 18 to 19 June 1846.
3. NLS MS 12241, f. 17, Lord Minto to William, 2 May 1847.
4. NLS MS 12016, f. 14, Gilbert's Journal, 24 May 1847.
5. Launched in 1819, HMS *Belleisle*, a third-rate ship of the line, had been converted into a 20-gun troopship in 1844.
6. NLS MS 11782, ff. 39–43, Gilbert to Harriet, 4 and 14 December 1847.
7. NLS MS 12016, f. 17, Gilbert's Journal, 23 April 1848.
8. NLS MS 11764, ff. 36–38, Gilbert to Harriet, 27 February 1848.
9. NLS MS 11901, ff. 175–176, Gilbert to Lady Minto, 4 May 1849.
10. NLS MS 11783, ff. 18–19, 27–28, Gilbert to Charlotte, 17 May 1849.
11. NLS MS 11901, ff. 169–170, Gilbert to Lady Minto, 4 August 1848.
12. NLS MS 11764, ff. 42–48, Gilbert to Charlotte, 22 December 1848.
13. NLS MS 13167, ff. 138–141, Harriet to Lady Mary, 14 May 1850.
14. NLS MS 11764, ff. 60–61, Lord Minto to Gilbert, 21 March 1850.
15. NLS MS 12016, f. 21, Gilbert's Journal, 27 April 1850.
16. NLS MS 12016, f. 22, Gilbert Elliot's Journal, 1 July 1850.
17. NLS MS 12016, f. 24, Gilbert Elliot's Journal, 11 July 1850.
18. NLS MS 12016, f. 25, Gilbert Elliot's Journal, 20 November 1850
19. Sir William H. Cope, *History of the Rifle Brigade*, chap. 9, pp. 286–289.
20. Ibid., pp. 290–91.
21. NLS MS 13091, ff. 1–11, Gilbert Elliot to George, 11 January 1853.
22. NLS MS 13091, ff. 13–14, Gilbert Elliot to George, 11 February 1853.
23. NLS MS 13091, ff. 16–18, Gilbert Elliot to George, 14 April 1853.
24. NLS MS 13091, ff. 19–23, Gilbert Elliot to George, 16 May 1853.
25. NLS MS 13091, ff. 24–26, Gilbert Elliot to George, 16 June 1853.
26. NLS MS 13091, ff. 27–30, Gilbert Elliot to George, 12 July 1853.
27. NLS MS13091, ff. 31–36 Gilbert Elliot to George, 12 September 1853.
28. Cope, *History of the Rifle Brigade*, chaps 9 and 10, pp. 296–97 and 298–303 respectively.
29. Gilbert's ship had been built for the Admiralty as the corvette HMS *Recruit*. She was purchased and renamed *Harbinger* when she was converted to being a troop transport in 1854.
30. NLS MS11765A, ff. 1–2, Gilbert Elliot to Charlotte, 31 August 1854.
31. NLS MS11765A, f. 3, Gilbert Elliot to Charlotte, 1 September 1854.
32. NLS MS 11765A, ff. 4–7, Gilbert Elliot to George, 17 September 1854.
33. Cope, *History of the Rifle Brigade*, chap. 10, p. 306.
34. Ibid., p. 309.
35. NLS MS 11765A, ff. 8–12, Gilbert Elliot to Charlotte, 21 September 1854.
36. NLS MS 11765A, ff. 13–14, Gilbert Elliot to George, 22 September 1854.
37. NLS MS 11765A, ff. 15–17, Gilbert Elliot to George, 2 October 1854.
38. NLS MS 11765A, ff. 18–20, Gilbert Elliot to George, 10 October 1854.
39. NLS MS 11765A, ff. 21–24, Gilbert Elliot to Harriet 22 October 1854.
40. NLS MS 11765A, ff. 25–26, Gilbert Elliot to George, 22 October 1854.
41. NLS MS 11765A, ff. 27–33, Gilbert Elliot to George, 27 October 1854.
42. On 5 November, General Sir George Cathcart, with whom Gilbert had been in South Africa, became involved in another fatal confusion which stemmed from the dispatch of contradictory orders, some of which he received and others which he did not. After the death of General Torrens almost as soon as an attack on Mount Inkerman had started, Cathcart was to say to a staff officer, 'I fear we are in a mess.' Minutes later he fell from his horse, shot through the heart.
43. NLS MS 11765A, ff. 34–35, Gilbert Elliot to George, 6 November 1854.
44. The Disbrowe referred to was one of Sir Edward Cromwell Disbrowe's two sons. His father had been British ambassador to the Netherlands. He died at The Hague in 1851.
45. NLS MS 11765A, ff. 36–39, Gilbert Elliot to Lotty, 7 November 1854.
46. NLS MS 11765A, ff. 40–41, Gilbert Elliot to Fanny, 7 November 1854.
47. NLS MS 11765A, ff. 44–50, Gilbert Elliot to George, 20/21 November 1854. For a fuller account of this exploit and the exchange of correspondence between Lord Raglan and General Canrobert, see Cope's *History of the Rifle Brigade*, pp. 322–327.
48. NLS MS 11765A, ff. 51–55, Gilbert Elliot to Lord Minto, 27 November 1854.
49. NLS MS 11765A, ff. 58–60, Gilbert Elliot to Lord Minto, 6 December 1854.
50. NLS MS 11765A, ff. 63–67, Gilbert Elliot to Henry, 16 December 1854.
51. NLS MS 11765, f. 7, Gilbert Elliot to Lord Minto, 15 January 1855.
52. NLS MS 11765 f. 17, Gilbert Elliot to Lotty, 21 January 1855.

53. NLS MS 11765 f. 37, Gilbert Elliot to Lotty, 28 January 1855.
54. Cope, *History of the Rifle Brigade*, Appendix IV, pp. 334 and 525.
55. NLS MS 11765A, ff. 69–70, Gilbert Elliot to Lotty, 9 July 1855.
56. NLS MS 11765A, ff. 71–73, Gilbert Elliot's Journal, 11–13 July 1855.
57. NLS MS 11765A, ff. 78–80, Gilbert Elliot's Journal, 19–20 July 1855.
58. NLS MS 11765A, ff. 81–83, Gilbert Elliot's Journal, 21–23 July 1855.
59. Cope, *History of the Rifle Brigade*, pp. 334–340.
60. NLS MS 11765A, ff. 87–88, Gilbert to Lotty, 9 November 1855.
61. NLS MS 11765A, f. 89, Gilbert to Lotty, 20 November 1855.
62. NLS MS 11765A, f. 90, Gilbert to Lotty, 24 December 1855.
63. NLS MS 11765A, f. 93, Gilbert to Lotty, 25 January 1856.
64. NLS MS 11765A, f. 94, Gilbert to Lotty, 15 February 1856.
65. NLS MS 11765A, f. 95, Gilbert to Lotty, 10 March 1856.
66. NLS MS 11765A, ff. 96–97, Gilbert to Lotty, 17 March 1856.
67. Count Alexander Nikolajewitsch von Lüders (1790–1874) commanded the Southern Russian army in the Crimean War.
68. NLS MS 11765A, ff. 98–99, Gilbert to Lotty, 18 April 1856.
69. NLS MS 11765A, f. 100, Gilbert to Lotty, 19 May 1856.
70. NLS MS 11765A, ff. 101–102, Gilbert to Lotty, 26 May 1856.
71. Cope, *History of the Rifle Brigade*, pp. 342–343.
72. The four privates in the 2nd Battalion of the Rifle Brigade who were awarded the Victoria Cross were Joseph Bradshaw, Francis Wheatley, Roderick McGregor and R. Humpston.
73. Little is known about Gilbert's wife Katherine except that she was one of eleven children and brought with her a dowry of £8,000. She died on 30 May 1895.
74. Lady Sarah Maitland's husband was Sir Peregrine Maitland (1777–1854). After serving in the Napoleonic Wars, he became lieutenant-governor of Upper Canada (1818), Nova Scotia (1828), and governor of the Cape of Good Hope (1844). He retired in 1852 and died at Eaton Place, West London, in May 1854. Sir Peregrine married firstly Harriet Crofton and secondly Lady Sarah Lennox, the daughter of the fourth Duke of Richmond. He had three sons and three daughters.
75. NLS MS 13091, ff. 37–38, Gilbert Elliot to George, 4 June 1859.
76. NLS MS 13091, ff. 40–43, Gilbert Elliot to George, 22 January 1860.
77. NLS MS 13091, ff. 44–47, Gilbert Elliot to George, 28 April 1860.
78. NLS MS 13091, ff. 48–51, Gilbert Elliot to George, 11 May 1860.
79. NLS MS 13091, ff. 52–55, Gilbert Elliot to George, 15 February 1861.
80. NLS MS 13091, ff. 56–57, Gilbert Elliot to George, 4 May 1864.
81. NLS MS 13091, ff. 58–60, Gilbert Elliot to George, 31 May 1864.
82. MacCarthy and Russell (eds), *Lady John Russell*, Fanny to Lady Georgians Russell, 21 September 1864.
83. NLS MS 13091, ff. 61–62, Gilbert Elliot to George, 16 August 1864.
84. NLS MS 13091, ff. 63–64, Gilbert Elliot to George, 31 January 1865.
85. NLS MS 13106, An account of the last days of the Hon. Gilbert Elliot by his wife, *c*. 1865.

## 13
## Captain Charles Elliot's Later Years (1845–1895)

1. NLS MS 13090, ff. 1–3, Charles to George, 1 June 1859.
2. NLS MS 13090, ff. 4–5, Charles to George, 15 July 1859.
3. NLS MS 13090, ff. 6–8, Charles to George, 23 and 24 July 1859.
4. NLS MS 13090, ff. 9–10, Charles to George, 17 September 1859.
5. NLS MS 13090, ff. 11–12, Charles to George, 12 November 1859.
6. NLS MS 13090, ff. 13–14, Charles to George, 17 December 1859.
7. NLS MS 13090, ff. 15–16, Charles to George, 2 and 7 February 1860.
8. NLS MS 13090, ff. 19–20, Charles to George, 24 March 1860.
9. NLS MS 13090, f. 24, Charles to George, 29 May 1860.
10. NLS MS 13090, ff. 25–26, Charles to George, 29 May 1860.
11. Rt Hon. Sir John Drummond Hay (1816–1893) became an attaché at the age of twenty-four at Constantinople, where he remained for four years until he was transferred to the court of Morocco, becoming consul-general. After negotiating a treaty with the Moroccan government in 1856, he became minister resident in 1862. He retired from the Foreign Service in 1886.
12. NLS MS 13090, ff. 27–28, Charles to George, 28 June 1861.
13. NLS MS 13090, ff. 31–32, Charles to George, 2 July 1861.
14. NLS MS 13090, ff. 33–36, Charles to George, 5 July 1861.
15. NLS MS 13090, ff. 37–39, Charles to George, 6 July 1861.
16. NLS MS 13090, ff. 42–45, Charles to George, 22 July 1861.

17. NLS MS 13090, ff. 46–47, Charles to George, 24 January 1863.

18. NLS MS 13090, ff. 48–49, Charles to George, 29 January 1863.

19. Ernst Leopold, fourth Prince of Leiningen, had been born at Amorbach, Bavaria, in 1830. He married Princess Marie Amelie of Baden at Karlsruhe in September 1858. They had two children, Alberta and Emich. Ernst served in the Second Anglo-Burmese War of 1851–52 and in the Crimean War. In 1880 the prince was selected for the post of second-in-command of the Channel squadron, but the Gladstone government came into office and rescinded the appointment In 1885 he was appointed commander at the Nore, which was his last service. He died in 1901.

20. NLS MS 13090, ff. 50–51, Charles to George, 9 February 1863.

21. Based on extracts from *The Times* published on the internet by Peter Davis, Zeist, Netherlands.

22. NLS MS 13090, ff. 52–55, Charles to George, 6 May 1864.

23. NLS MS 13090, ff. 56–60, Charles to George, 3 July 1864.

24. HMS *Actaeon* was a sixth-rate wooden sailing vessel of 620 tons which was in South America between 1838 and 1842 under the command of Captain Robert Russell.

25. NLS MS 13090, ff. 62–66, Charles to George, 3 July 1864.

26. NLS MS 13090, f. 67, Charles to George, 27 July 1864.

27. Hansard, 12 July 1864.

28. Venancio Flores (1809–1868) invaded Uruguay in 1863 for a third time but was defeated at Las Piedras on 16 August. When war between the republic and Brazil began, Flores, assisted by a Brazilian and Argentine force, blockaded Montevideo and forced Villalba, who had taken charge of the government, to enter into an arrangement by which Flores was elected president.

29. NLS MS 13090, ff. 67–68, Charles to George, 21 July 1864.

30. Isabel (de Bourbon e Braganca) married Louis Gaston, comte d'Eu, son of the Duke of Nemours, and Leopoldina (de Bourbon e Braganca) married Prince Ludwig August of Kohary of Saxe-Coburg-Gotha.

31. NLS MS 13090, ff. 69–70, Charles to George, 9 August 1864.

32. NLS MS 13090, ff. 72–75, Charles to George, 9 October 1864.

33. Edward (later Sir Edward) Thornton (1817–1906) was educated at King's College and Pembroke College, Cambridge. After initial service as a diplomat in Portugal he was attached to the mission at Turin in 1842. Three years later he went to the republic of Mexico where he was first a paid attaché and then, at the end of 1851, secretary of legation. For six months in 1853 he had been secretary to Sir Charles Hotham's special mission to the River Plate (1852–53) which drew up a convention for the free navigation of the Paraná and Uruguay rivers. In 1854 he became chargé d'affaires and consul-general at Montevideo, and minister plenipotentiary at Buenos Aires in 1859 and was accredited to the republic of Paraguay in 1863. In July 1865 he was sent on a special mission to Brazil for the renewal of diplomatic relations which had been broken off by the Brazilian government in 1863. Shortly afterwards, he became the British envoy at Rio de Janeiro.

34. NLS MS 13090, ff. 76–79, Charles to George, 30 October 1864.

35. William Bragge had built the first railway line in Argentina between 1855 and 1857 using a locomotive called *La Porteña* built in Leeds. It seems Admiral Elliot found time to travel a few miles on a railway under construction where along the whole length of some 60 or 70 miles the greatest elevation above the sea would be only 60 feet.

36. NLS MS 13090, ff. 81–84, Charles to George, 14 November 1864.

37. NLS MS 13090, ff. 85–88, Charles to George, 20 November 1864.

38. NLS MS 13090, ff. 89–93, Charles to George, 20 and 21 December 1864.

39. NLS MS 13090, ff. 94–101, Charles to George, 29 December 1864 and 9 January 1865.

40. NLS MS 13090, ff. 102–103, Charles to George, 14 January 1865.

41. NLS MS 13090, ff. 110–111, Charles to George, 29 January 1865.

42. NLS MS 13090, ff. 114–116, Charles to George, 14 February 1865.

43. NLS MS 13090, f. 123, Charles to George, 15 February 1865.

44. The subsequent account of the court-martial in February 1865 is based on that published in *The Times*.

45. Based on extracts of the proceedings of the court-martial in Portsmouth, February 1865, and published on the internet by Peter Davis, Zeist, Netherlands.

46. Francisco Solano López, the President of Paraguay, accurately assessed that Brazil's intervention in Uruguay had been seen as a slight against the region's lesser powers, but he wrongly concluded that the preservation of Uruguay's independence would be critical to his own nation's future. When Argentina did not react to Brazil's invasion of Uruguay, he invaded Mato Grosso in March 1865 and followed this by striking at Brazil's main force in Uruguay. The Argentine decided not to support Paraguay against Brazil, but when López requested permission for his army to cross Argentinian territory to attack the Brazilian province of Rio Grande do Sul, Argentina refused. Undeterred, he invaded – thereby setting the stage for Argentina, Brazil and Uruguay to sign a treaty which avowed the destruction of Paraguay.

47. NLS MS 13090, ff. 131–133, Charles to George, 14 April 1865.

48. Rumours originating from Rio de Janeiro suggested that Bolivia might act against Brazil but Peru, another candidate, had her own internal battles to attend to.

49. NLS MS 13090, ff. 134–137, Charles to George, 28 April 1865.

50. NLS MS 13090, ff. 145–148, Charles to George, 10 and 13 July 1865.

51. NLS MS 13090, ff. 149–154, Charles to George, 6 September 1865.

52. NLS MS 13090, ff. 159–161, Charles to George, 24 October 1865.

53. NLS MS 13090, ff. 162–165, Charles to George, 8 November 1865.

54. NLS MS 13090, ff. 166–170, Charles to George, 14 December 1865.

55. NLS MS 13090, ff. 173–175, Charles to George, 1 March 1866.

56. NLS MS 13090, ff. 178–181, Charles to George, 29 March 1866.

57. NLS MS 13090, ff. 182–186, Charles to George, 14 May 1866.

58. NLS MS 13090, ff. 187–190, Charles to George, 29 May 1866.

59. NLS MS 13090, ff. 191–192, Charles to George, 14 June 1866.

60. Lady Cecil, Dowager Marchioness of Lothian, died in 1877.

61. Charles and Louisa's visitors at this time may possibly have been Sir Walter George Stirling and his first wife Eliza Seymour from Faskine, a hamlet not far from Airdrie.

62. NLS MS 21230, ff. 34–46, Miscellaneous Papers relating to life at Bonjedward House 1867–70.

63. NLS MS 21228, ff. 1–5, Admiral Charles Elliot's Letter Book while at Sheerness Dockyard 1870–73.

64. NLS MS 12251, ff. 135–137, Charles to William, 13 December 1873.

65. NLS MS 12251, ff. 138–139, Charles to William, 23 December 1873.

66. John Pakington, first Baron Hampton, had twice been First Lord of the Admiralty and became president of the Institute of Naval Architects. He married three times and died in 1880.

67. NLS MS 12251, ff. 147–149, Charles to William, 1 January 1878.

68. The 1881 census shows that the Elliots had some six female servants and two domestic footmen.

69. NLS MS 12251, ff. 150–153, Charles to William, 26 February 1880.

70. Empress Eugénie (1826–1920) fled the Tuileries after Louis Napoleon's defeat by Prussia at Sedan and, having obtained a berth in a private British yacht, she arrived in Ryde on 8 September 1870. She was shortly afterwards joined by the aging Louis Napoleon, who had been released from a German prison and who was to die in 1873. The family, and a retinue of sixty, settled down at Camden Place, Chislehurst, Kent, and Napoleon Eugene (1856–1879), the Prince Imperial sometimes called Louis, joined the British Army, only to be killed in June 1879 during the Anglo-Zulu War. A heartbroken Empress Eugénie was on her way to make a pilgrimage to Sobuza's kraal when Admiral Charlie and Harriette offered their 'civilities'. It was the end of the Bonaparte claim to rule France.

71. NLS MS 12251, ff. 154–157, Charles to William, 26 March 1880.

72. NLS MS 12251, ff. 158–160, Charles to William, 27 May 1880.

73. NLS MS 13090, ff. 195–198, Charles to George, 29 May 1881.

74. NLS MS 12251, ff. 167–168, Charles to William, 30 October 1888.

75. NLS MS 12251, ff. 191–192, Charles to William, 13 October 1890.

76. NLS MS 12251, ff. 171–176, Charles to William, 30 August 1890.

77. NLS MS 12251, ff. 184–186, Charles to William, 23 February 1891.

78. NLS MS 12251, ff. 187–188, Charles to William, 24 April 1891.


## 14

## George Francis Elliot – A Brotherly Lawyer (1847–1901)

1. NLS MS 12252, ff. 7–9, George to William, 8 January 1840.

2. NLS MS 12252, ff. 10–11, George to William, 23 February 1840.

3. NLS MS 12252, ff. 12–13, George to William, September 1840.

4. NLS MS 12252, ff. 14–19, George to William, 9 November 1847.

5. NLS MS 12252, ff. 20–22, George to William, 19 December 1847.

6. NLS MS 12252, ff. 30–35, George to William, 15 March 1854.

7. MacCarthy and Russell (eds), *Lady John Russell*, Fanny to Lady Mary Abercromby, 14 February 1854.

8. Ibid., Fanny to Lady Elizabeth Romilly, 28 February 1854.

9. NLS MS 12252, ff. 38–41, George to William, 9 February 1856.

10. NLS MS 12252, ff. 42–48; George to William, 10 and 14 December 1858.

11. NLS MS 12252, ff. 49–50, George to William, 27 August 1859.

12. NLS MS 12252, ff. 51–54, George to William, 6 September 1859.

13. NLS MS 12252, ff. 55–59, George to William, 28 December 1859.

14. NLS MS 13091 (iii), ff. 151–152, William to George, 3 May 1865.

15. In 1866 Walter Elliot was created a Knight Commander of the Star of India and in 1877 he was elected a Fellow of the Royal Society. He spent the rest of his life at Wolfelee in Roxburghshire, becoming deputy lieutenant of the county and a magistrate. He died on 1 March 1887, the same day that he wrote to a Tamil scholar in praise of his translation of the Tamil Kural, remarking how his own interest in literature continued 'unabated'. He was survived by his wife and five of his children.

16. NLS MS 13092, ff. 1–2 and 3–4, Walter Elliot to George, 12 January and 24 March 1864.

17. NLS MS 12252, ff. 64–66, George to William, 23 October 1865.

18. NLS MS 13092, ff. 11–13, William Fraser to George, 14 November 1867.

19. NLS MS 13092, ff. 17–18, Dr Aitkin to George, 10 and 14 January 1868.

20. NLS MS 19471, ff. 13–14, William to George, 29 June 1868.

21. NLS MS 19471, ff. 26–27, Fanny to George, 1 July 1868.

22. NLS MS 19471, ff. 20–23, Lady Mary to George, 2 July 1868.
23. NLS MS 19471, ff. 28–29, Elizabeth (Lizzy) to George, 6 July 1868.
24. NLS MS 13092, ff. 21–22, Walter Elliot to George, 31 March 1871.
25. NLS MS 13092, ff. 25–26, Riddell-Carre to George, 10 June 1872.
26. NLS MS 13092, ff. 30–64, Ninion Elliot to George, 7 January to June 1876.
27. NLS MS 12252, ff. 67–69, George to William, 6 July 1876.
28. NLS MS 12252, ff. 70–73, George to William, 7 November 1876.
29. NLS MS 12252, ff. 74–75, George to William, 10 November 1876.
30. NLS MS 12252, ff. 76–77, George to William, 30 November 1876.
31. MacCarthy and Russell (eds), *Lady John Russell*, pp. 246–247.
32. Ibid., Queen Victoria to Fanny, 30 May 1878.
33. Ibid., Lady Minto to Lady Russell, 4 June 1878.
34. NLS MS 13092, ff. 70–77, Rev Ridlon to George, 23 March 1879 and a note of June 1879 from George.
35. NLS MS 13092, ff. 85–88, Robert Armstrong to George, 12 November and 2 December 1879.
36. The bill was the Metropolis Waterworks Purchase Bill.
37. Arthur's eldest brother was Gilbert, who was to become the fourth Earl Minto. Hugh and William were his other brothers. When he was only five years old Arthur had a fall and had to have his leg amputated. In consequence he did not go to school but his injury did not prevent him from climbing, riding to hounds and swimming. However, he went to Edinburgh University in 1863 and matriculated at Trinity College, Cambridge, in 1864, gained his BA in 1868 and was admitted to Lincoln's Inn in 1868 and the Temple, where he was called to the bar in 1870. After serving as MP for Roxburghshire until 1892, he represented Durham City between 1898 and 1906, becoming Financial Secretary to the Treasury in 1903.
38. Eustice Smith (1831–1903), who lived at Gosforth Park near Newcastle, was a member of one of Tyneside's most prosperous shipping families. He held the parliamentary seat there for the Liberals until 1885.
39. NLS MS 12252, ff. 80–81, George to William, 9 March 1880.
40. NLS MS 12252, ff. 82–83, George to William, 16 March 1880.
41. NLS MS 12252, ff. 84–85, George to William, 24 March 1880.
42. NLS MS 12252, ff. 86–87, George to William, 27 March 1880.
43. NLS MS 12252, ff. 88–89, George to William, 31 March 1880.
44. NLS MS 12252, ff. 90–92, George to William, 7 April 1880.
45. NLS MS 12252, ff. 93–96, George to William, 10 April 1880.
46. Henry Brand was in fact followed as Speaker in 1886 by Arthur Wellesley Peel, Sir Robert's youngest son.
47. Hugh Culling Eardley Childers (1827–1896) had been educated at Cheam School and both Wadham College, Oxford, and Trinity College, Cambridge. He started his career in Australia, returning to London in 1857 as agent-general for the state of Victoria. He became Liberal MP for Pontefract and in 1864 became a Civil Lord of the Admiralty and, in the following year, Financial Secretary to the Treasury when Gladstone was Chancellor of the Exchequer in Palmerston's administration. In 1868 Childers was appointed First Lord of the Admiralty in Gladstone's first administration, resigning in 1871 after the death of his son when HMS *Captain* sank in the Bay of Biscay. As Secretary for War in Gladstone's second administration he saw the Anglo-Transvaal War of 1881 and the Egyptian campaign of 1882.
48. NLS MS 12252, ff. 99–101, George to William. 30 April 1880.
49. NLS MS 13092, ff. 89–93, Robert Armstrong to George, 3 June, 23 August and 5 October 1880.
50. NLS MS 13092, ff. 120–130, Robert Armstrong to George, 28 May and 12 June 1881.
51. NLS MS 13091 (iii), ff. 153–154, William to George, 13 April 1881.
52. NLS MS 13091 (iii), ff. 155–157, William to George, 27 November 1886.
53. Hon. William Warren Vernon (1834–1919) was the son of the fifth Baron Vernon and Isabella Ellison. His elder brother, Augustus Henry, became the sixth Baron and died in 1883. William was educated at Eton and Christ Church, Oxford. On leaving university he was commissioned in the Staffordshire Militia. He was first married in 1855, his wife being Agnes Lucy, third daughter of Sir John Boileau, who died in 1881, His second wife, whom he married in 1884, was Annie Georgiana, daughter of Charles Eyre of Welford Park, Newbury. He had a son, Reginald William, by his first wife and two children by his second wife – Mary Ann (1885–1957) and Arnold (1887–1906). He was a student of medieval history and towards the end of his life he became a Dante scholar, publishing commentaries and translations of the *Divine Comedy*. He was to die aged eighty-five.
54. NLS MS 13092, ff. 144–149, Walter Elliot to George, 6 October 1884.
55. George Elliot, *Sir James Hudson and Earl Russell: An Historical Rectification*, p. 8.
56. Sir James Lacaita (1813–1895), born in Italy, settled in the 1850s in Edinburgh, where he married Maria Carmichael. He became an intimate friend of Lord John Russell and Fanny. He returned in late 1860 to Naples, where he had originally practised law. In 1876 he became a senator and a director of the Italian Southern Railway Company, dying in 1895 at Posilipo. As a Dante specialist with many articles to his name, he cooperated with Lord Vernon in the production of the latter's edition of the *Inferno*.
57. William Vernon, *Recollections of Seventy-Two Years*, p. 307.
58. NLS MS 12252, ff. 102–103, George to William, 5 June 1886.
59. NLS MS 12252, ff. 108–109, George to William, 2 November 1889.
60. NLS MS 12252, ff. 110–111, George to William, 19 March 1890.

61. Nathan Bailey first published his *Dictionarium Britannicum* in 1730. It contained some 48,000 words and proved very popular.

62. NLS MS 12252, ff. 112–114, George to William, 27 March 1890.

63. NLS MS 12252, ff. 115–116, George to William, 24 May 1890.

64. NLS MS 12252, ff. 120–121, George to William, 10 July 1890.

65. John Francis Stanley Russell's second marriage to Maria Cooke also ended in divorce in 1915, as did his third marriage to Mary Annette Beauchamp in 1919.

66. NLS MS 12252, ff. 124–125, George to William, 29 July 1890.

67. NLS MS 12252, ff. 126–127, George to William, 25 August 1890.

68. This may have been a reference to Colonel James Yule (1847–1920), who at that time would have been about to leave for an expedition to Burma.

69. NLS MS 12252, ff. 130–131, Laurence G. Holland to Rt Hon. Sir Henry George Elliot PC, GCB, 20 November 1890.

70. The strike on the North British Company ended on 29 January 1891, that on the Caledonian on 31 January and that on the Glasgow and South Western Railways on 31 December 1890. Some 8,000 men went on strike during this period and the effect on the industries of Scotland was immediate and serious. Stocks of coal were speedily exhausted and a 100,000 people were without work or wages.

71. MacCarthy and Russell (eds), *Lady John Russell*, Queen Victoria to Fanny, 1 January 1891.

72. BLO MS Eng.Lett.e.113, ff. 24–27. Fanny's letters to Rollo, 23 October 1891.

73. BLO MS Eng.Lett.e.113, ff. 28–29. Fanny's letters to Rollo, 19 November 1891.

74. Dunrozel, a property near Haslemere, had been bought by Rollo in the summer of 1883. It had been named after Rozel in Normandy, which was supposed to be the original home of the Russells.

75. NLS MS 13092, ff. 165–168, Robert Armstrong to George, 18 November 1892.

76. NLS MS 13092, ff. 180–183, Col. Robert Boyle to George, 8 December 1892.

77. NLS MS 13091 (iii), ff. 167–172, Hugh Elliot to George, 26 November 1892.

78. NLS MS 13092, ff. 206–214, Robert Armstrong to George, 16 and 24 November, also Robert Purdom to George, 23 November 1893.

79. NLS MS 13092, ff. 231–233, Archibald Dunbar to George, 13 December 1893.

80. BLO MS Eng.Lett.e.113, ff. 72–75, Fanny's letters to Rollo, 3 and 13 February 1894.

81. Bertrand Russell was to grow increasingly cold and irritable towards Alys and after several affairs and separation they were eventually divorced in 1921. He married his second wife Dora Black the same year, divorcing her in 1935. He married Patricia Spence in January 1936 and they were divorced in 1952. His fourth wife was Edith Finch, whom he married in 1952. He died in 1970.

82. BLO MS Eng.Lett.e.113, ff. 84–85, Fanny's letters to Rollo, 18 April 1895.

83. Arthur had lost his Roxburghshire seat in 1892 and was to be defeated in 1895 standing for the City of Durham, which he subsequently won in 1898, holding it until 1906. He became editor of the *Edinburgh Review* in 1895, writing some sixty articles, and in 1911 he published *The Life of George Joachim Goschen*.

84. NLS MS 13091 (iii), ff. 177–180, Arthur to George, undated and 27 February 1897.

85. NLS MS 13091 (iii), ff. 181–184, Arthur to George, late spring 1897.

86. Cecil Rhodes (1853–1902) was the colonial politician, Leander Starr Jameson (1853–1917) the leader of the raid of that name, and Digby Willoughby (1845–1901) a soldier, adventurer and member of the council of defence at Bulawayo.

87. BLO MS Eng.Lett.e.113, ff. 98–99, Fanny's letters to Rollo, 28 November 1895.

88. BLO MS Eng.Lett.e.113, ff. 121–122, Fanny's letters to Rollo, 23 February 1897.

89. MacCarthy and Russell (eds), *Lady John Russell*, p. 287.

90. Craig-Brown Collection, Scottish Borders Council, two letters from George to Craig-Brown, December 1897.

91. NLS MS 13091 (iii), ff. 191–192, Samuel Romilly to George, 4 December 1897.

92. NLS MS 13091 (iii), f. 193, Margaret Elliot to George, 4 December 1897.

93. NLS MS 13091 (iii), ff. 196–197, Katie Scott (one of Lotty's daughters) to George, 5 December 1897.

94. One of the many Trotters in the British Army married the Hon. Mary Catherine Elizabeth (d. 1908), the only child of Ralph Abercromby and Lady Mary, the second Earl Minto's eldest daughter.

95. NLS MS 13091 (iii), ff. 198–199, 'Mimi' Trotter to George, 5 December 1897.

96. NLS MS 13091 (iii), ff. 200–201, Rollo Russell to George, 5 December 1897.

97. NLS MS 13091 (iii), ff. 202–203, William Fitzwilliam to George, 5 December 1897.

98. NLS MS 13091 (iii), ff. 204–205, Fanny to George, 5 December 1897.

99. NLS MS 13091 (iii), ff. 206–207, Harriette Liddell to George, 6 December 1897.

100. NLS MS 13091 (iii), ff. 208–214, Charlotte to George, 6 and 18 December 1897.

101. NLS MS 13091 (iii), ff. 215–216, Sir Francis G. M. Boileau to George, 11 December 1897.

102. NLS MS 13091 (iii), ff. 219–220, Henry to George, 21 December 1897.

103. NLS MS 13091 (iii), ff. 234–235, Admiral George Elliot to George, 15 January 1898.

104. NLS MS 13091 (iii), ff. 240–241, Arthur Elliot to George, undated.

105. *A Scottish Border Clan* was published in a miscellany of articles and book reviews entitled *Selkirk Various*, pp. 485–521. See the Craig-Brown Collection, Scottish Borders Council.

106. Vernon, *Recollections*, pp. 360–363.

# SOURCES AND BIBLIOGRAPHY

MANUSCRIPTS

Bodleian Library, Oxford
MS Eng.Lett.e.113, Lady Fanny Russell's letters to Rollo 1891–1897.

British Library
Ac. 8248/72, Correspondence of George Baillie of Jerviswood.
Add. 70841, f. 117, Third Earl Minto, 15 May 1863.
Add. 48267, f. 63, Third Earl of Minto to Lord Morley, 8 May 1886.
Add. 48267, f. 122, Third Earl of Minto to Gladstone, 20 May 1886.

Edinburgh University Library
La.IV. ff. 300–301.
La.IV. ff. 302–303.
La.IV. f. 304.
La.IV. ff. 305–306, Four letters from Lord Minto to David Laing.

Glasgow University Library
Correspondence of James McNeil Whistler with Cyril Flower c. 1876.

Hampshire Record Office
MS 92m95/f3/3/1–10, Sir Francis Baring to Minto 1837–40.

National Archives, Kew
ADM 222/11, Symonds to Admiralty.

National Library of Scotland
MS 9140, ff. 131–164, Letters from William to John Hill Burton 1854–1878.
MS 11747, Correspondence of Admiral George Elliot 1790–1829.
MS 11748, Correspondence of Admiral George Elliot 1830–34.
MS 11479, ff. 2–5.
MS 11479, ff. 5–7.
MS 11479, ff. 9–12.
MS 11479, ff. 19–23.
MS 11479, ff. 25–26.
MS 11479, ff. 29–35.
MS 11479, ff. 40–45.
MS 11479, ff. 55–56.
MS 11479, ff. 59–63.
MS 11479, ff. 65–74.
MS 11479, ff. 84–93.
MS 11479, ff. 96–97.
MS 11750, ff. 4–6.
MS 11750, ff. 52–54.
MS 11750, ff. 68–69.

MS 11750, f. 74.

MS 11750, ff. 82–83.

MS 11750, ff. 96–103.

MS 11750, ff. 105–107.

MS 11750, ff. 112–115.

MS 11750, ff. 121–134.

MS 11751, Captain George Elliot's letters to Lord Minto, February 1837 to October 1845.

MS 11760, Letters from and to the Children.

MS 11764, ff. 36–38, Letters from George Gilbert to Harriet 1848.

MS 11764, ff. 42–48, Letters from George Elliot to Charlotte 1848.

MS 11765A, Letters from Gilbert Elliot to Charlotte and George from the Crimea.

MS 11782, ff. 39–43, Letters from Gilbert Elliot to Harriet 1847.

MS 11899A, Letters between Henry Elliot and Lord Minto 1842–1858.

MS 11901, ff. 169–171, Gilbert to Lady Minto 1848.

MS 11906, ff. 103–6, Catherine's travel expenses 1833.

MS 11906, ff. 109–11, Catherine writes to Lady Minto 1833.

MS 11906, ff. 96–98, 103–106, 109–111, 123–5, 153–157.

MS 11907, ff. 113–114, 126–129.

MS 11976, ff. 3–4v, Minto's visit to Blair Atholl 1808.

MS 11995, Lord Minto's Journal, January 1849 to June 1849.

MS 12014, ff. 1–70, Lady Harriet's Journal, October 1843 to July 1844.

MS 12015, ff. 1–13, Lady Harriet's Journal, 9 July to 10 August 1844.

MS 12063, ff. 1–282, Papers relating to the Admiralty 1834–41.

MS 12064, f. 62, Dinners given by Lady Minto at the Admiralty.

MS 12077–9, Sicilian Papers, February to April 1848.

MS 12241, ff. 9–303, Letters of Lord Minto to William 1847–1860.

MS 12249, ff. 10v, 12v, 14–15, 40–51.

MS 12272, William's Diary for 1853.

MS 12317 and 12319, Diaries of William, Third Earl Minto, 1889 & 1890.

MS 12252, ff. 1–134, Letters from George Elliot to his brother William 1832–1890.

MS 12358, ff. 73–74, 110–111, 112–114, 157–158, 177–181, 187–188, 189–190, 191–192, 201, 205–206, 225–226, 227–228, Letters to and from William 1835–1858.

MS 12360, ff. 63–64, William Elliot's Miscellaneous Political Correspondence 1870–1881.

MS 12263, ff. 127–128.

MS 13091 (iii), ff. 151–152, William to George, 3 May 1865.

MS 13108, ff. 58–60.

MS 13167, ff. 138–141, Harriet to Lady Mary 1850.

MS 13190, Robert Selby to Lord Minto 1830–5.

MS 13191, ff. 277–282, 352–353.

MS 13217.

MS 13342.

MS 13343.

MS 13415, Photograph of 'Uncle George Elliot' (not clarifying whether it is Admiral George Elliot (1784–1863) or George Francis Stewart Elliot (1822–1901))

MS 13415, f. 2, Unconfirmed photograph of William, Third Earl Minto.

MS 13425 (ii), Stobie Plan of Minto.

MS 19471, ff. 1–53, Letters to George F. S. Elliot from Lord Minto, his siblings and their families.

MS 19577 (I), Part of Court Report in the *Jamaica Despatch*.

MS 19577 (II), Substance of the Statement by the Rev Mr Gleig.

MS 21230, Miscellaneous papers relating to life at Bonjedward House 1867–70.

MS 31050, Catherine's Journal.

MS 31051, Letters to Miss McGilchrist and Lord Minto to Robert Selby 1835.

MS 31052, Catherine leaves Minto for London.

MS 31053.

MS 31054, Family in Paris and Switzerland.

MS 31055.

MS 31056, To Berlin.

MS 31057, Family in Berlin.

MS 31058.

MS 31059, Catherine's Poems and Artwork.

MS 31061, Catherine in Paris.

National Maritime Museum
NMM Caird Library ELL 220/221, Sir Charles Adam to Minto, September 1836.
NMM Caird Library ELL 220/221, Admiral George Elliot to Lord Minto, 26 December 1837.
NMM Caird Library ELL 220/221, Charles Elliot to his uncle, 15 April 1837.
NMM Caird Library ELL 220/221, Charles Elliot to Admiral George Elliot, 23 April 1838.
NMM Caird Library ELL 220/221, Commander Hon. H. A. Murray to Lord Minto, 30 April 1838.
NMM Caird Library ELL 220/221, Copies of two Minutes in regard to the *Modeste* by Sir William Parker, 8 October 1838.
NMM Caird Library ELL 220/221, Communication from Sir John Barrow at the Admiralty, 20 October 1838.
NMM Caird Library ELL 220/221, Admiral George Elliot to Lord Minto, 25 August 1838, 16 November 1838, 1 February 1839, 21 February 1839, 12 November 1839, 21 October 1840, 7 June 1841, 24 July 1841, 28 December 1841, 5 January 1842, 18 January 1842, 28 March 1842, 10 April 1842, 8 June 1842, 19 June 1842, 14 July 1842, 25 September 1842, 18 October 1842, 22 November 1842, 24 November 1842, 4 December 1842, 9 April 1843, 18 and 28 January 1843, 5 February 1843, 3 March 1843, 18 May 1843, 31 May 1843, 24 August and 6–10 September 1843, 30 October and 24 November 1843.
NMM Caird Library ELL 220/221, Captain George Augustus Elliot to Lord Minto, 3 March 1844.


Scottish Borders Council
Craig-Brown Collection, two letters from George to Thomas Craig-Brown, December 1897.


University of Southampton Hartley Library
Add. 48482, ff. 47, 57, 62, 67, 88, 94, 95, 104, 109, 113, 116 and 118, summaries of dispatches received by the Foreign Office.
MS GC/MI/62, Minto to Palmerston.
MS GC/MI/63.
MS GC/MI/64, Minto en route for Berlin.
MS GC/MI/65.
MS GC/MI/67, Minto presents his credentials.
MS GC/MI/68, October 1832.
MS GC/MI/69.
MS GC/MI/70.
MS GC/MI/71, Minto to Palmerston.
MS GC/MI/72, Minto fines himself.
MS GC/MI/75, Bresson reads Ancillon a lecture.
MS GC/MI/76, Minto suggests pressure on Bülow.
MS GC/MI/78.
MS GC/MI/79.
MS GC/MI/80, Minto hopes for reduction of Antwerp.
MS GC/MI/81, Ancillon lies about audience with king.
MS GC/MI/82.
MS GC/MI/83, Personal messengers.
MS GC/MI/84, No English mail.
MS GC/MI/85, The five powers united.
MS GC/MI/86, Alarm from German intrigues.
MS GC/MI/87, Ancillon all mildness and sincerity.
MS GC/MI/89.
MS GC/MI/90, Count Clam-Martinitz, minister in Berlin.
MS GC/MI/93.
MS GC/MI/95, Firm dates for conclusion of treaty needed.
MS GC/MI/97, Minto presses Adair.
MS GC/MI/98, Ancillon had not taken the king's orders.
MS GC/MI/99.
MS GC/MI/100, Ancillon threatened by harsh dispatch.
MS GC/MI/101.
MS GC/MI/102, Public feeling in Berlin against England.
MS GC/MI/103, No compromise on road and river duties.
MS GC/MI/104, Russian minister in Berlin bitterly disliked.
MS GC/MI/105.
MS GC/MI/106, Minto wishes Belgians out of Luxembourg.
MS GC/MI/107.
MS GC/MI/108, Operations against Antwerp quietly received.
MS GC/MI/109, Prussia pacific as ever.
MS GC/MI/110.
MS GC/MI/111, Slow progress at Antwerp.
MS GC/MI/114, Minto congratulates Palmerston.

MS GC/MI/115.
Add. 48482, f. 47, Mischievous articles in Prussian Gazette.
Add. 48482, f. 57, Rare approbation from Palmerston.
Add. 48482, ff. 52–53, Towards a final treaty.
Add. 48482, ff. 57–59.
Add. 48482, f. 60.
Add. 48482, f. 62, No objections from Prussia.
Add. 48482, f. 69.
Add. 48482, f. 72, A Belgian envoy received in Berlin.

Yale University, Beinecke Library
Osborn File 10316, Lord Minto to Murray.

## BOOKS AND ARTICLES

*Admissions to the College of St John the Evangelist in the University of Cambridge*, Part IV, Cambridge University Press, 1931.
ANDERSON, R. D., *Education and the Scottish People 1750–1918*, Oxford University Press, 1995.
ASHLEY, Evelyn, *The Life of Henry John Temple, Viscount Palmerston 1846–1865*, Richard Bentley & Son, London, 1876.
BELL, Professor Herbert C. F., *Lord Palmerston*, 2 vols, Longmans, Green & Co., London, 1936.
BENSON, A. C., Viscount ESHER and G. E. BUCKLE (eds) *The Letters of Queen Victoria*, 9 vols, John Murray, London, 1907–32.
BOURNE, Kenneth, *Palmerston: The Early Years 1784–1841*, Macmillan, London, 1982.
BRASSEY, Lord, *The Naval Annual 1886*, J. Griffin & Co., Portsmouth, 1886.
BUCHAN, John, *Lord Minto: A Memoir*, London, 1924.
BULWER, The Rt Hon. Sir Henry Lytton, *The Life of Henry John Temple, Viscount Palmerston*, Richard Bentley & Son, London, 1870.
CARROLL, Francis M.., *A Good and Wise Measure: The Search for the Canadian–American Boundary 1783–1842*, University of Toronto Press, 2001.
CHADWICK, Owen, *Victorian Miniature*, Hodder & Stoughton, London, 1960.
COLLEDGE, J. J. and B. WARLOW, *Ships of the Royal Navy*, Chatham Publishing, London, 2006.
CLOWES, William Laird, *The Royal Navy: A History from the Earliest Times to the Death of Queen Victoria*, 6 vols, Sampson Low, Marston & Co., London, 1903.
*Complete British Diplomatic and Consular Handbook*, Foreign Office List No. 5 1865–66, published by Harrison of Pall Mall.
COPE, Sir William H., *History of the Rifle Brigade 1800–1874*, Chatto & Windus, London, 1877.
DONALDSON, Gordon, *Sir William Fraser: The Man and His Work*, Edina Press, Edinburgh, 1985.
DREYER, Fred, 'Three Years in the Toronto Garrison: The Story of the Honourable Gilbert Elliot, 1847–1850', *Ontario History*, vol. 57 (1965).
DROZ, Jacques, *Europe between the Revolutions 1818–1848*, Fontana Press, London, 1967.
DUGGAN, Christopher, *Francesco Crispi 1818–1901: From Nation to Nationalism*, Oxford University Press, 2002.
ELLIOT, Eleanor Elizabeth, *A Memoir of the Right Honourable Hugh Elliot*, Edinburgh, 1868.
ELLIOT, Eleanor Elizabeth (ed.), *Life and Letters of Sir Gilbert Elliot, First Earl of Minto from 1751 to 1806*, 3 vols, Longmans, Green, and Co., London, 1874.
ELLIOT, Eleanor Elizabeth (ed.), *Lord Minto in India: Life and Letters of Gilbert Elliot, First Earl of Minto from 1807 to 1814*, Longmans, Green & Co., London, 1880.
ELLIOT, George Francis Stewart, *Sir James Hudson and Earl Russell: An Historical Rectification from Authentic Documents*, William Ridgway, London, 1866.
ELLIOT, George Francis Stewart, *The Border Elliots and the Family of Minto*, David Douglas, Edinburgh, 1897.
ELLIOT, George Francis Stewart, *Thoughts on Bribery and Corruption at Elections*, James Ridgway, London, and A. & C. Black, Edinburgh, 1853.
ELLIOT, Sir Henry George, *Some Revolutions and Other Diplomatic Experiences* (ed. Gertrude Elliot), John Murray, London, 1922.
ELLIOT, William Fitzwilliam, *The Trustworthiness of Border Ballads as Exemplified by Jamie Telfer i' the Fair Dodhead' and Other Ballads*, William Blackwood & Sons, Edinburgh and London, 1906.
ELLIS, Hamilton, *Railway Carriages in the British Isles from 1830 to 1914*, George Allen & Unwin Ltd, London, 1965.
GILL, Christopher J. and Gillian C., 'Nightingale in Scutari: Her Legacy Re-examined', *Clinical Infectious Diseases*, vol. 40, 2005.
GOOCH, G. P. (ed.), *The Later Correspondence of Lord John Russell 1840–1878*, 2 vols, London, 1925.
GUEDALLA, Philip, *Palmerston*, Ernest Benn Ltd, London, 1926.
GROVE, Eric J., *The Royal Navy since 1815*, Palgrave Macmillan, London, 2005.
HALL, Sir John Richard, *England and the Orleans Monarchy*, Smith, Elder & Co., London, 1912.

HAY, J. D., *A Memoir of Sir John Drummond Hay*, John Murray, London, 1896.

HEATHCOTE, T. A., *The British Admirals of the Fleet 1734–1995*, Leo Cooper, Barnsley, 2002.

HEPPER, David, *British Warship Losses in the Ironclad Era, 1816–1919*, Chatham Publishing, London, 2006.

HINDLE, Wilfred, *The Morning Post 1772–1937: Portrait of a Newspaper*, George Routledge & Sons Ltd, London, 1937.

*The Holland House Diaries 1831–1840*, ed. A. D. Kriegel, Routledge & Kegan Paul, London, 1977.

HORNER, Susan, *A Century of Despotism in Naples and Sicily*, Edmonston & Douglas, Edinburgh, 1860.

HUGGETT, Frank E., *Life Below Stairs*, Book Club Associates, London, 1977.

LAMBERT, A. D., *The Last Sailing Battle Fleet: Maintaining Naval Mastery, 1815–1850*, Conway Maritime Press, London, 1991.

LEE, Sidney, *Queen Victoria: A Biography*, John Murray, London, 1904.

LONGFORD, Elizabeth, *Queen Victoria*, Sutton Publishing, 1999.

MACCOLL, Rev. Malcolm, *Three Years of the Eastern Question*, Chatto & Windus, London, 1878.

MACCARTHY, Desmond, and Agatha RUSSELL (eds), *Lady John Russell: A Memoir with Selections from Her Diaries and Her Correspondence*, 3rd edn, Longmans, Green & Co., London, 1926.

MOSSLANG, Markus, Sabine FREITAG and Peter WENDE (eds), *British Envoys to Germany, 1816–1847*, Cambridge University Press, 2002.

MARTIN, Theodore., *Life of His Royal Highness the Prince Consort*, 3 vols, Smith Elder & Co., London, 1875–77.

MAVOR, James, 'The Scottish Railway Strike', *Royal Economic Society Journal*, March 1891, pp. 204–219.

MILLER, C., *The Canadian Career of the Fourth Earl of Minto: The Education of a Viceroy*, Wilfrid Laurier University Press, Waterloo, Ontario, 1980.

MITCHELL, Sally, *Daily Life in Victorian England*, Greenwood Press, Westport, Connecticut, 2009.

MULLEN, Richard, and James MUNSON, *The Smell of the Continent: The British Discover Europe*, Macmillan, London, 2009.

NAMIER, Lewis, and John BROOKE (eds) *The History of Parliament: The House of Commons 1754–1790*, 3 vols, HMSO, London, 1964.

OUCHTERLONY, John, *Chinese War: An Account of All the Operations of the British Forces from the Commencement to the Treaty of Nanking*, Saunders & Otley, London, 1844.

PENNELL, C. R., *Morocco since 1830: A History*, New York University Press, 2000.

PHILLIMORE, A., *The Life of the Admiral of the Fleet, Sir William Parker*, 3 vols, Harrison & Sons, London, 1876–80.

PHILLIMORE, G. G., 'Booty of War', *Journal of Society of Comparative Legislation*, vol. 3, no. 2, 1901, pp. 214–230.

PREST, John M., *Lord John Russell*, Macmillan, London, 1972.

RALSTON, Andrew G., 'The Development of Reformatory and Industrial Schools in Scotland, 1832–1872', *Scottish Economic and Social History*, vol. 8, 1988, pp. 40–55.

RAUGH, Jr., Harold E., *The Victorians at War 1815–1914*, ABC-Clio Inc., Santa Barbara, 2004.

RAY, Margaret, 'Administering Emigration: Thomas Elliot and Government-Assisted Emigration from Britain to Australia 1831–1855', PhD thesis, University of Durham, 2001.

REYNOLDS, K. D., *Aristocratic Women and Political Society in Victorian Britain*, Clarendon Press, Oxford, 1998.

SAUNDERS, Robert, 'Lord John Russell and Parliamentary Reform, 1848–67', *English Historical Review*, vol. 120, no. 489, 2005, pp. 1289–1315.

SCHERER, Paul, *Lord John Russell: A Biography*, Associated University Presses, London, 1999.

SCHROEDER, Paul, *The Transformation of European Politics 1863–1848*, Oxford University Press, 1994.

SEWELL, Robert, *Sir Walter Elliot of Wolfelee: A Sketch of His Life and a Few Extracts from His Note Books*, privately published, Edinburgh, 1896.

SHANNON, R. T., *Gladstone and the Bulgarian Agitation, 1876*, Thomas Nelson & Son, London, 1963.

SLETTAN, Bjørn, 'Ein engelsk gentleman i Holum', *Agder Historielag*, no. 66, Kristiansand, 1990.

SMITH, A. E., *Lord Grey, 1764–1845*, Clarendon Press, Oxford, 1990.

SPERBER, Jonathan, *The European Revolutions 1848–1851*, 2nd edn, Cambridge University Press, 2005.

THORNE, R. G. (ed.) *The History of Parliament: The House of Commons 1790–1820*, 5 vols, HMSO, London, 1986.

TREVELYAN, G. O., *The Life and Letters of Lord Macaulay*, 2 vols, Longmans, Green & Co., London, 1876.

VERNON, The Honourable William, *Recollections of Seventy-Two Years*, John Murray, London, 1917.

WEBSTER, Sir Charles, *The Foreign Policy of Palmerston 1830–1841*, G. Bell & Sons, London, 1951.

WHITAKER, Tina, *Sicily and England: Political and Social Reminiscences 1848–1870*, Archibald Constable & Co. Ltd, London, 1907.

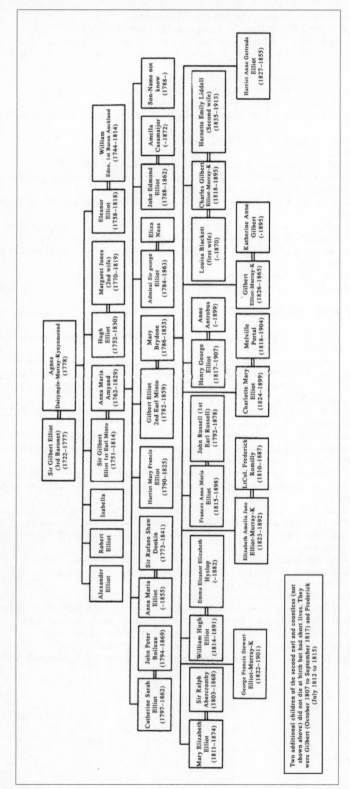

Principal members of the Elliot family in the eighteenth to twentieth centuries.

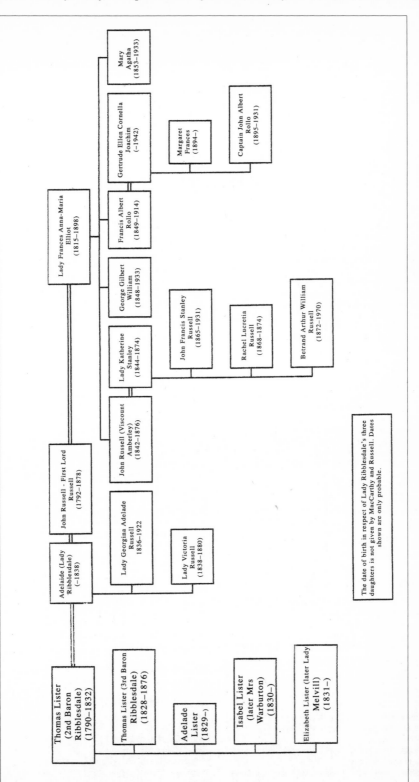

Descendants of John Russell, first Earl Russell.

# INDEX